Feminist Foundations

Gender & Society Readers

Sponsored by Sociologists for Women in Society

Gender & Society Readers address key issues in contemporary gender studies informed by feminist writing, theory, and research. Readers are based on articles appearing in, and special theme issues of, the scholarly journal *Gender & Society*, sponsored by Sociologists for Women in Society.

Titles in this series:

Judith Lorber and Susan A. Farrell (eds.)
THE SOCIAL CONSTRUCTION OF GENDER (1991)

Pauline B. Bart and Eileen Geil Moran (eds.)
VIOLENCE AGAINST WOMEN: The Bloody Footprints (1993)

Esther Ngan-ling Chow, Doris Wilkinson, Maxine Baca Zinn (eds.)
RACE, CLASS, AND GENDER: Common Bonds,
Different Voices (1996)

Kristen A. Myers, Cynthia D. Anderson, and Barbara J. Risman (eds.)
FEMINIST FOUNDATIONS: Toward Transforming Sociology (1998)

Feminist Foundations
*Toward
Transforming
Sociology*

Editors
Kristen A. Myers
Cynthia D. Anderson
Barbara J. Risman

 SAGE Publications
International Educational and Professional Publisher
Thousand Oaks   London   New Delhi

For information:

SAGE Publications, Inc.
2455 Teller Road
Thousand Oaks, California 91320
E-mail: order@sagepub.com

SAGE Publications Ltd.
6 Bonhill Street
London EC2A 4PU
United Kingdom

SAGE Publications India Pvt. Ltd.
M-32 Market
Greater Kailash I
New Delhi 110 048 India

Printed in the United States of America

Library of Congress Cataloging-in-Publication Data

Myers, Kristen A.
    Feminist foundations: Toward transforming sociology/edited by
Kristen A. Myers, Barbara J. Risman, Cynthia D. Anderson
        p. cm. — (Gender and Society readers; v. 3)
    Includes bibliographical references and index.
    ISBN 0-7619-0785-8 (cloth: alk. paper)
    ISBN 0-7619-0786-6 (pbk.: alk. paper)
    1. Feminist theory. 2. Feminist criticism. I. Risman, Barbara J., 1956–
II. Anderson, Cynthia D.
    HQ1190 .F457 1997
    305.42/01 21

This book is printed on acid-free paper.

98 99 00 01 02 03 10 9 8 7 6 5 4 3 2 1

Acquiring Editor:	Peter Labella
Editorial Assistant:	Corrine Pierce
Production Editor:	Sherrise M. Purdum
Production Assistant:	Denise Santoyo
Typesetter:	Marion Warren
Indexer:	Molly Hall
Print Buyer:	Anna Chin

Contents

Introduction: Bridging the Gaps in Feminist Sociology

I am not asking what sociology can do for women—for example by filling in the gaps in our knowledge about them, itself a significant contribution—but rather what women (and sympathetic male colleagues) can do for sociology.

Jessie Bernard

In discussing the four revolutions she experienced in the American Sociological Association, Bernard (Chapter 1, this volume) called for a feminist revolution in sociology so as to open the previously closed doors to new areas, new questions, and new paradigms that better capture the reality of *all* people. It is noteworthy that Bernard did not trust sociologists (a predominantly male group) to interpret women's situations and "fill in the gaps." She feared that such interpretations would be grounded in stereotypes (Note 13, p.15). Indeed, she considered the task of transforming sociology to be so overwhelming that she sought only to "nibble" at the problem. Twenty-five years later, sociology as a discipline has largely moved beyond such stereotypes, and a great deal of literature has been written by women (and sympathetic male colleagues) on the inequality between men and women in society. Yet gaps still remain in our intellectual understandings of gender inequality. Feminist scholarship—though remarkably more commonplace than during Bernard's career—remains at the margins of sociological theory. After all of these years, we are still filling in the intellectual gaps with feminist scholarship. This book is an illustrative overview of feminist thought through the years, beginning with Bernard's renowned indictment of sociology. With this book, we act as sociologists doing something for women; and we act as women doing something for sociology.

RECOGNIZING THE INTELLECTUAL GAPS IN SOCIOLOGY

The idea for this book grew out of a conversation on the Sociologists for Women in Society Internet list server during 1995. Many sociologists use this forum not only to discuss issues and announce upcoming conferences, but also to request references and discuss important scholarship—new and old. In ongoing dialogue, participants discussed key pieces of feminist scholarship in sociology that had particularly influenced their careers and their sociological thinking. They paid homage to their *foremothers* and advised each other of where to find more enlightening materials. The conversation highlighted the herstory of feminist scholarship in sociology. It also illuminated for us the absence of a comprehensive volume of feminist contributions to sociology. While list server discussions are stimulating, they leave no trace for future reference. We thought such discussions too important to lose in cyberspace.

Until the feminist influence on the academy, most sociology was a chronicle of men's writings, research, and theories. Classical theory courses still concentrate on our intellectual "fathers," Marx, Weber, and Durkheim. Contemporary theory courses focus primarily on neo-Marxists, neo-Weberians, and neo-Durkheimians, occasionally sprinkling in some interactionists, phenomenologists, and feminists. The "fathers'" ideas formed the foundation for sociological theories and research methods. While their work was necessarily informed by their European, white male standpoints (Sprague, 1997), we continue as a discipline to ground our most important and serious endeavors on this foundation. Even our subjects have traditionally been men (as well as white and middle class, for that matter [Sprague, 1997]).

Although some sociologists have compiled examples of feminist scholarship (Campbell & Manicom, 1995; England, 1993; Lorber & Farrell, 1991; Risman & Schwartz, 1989; Wallace, 1989), these books represent a drop in the bucket. More collections are desperately needed to ground our field in its own herstory, and to continue transforming the field itself. We feel the time has come to begin to mainstream feminist scholarship more completely. This book is designed to provide an overview of sociological feminist thought for students in required sociology theory courses at both the upper-division undergraduate and the graduate student level. This book chronicles feminist theories and research about gender, work, family, sexuality, culture, organizations, race, class, sociology, and myriad other embedded concepts. The articles bridge every level of analysis—individual, interactional, and institutional. Taken together, the authors show the dialectical nature of social forces: how individuals are shaped by their social context, and yet, how individuals shape their worlds themselves.

We are personally and intellectually committed to providing this resource for many groups of sociologists and students. For Cindy Anderson and

Kristen Myers, interest in a project like this one began early in graduate school. We were concerned about the lack of feminist theory and scholarship in our graduate theory classes. We had a strong feminist mentor in Barbara Risman, and we were fully steeped in critical scholarship in our inequality graduate specialization. However, we were concerned about the state of the other subdisciplines in sociology. We read Stacey and Thorne's discussion (Chapter 9, this volume) of a feminist revolution in sociology, looked at our own graduate curriculum (outside of the inequality area), and woefully agreed with their assessment. Together with Jammie Price, we decided to find out what students in other area sociology programs were learning about feminist theory. Because our university—North Carolina State University—was located in an area with other large sociology graduate programs, we were able to survey NCSU students as well as students from two other major universities in our home community—University of North Carolina and Duke University. We found that, overall, few students had been exposed to gender *as a concept,* let alone feminist theory and scholarship. Those students who had been exposed cited a great variety of scholarship as feminist, including work that used gender as a variable, work that considered gender only as a personality trait, and work that critically challenged structures of inequality in society (for more, see Anderson, Myers, & Price, 1995). We recognized a need in sociology for a book that provides an extensive overview of feminist theory and research. Editing this book is our first attempt at contributing to the field of sociology.

This book is for sociologists who had to dig long and hard to find any feminist work; for those whose graduate school committees would not allow them to study gender as a research topic; for those in departments who still "don't get it"; for those lucky sociologists of today who have access to various genres within gender sociology, but who are looking for an intellectual framework; and for those who teach contemporary theory and do not yet incorporate feminist thought.

GENRES OF FEMINIST THOUGHT

When we began this project, we conceptualized feminist scholarship as following a distinct, cumulative trajectory as it has attempted to transform traditional sociology (see Johnson & Risman, 1997). We expected to show how feminist scholarship has moved through the following stages: (a) from discovering the absence of women in theory and research; (b) to documenting the inequity of socially created sex differences; (c) to discovering that gender is not only about women and subsequently incorporating men; (d) to focusing on gender as a social structure rather than simply a characteristic of individuals; and, finally, (e) to the realization that gender is systematically and inextricably tied to other matrices of inequality, such as race, sexual orientation, and class. Our argument was not that each new stage supplanted the former. Instead, we believed that the stages built upon one another. In planning and organizing this book, however, we reconceptualized the process by which feminist theory and scholarship has developed in sociology. We realized as we collected articles, as you too will notice, that many of the articles in the different sections of this book were originally published in the same time period. For example, Rosenfeld (1980) and Kanter (1976) were writing in the same time period, even though we have included their work in different "stages" of development in feminist theory and research.

Organizing feminist scholarship in terms of "stages" presumes that the dominant model of evaluating theory and research applies to this marginalized genre in sociology. Karl Popper (1968) explains this dominant model of scholarly development as a process of falsification whereby one theory or paradigm rises to dominance in a discipline. Over time, other theorists will challenge the dominant paradigm by trying to falsify its claims, providing contrary evidence and arguments. As old theories are falsified, new paradigms become dominant. Popper is writing about the "hard" sciences, but other sciences, including sociology, have borrowed this process as the only legitimate means to transform disciplines over time. Although there is much debate over the politics and the efficacy of this model of scholarly development (see Feyerabend, 1978; Kuhn, 1970; Lakatos & Musgrave, 1970; Sprague, 1997), we believe that feminist scholarship has developed largely outside of this process. Because feminist work has traditionally been marginalized, feminist scholars have not had the benefit of building upon each others' work in the way mainstream researchers have been able to do. As many of the reflectors in this book explain, feminist scholars have often worked in a relative vacuum of previous scholarship.

Given the historic invisibility of feminist scholarship—except for within cloistered circles and feminist enclaves—we prefer to conceptualize the sections of this book as *intellectual genres* rather than stages of feminist development in sociology. Based on these intellectual genres, we have broken the book into these five sections: "The Fourth Revolution: Confronting Androcentrism in Sociology"; "Exposing the Gender Gap: Separate Is Never Equal"; "Theorizing What Gender Means"; "Gender in the Machine: Structured Inequality"; and "Panning to the Margins." Although they are diverse, many of the different ideas and concepts presented in this collection originated concomitantly in time. Clearly, though, some scholarship received attention from the mainstream before others. The differential recognition is undoubtedly tied to the political climate of society in general and sociology in particular, both of which are typically conservative on gender issues. We resist reifying the conservative development of sociology by defining discrete stages of feminist scholarship. To do so implies that the new and better theories replaced old, inaccurate ones. We hope to span traditional intellectual boundaries within feminist scholarship by situating this theoretical waxing and waning into the political climate at large. *All* of these genres have impacted feminist scholars. We celebrate the different genres and hope to underscore all of their contributions to the discipline and to individuals' careers and personal lives.

Overall, then, we stand by our early perceptions about how the field has changed over time—realizing, however, that this is a consequence of what sociologists were ready to hear, to cite, and to understand, not a result of when important ideas were first introduced. Women of color called attention to the margins a decade before white feminists began to look there. Perhaps the ability to understand these conceptual categories is cumulative—one can hardly see gender systematically built into organizations before one has noticed women are absent entirely from sociological thought.

While feminist scholarship has not benefited in the same ways as mainstream scholarship from a progressive development of ideas and findings, some feminist scholarship has emerged in direct response to previous research. For example, work on the social construction of gender developed by building on and reacting against sex role theory. Feminist scholars do elaborate on and reconceptualize previous feminist work. The problem is that this intellectual process takes place largely in the margins, where it has limited effect on the center. Likewise, the mood of the discipline affects which strains of thought come into vogue in different time periods. The progression of thought may be as much related to social politics as to scholarly importance of ideas. By incorporating many different intellectual genres here, we hope to bridge the gaps that divide feminist scholarship.

AN OVERVIEW OF THE ORGANIZATION OF THE BOOK

We organize the book according to the genres' chronological recognition in sociology. The first section is titled "The Fourth Revolution: Confronting Androcentrism in Sociology." Articles in this section were among the first in sociology to recognize that women's experiences were conspicuously absent from theory, methods, and data. They explain that men's experiences and perspectives are not generalizable to all people. They indict sociologists for being androcentric and call for future work to include women's experiences as well as men's. This may be the first body of work that elucidates the hegemony of patriarchy in sociology. The second section is called "Exposing the Gender Gap: Separate Is Never Equal." In these articles, feminist scholars empirically document inequality between women and men, bringing women into traditional stratification research and providing evidence of unequal outcomes. These scholars provide the methodological and theoretical groundwork for generations to come.

We have titled the third section of this collection "Theorizing What Gender Means." Feminists who fit into this intellectual genre critically assess the definition of gender. They argue—and demonstrate—that differences between women and men are not essential to either sex. They point out that men have gender, too, and they help make the social construction of gender a vital assumption of feminist research. In the fourth strain of thought, "Gender in the Machine: Structured Inequality," feminists begin to apply the assumption of social construction to the institutional level of analysis, arguing that gender is more than individual behavior or identity. These scholars show how gender is built into structures and how this helps to create and maintain gender inequality.

The fifth intellectual genre is one that has only recently been recognized in sociology, although much of the groundwork was laid decades ago. We call this section "Panning to the Margins." The efforts of these and other feminists who have traditionally been at the margins of mainstream society and academia have helped to alter the assumptions of many mainstream (i.e., white, middle/upper class) feminists. These challengers include people of color as well as gay, lesbian, and bisexual scholars. Today, more feminists validate a variety of experiences, as exemplified by standpoint theories. They make research more inclusive and responsive to diverse needs. We end the book with this intellectual genre because we feel it offers the best template for an integrative sociology in the future.

THE POLITICS OF PARTICIPATION

The hardest part of this project was deciding which articles to include. In making these decisions, we relied on our own sense of which intellectual traditions have impacted the discipline. We used citation indexes and listened to the women on the SWS list server. Even so, we have made substantive decisions as to what to include. Although occasionally our colleagues have jokingly referred to this volume as the "feminist canon book," we resist the label. Many of these articles are written by the "mothers" of feminist sociology; there are many other seriously important articles we did not have room to include. The articles included here are best seen as *illustrations* of the kinds of key theoretical perspectives in feminist sociology. For each article included, there are several others equally central that had to be omitted because of space. Despite the absence of many important works, we believe this book can play a critical role in beginning to integrate feminist scholarship into the mainstream of sociological discourse. Here, we provide one volume for professors who teach sociological theory to add to their syllabi to provide an overview of feminist discourse. We supply the conceptual frameworks and some illustrative articles to help understand the place of

feminist thought *in sociology*. Providing an overview for those yet uniniti-
ated is one of our goals; another goal is to provide feminist colleagues with
a set of conceptual frameworks upon which to build future scholarship.

REFLECTIONS BY FEMINIST SCHOLARS

A unique aspect of this book is the inclusion of reflectors at the end of
each section. In the spirit of the list server discussion, we invited feminist
scholars to comment and reflect upon each section. The reflectors each
discuss how the articles and perspectives they represent impacted them as
sociologists, as feminists, and as individuals. The reflectors add a human
element to the development of feminist scholarship. As sociologists, our
scholarship all too often tends towards abstraction from reality (Sprague,
1997). The reflectors help ground us in the social context in which feminist
scholarship takes place. They remind us of the emancipatory, transformative
goal of feminism, talking personally about feminist theory and research. The
reflectors illustrate that, for scholarship to develop, we require an intellectual
community. We hope this book will foster such a community of feminist
scholars. We encourage you to reflect on how these strains of feminist
thought affect you intellectually, politically, and personally. Taken together,
the articles and reflections in this book should act as a catalyst for future
feminist forums where intellectual growth can occur. We have included
electronic mail addresses for reflectors, and we have included them for
ourselves. We hope this will stimulate further development of feminist
thought through the interaction of readers, editors, and authors.

This volume will, at first glance, appeal mostly to feminist scholars and
sociologists who study gender. As this community is our own intellectual
home, we dedicate this work to the feminist sisterhood embodied in Sociologists for Women in Society—and this work is published in an SWS series.
We are pleased to be the birth mothers. But this "baby" will thrive only if
othermothers and otherfathers—like you—nurture the child, for our goal is
to help mainstream feminist thought into the discipline—to further transform
sociology. So we end our editorial musings with a challenge to every reader.
If you are a feminist sociologist, do you know if the students in your
departments (including the men) routinely encounter feminist scholarship in
their required contemporary theory courses? If not, take our challenge to do
your part to mainstream feminist discourse. Share this book with the (usually
male) instructor who determines what is the contemporary "core" of the
discipline presented to all students. Let him (or, less often, her) know that in
the next century no one can do good sociology without an appreciation for
the feminist re-visioning of intellectual thought. If you teach contemporary
theory, please think of your role sociologically; you *are* a gatekeeper to what

the next generation of scholars considers the center of intellectual discourse. Bring feminist thought from the margins to the center. Assign this book—or some other feminist theory. If you are a student, we encourage you to share this book with other students and even faculty. Together, we will move feminist sociology closer to the center of the discipline.

Part I

The Fourth Revolution: Confronting Androcentrism in Sociology

The scholars in this genre were the pioneers, the settlers of feminist sociology. They forged new intellectual frontiers, demanding that women be incorporated into research and theories. They braved the chill of exclusion by peers and superiors because their perspectives were unpopular, marginalized. As feminist sociologists today, we owe them a great debt. The works included here emerged when sociologists focused predominantly on male subjects, using primarily a functionalist, abstract, and conservative lens. These scholars emphasize that women's experiences are significantly different from men's, and that women should be studied in their own right. They call for an incorporation of women's perspectives—as theorists, researchers, and subjects of study. These are ideas that we take for granted today, thanks to the efforts of these scholars.

1 My Four Revolutions: An
Autobiographical History of the ASA[1]

JESSIE BERNARD
Pennsylvania State University

I am undoubtedly the only person, living or dead, who has participated in four revolutions in the American Sociological Association (ASA). The first in the 1920s, the second in the 1930s, the third in the 1950s, and the current, or fourth, in the 1970s.

In the early 1920s, a radical young sociologist at Columbia University by the name of W. F. Ogburn, who had himself, both in government service and in academia, participated in the burgeoning movement to quantify sociological research, had the mind-boggling idea that the annual meetings of the American Sociological Society ought to inject into their programs some papers on empirical research. Not, mind you, at the expense of the high-level papers the giants addressed to one another but as an interesting fillip. He proceeded with his idea and solicited papers based on empirical research. That was how I came to participate in the program in 1925, which I now see as far more revolutionary than it appeared to be then. At his invitation—imagine how barren the field must have been—I presented a paper based on my master's dissertation. I am not at all anxious to advertise it, so let that pass. The important thing was that the idea of papers based on empirical research was introduced and took hold. This revolution did not create the emphasis on empirical research; that had a long history.[2] But that first research program did open the door of the Society to the accelerating thrust of empirical research, give it official sanction, and provide it with a recognized forum. The rest is history. The research programs acquired prestige, proliferated into a veritable jungle, and all but overshadowed the theoretical papers. I leave

"My Four Revolutions: An Autobiographical History of the ASA" by Jessie Bernard, in *American Journal of Sociology,* Vol. 78, No. 4, pp. 11-29. © University of Chicago. All rights reserved. Reprinted with permission.

for the official historians of the ASA the job of assessing the impact of this first revolution on the discipline and tracing its implications.

My second revolution, in the 1930s, marked the emancipation of the Society from the fostering protection of the University of Chicago. Until that time, the University of Chicago had, in effect, owned the Society. It supplied the leadership, published the proceedings, and provided a home for the secretary treasurer. In the early 1930s, a group of rebels—led to a large extent by L. L. Bernard—stole the Society away.[3] The *American Journal of Sociology* was no longer to be its official journal. Again I leave for the official historians of the ASA the task of assessing the impact of this second revolution on the discipline and tracing its implications.

The third revolution, in the early 1950s, consisted of the declaration of independence of a group of rebels who, deploring the refusal of the parent organization to take a stand on any policy issue, established the Society for the Study of Social Problems (SSSP).[4] Our gripes were manifold. We objected to the elitist direction the ASA was following, its lack of interest in social problems and issues, its antiseptic "line" on research, its cronyism, and its complacent acceptance of the increasing trend of putting sociological research at the service of business and industry. We were concerned also with protecting academic freedom in the era of McCarthy. The SSSP's objectives were: (1) advancement of the study of social problems; (2) application of social science research to the formulation of social policies; (3) improvement of the opportunities and working conditions of social scientists; (4) protection of freedom of teaching, research, and publication; and (5) interdisciplinary cooperation in social science research.[5] Although some of the stars of the ASA agreed to front for us,[6] the actual leadership was in the hands of Alfred McClung Lee and Arnold Rose, who were not afraid to stand up to the conservative ASA elite. We embarrassed the ASA; it didn't know exactly how to deal with us.[7] For a long time, despite the shining stars—E. W. Burgess was the first president—we scared the elite by threatening to give sociology a bad name by taking positions on issues. But we were clearly in tune with the times. Before too many years had passed we became respectable. More's the pity, perhaps. The most elite members of the ASA not only joined but became active. Became officers, in fact. We were not co-opted but the ASA did take over all the "radical" innovations we had introduced, and you can hardly tell the two apart anymore except that there may be more beards and slightly longer hair in the SSSP.[8] Once more I leave to the official historians of the ASA and the SSSP the chore of assessing the impact of this third revolution on our discipline and tracing its implications.

My fourth—feminist—revolution came as something of a surprise to me. It should not have. For although, like my colleagues, I stand accused of not foretelling the uprisings of the 1960s—still, on the basis of research dealing with the feminine "life calendar," I did note "augurs of change" in my (1964, pp. 62-63) study of academic women. By the end of the decade, academic women in several disciplines were protesting their status in the profession. Led by Alice Rossi, the revolution in sociology surfaced in San Francisco in 1969. I was in London at the International Population Conference, so I did not have the privilege of taking part in the meetings at which the Women's Caucus under Alice Rossi's leadership got an astonishing list of resolutions accepted. But I was present the next year in Washington when the Women's Caucus began the process of transforming itself into Sociologists for Women in Society, and I was one of the midwives at the birth of that organization.[9]

The feminist revolution was a complex event. The tasks envisioned by the participants varied. Some were interested primarily in fighting discrimination in the profession. Some were concerned with fighting discrimination against women in society at large. Some wanted to liberate sociology from its establishmentarian bias to make it an instrument for total revolution.[10] And some sought mainly to counteract the sexist bias in the discipline. The last of these tasks is my own major concern and is the focus of the discussion here.

I am not attempting to account for any of my four revolutions. In each case, I am sure, "the time had come." This is a cliché that can never be disproved, a tautology; you know the time has come because the revolution occurs. Nor am I trying to explain why this is the time for the feminist revolution in sociology, why this is the time for an attack on sexism in our discipline.[11] Suffice to say that this is the time because the world to which sociology addresses itself has changed so much that a shift is required to take into account the anomalies resulting from "the novelties of fact"[12]—to use Thomas S. Kuhn's phrase—that modern life is introducing into the classic paradigms. Because it is now essential for us to bring our discipline up to date, to fill in the deficiencies its male bias has created. Because if we want sociology to have relevance for the world it is supposed to interpret, it has to look at this world through suitable paradigms. Because, in brief, sociology is in a state of crisis, a word which appears with increasing frequency in sociological discussions. Sociology is in crisis because the old paradigms are overburdened by anomalies and satisfactory new ones are not available. Whatever the reason may be, the fourth revolution is now.

"ASK NOT . . . "

I am concerned, as any fair-minded person must be, with the effects of sexism on the position of women in our profession and in our society; but I am also concerned, as any dedicated sociologist must be, with its effects on our discipline as well. Important as are the costs to women of the male bias in sociology, on which a considerable literature exists (Roby 1972; Rossi

1972), I am concerned here not with them but rather with the costs of this bias to the discipline itself. I am not, therefore, asking what sociology can do for women—for example, by filling in the gaps in our knowledge about them, itself a significant contribution[13]—but rather what women (and sympathetic male colleagues) can do for sociology. How they can correct some of its defects by overcoming deficiencies, broadening its perspective, opening up new areas, asking new questions, offering new paradigms; how, in brief, they can make sociology a better instrument for understanding, explaining, and interpreting the way modern societies operate.[14] Though I despair of my ability to do justice to the problem—a thoroughgoing attack would require a series of monographs—I can at least nibble at it here.

I have selected for comment (1) some of the antecedents of the fourth revolution; (2) critiques by women of such major concepts and paradigms as Parsonian functionalism, interactionism, socialization, and exchange theory; and (3) the attempt to expand sociology into a genuine science of society by including women as well as men.

ANTECEDENTS AND PRECURSORS

Even before the fourth revolution hit sociology, there was already a remarkable corpus of critical-polemical writing by women of the Women's Liberation Movement who came from a wide variety of backgrounds, from Maoist to Christian,[15] on a wide variety of sociological phenomena— functionalism, socialization, interaction, power, exploitation, oppression— which sought to show how the social sciences, especially sociology and psychology, had been used to bolster the power of men and justify discrimination and oppression. The Women's Liberation Movement had been nurtured in the New Left, a disproportionate number of whose members were sociology students, if not professional sociologists. It retained this New Left sociological stamp even when it seceded from the male matrix.

Thus in their written work these early leaders applied to women the same arguments and logic as those applied to the underclasses by their male prototypes. As the Sociology Liberation Movement had accused sociologists of cultivating a power-oriented sociology, creating not a science of society but a science of just one segment of society, honed to help it exploit the other segments, so, in a similar vein, these women charged that sociology was not a science of society but rather a science of male society and that it did not necessarily have great relevance for women. Just as the Sociology Liberation Movement charged that sociological research was on the side of the power structure, these women charged that it had been on the side of men.

These early leaders were almost certainly familiar with C. Wright Mills. Whether or not they had read *The Sociological Imagination,* they followed the tenets it laid down (1959, p. 196). Mills's (1959, pp. 225-26) last imperative—to reveal the human meaning of public issues by relating them to personal troubles—was especially salient in the process that came to be known as consciousness raising. Women who had always been blamed for their miseries, rebuked for mentioning them, and told that something was wrong with them were liberated when they came to see that they were not defective individuals but victims of oppressive institutions. Their method, like that of their male counterparts, has since been given the name of ethnomethodology (Garfinkel 1967). Young (1971, p. 279) defines it as a special type of conflict methodology which requires one to poke, probe, provoke, and puncture the social system in order to reveal its charac-teristics.[16] By such techniques, the writings of these early feminists led readers suddenly to become aware of a wide gamut of phenomena which they had always taken for granted. Their consciousness was raised.

THE FEMALE CRITIQUE: THEORY

The work of the present cohort of women critics of sociology has been largely normal science in nature, modifying, correcting, sharpening, or refining the classic paradigms and analyses of traditional sociology, often with the effect of exposing their male bias.

The criticism of *Parsonian functionalism* by women followed essentially the same logic as that of its male critics, namely, that, by implication if not by intention,[17] it had the effect of justifying the sexual status quo, as though a functionalist explanation of it supplied a scientific basis for it.[18] They pointed out that it is one thing to analyze the way social structures operate—including the way they allocate functions—but quite another to accept the sexual allocation of functions in any given system as intrinsic to social systems. As a result of this critique, few sociologists are likely to continue to justify the sexual status quo through functional analysis. This does not mean that they will all necessarily accept changes in the status quo; they will simply find other justifications for it.[19]

The work of women critics has also contributed to overcoming one of the weaknesses of *interactionism* as specified by Rose (1962, p. x), namely, neglect of power relationships.[20] Their analyses of the ways men exert power over women in everyday interaction as well as in sexual relationships has been one of their most important contributions (see Jones 1970; Mainardi 1970).

The explanatory value of both functionalism and interactionism in the form of role theory rests heavily on the paradigm of *socialization,* which the female critique has not only accepted but also greatly expanded. Socializa-tion has, in fact, been an all-but-overwhelming preoccupation of the women critics.[21] They have alerted us to aspects of it not previously recognized by male researchers, highlighting especially the processes by which women are socialized for weakness, dependency, fear of success (Horner 1969), and even mild mental illness (Broverman, Broverman, Charlson, Rosenkrantz, and Vogel 1970), and thus shaped for marriage (Bernard 1971a, pp. 94-95; 1972, chap. 3). The "adjustment" that brings stability of the status quo— which functionalism reports—by means of the techniques—which inter-actionism describes—becomes a dirty word.

Despite the fact that the whole *exchange* paradigm cries out for a feminist critique, no such analysis has yet been made.[22] Thus far exchange theory in the area of the relations between the sexes has been applied almost exclusively to mate selection or to the exchange of sex favors (see Blau 1964; or Elder 1969). The other kinds of relations between the sexes have not been encompassed in it.[23] The female critique has highlighted the asymmetry in most of these relations, noting that in almost every intersex exchange, "the woman pays," that she is on the losing side, and that she is even expected to accept the situation without complaint.[24] Free exchange under the conditions specified by Adam Smith leaves both parties better off, both having ex-changed something they value less for something they value more. But game theory has taught us that both parties can lose; or that one can win and the other lose. The women critics note that in our society the loser is most likely to be the woman. Losing, in fact, is written into her role script; she has a stroke deficit: "Women . . . are enjoined to give out more strokes than they receive by the dictates of their roles as women. The instruction to give more strokes than they receive and to be willing to settle for this disparity are essentially aspects of women's life scripts" (Wyckoff 1971); see also Bernard 1971b). In this "stroke economy," women may win an occasional battle, particularly when they are young and especially desirable, but they lose the wars. The presidential address of George Homans, a leading exponent of exchange theory, before the ASA was dedicated to "bringing men back in" to sociology. The feminist revolution calls for bringing women in too.

Women increasingly fault history also for its neglect of women, so that what history we have is almost exclusively a history of men. Male biases determine not only what is selected for study but also how it is interpreted. Turner's theory of the effect of the frontier on American character, for example, deals only with males (Chmaj 1971, p. 65). "Descriptions of the experiences of women servants, slaves, immigrants, pioneers, and factory workers remain buried in court records, journals, letters, travelogs, and newspapers," as yet unexploited for the knowledge they can make available about our society (Greenwald 1971, p. 152). Women also criticize the condescending and patronizing manner what history of women there is has been dealt with.

Much of the female critique to date is remedial, a patching up, merely a first installment of the potential contribution women can make. Still, I challenge any sociologist to read it thoughtfully and nondefensively and not find that a re-thinking of sociological paradigms is indeed in order. But that is not all. In addition to this theoretical critique, there is also a critique of the substantive questions raised by sociology and of the research methods used to answer them.

CAN SOCIOLOGY TRANSCEND SEX?

I once asked, "Can science transcend culture?" and gave an affirmative reply. Yes, I said, it could if the canons of scientific method were scrupulously observed (Bernard 1950). I am not so sure today.[25] But let that pass. What the fourth revolution asks today is, Can one particular science—sociology—transcend sex? With respect to both contents and methods? Can it become a science of society rather than a science of male society? Or than a male science of society?

To the charge leveled by the fourth revolution that the male bias of sociology to date has interfered with our knowledge-based understanding of the way our society operates, a plea of guilty is in order. There are questions about the functioning of our society that have not been raised or, if raised, not adequately attended to. As a result, we have a lopsided conceptualization of it. Hochschild (1970, p. 14) has reminded us how much our discipline suffers from the absence of the contribution of women. She specifies two kinds of costs, factual and paradigmatic, the first requiring that we figure out what is missing in our discipline, and the second that we get our heads straight.[26]

Sociology as a science of male society.—We can begin to figure out what is missing by looking at the kinds of questions the researcher asks, for, as we are becoming increasingly aware, they reveal his value as well as his acumen.[27] And so far men, of course have asked the questions.[28]

In a book on the future of marriage (Bernard 1972) I had occasion to summarize the large research literature on the so-called discrepant responses husbands and wives give to identical questions; they tend to agree on a few items such as number of children, but discrepancies occur on almost everything else. Some of the discrepancy can be attributed to selective perception. But, in addition, the "realities" of marriage—the complex institutional web of law, religion, custom, mores that constitute marriage—really are different for husbands and wives. As, indeed, are the "realities" of other institutions. Not only do men and women view a common world from different perspectives, they view different worlds as well. The fourth revolution demands that we include the world women inhabit.

The idea that men and women inhabit different worlds is an old one.[29] I have found it useful to characterize them in terms of the nature of the bonds between and among people, one a status world in which the bonds are on a love/duty basis and the other, one in which they are based on a cash nexus characterized by monetary exchange.[30] By and large, women have lived in a status world and men in a cash-nexus world.[31] Practically all sociology to date has been a sociology of the male world.[32] The topics that have preoccupied sociologists have been the topics that preoccupy men: power, work, climbing the occupational ladder, conflict, and sex—but not women—or women only as adjuncts to men. When women have been dealt with in this sociology of male society, it has usually been in a chapter or a footnote on "the status of women," thrown in as an extra, almost beside the point, rather than as an intrinsic component of a total society. Very little sociology deals with the nature, structure, and functioning of a female status world. When it is dealt with at all, it is analyzed at its point of intersection with the cash-nexus or work world, as in the instance of the conflicting roles of working wives and mothers. Even here, the results of the work done by men and by women differ markedly.[33]

There is also another way to look at the sexist bias in sociology; it has to do not with a status world but with women as a collective entity, as much a component of our society as other conceptual entities, such as for example, "labor," "ethnic groups," youth, and all the others which are stock-in-trade for sociological analysts and hence worthy of attention. The women now seen by our discipline are almost exclusively viewed in their relations to men as daughters, wives, and mothers or, simply, as sexual partners. There may have been a time when such a limited perspective was justified. If so, it is no longer. Women have become a collective entity and can no longer be viewed exclusively as separate adjuncts to men, the lesser member of a pair. They need instead to be seen as an entity, not, to be sure, in terms of mindless stereotypical generalizations like "women are such and such" or "women do so and so" but as a collectivity with common bonds and interests, as the entity which the concept of "sisterhood" has taught so many of them to see, a collectivity different to be sure from others but no less indispensable to any analysis of a modern society.

Is it so unreasonable to look forward to a time when introductory texts begin with the fundamental sociological datum that all societies include two collectivities, one in which the members are characteristically smaller, slower, less physically powerful, etc., the other in which members are characteristically less tolerant of sexual deprivation, etc., but both of which must live together in a common locale? What structural outcomes can then be predicted under given technological and other related circumstances? What form will the social processes within and between these collectivities take? If we started coldly, without tittering, to ask how the sexual nature of the bond between members of the two collectivities resembled, or differed from, other kinds of bonds between members of other collectivities, taking nothing for granted, we might see many things more clearly. I am not, of course, seriously proposing that we begin with this datum, but I would be happy if the idea produced even a minuscule shift in at least one person's perspective.

Sociology as a male science of society.—No attempt is made here to explain the male bias in the subject matter sociologists deal with except to note that it is not wholly due to selective perception or limited perspective. It seems to be related also to methodological and technical predilections, for, as we have been reminded so often, we tend to choose our problems on the basis of available techniques rather than on the basis of intrinsic importance. In sociology, as in psychology, a masculine bias has been embedded in the structure of inquiry; the most prestigious methods have tended to be those that yielded "hard" data. And thereby hangs a most interesting tale, a tale of the part played by what might well be called a *machismo* factor in research.

Carlson (1971), a psychologist, has found that the classification of research approaches proposed by Bakan (1972) into "agency" and "communion" can be validated on the basis of several studies she has made. Agency tends to see variables,[34] communion to see human beings. Agentic research tends to see sex as a variable, communal research to see women as people.[35] Agency has to do with separation, repression, conquest, and contract; communion with fusion, expression, acceptance, noncontractual cooperation. Agency operates by way of mastery and control; communion with naturalistic observation, sensitivity to qualitative patterning, and greater personal participation by the investigator (Carlson 1972). Nothing in this polarity is fundamentally new. For almost 50 years I have watched one or another version of it in sociology.[36]

What is new and illuminating, however, is the recognition of a *machismo* element in research. The specific processes involved in agentic research are typically male preoccupations; agency is identified with a masculine principle, the Protestant ethic, a Faustian pursuit of knowledge—as with all forces toward mastery, separation, and ego enhancement (Carlson 1972). The scientist using this approach creates his own controlled reality. He can manipulate it. He is master. He has power. He can add or subtract or combine variables. He can play with a simulated reality like an Olympian god. He can remain at a distance, safely invisible behind his shield, uninvolved. The communal approach is much humbler. It disavows control, for control spoils the results. Its value rests precisely on the absence of controls. Jane van Lawick-Goodall (1971), observing primates in their natural habitat, imposed no controls on their life-style. She dealt with a quite different reality from that of H. P. Harlow in his laboratory.

In psychology, the research topics for which the agentic approach is most suitable have been such characteristically male variables as ego strength, reality orientation, objectivity, and delay of gratification. Carlson found corroboration of this observation in a study comparing work by men and by women psychologists: men preferred the agentic, women the communal approach. These findings and insights help to explain why, for reasons no one has yet formally explicated but which, I believe, most of us intuit, the agentic approach which yields "hard" data tends to have more prestige than the communal, which yields "soft" data. Apart from the double entendre in "hard" and "soft" data, one reason is that, as in all societies, what men do is valued more highly than what women do. Problems for which the agentic approach is appropriate attract males and hence have higher status than those for which the communal approach is suitable. Until recently, in fact, many have argued that the agentic approach was the only scientific approach.[37]

There has been no analysis of sociological research comparable to Carlson's in psychology.[38] But in a paper on "The Methods of Sociology," Coleman (1969, pp. 109-10) is quite optimistic about such agentic research techniques as quantitative measures and indices, improved techniques, social indicators, and laboratory experiments. Unhappily, he is skeptical about the future of such communal techniques as observation of social behavior in situ. Like Carlson, Coleman (1969, p. 86) speaks of "missing research methods that truncate sociology, and cause some important problems of the discipline and other problems important to society, to languish relatively unexplored." He finds sociologists inhibited from asking themselves fundamental questions about what problems are important ones to sociology, their vision narrowly restricted, their horizons limited" (Coleman 1969, p. 113).[39]

The relevance of these comments lies in the fact that, since the agentic approach has more prestige, a disproportionately large amount of research has been invested in the sociology of sex as a variable and a correspondingly smaller amount in the sociology of women as a collectivity, or as simply people. A great deal of research focuses on men with no reference at all to women; but when research is focused on women, it is almost always with reference to men. If comparisons are not made with men, the research is viewed as incomplete. Research on women in their own right, without reference to a male standard, is not viewed as worthy of male attention. Notice how uniformly journals assign books about women to female reviewers.

I close this truncated discussion of the way research mode affects choice of topics and findings with a personal example of the moral it points. In my book on academic women, "controlling" as many variables as I could, I was unable, by the agentic method (which is peculiarly inappropriate for research on the subtleties of interaction between the sexes), to document discrimination against women (Bernard 1964, chap. 3). Later researchers, going beyond one of my major "controls"—proportion of women in the qualified pool—explained by way of the communal approach why there were, relatively, so few women in it in terms of all the hurdles women had to overcome to arrive at the qualified pool.[40]

The implications of these comments is not that only women can study female reality. Or even that all women can, for women have been so trained to accept the male definition of almost every situation, to accept the reality constructed by men, that it takes a considerable amount of consciousness raising to get them to construct their own, even to believe in it. And even when the "conversion" takes place, it requires reinforcement to maintain the new consciousness. For the present, only sociologists whose consciousness has been raised will be able to deal adequately with the realities so urgently demanding study. Among them there will doubtless be some men, especially among those who have been so assiduously studying how to "become"—reality constructionists, marijuana users, world savers, nudists, and deviants. It should be no harder for men to "become" feminists than for them to "become" deviant in other ways.

In the meanwhile, I agree with Carlson who concludes that "by achieving liberation from the constraints of 'agentic' modes of inquiry and developing the 'communal' aspects of content and method, women [and their male confreres] may succeed in bringing forth those new research paradigms needed for the scientific revolution" (Carlson 1972) which will make sociology a genuine science of society.

ENVOI

All four of my revolutions have been important, necessary, and, I believe, have had a benign effect on our discipline. In the case of the first three, the evidence is in. It was essential for sociology in the 1920s that the ASS give official recognition to the importance of empirical research along with the grand conceptualizing of the early giants. It was essential that sociology be emancipated from the control, however benign, of one university, that the American Sociological Society achieve independence from the University of Chicago, great as that university was and great as its role as alma mater had been. It was essential that the neglect of social problems and policy be corrected, that the uncritical placing of sociological research know-how at the disposal of industry be criticized, that sociologists be protected against McCarthyism in the 1950s, that the Society for the Study of Social Problems shake its fist at the American Sociological Association. The American Sociological Association is a better organization and sociology itself a more adequate discipline as a result of these three revolutions.

Returns on the success of the fourth revolution are not yet all in. So far as the activist phase in the profession is concerned, it has been remarkably successful. The Rossi resolutions were favorably received; a Committee on the Status of Women was appointed; a section on the sociology of sex roles was established which will provide the matrix for important contributions to the needed expansion of our discipline. Much of this knowledge will be useful in helping to free women in society from the handicaps of discrimi-nation. Now the question is, Will the harder phase—that of reorienting the paradigms to take account of women—be equally successful?

The reaction of sociologists, male and female, to the theoretical and methodological challenge of the fourth revolution will test the validity of its critique. Will they slough off the challenges as trivial, a passing fad, unwor-thy of serious professional attention? Will they impose a male test, namely, What will meeting the challenges add to our knowledge or potential for control and power? If not, why bother?

I would hope for at least some "conversions"; for a bemused "How about that?" or a friendly "They've got something there." And even if some reject the challenges, the fourth revolution will have achieved at least a modicum of success if it leads them to ask themselves if their writing would be any different if it included women; if, for example, instead of the generic "mankind," they had to say "humankind?" If, instead of the generic "man," they had to say "human being"?[41] If every generalization they made about the way societies operate had to include the ways the female component fit in?

Or if, on a more practical level, they remembered that the brilliant young women they talked to at meetings knew as much sociology as they did, if not more, so that they did not patronize them and, above all, did not try to co-opt them by flattery or put them down by ignoring them.

NOTES

1. This paper is not to be confused with another with a similar title (see Bernard 1966).

2. See Bernard and Bernard (1943, pts. 10-12).

3. Much of the documentary material on this revolution is available in the L. L. Bernard papers in the archives of Pennsylvania State University, in charge of Ronald Fillipelli.

4. The nucleus for this organization was a group of faculty members of Brooklyn College, esp. Alfred McClung Lee, Elizabeth Bryant Lee, Sylvia Fleis Fava, and Barbara Mintz Mishkin, all of whom invested great blocks of time as well as financial support. In a way, this revolution might be viewed as a corrective to oversuccess of the first.

5. In the early years there were several meetings with our counterparts in psychology and anthropology, the Society for the Psychological Study of Social Issues, and Applied Anthropol-ogy.

6. The journal, *Social Problems,* flaunted among its advisory editors such luminaries as the older Howard Becker, E. F. Frazier, John P. Gillin, A. Irving Hallowell, Otto Klineberg, Clyde Kluckhohn, Max Lerner, Abraham H. Maslow, Francis E. Merrill, Robert K. Merton, and Robin M. Williams, Jr. Although C. Wright Mills was the ideological patron saint—an award in his honor was later established—he was not actively involved in SSSP.

7. We demanded representation in the International Sociological Association, for example, and refused to accept second-class status in that body.

8. I fear that SSSP has run out of innovativeness. The New University Conference has come to preempt many of SSSP's issues and has shoved them to the left.

9. For a personal account of that organizational meeting, see my letter in the first issue of the *SWS Newsletter,* 1971.

10. Marlene Dixon was the leader of this group. Since in her view it was the duty of sociology to put research at the service of the oppressed instead of, as now, their oppressors, women, as among the oppressed, constituted an important area for research. Her success was so limited that, in a paper (1970) on "The Failure of the Sociology Liberation Movement," she washed her hands of sociology as an arm of revolution. Her disillusion was complete. The first public professional statement of the sociology-as-servant-of-the-ruling-class-against-the-oppressed was made by Jack Nicklaus at the Boston, 1968, meetings of the ASA. (It sounded strangely like Alfred McClung Lee's strictures in the SSSP almost 20 years earlier.) Dixon was bitterly disappointed in the sequelae. Clever strategy by power wielders, she concluded, had deflected the thrust of the radicals and turned radical sociology into a form of career hustling or radical profiteering which perpetuated the myth that one could have a career in sociology and still remain radical: "Our experience since the first Sociology Liberation Movement in Boston is clear: if you sleep with dogs you'll pick up fleas." (Like so many of the ephemera of radical writers, this mimeographed paper bears no date. It was distributed at the ASA meetings in 1970.) I must say that, abrasive as I find Dixon's style to be, I regret that the fourth revolution will not have the needling her polemics supply.

11. See Ferriss (1971, pp. 1-2) for possible reasons.

12. Some of the anomalies have to do with the changing sexual allocation of functions in our society (Bernard 1971*b,* passim).

13. Merely clearing up stereotypes about women is a major research contribution. Among the sources of the feminist movement that Ferris (1971) specifies are the studies of women made during the 1960s. They supplied polemic tracts with factual support.

14. Women psychologists also look for a similar revolution in their discipline (see Carlson 1972).

15. For a brief overview of the Women's Liberation Movement, see Bernard (1971*b,* pt. 5).

16. Young (1971, p. 279) illustrates its use in teaching students the invisible, taken-for-granted aspects of trust, for example, by challenging it in some relationship. Pioneer activists in the Women's Liberation Movement, similarly, challenged the invisible, taken-for-granted aspects of the relations between the sexes by violating them. They parodied some of them by outdoing men in the use of obscenities, in aggressive, nonsupportive responses. They refused to play according to the prescribed male script. Thus when David Susskind and Dick Cavett insisted that their women guests talk about the book they wanted them to talk about, women refused. They had become alerted to the conventionalized traps used to control them. The men were nonplussed because the women were not responding according to their design. The men were accustomed to prettily yielding women or prettily protesting women—equally flattering in either case. A woman's eyewitness description of the conventional scenario for relations even between professional sociologists is presented by Geraldine Mintz, pseud. (1967, pp. 158-59).

17. The intention may be quite hidden in the original assumptions and premises which make only the intended implications logical. Thus Parsons's (1959, pp. 262 ff.) analysis of the integration of the family and occupational systems rests on certain basic assumptions about the primary allegiance of men and women to their respective worlds, assumptions which lead logically to his conclusion that integration of the two worlds calls for role segregation. Coser and Rokoff (1971, p. 552) explore the possibilities which can occur if the basic assumption about the primary allegiances of the sexes is not granted. Their results are not the same as Parsons's.

18. Friedan (1963, p. 127) set the pattern for this critique of functionalism. For recent examples, see the August and October 1971 issues of *Journal of Marriage and the Family* and the November-December 1970 issue of *Trans-Action.*

19. Not all, though. In a brilliant tour de force, Gronseth (1971) showed point for point how the present sexual status quo is dysfunctional for society as a whole.

20. Caroline Rose makes the following comment here: "I don't think Arnold's criticism of interactionism as neglecting power applies to the example you give; interactionism would

certainly handle power and conflict relations between or among groups" (personal letter, June 30, 1972).

21. Hanisch (1971, p. 2) rejects this preoccupation with roles and socialization. She views it as a diversionary tactic, distracting attention from the real—power—basis for the position of women. She finds that male social scientists can cheerfully accept the socialization interpretation of the status of women because they gain greatly in substituting the socialization paradigm for a power paradigm. She specifies in detail the male gain from this substitution.

22. In their work on Blau's statement on exchange theory, Marie Osmond and Patricia Martin demonstrate the sexist bias in it by the use of simulation and, incidentally, show that "sexist behavior, regardless of social psychological attitudes, is a response to the structure of the game (social system) and the rules (norms) of play (interaction); and that a change in game structure and rules results in a change in game-behavior."

23. For a discussion of such relations, see Bernard (1968, passim).

24. Note, for example, the complacency of Parsons's (1949, p. 223) that "it is quite clear that in the adult feminine role there is quite sufficient strain and insecurity so that widespread manifestations are to be expected in the form of neurotic behavior." For his statement that "absolute equality of opportunity is clearly incompatible with any positive solidarity of the family" (Parsons 1949, p. 174).

25. Many of the paradigms developed in the West have not proved successful in the Third World (Bernard 1973, chap. 9).

26. Among the factual issues mentioned by her are knowledge of the undervalued role of fathers, the social origins of misogyny, female social mobility, the structured strain for women built into our society, the power relationships behind ordinary customs and personality traits, the change in sex differences in the several stages of the life cycle.

27. For example, white social scientists have asked the questions about blacks that concerned them: the female-headed family, out-of-wedlock births, sexual mores, control. Black men have asked questions about powerlessness, race pride, genocide. Do the data dredged up by the two lines of questioning constitute the same science in both cases? What if one asks how white people can maintain their power over blacks (Blalock 1967, pp. 153-54) and the other how black people can achieve power over whites? Will the same technique fit both questions? Will they arrive at the same kinds of generalizations?

28. Sociology is not alone in the male bias of its questions. Bart (1972) specifies areas in other disciplines dominated by a male perspective: research on contraception is overwhelmingly oriented to techniques which assign responsibility to women; the management of childbirth and breast-feeding; the psychoanalytic theory of depression; and field-independence-field-dependence research in psychology which assumes that field-independence, more characteristic of males, is superior to field-dependence in perception.

29. Kraditor (1968) has assembled some delineations of "women's sphere" in the 19th century; even today the idea of a "women's world" dominates the thinking of Madison Avenue. Sometimes the two worlds are delineated in terms of home or family and work (Henderson and Parsons 1947), sometimes in terms of subcultures (LeMasters 1957; Ann Battle-Sister 1971), and sometimes in terms of "place" (Epstein 1970).

30. Only by definition do interactions in a status world constitute exchanges. We speak glibly of the give-and-take of marriage, but research shows that women make more adjustments than men. Interesting to note is the superiority, according to Richard Titmuss, of the blood gathered and distributed on a love/duty basis as in England over blood in this country where it is bought and sold on an exchange basis.

31. A status world tends to be characterized by the first component of the five Parsonian variables: ascription, diffuseness, particularism, collectivity orientation, and affectivity; the cash-nexus world by their counterparts: achievement, specificity, universalism, self-orientation,

and emotional neutrality (Bernard 1971*b*, pp. 24-25). In the cash-nexus world competition is the preferred way to allocate rewards, and the best man wins; in the status world everyone's needs are taken care of to the extent possible.

32. Thus, for example, in a—deservedly—award-winning treatise on the American occupational structure, the two-fifths of the labor force constituted of women are excluded. Women appear only as contributors to husbands' careers (Blau and Duncan 1967, chap. 10. See also résumé of current research on the same topic by Mary Salpukas). A glance at the Parsons-Shils source book on sociological theories also shows how pervasive this one-sided orientation has been in sociology. From precursors like Hobbes, Locke, Rousseau, and even Adam Smith to recent times, one gets a picture of society as constituted entirely of men. "Man" does this; "men" believe that. Half of the human species is invisible. Men are furiously interacting with one another, but one catches hardly a glimpse of any woman. The economists have been more candid and forthright. They state at the outset that they deal only with the cash-nexus world. This permits them to exclude the enormous contribution that housewives make, not because these services are dispensable for the operation of the economy—they would have to be supplied by industry if housewives did not perform them—but because they are not monetized. Sociologists have not specified that most of their paradigms also fit only that cash-nexus world. Kenneth Boulding (in press) helps to fill in the gap with what he calls the "grants economy." Like all good economists he had always recognized that market economics was extremely limited; but unlike them he undertook to analyze the nonmarket or "grants economy," with interesting results: he re-discovered sociology. "The key to a theoretical approach to the grants economy . . . must lie . . . in the theory of the integrative structure of society. Grants fall into place as a perfectly normal, reasonable element of social life, once we realize that they give us a first-approximation measure of the structure of integrative relationships in society. We are familiar with the concept of 'an economy,' which is that part of the total social system that is organized by exchanges. We are less familiar with the concept of an 'integry,' which is that part of the total social system which deals with such concepts and relationships as status, identity, community, legitimacy, loyalty, love, trust, and so on. Nevertheless, this is a distinct segment of the social system with a dynamics of its own, and strong interactions with other elements of the social system" (Boulding 1969, p. 4). It is this "grants economy" which women for the most part inhabit and which has been neglected by male sociologists. Boulding develops the concept of the "sacrifice trap," showing how objects become sacred because they are sacrificed to rather than the other way round. All sacrifices are not grants, but all grants are sacrifices.

33. For example, when Parsons (1959, pp. 262 ff.) tackles the problem of how the two systems are integrated, he concludes that, because they are governed by such different norms, integration occurs only if just one member in a marriage participates in the work world. Coser and Rokoff (1971, p. 552) call instead for a redefinition of life goals. They conclude (as I have done also) that shared roles in marriage are not only possible but eufunctional and may actually increase family cohesion. Papanek's (1971) analysis of purdah in Pakistan is almost a model of viewing the status and the cash-nexus worlds as parts of a total society.

34. Bakan (1972, p. 28) refers to the variable approach as a fact-module approach which views human behavior "in terms of specific variables, each of which could be studied separately, yet which, in conjunction, would ultimately 'explain' man and predict his behavior. With statistical tests of significance, one presumably could identify the relationships among variables, factoring out the noise of other uncontrolled variables. It was believed that when psychologists identified all possible relationships, of course, all such noise would be eliminated."

35. Even as a variable, sex is usually seen in connection with variables that interest men more than women, such as aggression, achievement, and others having to do with power or control. There are far more studies on aggression and achievement than on love and tenderness. Females have thus been forced into inappropriate categories so that they have turned out to be merely

non-men, and "different" has been read as "deficient." Psychological inquiry has therefore been "constricted and manipulative" and precluded from studying individuals except as "carriers" of variables of immediate interest to the—usually male—experimenter (Carlson 1972).

36. For example: statistical vs. case method, quantitative vs. qualitative, knowledge vs. understanding or *verstehen,* tough-minded vs. tender-minded, and so on. These poles as related to methods have been paralleled by such conceptual polarities as *Gemeinschaft* and *Gesellschaft,* expressive and instrumental, status and cash nexus, and so on.

37. The small coterie with expertise in quantitative and, especially, in mathematical agentic techniques have been able to exert disproportionate influence on the direction of the social-and behavioral-science disciplines. Proponents of the communal approach tend to be on the defensive. Once the *machismo* factor in research was called to my attention, a host of illustrations of how it operates to intimidate others crowded my memory. For example, the social scientist reduced to a pulp at a committee meeting evaluating grant proposals, when he argued in favor of a "soft" project. His willingness to defend it was used to denigrate him by techniques which only a master of communal research like Erving Goffman could do justice to. Or the faculty member who voted to accept a "soft" dissertation made to feel, as he put it, utterly incompetent. Or the editor, intimidated by his agentic referee, who rejected a manuscript because the analysis was not "hard" enough—no multiple regression equations, for example. He was more afraid of the disapproval of his agentic than of his communal constituencies. A standard criticism of the communal approach is that the data it yields are less replicable because they depend so much on the unique personality of the researcher. Isn't it, the criticism continues, more like art, idiosyncratic, a unique "vision" more than a testable scientific observation? The initial "vision" or "insight" is, indeed, as in most scientific innovations, much like that of the artist. But beyond that the communal method is not uniquely different from established procedures. The freshman looking through the microscope can rarely see what his professor tells him he should see. The laboratory manual is not replicable. For all he can tell, the professor could be making it all up. It takes some learning—even consciousness raising—to be able to see what the professor wants him to see. Who, for example, was able to see "lurk-lines," "body gloss," "interaction synchrony," "loller's tuck" (my favorite), before Erving Goffman (1971), like the professor in the laboratory, taught us to see them. With these "sensitizing concepts," even the most dyed-in-the-wool practitioner of agentic techniques can learn to observe them. The analogy with research on women is clear. Until women made clear a score of behavioral patterns that were visible to them but not to men, it was impossible for men to research them. Once attention had been called to them, the evidence of "oppression"—the fact that avant garde women had to use such a pejorative concept is a good example of the inadequacy of our conceptual tool kit—could be made visible to everyone. And I do not doubt that the agentic approach will, in the not-too-distant future, be invoked to study it. Opening up this enormous area in interpersonal relations is one of the major contributions the fourth revolution can make to our discipline.

38. Except, perhaps, in the study of community power structure, in which the part played by research methods has been reported to be related to kinds of communities selected for study and hence to the results obtained (Bernard 1973, chap. 5).

39. Coleman (1969, pp. 105-6) illustrates what he calls "research lacunae" with such examples as changes in the relation of youth to adult society and the increasing age segregation of the age. But he has not a word about women. This oversight by a master research sociologist is thought provoking.

40. Much of this research is summarized in Roby (1972) and Rossi (1972). I hasten to save face by noting that I did recognize the importance of what I called the "stag effect" in accounting for scientific productivity (Bernard 1964, pp. 157, 302). I should add that my interest in that book was more in the sociology of knowledge than in the status of women in academia.

41. Or "men and women," as Mills (1959, p. 225) did in the passage noted above.

REFERENCES

Bakan, David. 1972. "Psychology Can Now Kick the Science Habit." *Psychology Today* 5 (March): 26, 28, 86-88.

Bart, Pauline. 1972. "Why Women's Studies?" In *Female Studies IV,* edited by Ray Siporin. Pittsburgh: KNOW.

Battle-Sister, Ann. 1971. "Conjectures on the Female Culture Question." *Journal of Marriage and the Family* 33 (August): 411-20.

Bernard, Jessie. 1950. "Can Science Transcend Culture?" *Scientific Monthly* 71 (October): 268-73.

————. 1964. *Academic Women.* University Park: Pennsylvania State University Press. Reprint. New York: Meridian Press, 1966.

————. 1966. "The Fourth Revolution." *Journal of Social Issues* 23 (April): 76-87.

————. 1968. *The Sex Game.* Englewood Heights, N.J.: Prentice-Hall. Reprint. New York: Atheneum Press, 1972.

————. 1971a. "The Paradox of the Happy Marriage." In *Women in Sexist Society,* edited by Vivian Gornick and Barbara Moran. New York: Basic Books.

————. 1971b. Women and the Public Interest: An Essay on Policy and Protest. Chicago: Aldine-Atherton.

————. 1972. *The Future of Marriage.* New York: World.

————. 1973. *The Sociology of Community.* Glenview, Ill.: Scott, Foresman.

Bernard, L. L., and Jessie Bernard. 1943. *Origins of American Sociology.* New York: Crowell. Reprint. New York: Russell & Russell, 1965.

Blalock, Hubert M., Jr. 1967. *Toward a Theory of Minority-Group Relations.* New York: Wiley.

Blau, Peter. 1964. *Exchange and Power in Social Life.* New York: Wiley.

Blau, Peter M., and Otis Dudley Duncan. 1967. *The American Occupational Structure.* New York: Wiley.

Boulding, Kenneth E. 1969. "The Grants Economy." *Michigan Academician* 1 (Winter): 4, 5.

————. In press. *The Economy of Love and Fear: A Preface to Grants Economics.* Belmont, Calif.: Wadsworth Publishing Company.

Broverman, Inge K., Donald M. Broverman, Frank E. Charlson, Paul S. Rosenkrantz, and Susan R. Vogel. 1970. "Sex-Role Stereotypes and Clinical Judgments of Mental Health." *Journal of Consulting and Clinical Psychology* 34 (February): 1-7.

Carlson, Rae. 1971. "Sex Differences in Ego Functioning: Exploratory Studies of Agency and Communion." *Journal of Consulting and Clinical Psychology* 37 (April): 267-77.

————. 1972. "Understanding Women: Implications for Personality Theory and Research." *Journal of Social Issues* 28(2).

Chmaj, Betty E. 1971. *American Women and American Studies.* Pittsburgh: KNOW.

Coleman, James S. 1969. "The Methods of Sociology. In *A Design for Sociology: Scope, Objectives, and Methods,* edited by Robert Bierstedt. Monograph no. 9, American Academy Political and Social Science. Philadelphia: American Academy of Political and Social Science.

Coser, Rose, and Gerald Rokoff. 1971. "Women in the Occupational World: Social Disruption and Conflict." *Social Problems* 18 (Spring): 535-54.

Dixon, Marlene. 1970. "The Failure of the Sociology Liberation Movement." Mimeographed.

Elder, Glen H., Jr. 1969. "Appearance and Education in Marriage Mobility." *American Sociological Review* 34 (August): 519-32.

Epstein, Cynthia. 1970. *Man's World Woman's Place.* Berkeley: University of California Press.

Ferriss, Abbott L. 1971. *Indicators of Trends in the Status of American Women.* New York: Russell Sage.

Friedan, Betty. 1963. *The Feminine Mystique*. New York: Norton.

Garfinkel, Harold. 1967. *Studies in Ethnomethodology*. Englewood Cliffs, N.J.: Prentice-Hall.

Goffman, Erving. 1971. *Relations in Public: Microstudies of the Public Order*. New York: Basic.

Greenwald, Maurine. 1971. "On Teaching Women's History." In *American Women and American Studies*, edited by Betty E. Chmaj. Pittsburgh: KNOW.

Gronseth, Eric. 1971. "The Dysfunctionality of the Husband Provider Role in Industrialized Societies." Paper prepared for International Sociological Association, Varna.

Hanisch, Carol. 1971. "Male Psychology: A Myth to Keep Women in Their Place." *Women's World* 1 (July-August): 2.

Henderson, A. M., and Talcott Parsons, trans. 1947. "Introduction." In *The Theory of Social and Economic Organization*, by Max Weber. New York: Free Press.

Hochschild, Arlie. 1970. "The American Woman: Another Idol of Social Science." *Trans-Action* 8 (November-December): 13-14.

Horner, Matina. 1969. "Fail: Bright Women." *Psychology Today* 3 (November): 36, 38, 69.

Jones, Beverley. 1970. "The Dynamics of Marriage and Motherhood." In *Sisterhood Is Powerful*, edited by Robin Morgan. New York: Vintage.

Kraditor, Aileen. 1968. *Up from the Pedestal*. Chicago: Quadrangle.

LeMasters, E. E. 1957. *Modern Courtship and Marriage*. New York: Macmillan.

Mainardi, Pat. 1970. "The Politics of Housework." In *Sisterhood Is Powerful*, edited by Robin Morgan. New York: Vintage.

Mills, C. Wright. 1959. *The Sociological Imagination*. New York: Oxford.

Mintz, Geraldine (pseud.). 1967. "Some Observations on the Function of Women Sociologists at Sociology Conventions." *American Sociologist* 2 (August): 158-59.

Osmond, Marie, and Patricia Martin. "From Closed to Open Systems: Game Simulation of Sex Role Behavior." Unpublished manuscript.

Papanek, Hanna. 1971. "Purdah in Pakistan: Seclusion and Modern Occupations for Women." *Journal of Marriage and Family* 33 (August): 517-30.

Parsons, Talcott. 1949. "Age and Sex in the Social Structure of the United States." In *Essays in Sociological Theory*. New York: Free Press.

———. 1959. "The Social Structure of the Family." In *The Family: Its Function and Destiny*, edited by Ruth Nanda Anshen. New York: Harper.

Roby, Pamela. 1972. "Institutional and Internalized Barriers to Women in Higher Education." In *Toward a Sociology of Women*, edited by Constantina Safilios-Rothschild. Lexington, Mass.: Xerox College Publishing.

Rose, Arnold, ed. 1962. "Preface." In *Human Behavior and Social Processes*. Boston: Houghton-Mifflin.

Rossi, Alice, ed. 1972. *Academic Women on the Move*. New York: Russell Sage.

Salpukas, Mary. 1972. "The Man Who Gets Ahead: Being Married Really Helps." *New York Times*, July 24.

van Lawick-Goodall, Jane. 1971. *In the Shadow of Man*. Boston: Houghton-Mifflin.

Wyckoff, Hogie. 1971. "The Stroke Economy in Women's Scripts." *Journal of Transactional Analysis* 1 (July): 3.

Young, T. R. 1971. "The Politics of Sociology: Gouldner, Goffman, and Garfinkel." *American Sociologist* 6 (November): 276-81.

2 Women and Social Stratification: A Case of Intellectual Sexism[1]

JOAN ACKER
University of Oregon

In the last 10 years, empirical studies and speculative discussions on the disadvantaged status of women have increased rapidly. Although social inequality is the subject matter of social stratification studies, little of this work on the position of women has been done by sociologists in the field of social stratification.[2] Indeed, sex has rarely been analyzed as a factor in stratification processes and structures,[3] although it is probably one of the most obvious criteria of social differentiation and one of the most obvious bases of economic, political, and social inequalities. Very few sociologists have even recognized that we have, with the exception of the study of the family, constructed a sociology that tends to deal with only the male half of humanity.

The inclusion of the female half of humanity and of sex as a central dimension in the study of society would lead to a more accurate picture of social structure and to a better understanding of process. However, serious consideration of sex as a central social factor will require reconceptualization in many areas of sociology. Problems of concept and method which arise in the field of social stratification when women are assumed to be significant participants in society are the subject of this paper. I discuss, first, the assumptions in stratification literature about the social position of women; second, some problems of reconceptualization; and, third, some contributions to the understanding of society which may result from studying women in the stratification system.

"Women and Social Stratification: A Case of Intellectual Sexism" by Joan Acker, in *American Journal of Sociology,* Vol. 78, No. 4, pp. 936-945. © 1973 by University of Chicago. Reprinted with permission.

ASSUMPTIONS ABOUT WOMEN AND STRATIFICATION

In stratification literature, six assumptions are made, sometimes explicitly and sometimes implicitly, about the social position of women. These are most clearly stated by the functionalists but are present also in the work of nonfunctionalists and Marxists.[4] These assumptions are:

1. The family is the unit in the stratification system.
2. The social position of the family is determined by the status of the male head of the household.
3. Females live in families; therefore, their status is determined by that of the males to whom they are attached.
4. The female's status is equal to that of her man, at least in terms of her position in the class structure, because the family is a unit of equivalent evaluation (Watson and Barth 1964).
5. Women determine their own social status only when they are not attached to a man.
6. Women are unequal to men in many ways, are differentially evaluated on the basis of sex, but this is irrelevant to the structure of stratification systems.

The first assumption, that the family is the unit in stratification, is basic to the other five. Together, these assumptions neatly dispense with the necessity for considering the position of women in studies of social stratification or considering the salience of sex as a dimension of stratification.[5] To put it another way, the fate of the female in the class system is determined by the fate of the male. Therefore, it is only necessary to study males.

How adequate are these assumptions? There are, I believe, deficiencies of both logic and validity which I will discuss briefly.

1. *The family is the unit in the stratification system.*—The choice of the family as the unit may be based on the belief that all persons live in families. This is obviously not true, since 11% of the population over age 18 is categorized as unattached individuals in 1970 data.[6] This assumption also rests on the validity of the other five assumptions, which I examine in the following paragraphs.

2. *The social position of the family is determined by the status of the male head of the household.*—This is a researchable question which has been little researched. Instead, empirical researchers often imply an answer to this question in their choice of indicators of class or status position. Thus, if family income is chosen as an indicator, there is an implication that total family resources determine standing. If class placement is measured by occupation alone or an index including occupation, the occupation of the

male head of household is invariably used, implying that his position does decide that of the family.[7]

There is one situation in which the second assumption is clearly invalid. The position of the family cannot be determined by the male head if there is no male head of the household. This is the case in a substantial proportion of American families. On the basis of the 1960 census, Watson and Barth (1964) estimated that approximately two-fifths of the households in the United States do not have a male head, in the sense implied by the traditional model of the small nuclear family. They found that two-fifths of the households were either "females or female headed households or husband-wife families in which the husband is retired or otherwise not in the labor force, is unemployed, or is working only part time."

3. *Females live in families; therefore, their status is determined by that of the males to whom they are attached.*—This assumption may be challenged on the grounds that all females do not live in families. Further, the assumption that a woman's status is determined by that of the man to whom she is attached implies that women have no status resources of their own. In a society in which women, as well as men, have resources of education, occupation, and income, it is obviously not true that women have no basis for determining their own status. If women do have such resources, why do we assume that they are inoperative if the woman is married? It is inconsistent to rank an unmarried woman on the basis of her education and occupation and then maintain that these factors are of no importance to her social status or class placement after she gets married the next day.[8] However, such an abrupt alteration of the criteria of class placement at the time of a shift in marital status is necessary if we are to accept the assumption that only women without men determine their own social status.

4. *The female's status is equal to that of her man.*—Once we question the assumption that the woman's status is determined by the man, we must also question the assumption that the status of the female is equal to that of her male. Of course, wife and husband may be equal, but equivalent evaluation can no longer be assumed.

Even if all females had no independent, status-creating resources, the equality of their status with that of their husbands would still be in question. Equality can be assessed on numerous dimensions. Prestige in the community, style of life, privileges, opportunities, association with social groups, income, education, occupation, and power might all be considered in evaluating the equality of husband and wife in the class structure. Occupation, equated by the functionalists with full-time, functionally important social role, is often used as the indicator of position for men. However, the full-time occupation of many women, that of housewife-mother, is never considered as a ranking criterion in stratification studies. Are we to conclude that this role is either not functionally important or not a full-time activity, or are we to conclude that only those activities which are directly rewarded financially can bestow status upon the individual or the family? Perhaps this is another question which could be explored through empirical research. There is some research evidence to suggest that housewives whose husbands work in a given occupation have less prestige than women who themselves are employed in the same occupation (Haavio-Mannila 1969). However, the evidence to support or refute the assumption of equal status in regard to the class structure is unfortunately sparse.

5. *Women determine their own social status only when they are not attached to a man.*—This assumption can be interpreted as a way of coping with the inconvenient fact that some women are not married or living in the household of a male relative.

6. *Women are at a disadvantage in hierarchies of wealth, power, and prestige, but this fact is irrelevant to the study of stratification systems.*— This assumption is implicit in the stratification literature. I draw this conclusion from, on the one hand, the scant attention to the situation of women in the stratification literature, and, on the other hand, the existence of ample evidence that women are excluded from the higher positions of power, that they earn less than men, and that they are present in very small proportions in the more prestigious occupations.

But, perhaps, the position of women is irrelevant to the structure of the larger system. I don't think so. For example, female-headed households account for almost 40% of those below the poverty line (Ferriss 1970). This statistic suggests that the economic and social disadvantages of being female may have an impact on class differentials in family structure. When stratification theorists talk about some classes, they are talking about women to a large extent. It is possible that some of the differences they discuss are sex rather than class differences. These differences may, for example, have an effect upon mobility patterns and the permeability of class boundaries, thus affecting the larger system in complex ways.

In sum, it is not adequate or useful to assume that females have no relevant role in stratification processes independent of their family roles and their ties to particular men. If this conclusion is reasonable, a reconsideration of sex status and stratification is indicated.

As a first step in such a reconsideration, I make the following assumptions:

1. Sex is an enduring ascribed characteristic which (*a*) has an effect upon the evaluation of persons and positions, and (*b*) is the basis of the persisting sexual division of labor and of sex-based inequalities.

2. The sex dichotomy cuts across all classes and strata. (This is also true of ethnicity and race.)

MODELS OF STRATIFICATION AND SEX

A number of conceptual issues arise when sex is considered a relevant stratification variable. One of these issues is, Can inequalities based on sex be integrated into a conceptual model of stratification systems? The traditional view of classes as aggregates occupying similar positions in relationship to the means of production or similar positions in one or more hierarchies of wealth, power, or prestige has made it difficult to deal with inequalities which cut across class lines. It has been easier to assume, as Watson and Barth point out, that the family is a unit, that all members of the family are equally evaluated, and that, therefore, it is not important to investigate the status of women.

Some current developments in the study of social stratification may make it easier to give serious consideration to sex inequalities. For example, there is a trend toward expanding the study of stratification to include a wide variety of structured social inequalities (Heller 1969). Similarly, there is a trend away from exclusive concern with the classic definitions of class and toward a concern with the individual as a unit. Although this trend began a number of years ago, it now seems to have establishment blessing even in the person of Parsons. A recent review article notes, "he [Parsons] also poses some serious objection to the relevance of classic definitions of class in the analysis of modern societies, arguing . . . that the unit of class stratification can no longer be usefully taken to be the family but a man's complex of ascribed and achieved collectivity memberships, including his organization memberships" (Laumann 1970).

Using the individual rather than the family as a unit, it may become possible to integrate sex into models of stratification systems in at least two ways: (1) as a dimension in stratification which cuts across class lines and produces two interrelated hierarchies of positions or persons, or (2) as a basis of evaluation which affects the placement of individuals in particular hierarchies.

An alternative solution to the problem of integrating sex-based inequalities into conceptual models of stratification systems would not require abandoning classic definitions of class. Females can be viewed as constituting caste-like groupings within social classes.[9] Female castes, using this approach, may have certain common interests and life-patterns. In addition, they may share certain disabilities and inequities. At the same time, female castes are imbedded in the class structure and each is affected by the class which envelops it. Class differences in ideology, life-chances, and life-style may obscure the identical nature of many structural factors affecting female castes.

STATUS AND CLASS:
CONCEPTUAL AND EMPIRICAL PROBLEMS

An additional conceptual problem can be stated as follows: If women are to be seen as persons rather than as appendages to males, how do we define their social status, particularly if they are not working for pay and cannot be categorized on the basis of their own occupation and income? Can value be assigned to productive work which is not paid labor?[10] This is a broader problem which also arises in trying to define the status of retired persons, of young people who are still students, of volunteers, and of the unemployed. It may eventually become a problem even in determining the status of adult men who are in the work force. If long-range predictions about the declining centrality of work and the increasing importance of nonwork activities in cybernated societies become reality, the relevance of paid occupation for class placement may decline, and other, unpaid activities may become more important as a source of social identity.

In the interim, one solution to the problem of defining women's social status is to view "housewife" as an occupation and to give it some sort of ranking in the hierarchy of occupations. Although the rankings of occupational status in current use, such as the North-Hatt Scale, do not include housewife as a category, new scales could be developed. I assume that this occupation would have a rather low ranking. This raises the interesting question of whether, and under what conditions, marriage constitutes downward social mobility and/or reduced mobility opportunities for women. At the same time, the value of "housewife" may vary with the socioeconomic stratum within which the position occurs. For example, the position of upper-class housewife may be much more highly valued in the overall structure than the position of lower-class housewife. It may be that the valuation of this position rises as its functions become more symbolic and less utilitarian.[11] Or, to put it another way, the value may rise as functions become centered more around consumption and less around productive activities. Within classes, however, the evaluation of housewife relative to other occupations open to females may vary in other ways.

Another partial solution to the problem of defining the status of women is to explore more thoroughly the notions of conferred status and deference entitlement (Shils 1968). Shils points out that "relative proximity to persons in powerful roles is [another] deference entitlement." Applied to the family, this means that the social position of the most powerful person in the family is, to an extent, reflected onto the other members of the family. Dependent women are among the most obvious recipients of this type of deference entitlement. This concept should not be confused with that of equivalent evaluation of all family members, based on the evaluation of the male head. There is no necessary implication that only the male family head determines status or class placement of family members. Some men may achieve entitlement to deference through their close relationship with a prestigious wife or mother. In addition, conferred status does not imply equivalent status. The status which is gained through close association with another person is probably a different order of deference entitlement than that which is gained more directly through characteristics or achievements of the individual herself. The recipient of conferred status in most cases probably does not have deference entitlements equivalent to those of the person whose proximity confers deference. With fewer status resources available, the recipient usually cannot reciprocate, and consequently as long as status is conferred must remain unequal to the person with greater resources.[12] This relationship between the bestower of status and the recipient is, in all probability, reflected in differential social evaluations.

To summarize, the position of the nonemployed wife may be determined by a combination of the ranking of housewife, conferred status, and pre-marriage deference entitlements belonging to the woman herself. The incorporation into sociology of the insight that sex does affect standing in the social structure would contribute to a more accurate picture of our society. Questions about social mobility and about power structures which are suggested when sex is taken as a salient variable illustrate this point.

Generalizations about social mobility patterns and trends on a societal level are based primarily on studies of white males (Blau and Duncan 1967). Since this group does not comprise even one-half of the population, the validity of the generalizations might be questioned. Of course, the choice of males as the proper subjects in the study of mobility is related to the assumption that female mobility is tied to male mobility. This derives from the assumptions discussed above and also pervades the literature. For example, Lopata (1971, p. 14) states, "The occupational ranking of the husbands of the women interviewed is generally higher than that of their fathers; thus the women had experienced upward mobility."

If the assumptions of female dependence were dropped, different patterns might emerge. For example, it would be interesting to look at intergenerational occupational mobility patterns of females, using the mother's status as the point of origin and using housewife as an occupational category. The findings from studies of this type might then be usefully combined with studies of mobility patterns and trends among white males to produce a much more complex and complete view of American mobility processes.

The few studies of intragenerational female mobility which have been made (Rubin 1968, 1969; Scott 1969; Elder 1969) focus on mobility through the contracting of a marriage. It would be just as reasonable to study mobility as the consequence of the dissolution of a marriage. Is there, for example, a greater probability of downward mobility for the woman who is divorced, deserted, or widowed than for the woman whose marriage is not disrupted? Some historical studies on this problem might also help to dissolve the notion that, even though the ideal nuclear family is not universal today, it was almost universal at some mythical time in our past. Although widespread divorce is a fairly recent phenomenon in the United States, dissolution of the nuclear family through death and desertion has probably always been with us. The deserving widow working hard in the boardinghouse to put her boys through school is a well-known mythical figure. It may be that the female-headed household was more prevalent in our past than we generally think. It may also be that, in some cases, this type of downward mobility for the woman contributed to the mobility strivings in her children.

A more complex and complete understanding of the structure of power and power relationships might also result from the recognition of the relevance of sex. For example, there may be a relationship between the position of women and the type of power system. This might be examined at the level of the local community as well as the level of the nation-state. In addition, cross-national comparisons of the position of women in societies which are undergoing rapid changes in class structure and the distribution of power might contribute to our understanding of larger social systems.

Conclusion: I have briefly indicated a number of conceptual and empirical questions which arise if we consider sex-based inequalities as salient to the structure of stratification systems. As the traditional nuclear family becomes less and less the dominant form in our country, the contribution which sex makes to the class and caste structure and to the social status of the individual will become more visible. In addition, as women become more powerful through greater participation in the labor force and through political organization as women, their position in the total social structure will become a more legitimate problem for the sociologist.

NOTES

1. Revision of a paper read at the annual meeting of the Southwestern Sociological Association (1971), Dallas, Texas.

2. Sociologists in other areas have made a number of recent contributions which are relevant to problems of stratification. For example, Epstein (1970) discusses the salience of sex status in the professional careers of women in the higher professions. Oppenheimer (1968) examines the basis for the sex labeling of jobs in the American work force. Wilensky (1968) explores the relationships between the position of women, economic growth, and democratic ideology. Etzioni (1969) investigates the relationship between sex status and occupation in the semiprofessions. Some earlier, but isolated, analyses were Hacker (1951) and Myrdal (1944, Appendix 5) both of whom discuss women as a minority group: Hughes (1949) who places nontraditional, career women in the role of "marginal men"; Ellis (1952) who studied correlates of mobility among career women; and Caplow (1954) who devotes a chapter to women in the world of work.

There have been other sociological discussions of the position of women (Komarovsky 1950, 1953; Bernard 1966, 1968), but these analyses have not been integrated into the studies of social stratification.

3. Lenski (1966) is one of the few who recognized this problem in the field of stratification. In *Power and Privilege* he states, "Another much neglected aspect of the distributive systems of modern societies is the class system based on sex." He also observes that, "in analyses of advanced industrial societies, it is impossible to ignore or treat as obvious the role of sex in the distributive process." Even Lenski, however, does little analysis. He concludes his brief discussion of the position of women (mentioned on 13 pages out of a total of 446 pages in the book) with the comforting thought that, "for the vast majority of women, the battle for equality has been won." There may be some contradiction between the statements that the battle for sex equality has been won and that sex is still an important factor in the distributive process. However, this book was published pre-women's lib, in 1966, when such inconsistencies, although frequent, were relatively invisible. This contradiction reflects the difficulties of stratification theory in dealing with the status of women.

4. See, e.g., two recent studies of class structure in Poland and Czechoslovakia (Machonin 1970; Wesolowski and Slomczyński 1968) which explicitly make the assumptions outlined here.

5. Lenski (1966) makes the same point: "This neglect [of women] has been due in large measure to the tendency of sociologists to treat families, rather than individuals, as the basic unit in systems of stratification" (p. 402).

6. Calculated from table 6, 8, and table 44, p. 36, *Statistical Abstract of the United States, 1971* (U.S., Bureau of the Census 1971).

7. Hofstetter (1970) explores this problem. She concludes that class self-placement by college student respondents may be determined by the combined resources of father and mother, rather than by those of father alone.

8. Many of these points have also been made by Watson and Barth in a penetrating critique of some assumptions in stratification theory and research published in 1964.

9. Both Myrdal (1944; Appendix 5) and Hacker (1951) drew the parallel between women and blacks, suggesting that women occupy a caste position similar to that of blacks. As noted above, their work, among that of others, has remained peripheral to the mainstream study of stratification in all theoretical perspectives.

10. Exercises along this line can be found in ladies' magazines and in women's lib literature. However, they have not been seriously pursued, so far as I know, by sociologists.

11. Thorstein Veblen, in *The Theory of the Leisure Class* ([1899] 1953), of course, makes the same point.

12. This idea derives most directly from Blau (1964).

REFERENCES

Bernard, Jessie. 1966. *Academic Women*. Cleveland: World.
———. 1968. *The Sex Game*. Englewood Cliffs, N.J.: Prentice-Hall.
Blau, Peter M. 1964. *Exchange and Power in Social Life*. New York: Wiley.
Blau, Peter M., and O. Dudley Duncan. 1967. *The American Occupational Structure*. New York: Wiley.
Caplow, Theodore. 1954. *The Sociology of Work*. Minneapolis: University of Minnesota Press.
Elder, Glenn H., Jr. 1969. "Appearance and Education in Marriage Mobility." *American Sociological Review* 34 (August): 519-32.
Ellis, Evelyn. 1952. "Social Psychological Correlates of Upward Mobility among Unmarried Career Women." *American Sociological Review* 17 (October): 558-63.
Epstein, Cynthia. 1970. "Encountering the Male Establishment: Sex Status Limits on Women's Careers in the Professions." *American Journal of Sociology* 75 (May): 965-82.

Etzioni, Amitai, ed. 1969. *The Semi-Professions and Their Organizations.* New York: Free Press.

Ferriss, Abbott L. 1970. *Indicators of Change in the American Family.* New York: Russell Sage.

Haavio-Mannila, E. 1969. "Some Consequences of Women's Emancipation." *Journal of Marriage and the Family* 31 (February): 123-34.

Hacker, Helen Mayer. 1951. "Women as a Minority Group." *Social Forces* 30 (October): 60-69.

Heller, Celia S. 1969. *Structured Social Inequality.* New York: Macmillan.

Hofstetter, Heather N. 1970. "The Problem of Family Status Arrangements in Stratification Analysis." Unpublished dissertation, University of Oregon.

Hughes, Everett C. 1949. "Social Change and Status Protest: An Essay on the Marginal Man." *Phylon* 10 (First Quarter): 58-65.

Komarovsky, Mirra. 1950. "Functional Analysis of Sex Roles." *American Sociological Review* 15 (August): 508-16.

———. 1953. *Women in the Modern World.* Boston: Little, Brown.

Laumann, Edward O., ed. 1970. "Stratification Theory and Research." *Sociological Inquiry* 4 (Spring): 3-12.

Lenski, Gerhard. 1966. *Power and Privilege.* New York: McGraw-Hill.

Lopata, Helena Z. 1971. *Occupation: Housewife.* New York: Oxford University Press.

Machonin, Pavel. 1970. "Social Stratification in Contemporary Czechoslovakia." *American Journal of Sociology* 75 (March): 725-41.

Myrdal, Gunnar. 1944. *An American Dilemma.* New York: Harper.

Oppenheimer, Valerie Kincade. 1968. "The Sex-Labeling of Jobs." *Industrial Relations* 7 (May): 219-34.

Rubin, Zick. 1968. "Do American Women Marry Up? *American Sociological Review* 33 (October): 750-60.

———. 1969. "Reply to Scott." *American Sociological Review* 34 (October): 727-28.

Scott, J. F. 1969. "A Comment on 'Do American Women Marry Up?' " *American Sociological Review* 34 (October): 725-27.

Shils, Edward. 1968. "Deference." In *Social Stratification,* edited by J. A. Jackson. Cambridge: Cambridge University Press.

U.S., Bureau of the Census. 1971. *Statistical Abstract of the United States, 1971.* Washington, D.C.: Government Printing Office.

Veblen, Thorstein. (1899) 1953. *The Theory of the Leisure Class.* New York: New American Library, Mentor Books.

Watson, Walter B., and Ernest A. Barth. 1964. "Questionable Assumptions in the Theory of Social Stratification." *Pacific Sociological Review* 7 (Spring): 10-16.

Wesolowski, Wlodzimierz, and Kazimierz Slomczyński. 1968. "Social Stratification in Polish Cities." In *Social Stratification,* edited by J. A. Jackson. Cambridge: Cambridge University Press.

Wilensky, Harold L. 1968. "Women's Work: Economic Growth, Ideology, Structure." *Industrial Relations* 7 (May): 235-48.

3 Equality Between the Sexes:
An Immodest Proposal

ALICE S. ROSSI

> . . . the principle which regulates the existing relations between the two sexes . . . is wrong in itself and [is] now the chief hindrance to human improvement; and . . . it ought to be replaced by a principle of perfect equality, admitting no power or privilege on the one side, nor disability on the other.
>
> John Stuart Mill, 1869

INTRODUCTION

When John Stuart Mill wrote his essay on "The Subjection of Women" in 1869, the two major things he argued for with elegance and persuasion were to extend the franchise to women, and to end the legal subordination of married women to their husbands. The movement for sex equality had already gathered considerable momentum in England and the United States by 1869, reaching its peak fifty years later, when the franchise was won by American women in 1920. In the decades since 1920, this momentum has gradually slackened, until by the 1960's American society has been losing rather than gaining ground in the growth toward sex equality. American women are not trying to extend their claim to equality from the political to the occupational and social arenas and often do not even seem interested in exercising the rights so bitterly won in the early decades of

AUTHOR'S NOTE: I wish to express my gratitude to Peter H. Rossi for his critical assessment of several drafts of this essay; to the Social Science Research Committee at the University of Chicago for a research grant that supported part of the research on which this essay is based; and to Stephen R. Graubard for his generosity of time and editorial skill.

"Equality Between the Sexes: An Immodest Proposal" reprinted by permission of *Daedalus,* Journal of the American Academy of Arts and Sciences, from the issue entitled "The Woman in America," Spring 1964, Vol. 93, No. 2.

the twentieth century in politics and higher education. The constitutional amendment on equal rights for men and women has failed to pass Congress for seventeen consecutive years, and today a smaller proportion of college graduates are women than was true thirty years ago.

There is no overt antifeminism in our society in 1964, not because sex equality has been achieved, but because there is practically no feminist spark left among American women. When I ask the brightest of my women college students about their future study and work plans, they either have none because they are getting married in a few months, or they show clearly that they have lowered their aspirations from professional and research fields that excited them as freshmen, to concentrate as juniors on more practical fields far below their abilities. Young women seem increasingly uncommitted to anything beyond early marriage, motherhood and a suburban house. There are few Noras in contemporary American society because women have deluded themselves that the doll's house is large enough to find complete personal fulfillment within it.

It will be the major thesis of this essay that we need to reassert the claim to sex equality and to search for the means by which it can be achieved. By sex equality I mean a socially androgynous conception of the roles of men and women, in which they are equal and similar in such spheres as intellec- tual, artistic, political and occupational interests and participation, comple- mentary only in those spheres dictated by physiological differences between the sexes. This assumes the traditional conceptions of masculine and femi- nine are inappropriate to the kind of world we can live in in the second half of the twentieth century. An androgynous conception of sex role means that each sex will cultivate some of the characteristics usually associated with the other in traditional sex role definitions. This means that tenderness and expressiveness should be cultivated in boys and socially approved in men, so that a male of any age in our society would be psychologically and socially free to express these qualities in his social relationships. It means that achievement need, workmanship and constructive aggression should be cultivated in girls and approved in women so that a female of any age would be similarly free to express these qualities in her social relationships. This is one of the points of contrast with the feminist goal of an earlier day: rather than a one-sided plea for women to adapt a masculine stance in the world, this definition of sex-equality stresses the enlargement of the common ground on which men and women base their lives together by changing the social definitions of approved characteristics and behavior for both sexes.

It will be an assumption of this essay that by far the majority of the differences between the sexes which have been noted in social research are socially rather than physiologically determined. What proportion of these sex differences are physiologically based and what proportion are socially based is a question the social and physiological sciences cannot really answer at the present time. It is sufficient for my present purposes to note that the opportunities for social change toward a closer approximation of equality between the sexes are large enough within the area of sex differences now considered to be socially determined to constitute a challenging arena for thought and social action. This is my starting point. I shall leave to speculative discourse and future physiological research the question of what constitutes irreducible differences between the sexes.

There are three main questions I shall raise in this essay. Why was the momentum of the earlier feminist movement lost? Why should American society attempt to reach a state of sex equality as I have defined it above? What are the means by which equality between the sexes can be achieved?

WHY FEMINISM DECLINED

I shall discuss three factors which have been major contributors to the waning of feminism. The chief goals of the early leaders of the feminist movement were to secure the vote for women and to change the laws affecting marriage so that women would have equal rights to property and to their own children. As in any social reform movement or social revolution, the focus in the first stage is on change in the legal code, whether this is to declare independence from a mother country, establish a constitution for a new nation, free the slaves, or secure the right of women to be equal citizens with men. But the social changes required to translate such law into the social fabric of a society are of a quite different order. Law by itself cannot achieve this goal. It is one thing to declare slaves free or to espouse a belief in racial equality; quite another matter to accept racial integration in all spheres of life, as many northern communities have learned in recent years. In a similar way, many people accept the legal changes which have reduced the inequality between men and women and espouse belief in sex equality, but resist its manifestation in their personal life. If a social movement rests content with legal changes without making as strong an effort to change the social institutions through which they are expressed, it will remain a hollow victory.

This is one of the things which occurred in the case of the feminist movement. Important as the franchise is, or the recent change in Civil Service regulations which prevents the personnel specification of "male only," the new law or regulation can be successful only to the extent that women exercise the franchise, or are trained to be qualified for and to aspire for the jobs they are now permitted to hold. There is no sex equality until women participate on an equal basis with men in politics, occupations and the family. Law and administrative regulations must permit such participation, but women must want to participate and be able to participate. In politics and the occupational world, to be able to participate depends primarily on whether home responsibilities can be managed simultaneously with work or political commitments. Since women have had, and probably will continue to have, primary responsibility for child-rearing, their participation in politics, professions or the arts cannot be equal to that of men unless ways are devised to ease the combination of home and work responsibilities. This is precisely what has not occurred; at the same time, since fewer women today choose a career over marriage, the result has been a reduction in women's representation in the more challenging and demanding occupations.

By itself, the stress on legal change to the neglect of institutional change in the accommodations between family and work does not go very far in explaining why the feminist movement has lost momentum. There is an important second factor which must be viewed in conjunction with this first one. The feminist movement has always been strongest when it was allied with other social reform movements. In the nineteenth century its linkage was with the antislavery movement, and in the early twentieth century it was allied to the social welfare movement. There is an interesting and a simple explanation of this: unlike any other type of social inequality, whether of race, class, religion or nationality, sex is the only instance in which representatives of the unequal groups live in more intimate association with each other than with members of their own group. A woman is more intimately associated with a man than she is with any woman.[1] This was not the case for lord-serf, master-slave, Protestant-Roman Catholic, white-Negro relationships unless or until the social groups involved reach a full equality. By linking the feminist cause to the antislavery or social welfare movement, women were able to work together with men of similar sympathies and in the process they enlisted the support of these men for the feminist cause. To a greater extent than any other underprivileged group, women need not only vigorous spokesmen and pacesetters of their own sex, but the support of men, to effect any major change in the status of women, whether in the personal sphere of individual relationships or on the level of social organization.[2] The decline of political radicalism and the general state of affluence and social conservatism in American society since World War II have contributed in subtle ways to the decline of feminism, for women are not joined with men in any movement affecting an underprivileged group in American society. At the present time, marriage remains the only major path of social mobility for women in our society.

The general conservatism of the total society has also penetrated the academic disciplines, with side effects on the motivation and ability of women to exercise the rights already theirs or to press for an extension of them. Feminism has been undermined by the conservatism of psychology and sociology in the postwar period. Sociologists studying the family have borrowed heavily from selective findings in social anthropology and from psychoanalytic theory and have pronounced sex to be a universally necessary basis for role differentiation in the family. By extension, in the larger society women are seen as predominantly fulfilling nurturant, expressive functions and men the instrumental, active functions. When this viewpoint is applied to American society, intellectually aggressive women or tender expressive men are seen as deviants showing signs of "role conflict," "role confusion," or neurotic disturbance. They are not seen as a promising indication of a desirable departure from traditional sex role definitions.[3] In a similar way, the female sphere, the family, is viewed by social theorists as a passive, pawnlike institution, adapting to the requirements of the occupational, political or cultural segments of the social structure, seldom playing an active role either in affecting the nature of other social institutions or determining the nature of social change.[4] The implicit assumption in problem after problem in sociology is that radical social innovations are risky and may have so many unintended consequences as to make it unwise to propose or support them. Although the sociologist describes and analyzes social change, it is change already accomplished, seldom anticipated purposive social change.[5] When the changes are in process, they are defined as social problems, seldom as social opportunities.

Closely linked to this trend in sociology and social anthropology, and in fact partly attributable to it, is the pervasive permeation of psychoanalytic thinking throughout American society. Individual psychoanalysts vary widely among themselves, but when their theories are popularized by social scientists, marriage and family counselors, writers, social critics, pediatricians and mental health specialists, there emerges a common and conservative image of the woman's role. It is the traditional image of woman which is popularized: the woman who finds complete self-fulfillment in her exclusive devotion to marriage and parenthood. Women who thirty years ago might have chosen a career over a marriage, or restricted their family size to facilitate the combination of family and work roles, have been persuaded to believe that such choices reflect their inadequacy as women. It is this sense of failure as a woman that lies behind the defensive and apologetic note of many older unmarried professional women, the guilt which troubles the working mother (which I suspect goes up in direct proportion to the degree to which she is familiar with psychoanalytic ideas), the restriction of the level of aspiration of college women, the early plunge into marriage, the closed door of the doll's house.

Our society has been so inundated with psychoanalytic thinking that any dissatisfaction or conflict in personal and family life is considered to require solution on an individual basis. This goes well with the general American value stress on individualism, and American women have increasingly resorted to psychotherapy, the most highly individualized solution of all, for the answers to the problems they have as women. In the process the idea has been lost that many problems, even in the personal family sphere, cannot be solved on an individual basis, but require solution on a societal level by changing the institutional contexts within which we live.

The consequences of this acceptance of psychoanalytic ideas and conservatism in the social sciences have been twofold: first, the social sciences in the United States have contributed very little since the 1930's to any lively intellectual dialogue on sex equality as a goal or the ways of implementing that goal. Second, they have provided a quasi-scientific underpinning to educators, marriage counselors, mass media and advertising researchers, who together have partly created, and certainly reinforced, the withdrawal of millions of young American women from the mainstream of thought and work in our society.[6]

WHY SEEK EQUALITY BETWEEN THE SEXES

This brings us to the second question: why should American society attempt to reach a state of sex equality? If women seem satisfied with a more narrowly restricted life pattern than men would be, why should we seek to disturb this pattern? To begin with, I do not think this question is really relevant to the issue. There have been underprivileged groups throughout history which contained sizable proportions of contented, uncomplaining members, whether slaves, serfs or a low status caste. But the most enlightened members of both the privileged and underprivileged groups in such societies came to see that inequality not only depressed the human potential of the subject groups but corrupted those in the superordinate groups. The lives of southern whites are as crippled by racial inequality as the lives of southern Negroes are impoverished. In the same way, many men spend their daytime hours away from home as vital cognitive animals and their nights and weekends in mental passivity and vegetation. Social and personal life is impoverished for some part of many men's lives because so many of their wives live in a perpetual state of intellectual and social impoverishment.

A second reason why American society should attempt to reach a state of full sex equality is that at the level our industrial society has now reached, it is no longer necessary for women to confine their life expectations to marriage and parenthood. Certain of the reasons for this have been increasingly stressed in recent years: with increased longevity, and smaller sized families, the traditional mother role simply does not occupy a sufficient portion of a woman's life span to constitute any longer the exclusive adult role for which a young woman should be prepared.[7] American girls spend more time as apprentice mothers with their dolls than they will as adult women with their own babies, and there is half a lifetime still ahead by the time the youngest child enters high school. Although studies have shown that women today are working in the home roughly the same number of hours a week as their mothers did,[8] this is not because they have to do so: techno-logical innovations in the production and distribution of food, clothing and other household equipment have been such that homemaking no longer requires the specialized skills and time-consuming tasks it did until early in our century. Contemporary women often turn what should be labor-saving devices into labor-making devices. In the light of the many time-consuming tasks the American mother fifty years ago had to perform, and the much longer work day for those in the labor force then, the woman in 1964 who holds down a full-time job will probably have as much or more time with her children as her grandmother had. Furthermore, most of the skills needed for adulthood are no longer taught within the family: child socialization is increasingly a shared enterprise between the parent and teachers, doctors, nurses, club leaders and instructors in an assortment of special skills.

These are perhaps all familiar points. What has not been seen is the more general point that *for the first time in the history of any known society, motherhood has become a full-time occupation for adult women.* In the past, whether a woman lived on a farm, a Dutch city in the seventeenth century, or a colonial town in the eighteenth century, women in all strata of society except the very top were never able to be full-time mothers as the twentieth-century middle class American woman has become. These women were productive members of farm and craft teams along with their farmer, baker or printer husbands and other adult kin. Children either shared in the work of the household or were left to amuse themselves; their mothers did not have the time to organize their play, worry about their development, discuss their problems. These women were not lonely because the world came into their homes in the form of customers, clients or patients in villages and towns, or farmhands and relatives on the farm; such women had no reason to complain of the boredom and solitude of spending ten-hour days alone with babies and young children because their days were peopled with adults. There were no child specialists to tell the colonial merchant's wife or pioneer farmer's wife that her absorption in spinning, planting, churning and preserving left her children on their own too much, that how she fed her baby would shape his adult personality, or that leaving children with a variety of other adults while she worked would make them insecure.

There are two important questions this analysis raises: why has full-time motherhood been accepted by the overwhelming majority of American women, and how successful has been the new pattern of full-time mother-hood of the past forty years or so? I believe the major answer to the first question is that the American woman has been encouraged by the experts to whom she has turned for guidance in child-rearing to believe that her children need her continuous presence, supervision and care and that she should find complete fulfillment in this role. If, for example, a woman reads an article by Dr. Spock on working mothers, she is informed that any woman who finds full-time motherhood produces nervousness is showing a "residue of difficult relationships in her own childhood"; if irritability and nervousness are not assuaged by a brief trip or two, she is probably in an emotional state which can be "relieved through regular counseling in a family social agency, or, if severe, through psychiatric treatment"; and finally, "any mother of a preschool child who is considering a job should discuss the issues with a social worker before making her decision."[9] Since the social worker shares the same analytic framework that Dr. Spock does, there is little doubt what the advice will be; the woman is left with a judgment that wanting more than motherhood is not natural but a reflection of her individual emotional disturbance.

The fundamental tenet of the theory underlying such advice is that the physically and emotionally healthy development of the infant requires the loving involvement of the mother with the child. If an infant does not receive stable continuous mothering there is almost invariably severe physical and emotional disturbance. There is apparently ample clinical evidence to support these points. Studies have suggested that prolonged separation from parents, and particularly from the mother, has serious effects upon infants and young children.[10] However, practitioners make unwarranted extrapolations from these findings when they advise that *any* separation of mother and child is risky and hazardous for the healthy development of the child.[11] Despite the fact that the empirical evidence stems from instances of prolonged, traumatic separation caused by such things as the death or serious illness of the mother, or the institutionalization of the child, this viewpoint is applied to the situation of an employed mother absent from the home on a regular basis. No one predicts that any dire consequences will flow from a woman's absence from home several afternoons a week to engage in a shopping spree, keep medical appointments or play bridge; nor is a father considered to produce severe disturbance in his young children even if his work schedule reduces contact with them to the daylight hours of a weekend. But women who have consulted pediatricians and family counselors about their resuming work are firmly told that they should remain at home, for the sake of their children's emotional health.[12]

What effect *does* maternal employment have upon children? Many sociologists of the family have raised this question during the past fifteen years, expecting to find negative effects as psychoanalytic theory predicted. In fact, the focus of most maternal employment studies has been on the effect of mothers' working upon the personalities of their children, somewhat less often on the tensions and strains between the mother role and the occupational role,[13] seldom on the question of how maternal employment affects the woman's satisfactions with herself, her home and marriage. To date, *there is no evidence of any negative effects traceable to maternal employment;*

children of working mothers are no more likely than children of non-working mothers to become delinquent, to show neurotic symptoms, to feel deprived of maternal affection, to perform poorly in school, to lead narrower social lives, etc.[14] Many of the researchers in the 1950's frankly admitted surprise at their negative findings. In a study reported in 1962,[15] the only significant difference found between working and non-working mothers was the mother's confidence about her role as mother: 42 per cent of the working mothers but only 24 per cent of the non-working mothers expressed concern about their maternal role, "often by explicit questioning and worry as to whether working is interfering with their relationships and the rearing of their children." Yet these working women did not actually differ from the at-home mothers in the very things that concerned them: there were no differences between these women in the emotional relationships with their children, household allocation of responsibilities, principles of child-rearing, etc. The working mothers appeared to share the prevailing view that their children would suffer as a result of their employment, though in fact their children fare as well as those of non-working mothers.[16]

It would appear, therefore, that the employment of women when their children are eight years of age or older has no negative effect on the children. What about the earlier years, from infancy until school age? In the American literature, there is little to refer to as yet which bears directly upon the effect of maternal employment on the infant or toddler, partly because employment of mothers with preschool children is so negligible in the United States, partly because the measurement of "effects" on young children is difficult and cannot be done with the research tools which have been used in most studies of maternal employment effects—questionnaires administered to mothers and to their school-age children.[17]

There is, however, one significant body of data which is of considerable relevance to the question of the effect of maternal employment upon infants and very young children. Maternal employment is a regular pattern of separation of mother and child: the Israeli kibbutzim are collective settlements with several decades of experience in precisely this pattern. On the kibbutz, infants live in children's houses where their physical care and training are largely handled. During the infancy months the mother visits the house to feed the infant; as toddlers, children begin a pattern of visiting with their parents for a few hours each day, living in the children's houses for the remaining portions of their days and nights. A number of studies have been conducted to investigate the effect of this intermittent multiple mothering on the young child.[18] They all point to essentially the same conclusion; the kibbutz child-rearing practices have no deleterious effects upon the subsequent personality development of the children involved. In fact, there are a number of respects in which the kibbutz-reared Israeli children exceed those reared in the traditional farm family: the kibbutz children showed a more accurate perception of reality, more breadth of interest and cultural background, better emotional control and greater overall maturity.

Continuous mothering, even in the first few years of life, does not seem to be necessary for the healthy emotional growth of a child.[19] The crux of the matter appears to be in the nature of the care which is given to the child.[20] If a child is reared by a full-time mother who is rejecting and cold in her treatment of him, or if a child is reared in an institutional setting lacking in warmth and stimulation and with an inadequate staff, both children will show personality disturbances in later years. If the loving care of the biological mother is shared by other adults who provide the child with a stable loving environment, the child will prosper at least as well as and potentially better than one with a good full-time mother.[21] In the section below on child care and careers, I shall suggest institutional innovations which would ensure good quality care for children and ease the combination of work and child-rearing for women.

Turning now to the second question raised above: how successful has the new pattern of full-time motherhood been? Are women more satisfied with their lives in the mid-twentieth century than in the past? Does motherhood fulfill them, provide them with a sufficient canvas to occupy a lifetime? Are contemporary children living richer lives, developing greater ego strength to carry them through a complex adulthood? Are children better off for having full-time mothers?

I think the answer to all the questions posed above is a firm *no*. Educators, child psychologists and social analysts report an increasing tendency for American middle-class children to be lacking in initiative, excessively dependent on others for direction and decision, physically soft.[22] Our children have more toys and play equipment than children in any other society, yet they still become bored and ask their mothers for "something to do." No society has as widespread a problem of juvenile delinquency and adolescent rebellion as the United States. Alcoholism, compulsive sex-seeking and adolescent delinquency are no longer social problems confined to the working class, socially disorganized sections of our cities, but have been on the increase in the middle-class suburb in the past twenty years, and involve more women and girls than in the past. There is a strong strand of male protest against the mother or "matriarch" in both our beatnik culture and our avant-garde literature: social and artistic extremes are seldom fully deviant from the middle range in a society, but show in an exaggerated heightened way the same though less visible tendencies in the social majority.

In a large proportion of cases, the etiology of mental illness is linked to inadequacy in the mother-child relationship. A high proportion of the psychoneurotic discharges from the army during World War II was traced to these young soldiers' overly dependent relationships to their mothers.[23] This has been the subject of much earnest discussion in the years since the war, but the focus has remained on the mother-son relationship, I suspect only because as a fighter, a professional man or a worker, male performance is seen to be more crucial for society than female performance. But dependence, immaturity and ego diffusion have been characteristic of daughters as well as sons. The only difference is that, in the case of daughters, this less often reaches the overt level of a social problem because young women move quickly from under their mothers' tutelage into marriage and parenthood of their own: female failures are therefore not as socially visible, for they are kept within the privacy of family life and psychoanalytic case records. It is a short-sighted view indeed to consider the immature wife, dominating mother or interfering mother-in-law as a less serious problem to the larger society than the male homosexual, psychoneurotic soldier or ineffectual worker, for it is the failure of the mother which perpetuates the cycle from one generation to the next, affecting sons and daughters alike.

Disturbing trends of this sort cannot all be traced to the American woman's excessive and exclusive involvement with home and family. We live in turbulent times, and some part of these trends reflects the impact of world tension and conflict. But there is no reason to assume that world tension is relevant to many of them. Emotional and physical difficulties after childbirth or during the menopause years, the higher incidence of college girl than college boy breakdowns, the shrunken initiative and independence of children, are clearly not explained by world conflict. Besides, vast sections of American society remain totally unmoved and unaffected by international political and military events until they directly impinge on their own daily lives. Since history is both written and produced more by men than by women, the fact that our writers are preoccupied with the relationship to the mother points to difficulties in our family system more than the course of world events.

It is a paradox of our social history that motherhood has become a full-time occupation in precisely the era when objectively it could, and perhaps should, be a part-time occupation for a short phase of a woman's life span. I suspect that the things women do for and with their children have been needlessly elaborated to make motherhood a full-time job. Unfortunately, in this very process the child's struggle for autonomy and independence, for privacy and the right to worry things through for himself are subtly and pervasively reduced by the omnipresent mother. As a young child he is given great permissive freedom, but he must exercise it under supervision. As an adolescent he is given a great deal of freedom, but his parents worry excessively about what he does with it. Edgar Friedenberg has argued that there is entirely too much parental concentration on adolescent children, with the result that it has become increasingly difficult to *be* an adolescent in American society.[24] He suggests that parents are interested in youth to the extent that they find their own stage of life uninteresting. Middle-class children are observed and analyzed by their mothers as though they were hothouse plants psychologically, on whose personalities any pressure might leave an indelible bruise. If a woman's adult efforts are concentrated exclusively on her children, she is likely more to stifle than broaden her children's perspective and preparation for adult life. Any stress or failure in a child becomes a failure of herself, and she is therefore least likely to truly help her child precisely when the child most needs support.[25] In myriad ways the mother binds the child to her, dampening his initiative, resenting his growing independence in adolescence, creating a subtle dependence which makes it difficult for the child to achieve full adult stature without a rebellion which leaves him with a mixture of resentment and guilt that torments him in his mother's declining years.

It seems to me no one has linked these things together adequately. Psychiatric counselors of college students frequently have as their chief task that of helping their young patients to free themselves from the entangling web of dependence upon their parents, primarily their mothers, and encouraging them to form stable independent lives of their own. In other words, if the patient is eighteen years old the analyst tries to help her free herself from her mother, but if the next patient is twenty-five years old with young children at home, the analyst tells her the children would suffer emotional damage if she left them on a regular basis to hold down a job. The very things which would reduce the excessive dependency of children before it becomes a critical problem are discouraged by the counselor or analyst during the years when the dependency is being formed. If it is true that the adult is what the child was, and if we wish adults to be assertive, independent, responsible people, then they should be reared in a way which prevents excessive dependence on a parent. They should be cared for by a number of adults in their childhood, and their parents should truly encourage their independence and responsibility during their youthful years, not merely give lip service to these parental goals. The best way to encourage such independence and responsibility in the child is for the mother to be a living model of these qualities herself. If she had an independent life of her own, she would find her stage of life interesting, and therefore be less likely to live for and through her children. By maintaining such an independent life, the American mother might finally provide her children with something she can seldom give when she is at home—a healthy dose of inattention, and a chance for adolescence to be a period of fruitful immaturity and growth.[26] If enough American women developed vital and enduring interests outside the family and remained actively in them throughout the child-bearing years, we might then find a reduction in extreme adolescent rebellion, immature early marriages, maternal domination of children, and interference by mothers and mothers-in-law in the lives of married children.

There remains one further general characteristic of our industrial society which has relevance to the question of why American society should achieve full sex equality. Our family unit is small, for the most part geographically if not socially isolated from its kin. This small family unit is possible because of the increased longevity in highly industrialized societies. In agricultural societies, with their high rate of mortality, many parents die before they have completed the rearing of their young. The extended family provided substitutes for such parents without disturbing the basic lines of kin affiliation and property rights of these children. In our modern family system it is an unusual event for women or men to be widowed while they have young dependent children. This also means, however, that American families must fend for themselves in the many emergencies less critical than the death of a spouse: army service, long business or professional trips, prolonged physical or emotional illness, separation or divorce often require that one spouse carry the primary responsibility for the family, even if this is cushioned or supplemented by insurance, government aid, paid helpers or relatives. The insurance advertisements which show fathers bending over a cradle and begin "what would happen if?" evoke a twinge of fear in their readers precisely because parents recognize the lonely responsible positions they would be in if serious illness or death were to strike their home. In our family system, then, it is a decided asset if men and women can quickly and easily substitute for or supplement each other as parents and as breadwinners. I believe these are important elements in the structure of our economy and family system which exert pressure toward an equality between men and women. It is not merely that a companionate or equalitarian marriage is a desirable relationship between wife and husband, but that the functioning of an urban industrial society is facilitated by equality between men and women in work, marriage and parenthood.

The conclusions I have drawn from this analysis are as follows: full-time motherhood is neither sufficiently absorbing to the woman nor beneficial to the child to justify a contemporary woman's devoting fifteen or more years to it as her exclusive occupation. Sooner or later—and I think it should be sooner—women have to face the question of who they are besides their children's mother.

A major solution to this quest would be found in the full and equal involvement of women in the occupational world, the culmination of the feminist movement of the last one hundred and fifty years. This is not to overlook the fact that involvement as a volunteer in politics or community organizations or a serious dedication to a creative art can be a solution for many women. These areas of participation and involvement provide innumerable women with a keen sense of life purpose, and women are making significant and often innovative contributions in these pursuits. A job *per se* does not provide a woman, or a man either, with any magical path to self-fulfillment; nor does just any community volunteer work, or half-hearted dabbling in a creative art.

Women are already quite well represented in volunteer organizations in American communities. However, broadening the range of alternatives open to women and chosen by women for their life patterns is still to be achieved in the occupational world. It is also true that at the most challenging reaches of both political and community volunteer work, the activities have become increasingly professionalized. Thus while many women have and will continue to make innovative contributions to these fields as volunteers, such opportunities have become limited. Furthermore, many such women often find themselves carrying what amounts to a full-time job as a "volunteer executive," yet neither the recognition nor the rewards are equivalent to what they would receive in comparable positions in the occupational system.[27] Hence, the major focus in this essay will be on the means by which the full and equal involvement of well-educated women in the occupational world may be achieved. For reasons which will become clear later, I believe that the occupational involvement of women would also be the major means for reducing American women's dominance in marriage and parenthood, and thus for allowing for the participation of men as equal partners in family life.

Of course there have already been changes in the extent and the nature of women's participation in the American labor force. Indeed, this is sometimes cited as proof that sex equality has been achieved in the United States. There are roughly twenty-three million American women in the labor force, and it is predicted that this will swell to thirty million by 1970. About three-fifths of these women are married, an increase of well over 20 per cent since 1940. It should be noted that this increase came predominantly from women between the ages of 35 and 54 years, after the child-rearing years and before the usual retirement age for workers. This is a major social change, to be sure, and people who still raise the question of whether married women should work are arguing after the fact, for such women are doing so at increasing rates. The point is, however, that most American women—65 per cent—do *not* work outside the home, and those who do are found largely in blue collar or low-skill white collar occupations. Men fill roughly 85 per cent of the very top professional and technical jobs in the United States. Furthermore, only a very small proportion of American wives work if their husbands are in the middle and top income brackets, or if they have young children. Finally, the distribution of the female labor force by age shows two major peaks of female participation, before and for a short time after marriage, and then for the fifteen years from their early forties through middle fifties. Withdrawal and re-entry many years later is now a common female work pattern in the United States. As long as this pattern continues, women will not increase their representation in the top professional and technical occupations.[28]

Over the past twenty years, women in many European countries have doubled or more their representation in the professional occupations. By comparison, American women constitute a smaller proportion of the professional world today than they did twenty years ago. That this reflects a lowering of ambition among American women is suggested by the fact that of all the women capable of doing college work, only one out of four do so, compared to one out of two men. This is the point at which we begin to tap a deeper root of women's motivations in the United States. Whether a woman works steadily throughout her marriage or returns to work after the child-rearing period, no significant increase of women in the professional and high-skill job categories will occur unless American women's attitude toward education and work is changed.[29] To study and to prepare for a future job "in case I have to work" is just as poor a preparation for occupational participation as the postponement of learning domestic skills "until I have to" is a poor preparation for the homemaker role. Both views reflect a digging in of the heels into the adolescent moment of a lifetime. In many ways the middle-class girl considers only the present, the here-and-now, as do most members of the working class, and not the future, as do her father, brothers and male friends. There is evidence to suggest that such an emphasis on the present is characteristic not only of the American woman at college age, but also more generally throughout her life span. Thus, Gallup's portrait of the American woman shows the same characteristic at all points during the younger half of the life cycle: young unmarried women as well as mature women with their children now entering high school give little thought to and no preparation for their life over forty years of age.[30]

The middle-class wife of a successful business executive or professional man has a special problem. To earn a salary in the occupational world, she will be judged by her own achieved merits without regard to her social position or her husband's influence. Unless she has had the education and experience necessary to hold a position of some prestige, she will experience social and personal barriers to entering the labor force. In the absence of such education and experience, she is qualified to be only the occupational subordinate of men who are her equals socially, a status incongruity few women are likely to tolerate. By contrast, no matter how menial, her service as a volunteer will be socially approved. Unless such women secure specialized training before marriage, or acquire it after marriage, there will be little increase in the proportion of working wives and mothers in the upper half of the middle class. Many such women with a flair for organization have found full scope for their independent fulfillment in volunteer work in politics, education, social welfare and the arts. Unfortunately, there are innumerable other women for whom such outlets have little attraction who realize they have missed their chance for independent self-fulfillment, and who have little opportunity for a second chance by their late forties.

It has been argued by some sociologists that the American marriage is already too fragile to sustain competition at comparable skill levels between spouses.[31] If this were true, and women were also reluctant to work at lower prestige jobs than their husbands, this would effectively freeze most middle-class women out of the occupational world. I would raise three points concerning this assumption. First, husbands and working wives are usually found in different segments of the occupational system, which makes comparison of success a difficult matter. For example, is an architect working for a large firm and earning $20,000 a year more or less successful than his wife who directs a large family welfare agency and earns $15,000 a year? Second, even were such achievements in nonfamily roles to provoke some competitive feeling between husband and wife, I think the consequences of this competition are far less potentially harmful to the marriage or to the children than the situation of the well-educated able woman who is not working and engages instead in a competition with her husband for the affections and primary loyalties of the children. If a woman is markedly more successful than her husband, it would probably create difficulty in the marriage, particularly if there are residues of traditional expectations of male breadwinner dominance on the part of either partner to the marriage. But competition does not necessarily mean conflict. It can be a social spice and a source of pride and stimulation in a marriage of equals. Last, one must face up to the fact that a new social goal exacts a price. A change toward sex equality may cause some temporary marital dislocations, but this is not sufficient reason to expect all women to remain enclosed in the past.

INSTITUTIONAL LEVERS
FOR ACHIEVING SEX EQUALITY

In turning to the problem of how equality between the sexes may be implemented as a societal goal, I shall concentrate on the three major areas of child care, residence and education. Institutional change in these areas in no sense exhausts the possible spheres in which institutional change could be effected to facilitate the goal of sex equality. Clearly government and industry, for example, could effect highly significant changes in the relations between the sexes. But one must begin somewhere, and I have chosen these three topics, for they all involve questions of critical significance to the goal of equality between men and women.

1. It is widely assumed that rearing children and maintaining a career is so difficult a combination that except for those few women with an extraordinary amount of physical strength, emotional endurance and a dedicated sense of calling to their work, it is unwise for women to attempt the combination. Women who have successfully combined child-rearing and

careers are considered out of the ordinary, although many men with far heavier work responsibilities who yet spend willing loving hours as fathers, and who also contribute to home maintenance, are cause for little comment. We should be wary of the assumption that home and work combinations are necessarily difficult. The simplified contemporary home and smaller sized family of a working mother today probably represent a lesser burden of responsibility than that shouldered by her grandmother.

This does not mean that we should overlook the real difficulties that are involved for women who attempt this combination. Working mothers do have primary responsibility for the hundreds of details involved in home mainte- nance, as planners and managers, even if they have household help to do the actual work. No one could suggest that child-rearing and a career are easy to combine, or even that this is some royal road to greater happiness, but only that the combination would give innumerable intelligent and creative women a degree of satisfaction and fulfillment that they cannot obtain in any other way. Certainly many things have to "give" if a woman works when she also has young children at home. Volunteer and social activities, gardening and entertaining may all have to be curtailed. The important point to recognize is that as children get older, it is far easier to resume these social activities than it is to resume an interrupted career. The major difficulty, and the one most in need of social innovation, is the problem of providing adequate care for the children of working mothers.

If a significant number of American middle-class women wish to work while their children are still young and in need of care and supervision, who are these mother-substitutes to be? In the American experience to date, they have been either relatives or paid domestic helpers. A study conducted by the Children's Bureau in 1958 outlines the types of child-care arrangements made by women working full time who had children under twelve years of age.[32] The study showed that the majority of these children (57 per cent) were cared for by relatives: fathers, older siblings, grandparents and others. About 21 per cent were cared for by nonrelatives, including neighbors as well as domestic helpers. Only 2 per cent of the children were receiving group care—in day nurseries, day-care centers, settlement houses, nursery schools and the like. Of the remainder, 8 per cent were expected to take care of themselves, the majority being the "latchkey" youngsters of ten and twelve years of age about whom we have heard a good deal in the press in recent years.

These figures refer to a national sample of employed mothers and concern women in blue collar jobs and predominantly low-skill white collar jobs. Presumably the proportion of middle-class working mothers who can rely on either relatives or their husbands would be drastically lower than this national average, and will probably decline even further in future years. Many of today's, and more of tomorrow's American grandmothers are going to be wage earners themselves and not baby-sitters for their grandchildren. In addition, as middle-class women enter the occupational world, they will experience less of a tug to remain close to the kinswomen of their childhood, and hence may contribute further to the pattern of geographic and social separation between young couples and both sets of their parents. Nor can many middle-class husbands care for their children, for their work hours are typically the same as those of their working wives: there can be little dovetailing of the work schedules of wives and husbands in the middle class as there can be in the working class.

At present, the major child-care arrangement for the middle-class woman who plans a return to work has to be hired household help. In the 1920's the professional and business wife-mother had little difficulty securing such domestic help, for there were thousands of first generation immigrant girls and women in our large cities whose first jobs in America were as domestic servants.[33] In the 1960's, the situation is quite different: the major source of domestic help in our large cities is Negro and Puerto Rican women. Assuming the continuation of economic affluence and further success in the American Negro's struggle for equal opportunity in education, jobs and housing, this reservoir will be further diminished in coming decades. The daughters of many present-day Negro domestic servants will be able to secure far better paying and more prestigeful jobs than their mothers can obtain in 1964. There will be increasing difficulty of finding adequate child-care help in future years as a result.

The problem is not merely that there may be decreasing numbers of domestic helpers available at the same time more women require their aid. There is an even more important question involved: are domestic helpers the best qualified persons to leave in charge of young children? Most middle-class families have exacting standards for the kind of teachers and the kind of schools they would like their children to have. But a working mother who searches for a competent woman to leave in charge of her home has to adjust to considerably lower standards than she would tolerate in any nursery school program in which she placed her young son or daughter, either because such competent help is scarce, or because the margin of salary left after paying for good child care and the other expenses associated with employment is very slight.

One solution to the problem of adequate child care would be an attempt to upgrade the status of child-care jobs. I think one productive way would be to develop a course of study which would yield a certificate for practical mothering, along the lines that such courses and certificates have been developed for practical nursing. There would be several important advantages to such a program. There are many older women in American communities whose lives seem empty because their children are grown and their grandchildren far away, yet who have no interest in factory or sales work, for they are deeply committed to life and work within the context of a home. Indeed, there are many older women who now work in factories or as cashiers or salesclerks who would be much more satisfied with child-care jobs, if the status and pay for such jobs were upgraded. These are the women, sometimes painfully lonely for contact with children, who stop young mothers to comment on the baby in the carriage, to talk with the three-year-old and to discuss their own distant grandchildren. I think many of these women would be attracted by a program of "refresher" courses in first aid, child development, books and crafts appropriate for children of various ages, and the special problems of the mother substitute-child relationship. Such a program would build upon their own experiences as mothers but would update and broaden their knowledge, bringing it closer to the values and practices of the middle-class woman who is seeking a practical mother for her family. Substitute motherhood for which she earns a wage, following active motherhood of her own, could provide continuity, meaning and variety to the life-span of those American women who are committed to the traditional conception of woman's role. Such a course of study might be developed in a number of school contexts—a branch of a college department of education, an adult education extension program or a school of nursing.

A longer-range solution to the problem of child care will involve the establishment of a network of child-care centers.[34] Most of the detailed plans for such centers must be left for future discussion, but there are several important advantages to professionally run child-care centers which should be noted. Most important, better care could be provided by such centers than any individual mother can provide by hiring a mother's helper, housekeeper or even the practical mother I have just proposed. In a child-care center, there can be greater specialization of skills, better facilities and equipment, and play groups for the children. Second, a child-care center would mean less expense for the individual working mother, and both higher wages and shorter hours for the staff of the center. Third, these centers could operate on a full-time, year-round schedule, something of particular importance for women trained in professional or technical fields, the majority of which can be handled only on a full-time basis. Except for the teaching fields, such women must provide for the afternoon care of their nursery school and kindergarten-age children, after-school hours for older children and three summer months for all their children. Fourth, a child-care center could develop a roster of home-duty practical mothers or practical nurses to care for the ill or convalescent child at home, in much the way school systems now call upon substitute teachers to cover the classes of absent regular teachers.

A major practical problem is where to locate such child-care centers. During the years of experimentation which would follow acceptance of this idea, they might be in a variety of places, under a variety of organizational auspices, as a service facility offered by an industrial firm, a large insurance company, a university, the federal or a state government. Community groups of women interested in such service might organize small centers of their own much as they have informal pooled baby-sitting services and cooperatively run nursery schools at the present time.

I believe that one of the most likely contexts for early experimentation with such child-care centers is the large urban university. As these universities continue to expand in future years, in terms of the size of the student body, the varied research institutes associated with the university and the expansion of administrative, technical and counseling personnel, there will be increasing opportunity and increasing need for the employment of women. A child-care center established under the auspices of a major university would facilitate the return for training of older women to complete or refresh advanced training, forestall the dropping out of younger graduate married women with infants and young children to care for, and attract competent professional women to administrative, teaching or research positions, who would otherwise withdraw from their fields for the child-rearing years. It would also be an excellent context within which to innovate a program of child care, for the university has the specialists in psychology, education and human development on whom to call for the planning, research and evaluation that the establishment of child-care centers would require. If a university-sponsored child-care program were successful and widely publicized, it would then constitute an encouragement and a challenge to extend child-care centers from the auspices of specific organizations to a more inclusive community basis. A logical location for community child-care centers may be as wings of the elementary schools, which have precisely the geographic distribution throughout a city to make for easy access between the homes of very young children and the centers for their daytime care. Since school and center would share a location, it would also facilitate easy supervision of older children during the after-school hours. The costs of such care would also be considerably reduced if the facilities of the school were available for the older children during after-school hours, under the supervision of the staff of the child-care center. There are, of course, numerous problems to be solved in working out the details of any such program under a local educational system, but assuming widespread support for the desirability of community facilities for child care, these are technical and administrative problems well within the competence of school and political officials in our communities.

I have begun this discussion of the institutional changes needed to effect equality between the sexes with the question of child-care provision because it is of central importance in permitting women to enter and remain in the professional, technical and administrative occupations in which they are presently so underrepresented. Unless provision for child care is made, women will continue to find it necessary to withdraw from active occupational involvement during the child-rearing years. However, the professional and scientific fields are all growing in knowledge and skill, and even a practitioner who remains in the field often has difficulty keeping abreast of new developments. A woman who withdraws for a number of years from a professional field has an exceedingly difficult time catching up. The more exacting the occupation, then, the shorter the period of withdrawal should probably be from active participation in the labor force. If a reserve of trained practical mothers were available, a professional woman could return to her field a few months after the birth of a child, leaving the infant under the care of a practical mother until he or she reached the age of two years, at about which age the child could enter a child-care center for daytime care. Assuming a two-child family, this could mean not more than one year of withdrawal from her professional field for the working mother.

2. The preferred residential pattern of the American middle class in the postwar decades has been suburban. In many sections of the country it is difficult to tell where one municipality ends and another begins, for the farm, forest and waste land between towns and cities have been built up with one housing development after another. The American family portrayed in the mass media typically occupies a house in this sprawling suburbia, and here too, are the American women, and sometimes men, whose problems are aired and analyzed with such frequency. We know a good deal about the characteristics and quality of social life in the American suburb[35] and the problems of the men and women who live in them. We hear about the changing political complexion of the American suburbs, the struggle of residents to provide sufficient community facilities to meet their growing needs. But the social and personal difficulties of suburban women are more likely to be attributed to their early family relationships or to the contradictory nature of the socialization of girls in our society than to any characteristic of the environment in which they now live. My focus will be somewhat different: I shall examine the suburban residence pattern for the limitations it imposes on the utilization of women's creative work abilities and the participation of men in family life. Both limitations have important implications for the lives of boys and girls growing up in the suburban home.

The geographic distance between home and work has a number of implications for the role of the father-husband in the family. It reduces the hours of possible contact between children and their fathers. The hour or more men spend in cars, buses or trains may serve a useful decompression function by providing time in which to sort out and assess the experiences at home and the events of the work day, but it is questionable whether this outweighs the disadvantage of severely curtailing the early morning and late afternoon hours during which men could be with their children.

The geographic distance also imposes a rigid exclusion of the father from the events which highlight the children's lives. Commuting fathers can rarely participate in any special daytime activities at home or at school, whether a party, a play the child performs in or a conference with a teacher. It is far less rewarding to a child to report to his father at night about such a party or part in a play than to have his father present at these events. If the husband-father must work late or attend an evening function in the city, he cannot sandwich in a few family hours but must remain in the city. This is the pattern which prompted Margaret Mead to characterize the American middle-class father as the "children's mother's husband," and partly why mother looms so oversized in the lives of suburban children.

Any social mixing of family-neighborhood and job associates is reduced or made quite formal: a work colleague cannot drop in for an after-work drink or a Saturday brunch when an hour or more separates the two men and their families. The father-husband's office and work associates have a quality of unreality to both wife and children. All these things sharpen the differences between the lives of men and women—fewer mutual acquaintances, less sharing of the day's events, and perhaps most importantly, less simultaneous filling of their complementary parent roles. The image of parenthood to the child is mostly motherhood, a bit of fatherhood and practically no parenthood as a joint enterprise shared at the same time by father and mother. Many suburban parents, I suspect, spend more time together as verbal parents— discussing their children in the children's absence—than they do actively interacting with their children, the togetherness cult notwithstanding. For couples whose relationship in courtship and early marriage was equalitarian, the pressures are strong in the suburban setting for parenthood to be highly differentiated and skewed to an ascendant position of the mother. Women dominate the family, men the job world.

The geographic distance between home and the center of the city restricts the world of the wife-mother in a complementary fashion. Not only does she have to do and be more things to her children, but she is confined to the limitations of the suburban community for a great many of her extrafamilial experiences. That suburban children are restricted in their social exposure to other young children and relatively young adults, mostly women and all of the same social class, has often been noted. I think the social restriction of the young wife to women of her own age and class is of equal importance: with very few older persons in her immediate environment, she has little first-hand exposure to the problems attending the empty-nest stage of life which lies ahead for herself. It is easy for her to continue to be satisfied to live each day as it comes, with little thought of preparing for the thirty-odd years when her children are no longer dependent upon her. If the suburban wife-mother had more opportunity to become acquainted with older widows and grandmothers, this would be pressed home to her in a way that might encourage a change in her unrealistic expectations of the future, with some preparation for that stage of life while she is young.[36]

If and when the suburban woman awakens from this short-range perspective and wants either to work or to prepare for a return to work when her children are older, how is she to do this, given the suburban pattern of residence? It is all very well to urge that school systems should extend adult education, that colleges and universities must make it possible for older women to complete education interrupted ten or more years previously or to be retrained for new fields; but this is a difficult program for the suburban wife to participate in. She lives far from the center of most large cities, where the educational facilities tend to be concentrated, in a predominantly middle-class community, where domestic help is often difficult to arrange and transportation often erratic during the hours she would be using it.

It is for these reasons that I believe any attempt to draw a significant portion of married women into the mainstream of occupational life must involve a reconsideration of the suburban pattern of living. Decentralization of business and industry has only partly alleviated the problem: a growing proportion of the husbands living in the suburbs also work in the suburbs. There are numerous shops and service businesses providing job opportunities for the suburban wife. Most such jobs, however, are at skill levels far below the ability potential and social status of the suburban middle-class wife. Opportunities for the more exacting professional, welfare and business jobs are still predominantly in the central sections of the city. In addition, since so many young wives and mothers in this generation married very young, before their formal education was completed, they will need more schooling before they can hope to enter the fields in which their talents can be most fruitfully exercised, in jobs which will not be either dull or a status embarrassment to themselves and their husbands. Numerous retail stores have opened suburban branches; colleges and universities have yet to do so. A woman can spend in the suburb, but she can neither learn nor earn.

That some outward expansion of American cities has been necessary is clear, given the population increase in our middle- to large-sized cities. But there are many tracts in American cities between the business center and the outlying suburbs which imaginative planning and architectural design could transform and which would attract the men and women who realize the drawbacks of a suburban residence. Unless there is a shift in this direction in American housing, I do not think there can be any marked increase in the proportion of married middle-class women who will enter the labor force. That Swedish women find work and home easier to combine than American women is closely related to the fact that Sweden avoided the sprawling suburban development in its postwar housing expansion. The emphasis in

Swedish housing has been on inner-city housing improvement. With home close to diversified services for schooling, child care, household help and places of work, it has been much easier in Sweden than in the United States to draw married women into the labor force and keep them there.

In contrast, the policy guiding the American federal agencies which affect the housing field, such as the FHA, have stressed the individual home, with the result that mortgage money was readily available to encourage builders to develop the sprawling peripheries of American cities. Luxury high-rise dwellings at the hub of the city and individual homes at the periphery have therefore been the pattern of middle-class housing development in the past twenty years. A shift in policy on the part of the federal government which would embrace buildings with three and four dwelling units and middle-income high-rise apartment buildings in the in-between zones of the city could go a long way to counteract this trend toward greater and greater distance between home and job. Not everyone can or will want to live close to the hub of the city. From spring through early fall, it is undoubtedly easier to rear very young children in a suburban setting with back yards for the exercise of healthy lungs and bodies. But this is at the expense of increased dependence of children on their mothers, of minimization of fathers' time with their youngsters, of restriction of the social environment of women, of drastic separation of family and job worlds and of less opportunity for even part-time schooling or work for married women.

3. Men and women must not only be able to participate equally; they must want to do so. It is necessary, therefore, to look more closely into their motivations, and the early experiences which mold their self-images and life expectations. A prime example of this point can be seen in the question of occupational choice. The goal of sex equality calls for not only an increase in the extent of women's participation in the occupational system, but a more equitable distribution of men and women in all the occupations which comprise that system. This means more women doctors, lawyers and scientists, more men social workers and school teachers. To change the sex ratio within occupations can only be achieved by altering the sex-typing of such occupations long before young people make a career decision.[37] Many men and women change their career plans during college, but this is usually within a narrow range of relatively homogenous fields: a student may shift from medicine to a basic science, from journalism to teaching English. Radical shifts such as from nursing to medicine, from kindergarten teaching to the law, are rare indeed. Thus while the problem could be attacked at the college level, any significant change in the career choices men and women make must be attempted when they are young boys and girls. It is during the early years of elementary school education that young people develop their basic

views of appropriate characteristics, activities and goals for their sex. It is for this reason that I shall give primary attention to the sources of sex-role stereotypes and what the elementary school system could do to eradicate these stereotypes and to help instead in the development of a more androgynous conception of sex role.[38]

The all-female social atmosphere of the American child has been frequently noted by social scientists, but it has been seen as a problem only in its effect upon boys. It has been claimed, for example, that the American boy must fight against a feminine identification this atmosphere encourages, with the result that he becomes overly aggressive, loudly asserting his maleness. In contrast, it is claimed that the American girl has an easy socialization, for she has an extensive number of feminine models in her environment to facilitate her identification as a female.

There are several important factors which this analysis overlooks. To begin with the boy: while it is certainly true that much of his primary group world is controlled by women, this does not mean that he has no image of the male social and job world as well. The content of the boy's image of man's work has a very special quality to it, however. Although an increasingly smaller proportion of occupations in a complex industrial society relies on sheer physical strength, the young boy's exposure to the work of men remains largely the occupations which do require physical strength. The jobs he can see are those which are socially visible, and these are jobs in which men are reshaping and repairing the physical environment. The young boy sees working class men operating trucks, bulldozers, cranes; paving roads; building houses; planting trees; delivering groceries. This image is further reinforced by his television viewing: the gun-toting cowboy, the bat-swinging ballplayer, the arrow-slinging Indian. Space operas suggest not scientific exploration but military combat, the collision and collusion of other worlds. In short, even if the boy sees little of his father and knows next to nothing of what his father does away from home, there is some content to his image of men's work in the larger society. At least some part of his aggressive active play may be as much acting out similar male roles in response to the cultural cues provided by his environment as it is an over-reaction to his feminine environment or an identification with an aggressor-father.

And what of the girl? What image of the female role is she acquiring during her early years? In her primary group environment, she sees women largely in roles defined in terms that relate to her as a child—as mother, aunt, grandmother, baby-sitter—or in roles relating to the house—the cleaning, cooking, mending activities of mother and domestic helpers. Many mothers work outside the home, but the daughter often knows as little of that work as she does of her father's. Even if her own mother works, the reasons for such working that are given to the child are most often couched in terms of the mother or housewife role. Thus, a girl is seldom told that her mother works because she enjoys it or finds it very important to her own satisfaction in life, but because the money she earns will help pay for the house, a car, the daughter's clothes, dancing lessons or school tuition.[39] In other words, working is something mothers sometimes have to do as mothers, not something mothers do as adult women. This is as misleading and distorted an image of the meaning of work as the father who tells his child he works "to take care of mummy and you" and neglects to mention that he also works because he finds personal satisfaction in doing so, or that he is contributing to knowledge, peace or the comfort of others in the society.

The young girl also learns that it is only in the family that women seem to have an important superordinate position. However high her father's occupational status outside the home, when he returns at night, he is likely to remove his white shirt and become a blue collar Mr. Fixit or mother's helper. The traditional woman's self-esteem would be seriously threatened if her husband were to play a role equal to her own in the lives and affections of her children or in the creative or managerial aspect of home management, precisely because her major sphere in which to acquire the sense of personal worth is her home and children.[40] The lesson is surely not lost on her daughter, who learns that at home father does not know best, though outside the home men are the bosses over women, as she can see only too well in the nurse-doctor, secretary-boss, salesclerk-store manager, space Jane-space John relationships that she has an opportunity to observe.

The view that the socialization of the girl is an easy one compared with the boy depends on the kind of woman one has in mind as an end-product of socialization. Only if the woman is to be the traditional wife-mother is present-day socialization of young girls adequate, for from this point of view the confinement to the kinds of feminine models noted above and the superordinate position of the mother in the family facilitate an easy identification. If a girl sees that women reign only at home or in a history book, whereas outside the home they are Girl Fridays to men, then clearly for many young girls the wife-mother role may appear the best possible goal to have. It should be noted, however, that identification has been viewed primarily as an either-or process—the child identifies either with the mother or the father—and not as a process in which there is a fusion of the two parent models such that identification involves a modeling of the self after mother in some respects, father in others. It is possible that those women who have led exciting, intellectually assertive and creative lives did not identify exclusively with their traditional mothers, but crossed the sex line and looked to their fathers as model sources for ideas and life commitments of their own. This is to suggest that an exclusively same-sex identification between parent and child is no necessary condition for either mentally healthy or creative adults.

If I am correct about the significance of the father in the childhoods of those women who later led creative adult lives, then an increased accessibility of the middle-class father to his daughters and greater sharing of his ideas and interests could help to counteract the narrow confines of the feminine models daughters have. Beyond this, young girls need exposure to female models in professional and scientific occupations and to women with drive and dedication who are playing innovative volunteer roles in community organizations; they need an encouragement to emulate them and a preparation for an equalitarian rather than a dominant role in parenthood. Only if a woman's self-esteem is rooted in an independent life outside her family as well as her roles within the home can she freely welcome her husband to share on an equal basis the most rewarding tasks involved in child-rearing and home maintenance.

What happens when youngsters enter school? Instead of broadening the base on which they are forming their image of male and female roles, the school perpetuates the image children bring from home and their observations in the community. It has been mother who guided their preschool training; now in school it is almost exclusively women teachers who guide their first serious learning experiences. In the boy's first readers, men work at the same jobs with the same tools he has observed in his neighborhood— "T" for truck, "B" for bus, "W" for wagon. His teachers expect him to be rugged, physically strong and aggressive. After a few years he moves into separate classes for gym, woodworking and machine shop. For the girl, women are again the ones in charge of children. Her first readers portray women in aprons, brooms in their hands or babies in their arms. Teachers expect her to be quiet, dependent, with feminine interests in doll and house play and dressing up. In a few years she moves into separate classes for child care, cooking and practical nursing. In excursions into the community, elementary school boys and girls visit airports, bus terminals, construction sites, factories and farms.

What can the schools do to counteract these tendencies to either outmoded or traditional images of the roles of men and women? For one, class excursions into the community are no longer needed to introduce American children to building construction, airports or zoos. Except for those in the most underprivileged areas of our cities, American children have ample exposure to such things with their car- and plane-riding families. There are, after all, only a limited number of such excursions possible in the course of a school year. I think visits to a publishing house, research laboratory, computer firm or art studio would be more enriching than airports and zoos.

Going out into the community in this way, youngsters would observe men and women in their present occupational distribution. By a program of bringing representatives of occupations into the classroom and auditorium, however, the school could broaden the spectrum of occupations young children may link to their own abilities and interests regardless of the present sex-typing of occupations, by making a point of having children see and hear a woman scientist or doctor; a man dancer or artist; both women and men who are business executives, writers and architects.[41]

Another way in which the elementary schools could help is making a concerted effort to attract male teachers to work in the lower grades. This would add a rare and important man to the primary group environment of both boys and girls. This might seem a forlorn hope to some, since elementary school teaching has been such a predominantly feminine field, and it may be harder to attract men to it than to attract women to fields presently considered masculine. It may well be that in the next decade or so the schools could not attract and keep such men as teachers. But it should be possible for graduate schools of education and also school systems to devise ways of incorporating more men teachers in the lower grades, either as part of their teacher training requirements or in the capacity of specialized teachers: the science, art or music teacher who works with children at many grade levels rather than just one or two contiguous grade levels.[42] His presence in the lives of very young children could help dispel their expectation that only women are in charge of children, that nurturance is a female attribute or that strength and an aggressive assault on the physical environment is the predominant attribute of man's work.

The suggestions made thus far relate to a change in the sex-linking of occupations. There is one crucial way in which the schools could effect a change in the traditional division of labor by sex within the family sphere. The claim that boys and girls are reared in their early years without any differentiation by sex is only partially true. There are classes in all elementary schools which boys and girls take separately or which are offered only to one sex. These are precisely the courses most directly relevant to adult family roles: courses in sex and family living (where communities are brave enough to hold them) are typically offered in separate classes for boys and for girls, or for girls only. Courses in shop and craft work are scheduled for boys only; courses in child care, nursing and cooking are for girls only. In departing from completely coeducational programs, the schools are reinforcing the traditional division of labor by sex which most children observe in their homes. Fifteen years later, these girls find that they cannot fix a broken plug, set a furnace pilot light or repair a broken high chair or favorite toy. These things await the return of the child's father and family handyman in the evening. When a child is sick in the middle of the night, his mother takes over; father is only her assistant or helper.

These may seem like minor matters, but I do not think they are. They unwittingly communicate to and reinforce in the child a rigid differentiation of role between men and women in family life. If first aid, the rudiments of child care and of cooking have no place in their early years as sons, brothers and schoolboys, then it is little wonder that as husbands and fathers American men learn these things under their wives' tutelage. Even assuming these wives were actively involved in occupations of their own and hence free of the psychological pressure to assert their ascendancy in the family, it would be far better for all concerned—the married pair and the children as well—if men brought such skills with them to marriage.

This is the point where the schools could effect a change: if boys and girls took child care, nursing, cooking, shop and craft classes together, they would have an opportunity to acquire comparable skills and pave the way for true parental substitutability as adults. They would also be learning something about how to complement each other, not just how to compete with each other.[43] Teamwork should be taught in school in the subjects relevant to adult family roles, not just within each sex on the playground or in the gymnasium. In addition to encouraging more equality in the parental role, such preparation as school children could ease their adjustment to the crises of adult life; illness, separation due to the demands of a job or military service, divorce or death would have far less trauma and panic for the one-parent family— whether mother or father—if such equivalence and substitutability were a part of the general definition of the parental role.

A school curriculum which brought boys and girls into the same classes and trained them in social poise, the healing skills, care of children, handling of interpersonal difficulties and related subjects would also encourage the development of skills which are increasingly needed in our complex economy. Whether the adult job is to be that of a worker in an automated industry, a professional man in law, medicine or scholarship, or an executive in a large bureaucratic organization, the skills which are needed are not physical strength and ruggedness in interpersonal combat but understanding in human dealings, social poise and persuasive skill in interpersonal relations.[44] All too often, neither the family nor the school encourages the development of these skills in boys. Hundreds of large business firms look for these qualities in young male applicants but often end up trying to develop them in their young executives through on-the-job training programs.

I have suggested a number of ways in which the educational system could serve as an important catalyst for change toward sex equality. The schools could reduce sex-role stereotypes of appropriate male and female attributes and activities by broadening the spectrum of occupations youngsters may consider for themselves irrespective of present sex-linked notions of man's work and woman's work, and by providing boys as well as girls with training in the tasks they will have as parents and spouses. The specific suggestions for achieving these ends which I have made should be viewed more as illustrative than as definitive, for educators themselves may have far better suggestions for how to implement the goal in the nation's classrooms than I have offered in these pages. Equality between the sexes cannot be achieved by proclamation or decree but only through a multitude of concrete steps, each of which may seem insignificant by itself, but all of which add up to the social blueprint for attaining the general goal.

SUMMARY PROFILE

In the course of this essay I have suggested a number of institutional innovations in education, residence and child care which would facilitate equality between the sexes. Instead of a more conventional kind of summary, I shall describe a hypothetical case of a woman who is reared and lives out her life under the changed social conditions proposed in this essay.

She will be reared, as her brother will be reared, with a combination of loving warmth, firm discipline, household responsibility and encouragement of independence and self-reliance. She will not be pampered and indulged, subtly taught to achieve her ends through coquetry and tears, as so many girls are taught today. She will view domestic skills as useful tools to acquire, some of which, like fine cooking or needlework, having their own intrinsic pleasures but most of which are necessary repetitive work best gotten done as quickly and efficiently as possible. She will be able to handle minor mechanical breakdowns in the home as well as her brother can, and he will be able to tend a child, press, sew, and cook with the same easy skills and comfortable feeling his sister has.

During their school years, both sister and brother will increasingly assume responsibility for their own decisions, freely experiment with numerous possible fields of study, gradually narrowing to a choice that best suits their interests and abilities rather than what is considered appropriate or prestigeful work for men and women. They will be encouraged by parents and teachers alike to think ahead to a whole life span, viewing marriage and parenthood as one strand among many which will constitute their lives. The girl will not feel the pressure to belittle her accomplishments, lower her aspirations, learn to be a receptive listener in her relations with boys, but will be as true to her growing sense of self as her brother and male friends are. She will not marry before her adolescence and schooling are completed, but will be willing and able to view the college years as a "moratorium" from deeply intense cross-sex commitments, a period of life during which her identity can be "at large and open and various."[45] Her intellectual aggressiveness as well as her brother's tender sentiments will be welcomed and accepted as *human* characteristics, without the self-questioning doubt of latent homosexuality that troubles many college-age men and women in our era when these qualities are sex-linked.[46] She will not cling to her parents, nor they to her, but will establish an increasingly larger sphere of her own independent world in which she moves and works, loves and thinks, as a maturing young person. She will learn to take pleasure in her own body and a man's body and to view sex as a good and wonderful experience, but not as an exclusive basis for an ultimate commitment to another person, and not as a test of her competence as a female or her partner's competence as a male. Because she will have a many-faceted conception of her self and its worth, she will be free to merge and lose herself in the sex act with a lover or a husband.[47]

Marriage for our hypothetical woman will not mark a withdrawal from the life and work pattern that she has established, just as there will be no sharp discontinuity between her early childhood and youthful adult years. Marriage will be an enlargement of her life experiences, the addition of a new dimension to an already established pattern, rather than an abrupt withdrawal to the home and a turning in upon the marital relationship. Marriage will be a "looking outward in the same direction" for both the woman and her husband. She will marry and bear children only if she deeply desires a mate and children, and will not be judged a failure as a person if she decides against either. She will have few children if she does have them, and will view her pregnancies, childbirth and early months of motherhood as one among many equally important highlights in her life, experienced intensely and with joy but not as the exclusive basis for a sense of self-fulfillment and purpose in life. With planning and foresight, her early years of child bearing and rearing can fit a long-range view of all sides of herself. If her children are not to suffer from "paternal deprivation," her husband will also anticipate that the assumption of parenthood will involve a weeding out of nonessential activities either in work, civic or social participation. Both the woman and the man will feel that unless a man can make room in his life for parenthood, he should not become a father. The woman will make sure, even if she remains at home during her child's infancy, that he has ample experience of being with and cared for by other adults besides herself, so that her return to a full-time position in her field will not constitute a drastic change in the life of the child, but a gradual pattern of increasing supplementation by others of the mother. The children will have a less intense involvement with their mother, and she with them, and they will all be the better for it. When they are grown and establish adult lives of their own, our woman will face no retirement twenty years before her husband, for her own independent activities will continue and expand. She will be neither an embittered wife, an interfering mother-in-law nor an idle parasite, but together with her husband she will be able to live an independent, purposeful and satisfying third act in life.

NOTES

1. This is one among many points of crucial and still relevant significance to be found in John Stuart Mill's essay "The Subjection of Women" (London, 1869).

2. In recent years of acute manpower shortages in scientific, professional and technical fields, there has been a growing awareness of the fact that women constitute the only sizable remaining reservoir of such talent. Many men whose administrative or policy responsibilities alert them to this fact have been eagerly exploring the ways by which female brainpower could be added to the national pool of skilled manpower. The contemporary period is therefore ripe with opportunities for talented women, and women can anticipate a welcome from male colleagues and employers. I shall not discuss any further the current societal need for women in the labor force, because I would argue for an extension of female participation in the higher levels of occupations even in an era with *no* pressing manpower shortages, on the grounds of the more general principles to be developed in this essay.

3. Often the conclusion that sex differentiation is a basic and universal phenomenon is buttressed by pointing to a large number of societies, all of which manifest such sex differentiation. Since Americans are easily impressed by large numbers, this does indeed sound like conclusive evidence against the likelihood of any society's achieving full sex equality. Closer examination of such samples, however, reveals two things: very little representation of numerous African societies in which the instrumental-expressive distinction is simply *not* linked to sex in the predicted direction, and second, they are largely primitive societies, a half dozen of which might equal the size of a very small American city. Such cultural comparisons assume every possible kind of societal arrangement is represented, but this is not the case: Sweden, China, Yugoslavia, the Soviet Union, Israel are not represented on such a continuum. I believe we may learn more that is of relevance to a future America by studying family patterns in these societies than from a study of all the primitive societies in the world. Unfortunately, most of contemporary sociology and social anthropology is far less concerned with the future than the present as molded by the past.

4. A rare exception is the recent work by William J. Goode, who has focussed precisely on the active role of the family in determining the course of social change in the non-family segments of social structure. See his *World Revolution and Family Patterns* (Glencoe: The Free Press, 1963).

5. When the sociologist finds, for example, that the incidence of divorce is higher for those who marry outside their religion than for those who do not, he concludes that intermarriage is "bad" or "risky"; he does not say such marital failures may reflect the relative newness of the social pattern of intermarriage, much less suggest that such failures may decline once this pattern is more prevalent. In fact, the only aspect of intermarriage which is studied is the incidence of its failure. Sociologists have not studied *successful* intermarriages.

6. A full picture of this post-World War II development is traced in Betty Friedan's *The Feminine Mystique* (New York: W. W. Norton, 1963). See particularly Chapters 6 and 7 on the "Functional Freeze" and the "Sex-Directed Educators."

7. Demographic changes in the family life cycle between 1890 and 1950 are shown in great detail in Paul Glick's *American Families* (New York: John Wiley, 1957). It should also be noted that even in contemporary families with four or five children, child-bearing occupies a far shorter portion of a woman's life span than it did to achieve this size family fifty years ago, because infant mortality has been so drastically reduced.

8. Cowles and Dietz, Myrdal and Klein, and Jean Warren have shown that there has been very little change in the past quarter century in the total working time per week devoted to homemaking activities. May L. Cowles and Ruth P. Dietz, "Time Spent in Homemaking Activities by a Selected Group of Wisconsin Farm Homemakers," *Journal of Home Economics,* 48 (January, 1956), 29–35; Jean Warren, "Time: Resource or Utility," *Journal of Home Economics,* 49 (January, 1957), 21 ff; Alva Myrdal and Viola Klein, *Women's Two Roles: Home and Work* (London: Routledge and Kegan Paul, 1956).

9. Benjamin Spock, "Should Mothers Work?" *Ladies' Home Journal,* February, 1963.

10. See Anna Freud and Dorothy T. Burlingham, *Infants Without Families* (New York: International University Press, 1944); William Goldfarb, "Psychological Deprivation in Infancy and Subsequent Adjustment," *American Journal of Orthopsychiatry,* 15 (April, 1945), 247–255; John Bowlby, *Maternal Care and Mental Health* (Geneva: World Health Organization, 1952); John Bowlby, *Child-Care and the Growth of Love* (London: Pelican Books, 1953); and James Bossard, *The Sociology of Child Development* (New York: Harper, 1954).

11. A few authors have seen this claim that all separation of the child from the biological mother or mother surrogate, even for a few days, is inevitably damaging to the child, as a new and subtle form of anti-feminism, by which men, under the guise of exacting the importance of maternity, are tying women more tightly to their children than any real clinical or cultural evidence indicates is necessary. See Hilde Bruch, *Don't Be Afraid of Your Child* (New York: Farrar, Straus & Young, 1952); and Margaret Mead, "Some Theoretical Considerations on the Problem of Mother-Child Separation," *American Journal of Orthopsychiatry* (1954), 24: 471–483.

12. It is interesting in this connection that studies concerning the separation of the mother and child are frequently cited as cases of *maternal deprivation,* but those concerning the separation of the father and child are cited more neutrally as cases of *father absence,* never as *paternal deprivation.*

13. Social scientists raise the question of whether there are not such diametrically opposed requirements of an occupational role from the mother role as to involve great strain between the two. It is argued that because of this contrast between the two spheres, one or the other role must "suffer," there will be "role conflict." The researchers were not prepared to find either that women could slip back and forth between these two spheres just as men have done for decades without any of the same difficulty predicted for women, or that the mother role may be subtly changed in the direction of more rationality, greater stress on independence and autonomy in children than is found in the child-rearing values of non-working mothers (See Faye VonMering, "Professional and Non-Professional Women as Mothers," *Journal of Social Psychology* [August, 1955], 42: 21–34). Rather, the researcher expected to find maternal neglect, negative effect on children's personality, or inadequacy in occupational roles, such as absenteeism, overly personal view of work relationships, etc. As in many areas in which role conflict has been predicted, human beings have a greater tolerance for sharp contrasts in role demands than social scientists credit them with.

14. Burchinal and Rossman found no significant relationships between any kind of employment and personality characteristics or social interaction of children in the 7th and 11th grades in school—Lee G. Burchinal and Jack E. Rossman, "Relations among Maternal Employment Indices and Developmental Characteristics of Children," *Marriage and Family Living,* 23 (November, 1961), 334–340. Nye administered questionnaires to over two thousand high school students and found no significant relationships between maternal employment and educational achievement or neurotic symptoms—F. Ivan Nye, "Employment Status of Mothers and Adjustment of Adolescent Children," *Marriage and Family Living,* 21 (August, 1959), 240–244. Using scales to tap nervous symptoms, antisocial and withdrawing tendencies, Perry found no significant differences between children with working and non-working mothers—Joseph B. Perry, "The Mother Substitutes of Employed Mothers: An Exploratory Inquiry," *Marriage and Family Living,* 23 (November, 1961), 362–367. Kligler found that employed mothers reported their maternal role suffered least from their occupations—Deborah S. Kligler, "The Effects of the Employment of Married Women on Husband and Wife Roles." Unpublished. Ph.D. dissertation, Department of Sociology, Yale University, 1954. Roy found no consistent effects of maternal employment on the social life and participation of children or their academic performance, or the affection, fairness of discipline and cooperation in the family—Prodipto Roy, "Maternal Employment and Adolescent Roles: Rural-Urban Differentials," *Marriage and Family Living,*

23 (November, 1961), 340–349. Peterson found no significant differences on employment of mothers and maternal interest in and supervision of their adolescent daughters—Evan T. Peterson, "The Impact of Maternal Employment on the Mother-Daughter Relationship," *Marriage and Family Living*, 23 (November, 1961), 355–361. In Eleanor Maccoby's reanalysis of data from the Gluecks' study of working mothers and delinquency, she shows that working or not working has little effect once the quality of child care is taken into account—Eleanor Maccoby, "Effects Upon Children of their Mothers' Outside Employment," in National Manpower Council, *Work in the Lives of Married Women* (New York: Columbia University Press, 1958), pp. 150–172. General reviews of the literature are found in: Lois M. Stolz, "Effects of Maternal Employment on Children: Evidence from Research," *Child Development*, 31 (December, 1960), 749–782; Eli Ginzberg (ed.), *The Nation's Children*, Vol. 3, *Problems and Prospects* (New York: Columbia University Press, 1960) in the chapter by Henry David on "Work, Women and Children," pp. 180–198; and Elizabeth Herzog, *Children of Working Mothers* (Washington, D.C.: U. S. Department of Health, Education and Welfare, Children's Bureau Publication #382, 1960); and most recently, a volume of research papers on the employed mother by F. Ivan Nye and Lois W. Hoffman, *The Employed Mother in America* (Chicago: Rand McNally, 1963).

15. Marian Radke Yarrow, Phyllis Scott, Louise de Leeuw, and Christine Heinig, "Child-rearing in Families of Working and Non-working Mothers," *Sociometry*, 25 (June, 1962), 122–140.

16. Only in recent years has there been a shift in the discussion and research on maternal employment: investigators have begun to explore the *positive* effects of maternal employment. For example, Urie Bronfenbrenner has suggested that employed mothers may have a positive effect upon adolescent children by giving them a chance to develop responsibility for their own behavior—Urie Bronfenbrenner, "Family Structure and Personality Development: Report of Progress" (Ithaca, New York: Cornell University, Department of Child Development and Family Relationships, 1958 mimeographed). Ruth Hartley has suggested that the working mother may have "stretching effects" upon a child's perceptions and social concepts—Ruth E. Hartley, "What Aspects of Child Behavior Should be Studied in Relation to Maternal Employment," *Research Issues Related to the Effects of Maternal Employment on Children* (New York: Social Science Research Center, The Pennsylvania State University, 1961), p. 48.

17. The Burchinal-Rossman research cited previously did give special attention to employment of mothers during the child's early years. Their 7th- and 11th-grade students were divided according to when the maternal employment occurred—i.e., whether during the first three years of the child's life, second three, between the ages of 1 and 6, only within the previous 30 months or for the child's entire life. How long the mother has been working, or when in the growth of the child she began work, showed no significant effect upon the children's development: those whose mothers were working when they were under three years of age did not differ from those whose mothers began working when they were adolescents.

18. A. I. Rabin, "Infants and Children under Conditions of 'Intermittent' Mothering in the Kibbutz," *American Journal of Orthopsychiatry*, 28 (1958), 577–584; Rabin, "Personality Maturity of Kibbutz and Non-Kibbutz Children as Reflected in Rorschach Findings," *Journal of Projective Techniques*, 21 (1957), 148–153; Rabin, "Attitudes of Kibbutz Children to Family and Parents," *American Journal of Orthopsychiatry*, 29 (1959), 172–179; Rabin, "Some Psychosexual Differences between Kibbutz and Non-Kibbutz Israeli Boys," *Journal of Projective Techniques*, 22 (1958), 328–332; H. Faigin, "Social Behavior of Young Children in the Kibbutz," *Journal of Abnormal and Social Psychology*, 56 (1958), 117–129. A good overview of these studies can be found in David Rapaport, "The Study of Kibbutz Education and its Bearing on the Theory of Development," *American Journal of Orthopsychiatry*, 28 (1958), 587–599.

19. There are of course other instances of infant and toddler care by persons supplementing the biological mother, notable among them being the creche and nursery school systems in the Soviet Union. What effect these early experiences of creche care have upon the subsequent

personality development of Soviet young people is not known. Western observers who have visited them during the past several years have been impressed with the facilities, quality of staff personnel, and general happy mood of the children seen in them, but there is no rigorous evidence to substantiate these impressions, or assess the effect of such early separation from the mother upon personality.

20. In this analysis, I am placing primary emphasis on the quality of the care given to the children. Another specification of maternal employment involves introducing the motivations and satisfactions of working and non-working mothers: many women work who do not wish to work, and many women are at home who do not wish to be at home. One recent study which took these factors into consideration found that the non-working mothers who are dissatisfied with not working (who want to work but, out of a sense of "duty," do not work) show the greatest problems in child rearing—more difficulty controlling their children, less emotional satisfaction in relationships to their children, less confidence in their functioning as mothers. Cf. Marian Radke Yarrow *et al., op. cit.*

21. This shifts the ground of the problem of maternal employment to a very different level from the one on which it is usually discussed. As a research problem, the crucial question is not whether the mother is employed or not, but what is the quality of the care given to the children—whether by the mother alone or a combination of other adults. Since full-time mothers vary from loving care to rejecting neglect, and mother substitutes may be presumed to vary in the same way, it is scarcely surprising that maternal employment *per se* shows very little effect upon the personality of children. Social scientists have uncritically borrowed the assumption of the psychoanalysts that the mental health of the child is possible only with continuous care by the biological mother. What is clearly called for is a shift in research definition from maternal employment versus full-time motherhood, to the quality of the care the child receives under conditions of full- and part-time working or non-working mothers. There is also a need for research which is based on a clear conceptualization of the variables of both "maternal care" and "maternal deprivation." For a careful review of crucial dimensions of maternal care and their effect upon infants, see Leon J. Yarrow, "Research in Dimensions of Early Maternal Care," *Merrill-Palmer Quarterly,* 9 (April, 1963), 101–114. The same author has written a careful re-evaluation of the concept of maternal deprivation: "Maternal deprivation: toward an empirical and conceptual re-evaluation," *Psychological Bulletin,* 58 (1961), 459–490.

22. This passivity and softness in American young people has been noted in the following works: David Riesman, Introduction to Edgar Friedenberg, *The Vanishing Adolescent* (Boston: Beacon Press, 1959); Paul Goodman, *Growing Up Absurd* (New York: Random House, 1960); Marjorie K. McCorquodale, "What They Will Die for in Houston," *Harper's,* October, 1961; the *Dædalus* issue on *Youth: Change and Challenge,* Winter 1962. The White House attempt in recent years to revitalize physical education has been in part a response to the distressing signs of muscular deterioration and physical passivity of American youth.

23. Edward A. Strecker, *Their Mothers' Sons* (Philadelphia: Lippincott, 1946).

24. Friedenberg, *The Vanishing Adolescent.*

25. Numerous authors have analyzed the effect of women's focus on their children as their chief achievement: John Spiegel, "New Perspectives in the Study of the Family," *Marriage and Family Living,* 16 (February, 1954), 4–12; Bruno Bettelheim, "Growing Up Female," *Harper's,* October, 1962. The effects of such exclusive maternal focus on children upon relations with married children are shown in: Marvin Sussman, "Family Continuity: Selective Factors which Affect Relationships between Families at Generational Levels," *Marriage and Family Living,* 16 (May, 1954), 112–130; Paul Wallin, "Sex Differences in Attitudes toward In-Laws," *American Journal of Sociology,* 59 (1954), 466–469; Harvey Locke, *Predicting Adjustment in Marriage* (New York: Holt, 1951); Evelyn M. Duvall, *In-Laws: Pro and Con* (New York: Associated Press, 1954); and Frances Jerome Woods, *The American Family System* (New York: Harper and Brothers, 1959), pp. 265–266. These authors discuss the strains with mothers-in-law stemming

from too exclusive a focus of women on their children and their subsequent difficulty in "releasing" their children when they are grown.

26. This has been argued by Eric Larrabee, though he does not suggest the employment of the mother as the way to make the older woman's life more interesting. See Eric Larrabee, "Childhood in Twentieth Century America," Eli Ginzberg (ed.), *The Nation's Children,* Vol. 3, *Problems and Prospects* (New York: Columbia University Press, 1960), pp. 199–216.

27. See Margaret Cussler's profile of the "volunteer executive" in her study *The Woman Executive* (New York: Harcourt, Brace, 1958), pp. 111–118.

28. Viola Klein's study of English working women shows the same pattern: withdrawal and return to work at a later age is paid for by a loss of occupational status. See Viola Klein, *Working Wives,* Occasional Papers No. 15 (London: Institute of Personnel Management, 1960), pp. 21–24.

29. Myrdal and Klein, *Women's Two Roles: Home and Work,* pp. 33–64; National Manpower Council, *Womanpower* (New York: Columbia University Press, 1957); Florence Kluckhohn, *The American Family: Past and Present and America's Women* (Chicago: The Delphian Society, 1952), p. 116; and Rose Goldsen et al., *What College Students Think* (Princeton: D. Van Nostrand, 1960), pp. 46–59, 81–96.

30. Florence Kluckhohn, "Variations in Basic Values of Family Systems," in Norman W. Bell and Ezra F. Vogel, *A Modern Introduction to the Family* (Glencoe, Illinois: The Free Press, 1960), pp. 304–316; and George Gallup and Evan Hill, "The American Woman," *The Saturday Evening Post,* December 22, 1962, pp. 15–32.

31. Talcott Parsons, *Essays in Sociological Theory Pure and Applied* (Glencoe, Illinois: The Free Press, 1949), pp. 222–224 and 243–246.

32. Henry C. Lajewski, *Child Care Arrangements of Full-Time Working Mothers* (Washington, D.C.: U.S. Department of Health, Education and Welfare, Children's Bureau Publication No. 378, 1959); and Herzog, *Children of Working Mothers.*

33. In one study conducted for the Bureau of Vocational Information in 1925, Collier found that 42% of the one hundred professional and business mothers she interviewed had two or more full-time domestic servants to maintain their homes and care for their children during the day; only 9 of these 100 women had no full-time servants, five of whom had their mothers living with them. Virginia MacMakin Collier, *Marriage and Careers: A Study of One Hundred Women who are Wives, Mothers, Homemakers and Professional Women* (New York: The Channel Bookshop, 1926), pp. 59 and 74.

34. Child-care centers would not be an entirely new phenomenon in the United States, for there were a number of municipal day-care centers established during World War II when the need for womanpower in factories engaged in war production made them necessary to free women to accept employment. There have also been continuing debates about the provision of child-care centers for other mothers, such as the ADC mother, the problem revolving about whether such women should be given sufficient money from municipal funds to stay at home and care for her children, or to establish child-care centers and thus enable such women to hold down jobs and at least partially support their children. In either case, the focus has been upon working-class women. Child-care centers as an institutional device to facilitate the combination of job and family by women in professional and technical occupations in the middle class are very rare, and are largely confined to small private ventures in the large metropoli.

35. William Whyte, *Organization Man* (New York: Simon and Schuster, 1956); Robert Wood, *Suburbia, Its People and Their Politics* (Boston: Houghton Mifflin, 1959); John Keats, *The Crack in the Picture Window* (Boston: Houghton Mifflin, 1956); A. C. Spectorsky, *The Exurbanites* (Philadelphia: J. B. Lippincott, 1955); and Nanette E. Scofield, "Some Changing Roles of Women in Suburbia: A Social Anthropological Case Study," *Transactions of the New York Academy of Sciences,* 22 (April, 1960), 6.

36. George Gallup and Evan Hill, "The American Woman," *The Saturday Evening Post,* December 22, 1962. One must read this survey very carefully to get behind the gloss of the

authors' rosy perspective. Gallup reports that almost half of the married women in the sample claimed that childbirth was the "most thrilling event" in their lives. He gives two quotes to illustrate why these women were so fascinated by childbirth: one stresses the point that it was "the one time in my life when everything was right"; the other points out "you've done something that's recognized as a good thing to do, and you're the center of attention." If these are truly typical, it tells us a good deal about the underlying attitude toward the thousands of days on which no child is born: things are *not* all right, and there must be some sense of being on the sidelines, of having a low level of self-esteem, if childbirth is important because "society views it as good" and it is the only time in her life that she is the important center of attention. In other parts of the article, which generally stresses the central importance of children to women, and their high satisfaction with marriage, we learn that a large proportion of American women wish the schools would do more of the socializing of these children—teach them good citizenship, how to drive, sex education; and if these women were so satisfied with their lives, why does only 10% of the sample want their daughters to live the same lives they have? Instead, these women say they want their daughters to get more education and to marry later than they did. If marriage is the perfect female state, then why wish to postpone it, unless there are unexpressed sides of the self which have not been fulfilled?

The only strong critical point made is the following: "with early weddings and extended longevity, marriage is now a part-time career for women, and unless they prepare now for the freer years, this period will be a loss. American society will hardly accept millions of ladies of leisure, or female drones, in their 40's" (p. 32). But only 31% of the sample reported they are "taking courses or following a plan to improve themselves," a third of these involving improvement of their physical shape or appearance. The photographs accompanying this article reveal the authors' own focus on the years of youth rather than of maturity: of 29 women appearing in these pictures, only 2 are clearly of women over 45 years of age.

37. The extent of this sex-typing of occupations is shown dramatically in a study of the June, 1961 college graduates conducted by the National Opinion Research Center at the University of Chicago. Although the women in this sample of college graduates showed a superior academic performance during the college years—only 36% of the women in contrast to 50% of the men were in the "bottom half" of their class—their career aspirations differed markedly from those of men. Of those who were going on to graduate and professional schools in the fall of 1961, only 6% of those aspiring to careers in medicine were women; 7% in physics, 7% in pharmacology, 10% in business and administration, 28% in the social sciences. In contrast, women predominated in the following fields: 51% in humanities, 59% in elementary and secondary education, 68% in social work, 78% in health fields such as nursing, medical technology, physical and occupational therapy. In a sample of 33,782 college graduates, there were 11,000 women who expected to follow careers in elementary and secondary education, but only 285 women who hoped to enter the combined fields of medicine, law and engineering. See James A. Davis and Norman Bradburn, "Great Aspirations: Career Plans of America's June 1961 College Graduates," National Opinion Research Center Report No. 82, September, 1961 (mimeographed). Davis and Bradburn report that some 40% of the graduates had changed their career plans during their college years (p. 40).

38. My attention in this section will be largely on the early years of schooling. There is a great need, however, for a return of the spirit that characterized high school and college educators of women in the 1930's. It has seemed to me that there is an insidious trend at this level of education toward discouraging women from aspiring to the most demanding and rewarding fields of work and thought. Dr. Mary Bunting, noteworthy for the imaginative Radcliffe Institute for Independent Study, now urges women to work on the "fringes" of the occupational system, away from the most competitive intellectual market places. In her first public address upon assuming the presidency of Barnard College, Dr. Rosemary Park stated that in her view college education of women in the United States should have as its goal the creation of "enlightened laymen." High

school and college counselors give hearty approval if women students show talent and interest in elementary school teaching, nursing, social work; their approval is all too often very lukewarm if not discouraging, if women students show interest in physics, medicine or law.

39. Although her sample was upper-middle-class mothers of girls in progressive schools in New York City, Ruth Hartley reports that the working mothers in her sample told their children they were working out of the home because of financial need: "They express guilt about their working and appear to hold quite traditional concepts of appropriate 'feminine' behavior which they feel they are violating." An example is provided by a well-to-do working mother who obviously loves her work but told her daughter that she works because of financial necessity. When asked why she doesn't let her daughter know she enjoys her work, she answered, "well, then what excuse would I have for working?" Ruth Hartley and A. Klein, "Sex Role Concepts among Elementary School-Age Girls," *Marriage and Family Living*, 21 (February, 1959), 59–64.

40. Women enhance their own self-esteem when they urge their children to "be good when father gets home" because he is tired and needs to rest. They are not only portraying an image of the father as a fragile person, a "Dresden cup" as Irene Joselyn expresses it, but by expanding their maternalism to include the father, they are symbolically relegating him to the subordinate position of the child in the family structure. See Irene Joselyn, "Cultural Forces, Motherliness and Fatherliness," *American Journal of Orthopsychiatry*, 26 (1956), 264–271.

41. In a large metropolis, resource persons could be invited through the city business and professional organizations, the Chamber of Commerce, art, music and dancing schools, etc. This could constitute a challenging program for PTA groups to handle; or a Community Resources Pool could be formed similar to that the New World Foundation has supported in New York City whereby people from business, the arts and sciences and the professions work with the public schools. Many educators and teachers might hesitate to try such a project in anticipation of parent-resistance. But parent-resistance could be a good opportunity for parent-education, if teachers and school officials were firm and informed about what they are trying to do.

42. Though predominantly a feminine field, there is one man to approximately every two women planning careers in teaching. In the "Great Aspirations" study, there were 11,388 women students planning to teach in elementary and secondary schools, but also 5038 men. The problem may therefore not be as great as it seems at first: schools of education could surely do more to encourage some of these men to work in the lower grades, in part or for part of their teaching careers.

43. Bruno Bettelheim makes the point that American boys and girls learn to compete with each other, but not how to complement each other. He sees this lack of experience in complementarity as part of the difficulty in achieving a satisfactory sexual adjustment in marriage: the girl is used to "performing with males on equal grounds, but she has little sense of how to complement them. She cannot suddenly learn this in bed." See Bruno Bettelheim, "Growing Up Female," *Harper's*, November, 1962, p. 125.

44. These are the same skills which, when found in women, go by the names of charm, tact, intuition. See Helen Mayer Hacker, "The New Burdens of Masculinity," *Marriage and Family Living*, 19 (August, 1957), 227–233.

45. Eric Erikson, *Childhood and Society* (New York: W. W. Norton, 1950).

46. David Riesman has observed that this latent fear of homosexuality haunts the Ivy League campuses, putting pressure on many young men to be guarded in their relations with each other and with their male teachers, reflecting in part the lag in the cultural image of appropriate sex characteristics. See David Riesman, "Permissiveness and Sex Roles," *Marriage and Family Living*, 21 (August, 1959), 211–217.

47. It goes beyond the intended scope of this essay to discuss the effects of a social pattern of equality between men and women upon their sexual relationship. A few words are, however, necessary, since the defenders of traditional sex roles often claim that full equality would so feminize men and masculinize women that satisfactory sexual adjustments would be impossible

and homosexuality would probably increase. If the view of the sex act presupposes a dominant male actor and a passive female subject, then it is indeed the case that full sex equality would probably be the death knell of this traditional sexual relationship. Men and women who participate as equals in their parental and occupational and social roles will complement each other sexually in the same way, as essentially equal partners, and not as an ascendant male and a submissive female. This does not mean, however, that equality in non-sexual roles necessarily de-eroticizes the sexual one. The enlarged base of shared experience can, if anything, heighten the salience of sex *qua* sex. In Sweden, where men and women approach equality more than perhaps any other western society, visitors are struck by the erotic atmosphere of that society. Sexually men and women do after all each lack what the other has and wishes for completion of the self; the salience of sex may be enhanced precisely in the situation of the diminished significance of sex as a differentiating factor in all other areas of life. It has always seemed paradoxical to me that so many psychoanalysts defend the traditional sex roles and warn that drastic warping of the sexual impulses may flow from full sex equality; surely they are underestimating the power and force of the very drive which is in so central a position in their theoretical framework. Maslow is one of the few psychologists who has explored the connections between sex experience and the conception of self among women. With a sample of one hundred and thirty college-educated women in their twenties, he found, contrary to traditional notions of femininity and psychoanalytic theories, that the more "dominant" the woman, the greater her enjoyment of sexuality, the greater her ability to give herself freely in love. Women with dominance feelings were free to be completely themselves, and this was crucial for their full expression in sex. They were not feminine in the traditional sense, but enjoyed sexual fulfillment to a much greater degree than the conventionally feminine women he studied. See A. H. Maslow, "Dominance, Personality and Social Behavior in Women," *Journal of Social Psychology,* 10 (1939), 3–39; and "Self-Esteem (Dominance Feeling) and Sexuality in Women," *Journal of Social Psychology,* 16 (1942), 259–294; or a review of Maslow's studies in Betty Friedan, *The Feminine Mystique,* pp. 316–326.

Jobs and the Gender Gap:
Bringing Women Into the Workplace

CHRISTINE E. BOSE

In assessing the impact of these three pieces, I inevitably use a contemporary lens, but, at the same time, in rereading them, I cannot avoid being pulled back to memories of my own professional choices and the past. To understand my vantage point in 1973, the year two of these chapters were published, I was a 25-year-old graduate student finishing my dissertation at Johns Hopkins University. That spring, three graduate student colleagues and I were co-teaching the second course on women ever taught at Johns Hopkins, titled "Women in the Social Structure," and, in order to have enough materials for it, we had drawn on literature from psychology, anthropology, economics, and political science, as well as sociology. This must sound strange to contemporary graduate students who now are able to take specialty exams in sociology of gender, especially as it has become difficult to keep up with the literature in even a small subarea of gender studies. Yet it indicates significant changes in our field during the past 20 to 25 years, and how much we had to find our own way back then. Indeed, there was a rarely acknowledged androcentric bias in social science research that meant that women were frequently missing from it, especially outside of family or deviance studies, and much of the published literature seemed to me to be conservative, stereotyped, or both. We were, of course, aware of Rossi's 1964 article (Chapter 3, this volume) and had assigned it, but the arrival of the *AJS* special issue with articles by Acker, Bernard, and others was an invaluable addition, covering a sorely needed diversity of issues. The whole volume reflected many of my experiences and concerns and greatly expanded the resources for our class lectures. I was fortunate later in 1973 to become part of a Northwest regional group of feminist sociologists, including Joan Acker, Nona Glazer, Dorothy Smith, and others when I moved to the University of Washington as an assistant professor. I knew Alice Rossi, as well, since Peter Rossi was my dissertation advisor at Johns Hopkins, and a group of us would occasionally visit their home. Jessie Bernard, I only knew through ASA activism.

Joan Acker's review of the literature on women and stratification clearly paralleled my research and political interests. Although Acker's review appeared after I had collected the data, my dissertation on women and occupational prestige, titled *Jobs and Gender,* was already intended to answer some of the questions she was raising: What is the prestige score of a housewife? How does it compare to other traditional women's jobs or to the status of other unpaid roles such as being unemployed or on welfare? Does the rating vary with the social class of the rater? Does a woman holding a job affect its occupational prestige? I assumed, as did she, that women had status resources of their own and were not always located in male-headed families (or in families at all). I even used the same focus on the effects of sex as an ascribed characteristic on the evaluation of people. At the time, the ascribed versus achieved dichotomy was one of the best, sociologically legitimate angles to use to incorporate women into stratification studies. Now, of course, our discourse is opposed to the use of any simple dichotomy such as this. Furthermore, we recognize that the ascribed characteristic of sex really has meaning only as a socially constructed gender role or in a gendered organization (see Acker, Chapter 12, this volume).

Acker highlighted a second trend that could help incorporate women into models of stratification systems: Using the individual, rather than the family, as the unit of analysis would allow us to see gender as a dimension that "cuts across class lines and produces two interrelated hierarchies" (p. 25). Alternatively, she suggested that women could be seen as "constituting caste-like groupings within social classes" (p. 25). In fact, her first prediction proved correct, since the model used by Blau and Duncan (1967) to study male occupational mobility achieved ascendance and was later applied to women, and because computers allowed us to analyze previously unthinkable massive quantities of individual data. Indeed, my own dissertation on women's status was based on respondent ratings of individual men's and women's occupational prestige—not of people in family groupings—ultimately assigning a score between 0 and 100 to each job (both with and without male and female incumbents). It was much easier to score the women separately this way but, as Acker suggests, the drawback was to move away from classic discrete measures of social class to one based on a continuum—one that ultimately ignores class boundaries or differences almost entirely. I was never happy about this feature, and therefore delayed several years before publishing my thesis as a book. Acker also continued to struggle with how to sensibly reveal the knotted links between stratification theory on class and on gender. Yet in her 1980 follow-up review article on stratification literature, she felt that, in spite of the burgeoning literature on women, we still did not have a "sex-integrated treatment of class stratification." We had begun to study women of many different classes, but this was not the same thing. Perhaps we have yet to succeed in this endeavor, as indicated by friends' descriptions of my current project, in which I am developing a model of race, ethnicity, class, and gender in turn-of-the-century U.S. political economy, as part of an attempt to "bring class back in."

The controversy over the appropriate unit of analysis remains with us, although the pendulum has swung in the direction of looking at the household, rather than the family or the individual, as an economic unit in which contributions could be varying and diverse. This model has been used in U.S. historical studies of women's work and especially in the area of women and development. At its best, the model assumes that a household's economic options are structured by the local and national economies as well by its own composition and human resources, and neither a particular household division of labor nor a harmonious decision-making process are presupposed. Such a perspective must consider the gendered identities of the household's members and the power relations among them, and it may function best when women are placed at the center of the analysis.

Many of the various directions Acker suggests for future research were followed by others. Throughout the 1970s, intergenerational mobility studies began to incorporate women: comparing women's occupational mobility to men's, comparing women to their mothers instead of their fathers, and ultimately noting that even though the variables of the mobility model—such as parental education, income, or status—might move in the same direction for men and women, the outcomes were not really the same due to occupational segregation. Prior intragenerational studies of women's social mobility through marriage were complemented by studies of downward mobility in divorce, as well as by research on blockades to women's upward occupational mobility. Ultimately, all of these studies showed the drawbacks to stratification approaches that focused on the individual: There were too many gendered labor force institutions such research could not consider—lack of significant child care or maternity benefits, segregation within firms, glass ceilings, segregated career ladders and internal labor markets, and so on. Undoubtedly, this is why Acker's 1980 stratification literature review concluded that "a theory that includes women will have to conceptually bridge the gap between women's unpaid and paid labor and bring structural sources of sex inequality into the analysis" (p. 33). Indeed, this was one of the two directions gender research on stratification began to take. Furthermore, Acker also had correctly identified the trend to incorporate a wide variety of structured social inequalities. Race, ethnicity, age, and sexual preference have all been raised as separate bases of stratification and as elements differentiating women. The continuing struggle is to understand the interplay of these factors in a non-additive form.

There were almost two generations' difference in age between Jessie Bernard and myself, and I entered the sociological profession at the time of her fourth revolution. Yet it was easy to feel close to her, both because of her own energy and ability to be in touch with the important issues and because my professional life and politics were shaped by three of her four revolutions. As an undergraduate I had been a mathematics major with a sociology minor. I had participated in the 1969 strikes at Columbia University and, having lived my teenage years in the suburbia of the 1950s and feeling suffocated by it, I was just waiting for the women's movement to give a theoretical and activist content to my personal discontent with women's limited options. I wanted to be "relevant." So, when a faculty mentor suggested that "sociology needed me" in its quest to be more quantitative, I applied to graduate school, planning to work with Jim Coleman, who had just published *Mathematical Sociology*. Ultimately, I found those math models too abstracted from the "real" world and shifted to survey research, working with Peter Rossi. So I was and am a product of the escalating empirical movement Jessie identified. Furthermore, as a graduate student I was active in the anti-Vietnam War movement, the Left, radio production, and women's caucuses, and had joined the very New University Conference that Bernard said helped push the SSSP to the left in the early 1970s (see Chapter 1, p. 4). In fact, the business meetings of the ASA were much more fun then, as we strategized about how to pass motions about the war or marched in protest right in the middle of the session. I enjoyed the third revolution!

The fourth revolution did not catch me off guard. I had pursued my education, at least in part, because I expected to and wanted always to support myself. I represented a different cohort, one that had benefited from affirmative action and the women's movement. The fact that our cohort numerically included many more women, represented the beginnings of a removal of androcentric bias. As Bernard indicates, we felt it was our job to raise the questions that had not been asked before and to challenge the assumptions that previously had limited women's access to many male-domi-nated institutions. But as a generation honed by social movements, we were more ready to see the problems as institutional, and readily challenged any perspective that blamed women's problems on ourselves. It was no surprise that at the end of my first year of graduate school in 1970, I found myself sitting in sessions of both the radical and the women's caucuses at the Washington, D.C., ASA meetings, which variously included many authors in this volume. In the beginning I watched, learned, and demonstrated; over the next few years attending the birth of Sociologists for Women in Society and the Sex and Gender section of the ASA, as well as the Marxist section. However, my participation was conflicted, because at that point I thought we might be "selling out" by becoming institutionalized. Little did I know that SWS and Sex and Gender would attain the key places they now hold in sociology, and it was hard to imagine then that many of us would be elected to the very same officer slots whose political positions we were then protesting.

Bernard highlighted many important issues, some of which became the source of feminist debate and contention. Among these is the idea of women as a collective entity, with common bonds and interests. Bernard correctly observed that women are often viewed in sociology only in relation to men (as daughters, wives, or mothers), and that the concept of sisterhood had allowed (some) women to see ourselves as mutually allied. One problem with this standpoint was raised by women of color, who argued that women were not a single entity, and that our needs and interests are different, although frequently overlapping. A second problem, only recognized in an intermittent fashion, was pointed out by Rossi (Chapter 3, p. 34): "sex is the only instance in which representatives of the unequal groups live in more intimate association with each other than with members of their own group." Her solution was for feminist movements to be allied with other social reform movements. However, lesbian feminists of the mid-1970s suggested a more effective solution could be found in the short-term advantages of female separatism, which allowed women independently to form our own paradigms; more recently, different analyses have been offered by the development of queer theory.

Bernard also invited discussion about the appropriate research methods by which to put women at the center of analyses. She felt that "agentic" methods were more likely to be funded and less likely to address women's concerns than were "communal" methods. Her suggestions were the beginnings of future complaints about the "add women and stir" approach to studying gender as merely the variable "sex," as well as hints of debates-to-come about the relative usefulness of quantitative and qualitative methods that are only now settling down into some meld of the two approaches. Retrospectively, it feels odd to read objections to men's agentic research, which were later followed by discussions of the importance of women's agency in research.

Bernard ends her chapter, asking if the fourth revolution will move from addressing androcentric bias to an actual re-orientation of our paradigms to include women. It took until the mid-1970s, with the socialist feminist movement, to develop newer paradigms that tried to meld the best of class and gender analysis into one form; it took longer still to add race and ethnicity in a meaningful way. In their 1985 article (see Chapter 9 in this volume), Judy Stacey and Barrie Thorne felt we had been less successful than history and anthropology, but more successful than economics and political science, in this endeavor. More recently, they have suggested that a feminist revolution in sociology might be a contradiction in terms, given both the transdisciplinary and activist nature of feminism.

While contemporary paradigm shifts sometimes may feel confined more to the sociology of sex and gender than located in any other realm of the discipline, Rossi's chapter illustrates how far feminist approaches had already shifted between 1964 and 1973. That 1964 article reflected its time, just as it was progressive for it. The year before, Betty Friedan published *The Feminine Mystique* and the Equal Pay Act was passed, followed by Title VII of the Civil Rights Act in 1964. Middle-class women, living in the suburbs and employed only before the birth of their children or after those children had graduated, were beginning to articulate Friedan's "problem that had no name." Rossi's chapter describes that predominantly white, middle-class world and its injustices, blaming sociology and psychology for their conservative stances in creating motherhood as a full-time occupation and suggesting institutional changes that could free women from the home: child care, middle-class residences near urban employment, and reducing stereotyping in the schools. Notwithstanding this progressive approach, she is forced to address the conservative nature of the times on its own terms. For example, in arguing for "sex equality," she must assert that women do not need to confine themselves to the home and address beliefs that employed mothers might harm their children. The arguments she makes for women's employment, based on the need for their underutilized skills in the workforce, the psychological costs of full-time mothering, and the importance of seeking satisfaction, are supplanted in the early 1970s by discussions of occupational segregation, the pull of service industry jobs on women, and the rather different problems of working-class or racial/ethnic women. By the 1980s, the decline of the family wage and the need for the two-income family had entirely changed the answers to the question of the factors that would ultimately create gender equality.

Hence, the early focus on androcentric, male-centered models contained the seeds for many of the future conceptual, theoretical, and methodological debates, but also represented the problems of the general political economy of the time, as well as those of the discipline and the professional women who had only grudgingly been allowed to enter it at that point.

The Fourth Revolution: Reflection on Three Pioneers in the Transformation of American Sociology

DORIS WILKINSON

With the political discourse and the civil rights and liberation protests of the 1960s and early 1970s, a national collective movement to re-organize the way sociologists viewed and interpreted the social world evolved. I was an observer and participant in this dynamic era. A new breed of sociologists began revisiting conflict models and power arrangements in the society as well as in the profession. They were women trained in the discipline who were not, at the time, significantly represented as members of the intellectual elite. These early feminists played a major role in the latter part of the 20th century in reframing the content of the sociological imagination. Given my own professional biography, I was delighted with the invitation to contribute to this important volume. I was especially pleased to have been granted an oppor-tunity to comment on the work of three outstanding feminist scholars in the field whom I have known not only as imaginative pioneers in the reformulation of "doing sociology," but as friends.

Rossi, whose penetrating assessment of "Equality Between the Sexes: An Immodest Proposal" was published in a period of rapid social changes, critically appraised the profession and the society. She characterized the prevailing state of intellectual activism: "There is no overt anti-feminism in our society in 1964, not because sex equality has been achieved, but because there is practically no feminist spark left among American women" (Rossi, Chapter 3 in this volume, p. 32). Historically, where women had joined men in movements for social reform, their cause had been more easily articulated. Following World War II and the gradual unfolding of the Civil Rights Move-ment, politically reactionary theories in the social and behavioral sciences affected the direction and scope of feminism. With extraordinary skill and perceptiveness, Rossi pointed out that in the United States at the time of her writing, the social sciences had not produced much since the post-Depression with respect to "sex equality as a goal or the ways of implementing that goal" (Rossi, p. 36). Much has changed since then.

I was a graduate student when Alice began writing about sex equality in the mid-1960s. At the time, she felt that "young women [seemed] increasingly uncommitted to anything beyond early marriage, motherhood and a suburban house." The guiding thesis of her reasoning was the societal necessity for "sex equality and [a] search for the means by which it can be achieved." By demarcating a rational conception of sex equality, she reframed sociological thinking about female and male role expectations. She expressed that the standard ways of delimiting masculine and feminine roles would not fit the post-industrial order nor its political culture. Reflecting on our indoctrination into fixed imagery of males and females, she asserted that "the majority of the differences between the sexes which have been noted in social research are socially rather than physiologically determined" (Rossi, p. 32). In exploring issues revealed in an earlier feminist voice and the rationale for aspiring to "a state of sex equality" (Rossi, p. 33), she maintained that "inequality not only depressed the human potential of the subject groups but corrupted those in the superordinate groups" (p. 36).

By the 1980s, Alice began to broaden her focus. I presided over a session in Washington, D.C. where she spoke on "Women in Politics in the 1980's." At the time, I was president of the District of Columbia Sociological Society, and Alice was president of the American Sociological Association. Joining together, the Capital Area chapter of SWS and the DCSS co-sponsored her presentation at our January meeting. That was an exciting moment: Within 20 years, she had been elected president of the organization that she once challenged. We described her as a "leading scholar, activist, and prolific writer on women's issues."

For the historical period in which Alice was writing, her insights were powerful and revolutionary. She offered several creative resolutions to attain the societal goal of sex equality: creating a cluster of child care centers, exploring possibilities for university-affiliated child care centers, replacing existing suburban residential arrangements because of the constraints imposed on families, and modifying self-images and the gender typing of jobs.

SWS brought me in contact with Alice—who was president at the time when I joined—Jessie, and Joan, another of the critical interpreters and molders of early feminist thought who outlined new ways to conceptualize social class. Acker's insightful clarification of "Women and Social Stratification: A Case of Intellectual Sexism," published in the *American Journal of Sociology,* contributed much to our grasp of the female condition in the 1960s and 1970s. She introduced an essential and logical argument against the systematic exclusion of sex as a variable in sociological analyses of stratification processes and structures. Using rational thinking and her comprehension of the social order, she reinforced an empirical reality—that sex "is probably one of the most obvious criteria of social differentiation and one of the most obvious bases of economic, political, and social inequalities" (Acker, Chapter 2 in this volume, p. 21). Sociology deserved criticism, because the field had based its entire theoretical premises and research analyses principally on male conceptions and "the male half of humanity" (p. 21). Joan maintained that the inclusion of "sex as a central dimension in the study of society would lead to a more accurate picture of social structure and to a better understanding" (p. 21) of the system of stratification.

Proposing a feminist reconstruction of American sociology, Joan explored dominant themes in stratification studies. The prominent conceptions were anchored solidly in the functionalist model that had formed sociological theory and research. She outlined typical assumptions such as: "The family is the unit in the stratification system. . . . The social position of the family is determined by the status of the male head of the household. . . . Females live in families; therefore, their status is determined by that of the males to whom they are attached" (Chapter 2, p. 21). Each of these claims was thoughtfully discussed and critically assessed. She reasoned, for example, that since not everyone lives in a family, significant numbers in the population were excluded from sociological analyses. The assertion that families make up the basic units in the stratification system rests on the validity of the other premises. Reliance on an idealistic formula for a nuclear family with husband-wife called into question theories regarding the family as the central unit of the social class hierarchy.

Joan's probing dissection of the social location of women helped to set in motion new principles for translating the structure of class in sociology. Arguments that women had no "relevant role in stratification processes independent of the family roles and their ties to particular men" did not permit realistic explanations nor thorough understanding of the nature of the social class system. Joan pointed out that "sex is an enduring ascribed characteristic which (a) has an effect upon the evaluation of persons and positions, and (b) is the basis of the persisting sexual division of labor and of sex-based inequalities" (Acker, p. 24).

A gentle but persistent forerunner of feminist thought in American sociology, Jessie Bernard was one of those rare personalities whose extraordinarily productive life spanned many intellectual and political decades. I was deeply saddened to learn of her recent passing; she was indeed a great lady. I have been most fortunate to have known her not only to talk to briefly at annual meetings but to have interacted with her over many years at informal social gatherings and at dinners on numerous occasions in Washington, D.C., in the company of our friends—Muriel Cantor and Jean Lipman-Blumen. I was also present when Jessie celebrated her 80th birthday, which was held at the same time as the celebration of the ending of my term as an employee of the American Sociological Association. Of her "Four Revolutions: An Autobiographical History of the ASA," Jessie informed the reader that she probably was "the only person, living or dead, who has participated in four revolutions in the American Sociological Association" (Bernard, Chapter 1 in this volume, p. 3).

For four decades, Jessie had observed the changes in the profession and in the discipline from efforts to quantify research to the collective protests to "bring women in." The second revolution that she experienced was an organizational transformation—the "emancipation of the Society from the fostering protection of the University of Chicago." Up to the 1930s, the American Sociological Association had been under the direct influence of the University of Chicago, which had "supplied the leadership, published the proceedings, and provided a home for the secretary-treasurer." As the 1950s evolved, sociologists began to recognize their ideological diversity. As a result, a different professional association was born—the Society for the Study of Social Problems. One principal catalyst for this radical structural move was that the "parent organization did not take a stand on any policy issue." Of her own participation in this revolutionary process, Jessie stated:

> We objected to the elitist direction the ASA was following, its lack of interest in social problems and issues, its antiseptic "line" on research, its cronyism, and its complacent acceptance of the increasing trend of putting sociological research at the service of business and industry. We were concerned also with protecting academic freedom in the era of McCarthy. (p. 4)

Jessie's fourth revolution was the feminist transition, which surprised her. Jessie expressed that at the time her concern was not with "what sociology can do for women . . . but rather what women . . . can do for sociology." A key emphasis in her thinking centered on converting the field into an authentic science that would include women and men. She documented the complexity of the "fourth revolution" and the multiple tasks confronting its principal representatives in Washington in 1970. Understandably, there was not consensus among them. As she wrote,

> some were interested primarily in fighting discrimination in the profession. Some were concerned with fighting discrimination against women in society at large. Some wanted to liberate sociology from its establishmentarian bias to make it an instrument for total revolution. And some sought mainly to counteract the sexist bias in the discipline. (p. 5)

Like Alice and Joan, Jessie, who enhanced our awareness of "the female world," was a significant participant in the fourth revolution through her presence, friendship, scholarship, her direct and principled actions and mentoring of so many of us. In 1972, when the ASA met in New Orleans, she was among those who "sat in" to challenge a restaurant's policy of not serving women. I watched with many others from the hotel window as policemen were called in. That was a rare moment in the evolution of women sociologists' participation in structural change *outside* the academy. The model for such activism had its roots in the civil rights protests of the 1960s, which Black sociologists emulated when seeking entry into the structure of the ASA (Blackwell, 1992; Roby, 1992).

Reflecting on the far-reaching influence of Joan, Jessie, and Alice—three exceptional women sociologists whom I have been fortunate to know—it is quite evident that their creative insights were highly instrumental in preparing the stage for contemporary intellectual discourse. Their imaginations shaped today's thought and other forms of social theory within the discipline. Each recognized that "a masculine bias ha[d] been embedded in the structure of inquiry" (p. 11) that prevented dealing "adequately with the realities so urgently demanding study. . . . The American Sociological Association [has been] a better organization and sociology itself a more adequate discipline as a result of these" four revolutions (p. 13) and others that have expanded the profession's boundaries to include all trained in the discipline.

Part II

Exposing the Gender Gap:
Separate Is Never Equal

This genre goes a step further: Once we are able to examine women's experiences, we see more than *gender differences;* we see *gender inequality*. These authors attract the attention of sociologists who previously ignored the important social differences between women and men, and they then show that separate is not equal. The works included here document that men have more structural advantages than women. As such, women and men have different access to rewards and opportunities. These scholars theorize about the roots and the perpetuation of this inequality. They conclude that men as a group benefit from gender inequality, and they examine the ways in which these benefits are guaranteed over time.

4 Trends in Gender Stratification, 1970–1985

JOAN HUBER
The Ohio State University

This paper addresses causes and consequences of sociological interest in gender stratification after 1970. The most recent women's movement spurred empirical research on the topic but development of a general theory was slowed by accidents of disciplinary history. A theory of preindustrial gender stratification that leans on anthropology is therefore used to interpret trends that occur during industrialization. This analysis helps to explain why trends in mortality, education, fertility, women's labor force participation, and men's household participation should continue to improve women's status relative to the status of men.[1]

With a few exceptions (Rossi, 1964; Blake, 1965), interest in gender stratification before 1970 was little above zero. Except in the sociology texts' chapters on marriage and family, women were rarely mentioned and their absence went unnoticed. Nor was there a sociological theory of gender stratification; most of the social and economic differences between men and women were thought to be of biological origin. From a scholarly perspective, the analysis of the causes of gender inequality became a principal consequence of its discovery. I therefore begin by sketching the events that led sociologists to discover gender stratification. I then use a relatively unfamiliar theory of preindustrial gender stratification to interpret the bulk of post-1970 research.

In order to convey what sociology was like in the pre-1970 period, I note two assessments that represent the best the discipline had to offer a generation ago. I call attention to this research with humility for these sociologists are ourselves, seen with the clarity of hindsight.

"Trends in Gender Stratification, 1970–1985" by Joan Huber, in *Sociological Forum*, Vol. 1, No. 3. © 1986 by The Eastern Sociological Society. Reprinted with permission.

When *Sociology Today* appeared in 1959, it included twenty-five papers presented at the Annual Meeting of the American Sociological Society in 1957. The papers, intended to address the discipline's strategic problems, were edited by the Society's president and the editors of its two journals, Merton, Broome, and Cottrell. They were written by twenty-seven men and two women, both of whom were co-authors. Most references to humans are implicitly to men, for example, Parsons's analysis of the part schools play in socialization. During college years, he says, a cohort of high achievers is sorted out. "Again, with many qualifications, the high achievers go on to further formal training, this time to graduate schools" (Parsons, 1959:34). There is no hint that the fate of talented youth differs by sex.

As expected, women appear as actors in the family chapter but the author claims that the area lacks theory (Goode, 1959:159). These examples suggest that where there is theory, women are invisible. Where women are visible, there is no theory. In sum, the discipline had no theory about women's place.

Sociology, Progress of a Decade appeared in 1961. It was intended to sample major trends as they unfolded in the journals (Lipset and Smelser, 1961:v). The authors included seventy-four men and five women; all of the women were co-authors save one psychologist. Except for a content analysis of the comic strip "Little Orphan Annie" and the analysis of "The House-maid, an Occupational Field in Crisis," women are even less visible than in *Sociology Today*. One reason is that family research rated only one article, seven of the book's 635 pages.

What happened to create an interest in gender stratification? The immediate stimulus was a new wave of the women's movement about 1970—which leads to a more basic question: What caused the women's movement itself? What long-term factors so changed the conditions of women's lives in the United States that their sense of grievance captured public attention? I first discuss how the movement developed during the 1960s and its subsequent impact on the discipline in the early seventies. Then, after outlining a theory of preindustrial gender stratification, I argue that the principles of this theory can be used to interpret trends that followed industrialization that have differentially affected the roles of men and women.

THE MOST RECENT WOMEN'S MOVEMENT

The most recent wave of the women's movement, by Freeman's (1973) account, involved two age groups. Each bore marks of having come of age in a given period. The older group, which organized first, was set in motion by the establishment of the President's Commission on the Status of Women in 1961. Subsequently fifty state commissions were established to do similar research. The commissions, composed of politically active and knowledge-able women, unearthed ample evidence of women's economic and legal problems, thereby creating an expectation of action. Awareness of these problems was further stimulated by Betty Friedan's *The Feminine Mystique* (1963), which became a bestseller overnight. Her analysis of the housewife's status struck a nerve.

In 1964 the category of sex was added to Title VII of the Civil Rights Act. The Equal Employment Opportunity Commission treated sex discrimination as a joke. This angered the women attending the Third National Conference of Commissions on the Status of Women and led to the formation of the National Organization for Women (NOW) in 1966. This became the core of the older women's group; members came primarily from the professions, government, and communications.

Later in the 1960s the consciousness of the younger women began to stir. Mostly white and college-educated like their older counterparts, this cohort of younger women activists was deeply influenced by the passionately egalitarian movements of the 1960s: the New Left, Civil Rights, and, later, resistance to the Viet Nam draft. The larger radical movements of the 1960s were dominated by men who were often insensitive to the need for equality between the sexes, both within their organizations and for society at large. As they discovered this, many young women left, disappointed and disillusioned, to form a movement of their own (Weinbaum, 1978; Evans, 1980). Like their male counterparts, they distrusted hierarchical organizations, formal rules of procedure, leadership, and people over thirty. The younger branch coalesced into fluid small groups devoted to raising members' consciousness through continual self-examination and confession.

In 1969 the women's movement surfaced at the annual meeting of the American Sociological Association. A number of women graduate students and faculty caucused, airing grievances for the first time. The graduate students came from major departments; the faculty did not, thereby exemplifying a potential strain.

A second caucus at the 1970 annual meeting led to the establishment of a permanent organization, launched in 1971 with Alice Rossi as president. One goal was to increase the quantity and quality of research on women's status. These events challenged traditional perspectives and helped to set the stage for a rapid increase in research on sex roles, as the new area was called. Several factors influenced the direction it would take.

INFLUENCES ON GENDER RESEARCH

First, since women were more likely than men to enter the new area, sex-roles research tended to reflect the substance and methods of the subareas in which women most often worked. The 1970 ASA Directory showed that women tended to cluster in the less quantitative areas. For example, women comprised only a twelfth of the persons who listed mathematical sociology as a primary research area and a sixth of those who listed methods, statistics, or demography. In contrast, about a third of those who listed medical sociology and more than a third of those who listed marriage and the family were women. I have the impression (but no data) that women tend to be attracted to areas that require interpretation of daily minutiae, a skill that subordinated groups develop because it is useful to them (see, for example, Epstein, 1983; Richardson, 1985; Daniels, 1986). These factors gave a social psychological and nonquantitative stamp to much of the sex-roles research produced by women.

A second influence on gender research resulted from change in the study of social stratification. Since the forties stratification research had been dominated by a Weberian perspective. By the mid-sixties a new school of stratification research emerged with the development of path analytic techniques. Focused primarily upon the precise measurement of the effect of father's status on son's educational and occupational attainment, this new perspective soon dominated the study of stratification. As models of status attainment were extended to women, researchers were surprised to discover that men and women appear to experience similar rates of occupational mobility, although women's earnings were lower than men's (Treiman and Terrell, 1975). Part of the puzzle was resolved with the discovery that the conventional occupational prestige and socioeconomic indices do not tap the distinctive attributes of sex-typed occupations (Bose and Rossi, 1983).

During the 1970s stratification models developed in two streams. One, more structural, broadened the range of explanatory variables to include organizational features that helped to explain sex wage differentials (Baron and Bielby, 1985:234). The other was the more psychological life-span perspective. It included family-related career issues, biopsychological factors (Rossi, 1985:xiii), aging (Riley, 1981), the social history of family relations and human development (Elder, 1978), and psychometric intelligence (Featherman, 1983:1).

Early sex-roles research tended to be descriptive. For example, gender stereotyping was found in children's books, where boys were pictured as being strong, independent, brave, and imaginative leaders, while girls were shown as dependent, timid, pretty, and sweet followers. A mountain of subsequent research found images of adult sex roles that followed much the same prescriptions.

As awareness of feminist issues began to infuse the social sciences, the agenda of research was broadened. To show where questions about gender roles fit in the mainstream of sociological research, I integrate my discussion around a substantive question: Why did the U.S. women's movement reappear around 1970? This question is important because sociology itself originated as a response to an older but parallel question: Why did a men's movement sweep Europe and North America during the nineteenth century?

Theorists do not emphasize the dominance of men in early political movements, but speak instead of social movements that were engendered by the social forces and structure of European industrialization.

These revolutionary changes in technology and social organization stimulated the development of the social sciences, the new scholarship on men, more than a century ago. Received explanations of the human condition lost their meanings. As erstwhile peasants and serfs shifted from agriculture to urban wage labor, masses of men struggled for a fair share of a rapidly increasing surplus. Traditional scholars saw these struggles as part of worldwide populist, socialist or labor movements aimed at overturning or at least redoing the class system. But it would be more accurate to call these collective efforts the men's movement. Women were virtually excluded. Early industrialization had thrown the class system into relief but it left gender patterns obscure, even though forces that would lead to change were already at work.

Nineteenth-century theorists were preoccupied only with the social (class) division of labor. They ignored the domestic division of labor. For example, Durkheim noticed that married men killed themselves less often than did single men while married women killed themselves more often than did single women. But he drew no implications from these facts (Tiryakian, 1981). Nor did anyone else. Four macrolevel trends would run their courses before ongoing economic development would transform housewives into wage earners as it had earlier transformed peasants into urban laborers.

Before discussing these trends that changed women's lives, I outline a theory of gender stratification drawn from the preindustrial period. This theory helps to make sense of macrolevel changes in women's roles that industrialization brought about.

PREINDUSTRIAL GENDER STRATIFICATION

The following theory assumes that the division of labor spawns the system of social stratification. The division of labor depends, in part, on the interaction of the environment with available tools. Lenski (1970) noted that the evolution of subsistence tools permitted certain forms of social organization. Friedl (1975) extended this hypothesis with her analysis of the effect of subsistence tools on patterns of sex stratification in foraging and hoe cultures. From Friedl's work (1975:8), three principles emerge to guide the study of cross-cultural sex stratification.

Two principles apply at the family level. First, producers tend to have more power and prestige than consumers. Whoever can put more bread on the table has more power in the household.

Second, the tasks women do are determined by the way productive roles can be meshed with the conditions of pregnancy and lactation. In other words, gender stratification arises from the way child bearing and rearing mesh with daily work routines.

The third principle is societal-level. Prestige and power tend to accrue to those who control the distribution of valued goods beyond the family. The question is, what kind of positions give their incumbents such control and how do their tasks mesh with pregnancy and lactation? To answer it, we can look at societies that depend on foraging, the hoe, or the plow for subsistence. These sketches suggest how such principles apply to the current scene.

In foraging societies, men hunted; women gathered. Men could distribute large animals to the group. Women could distribute nuts and berries only to the family. Hunters therefore outranked gatherers. Women could acquire hunting skills but could not carry a nursing child (up to age four) while tracking game days from camp. Since pregnancy and lactation were common conditions to most adult women—given the societal need for moderately high fertility in foraging societies—the consequence of the gender division of labor meant that women were generally barred from the tasks that yielded the most prestige and power (Friedl, 1975).

In hoe cultures women produced about half of the food supply. The use of the hoe in a nearby plot meshed well with pregnancy and lactation. Men monopolized land clearing but this gave them less advantage than did hunting in distributing valued goods beyond the family. Relative to men, women's status may have been higher in hoe than in foraging societies. More hoe cultures were matrilineal or matrifocal than any other types. The divorce rate was very high. Divorce did not interfere with the subsistence of either of the spouses or their children (Friedl, 1975).

The plow increased the food supply many fold. Paradoxically, in agricultural societies, the majority were worse off than their hunting and gathering ancestors (Lenski, 1970). The presence of a food surplus in the countryside coupled with the availability of iron weapons allowed elites to extract as much as possible from impoverished peasants.

Men monopolized the plow. Larger fields further from home make it hard to arrange work to suit a nursling (Blumberg, 1978:50). Women therefore produced less food than men did. The plow further depressed women's status by making land the chief form of wealth. With the technology of the hoe, people had to move frequently as the soil becomes exhausted. The plow permits a longer period of continued farming on the same land, hence land values increase. Since land is an impartible inheritance (at a given level of technology it supports only a given number of persons), the number of legal heirs must be controlled. Monogamy therefore prevails. Divorce becomes nearly impossible. Women's sexual behavior is controlled lest a man's property go to another man's child—the concern with women's sexual purity derives from their status as transmitters of male property (Goody, 1976:15, 97).

Recent research suggests that European women were less constrained than Asian ones, which may be an unexpected result of Church efforts to acquire land. The Church controlled marriage and the legitimation of children in order to control inheritance patterns (Goody, 1983:221). It reduced the supply of close relatives by encouraging celibacy, prohibiting close cousin marriage and adoption (all widespread in Biblical and Roman times), condemning polygyny and divorce, and discouraging remarriage. These measures induced testators to leave property to the Church. Child marriage was discouraged by the Church's emphasis on mutual consent as a requirement, making it harder for a marriage to serve family interests. Women could inherit land and avoid marriage by becoming nuns. This increased their control over property and the Church's chances of inheriting it.

The increase in Church lands is well known. Other questions merit much study. Did such measures enable European women to adapt to change more easily than Asian ones? Did such measures affect readiness for change? For example, west of a line from Leningrad to Trieste the age of first marriage was higher than east of it—hence birth rates were lower—well before industrialization (Hajnal, 1965), a pattern that could conceivably have been affected by Church practice.

Industrialization ended the plow era in Europe. Pregnancy, lactation, and child rearing had to mesh with new ways of producing and distributing goods. I first outline sequential macrolevel trends. Then, applying the three stratification principles, I show how these trends eventually increased women's economic productivity, reduced time spent in child care, and allowed limited entry to elite jobs.

FROM AGRICULTURAL TO
INDUSTRIAL GENDER STRATIFICATION

The first two trends to affect gender stratification in Western plow societies occurred at about the same time. Mortality, primarily of infants, declined; levels of education rose. By 1880 schooling was compulsory in most of the West. These two trends induced a third—a fertility decrease—and set the stage for the nineteenth-century women's movement, an attempt to gain the civil and legal rights of propertied men (Rupp and Taylor, 1986). Preconditions for a more broadly based movement exist only when, given the other three trends, a high demand for female labor induces married women into the workforce in large numbers. The proportion of married women in the workforce had increased at a steady rate since the turn of the century (Davis, 1984) but not till the 1950s was the base large enough for the increase to involve large numbers. Mature married women are more likely than young unmarried women to perceive discrimination. The 1970s threw men's participation in household labor into relief, launching a fifth trend. I now discuss each one in more detail.

Mortality. In the West death rates responded in turn to improved nutrition, reduced exposure to disease and medical measures. In England and Wales, for example, lowered death rates from 1700 to 1870 resulted from better diet, and from 1870 to 1935, from reduction in exposure to infectious and parasitic disease. Medical measures became effective after 1935 (McKeown, 1976).

Education. The spread of public education deeply affected women's status. For individual women, it provided a taste of the world beyond the household and increased the opportunity cost of being a housewife, thereby increasing the allure of paid work.

However, education most profoundly affects both family and society through its effects on fertility. The shift from agriculture to industry reduces the ratio of physical to human capital. The spread of public education therefore can reverse the direction of generational wealth flows. In traditional societies the net flow is from child to parent. Then there is a great divide where the intergenerational flow of wealth is reversed and children become a net drain on parental resources. High fertility then becomes irrational (Caldwell, 1976, 1980). The ensuing fertility decline dramatically reduces women's time spent in childcare over the life span.

Fertility. After the spread of mass education, marital fertility declined from about seven to fewer than three children. The decline was first apparent in France in 1830. It reached the U.S. in 1900, slowed by the mix of young immigrants in the American population (United Nations, 1973:65, 68). Reduced fertility was preceded by a pattern of marrying late or never. Unmarried adults were absorbed as servants in household production (Hajnal, 1982:470).

In every developing country abortion has been important until women learn contraceptive techniques (McLaren, 1983:137). Abortion was common for middle-class women in the U.S. from 1840 to 1860 (Tietze, 1981:21). It was illegal by 1880 and again became a last resort of poor women. Legislators feared that middle-class white women's birth rates would let "foreigners" swamp the "true" American population (Mohr, 1978:240).

The Western fertility decline yields insights of importance today. People respond to economic stimuli even when psychological costs—abortion, for example—seem high. Birth control also faced strong opposition from all churches, from the state, and from political parties, right, center, and left. Moreover, when legislators (except in the U.S.), fearing depopulation, provided child or maternal allowances to encourage growth, these benefits apparently had little or no demographic effect (Westoff, 1978:81).

Women's Labor Force Participation. During most of the nineteenth century in the West women who worked for pay were in agriculture, household employment, service occupations, and the new industrial sector. Although fertility was falling, the laws and customs that emerged to govern women's work responded to pre-transition birth expectations. Until 1880 only France and Ireland had achieved low fertility (the latter by late marriage and a high level of celibacy). It was not clear that fertility would finally decline in all classes throughout the West. Thus women's exclusion from high-wage jobs was readily justified: their children needed them at home.

The mechanisms that excluded them included employers' refusal to hire them, unions' refusal to admit or organize them and legislation that "protected" their maternal status by restricting their hours and conditions of employment, excluding them for seniority and overtime pay.

Did such protection spare women from night work and lifting heavy objects? Did it protect men's dominance at home? Did it give employers a low-wage labor reserve? Or some of each? A minority view (Baker, 1925) held that protective legislation drove women's low wages even lower. The U.S. Department of Labor (1928) took the majority view: Restricting women's hours did not harm them. As late as 1972 the AFL-CIO opposed the Equal Rights Amendment because it would wipe out protective labor legislation.

From 1890 to 1920 the proliferation of clerical occupations opened up white collar jobs to women. Their wages, which increased sharply, were relatively higher in 1920 than in 1980 (Smith and Ward, 1984: viii). White collar jobs were rapidly feminized, that is, their wages fell too low to attract men qualified to do the work. Women with high school degrees worked in clerical and sales jobs; with college degrees, as teachers, nurses, social workers, or librarians. Few women worked as physicians, lawyers, college professors, or administrators in business or government. The mechanisms that excluded them have been well documented (Chafetz and Dworkin, 1986). However, one factor alone can suffice to lower the proportion of women in elite positions: the division of household labor. It had long been perceived as a constant. It became a variable after the reappearance of the women's movement highlighted the changes that had been occurring in work and family life.

GENDER STRATIFICATION AFTER 1950

In 1950 predicting change in gender stratification on the basis of trends in mortality, education, fertility, and female employment would have seemed risky. Complementary-role marriage surely seemed here to stay.

By 1950 mortality rates were relatively low. Further rapid progress seemed unlikely.

High school completion rates continued to rise and women were more likely than men to graduate. College completion rates also continued to rise but women did not gain as rapidly as men. In 1940 the college completion rate of women was about three-fourths that of men. By 1950 the ratio plummeted to one-third, a result of legislation that gave veterans, mostly men, a free college education. Thus, among young middle-class couples in the 1950s, wives tended to have lower human capital than their spouses—a characteristic which influenced the relative potential earnings of husbands and wives. The ratio of female to male college completion was returned to the 1940 level only by 1970 (U.S. Bureau of the Census, 1975:385).

Fertility trends had turned around. The postwar baby boom reversed a long-term secular decline. Although the baby boom turned out to be an accident of history that resulted from the confluence of several factors all of which exerted upward pressure on fertility, no one knew that in 1950.

With the exception of the World War II years, the changes in female labor force participation were relatively modest up to 1950. Since 1900, the level of participation had increased from 20 percent to 30 percent but the life-span pattern was much the same. Young women typically worked for pay until they married, then they left the labor force never to return, unless their husbands could not support them. The proportion of married women in the labor force had actually been increasing at a steady rate for fifty years (Davis, 1984) but the original base had been so small that even by 1950 the total number seemed modest.

Male household participation occurred only in the imagination of dreamers like Charlotte Perkins Gilman (1972). But by 1950 all of her works were out of print, and her ideas seemed lost to popular consciousness.

However, forces that would bring change were already at work. A postwar expansion in service occupations raised the demand for women workers. The traditional supply of female workers—young and unmarried—fell short owing to low birth rates during the Depression, an increase in rates of post-secondary education, and a trend towards earlier marriage and child-bearing. With a demand for female workers that exceeded the traditional supply, married women with school-age children were pulled into the work force in increasing numbers, dramatically changing the life-span pattern of participation (Oppenheimer, 1973). The trend continues. It laid the foundations for a more broadly-based women's movement: Women who intend to be employed most of their adult lives are more likely to compare their opportunities to those of male counterparts and feel that unequal conditions ought to be changed.

The comparisons suggested that the forces of particularism were at work. In all developed countries the earnings of full-time women workers had long hovered at about three-fifths those of men (Lydall, 1968), even in the Soviet Union (Swafford, 1978). In the U.S. the gap was even greater from 1920 to

1980 (Smith and Ward, 1984). Education yields lower earnings for female than male white collar workers. Skill attainment yields lower earnings for female than male blue-collar workers (Form, 1985). A sizeable literature in sociology and economics asks why (see references in Reskin, 1984).

Two types of answers have emerged. Both supply some elements for a general theory of gender stratification. The sociological interpretation is diffuse, dealing with human capital, structural, and opinion variables. Women's lower earnings result from lower rates of labor force participation owing to household duties, from segregation into lower wage occupations, and direct wage discrimination. Women work in heavily feminized occupations (Rytina and Bianchi, 1984:15). Difference in pay scales for job classifications by sex accounts for much of the wage gap (Bielby and Baron, 1984:27).

Another type of answer comes from neoclassical economics, for example, Gary Becker's (1976, 1981) work and the school known as the New Home Economics. Women's earnings are lower than men's because their stock of human capital is lower. They invest in less human capital because they expect to marry and rear children. Marriage yields higher economic gains if spouses specialize in complementary activities, i.e., the husband in the market, the wife at home. The wife will therefore acquire less human capital and her labor force attachment will be weaker. As an economist, Becker holds constant the variables that sociologists study, such as sex-role norms and labor market discrimination. From a strictly scientific point of view, a theory need not explicitly deal with every aspect of social reality. However, some of the variables that Becker ignores appear to have been critical determinants of the changes in women's employment of the last few decades.

Blau and Ferber (1986) also use neoclassical theory but their assumptions take account of recent changes in behaviors and beliefs. For example, rather than assuming just one household utility function, they assume that spouses' preferences may differ. Thus, they see specializing in homemaking as a particularly high risk undertaking. The value of home production peaks early in the life cycle. Market skills decline when a person remains out of the labor force. Therefore, the homemaker's bargaining power in the family tends to decline over time, and she will find it hard to manage on her own, should need arise (Blau and Ferber, 1986:51).

A recent neoclassical study explains the persistence of the wage gap and predicts much change in the next two decades (Smith and Ward, 1984). The gap has occurred because the educational level of employed women has been lower than that of employed men. For most of this century the women most likely to be employed had less education than all women; the women least likely to be employed had more education than all women. The reason was that women with high levels of education tended to marry comparably educated men, whose earnings reduced wives' interest in working for pay.

This historic situation is now reversing. Recently, employment has increased rapidly among well educated women. By the year 2000 the relative wages of young women workers should rise about 15 percent faster than those of their male counterparts. This projection is probably too conservative because it is based on parameters and behaviors that represent averages over the last thirty years. Early indicators suggest that participation rates will continue to rise at the more rapid pace of the 1970s (see Mott, 1982) for those cohorts of women who first enter the market in the last years of the century (Smith and Ward, 1984).

If women's wages do improve, this should, in turn, increase the proportion of daily bread women can put on the table. According to the theoretical principles expressed earlier in my paper, this change should also mean that women's household influence will rise.

What are current prospects for fertility? Western Europe and the U.S. experienced a "spectacular" fertility decline in the early 1960s (Tabah, 1980). In the U.S. the decline leveled off in 1973. Since then the total fertility rate (the average lifetime fertility implied by age-specific child bearing patterns of a given year) has been 1.8 or 1.9. The projected proportion of women who will never have a first birth is increasing across cohorts and may end up as high as 20 to 25 percent of recent nonwhite and white cohorts (Bloom, 1982:370). There have been small increases in the absolute number of annual births during the past decade. However, these increases are almost entirely due to the presence of a large number of women in childbearing ages (U.S. Bureau of the Census, 1985b:2). There has not been a rise in the birth rate. Moreover a future rise in the birth rate seems unlikely for several reasons.

First, the conditions that made the baby boom possible are not on the current horizon. The baby boom was partially a product of the unique conditions following a long period of depression and war. Middle-aged persons "made up" for postponed marriages and births. Young people married earlier because the labor market was booming and they were educationally advantaged over older cohorts. The young adults who entered the labor force in the 1940s benefited from a rise in high school completion rates, from 29 percent in 1930 to 49 percent in 1940 (U.S. Bureau of the Census, 1975:357), a year that marked the beginning of a long economic boom. Real earnings per worker rose only 22 percent from 1920 to 1939 but then rose 215 percent from 1940 through 1959 (Spitze and Huber, 1980).

From a different perspective, however, Easterlin (1980) predicts a cyclical baby boom when the children born in the 1970s reach reproductive age. He posits that the relative scarcity of younger male workers should favorably affect their employment opportunities. If the economic prospects for young men are good, Easterlin thinks this will lead to higher fertility. Ryder (1979:360) questions this interpretation and warns that demographers who have been betrayed by a trend theory that ignored fluctuations ought not to accept a fluctuation theory that ignores trends. His interpretation and that of many other demographers is that low fertility is here to stay.

Second, the direct cost of child rearing continues to rise. In constant 1982 dollars it will take $226,000 to raise a first-born son to age twenty-two; $247,000 to raise a daughter (Olson, 1982).

Third, the opportunity cost of the mother's time is high and there is no reason to expect a decline. It would increase if college completion rates rise.

Fourth, the prospect and experience of divorce lowers fertility (Becker, 1981:250). Divorce occurs often. A newborn today is as likely to spend some time in a one-parent family as to have an entire childhood with natural parents, and the one-parent experience is seldom brief (Bumpass, 1984:80).

Fifth, changes in the propensity to marry signal negative effects for fertility. Marriage has been declining as a social institution since 1960, as indicated by postponement, fewer people ever marrying, a lower proportion of life spent in wedlock, and shorter duration (Espenshade, 1985:195). For women the mean age of first marriage is at its highest level since 1890. The proportion of never-married persons under forty has doubled since 1970 (U.S. Bureau of the Census, 1985a). Remarriage occurs more often but this is due to the increased number of divorced persons, not to an increasing propensity to remarry. Between 1940 and 1980 the remarriage rate decreased. The fading centrality of marriage is even more noticeable among blacks (Espenshade, 1985:208). The institution of the family appears to be in flux. The demographic transition and recent changes in family formation and procreation successively signal a long-term shift in the Western ideational system whose underlying dimension is the increasing centrality of individual goal attainment (Lesthaeghe, 1983:416, 429).

Sixth, the economic benefits of child rearing have decreased in the West. Government and private retirement programs maintain incomes of people who are too old or too sick to work (except for those in noncovered, low-wage jobs). Americans want to be independent of their children in old age.

Seventh, the psychological rewards for parenthood seem too low to offset the presence of strong disincentives to reproduce. A number of studies report that children negatively affect women's mental health (Kessler and McRae, 1981:44). A survey of studies on childlessness reports that its effects on mental health are nil or favor the childless (Veevers, 1979). National surveys show that children's effect on parental happiness and satisfaction is negative (Campbell, Converse and Rogers, 1976:423) or nil; furthermore, most people reject the idea that married couples who do not want children are being selfish (Huber and Spitze, 1983:138). General Social Survey data, 1972–1975, indicate that children negatively affect parental happiness net of age, family income, years of school, or marital status (Glenn and Weaver, 1979). A survey of cross-sectional, longitudinal, and retrospective U.S. studies reports increased parental well-being after children leave home; for older respondents there were no compensating effects for earlier unhappiness (Glenn and McLanahan, 1981:418). Another national survey reports that hardly anyone expects to turn to grown children for help with personal problems (Veroff, Douvan, and Kulka, 1981:495).

All of these factors not only encourage lower fertility, but also make possible a weakening of social supports for children in society. Many examples of such trends can be cited: the rise in the number of housing units that exclude children (Sullivan, 1983:61); the decrease in the quality of public education; the number of children in poverty (Preston, 1984). Although many couples still plan to have children in modern industrial society, they will have to cope with the growing disincentives for childbearing.

Historically, nations have been wary of depopulation. Armies needed bodies. Today concern about declining fertility will be spurred by the need to maintain retirement programs. When that concern reaches a critical point, it will likely be discovered that programs to increase fertility pose prickly political problems. Fuchs (1983:42) points out that there are three general ways to increase fertility: to increase the cost and difficulty of avoiding births; to replace much social welfare legislation with pro-child measures; or to decrease individual costs of rearing children. None of these is attractive to cost-conscious politicians. Moreover, most measures that would benefit children would also benefit mothers, some of whom are unmarried. More important, benefits to children pay off only in the long run. Politicians get elected in the short run. I conclude that it is very unlikely that fertility will rise much from current low levels.

A NEW VARIABLE:
THE DIVISION OF HOUSEHOLD LABOR

Perhaps the most significant phenomenon in gender stratification after 1950 is the emergence of a new variable: the division of household labor. It was preceded by research on family power (household decision-making), which reported that wives had fairly equal power. Then post-1970 feminism highlighted the futility of studying family power when all women were disadvantaged in society (Gillespie, 1971). Research emphasis shifted to the division of household labor (see references in Berk, 1985). This focus highlights the parallels between the effects of industrialization on men and, later, on women. Nineteenth-century theory focused on the division of labor as source of *class* stratification. Late twentieth-century theory now focuses on the division of household labor as a primary source of *gender* stratification.

Much housework has been mechanized. However, despite improvement in tools, time spent in housework had long held steady, even for employed women. Standards rose instead. The first report of a decrease in time appeared in 1980: employed women spent two-thirds the time of nonemployed women (Robinson, 1980). Although diverse samples and measures have yielded inconsistent findings, an extensive literature review reports that husbands' housework has recently increased—but not much (Pleck, 1983:263), leading Miller and Garrison (1982) to suggest that studies of the division of household labor could be dubbed "Much Ado About Nothing."

However, beliefs in the United States about housework may be changing. Most respondents to a national survey agreed that if both spouses are employed, then housework should be equally shared. Married women were less likely to consider divorce to the extent that their husbands shared housework (Huber and Spitze, 1983) and both spouses were least depressed if the wife was employed and housework was equally shared (Ross, Mirowsky, and Huber, 1983).

Incentives to share housework should be strongest for husbands with well educated and well paid wives. Having a well paid wife gives a man choices: Her wages can cover the cost of hiring help to do the work, reducing the amount to be shared. If he prefers to spend more time on housework, he can avoid the expense of joining a health club to lower his cholesterol and increase his cardiac output. The savings can be invested in tax-free municipals, always attractive to dual-earner couples whose marginal tax rates tend to be high.

DISCUSSION

This paper addressed causes and consequences of research interest in gender stratification. About 1970 a resurgent women's movement made sociologists aware of the social aspects of gender stratification. The ensuing search for causes was influenced by extant methods and approaches in three critical subareas. For different reasons, the situation in each one tended to slow the development of general gender theory.

First, women (typically more interested in the topic than men are) tended to be in family and medical sociology more than in other subareas. Both subareas (but especially family) tend to use social psychological perspectives that make little use of fertility or employment status variables, both of which are basic to gender theory. Second, demography provided basic data but this subarea still tended to be empirical rather than theoretical. The baby boom (which their theory did not predict) had shattered demographers' morale (Ryder, 1979). Third, the Weberian approach to stratification had been swamped temporarily by the modest but precise theory of the status attainment model, which could not readily handle the historical and comparative data needed for a general theory.

The theory outlined above therefore derives from the preindustrial stratification theory suggested by Lenski's (1970) analysis of the effect of technology on social organization and, especially, by Friedl's (1975) analysis of the interaction of work and child care practices in foraging and hoe cultures. The theory poses three basic principles. At the family level, producers outrank consumers. At the societal level, the most power and prestige accrue to those who control the distribution of valued goods beyond the family. Women's involvement in tasks that would enable them to supply subsistence needs or control distribution beyond the family is determined by the way such tasks mesh with child rearing.

These principles help to interpret five trends that have occurred or are occuring in developed societies: in mortality, education, fertility, women's labor force participation, and men's household participation. The analysis explains why, over time, women's levels of power and prestige have become more akin to men's.

First, trends in infant mortality and fertility have drastically reduced the proportion of women's life span spent in rearing children. Moreover, technology has made it possible to separate child bearing from child rearing. Since about 1910 safe methods of artificial feeding enable a baby to survive whether or not it is nursed by its biological mother. I am not arguing that it is "better" for children to be fed by fathers, nannies, or by other caretakers, or to be socialized by someone other than the biological mother. I argue only that children so reared can live to grow up.

Second, trends in education and women's labor force participation have enabled women to provide a substantial share of subsistence needs today. It is even possible that their productivity (compared to men's) is higher today than in any societies except horticultural ones. Women's ability to supply family needs in the industrial age has been nonlinear. Early on, home production was substantial. Later, needed items were produced in factories. Women became housewives and consumers. In the last years of this century women's "production" of earnings will come closer to men's.

A fifth trend is barely underway. Women remain underrepresented in top positions. Men's equal representation in the household is a condition for change. This is rather a large order. Yet, as Komarovsky (1985:336) noted, if pious egalitarian proclamations are to be realized, then several institutions need to be profoundly overhauled. Whether population replacement would be possible under such conditions is unknown, as Lorber (1975) implied a decade ago. It is tempting to take an optimistic view but it is much too early to know.

NOTE

1. The original version of this paper, sponsored by the National Academy of Science Committee on Scholarly Communication with the People's Republic of China, was presented in August 1985 at Airlie House, Warrenton, Virginia. I am grateful to Lisa Ransdell for research

assistance, to William Form, and two anonymous readers for helpful comments, and to Judith Essig for clerical help.

REFERENCES

Baker, Elizabeth Faulkner. 1925. *Protective Labor Legislation*. New York: Columbia University Press.

Baron, James and William Bielby. 1985. "Organizational barriers to gender equity." In Alice Rossi (ed.), *Gender and the Life Course:* 233–252. New York: Aldine.

Becker, Gary. 1976. *The Economic Approach to Human Behavior.* Chicago: University of Chicago Press.

———. 1981. *A Treatise on the Family.* Cambridge, MA: Harvard University Press.

Berk, Sarah Fenstermaker. 1985. *The Gender Factory.* New York: Plenum.

Bielby, William and James Baron. 1984. "Sex segregation within organizations." In B. Reskin (ed.), *Sex Segregation in the Workplace:* 27–55. Washington: National Academy Press.

Blake, Judith. 1965. "Demographic science and the redirection of population policy." In M. Sheps and J. C. Ridley (eds.), *Public Health and Population Change:* 41–69. Pittsburgh: University of Pittsburgh Press.

Blau, Francine and Marianne Ferber. 1986. *The Economics of Women, Men and Work.* Englewood Cliffs, NJ: Prentice-Hall.

Bloom, David. 1982. "What's happening to age at first birth in the United States." *Demography* 19:351–370.

Blumberg, Rae Lesser. 1978. *Stratification.* Dubuque, IA: W. C. Brown.

Bose, Christine and Peter Rossi. 1983. "Prestige standings of occupations as affected by gender." *American Sociological Review* 48:316–330.

Bumpass, Larry. 1984. "Children and marital disruption." *Demography* 21:71–82.

Caldwell, John. 1976. "Toward a restatement of demographic transition theory." *Population and Development Review* 2:321–366.

———. 1980. "Mass education as a determinant of the timing of the fertility decline." *Population and Development Review* 6:225–256.

Campbell, Angus, Philip Converse, and Willard Rogers. 1976. *The Quality of American Life.* New York: Russell Sage Foundation.

Chafetz, Janet and Gary Dworkin. 1986. *Female Revolt.* Totowa, NJ: Rowman & Allanheld.

Daniels, Arlene Kaplan. 1986. *Invisible Careers.* Chicago: University of Chicago Press.

Davis, Kingsley. 1984. "Wives and work: Consequences of the sex role revolution." *Population and Development Review* 10:397–418.

Easterlin, Richard. 1980. *Birth and Fortune.* New York: Basic Books.

Elder, Glen. 1978. "Family history and the life course." In Tamara Hareven (ed.), *Family and Life Course in Historical Perspective:* 17–64. New York: Academic Press.

Epstein, Cynthia Fuchs. 1983. *Women in Law.* New York: Anchor Press.

Espenshade, Thomas. 1985. "Marriage trends in America." *Population and Development Review* 11:193–245.

Evans, Sara. 1980. *Personal Politics.* New York: Random House.

Featherman, David. 1983. "Life-span perspectives in social science research." In Paul Baltes and Orville Brim (eds.), *Life-Span Development and Behavior:* 1–57. New York: Academic Press.

Form, William. 1985. *Divided We Stand.* Urbana: University of Illinois Press.

Freeman, Jo. 1973. "The origins of the women's movement." In J. Huber (ed.), *Changing Women in a Changing Society:* 30–49. Chicago: University of Chicago Press.

Friedl, Ernestine. 1975. *Women and Men: An Anthropologist's View.* New York: Holt, Rinehart and Winston.

Fuchs, Victor. 1983. *How We Live*. Cambridge, MA: Harvard University Press.

Gillespie, Dair. 1971. "Who has the power? The marital struggle." *Journal of Marriage and the Family* 33:445–448.

Gilman, Charlotte Perkins. 1972. *The Home*. (1903*) Urbana: University of Illinois Press.

Glenn, Norval and Charles Weaver. 1979. "Family situation and global happiness." *Social Forces* 57:960–967.

Glenn, Norval and Sara McLanahan. 1981. "The effects of offspring on the psychological well-being of older adults." *Journal of Marriage and the Family* 43:409–421.

Goode, William. 1959. "The sociology of the family." In R. Merton, L. Broome, L. Cottrell (eds.), *Sociology Today:* 178–196. New York: Basic Books.

Goody, Jack. 1976. *Production and Reproduction*. Cambridge: Cambridge University Press.

———. 1983. *The Development of Family and Marriage in Europe*. Cambridge: Cambridge University Press.

Hajnal, John. 1965. "European marriage patterns in perspective." In D. Glass and D. Eversley (eds.), *Population in History:* 101–143. London: Methuen

———. 1982. "Two kinds of preindustrial household formation system." *Population and Development Review* 8:449–494.

Huber, Joan and Glenna Spitze. 1983. *Sex Stratification*. New York: Academic Press.

Kessler, Ronald and James McRae. 1981. "Trends in the relation between sex and psychological distress, 1957–1976." *American Sociological Review* 46:443–452.

Komarovsky, Mirra. 1985. *Women in College: Shaping Basic Identities*. New York: Basic Books.

Lenski, Gerhard. 1970. *Human Societies*. New York: McGraw-Hill.

Lesthaeghe, Ron. 1983. "A century of demographic and cultural change in Western Europe." *Population and Development Review* 9:411–435.

Lipset, Seymour Martin and Neil Smelser. 1961. *Sociology: Progress of a Decade*. Englewood Cliffs, NJ: Prentice-Hall.

Lorber, Judith. 1975. "Beyond equality of the sexes: The question of the children." *The Family Coordinator* 24:465–472.

Lydall, Harold. 1968. *The Structure of Earnings*. London: Oxford Clarendon Press.

McKeown, Thomas. 1976. *The Modern Rise of Population*. New York: Academic Press.

McLaren, Angus. 1983. *The Debate over the Fertility of Women and Workers in France*. New York: Holmes & Meier.

Merton, Robert, Leonard Broome, and Leonard Cottrell, Jr. (eds.) 1959. *Sociology Today: Problems and Prospects*. New York: Basic Books.

Miller, Joanne and Howard Garrison. 1982. "Sex roles: The division of labor at home and in the work place." *Annual Review of Sociology* 9:237–262.

Mohr, James. 1978. *Abortion in America*. New York: Oxford University Press.

Mott, Frank (ed.) 1982. *The Employment Revolution*. Cambridge, MA: MIT Press.

Olson, Lawrence. 1982. *Costs of Children*. Lexington, MA: Lexington Books. (Quoted in Intercom 10(11/12):6.)

Oppenheimer, Valerie Kincade. 1973. "Demographic influences on female employment and the status of women." In Joan Huber (ed.), *Changing Women in a Changing Society:* 184–199. Chicago: University of Chicago Press.

Parsons, Talcott. 1959. "General theory in sociology." In R. Merton, L. Broome, and L. Cottrell (eds.), *Sociology Today:*3–38. New York: Basic Books.

Pleck, Joseph. 1983. "Husbands' paid work and family roles." In H. Lopata and J. Pleck (eds.), *Research in the Interweave of Social Roles:*251–333. Greenwich, CT: JAI Press.

Preston, Samuel. 1984. "Children and the elderly: Divergent paths for America's dependents." *Demography* 21:435–457.

Reskin, Barbara (ed.) 1984. *Sex Segregation in the Workplace*. Washington, DC: National Academy Press.

Richardson, Laurel. 1985. *The Other Woman.* New York: The Free Press.

Riley, Matilda White. 1981. "Age and aging." In H. B. Blalock (ed.), *Sociological Theory and Research:*339–348. New York: The Free Press.

Robinson, John. 1980. "Household technology and household work." In S. F. Berk (ed.), *Women and Household Labor* 5:53–67. Beverly Hills, CA: Sage.

Ross, Catherine, John Mirowsky, and Joan Huber. 1983. "Dividing work, sharing work, and in-between: Marriage patterns and depression." *American Sociological Review* 48:809–823.

Rossi, Alice. 1964. "Equality between sexes: A modest proposal." *Daedalus* 93:602–652.

Rossi, Alice (ed.) 1985. *Gender and the Life Course.* New York: Aldine.

Rupp, Leila and Verta Taylor. 1986. *Feminism in the Fifties.* New York: Oxford.

Ryder, Norman. 1979. "The future of American fertility." *Social Problems* 26:359–370.

Rytina, Nancy and Suzanne Bianchi. 1984. "Occupational reclassification and changes in distribution by gender." *Monthly Labor Review* 107:11–17.

Smith, James P. and Michael Ward. 1984. "Women's wages and work in the twentieth century." R-3119-NPCHD. Santa Monica, CA: Rand.

Spitze, Glenna and Joan Huber. 1980. "Changing attitudes toward women's nonfamily roles, 1938–1978." *Work and Occupations* 7:317–335.

Sullivan, Teresa. 1983. "Family mortality and family morality." In W. D'Antonio and J. Aldous (eds.), *Families and Religious Conflict.* Beverly Hills, CA: Sage.

Swafford, Michael. 1978. "Sex differences in Soviet earnings." *American Sociological Review* 43:657–673.

Tabah, Leon. 1980. "World population trends: A stocktaking." *Population and Development Review* 6:355–389.

Tietze, Christopher. 1981. *Induced Abortion: A World Review.* New York: The Population Council.

Tiryakian, Edward. 1981. "Sexual anomie and social change." *Social Forces* 59:1025–1053.

Treiman, Donald and Kermit Terrell. 1975 "Sex and status attainment." *American Sociological Review* 40:174–200.

United Nations. 1973. *Determinants and Consequences of Population Trends.* New York: Department of Economic and Social Affairs, Population Studies 50.

U.S. Bureau of the Census. 1975. *Historical Statistics of the United States. Part I.* Washington, DC: Government Printing Office.

————. 1985a. "Marital status and living arrangements: March 1984." *Current Population Reports. Population Characteristics. Series P-20, 399.* Washington, DC: Government Printing Office.

————. 1985b. "Estimates of the US population by age, sex, and race, 1980 to 1984." *Current Population Reports. Series P-25, 965.* Washington, DC: Government Printing Office.

U.S. Department of Labor. 1928. *Women's Bureau Summary: The Effects of Labor Legislation on Women's Employment Opportunities. Bulletin 68.* Washington, DC: Government Printing Office.

Veevers, Jean. 1979. "Voluntary childlessness." *Marriage and Family Review* 2:1–26.

Veroff, Joseph, Elizabeth Douvan, and Richard Kulka. 1981. *The Inner American.* New York: Basic Books.

Weinbaum, Batya. 1978. *The Curious Courtship of Women's Liberation and Socialism.* Boston: South End Press.

Westoff, Charles. 1978. "Some speculations on the future of marriage and fertility." *Family Planning Perspectives* 10:79–83.

* For reprinted publications, the date in parentheses is the original publication date.

5 Sex Differences in the Games Children Play

JANET LEVER
Northwestern University

The world of play and games has been relegated to a minor position in the study of childhood socialization. This study accords a more important role in the socialization process to the games children play. It asks: are there sex differences in the organization of children's playtime activities? A large body of new empirical data on the leisure patterns of fifth-grade schoolchildren suggests six important differences. After describing these differences, the author speculates on their possible consequences. It is suggested that play and games contribute to the preservation of traditional sex-role divisions in society by equipping boys with the social skills needed for occupational careers while equipping girls with the social skills better suited for family careers.

Children's socialization is assumed to have consequences for their adult lives. When sex differences in socialization are considered, a chief concern is the extent to which one group (men) is advantaged over another (women). Assuming that girls' socialization equips them less well for occupational careers than boys', the question becomes, "what is it about socialization that has this effect?" Typically, the answers have focused on institutional agents, primarily the family but also the school, and on the values, attitudes, and bodies of knowledge imparted by them.

In this paper, I take a different tack. I examine the peer group as the *agent* of socialization, children's play as the *activity* of socialization, and role-skills as the *product* of socialization. Despite the importance attributed to peers during adolescence, the peer group and playtime have been relatively neglected in the study of child development. Perhaps social scientists have ignored the subject because they feel that sex differences in the preferred

"Sex Differences in the Games Children Play" by Janet Lever, in *Social Problems,* Vol. 23, No. 4, pp. 478-487. © 1976. Reprinted with permission.

activities of children are obvious. Or maybe no one pauses to reflect upon the consequences of children's leisure activities because of the general tendency to view play as trivial. Yet it is during play that we have an opportunity to observe the development of precisely those role skills that are crucial for success in modern society.

Mead and Piaget are the foremost authorities who have recognized the social value of play and game participation. Mead (1934) suggests that the game experience is important as a situation in which the child can develop a sense of "self as object" and learn the complex role-playing skills relevant to later life. Mead illustrates his point by referring to the boys' games of baseball, but he does not tell us how girls, who are less familiar with team play, learn these critical lessons. Piaget (1965), through a close study of the game of marbles, meticulously explains how children develop moral values while they play rule-bounded games.[1] He mentions almost as an afterthought that he did not find a single girls' game that has as elaborate an organization of rules as the boys' game of marbles. If we believe that games can be rich learning environments, then we must give serious attention to the differential exposure of boys and girls to certain types of play.[2] The research question then becomes: Are there sex differences in the organization of children's playtime activities?

Methodology

I used a variety of methods to gather as much data as possible in one year, 1972. 181 fifth-grade children, aged 10 and 11, were studied. Half were from a suburban school and the other half from two city schools in Connecticut. The entire fifth grade of each school was included in the study. I selected three schools whose student populations were predominantly white and middle-class—a choice made deliberately because I believe that race and class distinctions would only confound the picture at this stage of exploratory research.

Four techniques of data collection were employed: observation of school-yards, semi-structured interviews, written questionnaires, and a diary record of playtime activities. The diary was a simple instrument used to document where the children had actually spent their time for the period of one week. Each morning I entered the classrooms and had the children fill out a short form on which they described *what* they had done the previous day after school, *who* they did it with, *where* the activity took place, and *how long* it had lasted. Half the diaries were collected in the winter and half in the spring. Over two thousand diary entries were recorded. The questionnaire, designed to elicit how children spend their time away from school, was also administered by me inside the classroom. I conducted semi-structured interviews with one-third of the sample. Some were done in order to help me design the questionnaire and diary; others were done later to help me interpret the results. I gathered the observational data while watching children's play activity during recess, physical education classes, and after school.[3]

The Distribution of Play in Space and Time

Children spend an extraordinary proportion of their day at play. For this reason alone the subject is worthy of serious investigation. Boys and girls alike spent only 24% of their free time (i.e., outside school) activities engaged in *non-play*. The activities most frequently mentioned were household chores, doing homework, and going to religious services.[4]

Another 24% of the activities listed in the diaries were neither "play" nor "non-play," but rather *vicarious pastimes*. The most important pastime, by far, was watching TV. Again, virtually no sex differences were found; both boys and girls watched TV from 15 to 20 hours per week. However, there were strong differences in the types of shows preferred by each sex. Generally speaking, girls preferred family-oriented situation comedies and boys preferred adventure shows.

Looking now at the 52% of the activities representing *real play,* the differences between boys and girls become clear and strong. Following are six differences I observed:

First, boys play outdoors far more than girls. Many of the preferred activities of girls—like playing with Barbie dolls or board games—are best played indoors. Many of the boys' preferred activities—like team sports or fantasy games like "War"—have to be played outdoors. According to the diaries, 40% of the girls compared to 15% of the boys spent less than one quarter of their playtime outdoors. This sex difference has several important implications. Girls, playing indoors, are necessarily restricted in body movement and vocal expressions. Boys, playing outdoors, move in larger, more open spaces and go farther away from the home which, undoubtedly, is part of their greater independence training. We can think of girls' indoor games (usually played behind closed doors) as *private* affairs whereas boys' outdoor games are *public* and open to surveillance.

Second, even though boys and girls spent the same amount of their playtime alone (approximately 20%), when they were involved in social play, *boys more often played in larger groups.* This second sex difference is related to the first, for indoor environments place structural limitations on the maximum number of participants that can join in play. But this finding is also independent of the first point, for, according to the diary data, girls played in smaller groups even when they were outdoors. The nature of boys' games is such that a larger number of participants is required for proper play. For example, team sports require a larger number of players than activities like tag, hopscotch, or jumprope. On the questionnaire, 72% of the boys compared to 52% of the girls reported that their neighborhood games usually include four or more persons. Diary and observational data ran in the same direction, although the sex differences reflected were slightly weaker.[5]

Third, boys' play occurs in more age-heterogeneous groups. Children between ages 8 and 12 prefer to play in sex-segregated and age homogeneous groups. But if boys' games require a larger number of participants, the limited availability of their age-peers necessitates allowing some younger children to join the game. The implicit understanding is that "you're better off with a little kid in the outfield than no one at all."

For example, I witnessed numerous ice hockey games where ages ranged from 9 to 15 or 16. The youngest children tried their best to keep up with the older ones or dropped out. They learned to accept their bruises, stifle their frustrations, or not be invited to play again. The very few times I observed girls in age-mixed play was at summer camp when the 10–12 year olds used much younger children of 5 and 6 as "live dolls," leading them in circle songs like "ring around the rosy" or versions of tag like "duck, duck, goose." Here the oldest girls had to play on the level of the youngest instead of vice versa. The implications of this female play pattern for learning child care/nurturance skills are so obvious as to require little comment.[6]

Fourth, girls more often play in predominantly male games than boys play in girls' games. We would expect more girls to be included in boys' games in accordance with the same principle: "you're better off with even a girl in the outfield than no one at all." Besides, there are theoretical reasons to make this prediction. It is believed that girls are neither punished as early nor as severely for sex-inappropriate behavior (Lynn, 1966).

The evidence for this proposition is mixed. In each of the three schools, there were one or two girls who were skilled enough to be included as regular members of the boys' basketball or baseball teams. On the other hand, there were many occasions when boys were seen playing girls' games like hopscotch or jumprope too. They did this without being censured, for they entered the game in the role of "buffoon" or "tease"—there to interrupt and annoy the girls and not be taken as serious participants. This is a clear example of what Goffman (1961) calls "role distance." The point to be made here is that girls playing boys' games had to do so as serious participants and suffered the consequence of being labelled a "tomboy," whereas the boys had a convenient protective device available to soften the consequences of sex-inappropriate play behavior.

Fifth, boys play competitive games more often than girls. For the purposes of analysis, a distinction was made between play and games.[7] *Play* was defined as a *cooperative* interaction that has no explicit goal, no end point, and no winners. To the contrary, formal *games* are *competitive* interactions, governed by a set body of rules, and aimed at achieving an explicit, known goal (e.g., baskets, touchdowns). Formal games have a predetermined end point (e.g., when one opponent reaches so-many points, or at the end of the ninth inning) that is simultaneous with the declaration of a winner. Some activities may be organized as either play or game. For instance, just riding bikes is play whereas racing bikes is a game. Sixty-five percent of the play activities boys reported in their diaries were formal games, compared to 35% of the girls' activities.

In other words, *girls played more* than boys and *boys gamed more* than girls. Boys' greater involvement in team sports accounts for much of the strength of this sex difference in competitiveness, as well as the other sex differences described. But team sports constituted only 30% of the boys' play activities; if they were excluded from the analysis, the sex differences reported above would be weakened but by no means would they disappear. For example, eliminating team sports for both sexes, 54% of the boys' activities and 30% of the girls' activities are competitively structured. That is to say, if there were no team sports, we would still find important differences in the nature of the games boys and girls play.

Sixth, boys' games last longer than girls' games. According to the diary data, it was found that 72% of all boys' activities lasted longer than 60 minutes while only 43% of the girls' play activities did so. This finding was supported by recess observations. Boys' games lasting the entire period of 25 minutes were common, but in a whole year in the field, I did not observe a single girls' activity that lasted longer than 15 minutes.

There are several possible explanations for this sex difference. The most obvious is that the *ceiling of skill*[8] is higher in boys' games. A group of eight-year-olds find the game of baseball fun and challenging, and those same boys at twelve years of age can play the game and enjoy it just as much because the requisite skills have been developing all along; thus, the element of challenge remains. By contrast, girls who could play the games of jumprope and tag in the first grade are still playing them in the fifth-grade but find them "boring" now. To be sure, they are better jumpers and runners, but the ceiling of skill was reached long ago. Moreover, girls' games have less structured potential for surprise, such as stealing bases or bunting as in the game of baseball. In short, it is likely that boys find their games more challenging and, therefore, have a longer span of attention.

Even when girls play games with a high ceiling of skill, the games often end shortly after they begin because the players have not developed the motor skills necessary to keep the action exciting. Some girls I watched could not catch or throw a volleyball. The one spontaneous girls' sports games I observed—a game of kickball—ended after fifteen minutes because the fielders had not succeeded in getting a single player out, and they were both frustrated and bored.

Another reason that boys' games continued for a longer period of time than girls' games is because boys could resolve their disputes more effectively. During the course of this study, boys were seen quarrelling all the time, but not once was a game terminated because of a quarrel, and no game was interrupted for more than seven minutes. In the gravest debates, the final word was always to "repeat the play," generally followed by a chorus of "cheaters proof." The P.E. teacher in one school noted that his boys seemed to enjoy the legal debates every bit as much as the game itself. Even players who were marginal because of lesser skills or size took equal part in these recurring squabbles. Learning to deal with disputes may have been facilitated by the model set by the older boys during the age-mixed play referred to earlier.[9] Piaget argues that children learn respect for rules by playing rule-bounded games; Kohlberg (1964) adds that these lessons are greatest where there are areas of ambiguity and the players experience dissonance.

If Kohlberg is right, the moral lessons inherent in girls' play are fewer since there are almost no areas of ambiguity comparable to a player sliding into first base. Traditional girls' games like jumprope and hopscotch are *turn-taking* games where the nature of the competition is *indirect* (that is, there is pre-ordained action: first my turn, then your turn, finally we compare achievements). "Hogging" is impossible when participation is determined by turn-taking; nor can personal fouls occur when competition is indirect. These turn-taking games do not contain contingent rules of strategy as in sport games; rather they are regulated by invariable rules of procedure. Given the structure of girls' games, disputes are not likely to occur. Thus, girls gain little experience in the judicial process. This lack of experience shows dramatically when they do play games where rule interpretation and adjudi-cation are important. Most girls interviewed claimed that when a quarrel begins, the game breaks up, and little effort is made to resolve the problem. As I observed almost no examples of self-organized sports games, let me quote one interviewee, the captain of the girls' after-school soccer team, for a description of what occurs:

> Girls' soccer is pretty bad because most of the girls don't show up every time. We have to keep changing our teams to make them even. Then pretty soon we start arguing over whether something was fair or not. And then some girls quit and go home if they don't get their way. Sometimes calling them "babies" helps to get them to stay and play a while longer.

Other girls concurred, and some complained that their friends could not resolve the basic issues of choosing up sides, deciding who is to be captain, which team will start, and sometimes not even what game to play!

The most striking example of boys' greater consciousness and experience with rules was witnessed in a gym class when the teacher introduced a game called "newcombe," a variation on volleyball. The principle rule was that the ball had to be passed three times before it could be returned to the other side of the net. Although this game was new to both the boys and the girls, the boys did not once forget the "3-pass" rule, yet the girls forgot it on over half the volleys that first day.

DISCUSSION

Even though barriers still exist, many forms of discrimination against women are beginning to be eliminated. Some social scientists have oriented their research to answer the question: If we succeed in ending all forms of discrimination on the basis of sex, is there anything about the way we raise our daughters that will present obstacles to their pursuance of any occupational choice, including the professions and higher levels of business administration? The answers have been in the affirmative; the focus has been on personality and motivation. Some have examined aspects of childhood socialization that produce dependent, passive, obedient personalities in girls (Bronfenbrenner, 1961; Kagan, 1964). Others have stressed aspects of training that limit girls' motivation for success in the occupational world (Horner, 1972).

My own observations, however, lead me to stress a rather different theme, namely, that the differences in leisure patterns of boys and girls lead to the development of particular *social skills* and capacities. These skills, in turn, are important for the performance of different adult roles. Specifically, I suggest that boys' games may help prepare their players for successful performance in a wide range of work settings in modern society. In contrast, girls' games may help prepare their players for the private sphere of the home and their future roles as wives and mothers.

Boys' games provide many valuable lessons. The evidence presented here suggests that boys' games further independence training, encourage the development of organizational skills necessary to coordinate the activities of a numerous and diverse group of persons, and offer experience in rule-bounded events and the adjudication of disputes. Mead offered us the insight that team sports teach young children to play a role at the same time as they take into account the roles of other players.

Furthermore, boys' experience in controlled and socially approved competitive situations may improve their ability to deal with interpersonal competition in a forthright manner. And experience in situations demanding interdependence between teammates should help boys incorporate more general cooperative skills, as well as giving some team members (especially the older boys during age-mixed play) very specific training in leadership skills. The social and organizational skills learned in large play groups may generalize to non-play situations.

On the other hand, girls' games may provide a training ground for the development of delicate socio-emotional skills. We have seen that girls' play occurs in small, intimate groups, most often the dyad. It occurs in private places and often involves mimicking primary human relationships instead of playing formal games. Their age-mixed play is the type that helps girls to develop nurturance skills. Finally, girls' play, to a large extent, is spontaneous and free of structure and rules; its organization is cooperative more often than competitive.

The qualitative data collected through interviews and observation present a more convincing picture of girls' early friendships as a training ground for their later heterosexual courtship relations. The girls in this study claimed to feel more comfortable in pairs, less so in a triad, and least comfortable in groups of four or more. Most girls interviewed said they had a single "best" friend with whom they played nearly every day. They learn to know that person and her moods so well that through non-verbal cues alone, a girl understands whether her playmate is hurt, sad, happy, bored, and so on. There is usually an open show of affection between these little girls—both physically in the form of hand-holding and verbally through "love notes" that reaffirm how special each is to the other. Sharing secrets binds the union together, and "telling" the secrets to outsiders is symbolic of the "break-up." Such friendships may vary from two weeks to two years or more in duration. These girls experience the heartbreak of serial monogamy long before heterosexual dating begins some three to six years later.

Simmel's (1950:123) reflections on the dyad explain the precarious nature of these special relationships and why the larger play groups of boys are more stable:

> The dyad has a different relation to each of its two elements than have larger groups to their members. . . . The social structure here rests immediately on the other of the two, and the secession of either would destroy the whole. The dyad, therefore, does not attain that super-personal life which the individual feels to be independent of himself.

There can be no shift from the person to the role, let alone from the role to the collectivity, for the dyadic relationship is characterized by the *unique* interaction between two individuals. A girl engaged in pastimes with one of a series of "best friends" may be gaining training appropriate for later dating experiences where sensitivity skills are called for, but she is less likely than her sports-oriented brother to learn organizationally relevant skills. Returning to Meadian terms, boys develop the ability to take the role of the *generalized other,* whereas girls develop empathy to take the role of the *particular other.*

To be sure, boys also have strong friendships, and the interpersonal skills they learn through their games are many. But these interpersonal skills are more instrumental than expressive. A boy and his best friend often find themselves on opposing teams. They must learn ways to resolve disputes so that the quarrels do not become so heated that they rupture friendships. Boys must learn to "depersonalize the attack." Not only do they learn to compete against friends, they also learn to cooperate with teammates whom they may or may not like personally. Such interpersonal skills have obvious value in organizational milieu. Boys learn to share the limelight, for they are told that team goals must be put ahead of opportunities for self-glorification. The lessons in emotional discipline are repeated daily: boys must restrain their energy, temper, and frustration for the cohesiveness of the group. Self-control, rather than self-expression, is valued highly. Good-natured participation in any activity the majority elects to pursue is expected from all. In other words, boys must develop the social skills of "gregariousness" and "amiability"—social skills which Riesman (1961) claims are more closely linked to modern organizational life than are technical skills.[10]

The above thoughts are speculative. To the extent that my assessment of the consequences is true, it means that the world of play and game activity may be a major force in the development and perpetuation of differential abilities between the sexes—differences that reinforce the preparation of girls for traditional socio-emotional roles. It might be wise to review educational policy with these thoughts in mind. Perhaps we should support a broadening of physical education programs for girls to include learning opportunities now found primarily in boys' play activities. Since deeply-ingrained patterns are slow to change, alternate opportunities might be developed in non-play situations—for example, encouraging teachers to design group projects in which girls can gain experience in specialization of labor, coordination of roles, and interdependence of effort. At the same time, males have roles as husbands and fathers as well as occupational roles. A fully considered social policy will have to assess the extent to which emphasis on large-scale, organized sports for boys means systematic under-exposure to activities in which delicate socio-emotional skills are learned.

Children's play patterns are part of that vast behavioral repertoire passed on from generation to generation. American parents have always encouraged their boys to play contact team sports because they believe the "male nature" requires rough and tumble action, and organized competition is the best outlet for this surplus energy. Parents believe their girls are frail and less aggressive, and therefore do not enjoy serious competition; rather, they believe girls feel their maternal instincts early and prefer playing with dolls and reconstructing scenarios of the home. But parents give little thought to the structural components of those games and to the lessons inherent in each type of play. Yet it is perfectly clear that if the very different organization of children's play has *any* impact on the performance of adult roles, that influence must be a conservative one, serving to protect the traditional sex-role divisions within our society.

NOTES

* This paper is drawn from my Ph.D. dissertation (Lever, 1974). The research was supported by an N. I. M. H. Fellowship. I would like to thank Stanton Wheeler, Louis W. Goodman, and R. Stephen Warner for their advice and encouragement throughout this project.

1. Sometimes the word "rule" is used to refer to game norms or customs. Here the term "rule-bounded" is used in the narrower sense and refers to games in which the rules are known to all players before the game begins and remain reasonably constant from one game situation to the next and in which the infraction of those rules carries penalties (Eifermann, 1972).

2. Among others who have recognized the importance of play are Huizinga, 1955; Moore and Anderson, 1969; and Stone, 1965.

3. Further details on data collection can be found in Lever, 1974. As a contribution to the folklore of strategies of field research, I should mention that I sat in my car near a schoolyard every lunch hour for a month before formally beginning this study. I doubt a male researcher could have lasted three days before being questioned.

4. It should be said that the distinction between play and work for children is even fuzzier than it is for adults. A child walking to school appears to us only to be walking, but she may be involved in a private game like avoiding stepping on cracks; or, the newspaper boy making his deliveries appears to be working, which he is, yet simultaneously he may be immersed in a game of target practice with each shot at our doors. Some things we adults consider work—like cooking and baking—the children clearly defined as play, and were so categorized in my study, while there was no doubt that boys and girls alike saw making beds and washing dishes as work.

5. One of the important features of using different measures is that one gets a feel for what different measures produce. In this study, the children's statements of what they *usually* do and what they *prefer* to do (i.e., the questionnaire and interview data) showed the strongest sex differences. My own observations of what children did in the arena of the public schoolyard reflected differences of intermediate strength. The diary data i.e., what children *actually* do when away from the eyes of parents, teachers, and peers of the opposite sex—showed the weakest differences. In other words, the diary data were furthest from the cultural stereotypes of what boys and girls *ought to be doing*. Nevertheless, sex differences reported in the diaries are often strong.

6. The opportunity for age-mixed play is different for fifth-grade boys and girls. While boys' sports continue to be of interest through the teens and beyond, girls have already dropped out of the game culture by the time they reach age 13 or 14. Psychologists who have noted an earlier decline in girls' participation in schoolyard play believe it is due to girls' earlier maturation rate and superior verbal skills. The accepted argument is that girls are able to exchange games for conversation earlier and with more satisfaction (Eifermann, 1968:76). Leaving aside the empirical question of differential skills, I suggest a reversal in the causal model. Based on evidence presented in this paper, we can conclude that our culture is deficient in non-sport games that are sufficiently sophisticated and challenging for older girls, thereby forcing them to drop out of playground activity. Development of verbal skills may be seen as a consequence, rather than a cause, of this pattern.

7. This distinction is consistent with that made by G. H. Mead (1934), as well as the classificatory schemes of contemporary observers of play and games (Sutton-Smith *et al.,* 1963).

8. Csikzentmihalyi and Bennett (1971) coined this term.

9. Wheeler (1966:60) points out the advantages of being part of a system with *serial* rather than disjunctive socialization. In this case, it means that when older boys permit younger ones to join them in their games, they in effect teach their juniors a great deal about the setting, not only in terms of the requisite physical skills but the social ones as well. In this context, such lessons are more often due to sheer exposure than to self-conscious instruction.

10. In another article, I develop and test the hypothesis that boys' games are more *complex* than girls' games. Game complexity has been defined in many ways. I have chosen to define it as a constellation of six dimensions that emerged from a reading of the sociological literature on complexity in large-scale formal organizations. See Chapter Four in Lever (1974).

REFERENCES

Bronfenbrenner, Urie. 1961. "The changing American child: a speculative analysis." *Merrill-Palmer Quarterly* 7:73–83, 89.

Csikszentmihalyi, M. and S. Bennett. 1971. "An exploratory model of play." *American Anthropologist,* 73:45–58.

Eifermann, Rivka. 1968. "School children's games." U.S. Office of Education, Bureau of Research. (Mimeographed Report).

———. 1972. "Free social play: a guide to directed playing." Unpublished paper.

Goffman, Erving. 1961. *Encounters.* Indianapolis: Bobbs-Merrill Co.

Horner, Matina. 1972. "Toward an understanding of achievement-related conflicts in women." *Journal of Social Issues,* 28:157–175.

Huizinga, Johan. 1955. *Homo Ludens: A Study of the Play-Element in Culture.* Boston: Beacon Press.

Kagan, Jerome. 1964. "Acquisition and significance of sex typing and sex-role identification." Pp. 137–67 in M. L. Hoffman and L. W. Hoffman (eds.), *Review of Child Development Research, Vol. I,* New York: Russell Sage Foundation.

Kohlberg, Lawrence. 1964. "Development of moral character and moral ideology." Pp. 383–431 in M. L. Hoffmann and L. W. Hoffmann (eds.), *Review of Child Development Research, Vol. I.* New York: Russell Sage Foundation.

Lever, Janet. 1974. *Games Children Play: Sex Differences and the Development of Role Skills.* Unpublished Ph.D. dissertation, Department of Sociology, Yale University.

Lynn, David B.. 1966. "The process of learning parental and sex-role identification." *Journal of Marriage and the Family,* 28:466–470.

Mead, George Herbert. 1934. "Play, the game and the generalized other." Pp. 152–164 in *Mind, Self and Society.* Chicago: University of Chicago Press.

Moore, O. K. and A. R. Anderson. 1969. "Some principles for the design of clarifying educational environments." Pp. 571–613 in David A. Goslin (ed.) *Handbook of Socialization Theory and Research.* Chicago: Rand McNally.

Piaget, Jean. 1965. *The Moral Judgment of the Child.* New York: Free Press.

Riesman, David. 1961. *The Lonely Crowd.* New Haven: Yale University Press.

Simmel, Georg. 1950. *The Sociology of Georg Simmel.* Trans., and ed. by Kurt H. Wolff. New York: Free Press.

Stone, Gregory P. 1965. "The play of little children." *Quest* 4:23–31.

Sutton-Smith, B., B. G. Rosenberg, and E. F. Morgan, Jr. 1963. "Development of sex differences in play choices during pre-adolescence." *Child Development* 34:119–126.

Wheeler, Stanton. 1966. "The structure of formally organized socialization settings." Pp. 53–116 in Orville G. Brim, Jr., and Stanton Wheeler (eds.), *Socialization After Childhood.* New York: John Wiley and Sons.

6   Race and Sex Differences in Career Dynamics*

RACHEL A. ROSENFELD
McGill University; and the National Opinion
Research Center, University of Chicago

In this paper, career differences by race and sex are analyzed. Careers are defined as trajectories of socioeconomic status and wages and are described by a linear differential equation model. It is assumed that the different groups defined by race and sex tend to be in different labor markets and economic sectors and to face different opportunity structures even within labor market divisions. This assumption guides predictions for and interpretation of results with respect to various aspects of career inequality: initial status and wage level; potential status and wage levels; effects of human capital, family background, and family of procreation variables on initial and potential wage and status levels; speed of advancement. Pooling of cross-sections and time-series techniques are used to estimate the model, with data from the National Longitudinal Surveys of the Labor Market Experience of Young Men and Women.

In the last decade, sociologists have made extensive use of the status attainment approach, which focuses on the effects of individual-level characteris-

AUTHOR'S NOTE: * Direct all communications to: Rachel A. Rosenfeld; National Opinion Research Center; University of Chicago; 6030 South Ellis; Chicago, IL 60637.

An earlier version of this paper was presented at the Annual Meeting of the American Sociological Association, Boston, Mass., August, 1979. This research was supported in part by Canada Council grant 410-77-0530 and by National Institute for Mental Health grant 5-T32 MH 15163-02. I am grateful to Edward Withers, Carol Welch, and F. Yvonne McDonald for their assistance with the data analysis and to François Nielsen, Dennis Hogan, and anonymous reviewers for their helpful comments.

tics on achievement, to monitor racial and sexual inequality. (See, for example, the papers in Hauser and Featherman, 1977.) Even more recently, sociologists have begun to investigate the extent to which differences in labor market positions result in the observed inequality by sex and race (e.g., Bibb and Form, 1977; Beck et al., 1978a; 1978b). Spilerman has suggested (1977:551) "the notion of the career [job history] as a strategic link between structural features of the labor market and the socioeconomic attainments of individuals."

With few exceptions (e.g., Sørensen and Tuma, 1978), however, the empirical research on socioeconomic inequality by race and sex, with or without reference to labor market structures, has been done using models and methods developed for the analysis of achievement in cross-section, rather than for the analysis of careers. The purpose of this paper is to contribute to the small body of empirical research on career dynamics. Following Sørensen (1975; 1977), careers are defined as levels of status and wages individuals attain over their work lives and are modeled using a simple linear differential equation.[1]

In the next section, the literature on labor markets is used to develop hypotheses that are to be tested in this paper about sex and race differences in careers. Following this, the model of career trajectories is explained. The career model is then estimated by pooling of cross-sections and time-series methods, using data from the National Longitudinal Surveys of Labor Market Experience of Young Men and Young Women. The results of this estimation are discussed, and conclusions drawn, in the final sections.

SEX, RACE, LABOR MARKETS,
AND CAREERS: HYPOTHESES

Careers take place over time. They have beginnings, from which people, on the average, move up.[2] Between the time of their entry into the work force and of their retirement or withdrawal from it, people's income, status, and other rewards change. This change takes place with a certain speed, which may vary across groups with different characteristics and in different types of labor markets. People with given characteristics in given labor markets will, as they live their work lives, approach some highest possible career level—or potential—which they may or may not actually reach, depending on the speed of their mobility.

This process is perhaps most easily grasped in the context of a career within a given firm. The firm has a job hierarchy. An individual entering the firm has credentials enabling him/her to qualify for some position or positions within the firm that, without a change in credentials, will be the highest to which he/she can aspire. To reach such a position usually requires time in the firm, as well as formal credentials. Some people formally qualified for a given position will actually reach that position, others will not. Those with different types of qualifications may have the same potential for a position but reach it with different speeds. For example, those with higher education may be able to go almost directly to their highest possible position while those without the credentials require some time to work their way up. (See Rosenbaum, 1979, for an analysis of such mobility within a firm.) Also, those equally qualified formally—but having different ascribed characteristics—may have access to different career lines and may take more, or less, time to advance. For example, Blau (1977) hypothesizes that, even within internal labor markets, women will have different kinds of career ladders open to them, and that, when those career-ladder positions are also held by men, women will advance more slowly up them than will men.

Although it is easy to visualize the career process by thinking of mobility within a firm, and, although some people do have such careers, average career profiles show the general pattern (of upward mobility approaching some potential) to emerge without the mobility being all within one firm (Sørensen, 1975; 1977). The hypotheses and model developed here refer to the average careers for men and women, by race, regardless of whether these take place totally within particular firms. The model developed in the next section enables us to look directly at (1) initial achievement, (2) factors affecting initial achievement, (3) potential achievement, (4) factors affecting potential achievement, and (5) the speed at which the potential is approached. Hypotheses about race and sex differences along these dimensions are also developed in this section.

Although this paper does not directly use the concept of dual labor markets or segmented economy to investigate differences in opportunity by race and sex, it takes the labor market and segmented economy literature as suggestive of the sorts of differences in opportunity by race and sex that might be behind differences in careers. Various typologies of labor markets and the economy have been offered: primary and secondary markets (Doeringer and Piore, 1971); male and female markets (Oppenheimer, 1970); monopoly, competitive, and state sectors of the economy (see development by Hodson, 1978); core and periphery sectors (Bluestone, 1970, used by Beck et al., 1978a; 1978b); open and closed employment relationships (Sørensen and Tuma, 1978). (See Kalleberg and Sørensen, 1979, for a review of the labor market literature.) Women and blacks have been found to be overrepresented in the secondary labor markets and in the competitive or periphery sector—that is, in those labor market positions that offer generally lower rewards and less chance for advancement (Hodson, 1978; Bibb and Form, 1977; Beck et al., 1978a; 1978b; Boyd and Humphreys, 1979). Further, within sectors and labor markets, there is additional sorting by sex and race (Hodson, 1978; Beck et al., 1978a), with the process of this sorting resembling the general sorting into labor markets (Blau, 1977; Dussault and Rose-Lizée, 1979).

Thus, even within markets and sectors, women and blacks are often barred from high-reward, high-opportunity jobs.

No one typology of labor markets or economic sectors will be able to capture the extent to which there are overall differences in opportunities by sex and race, given the sorting that also goes on *within* industries, occupations, and firms as well as between labor market divisions. This argues for continuing attention to studies of firms, as well as for continuing refinement of typologies of the ways in which labor markets are segmented. These activities are, however, beyond the scope of this paper. Here, instead, differences in careers by sex and race are predicted by using what has been theorized and discovered about the workings of opportunity structures by sex and race among and within markets.[3] I will argue that the estimated parameters of the career model can be used as social indicators of the general position of sex and race groups, summarizing the effects of between- and within-market sorting.[4]

Initial and Potential Levels
of Job Rewards

As careers are viewed here, they have beginnings, at entry to the labor market, the levels of which are determined by the labor market in which persons are moving and their qualifications and background. They also have potential levels, which might or might not be reached, likewise determined by the labor market structure and the characteristics of the individuals. Most sex and race comparisons have been done cross-sectionally. Even when beginning job is treated separately, the average current job reward for any given group averages over those near the beginning of their careers, those approaching their potential, and those somewhere in between. When this is done, the differences among average job rewards for the different groups will depend on the career-stage composition of the groups as well as on the levels of rewards they receive at comparable career stages. This paper looks separately at the levels of job rewards at the beginning of the career, six years later (the last year in which observations were actually made, as will be discussed in the next section), and at the potential. Discussions in the labor market literature and existing over-time comparisons suggest several hypotheses about initial and potential wage and status differences, by race and sex.

(1) All women and nonwhite men will have lower average initial and potential wages. Given the wage structure evidenced in core versus periphery or primary versus secondary markets, and the overrepresentation of women and minority members in just those markets offering lower rewards and less opportunity to advance, plus the nature of sorting by sex and race within markets, I expect all women and nonwhite men to start their careers at a

disadvantage (as Gordon, 1972:115 suggests), and to have lower potential
wage levels than white men.

*(2) The gap in average wages between white men and other groups will
increase over the work life.* Hoffman (1978) discusses the increase in wage
differences between black and white males over the life cycle. Nonwhite men
(and women generally) might be denied access to jobs that motivate and
provide training and advancement and, thus, the chance for higher wages;
and so they fall farther and farther behind white men. It is to be expected,
then, that the wage differences between white men and other race/sex groups
would be greater at their potentials than initially, and that the distance
between starting and ending (or potential) wages would be greater for white
men than for other groups.

*(3) The average status of nonwhite men will be lower initially and at their
potential than status of white men, although the average status of white
women will be about the same as that of white men at their potential and
perhaps even slightly higher at career entry.* Given the sorting into occupations, by race, that occurs within and between markets and sectors, I would
expect the status of jobs held at any career stage by nonwhite men to be, on
the average, lower than that of jobs held by white men. For women, especially
white women, this sorting into occupations on the basis of sex has been
found, in cross-section, to lead to jobs with average status about the same as
that for men, as women are concentrated in lower white-collar jobs which
have fairly high status (although low wages). (See Oppenheimer, 1970;
Treiman and Terrell, 1975; see also Nilson, 1976, and Bose, 1973, for
discussion of the determination of prestige by sex.) Although nonwhite
women have been found more often in service jobs—with both low status
and low pay—than in clerical jobs, recently there have been shifts of
nonwhite women into the traditionally female positions (Jusenius, 1975;
Allen, 1979). For young nonwhite women, average status profiles are expected to be somewhere between white women's and nonwhite men's,
because they will represent a mix of lower white-collar, service, and blue-
collar jobs.

*(4) The status distance to be covered, on average, by white men will be
greater than that covered by women or nonwhite men.* Women and nonwhite
men tend to be in those jobs with restricted opportunity to move up. Workers
in such jobs are not expected to remain with the job, are not given much
on-the-job training, and perhaps do interrupt their employment; thus, they
remain at roughly the same occupational level. White men are supposed to
be especially likely to be operating in internal labor markets, where one
enters a firm at a particular entry port and continues up the career ladder
within the firm, protected to a large extent from competition with outsiders

(Doeringer and Piore, 1971). I would expect such men to have a greater potential distance to cover than those without such career ladders. Further, Blau (1977) has found that even when women are in internal markets the career ladders in which they predominate tend to be flatter than those for men. Generalizing to all groups sorted into disadvantageous labor market positions, women and nonwhite men are expected to have less actual and potential status mobility than white men. Empirical evidence on the status distance between first and current jobs, by sex and race, is consistent with this hypothesis (see Duncan et al., 1972; Rosenfeld, 1978; Wolf, 1976; Sewell et al., 1977).

Return to Resources

Of course, differences in status and income levels could be due to differences in the characteristics of different groups rather than to segregation in a particular type of labor market and sector. Indeed, those in secondary labor markets and in the competitive sector have been characterized by (and found to have) lower educational and skill levels (Beck et al., 1978b; Hodson, 1978; Doeringer and Piore, 1971; Gordon, 1972; Boyd and Humphreys, 1979). One needs to know, then, about the *returns* to various work-related resources across groups. If returns are the same across groups, then differences in level of achievement would be the result simply of differences in levels of resources (although the chances or motivation to get additional training, education, and so forth, could also be influenced by labor market location).

Also of interest is whether supposedly nonwork-related characteristics are evaluated differently for different groups. The overrepresentation of women and nonwhite men in the less desirable labor market positions has been explained, in part, by the idea of "statistical discrimination," whereby the core or primary market employers reduce their risk of hiring unstable or untrainable employees by using easily visible characteristics—such as race and sex—as screening devices. Any one individual with these traits will not necessarily be a bad risk, but, on the average at least, some employers believe that these group members will be less desirable employees (Phelps, 1972; Thurow, 1975). Spence (1974) has shown how this sort of screening can pay off for the employer even when the trait used to screen is *not* related to productivity. The analysis here is conducted separately, by race and sex groups, to capture such effects of screening on these traits. There may, however, be other easily observed traits, such as marital status, that are used to further channel people into more or less desirable positions. This screening can appear as differences in the effects of these traits for those assumed to be in different positions within the labor market if the screening works differently in different labor markets.

With respect to returns to resources and other traits, I suggest the following hypotheses.

(1) The wage returns to education, training, and other resources will be lower for women and nonwhite men than for white men. The returns to resources are expected to increase over the work life for white men, but not for other groups. The training and skill of workers are important in the more desirable labor market positions. People may be selected into the primary market and competitive sector on the basis of their credentials. Higher returns to education, then, would show up as a result of this selection. Thurow and Lucas (1972) suggest that education inversely represents to the employer the firm's cost in training a worker rather than the ability of a worker to perform a certain job. If this is the case, then the returns to education should increase for those who are in careers where training occurs and promotion is possible—that is, for white men especially. Further, Beck et al. (1978a) have suggested that, for minority group members in the better parts of the labor market, credentials are evaluated differentially, as the employer's protection against making a mistake in hiring (because it is more difficult and costly to fire a mistake in these sectors than in the secondary or periphery areas). Women and nonwhite men would have to be overqualified to get the same positions as white men and, thus, have lower returns to their resources. This might be especially true for blacks, the quality of whose education might be doubtful in the mind of the employers. Beck et al. (1978a) show that minority workers (nonwhite men and both nonwhite and white women) received lower earnings in relation to their education and experience than did white men, especially within the core sector. Bibb and Form (1977) also found differences between blue-collar women and men in wage returns to their education and tenure, even after roughly controlling for sector.

(2) The differences between white men and women, generally, in returns to resources will be less when career position is measured by status than when it is measured by wages. Gordon (1972:117) has said:

> One would expect more evident patterns of returns to education among women, both because stronger discriminatory patterns against women within the labor market help reduce the bargaining strength of women (and permit employers to reward the more educated without fearing for greater mobility), and because many women work in a variety of white-collar clerical jobs for which some general educational skills are useful.

This statement might be more relevant with respect to status than with respect to wages, however. Treiman and Terrell (1975), Featherman and Hauser (1976), and Sewell et al. (1977) provide evidence of greater similarity between women and men in status returns than in wage returns to education and other resources. Some increase over the career in status returns to resources is still expected for white men but not for white or nonwhite women, given the restrictions on women's opportunity.

(3) Marital status and number of children will be used as additional screening traits for men but not for women. Being married and having children will increase status and wages for men, but will have no effect for women. Although, in principle, family of procreation characteristics are not related to productivity, they may be used as indicators of stability by employers. If this is true, there should be effects of marital status and number of children for men but not for women in the analysis of this paper, which uses data from samples of workers continuously employed. Although some have argued that because—for women—being married and having children constrain both employment and career advancement, there is evidence that these variables are primarily proxies for employment history, with effects on career gains that tend to disappear when extent of employment is explicitly included in a model of status mobility (Rosenfeld, 1978; Boyd, 1977). Controlling for employment, marital status, and number of children would not be of much use to an employer in screening women from jobs with long career ladders. If a woman *is* married, she may be seen as lacking commitment to the labor force; if she is not married (or is married and does not have children), she may be seen as unstable because she *will get* married or *will have* children.

For men, in contrast, having a family may represent both the incentive to go after higher income and status and the signal to an employer that a man is going to be a good employee. This is probably true especially for young white men, just beginning their careers, who potentially have access to jobs with longer career ladders and who cannot use their past employment records as evidence of their stability. The drop in youth unemployment with marriage for young men is one basis for suspecting that marital status for men is, indeed, related to employment patterns. The results in Duncan et al. (1972, chap. 8) are consistent with the hypothesis.

Tests of hypotheses about the levels of status and wages, by race and sex, and about returns to various resources, have been carried out in research from both the status-attainment and the labor-market/economic-sector perspectives. The career model adds to this research primarily by focusing attention on both initial and potential levels of attainment. In cross-section, one cannot be sure at what stage careers are being observed. The attainments of various groups and the effects of independent variables on these attainments will depend on the stage of the process for the different groups. Careers are dynamic—they occur over time—and this dynamism affects even their "static" component.

Speed of Achievement

Perhaps even more important than correct estimation of these cross-sectional aspects of careers is the ability to estimate, directly, the dynamic aspect with this model. That is, one can estimate the speed with which the distance between initial and potential attainments is covered.

Assuming that white men are overrepresented in labor market positions that offer the greatest job mobility opportunities, I hypothesize that:

White men will reach their potential earning more slowly than other groups, but they may reach their potential status more quickly. White men would be expected to reach their maximum earnings more slowly than other groups because of the greater number of rungs on their career ladders (Sørensen, 1977). Essentially, their peak earnings would occur later in their work lives. Women and nonwhite men would be expected to reach their maximum earning ceilings more quickly. White men are thus expected to have greater opportunity for earnings *mobility* over their work life, while other groups are expected to have greater opportunity to *reach* their potential. Oppenheimer's (1974) discussion of career profile differences is consistent with this hypothesis. Looking at age differences in earnings of white men within occupational categories defined by level of peak earnings, she reports that, although young men (18 to 24) tend to be similar in their levels of income regardless of occupational category, their patterns of earnings, by age, differ considerably by occupation—with two general patterns emerging: Earnings for men in most blue-collar and middle- and low-level white-collar occupations peak early, before age 45; but high-level professional, managerial, and sales occupations seem to peak later, after age 45. The late-peaking occupations are those in which white men are most likely to be represented, and from which both women and nonwhite men are likely to be excluded.

For socioeconomic status, the predictions about relative ordering are reversed. Status is a relatively rough measure of level of job. Males entering internal labor markets might be expected to obtain, rather quickly, the highest occupational category they will obtain. Women and black men, who are restricted in the career ladders to which they can gain access, might have some possibility of upward mobility in status, but only after "proving" themselves by extended occupancy in a stereotypic occupation. In this case, they would slowly reach their potential status. If, however, there were no possibility at all of moving up from a typically black or female job (which most often would be in the secondary labor market and/or competitive sector), then it could be that women and blacks would reach their maximum statuses even more quickly than white men.

In summary, I expect to find that: women generally and nonwhite men have lower average initial and potential levels of income and at least nonwhite women and nonwhite men have lower average initial and potential status levels than white men; on average, the status and wage distance to be covered by nonwhite men and by all women will be shorter than that to be covered by white men; education and other resources should give fewer returns in the form of initial and potential levels of income and status to all women and to nonwhite men than to white men, while men (perhaps, particularly, white men) will benefit from having their own families, especially early in their careers; and the speed at which the maximum earnings level is attained will be slower for white men than for other groups, while the relative speed with which maximum status is reached will possibly be slower for women generally and for nonwhite men.

The Career Model

Careers have been described in the previous section as the process whereby people move up in status or in wages, over their work lives, to approach some potentially highest position. A fairly simple model of this sort of process is a partial adjustment model (see, for example, Doreian and Hummon, 1974; 1976):

$$dY/dt = -b(Y^* - Y). \qquad (6.1)$$

Here, Y is either status or income achieved, and Y^* is the potential level of status or income. The rate of change in Y (dY/dt) is proportional (by $-b$, which is positive because, here, $b < 0$, as explained below) to the gap that exists between the achieved level of Y and the potential level. If the potential is reached, then change in status or income will cease.[5]

The criterion Y^* could be set in any of a number of ways. Here, it is assumed that the criterion will be a linear function of the individual's characteristics—both job-relevant and others—with the weights associated with the characteristics varying according to the labor market position of the group to which the person belongs:

$$Y^* = a_0 + a_1 X_1 + \ldots + a_K X_K \qquad (6.2)$$

where there are K individual characteristics. This definition of the potential is consistent with the work that has been done to date from both the status attainment and labor market perspectives.

Substituting the right side of Equation 6.2 for Y^* in Equation 6.1, and multiplying Equation 6.1 through, gives a simple linear differential equation, which is easily solved (Coleman, 1968) to yield an equation defining the career trajectory—that is, the levels of Y over time:

$$Y_1 = e^{bt} Y_0 + a_0(1 - e^{bt}) + a_1(1 - e^{bt}) X_1 \qquad (6.3)$$
$$+ \ldots + a_K(1 - e^{bt}) X_K,$$

where Y_0 is initial income or status.

The potential Y^* as defined here need not be some fixed level. It can change in response to changes in individual characteristics. In socioeconomic achievement terms, this would mean that people could continue to improve their potential position by increasing job-relevant or other resources or could suffer a decrease in ultimate achievement because of depreciation of a resource or an increase in a liability. If, for the sake of simplicity, one assumes that the change in some individual characteristics is linear and occurs independently of changes in job rewards, then allowing for such change is straightforward (see Coleman, 1968, for the general form). If, say, X_1 were to change linearly and independently of Y, then the solution to Equation 6.1, when the criterion Y^* is defined as in Equation 6.2, would be:

$$Y_1 = e^{bt}Y_0 + a_0(1 - e^{bt}) + a_1(1 - e^{bt})X_1$$
$$+ \; a_1 \left\{ \frac{1 - e^{bt}}{bt} - 1 \right\} \Delta X_1 + \; \ldots$$
$$+ \; a_K(1 - e^{bt})X_K \tag{6.4}$$

Including the change term does not change the relationship among the other parameters of the model, but adds extra information about the model and its fit (Coleman, 1968:441–3).

As it is stated here, the model has face validity in that, when b is less than 0 and entry level is less than potential level, it predicts a career trajectory that is like that observed, at least for men: one in which there is rapid increase in reward levels early in the career and then a levelling-off (Ornstein and Rossi, 1970; Sørensen, 1975; Rosenfeld, 1978).[6] The speed with which the distance between some entry level and the potential level is covered is indicated by b: the larger b is in absolute value, the more quickly the gap between achieved and potential level is reduced. One could say that groups with a higher absolute value of b have a greater opportunity to reach their potential, while groups with lower absolute values of b have greater opportunities to be mobile (see Rosenfeld and Nielsen, 1978; Rosenfeld, 1979).

To complete the model, one can add an explicit formulation of the way in which individual characteristics determine Y_0:

$$Y_0 = c_0 + c_1X_1 \ldots + c_KX_K. \tag{6.5}$$

The individual characteristics determining the initial reward levels need not be the same as those determining the potential.

The assumption that changes in individual characteristics occur independently of changes in reward level is made for simplicity, and is probably not a realistic assumption. Ideally, one would simultaneously model changes in employment, in rewards received for employment, and in resources and family circumstances. Some attempts have been made in this direction (Doreian and Hummon, 1974; Tachibanaki, 1979), but there is still need for more thought about the conceptual and methodological problems involved in such models. The model presented in this paper is, thus, a first approximation of a dynamic model of careers, valuable in demonstrating the need for attention to the time component of careers and the further steps such attention should take. (See Blalock, 1969; Coleman, 1968; and Hannan and Tuma, 1979, for discussion of multiequation models.) In this paper, after a description of the data and estimation techniques, the model represented by Equations 6.1 and 6.5 will be estimated and the various components of the careers will be compared by sex and race.

DATA AND METHOD

The data with which to test the hypotheses about sex and race differences in career dynamics are from the National Longitudinal Surveys of Labor Market Experience (NLS) of Young Women (1968–1975) and of Young Men (1966–1973). The samples were chosen to represent the civilian noninstitutionalized population of the United States aged 14 to 24 at the time of the first survey for each group. Each sample initially included approximately 5,000 individuals, of whom approximately 1,500 were nonwhite. Detailed employment and educational histories were collected over the years of the surveys (which are still in progress). Such longitudinal data are essential if dynamic models are to be estimated. (See the National Longitudinal Surveys Handbook, CHRR, 1979, for further details.)

From each sample, only those who were still employed at the time of every survey date after the first (1967, 1968, 1969, 1970, 1971, and 1973 for the young men; 1969, 1970, 1971, 1972, 1973, and 1975 for the young women) were included in the analysis so that the greatest number of observations could be used in pooling of cross-sections and time-series to estimate the parameters of the model.

This selection of cases implies potential bias. The young women selected are likely to have a greater commitment to the labor market than other young women of comparable age. They are, therefore, more likely to be the ones who have "careers" in the sense of longer career ladders. (See Rosenfeld, 1977, for a comparison of women with and without employment breaks, using data on an older NLS cohort.) To the extent that this is true, differences between the women and men will be attenuated. Although this selection procedure is the result of the conceptual difficulties in measuring the socioeconomic attainments of women not in the labor force, it might be seen as a response to the argument that the reason women have flatter career profiles than men is that they spend less time in, and are less committed to, the workplace.[7] If there are still sex differences now, it will probably not be because of lesser employment experience for the women.

The selection affects the young men in that those in the military during this period (which covers the height of the Vietnam war) are excluded. During the Vietnam era, those with higher educational attainments were less likely to serve, as were those with lower ability and poor health. Black high school graduates, who might be seen as those blacks most likely to be successful in the labor market, were disproportionately likely to serve during the Vietnam period, but, relative to whites, blacks reporting health limitations were also more likely to serve (see Shields, 1977). To some extent, then, whites with better career chances and blacks with poorer career chances might be included. However, given the nature of occupational deferments, the white men in the sample might have made career choices different from those of a cohort entering the labor market during a period of relatively low exposure to the draft. For example, more college-educated young men might have entered teaching than would have, ordinarily. Given sex differences in careers, however, these men might still have an advantage over women in their chances for promotion. Further, counter-balancing the selection of nonwhite men with worse career chances is the selection of those with continuous employment in the face of very high unemployment rates for young black men relative to other groups (Winship and Rosenfeld, 1979).

Comparing the 1970 characteristics of members of the NLS who were employed all years with the 1970 Census description of people having the same sex, race, and age ranges shows the sort of bias in the subsample: members of the subsample of the NLS providing data for the analysis of this paper are more likely than the general population to have gone to college, given that they have at least a high school diploma; the men in the sample are more likely—and the women (especially the nonwhite women), less likely—to be married than the comparable United States population; while both men and women in the subsample are less likely to be doing service work, the women are also somewhat more likely than the general female population to be professionals, clericals, or operatives, and though the men are less likely to be clericals they are more likely to be managers (if they are white) or farm workers (if they are nonwhite) (U.S. Bureau of the Census, 1970).

Careers will be indexed by two variables: by socioeconomic status (SEI, see Duncan, 1961) and by hourly earnings on main job (in 1972 cents, with wages adjusted using personal consumption expenditures implicit price deflators in the Economic Report of the President, 1977). Three different sorts of individual-level characteristics will be used to predict the trajectories of SEI and wage: human capital variables, family of origin status, and family of procreation characteristics.

The first set of variables includes human capital variables, which influence an individual's productivity and/or the employer's perception of productivity. As already mentioned, the effects of such variables are expected to be greatest for those with jobs offering the greatest opportunities for advancement—that is, especially for white men. Education is one of the most important of these variables. Highest grade completed by the beginning of a two-year period (e.g., by 1967, 1969, and 1971, for the young men) is one measure of this. Change in this level over each two-year interval is also included. Formal training outside regular school is another way in which people can increase their human capital. Measures of whether training related to white-collar work (1 for professional, technical, clerical, sales, or general course outside regular school, 0 otherwise) or to blue-collar work (1 for skilled or other manual training, 0 otherwise) had been taken by the beginning of a two-year interval, and of whether or not there was additional training of either sort during the two years, were also included.[8] In addition to these measures of formal schooling and training, whether or not the individual reported that a health problem limited her/his extent or type of work (1 for some limitation, 0 for none) was included as a third measure of human capital. Health was assumed to remain relatively constant over an interval and was measured in about the middle of each two-year interval.

The second set of variables includes measures of socioeconomic background. Such factors have been a central concern of status attainment research, which endeavors to test the extent to which characteristics of one's family of origin, as compared with achievements of the individual, affect later achievements. Thinking in terms of intergenerational transmission of access to labor markets, one can imagine that a well-placed father could help a child get on a good career ladder by having knowledge of—and connections with—a firm, trade, or profession. If so, the positive effects of "good" family background would be expected to be especially strong for white men. Generally, though, effects of family background have been found to be largely mediated by education, which is included in the career model (Blau and Duncan, 1967; Duncan et al., 1972; Kelley, 1973; Sewell and Hauser, 1975; Sewell et al., 1977). The measures of family background included in the analysis to be presented here are SEI of father (or head of household) when the respondent was 14, mother's education (in years), and number of siblings reported in 1966 (men) or 1968 (women). All family background variables have values constant over time.[9]

The third set of variables is that of family of procreation characteristics. These include marital status and number of children (for women) or dependents (for men). (Marital status is coded 1 if the individual is currently married, 0 otherwise.) Marital status is assumed to have an effect which is constant over a two-year interval. Number of dependents (for men) and number of children (for women) are measured at the beginning of each interval. Change in the number of dependents or children over the two years is also measured. Responsibilities within the home are measured differently for men and women (dependents versus children) to capture differences in the ways such responsibilities may act on, or be imagined to act on, workers of different sexes.

Means and standard deviations for these variables by sex and race are shown in Table 6.1.

As mentioned above, longitudinal data are necessary for any study of careers. One problem with the use of longitudinal data, however, is finding a methodology by which to take advantage of the amount of information available in them. To estimate the parameters needed to compare the speed of career development, the potential levels, and the effects of individual characteristics on this potential, one can estimate

$$Y_t = a_0{}^* + b{}^*Y_{t-1} + a_1{}^*X_1 \ldots + a_k{}^*X_k + e \qquad (6.6)$$

(where some of the independent variables could be change variables) and transform these estimates to obtain the parameters in equations (6.1) and (6.2), for example, $\ln b^* = b$, $a_1{}^*/(1 - b^*) = a_1$.[10] One could choose any two observation times within which to estimate these parameters, adjusting the estimates for the length of the interval. This, however, seems to waste information on the other periods for which one has income and status observations. Another solution is to pool the pairs of observations, so that the data from which the estimates are made consist of more than one set of observations for each individual. Using a two-year lag, there are three sets of years for each individual.

One can imagine estimating Equation 6.6 using ordinary least squares regression (OLS). However, lagged dependent variables often mean serious violations of the assumptions of OLS. If the model is misspecified (as is usually the case with predictions of individual socioeconomic achievement) and the excluded variables are relatively stable or systematically related over time, the error terms will include the effect of these excluded variables and will be correlated over time (autocorrelated)—that is, $E(e_t e_t - 1) \neq 0$. Further, the error term will be correlated with a regressor, since the lagged dependent variable at one time is the dependent variable another time. The OLS estimators will be both inefficient and inconsistent. The bias is especially great in the OLS estimator of the coefficient for the lagged dependent variable. Such bias can affect all the conclusions from the analysis, since b^* is not only of interest in its own right but also enters into the calculations of all the coefficients of the career model.

To reduce the problems of bias, one models the structure of the errors and then uses an estimating technique that takes into account the modeled error structure. The error term can be hypothesized to be as follows:

$$e = \mu_i + \tau_t + \upsilon_{it} \qquad (6.7)$$

where the components are independently distributed with zero means and constant variances. The component for constant individual factors not included explicitly in the general model is μ_i; τ_t is the component for time

(text continues on page 132)

TABLE 6.1. Descriptive Statistics for Career Profiles by Race and Sex

Variables	Whites Mean	(Standard Deviation)	Nonwhites Mean	(Standard Deviation)
A. *Young men employed 1967–1973:*				
Age, 1966	(N = 707) 20.252	(2.989)	(N = 160) 20.088	(2.953)
Mother's education	10.380	(2.839)	7.594	(3.320)
Father's (or household head's) SEI when R was 14	33.298	(23.830)	29.950	(23.311)
Number of siblings	2.761	(2.131)	5.200	(3.104)
Highest grade completed, 1967	12.132	(2.218)	10.531	(2.678)
Change in highest grade, 1967–69	.390	(.702)	.156	(.483)
Highest grade completed, 1969	12.522	(2.281)	10.688	(2.761)
Change in highest grade, 1969–71	.181	(.514)	.088	(.362)
Highest grade completed, 1971	12.703	(2.408)	10.775	(2.835)
Change in highest grade, 1971–73	.303	(.638)	.350	(.711)
White-collar training as of 1967[a]	.209	(.407)	.088	(.284)
Blue-collar training as of 1967	.137	(.344)	.088	(.284)
Additional white-collar training 1967–69	.256	(.437)	.144	(.352)
Additional blue-collar training, 1967–69	.134	(.341)	.113	(.317)
White-collar training as of 1969	.376	(.485)	.213	(.410)
Blue-collar training as of 1969	.231	(.422)	.163	(.370)
Additional white-collar training 1969–71	.283	(.451)	.150	(.358)
Additional blue-collar training, 1969–71	.123	(.329)	.094	(.292)
White-collar training as of 1971	.485	(.500)	.288	(.454)
Blue-collar training as of 1971	.287	(.453)	.219	(.415)
Additional white-collar training 1971–73	.257	(.438)	.150	(.358)
Additional blue-collar training 1971–73	.058	(.234)	.050	(.219)
White-collar training as of 1973	.557	(.497)	.350	(.478)
Blue-collar training as of 1973	.303	(.460)	.244	(.431)
Health limitation, 1968[b]	.092	(.289)	.056	(.231)
Health limitation, 1970	.076	(.266)	.056	(.231)
Health limitation, 1971	.061	(.239)	.063	(.243)

128

Marital status, 1967[c]	.536	(.499)	.431	(.497)
Marital status, 1969	.683	(.466)	.594	(.493)
Marital status, 1971	.777	(.417)	.688	(.465)
Marital status, 1973	.823	(.382)	.719	(.451)
Number of dependents, 1967	.552	(.867)	.744	(1.172)
Change in number of dependents, 1967–69	.372	(.622)	.556	(.916)
Number of dependents, 1969	.924	(1.055)	1.300	(1.350)
Change in number of dependents, 1969–71	.290	(.673)	.288	(.934)
Number of dependents, 1971	1.214	(1.188)	1.588	(1.438)
Change in number of dependents, 1971–73	.235	(.756)	.275	(.931)
SEI67	37.082	(22.900)	20.706	(16.946)
SEI68	39.085	(23.270)*	22.716	(19.024)**
SEI69	39.922	(23.703)	25.269	(24.462)
SEI70	41.761	(23.809)*	25.936	(20.981)**
SEI71	42.745	(24.251)	26.456	(21.699)
SEI73	44.197	(24.296)	27.513	(20.615)
Hourly wages 67[d]	309.646	(130.382)	237.323	(104.079)
Hourly wages 68	350.983	(130.365)*	261.206	(94.308)**
Hourly wages 69	383.706	(143.084)	280.417	(106.137)
Hourly wages 70	418.183	(187.841)*	294.291	(117.433)**
Hourly wages 71	427.973	(174.190)	299.987	(128.898)
Hourly wages 73	487.452	(225.578)	331.671	(170.496)

  * Based on N = 699.
  ** Based on N = 155.

129

TABLE 6.1 Continued

Variables	Whites Mean	(Standard Deviation)	Nonwhites Mean	(Standard Deviation)
B. *Young women employed 1969–75:*	(N = 304)		(N = 86)	
Age	19.799	(2.816)	20.698	(2.657)
Mother's education	10.921	(2.646)	8.919	(3.073)
Father (or household head's) SEI when R was 14	35.299	(23.518)	19.756	(16.684)
Number of siblings	3.000	(2.217)	4.756	(2.886)
Highest grade completed, 1969	12.309	(1.837)	12.279	(1.643)
Change in highest grade, 1969–71	.378	(.712)	.221	(.562)
Highest grade completed, 1971	12.688	(1.803)	12.500	(1.679)
Change in highest grade, 1971–73	.158	(.482)	.093	(.395)
Highest grade completed, 1973	12.845	(1.886)	12.593	(1.778)
Change in highest grade, 1973–75	.227	(.537)	.279	(.607)
White-collar training as of 1969[a]	.319	(.467)	.337	(.467)
Blue-collar training as of 1969	.026	(.160)	.023	(.152)
Additional white-collar training, 1969–71	.270	(.445)	.233	(.425)
Additional blue-collar training, 1969–71	.040	(.195)	.081	(.275)
White-collar training as of 1971	.467	(.500)	.488	(.503)
Blue-collar training as of 1971	.059	(.236)	.105	(.308)
Additional white-collar training, 1971–73	.336	(.473)	.256	(.439)
Additional blue-collar training, 1971–73	.030	(.170)	.000	(.000)
White-collar training as of 1973	.599	(.491)	.547	(.501)
Blue-collar training as of 1973	.082	(.275)	.105	(.308)
Additional white-collar training, 1973–75	.237	(.426)	.209	(.409)
Additional blue-collar training, 1973–75	.010	(.099)	.000	(.000)
White-collar training as of 1975	.655	(.476)	.605	(.492)
Blue-collar training as of 1975	.089	(.285)	.105	(.308)
Health limitation, 1968[b]	.049	(.217)	.012	(.108)
Health limitation, 1971	.066	(.248)	.023	(.152)
Health limitation, 1973	.056	(.230)	.047	(.212)

Marital status, 1969[c]	.322 (.468)	.267 (.445)
Marital status, 1971	.457 (.499)	.395 (.492)
Marital status, 1973	.572 (.496)	.430 (.498)
Marital status, 1975	.674 (.469)	.454 (.501)
Number of children, 1969	.250 (.600)	.651 (.955)
Change in number of children, 1969–71	.089 (.401)	.174 (.439)
Number of children, 1971	.339 (.690)	.826 (1.098)
Change in number of children, 1971–73	.115 (.320)	.151 (.392)
Number of children, 1973	.454 (.756)	.977 (1.095)
Change in number of children, 1973–75	.188 (.502)	.140 (.489)
SEI69	44.211 (18.481)	36.454 (21.922)
SEI70	46.296 (18.773)*	36.541 (19.718)**
SEI71	47.980 (18.263)	38.279 (21.695)
SEI72	48.272 (17.864)*	39.977 (20.942)**
SEI73	49.355 (18.286)	38.616 (20.967)
SEI75	49.993 (19.506)	40.942 (23.347)
Hourly wages 69[d]	232.066 (10.706)	211.339 (81.705)
Hourly wages 70	256.573 (92.630)*	244.769 (86.625)*
Hourly wages 71	278.986 (114.227)	262.759 (97.623)
Hourly wages 72	296.619 (100.995)*	276.165 (111.541)**
Hourly wages 73	311.147 (110.464)	284.955 (100.685)
Hourly wages 75	315.990 (111.904)	296.415 (111.054)

  * Based on N = 294.
 ** Based on N = 85.

SOURCE: National Longitudinal Surveys of Labor Market Experience of Young Men (1966–1973) and Women (1968–1975).

NOTES: a. Training. White-collar training = 1 if professional, technical, clerical, sales training or general courses not leading to a degree have been taken by the date specified, 0 otherwise (see note 4 for further explanation). Additional white-collar training = 1 if any such training had been taken in a given two-year interval beyond that reported by the beginning of the interval, 0 otherwise. Blue-collar training = 1 if any skilled or other manual training has been taken by the specified date, 0 otherwise. Additional blue-collar training = 1 if such training has been taken over a two-year interval in addition to that reported at the beginning of the interval, 0 otherwise.

b. Health limitation = 1 if respondent reported health as limiting extent or kind of work, 0 otherwise (see note 5 for further explanation).

c. Marital status = 1 if presently married, 0 otherwise.

d. Hourly wages: in constant 1972 cents.

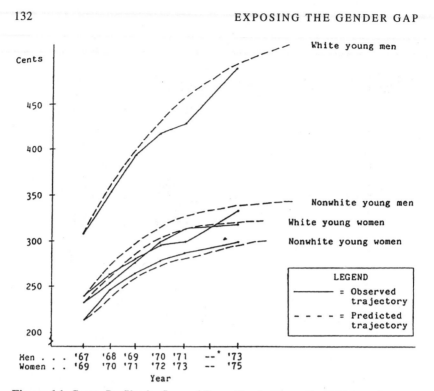

Figure 6.1. Career Profiles by Sex and Race: Hourly Wages (in 1972 Cents) over Time for Those Employed 1967-1973 (Young Men) or 1969-1975 (Young Women)
NOTE: * No observation made this year.

effects; and v_{it} is the usual well-behaved random error term. Substantively, μ_i would represent unmeasured traits affecting achievement, such as intelligence, motivation, and energy, which differ across individuals but are relatively constant over time. τ_t represents unobserved variables that vary over time and in roughly the same way for all individuals, such as the effects of the economy on socioeconomic achievement. With more than one observation per individual over more than one time, there is the possibility of estimating the various components of variance and controlling for them in estimating the other coefficients of the model.

An approach to estimation that takes the error structure into account is that of modified generalized least square (MGLS). This class of estimators is consistent and asymptotically efficient.[11] The small sample properties of GLS and MGLS have been examined by Hannan and Young (1977) (see also Hannan and Tuma, 1979). The particular MGLS estimator used in this paper is the one developed by Fuller and Battese (1974), which uses the fitting-of-constants method to estimate the covariance matrix (Henderson,

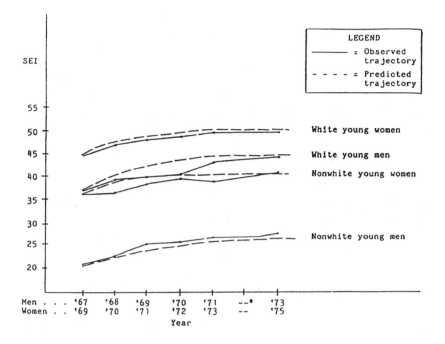

Figure 6.2. Career Profiles by Sex and Race: SEI over Time for Those Employed 1967-1973 (Young Men) or 1969-1975 (Young Women)
NOTE: * No observation made this year.

1952; Searle, 1971). This method is appropriate for this situation, in which some of the exogenous variables do not change over time. This algorithm has been included as part of the SAS computing package (Drummond and Gallant, 1977).[12]

RESULTS

Observed Career Profiles

Figures 6.1 and 6.2 show the observed career profiles (in solid lines) for white and nonwhite women and men. The data from which these profiles were drawn are in Table 6.1. The first time-point (1967 for young men, 1969 for young women) is the time of first job for many of these people and close to it for others, and will be discussed as approximately Y_0. Starting wages in 1972 cents vary as predicted: white men have the highest hourly wages, followed by nonwhite men, white women, and nonwhite women. The ordering of wages is first by sex and then, within sex, by race. The relative positions with respect to income remain the same six years later. Further, over the period observed, white men gain more in wages than nonwhite men, who in turn gain more than white women, who gain more than nonwhite women. The career profiles in Figure 6.1 show, however, that women and nonwhite men have very similar career profiles, while white men belong to a distinctly different pattern. Differences between white men and the other groups increase over the time observed. At the same time, the careers of men by race are parallel, and those of women by race are parallel.[13]

The story changes with respect to status. Here status is determined first by race and then, within race, by sex—but with women having the advantage. White women have the highest status profiles, nonwhite men the lowest; and white men and nonwhite women fall in between. Over the period observed, though, white men gain more in status than any other group, and nonwhite women gain the least (4.5 points), in line with what was expected.

The differences in wage and status curves cannot be explained completely by sex and race differences in the levels of resources and constraints. Nonwhite men do have: a noticeably lower level of education and training (especially white-collar training); mothers with less education and fathers with lower status jobs; more siblings and dependents; and somewhat less stability as indicated by marriage. If all these variables affect achievement— and if these effects do not vary by race—we would expect lower achievement for nonwhite men on the basis of their personal characteristics. The case is not so clear for women, however. The women, here, are approximately as well educated as the men. They have higher rates of white-collar training, although less blue-collar training. White women, on the average, come from socioeconomic backgrounds similar to those of white men, while nonwhite women, like nonwhite men, come from families with lower levels of parental education and status and larger number of siblings (which, perhaps, makes their educational comparability with whites even more remarkable). The women, here, who have been employed fairly consistently over the six years observed, have lower rates of marriage than the men and have fewer children than do men, on the average, have dependents. This is true despite the tendency of women, in general, to marry at lower ages than men. They may, indeed, have chosen to commit themselves to work rather than to raising families, at least for a while. And, if anything, these women are healthier than the men, although only a very small proportion of any group reports health limitations.

Effects of Individual Characteristics:
Initial Job

Returns to various resources, and constraints in early wages and status, are shown in Table 6.2. For all groups, education is important for early attainment. White men and women get approximately the same wage and status returns to their education at this stage of their work lives. Nonwhite women also receive returns comparable to those of white men—and much higher than those of nonwhite men. The location of these white and nonwhite women in lower white-collar jobs and of white men in positions where education, perhaps, is used to screen applicants, would seem to contrast with the position of nonwhite men who may be in exactly those positions for which education credentials are less important, as speculated before. Formal training is also of importance for the rewards received in early jobs. White-collar training increases the status of men and, to a lesser extent, of white women (some of whom have taken clerical courses within regular school). Blue-collar training also increases wages, significantly for all groups except nonwhite women. The effect is greatest for nonwhite men, for whom formal white- or blue-collar training perhaps is seen as a more reliable credential than education received in public schools of perceived dubious quality.

The returns to resources can be summarized by calculating returns to education and training using each group's coefficients and white men's average resources. If all groups had the average characteristics of white men, white men would receive the highest status returns to their resources, with white women and nonwhite women close behind. White men, with average white male education and training, would receive 65 status points on the basis of those resources. On the basis of their coefficients in Table 6.2 and the white men's means, white women would receive 61 points; nonwhite women, 57. Nonwhite men would receive the lowest returns to all their resources: only 35 status points.

With respect to wages, nonwhite men with average white male education and training are, still, the group with the lowest return to their resources: $1.31/hour on the basis of education and training alone. White women actually receive the greatest return to their human capital at this career stage: $3.02, compared with $2.72 for nonwhite women and $2.47 for white men.

Health limitations, which might be viewed as negative human capital, have no effects for men, but significant negative effects for white women. (See Corcoran and Duncan, 1979, for a more detailed comparison of the human capital returns to men and women.) Nonwhite women have an unexpectedly positive return to health limitations. Since only 1 of the 86 nonwhite women has any health limitations, this probably reflects an idiosyncratic case.

As expected, effects of family of origin are largely mediated by education (as demonstrated also by regressions, not shown), with some small effects for nonwhite women and men. Family of procreation variables have effects primarily for men. For them, being married has a positive effect on both status and wages. For women, there is essentially no effect on marital status. For men at this career stage, it is possible that marriage represents either actual or perceived stability, while for women, as speculated before, the stereotype may be such that they cannot win. However, white women do

TABLE 6.2 Prediction of "First" (1967 for Young Men, 1969 for Young Women) SEI and Hourly Wage by Sex and Race[a]

A. Young Men Employed 1967–1973

Dependent Variable Independent Variable	SEI 1967				Hourly Wage 1967			
	Whites		Nonwhites		Whites		Nonwhites	
	Metric Coefficient	s.e.	Metric Coefficient	s.e.	Metric Coefficient	s.e.	Metric Coefficient	s.e.
Mother's education	-.031	.265	.650	.388	.320	1.601	4.539	2.477
Father's SEI	.003	.029	.044	.049	-.022	.174	.752*	.310
Siblings	-.187	.344	-.381	.372	-1.550	2.079	-3.607	2.377
Highest grade, 1967	5.200**	.504	2.712**	.498	19.481**	2.147	8.870**	3.183
White-collar training	10.172**	1.758	8.762*	4.112	21.068*	10.617	90.965**	26.288
Blue-collar training	-2.024	2.047	4.265	3.887	48.119**	12.367	31.587	24.850
Health limitations, 1966	-1.676	1.996	4.794	4.272	-4.594	12.054	-22.003	27.311
Marital status, 1967	6.251**	1.729	7.252*	2.925	81.941**	10.446	67.248**	18.699
Number of dependents, 1967	-1.440	.988	-1.752	1.236	8.472	5.968	-3.556	7.902
Constant	-29.457		-15.463		16.027		70.244	
R²	.377		.387		.298		.336	
N	707		160		707		160	

TABLE 6.2 Continued

B. Young Women Employed 1969–1975

Dependent Variable Independent Variable	SEI 1969				Hourly Wage 1969			
	Whites		Nonwhites		Whites		Nonwhites	
	Metric Coefficient	s.e.	Metric Coefficient	s.e.	Metric Coefficient	s.e.	Metric Coefficient	s.e.
Mother's education	-.548	.387	.349	.715	-2.121	2.467	-.749	2.972
Father's SEI	.074	.042	.346*	.122	.071	.270	.281	.508
Siblings	-.428	.426	-.089	.782	2.914	2.718	-.834	3.254
Highest grade, 1969	4.940**	.536	4.937**	1.484	23.849**	3.422	21.562**	6.173
White-collar training	4.481*	1.994	-.302	4.230	45.017**	12.731	30.385	17.591
Blue-collar training	3.081	5.644	-21.210	13.463	22.261	36.026	27.638	55.994
Health limitations, 1968	-9.535*	4.170	46.326*	18.769	-30.705	26.619	-68.915	78.061
Marital status, 1969	-.828	2.315	2.864	5.333	8.529	14.775	10.551	22.180
Number of children, 1969	-1.758	1.794	-4.270	2.594	23.370*	11.452	4.791	10.789
Constant	-12.269		-31.627		-71.166		-64.359	
R²	.317		.389		.224		.239	
N	304		86		304		86	

a. These are ordinary least squares estimates, since there is no lagged dependent variable.
* .01 ≤ p ≤ .05; ** p < .01.

receive some small positive returns to number of children, perhaps because this variable represents perceived stability and motivation to earn, as was hypothesized for men.

At this point in the work life, soon after entry into the work force, women and white men do at least equally well in returns to their human capital resources, while nonwhite men get the low returns predicted for those in secondary labor markets and in the periphery sector. Marriage is effective in demonstrating stability (or being associated with other positive traits) only for men.

The analysis so far has not used the dynamic career model to look at speed of achievement or to go beyond the observed data to the potential level of achievement. It only forms the basis for comparison with this potential and effects on it. We can now turn to results from the dynamic career model.

Estimated Potential Achievement

Table 6.3 presents the estimates for the difference equation in Equation 6.6, with error structure such as in Equation 6.7. In all cases, the individual specific component of the variance is relatively large. Ignoring this would lead to biased coefficients and would have resulted in misleading inferences, with a confounding of the b, an indicator of opportunity structure, with the effects of individual-level characteristics, such as motivation to search for a "good" job. The time-specific component, however, is relatively small. From these estimates, we can calculate estimates of the parameters of the differential equation model. The results of doing this are shown in Table 6.4.[14]

We can now go beyond the observed data to comparison of potential reward levels. Potential is calculated for each group as

$$a_0 + a_1(\overline{X}_1) + a_2(\overline{X}_2) + \ldots a_K(\overline{X}_K) \qquad (6.8)$$

using estimated parameters a_i in Table 6.4 (derived from estimates in Table 6.3) and the last observed means for each group (generally from 1973 for the men and from 1975 for the women).[15]

At their potential, white women would, still, be expected to have the highest average status (50.3, compared with 44.8 for white men, 26.7 for nonwhite men, and 41.4 for nonwhite women), having gained on the average a bit over 6 status points since their "first" jobs. This gain in status is in contrast to the lack of status gain found in data for women, generally (Rosenfeld, 1978; Wolf, 1976). This provides further evidence that to some extent women, in general, fail to gain in status over time because of discontinuities in their employment. When employed as are men, they do experience some gains. The white men have, however, gained slightly more than have the women (and the nonwhite men). Although their expected potential status is, still, lower than that of white women, it is now higher than that of nonwhite women. This probably reflects the greater heterogeneity in the jobs held by men over their work lives. As a group, they would show more mobility, as some white men get sorted into higher-level jobs over time in the work force. Nonwhite men, while experiencing a somewhat greater gain in status than nonwhite women, remain at the lowest status level.

The situation with respect to wages shows much greater contrast between white males and other groups than is true of status potential. At their potential level, white men would be expected to earn over $5.50 an hour, having experienced an increase in wages of over $2.50. Women and nonwhite men have gained, on the average, less than $1.00 in hourly earnings, receiving under $3.50 an hour in 1972 dollars. Nonwhite men continue to have average earnings somewhat higher than white women, who earn about $.15 more an hour than nonwhite women. This result suggests that lack of wage increase for women is *not* related to employment continuity.[16]

Effects of Individual Characteristics:
Potential Achievement

The coefficients (after the first line) in Table 6.4 represent estimates of the a_i, the effects of individual characteristics on potential achievement. At their potential, white men receive greater returns to their human capital than white women. They receive higher returns in terms of both status and wages to their years of formal schooling; get greater returns, in terms of status, to their white-collar training; suffer less of a status disadvantage from having some formal preparation for a blue-collar job; and receive considerably greater wage returns from both types of training but, especially, blue-collar training. The difference in returns to white-collar vs. blue-collar training is consistent with the idea of the rich plumber—that is, that many craftsmen and skilled manual laborers receive rather high pay for their valuable skills. While nonwhite men receive lower human capital returns than white men, they actually do better than white women, with the exception of somewhat lower wage returns to education. Nonwhite men, as compared with white men, continue to benefit in wages much more from white-collar training and less from blue-collar training and schooling, perhaps because of difficulty in having their educational certification (at least for secondary school) recognized as having any value, and because of difficulty in gaining access to jobs on which to use formal blue-collar training (which is perhaps the result of union control). Nonwhite women, the "double minority," receive higher status returns to their education than does any other group, and wage returns almost as high as those of white men. The returns they receive for formal training, however, are as low as for white women. Poorly educated nonwhite

(text continues on page 143)

TABLE 6.3 Models of SEI and Wage Change by Sex and Race: Modified Generalized Least Squares Estimates

Dependent Variable Independent Variable	SEI at t				Hourly Wages at t			
	Whites		Nonwhites		Whites		Nonwhites	
	Metric Coefficient	s.e.	Metric Coefficient	s.e.	Metric Coefficient	s.e.	Metric Coefficient	s.e.
A. Young men employed 1967–1973:								
SEI or wage at t − 2	.299**	(.020)	.395**	(.045)	.638**	(.024)	.463**	(.053)
Mother's education	.061	(.182)	−.200	(.305)	2.190	(1.429)	3.038	(2.030)
Father's SEI	−.006	(.020)	.007	(.038)	.030	(.155)	.629*	(.252)
Siblings	−.514*	(.236)	.723*	(.285)	−.182	(1.846)	.710	(1.876)
Highest grade at t − 2	4.053**	(.250)	2.256**	(.421)	10.720**	(1.894)	7.584**	(2.740)
Change in highest grade t − 2 to t	2.327**	(.554)	3.796**	(1.106)	9.628*	(4.832)	.121	(8.336)
White-collar training at t − 2	2.427**	(.875)	1.330	(2.027)	10.979	(7.338)	52.244**	(14.452)
Blue-collar training at t − 2	−2.206*	(1.012)	−1.999	(2.036)	30.587**	(8.435)	10.278	(14.316)
Additional white-collar training	4.008**	(.805)	5.329**	(1.967)	11.481	(6.873)	48.347**	(13.958)
Additional blue-collar training	−.128	(1.125)	.836	(2.307)	5.367	(9.660)	−2.090	(16.720)
Health limitations	−2.349	(1.301)	−4.922	(2.939)	−6.117	(11.124)	−17.641	(21.007)
Marital status at t − 2	1.998*	(.934)	−1.189	(1.652)	10.261	(8.046)	11.538	(11.801)
Number of dependents t − 2	.174	(.460)	.131	(.699)	.424	(3.862)	3.003	(4.884)
Change in number of dependents	.732	(.493)	.234	(.679)	−.763	(4.265)	.718	(4.950)
Constant	−22.764**	(3.384)	−2.953	(4.496)	14.390	(32.381)	30.333	(31.813)
Variance components:								
individual specific	85.738		62.047		4732.790		2253.860	
time specific	.096		0.		879.142		302.287	
random error	136.320		116.907		11433.134		7011.838	
Regression MSE	161.342		133.458		12760.666		7605.960	

NOTE: Whites: 707 cross-sections, 3 time series.
Nonwhites: 160 cross-sections, 3 times series.

B. *Young Women Employed 1969–1975:*

	(1)		(2)		(3)		(4)	
SEI or wage at t – 2	.295**	(.032)	.117*	(.053)	.387**	(.031)	.556**	(.061)
Mother's education	.298	(.285)	-.352	(.543)	-1.520	(1.696)	-1.384	(2.131)
Father's SEI	-.014	(.030)	.083	(.095)	.371*	(.180)	.370	(.373)
Siblings	-.729*	(.303)	-.495	(.599)	-1.528	(1.797)	-1.756	(2.363)
Highest grade at t – 2	2.587**	(.401)	7.533**	(.983)	11.866**	(2.336)	12.101**	(4.288)
Change in highest grade t – 2 to t	.678	(.806)	4.041*	(1.739)	1.034	(4.875)	11.121	(9.125)
White-collar training at t – 2	1.186	(1.113)	.749	(2.327)	2.712	(6.781)	-1.935	(11.004)
Blue-collar training at t – 2	-4.671*	(2.373)	1.011	(5.153)	5.225	(14.182)	4.366	(20.819)
Additional white-collar training	1.873	(1.006)	2.331	(2.070)	18.502**	(6.068)	25.349*	(10.722)
Additional blue-collar training	-6.362*	(2.738)	4.005	(6.129)	22.698	(16.463)	38.476	(28.135)
Health limitations	-1.176	(2.024)	2.754	(4.961)	-13.203	(12.103)	-21.189	(26.561)
Marital status at t – 2	-.426	(1.145)	-2.458	(2.304)	2.219	(6.923)	.275	(11.373)
Number of children t – 2	-1.190	(.948)	2.050	(1.482)	5.498	(5.691)	.272	(6.422)
Change in number of children	-.033	(1.035)	3.419	(1.848)	2.933	(6.239)	-6.474	(9.740)
Constant	1.849	(5.002)	-58.383	(13.651)	-44.663	(31.314)	-3.973	(58.567)
Variance components:								
individual specific	71.532		129.066		2460.448		1539.760	
time specific	.463		0		211.844		123.718	
random error	98.895		86.344		3566.962		2876.207	
Regression MSE	118.646		106.706		4326.184		3393.626	

NOTE: Whites: 304 cross-sections, 3 time series.
Nonwhites: 86 cross-sections, 3 times series.
* .01 ≤ p < .05; ** p < .01.

141

TABLE 6.4 Estimated Parameters for Differential Equation Models[a]

	SEI		Hourly Wage	
A. Young Men Employed 1967–1973				
Variable	Whites	Nonwhites	Whites	Nonwhites
SEI or wage at t – 2 dynamic coefficient	–.604	–.464	–.225	–.385
Potential level coefficient for:				
Mother's education	.087	–.331	6.050	5.657
Father's SEI	–.009	.012	.083	1.171
Siblings	–.733	–1.195	–.503	–1.322
Highest grade completed	5.782	3.729	29.613	14.123
White-collar training	3.462	2.198	30.329	97.289
Blue-collar training	–3.147	–3.304	84.494	19.140
Health limitations	–3.351	–8.136	–16.898	–32.851
Marital status	2.850	–1.965	28.345	21.486
Number of dependents	.248	.217	1.171	5.592
Intercept	–32.474	–4.881	39.751	56.486
Potential predicted using means from 1971–1973	44.781	26.676	555.561	347.277
B. Young Women Employed 1969–1975				
SEI or wage at t – 2 dynamic coefficient	–.610	–1.073	–.475	–.293
Potential level coefficient for:				
Mother's education	.423	–.399	–2.480	–3.117
Father's SEI	–.020	.094	.605	.833
Siblings	–1.034	–.561	–2.493	–3.955
Highest grade completed	3.670	8.531	19.357	27.255
White-collar training	1.682	.848	4.424	–4.358
Blue-collar training	–6.626	1.145	8.524	9.833
Health limitations	–1.668	3.119	–21.538	–47.723
Marital status	–.604	–2.784	3.620	.619
Number of children	–1.688	2.322	8.969	.613
Intercept	2.623	–66.119	72.860	–8.948
Potential predicted using means from 1973–1975	50.337	41.432	323.336	308.843

NOTE: a. Formulate used are: dynamic parameter = ln lag coefficient/Δt (where $\Delta t = 2$); potential coefficients = regression coefficient/(1 – lag coefficient). Lag and other regression coefficients are shown in Table 6.3.

women receive very low status, while well-educated nonwhite women (and, on the average, these women *do* have education beyond high school) have their credentials recognized. For them, education seems to be the key to high attainment. (The status returns on education for nonwhite women compared with other groups are consistent with Treiman and Terrell, 1975.)

Overall, if all groups had the 1973 resources of white men, white men and nonwhite women would receive the highest status returns (76.1 and 111.8) and white women and nonwhite men the lowest (46.7 and 48.7). With respect to wage returns, white men would gain the most ($4.28/hour) for having average education and training, followed by nonwhite women ($3.33), and then white women and nonwhite men ($2.57 and $2.44). In general, white men, who might be expected to have the greatest access to the better labor markets, receive the greatest returns from their educational and training credentials.

Family of origin effects are small but still evident at potential reward levels. If anything, they are somewhat stronger, here, when occupational differentiation is greater and sorting on the basis of family background might be more apparent, in contrast to the early career stage, when there is less differentiation. Having a large number of siblings, perhaps causing competition for attention and material support, negatively affects status and wage returns, significantly so in the status difference equation for both groups of men and white women. Having a higher-status father significantly, although very slightly, increases wages of white women and nonwhite men. Family of procreation variables, however, have almost no effect here, in contrast with the situation earlier in the career. Only in the status difference equation for white men does marital status reach significance.

This further confirms the idea that characteristics of family of procreation act primarily as screening signals for employers and that these are most important early in the careers of men, when on-the-job behavior is most in question.

In contrast with a time early in the work life, both white women and nonwhite men do worse than white men in the evaluations of their human capital. The change in the position of white women may be due to their more static occupational position. They remain in lower white-collar jobs that do not lead to positions giving greater rewards to education and training credentials. As one can see from comparing Tables 6.2 and 6.4, the value of their credentials actually deteriorates slightly after they have entered the labor force. Nonwhite men, in contrast, do get increased returns to their education as compared with their early careers, as well as greater wage returns to their training, although the returns to their education remain relatively low. Nonwhite women, while not receiving returns to their formal training, get greater benefit from education at their potential than they did earlier in their careers, returns in some cases greater than those for white men. Of course, it must be kept in mind that the nonwhite women here are exceptions, in that they had jobs on each survey date. The small N for nonwhites, compared with those for whites, indicates the extent to which this is true. Beck et al. (1978a) found that nonwhite women received lower returns to human capital compared with white men, using an income indicator that took into account extent of unemployment. As emphasized before, this paper does not take race and sex as absolute indicators of labor market location. Some groups of women and nonwhite men will be more likely than others to be in the more desirable opportunity structures. Indeed, steady employment might be a sign of being in other than the secondary market. At the same time, one needs to keep in mind the values of the other components of the career model for nonwhite women. If nothing else, levels of wages for nonwhite women are below those of even nonwhite men.

With respect to the other types of variables included in the model, the findings are that family of origin has small effects that are, nonetheless, larger than those earlier in the career, perhaps because sorting into occupational levels was too far from complete for such effects to become apparent earlier. Family of procreation effects are smaller than earlier, perhaps because these variables are no longer needed to screen job applicants.

Speed of Achievement

Potential reward level, without changing resources and liabilities, is reached only as time reaches infinity—which is a longer time than anyone, to date, has spent in the labor force. The speed at which the potential is reached is, therefore, as important as the eventual level and is an indicator of the structure of opportunity. The first line for each sex in Table 6.4 gives estimates of the speed of mobility. Nonwhite women reach their status potential most quickly ($|b|$ of 1.073 is the greatest). White men and women attain their status potential at about the same speed ($|b| = .610$ and $.604$). Nonwhite men reach potential status most slowly, perhaps because of a possibility of advancement that is not always realized.[17] With respect to wages, white men, as predicted, reach their high potential most slowly, while white women reach their highest wages most quickly of all race/sex groups. For nonwhites, the ordering by sex is reversed.

The results concerning the speed with which the different groups reach their potentials in the two job rewards are consistent with what has been found by examining age differences in cross-section. In such examination, status potential is reached more quickly than wage potential. Occupation may stop changing while wages continue to change, even within the same occupation or general type of occupation. Otto and Haller (1979), although lacking good longitudinal data, show results suggesting that maximum status differentiation for men has been reached by age 35, while maximum income differentiation is not reached until about age 45.

In Figures 6.1 and 6.2, the estimated model is used to predict career trajectories, showing, in general, close fit to observed trajectories (the curves for nonwhite men's wages being an exception). The predicted values over time were estimated using

$$\hat{Y}_t = (e^{\hat{b}t})\overline{Y}_0 + (1 - e^{\hat{b}t})\hat{Y}^*, \qquad (6.9)$$

where Y_0 = 1967 (for men) or 1969 (for women) status or wages, Y^* is the predicted potential shown in Table 6.4 and b is the "dynamic" coefficient in Table 6.4.

CONCLUSIONS

This paper analyzes career differences by race and sex, with careers defined as trajectories of socioeconomic status and income over the work life. It was assumed that the different groups tend to be in different labor markets and economic sectors and to experience different opportunities even within labor market segments, and this assumption guided predictions for (and interpretation of) results. The simple differential equation model describing careers allowed examination of various elements of inequality within the work force: entry level of status and wages; potential status and wage levels; effects of human capital, family of origin, and family of procreation variables on initial and potential reward levels; and the speed at which potential status and wages are approached. The dynamic nature of this model required longitudinal data and an estimation technique that could avoid the confounding of state dependence with unmeasured individual or time effects. The data from the National Longitudinal Survey of Labor Market Experience of Young Men and Women provided six years of work history for the analysis. These data were analyzed using a variance components model that controlled for unobserved variables constant over time for individuals and constant over individuals for each time. The results of this analysis showed the general advantage of white men in many aspects of careers, including wage levels and returns to human capital. Further, it showed the differences in effects of education and training, marital status, and parental socioeconomic status early in the career versus at the career stage when change has ceased to occur. The differences in speed with which equilibrium is reached for the two socioeconomic position variables and for the four groups give clues to the nature of the job structure through which men and women and blacks and whites move, over the course of their work lives.

The career model estimated here involves time, yet assumes some constancy. Basically, it assumes that once the trajectory begins it continues smoothly along as described by the equation. This seems not unreasonable.

It may be that the economic conditions under which, and the particular position in which, one begins a career determines to a large extent where one goes from there. The small magnitude of the time-variance component is consistent with this speculation. With the longitudinal data currently and potentially available, however, one can look for period, cohort, and age effects. Using later panels from the group whose work histories were analyzed here, one could go on to see whether their careers in the next decade are as predicted by the model. Comparisons with the careers of young men and women beginning their work lives in the early 1980s (data on which will be gathered by a new National Longitudinal Survey of Labor Market Experience, and by High School and Beyond, 1980) might help answer the question of how the threat of the draft (as compared with the threat of a recession) affects career beginnings and trajectories. Comparisons of the effects of various economic shocks on different cohorts might suggest the nature of period effects vs. age effects. In general, then, the use of a simple career model such as the one estimated here enables one to use effectively the longitudinal data on labor market histories that have been and are being gathered to investigate change over and within lifetimes.

A model such as this provides an overview of careers: where a group came from, where it is going, and how fast it is getting there. As such, it is useful in giving us a variety of social indicators for the position of a given group. Understanding more fully what is behind the group differences, however, requires a closer examination of the nature of jobs held over time and of the types of job shifts occurring at the individual level. Further, to capture the extent of inequality in economic position, movement into and out of the work force must be analyzed. Although some of this work is in progress (see, for example, Winship and Rosenfeld, 1979), the interest in understanding the workings of labor markets and their effects on inequality has opened large areas of research problems that have not yet been addressed. This paper shows one—but only one—model and technique for analyzing the process of inequality.

NOTES

1. This definition of careers is similar to that used by Form and Miller (1949) and Lipset and Bendix (1952) and is more general than definitions of careers as a succession of related jobs in a hierarchy of prestige through which one moves in an ordered, predictable sequence (Wilensky, 1960) or as jobs within a particular firm (Rosenbaum, 1979; Halaby, 1979). See Spilerman (1977) for an extended discussion of the term "career."

2. As Goldner (1965) has shown, not all career mobility is upward. In some managerial situations, downward mobility after a certain age is even considered the norm, as older people lose out in competition with younger. This can be treated as a change in the underlying career model, with a change from a growth to a decline model, or as a change in potential, the result

of a change in the individual's characteristics. This will be discussed further in the context of the specific model to be estimated in this paper.

3. Four groups are being compared here: white men, white women, nonwhite men, and nonwhite women. Most of the nonwhites are black. Much of the prediction will involve a contrast between two groupings of these four categories—for example, what is expected for white men on the one hand, and for nonwhite men, white women, and nonwhite women on the other. Although some work has been done that examines race and sex simultaneously, it is still difficult to find the basis for ordering all four groups with respect to each dimension of careers. This ordering is the end product of the empirical analysis in this paper.

4. One would expect that the type of socioeconomic reward used to define the job level over time would affect the comparisons made of careers. Socioeconomic status changes only with occupation (and such change is a necessary—but not a sufficient—condition for change in status). Income, in contrast, can change without a change in occupation, as typically measured by three-digit census codes. Admittedly, both measures are rough. The use of socioeconomic status and income together, however, may be suggestive of the ways in which careers are structured, in general, for different groups.

5. I wish to thank an anonymous reviewer for pointing out that the explanation of the model and of the results would be simpler if I explicitly used the partial adjustment form. An earlier version of this paper presented the model as the "negative feedback" model, which Coleman (1968) describes and Sørensen (1975; 1977) uses. The "negative feedback" model specifies the rate of change in Y as a linear function of the level of Y itself and of the values of exogenous variables. The two models are mathematically the same when the criterion Y* is completely determined by the exogenous variables (ignoring for the moment the problems of misspecification and measurement error). See Rosenfeld and Nielsen (1978), Rosenfeld (1979), and Hannan and Tuma (1979) for a discussion of the two approaches.

6. The condition $b < 0$ is necessary because, if b were greater than 0, the trajectory would move from this maximum level at an accelerating rate, which does not make sense substantively. As will be seen later, the income and status trajectories of the sample studied here are like those predicted by Equation 6.3 or 6.4 with b less than 0 and initial position less than the maximum.

7. However, Fligstein and Wolf's (1978) results suggest that the *effects* of resources on attainment are not severely biased by selection of currently employed women.

8. For the initial survey year (1966 for men, 1968 for women), all types of training taken outside regular school up to that date were reported. In each year after the first, however, respondents were asked about type of training taken *longest* in the time since the last survey. The rough measure formed from these questions may thus underestimate somewhat the proportion of persons with a given type of training.

9. In more complete models of effects of family socioeconomic status, other variables, such as father's education and rural origin, are also included. These three variables were chosen to represent the range of effects family background has while minimizing problems of multicollinearity and missing data.

10. As one anonymous reviewer correctly pointed out, given the interdependence of estimators—and, thus, estimates of speed of mobility (b), level of potential (Y*), and effect of traits on this potential (a)—it is not really possible to test independent hypotheses about all three dimensions of careers. I have done so here because of the conceptual independence of the components and because of the need to demonstrate how to interpret findings with respect to each.

11. Unfortunately, unlike maximum likelihood estimators, the parameter estimates obtained by MGLS do not necessarily retain their desirable properties under nonmonotonic transformations, such as those by which one calculates the parameters of the career mode.

12. I wish to thank Andrew Kolsted for bringing this program to my attention.

13. The abrupt rise between 1971 and 1973 for young men may reflect measurement error. The 1973 wage for young men was not calculated by CHRR, but had to be constructed by me

for this analysis, using the reported CHRR procedures. Thus, this measure may be less clean than theirs.

14. With information on change in some of the exogenous variables, there are two ways in which coefficients for those variables could be calculated. One is the way used here. The second way is to use the more complicated formula in Coleman (1968), which utilizes information from the change variables as well. If the assumption of linear change in the exogenous variable is reasonable and if there is not too much measurement error, the estimates calculated in these two ways should give approximately the same result. As might be expected, although education seemed to vary linearly according to the tests in Coleman (1968), other variables did not. Since there is no compelling reason to seek another solution to the differential equation—because the overall result of including the possibility of exogenous change in X_i "leaves the original relationships between observations and coefficients of the model undisturbed" (Coleman, 1968:443)—the simpler formulation is used in Table 6.4.

15. These estimates, as explained earlier, will change as members of the different groups increase their resources and liabilities. The qualitative implications will probably not change too much over time, however, as changes in education and training—two very important factors which determine potential—should occur at a decreasing rate, according to predictions of human capital theory and to empirical results. Marital status and number of children (dependents) may continue to change over a longer period of time. However, these factors are not large contributors to the potential level.

16. Sandell and Shapiro, 1978, and Corcoran and Duncan, 1979, estimate that only 25% to 30% of the wage gap between white men and women can be accounted for by work history.

17. Sørensen, 1979, argues that SEI is not a good metric with which to test such hypotheses because its distribution does not make sense as a distribution of socioeconomic reward. Transforming SEI in such a manner that he obtains an exponential distribution of attainment, he finds orderings, on b, of blacks and whites and of men and women that do not correspond exactly to the orderings obtained by using the usual SEI metric. I have not yet tried these models with his transformation, although I have such work in progress. One should keep in mind, however, that Sørensen used OLS, which means that his estimates are biased. As Table 6.3 shows, the extent of bias will differ across groups, making OLS comparisons suspect.

REFERENCES

Allen, Walter R. 1979. "Family roles, occupational statutes, and achievement orientations among black women in the United States." *Signs* 4:670–856.

Beck, E. M., Patrick M. Horan, and Charles M. Tolbert II. 1978a. "Labor market discrimination against minorities: a dual economy approach." Revision of paper presented at the annual meetings of the American Sociological Association, San Francisco.

————. 1978b. "Stratification in a dual economy: a sectoral model of earnings determination." *American Sociological Review* 43:704–20.

Bibb, Robert, and William H. Form. 1977. "The effects of industrial, occupational, and sex stratification on wages in blue-collar markets." *Social Forces* 55:974–96.

Blalock, Hubert M. 1969. *Theory Construction: From Verbal to Mathematical Formulations.* Englewood Cliffs: Prentice-Hall.

Blau, Francine. 1977. *Equal Pay in the Office.* Lexington, Mass.: Lexington Books.

Blau, Peter M., and Otis Dudley Duncan. 1967. *The American Occupational Structure.* New York: Wiley.

Bluestone, Barry. 1970. "The tripartite economy: labor markets and the working poor." *Poverty and Human Resources Abstracts* 5:15–35.

Bose, Christine E. 1973. *Jobs and Gender: Sex and Occupational Prestige.* Baltimore: Center for Metropolitan Planning and Research, The Johns Hopkins University.

Boyd, Monica. 1977. "Occupational attainment of native born Canadian women." University of Wisconsin-Madison: Center for Demography and Ecology Working Paper 77–26.

Boyd, Monica, and Elizabeth Humphreys. 1979. "Sex differences in Canada: incomes and labour markets." Paper presented at the Conference on Canadian Incomes, Winnipeg, Manitoba, May 9–12, sponsored by the Economic Council of Canada.

Center for Human Resources Research. 1979. *The National Longitudinal Surveys Handbook.* Columbus, Ohio.

Coleman, James S. 1968. "The mathematical study of change." Pp. 428–78 in H. M. Blalock (ed.), *Methodology in Social Research.* New York: McGraw-Hill.

Corcoran, Mary, and Greg J. Duncan. 1979. "Work history, labor force attachment, and earnings differences between races and sexes." *Journal of Human Resources* 14:3–20.

Doreian, Patrick and Norman P. Hummon. 1974. "Models of stratification processes." *Quality and Quantity* 8:327–45.

————. 1976. *Modeling Social Processes.* New York: Elsevier.

Doeringer, Peter, and Michael Piore. 1971. *Internal Labor Markets and Manpower Analysis.* Lexington, Mass.: D. C. Heath and Co.

Drummond, Douglas and A. Ronald Gallant. 1977. "The TSCSREG procedure." Pp. 155–67 in Jane T. Helwig (ed.), *SAS Supplemental Library User's Guide.* Raleigh, N.C.: SAS Institute Inc.

Duncan, Otis Dudley. 1961. "A socioeconomic index for all occupations." Pp. 109–38 in Albert J. Reiss, Jr., *Occupations and Social Status.* New York: Free Press of Glencoe.

Duncan, Otis Dudley, David L. Featherman, and Beverly Duncan. 1972. *Socioeconomic Background and Achievement.* New York: Seminar Press.

Dussault, Ginette, and Ruth Rose-Lizée. 1979. "Discrimination against women and labour market segregation: the case of office workers in Montreal." Paper presented at the Conference on Canadian Incomes, Winnipeg, Manitoba, May, sponsored by the Economic Council of Canada.

Economic Report of the President. 1977. Washington, D.C.: U.S. Government Printing Office.

Featherman, David L., and Robert M. Hauser. 1976. "Sexual inequalities and socioeconomic achievement in the U.S., 1962–73." *American Sociological Review* 41:462–83.

Fligstein, Neil, and Wendy Wolf. 1978. "Sex similarities in occupational status attainment: are the results due to the restriction of the sample to employed women?" *Social Science Research* 7:197–212.

Form, William H., and Delbert C. Miller. 1949. "Occupational career pattern as a sociological instrument." *American Journal of Sociology* 54:317–29.

Fuller, Wayne, and George Battese. 1974. "Estimation of linear models with crossed error structure." *Journal of Econometrics* 2:67–78.

Goldner, Fred. 1965. "Demotion in industrial management." *American Sociological Review* 30:714–24.

Gordon, David. 1972. *Theories of Poverty and Underemployment.* Lexington, Mass.: Lexington Books, D. C. Heath and Co.

Halaby, Charles. 1979. "Sexual inequality in the workplace: an employer specific analysis of pay differences." *Social Science Research* 8:79–104.

Hannan, Michael, and Nancy Tuma. 1979. *Methods of Dynamic Analysis.* Unpublished manuscript, Stanford University.

Hannan, Michael T., and Alice Young. 1977. "Estimation in panel models: results on pooling cross-sections and time series." Pp. 52–83 in David Heise (ed.), *Sociological Methodology* 1977. San Francisco: Jossey-Bass.

Hauser, Robert M., and David L. Featherman. 1977. *The Process of Stratification: Trends and Analyses.* New York: Academic Press.

Henderson, Charles R., Sr. 1952. "Specific and general combining ability." Pp. 352–70 in John W. Gowen (ed.), *Heterosis*. Ames: Iowa State College Press.

Hodson, Randy. 1978. "Labor in the monopoly, competitive, and state sectors of production." University of Wisconsin-Madison: Center for Demography and Ecology Working Paper 78-2.

Hoffman, Saul. 1978. "Black-white earnings differences over the life cycle." Chap. 7, pp. 247-71 in Greg J. Duncan and James N. Morgan (eds.), *Five Thousand American Families—Patterns of Economic Progress, Vol. VI*. Ann Arbor, Mich.: Survey Research Center, Institute for Social Research, University of Michigan.

Jusenius, Carol. 1975. "Occupational change, 1967–1971." Pp. 21–35 in Herbert Parnes, Carol Jusenius, and Richard Shortlidge, Jr., *Dual Careers, Vol. 3*. Manpower Research and Development Monograph 21. Washington, D.C.: U.S. Government Printing Office.

Kalleberg, Arne, and Aage B. Sørensen. 1979. "The sociology of labor markets." *Annual Review of Sociology* 5:351–79.

Kelley, Jonathan. 1973. "Causal chain models for the socioeconomic career." *American Sociological Review* 38:481–93.

Lipset, Seymour M. and Reinhard Bendix. 1952. "Social mobility and occupational career patterns: I. stability of job holding." *American Journal of Sociology* 57:366–74.

Nilson, Linda. 1976. "The occupational and sex related components of social standing." *Sociology and Social Research* 60:328–36.

Oppenheimer, Valerie. 1970. *The Female Labor Force in the United States: Demographic and Economic Factors Governing its Growth and Changing Composition*. Population Monograph Series, No. 5. Berkeley: University of California.

———. 1974. "The life-cycle squeeze: the interaction of men's occupational and family life cycles." *Demography* 11:227–45.

Ornstein, Michael and Peter H. Rossi. 1970. "Going to work: an analysis of the determinants and consequences of entry into the labor force." Report No. 75. Baltimore: The Center for the Study of the Social Organization of Schools, Johns Hopkins University.

Otto, Luther and Archibald Haller. 1979. "Evidence for a social psychological view of the status attainment process: four studies compared." *Social Forces* 57:887–914.

Phelps, Edmund. 1972. "The statistical theory of racism and sexism." *American Economic Review* 62:659–61.

Rosenbaum, James. 1979. "Organizational career mobility: promotion chances in a corporation during periods of growth and contraction." *American Journal of Sociology* 85:21–49.

Rosenfeld, Rachel A. 1977. "Breaks in women's employment and labor market re-entry." Paper presented at the annual meetings of the Canadian Sociology and Anthropology Association, Fredericton, New Brunswick.

———. 1978. "Women's employment patterns and occupational achievements." *Social Science Research* 7:61–80.

———. 1979. "Dynamic models of socioeconomic achievement." Unpublished manuscript, National Opinion Research Center, University of Chicago.

Rosenfeld, Rachel, and François Nielsen. 1978. "Differential equations models of structural change." Paper presented at the 9th World Congress of Sociology, Uppsala, Sweden, August 14.

Sandell, Steven, and David Shapiro. 1978. "The theory of human capital and the earnings of women: a re-examination of the evidence." *Journal of Human Resources* 13:103–17.

Searle, S. R. 1971. "Topics in variance component estimation." Biometrics 27:1–76.

Sewell, William, and Robert Hauser. 1975. *Education, Occupation and Earnings*. New York: Academic Press.

Sewell, William, Robert Hauser, and Wendy C. Wolf. 1977. "Occupational achievement to mid-life of male and female high school graduates." Paper presented at the annual meeting of the American Sociological Association, September 6, Chicago.

Shields, Patricia. 1977. "The determinants of service in the armed forces during the Vietnam era." Columbus, Ohio: Center for Human Resource Research, Ohio State University.

Sørensen, Aage B. 1975. "The structure of intragenerational mobility." *American Sociological Review* 40:456–71.

———. 1977. "The structure of inequality and the process of attainment." *American Sociological Review* 42:965–78.

———. 1979. "A model and a metric for the analysis of the intragenerational status attainment process." *American Journal of Sociology* 85:361–84.

Sørensen, Aage B., and Nancy B. Tuma. 1978. "Labor market structure and job mobility." Paper presented at the 9th World Congress of Sociology, Uppsala, Sweden, August. Also University of Wisconsin-Madison: Institute for Research on Poverty Discussion Paper 505-78.

Spence, A. Michael. 1974. *Market Signaling: Information Transfer in Hiring and Related Screening Processes*. Cambridge, Mass.: Harvard University Press.

Spilerman, Seymour. 1977. "Careers, labor market structures and socioeconomic achievement." *American Journal of Sociology* 83:551–93.

Tachibanaki, Toshiak. 1979. "Models for educational and occupational achievement over time." *Sociology of Education* 52:156–62.

Thurow, Lester. 1975. *Generating Inequality*. New York: Basic Books.

Thurow, Lester C., and Robert E. B. Lucas. 1972. *The American Distribution of Income: A Structural Problem*. U.S. Government Printing Office: Washington, DC.

Treiman, Donald J., and Kermit Terrell. 1975. "Sex and the process of status attainment: a comparison of working women and men." *American Sociological Review* 40:174–200.

U.S. Bureau of the Census. 1970. *Census of the Population: 1970. Volume 1, Characteristics of the Population; Part 1: U.S. Summary, Section 2*. Washington, D.C.: U.S. Government Printing Office.

Wilensky, Harold. 1960. "Work, careers, and social integration." *International Social Science Journal* 12:543–60.

Winship, Christopher, and Rachel Rosenfeld. 1979. "Youth unemployment and job mobility." Proposal submitted to the National Science Foundation, Applied Research Division. University of Chicago: National Opinion Research Center.

Wolf, Wendy C. 1976. "Occupational attainment of married women: do career contingencies matter?" Madison, Wisconsin: Center for Demography and Ecology Working Paper 76-3.

Using the "Master's Tools" and Beyond: Reconstructing Difference

TONI M. CALASANTI

"Why is a gerontologist reflecting upon the articles in this section?" Part of the answer to this question is dependent upon recognizing aspects of the life course that are continuous—that systems of privilege/oppression, including but not limited to gender, influence us throughout our lives, exacerbating or attenuating problems and resources that are attendant with age. Another part of the answer derives from the kind of aging research that I do: examining diversity in relation to the work/retirement nexus. As a result, my work has not been confined to only the later part of life; in addition, it has often drifted into exploring differences in paid and unpaid, formal and informal labor. How I ended up with this research agenda has much to do with the substance and influence of these chapters—on me and on the field in general.

In essence, much of my decision to specialize in the area of aging relates to what was going on during the time period in which most of these works appeared. Sociological interest in gender had increased, enough so that I could explore gender issues in my research, but not sufficiently to allow me actually to specialize in this area. In fact, it never occurred to me to concentrate in gender relations when I began graduate work, or to wonder why I could not. Concern with social inequality is what spurred my interest in sociology, but social inequality still typically translated into a consideration of class; other inequities could be examined but were somehow secondary or epiphenomenal to class relations. When I began my work in aging, then, it served as a vehicle for exploring class and, increasingly, gender inequalities. Ultimately, I found myself most interested in retirement because of its obvious relationship with paid work and hence class relations; in order to understand diverse retirement experiences, I had to examine gender differences in the workplace. Not coincidentally, this also provided me an avenue for exploring my own workplace experiences. My research, and teaching, have thus revolved around diverse experiences of aging and workplace/retirement issues.

In many respects, my professional road is paralleled in these chapters. First, I entered research in gender "through the back door"—primarily on my own, through the field of aging, and by expanding what was "already out there," both theoretically and methodologically. Second, when I think about my graduate school experiences and the first few years as a new professional, what appears most salient were my needs to establish legitimacy and credibility: for research on women (and, eventually, gender), and for women engaged in paid labor—myself included. Similarly, the authors of these chapters had no strong feminist sociological research tradition to draw from or fall back on. Instead, they used what was there—and ended up representing some of the most innovative work available. Also, their use of mainstream perspectives was critical in justifying a concern with gender—both in terms of examining gender within sub-areas of sociology and as a legitimate focus of study itself. Further, in enhancing our knowledge of gender stratification in general, they also gave us the insights to begin to critique masculine perspectives. To a great extent, each used the dominant, masculine paradigms to shake the foundations of mainstream sociology—to demonstrate either the omission of, or inability to, explain gender (and, in Rosenfeld's case, racial) stratification.

These three chapters run the gamut of different aspects of gender stratification, ranging from Huber's macro-level, global theorizing on gender stratification to Lever's micro-level of interaction, where socialization reproduces the gender order. Although published over a 10-year span, with the most recent appearing in 1986, they are reflective of the state-of-the-art approaches to stratification within their areas. Although we have moved beyond these approaches to some degree in the subsequent decade(s), they laid the groundwork that enabled us to do so. Pointing to where and how we have advanced is not offered as a criticism but as an implicit acknowledgment of how these chapters took the necessary first steps. In essence, it is a tribute to the creativity and clarity of the arguments made: To transcend these works required the solid foundations they erected so that we could move ahead and not retrace our steps.

Further, there is a clear continuity between much of what appeared in these chapters and where we are now. Many of the theoretical insights and research findings of these feminist scholars have not been superseded or (sometimes unfortunately) rendered irrelevant. For example, Lever's work both legitimated and spawned a wide variety of important research and theory concerning the ways in which socialization, particularly in relation to children's play and the educational system, perpetuates gender stratification. Regrettably, much of what she documented in 1976 persists in 1996, as subsequent research and my experience with my own school-age daughters continually attest.

It is not merely because of the significance of these chapters for the development of theories and careers of researchers such as myself that makes it difficult for me to be very critical of these works. Indeed, I cannot be, once I consider the context in which they were written. We have moved forward so rapidly that it is difficult sometimes to remember/imagine what the state of feminist sociology was like before these chapters emerged. But when we do remember, the insights presented by these women are all the more remarkable.

The easiest way for me to discuss the importance of these chapters for fostering feminist theory and research is to view them in terms of their relationship to mainstream sociology and in the context of the arguments put forward regarding gender. Of course, this depiction is through my eyes—the eyes of someone "coming of age" in sociology at a time when these chapters spoke to my own struggle to make sense of gender inequality. My heuristic characterization of these works, which is admittedly oversimplified and not uniformly applicable, is that they all represent some variant of liberal feminism in the sense that they—and I—assumed that men and women were fundamentally similar and that differences were structurally induced. To the extent that this was the case, the argument was that, with equal opportunity, women and men would be the same. The quest, then, was to reveal the structural impediments to this equality; we did not question the patriarchal nature of the structures themselves, nor the androcentrism of stratification literature and theories themselves. But these works did give us the tools we needed to undertake the next level of questioning.

For example, whether or not we ultimately agree with part or all of Huber's argument, what makes it so noteworthy is her brilliant use of the grand-scale theories and tools of the androcentric stratification literature to demonstrate quite clearly the necessity and possibilities of the inclusion of gender in these perspectives. Regardless of the creativity and scope of Huber's theorizing, she does not question the assumptions of the role theory or functionalist approaches embedded in her work. Rose Laub Coser (1975) has provided an insightful analysis of the roles men and women play is somehow "power-neutral"; while there is an acknowledgment that some roles have more or less power, how this comes to be is not at issue. Instead, to some degree, gender inequality is seen to be a problem of role inequities, an assumption Huber's theory of gender stratification shares. That is, gender relations, as power relations, are not considered. Similarly, Lever is concerned with understanding how it is that boys and girls come to play different roles; given the timing of her research, her work is really quite remarkable, both theoretically and methodologically. Despite the mainstream theoretical emphasis, she does not "blame the victim" by saying that the different socialization processes boys and girls undergo causes gender inequality but rather that, if we eliminate structural bias, we also need to change how we raise children. Implicitly, she is concerned with both structure and agency, but without a strong feminist theoretical critique from which to draw—a critique that was not yet elucidated—she was left with a masculinist, role theory perspective.

In terms of my own professional development, I was most strongly influenced by Rachel Rosenfeld's piece for somewhat obvious reasons. Given that my work sought to explore the ways in which labor market and economic/industrial structures influence gender inequality and, eventually, retirement, her work at once provided both the tools and the credibility that a well-placed publication lends to such "marginal" work. To be sure, there was—and still is—a critical tradition in workforce stratification literature, but it stressed—and still does, too often—class, at the expense of other power relations. I had been able to draw suggestions from the similar yet theoretically disparate dual economic, dual labor market, and labor market segmentation literatures, but these perspectives contained little theoretical discussion of, or research interest in, gender inequalities.

Like everyone else in my cohort, I was trained to be a "good sociologist." This meant, first, either being a positivist or, if not, having an appreciation for positivism. Even more obliquely, it meant accepting the underlying masculine paradigm that virtually all sociologists heeded, regardless of their theoretical or methodological bent. Second, this meant that one's "career" was critical, and that all else in one's life was to be secondary. I was always uncomfortable with the positivist/masculine perspective, but with the kind of quiet "dis-ease" that does not generally interfere with one's work. Instead, it periodically reared its head in quiet, unexpected ways; for me, it was the academic equivalent of the "problem that has no name." Somehow, things just did not "fit," but I was unable to figure out why—except to speculate that either I lacked a sufficient understanding of theories, or that I myself did not "fit." Casting around for a different theoretical lens that fit my (often as much gut-level as intellectual) rejection of positivism, I aligned myself with a critical perspective. This left me feeling somewhat better, but still not satisfied. Given the inroads, or lack thereof, of feminist sociology at this point in time, my experiences were of no surprise.

It is in this context that I read Rosenfeld's article, and for me, it was a breath of fresh air—even more, a vindication. Though I still had further transitions to make, as neither Rosenfeld nor others had yet challenged the masculine assumptions of the theories they used, they supported both the type and subject of the research I wanted to conduct. In rereading her article for the purposes of this volume, I found myself still in awe of the skill Rosenfeld displayed in formulating and researching her problem—successfully operationalizing incredibly complex issues; using the most current literature and

quantitative techniques in adopting, and implicitly critiquing, the status attainment models. To paraphrase a well-known phrase by Audre Lorde, she used
the master's tools, if not to dismantle his house, then at least to knock out a
few walls. What her chapter—and the others in this section—remind us of is
that it is crucial to be able to critique paradigms from within as well as from
without. In fact, from a practical standpoint, it can be far more powerful, when
one is an "outsider," to use the dominant paradigm in pointing to its inadequacy. Certainly, this is the first step in mounting an attack against a dominant
view. Rosenfeld did just this: She turned status attainment research back on
itself.

    Like the authors in this section and many others at the time, my inclination
was to argue against gender stratification that was based on essentialist
notions of women and men. Gender differences were not natural, but social.
Thus I was concerned to show that women and men were the same, justifying
the call for equality. With this underlying agenda, then, my dissertation was
designed to examine the ways in which gender influenced the sources of
satisfaction with retirement, with the explicit assumption that the differences
between men and women would be attributable to their disparate labor force
experiences, or so I hoped. Through a combination of qualitative analysis of
interviews and quantitative manipulation of a national data set, I expected to
find that placement in different segments of the labor force and sectors of the
economy would result in men and women developing different sources of job
satisfaction, self-concepts, and, ultimately, sources of retirement satisfaction.
Indeed, I did find that men tended to have jobs high in autonomy and task
differentiation that encouraged them to develop self-concepts that stressed
efficacy while women, whose job experiences tended to be far more constrained, focused on their relational aspects—their "sociability." Furthermore,
my interview data revealed that men who held jobs that were structured in
ways similar to women's (only one woman had a job that was high in autonomy
and task differentiation, a situation that reflected the reality of jobs in the area)
also stressed such things as their interaction with co-workers as important
sources of job satisfaction.

    At the same time, both types of data revealed something I had hoped not
to find: that gender still mattered. In the multiple regression equations, gender
still differentiated between men and women of similar work backgrounds.
Similarly, in the interview data, I consistently found that women and men
responded differently to some of the same questions. For example, in an effort
to enhance my ability to interpret the quantitative data, I used some of the
exact same questions in my interviews. One of the most interesting in this
regard was the question that asked about the level of satisfaction retirees
derive from "leisure, i.e., non-work activities." Invariably, women would ask
me if housework was included in that category. As a measure of my own (lack

of) consciousness, I had not even thought about this possibility before I went into the field. What, then, was work?

Ultimately, what I concluded then and spent the next years trying to sort out theoretically, was that—like it or not—gender *did* matter. Equality did not mean "sameness." Both personally and professionally, the social construction and importance of gender differences, and the androcentrism of the sociological conceptions of "work" and "retirement" were, quite literally, brought home to me. Having completed my dissertation research while teaching two or three classes a term and raising a small child, the tension wrought by gender inequality heightened as I fought to balance a new job and the birth of my second child. Teaching a graduate-level course on women and work brought the contradictions to the surface. I understood, all too well, the intent of readings that discussed the work/family relationship and gender relations. Both in the office and at home, my lack of power was apparent: I was warned about the dangers of not publishing in "real" sociology journals about "real" sociological issues if I wanted to receive tenure; the lack of child care facilities available on campus meant that I spent a good portion of my day on the road, driving back and forth between day care and the office in order to nurse my child; and I was unable to effect any substantial change in the division of domestic labor.

Out of anomalous research findings and the frustrations I experienced as a relatively privileged, heterosexual, working woman with children, I have come to understand the meaning of gender relations and difference, work/family and retirement/family in a new way. Critical as the feminist works in this section have been to my own personal and professional development, they did not ask why labor markets are gendered, or why different gender "roles" matter. To be sure, labor market structures did and do matter, as do the variety of other social influences indicated by the three articles reprinted here. Hand in hand with these social processes and institutions, however, is the previously unrecognized social institution of gender itself—power relations that dictate continued differences between men and women.

Thus, since these articles were published, feminist sociologists—including myself—have come back around to the difference/sameness debate, but on a different plane, one that was facilitated by this pioneering research. We can now say that gender does matter, but the connotations are quite different from before. This ability to examine difference, and uncover the biases of the privileged in sociological theory, has opened my eyes to the existence of my own classism, racism, and heterosexism. In particular, and especially important in my life personally and as a feminist scholar/activist, I have come to appreciate differences. In my quest to show—and to be—"just as good" as the men by demonstrating our "sameness," I had uncritically accepted an androcentric standard by which to judge our similarity. Though, to the uninformed, praising difference seems to be a step backward, away from equality, the palpable relief and pride expressed by women students and colleagues supports me in my beliefs. Such "permission" to be who you are is still a struggle, all the more so for those who experience multiple oppressions; the process is ongoing.

We still have a long way to go. Recently, I sat on a doctoral committee in management in which the (thankfully, strong-minded) African American woman doctoral candidate was chastised by her cochair for being "biased": Her theoretical perspective (which was well documented) assumed that workplace organizations were gendered and racialized. The fact that the women on her committee successfully outmaneuvered him, resulting in his great pride for the accomplishments of "his student," does not detract from the months of suffering she endured, the emotional energy we expended, or the reality of patriarchy (not to mention racism) in academia.

I still often feel marginalized as well: by sociologists, who see the fields of aging and gender (and my increased interest in race/ethnicity) as "special-ized" and not "real sociology"; by feminist sociologists, who, despite the presumed interest in aging (read: menopause), still relegate age relations to the "et cetera" category; by gerontologists, who see the world of aging and especially retirement as one that is "gender-neutral" (read: white, middle-class male). The wealth of possibilities that women such as these three have opened up for many of us allows us to pursue these critical lines of research and to do so in ways that also allow us to demand our due.

From where I sit, a "classic" is not work that has uncovered Truths that "withstand the test of time." Such a notion inherently denies the dynamics of history and human agency. Instead, I would regard as "classic" those works that spur me to forge ahead—excite and ignite my imagination, and give me what I need to move forward. In addition, given the marginal status of feminist research, scholarship in which one is able to see oneself is also a part of what would constitute a classic. To me, then, the ultimate compliment would be to say that these articles are "classics" in the sense that they have been transcended dialectically—many of their intentions or insights are expressed in a new form.

From Sex/Gender Roles to Gender Stratification: From Victim Blame to System Blame

JANET SALTZMAN CHAFETZ

In the late 1960s, when feminist activism awoke from a 35-year slumber, I was a brand new PhD just beginning an academic career in sociology. I and a still rather small number of other female sociologists ran to catch up with and incorporate the heady insights of the "Women's Liberation Movement" into the androcentric sociological perspectives we had imbibed in graduate school. We clamored for the right to develop and teach classes on gender, and many students eagerly flocked to them. The problem was that we lacked not only textbooks and other teaching materials, but a *sociological* vocabulary to talk about the issues the Women's Movement was raising, one that might enable us to legitimate the subject in the eyes of our overwhelmingly male colleagues and university administrations. We used movement publications and terminology, but we also relied heavily on an already-available academic concept: sex (or gender) role. This concept came from the work of Talcott Parsons, a then-aged and very famous sociological theorist, whose theories both feminists and other sixties radicals castigated and rejected as hopelessly conservative. For several years, most of us blithely ignored the discrepancy between our rejection of Parsons's theories and our use of his terminology as the central concept defining our new sociological specialty.

The term "sex/gender roles" refers to the idea that there are two very different, overarching sets of normative expectations about how to behave and comport oneself: one feminine and the other masculine. Presumably, based on their biological sex as defined at birth, most people learn their "appropriate" sex/gender role (and corresponding self-concept) in very early childhood and display it in virtually all contexts for the remainder of their lives.

159

Moreover, as adults, people expect others to behave in gender-normative ways and respond negatively to any "deviance" from gender roles. As feminists, we recognized that these "roles"—or at least their outcomes—are not equal. Nonetheless, given its origins in a specific, ideologically conservative theory, the term sex/gender role implicitly emphasizes *difference* much more than it does inequality. This fact was not altogether clear to many of us until Stacey and Thorne (1985) later pointed it out, although we had begun to wonder why gender, but not other forms of inequality, such as racial/ethnic and class, was conceptualized in terms of "roles" (no one spoke of "black" and "white" race roles!). As sociologists, we should also have been more aware of the fact that individuals do not behave the same way in all contexts; that specific situations elicit very different kinds of behaviors (a point made explicit by Lopata & Thorne, 1978). For instance, women do not behave the same way as mothers (e.g., exercising discipline and authority) and as someone's secretary (behaving deferentially), nor do men as traditional husbands (dominating and authoritative) and as factory workers (submissive to authority). How, then, could we claim (as we did) that submissiveness and deference are parts of the feminine sex role, authoritative and domineering behavior parts of the masculine one?

Much of the research done by feminist sociologists during the 1970s (and into the 1980s) concerned the myriad ways by which children learn behaviors, cognitive and interpersonal skills, values, and preferences that are socially defined as appropriate to their sex role. It especially emphasized how these attributes later advantage males in the labor force and train females for domestic life (and a few traditionally female occupations). Because most feminists assume that the gender division of labor stands at the root of inequality, this approach implicitly incorporated the idea that gender roles produce inequality, not just difference. Janet Lever's chapter is an excellent example of this literature. It focuses on the role of play in the childhood socialization process, a classic symbolic interaction theory theme. From this general theoretical perspective, play teaches children skills that prepare them for adult roles. Lever describes the profound differences between boys' and girls' characteristic types of play and concludes that for boys, play encourages the development of skills that will be assets later in a competitive labor market, while girls' play teaches skills that prepare them for future roles as wives and mothers.

Although Lever published her article after I first published my undergraduate text on sex roles in 1974, our perspectives were similar. Indeed, one chapter of my rather short (six-chapter) book was explicitly devoted to childhood socialization and another to student-based research on the attributes Americans associate with femininity and masculinity. My chapter on employment emphasized how sex role attributes disadvantage women in the labor force, and the one concerning interpersonal relationships emphasized the disadvantageous outcomes of the masculine sex role. Four years later, when I wrote a second edition of that text (Chafetz, 1978), I included Lever's work in the chapter on socialization. Yet later (in 1988), when I wrote an undergraduate text about feminist theories in sociology, I discussed the same article as an important contributor to the gender socialization literature, and I have very recently done so yet again in two book chapters that review the varieties of feminist/gender theory in sociology (Chafetz, 1997, in press).

Along with most feminist sociologists, I have long since abandoned the concept of sex/gender role in research and teaching. Unlike many contemporary feminist scholars, I also radically de-emphasize the importance of childhood learning and experience for understanding both the behavior of men and women as individuals and systemic gender inequality. In fact, I tell students in my gender classes that they cannot use the "S word" (socialization) to explain anything until they have exhausted all other possible explanations. I do this for two reasons. First, when childhood learning is said to influence strongly all adult behavior, it becomes difficult, if not impossible, to explain change. I have lived long enough to see that a very large number of women my age (including me) do not behave in the ways we were taught and expected to during our childhoods in the heyday of the "feminine mystique" (the 1950s). I believe that our behavior differs from that of our mothers and the expectations we were taught as children primarily because the nature of the opportunity and constraint structure for women in our society has changed in the interim. As a feminist, I am committed to change and I want to use theories that more explicitly recognize its possibility. Second, as a sociologist, not a psychologist, I am committed to looking to the structure of situations and relationships, to the opportunities and constraints people experience in the present and near-past, in order to understand present behaviors, aspirations, choices, even self-concepts. But these understandings mostly evolved later for me—in the 1980s. In the 1970s, I and most other feminist sociologists talked primarily about inequitable sex/gender roles, about how children are socialized into them and adults are punished for their violation, and about how they explain our problems as women. Our faith was that through collective consciousness-raising and sisterly support, women could overcome the disadvantages of our sex role socialization primarily by changing our selves, and indeed, many of us (including me) ran our early courses in "sex roles" more or less as consciousness-raising groups.

As the 1970s gave way to a new decade, feminist sociologists began to publish more and more research that focused on the specific inequities that women confront in all institutional arenas and especially in the economy. Some data of this kind had been published earlier, but with the significant increase in the number of female PhDs in sociology, beginning in the 1970s, came more "hands" (actually, "minds") to do the careful research necessary to fully document structured gender inequality. It was during the 1980s that our specialty area, as defined by a formal section of the American Sociological Association (ASA), recognized a shift in emphasis by changing its name from "Sex Roles" to "Sex and Gender" (and rapidly grew to be the largest section within ASA). It was also during the 1980s that the national feminist sociological organization, Sociologists for Women in Society (SWS), began to publish its own scholarly journal, *Gender & Society.* This journal was begun because of the increasing perception by feminist sociologists that the two major existing ones short-shifted feminist social structural analysis: *Sex Roles* was too psychological and *Signs* was too heavily geared to the humanities. Although I claim no credit for the development of *Gender & Society,* I was fortunate to be SWS president during the exciting year that we finalized plans for its publication.

The shift from sex/gender roles to gender stratification de-emphasized individual-level traits of females and males, by which "victims" (women) are subtly blamed for their problems and disadvantages. It emphasized instead the gendered and unequal nature of the social structural arrangements that women confront daily. Rachel Rosenfeld's chapter is an excellent example of this new emphasis. She used what were then state-of-the-art statistical procedures on an excellent, national data set to compare the career trajectories of four categories of workers: white male, white female, nonwhite male, and nonwhite female. Her work demonstrates that after one controls for differences in "human capital" (work-related skills and attributes that make individuals more or less valuable to employers), there are still substantial gender and racial inequities in the labor market outcomes of status and income mobility, to the disadvantage of women and non-whites, and especially non-white women. As one of the first articles about gender to appear in the American Sociological Association's premier general journal, and as one of the earliest papers anywhere to examine systematically the simultaneous effects of race and gender, Rosenfeld's contribution was truly groundbreaking.

Joan Huber's chapter exemplifies this same general structural emphasis as it was being developed theoretically during the 1980s. This chapter theorizes the major societal forces that affect changes in the level of gender stratification from the earliest, foraging type of societies, through hoe- and plow-based, to modern industrial ones. In addition to the economic and domestic division of labor along gendered lines, Huber focuses on two demographic variables, mortality and fertility rates, as well as on average educational levels, in explaining recent changes in response to shifts in large, macrostructural forces that especially shape the payoffs for high fertility levels, the economic demand for female workers, and the interaction between the two forms of work—domestic and labor market—in which women might engage.

I had been trained as a graduate student primarily in the specialties of social stratification and classical sociological theory. During the 1970s, I had largely ignored these totally androcentric subjects, caught up in the social-psychological sex/gender role perspective of my new field. In the early 1980s, under the influence of an avalanche of structurally oriented research and theory on gender, I revisited my original interests but now from a feminist perspective. I changed the name of my class from the "Sociology of Sex Roles" to the "Sociology of Gender" and added one on "Women and Work." In doing so, I began to emphasize how gender permeates all social institutions (e.g., the economy, polity, educational systems, health care delivery, religious institutions, and, of course, the family) in ways that systematically reproduce female disadvantage. In my research, I first attempted to develop a structural theory (akin to Huber's) explaining variation, historically and across societies, in the level of gender stratification, which I defined as the extent to which, on average, males enjoy more access to an array of socially valued resources and opportunities than females do in their society (Chafetz, 1984). By the end of the decade, I had enlarged this project to a theory explaining how systems of gender stratification are maintained and changed (Chafetz, 1990). Along the way, I also worked with a colleague to develop a theory that explains how macro-structural shifts in women's opportunities spur the development of feminist consciousness and movements (Chafetz & Dworkin, 1986). In both my teaching and research, my main emphasis now centered on the effects of the gendered division of labor within the family and in the economy, using data such as those in the Rosenfeld chapter, and developing theoretical ideas very similar to those in the Huber one. Also, beginning in the late 1970s, I became personally friendly with Joan Huber, seeing her annually at professional meetings and sometimes corresponding with her in the interim. Probably as a partial result of these personal contacts, and of reading one another's published work, our theoretical ideas are remarkably similar, although we did not collaborate directly in their development (see, in addition to the chapter in this volume, Huber, 1976, 1988, 1991).

The three chapters included in this section of the book all reflect the influence of the Women's Movement on feminist sociologists by focusing on gender outcomes as unequal—not just different. Yet they also exemplify an important transition between the 1970s and 1980s, a transition clearly reflected in my own work. We moved from viewing inequality between men and women as the outcome of deep-seated (albeit socially produced) differences between them that are developed in early life and express themselves in virtually all aspects of adult life, to explaining gender inequality primarily as the outcome of opportunity and constraint structures that disadvantage women regardless of their personal "traits." By no longer locating women's disadvantages primarily in "inadequacies" they develop as children, we no longer assumed that to resolve gender inequality females had to alter their very selves. The new view located women's disadvantages in a set of social structural arrangements and, therefore, it identified structural change as necessary for the eradication of gender inequality. The practical outcome was a change from implicitly blaming the victims to explicitly blaming the system for gender stratification.

Part III

Theorizing What Gender Means

Feminists who fit into this intellectual genre critically assess the definition of gender. In this genre, gender is more than an individual trait or set of roles. These scholars argue—and demonstrate—that differences between women and men are not essential to either sex. They challenge a dichotomous conceptualization of gender, asserting that there is more than one way to be a woman and more than one way to be a man: There are multiple masculinities and femininities. They point out that men have gender, too. These writers have helped make the social construction of gender a vital assumption of sociological research. They show us how people *participate* in gender inequality when they adopt dichotomous assumptions and enact expected gendered behaviors on a daily basis. These chapters together illustrate the dialectical nature of gendered processes in society.

7 Doing Gender

CANDACE WEST
University of California, Santa Cruz

DON H. ZIMMERMAN
University of California, Santa Barbara

The purpose of this article is to advance a new understanding of gender as a routine accomplishment embedded in everyday interaction. To do so entails a critical assessment of existing perspectives on sex and gender and the introduction of important distinctions among sex, sex category, and gender. We argue that recognition of the analytical independence of these concepts is essential for understanding the interactional work involved in being a gendered person in society. The thrust of our remarks is toward theoretical reconceptualization, but we consider fruitful directions for empirical research that are indicated by our formulation.

In the beginning, there was sex and there was gender. Those of us who taught courses in the area in the late 1960s and early 1970s were careful to distinguish one from the other. Sex, we told students, was what was ascribed by biology: anatomy, hormones, and physiology. Gender, we said, was an achieved status: that which is constructed through psychological, cultural, and social means. To introduce the difference between the two, we drew on singular case studies of hermaphrodites (Money 1968, 1974; Money and

AUTHORS' NOTE: This article is based in part on a paper presented at the Annual Meeting of the American Sociological Association, Chicago, September 1977. For their helpful suggestions and encouragement, we thank Lynda Ames, Bettina Aptheker, Steven Clayman, Judith Gerson, the late Erving Goffman, Marilyn Lester, Judith Lorber, Robin Lloyd, Wayne Mellinger, Beth E. Schneider, Barrie Thorne, Thomas P. Wilson, and most especially, Sarah Fenstermaker Berk.

Ehrhardt 1972) and anthropological investigations of "strange and exotic tribes" (Mead 1963, 1968).

Inevitably (and understandably), in the ensuing weeks of each term, our students became confused. Sex hardly seemed a "given" in the context of research that illustrated the sometimes ambiguous and often conflicting criteria for its ascription. And gender seemed much less an "achievement" in the context of the anthropological, psychological, and social imperatives we studied—the division of labor, the formation of gender identities, and the social subordination of women by men. Moreover, the received doctrine of gender socialization theories conveyed the strong message that while gender may be "achieved," by about age five it was certainly fixed, unvarying, and static—much like sex.

Since about 1975, the confusion has intensified and spread far beyond our individual classrooms. For one thing, we learned that the relationship between biological and cultural processes was far more complex—and reflexive—than we previously had supposed (Rossi 1984, especially pp. 10–14). For another, we discovered that certain structural arrangements, for example, between work and family, actually produce or enable some capacities, such as to mother, that we formerly associated with biology (Chodorow 1978 versus Firestone 1970). In the midst of all this, the notion of gender as a recurring achievement somehow fell by the wayside.

Our purpose in this article is to propose an ethnomethodologically informed, and therefore distinctively sociological, understanding of gender as a routine, methodical, and recurring accomplishment. We contend that the "doing" of gender is undertaken by women and men whose competence as members of society is hostage to its production. Doing gender involves a complex of socially guided perceptual, interactional, and micropolitical activities that cast particular pursuits as expressions of masculine and feminine "natures."

When we view gender as an accomplishment, an achieved property of situated conduct, our attention shifts from matters internal to the individual and focuses on interactional and, ultimately, institutional arenas. In one sense, of course, it is individuals who "do" gender. But it is a situated doing, carried out in the virtual or real presence of others who are presumed to be oriented to its production. Rather than as a property of individuals, we conceive of gender as an emergent feature of social situations: both as an outcome of and a rationale for various social arrangements and as a means of legitimating one of the most fundamental divisions of society.

To advance our argument, we undertake a critical examination of what sociologists have meant by *gender*, including its treatment as a role enactment in the conventional sense and as a "display" in Goffman's (1976) terminology. Both *gender role* and *gender display* focus on behavioral aspects of being a woman or a man (as opposed, for example, to biological differences between the two). However, we contend that the notion of gender as a role obscures the work that is involved in producing gender in everyday activities, while the notion of gender as a display relegates it to the periphery of interaction. We argue instead that participants in interaction organize their various and manifold activities to reflect or express gender, and they are disposed to perceive the behavior of others in a similar light.

To elaborate our proposal, we suggest at the outset that important but often overlooked distinctions be observed among *sex, sex category,* and *gender. Sex* is a determination made through the application of socially agreed upon biological criteria for classifying persons as females or males.[1] The criteria for classification can be genitalia at birth or chromosomal typing before birth, and they do not necessarily agree with one another. Placement in a *sex category* is achieved through application of the sex criteria, but in everyday life, categorization is established and sustained by the socially required identificatory displays that proclaim one's membership in one or the other category. In this sense, one's sex category presumes one's sex and stands as proxy for it in many situations, but sex and sex category can vary independently; that is, it is possible to claim membership in a sex category even when the sex criteria are lacking. *Gender,* in contrast, is the activity of managing situated conduct in light of normative conceptions of attitudes and activities appropriate for one's sex category. Gender activities emerge from and bolster claims to membership in a sex category.

We contend that recognition of the analytical independence of sex, sex category, and gender is essential for understanding the relationships among these elements and the interactional work involved in "being" a gendered person in society. While our primary aim is theoretical, there will be occasion to discuss fruitful directions for empirical research following from the formulation of gender that we propose.

We begin with an assessment of the received meaning of gender, particularly in relation to the roots of this notion in presumed biological differences between women and men.

PERSPECTIVE ON SEX AND GENDER

In Western societies, the accepted cultural perspective on gender views women and men as naturally and unequivocally defined categories of being (Garfinkel 1967, pp. 116–18) with distinctive psychological and behavioral propensities that can be predicted from their reproductive functions. Competent adult members of these societies see differences between the two as fundamental and enduring—differences seemingly supported by the division of labor into women's and men's work and an often elaborate differentiation of feminine and masculine attitudes and behaviors that are prominent features of social organization. Things are the way they are by virtue of the fact that men are men and women are women—a division perceived to be natural and rooted in biology, producing in turn profound psychological, behavioral, and social consequences. The structural arrangements of a society are presumed to be responsive to these differences.

Analyses of sex and gender in the social sciences, though less likely to accept uncritically the naive biological determinism of the view just presented, often retain a conception of sex-linked behaviors and traits as essential properties of individuals (for good reviews, see Hochschild 1973; Tresemer 1975; Thorne 1980; Henley 1985). The "sex differences approach" (Thorne 1980) is more commonly attributed to psychologists than to sociologists, but the survey researcher who determines the "gender" of respondents on the basis of the sound of their voices over the telephone is also making trait-oriented assumptions. Reducing gender to a fixed set of psychological traits or to a unitary "variable" precludes serious consideration of the ways it is used to structure distinct domains of social experience (Stacey and Thorne 1985, pp. 307–8).

Taking a different tack, role theory has attended to the social construction of gender categories, called "sex roles" or, more recently, "gender roles" and has analyzed how these are learned and enacted. Beginning with Linton (1936) and continuing through the works of Parsons (Parsons 1951; Parsons and Bales 1955) and Komarovsky (1946, 1950), role theory has emphasized the social and dynamic aspect of role construction and enactment (Thorne 1980; Connell 1983). But at the level of face-to-face interaction, the application of role theory to gender poses problems of its own (for good reviews and critiques, see Connell 1983, 1985; Kessler, Ashendon, Connell, and Dowsett 1985; Lopata and Thorne 1978; Thorne 1980; Stacey and Thorne 1985). Roles are *situated* identities—assumed and relinquished as the situation demands—rather than *master identities* (Hughes 1945), such as sex category, that cut across situations. Unlike most roles, such as "nurse," "doctor," and "patient" or "professor" and "student," gender has no specific site or organizational context.

Moreover, many roles are already gender marked, so that special qualifiers—such as "female doctor" or "male nurse"—must be added to exceptions to the rule. Thorne (1980) observes that conceptualizing gender as a role makes it difficult to assess its influence on other roles and reduces its explanatory usefulness in discussions of power and inequality. Drawing on Rubin (1975), Thorne calls for a reconceptualization of women and men as distinct social groups, constituted in "concrete, historically changing—and generally unequal—social relationships" (Thorne 1980, p. 11).

We argue that gender is not a set of traits, nor a variable, nor a role, but the product of social doings of some sort. What then is the social doing of gender? It is more than the continuous creation of the meaning of gender through human actions (Gerson and Peiss 1985). We claim that gender itself is constituted through interaction.[2] To develop the implications of our claim, we turn to Goffman's (1976) account of "gender display." Our object here is to explore how gender might be exhibited or portrayed through interaction, and thus be seen as "natural," while it is being produced as a socially organized achievement.

GENDER DISPLAY

Goffman contends that when human beings interact with others in their environment, they assume that each possesses an "essential nature"—a nature that can be discerned through the "natural signs given off or expressed by them" (1976, p. 75). Femininity and masculinity are regarded as "proto-types of essential expression—something that can be conveyed fleetingly in any social situation and yet something that strikes at the most basic charac-terization of the individual" (1976, p. 75). The means through which we provide such expressions are "perfunctory, conventionalized acts" (1976, p. 69), which convey to others our regard for them, indicate our alignment in an encounter, and tentatively establish the terms of contact for that social situation. But they are also regarded as expressive behavior, testimony to our "essential natures."

Goffman (1976, pp. 69–70) sees *displays* as highly conventionalized behaviors structured as two-part exchanges of the statement-reply type, in which the presence or absence of symmetry can establish deference or dominance. These rituals are viewed as distinct from but articulated with more consequential activities, such as performing tasks or engaging in discourse. Hence, we have what he terms the "scheduling" of displays at junctures in activities, such as the beginning or end, to avoid interfering with the activities themselves. Goffman (1976, p. 69) formulates *gender display* as follows:

> If gender be defined as the culturally established correlates of sex (whether in consequence of biology or learning), then gender display refers to convention-alized portrayals of these correlates.

These gendered expressions might reveal clues to the underlying, funda-mental dimensions of the female and male, but they are, in Goffman's view, optional performances. Masculine courtesies may or may not be offered and, if offered, may or may not be declined (1976, p. 71). Moreover, human beings "themselves employ the term 'expression,' and conduct themselves to fit their own notions of expressivity" (1976, p. 75). Gender depictions are less a consequence of our "essential sexual natures" than interactional portrayals of what we would like to convey about sexual natures, using conventional-ized gestures. Our *human* nature gives us the ability to learn to produce and recognize masculine and feminine gender displays—"a capacity [we] have by virtue of being persons, not males and females" (1976, p. 76).

Upon first inspection, it would appear that Goffman's formulation offers an engaging sociological corrective to existing formulations of gender. In his view, gender is a socially scripted dramatization of the culture's *idealization* of feminine and masculine natures, played for an audience that is well schooled in the presentational idiom. To continue the metaphor, there are scheduled performances presented in special locations, and like plays, they constitute introductions to or time out from more serious activities.

There are fundamental equivocations in this perspective. By segregating gender display from the serious business of interaction, Goffman obscures the effects of gender on a wide range of human activities. Gender is not merely something that happens in the nooks and crannies of interaction, fitted in here and there and not interfering with the serious business of life. While it is plausible to contend that gender displays—construed as conventionalized expressions—are optional, it does not seem plausible to say that we have the option of being seen by others as female or male.

It is necessary to move beyond the notion of gender display to consider what is involved in doing gender as an ongoing activity embedded in everyday interaction. Toward this end, we return to the distinctions among sex, sex category, and gender introduced earlier.

SEX, SEX CATEGORY, AND GENDER

Garfinkel's (1967, pp. 118–40) case study of Agnes, a transsexual raised as a boy who adopted a female identity at age 17 and underwent a sex reassignment operation several years later, demonstrates how gender is created through interaction and at the same time structures interaction. Agnes, whom Garfinkel characterized as a "practical methodologist," developed a number of procedures for passing as a "normal, natural female" both prior to and after her surgery. She had the practical task of managing the fact that she possessed male genitalia and that she lacked the social resources a girl's biography would presumably provide in everyday interaction. In short, she needed to display herself as a woman, simultaneously learning what it was to be a woman. Of necessity, this full-time pursuit took place at a time when most people's gender would be well-accredited and routinized. Agnes had to consciously contrive what the vast majority of women do without thinking. She was not "faking" what "real" women do naturally. She was obliged to analyze and figure out how to act within socially structured circumstances and conceptions of femininity that women born with appropriate biological credentials come to take for granted early on. As in the case of others who must "pass," such as transvestites, Kabuki actors, or Dustin

Hoffman's "Tootsie," Agnes's case makes visible what culture has made invisible—the accomplishment of gender.

Garfinkel's (1967) discussion of Agnes does not explicitly separate three analytically distinct, although empirically overlapping, concepts—sex, sex category, and gender.

Sex

Agnes did not possess the socially agreed upon biological criteria for classification as a member of the female *sex*. Still, Agnes regarded herself as a female, albeit a female with a penis, which a woman ought not to possess. The penis, she insisted, was a "mistake" in need of remedy (Garfinkel 1967, pp. 126–27, 131–32). Like other competent members of our culture, Agnes honored the notion that there *are* "essential" biological criteria that un-equivocally distinguish females from males. However, if we move away from the commonsense viewpoint, we discover that the reliability of these criteria is not beyond question (Money and Brennan 1968; Money and Erhardt 1972; Money and Ogunro 1974; Money and Tucker 1975). Moreover, other cultures have acknowledged the existence of "cross-genders" (Blackwood 1984; Williams 1986) and the possibility of more than two sexes (Hill 1935; Martin and Voorhies 1975, pp. 84-107; but see also Cucchiari 1981, pp. 32–35).

More central to our argument is Kessler and McKenna's (1978, pp. 1–6) point that genitalia are conventionally hidden from public inspection in everyday life; yet we continue through our social rounds to "observe" a world of two naturally, normally sexed persons. It is the *presumption* that essential criteria exist and would or should be there if looked for that provides the basis for sex categorization. Drawing on Garfinkel, Kessler and McKenna argue that "female" and "male" are cultural events—products of what they term the "gender attribution process"—rather than some collection of traits, behaviors, or even physical attributes. Illustratively they cite the child who, viewing a picture of someone clad in a suit and a tie, contends, "It's a man, because he has a pee-pee" (Kessler and McKenna 1978, p. 154). Translation: "He must have a pee-pee [an essential characteristic] because I see the *insignia* of a suit and tie." Neither initial sex assignment (pronouncement at birth as a female or male) nor the actual existence of essential criteria for that assignment (possession of a clitoris and vagina or penis and testicles) has much—if anything—to do with the identification of sex category in everyday life. There, Kessler and McKenna note, we operate with a moral certainty of a world of two sexes. We do not think, "Most persons with penises are men, but some may not be" or "Most persons who dress as men have penises." Rather, we take it for granted that sex and sex category are congruent—that knowing the latter, we can deduce the rest.

Sex Categorization

Agnes's claim to the categorical status of female, which she sustained by appropriate identificatory displays and other characteristics, could be *discredited* before her transsexual operation if her possession of a penis became known and after by her surgically constructed genitalia (see Raymond 1979, pp. 37, 138). In this regard, Agnes had to be continually alert to actual or potential threats to the security of her sex category. Her problem was not so much living up to some prototype of essential femininity but preserving her categorization as female. This task was made easy for her by a very powerful resource, namely, the process of commonsense categorization in everyday life.

The categorization of members of society into indigenous categories such as "girl" or "boy," or "woman" or "man," operates in a distinctively social way. The act of categorization does not involve a positive test, in the sense of a well-defined set of criteria that must be explicitly satisfied prior to making an identification. Rather, the application of membership categories relies on an "if-can" test in everyday interaction (Sacks 1972, pp. 332–35). This test stipulates that if people *can be seen* as members of relevant categories, *then categorize them that way*. That is, use the category that seems appropriate, except in the presence of discrepant information or obvious features that would rule out its use. This procedure is quite in keeping with the attitude of everyday life, which has us take appearances at face value unless we have special reason to doubt (Schutz 1943; Garfinkel 1967, pp. 272–77; Bernstein 1986).[3] It should be added that it is precisely when we have special reason to doubt that the issue of applying rigorous criteria arises, but it is rare, outside legal or bureaucratic contexts, to encounter insistence on positive tests (Garfinkel 1967, pp. 262–83; Wilson 1970).

Agnes's initial resource was the predisposition of those she encountered to take her appearance (her figure, clothing, hair style, and so on), as the undoubted appearance of a normal female. Her further resource was our cultural perspective on the properties of "natural, normally sexed persons." Garfinkel (1967, pp. 122–28) notes that in everyday life, we live in a world of two—and only two—sexes. This arrangement has a moral status, in that we include ourselves and others in it as "essentially, originally, in the first place, always have been, always will be, once and for all, in the final analysis, either 'male' or 'female' " (Garfinkel 1967, p. 122).

Consider the following case:

> This issue reminds me of a visit I made to a computer store a couple of years
> ago. The person who answered my questions was truly a *salesperson*. I could
> not categorize him/her as a woman or a man. What did I look for? (1) Facial

hair: She/he was smooth skinned, but some men have little or no facial hair. (This varies by race, Native Americans and Blacks often have none.) (2) Breasts: She/he was wearing a loose shirt that hung from his/her shoulders. And, as many women who suffered through a 1950s' adolescence know to their shame, women are often flat-chested. (3) Shoulders: His/hers were small and round for a man, broad for a woman. (4) Hands: Long and slender fingers, knuckles a bit large for a woman, small for a man. (5) Voice: Middle range, unexpressive for a woman, not at all the exaggerated tones some gay males affect. (6) His/her treatment of me: Gave off no signs that would let me know if I were of the same or different sex as this person. There were not even any signs that he/she knew his/her sex would be difficult to categorize and I wondered about that even as I did my best to hide these questions so I would not embarrass him/her while we talked of computer paper. I left still not knowing the sex of my salesperson, and was disturbed by that unanswered question (child of my culture that I am). (Diane Margolis, personal communication)

What can this case tell us about situations such as Agnes's (cf. Morris 1974; Richards 1983) or the process of sex categorization in general? First, we infer from this description that the computer salesclerk's identificatory display was ambiguous, since she or he was not dressed or adorned in an unequivocally female or male fashion. It is when such a display *fails* to provide grounds for categorization that factors such as facial hair or tone of voice are assessed to determine membership in a sex category. Second, beyond the fact that this incident could be recalled after "a couple of years," the customer was not only "disturbed" by the ambiguity of the salesclerk's category but also assumed that to acknowledge this ambiguity would be embarrassing to the salesclerk. Not only do we want to know the sex category of those around us (to see it at a glance, perhaps), but we presume that others are displaying it for us, in as decisive a fashion as they can.

Gender

Agnes attempted to be "120 percent female" (Garfinkel 1967, p. 129), that is, unquestionably in all ways and at all times feminine. She thought she could protect herself from disclosure before and after surgical intervention by comporting herself in a feminine manner, but she also could have given herself away by overdoing her performance. Sex categorization and the accomplishment of gender are not the same. Agnes's categorization could be secure or suspect, but did not depend on whether or not she lived up to some ideal conception of femininity. Women can be seen as unfeminine, but that does not make them "unfemale." Agnes faced an ongoing task of *being* a woman—something beyond style of dress (an identificatory display) or allowing men to light her cigarette (a gender display). Her problem was to produce configurations of behavior that would be seen by others as normative gender behavior.

Agnes's strategy of "secret apprenticeship," through which she learned expected feminine decorum by carefully attending to her fiancé's criticisms of other women, was one means of masking incompetencies and simultaneously acquiring the needed skills (Garfinkel 1967, pp. 146–147). It was through her fiancé that Agnes learned that sunbathing on the lawn in front of her apartment was "offensive" (because it put her on display to other men). She also learned from his critiques of other women that she should not insist on having things her way and that she should not offer her opinions or claim equality with men (Garfinkel 1967, pp. 147–148). (Like other women in our society, Agnes learned something about power in the course of her "education.")

Popular culture abounds with books and magazines that compile idealized depictions of relations between women and men. Those focused on the etiquette of dating or prevailing standards of feminine comportment are meant to be of practical help in these matters. However, the use of any such source *as a manual of procedure* requires the assumption that doing gender merely involves making use of discrete, well-defined bundles of behavior that can simply be plugged into interactional situations to produce recognizable enactments of masculinity and femininity. The man "does" being masculine by, for example, taking the woman's arm to guide her across a street, and she "does" being feminine by consenting to be guided and not initiating such behavior with a man.

Agnes could perhaps have used such sources as manuals, but, we contend, doing gender is not so easily regimented (Mithers 1982; Morris 1974). Such sources may list and describe the sorts of behaviors that mark or display gender, but they are necessarily incomplete (Garfinkel 1967, pp. 66–75; Wieder 1974, pp. 183–214; Zimmerman and Wieder 1970, pp. 285–98). And to be successful, marking or displaying gender must be finely fitted to situations and modified or transformed as the occasion demands. Doing gender consists of managing such occasions so that, whatever the particulars, the outcome is seen and seeable in context as gender-appropriate or, as the case may be, gender-*in*appropriate, that is, *accountable*.

GENDER AND ACCOUNTABILITY

As Heritage (1984, pp. 136–37) notes, members of society regularly engage in "descriptive accountings of states of affairs to one another," and such accounts are both serious and consequential. These descriptions name, characterize, formulate, explain, excuse, excoriate, or merely take notice of some circumstance or activity and thus place it within some social framework (locating it relative to other activities, like and unlike).

Such descriptions are themselves accountable, and societal members orient to the fact that their activities are subject to comment. Actions are often designed with an eye to their accountability, that is, how they might look and how they might be characterized. The notion of accountability also encompasses those actions undertaken so that they are specifically unremarkable and thus not worthy of more than a passing remark, because they are seen to be in accord with culturally approved standards.

Heritage (1984, p. 179) observes that the process of rendering something accountable is interactional in character:

> [This] permits actors to design their actions in relation to their circumstances so as to permit others, by methodically taking account of circumstances, to recognize the action for what it is.

The key word here is *circumstances*. One circumstance that attends virtually all actions is the sex category of the actor. As Garfinkel (1967, p. 118) comments:

> [T]he work and socially structured occasions of sexual passing were obstinately unyielding to [Agnes's] attempts to routinize the grounds of daily activities. This obstinacy points to the *omnirelevance* of sexual status to affairs of daily life as an invariant but unnoticed background in the texture of relevances that compose the changing actual scenes of everyday life. (italics added)

If sex category is omnirelevant (or even approaches being so), then a person engaged in virtually any activity may be held accountable for performance of that activity as a *woman* or a *man,* and their incumbency in one or the other sex category can be used to legitimate or discredit their other activities (Berger, Cohen, and Zelditch 1972; Berger, Conner, and Fisek 1974; Berger, Fisek, Norman, and Zelditch 1977; Humphreys and Berger 1981). Accordingly, virtually any activity can be assessed as to its womanly or manly nature. And note, to "do" gender is not always to live up to normative conceptions of femininity or masculinity; it is to engage in behavior *at the risk of gender assessment.* While it is individuals who do gender, the enterprise is fundamentally interactional and institutional in character, for accountability is a feature of social relationships and its idiom is drawn from the institutional arena in which those relationships are enacted. If this be the case, can we ever *not* do gender? Insofar as a society is partitioned by "essential" differences between women and men and placement in a sex category is both relevant and enforced, doing gender is unavoidable.

RESOURCES FOR DOING GENDER

Doing gender means creating differences between girls and boys and women and men, differences that are not natural, essential, or biological. Once the differences have been constructed, they are used to reinforce the "essentialness" of gender. In a delightful account of the "arrangement between the sexes," Goffman (1977) observes the creation of a variety of institutionalized frameworks through which our "natural, normal sexedness" can be enacted. The physical features of social setting provide one obvious resource for the expression of our "essential" differences. For example, the sex segregation of North American public bathrooms distinguishes "ladies" from "gentlemen" in matters held to be fundamentally biological, even though both "are somewhat similar in the question of waste products and their elimination" (Goffman 1977, p. 315). These settings are furnished with dimorphic equipment (such as urinals for men or elaborate grooming facilities for women), even though both sexes may achieve the same ends through the same means (and apparently do so in the privacy of their own homes). To be stressed here is the fact that:

> The *functioning* of sex-differentiated organs is involved, but there is nothing in this functioning that biologically recommends segregation; *that* arrangement is a totally cultural matter . . . toilet segregation is presented as a natural consequence of the difference between the sex-classes when in fact it is a means of honoring, if not producing, this difference. (Goffman 1977, p. 316)

Standardized social occasions also provide stages for evocations of the "essential female and male natures." Goffman cites organized sports as one such institutionalized framework for the expression of manliness. There, those qualities that ought "properly" to be associated with masculinity, such as endurance, strength, and competitive spirit, are celebrated by all parties concerned—participants, who may be seen to demonstrate such traits, and spectators, who applaud their demonstrations from the safety of the sidelines (1977, p. 322).

Assortative mating practices among heterosexual couples afford still further means to create and maintain differences between women and men. For example, even though size, strength, and age tend to be normally distributed among females and males (with considerable overlap between them), selective pairing ensures couples in which boys and men are visibly bigger, stronger, and older (if not "wiser") than the girls and women with whom they are paired. So, should situations emerge in which greater size, strength, or experience is called for, boys and men will be ever ready to display it and girls and women, to appreciate its display (Goffman 1977, p. 321; West and Iritani 1985).

Gender may be routinely fashioned in a variety of situations that seem conventionally expressive to begin with, such as those that present "helpless" women next to heavy objects or flat tires. But, as Goffman notes, heavy, messy, and precarious concerns can be constructed from *any* social situation, "even though by standards set in other settings, this may involve something that is light, clean, and safe" (Goffman 1977, p. 324). Given these resources, it is clear that *any* interactional situation sets the stage for depictions of "essential" sexual natures. In sum, these situations "do not so much allow for the expression of natural differences as for the production of that difference itself" (Goffman 1977, p. 324).

Many situations are not clearly sex categorized to begin with, nor is what transpires within them obviously gender relevant. Yet any social encounter can be pressed into service in the interests of doing gender. Thus, Fishman's (1978) research on casual conversations found an asymmetrical "division of labor" in talk between heterosexual intimates. Women had to ask more questions, fill more silences, and use more attention-getting beginnings in order to be heard. Her conclusions are particularly pertinent here:

> Since interactional work is related to what constitutes being a woman, with what a woman *is,* the idea that it *is* work is obscured. The work is not seen as what women do, but as part of what they are. (Fishman 1978, p. 405)

We would argue that it is precisely such labor that helps to constitute the essential nature of women *as* women in interactional contexts (West and Zimmerman 1983, pp. 109-11; but see also Kollock, Blumstein, and Schwartz 1985).

Individuals have many social identities that may be donned or shed, muted or made more salient, depending on the situation. One may be a friend, spouse, professional, citizen, and many other things to many different people—or, to the same person at different times. But we are always women or men—unless we shift into another sex category. What this means is that our identificatory displays will provide an ever-available resource for doing gender under an infinitely diverse set of circumstances.

Some occasions are organized to routinely display and celebrate behaviors that are conventionally linked to one or the other sex category. On such occasions, everyone knows his or her place in the interactional scheme of things. If an individual identified as a member of one sex category engages in behavior usually associated with the other category, this routinization is challenged. Hughes (1945, p. 356) provides an illustration of such a dilemma:

> [A] young woman . . . became part of that virile profession, engineering. The designer of an airplane is expected to go up on the maiden flight of the first

> plane built according to the design. He [sic] then gives a dinner to the
> engineers and workmen who worked on the new plane. The dinner is naturally
> a stag party. The young woman in question designed a plane. Her co-workers
> urged her not to take the risk—for which, presumably, men only are fit—of
> the maiden voyage. They were, in effect, asking her to be a lady instead of an
> engineer. She chose to be an engineer. She then gave the party and paid for it
> like a man. After food and the first round of toasts, she left like a lady.

On this occasion, parties reached an accommodation that allowed a woman
to engage in presumptively masculine behaviors. However, we note that in
the end, this compromise permitted demonstration of her "essential" femininity, through accountably "ladylike" behavior.

Hughes (1945, p. 357) suggests that such contradictions may be countered
by managing interactions on a very narrow basis, for example, "keeping the
relationship formal and specific." But the heart of the matter is that even—
perhaps, especially—if the relationship is a formal one, gender is still
something one is accountable for. Thus a woman physician (notice the
special qualifier in her case) may be accorded respect for her skill and even
addressed by an appropriate title. Nonetheless, she is subject to evaluation
in terms of normative conceptions of appropriate attitudes and activities for
her sex category and under pressure to prove that she is an "essentially"
feminine being, despite appearances to the contrary (West 1984, pp. 97–101).
Her sex category is used to discredit her participation in important clinical
activities (Lorber 1984, pp. 52–54), while her involvement in medicine is
used to discredit her commitment to her responsibilities as a wife and mother
(Bourne and Wikler 1978, pp. 435–37). Simultaneously, her exclusion from
the physician colleague community is maintained and her accountability *as
a woman* is ensured.

In this context, "role conflict" can be viewed as a dynamic aspect of our
current "arrangement between the sexes" (Goffman 1977), an arrangement
that provides for occasions on which persons of a particular sex category can
"see" quite clearly that they are out of place and that if they were not there,
their current troubles would not exist. What is at stake is, from the standpoint
of interaction, the management of our "essential" natures, and from the
standpoint of the individual, the continuing accomplishment of gender. If, as
we have argued, sex category is omnirelevant, then any occasion, conflicted
or not, offers the resources for doing gender.

We have sought to show that sex category and gender are managed
properties of conduct that are contrived with respect to the fact that others
will judge and respond to us in particular ways. We have claimed that a
person's gender is not simply an aspect of what one is, but, more fundamentally, it is something that one *does,* and does recurrently, in interaction with
others.

What are the consequences of this theoretical formulation? If, for example, individuals strive to achieve gender in encounters with others, how does a culture instill the need to achieve it? What is the relationship between the production of gender at the level of interaction and such institutional arrangements as the division of labor in society? And, perhaps most important, how does doing gender contribute to the subordination of women by men?

RESEARCH AGENDAS

To bring the social production of gender under empirical scrutiny, we might begin at the beginning, with a reconsideration of the process through which societal members acquire the requisite categorical apparatus and other skills to become gendered human beings.

Recruitment to Gender Identities

The conventional approach to the process of becoming girls and boys has been sex-role socialization. In recent years, recurring problems arising from this approach have been linked to inadequacies inherent in role theory *per se*—its emphasis on "consensus, stability and continuity" (Stacey and Thorne 1985, p. 307), its ahistorical and depoliticizing focus (Thorne 1980, p. 9; Stacey and Thorne 1985, p. 307), and the fact that its "social" dimension relies on "a general assumption that people choose to maintain existing customs" (Connell 1985, p. 263).

In contrast, Cahill (1982, 1986a, 1986b) analyzes the experiences of preschool children using a social model of recruitment into normally gendered identities. Cahill argues that categorization practices are fundamental to learning and displaying feminine and masculine behavior. Initially, he observes, children are primarily concerned with distinguishing between themselves and others on the basis of social competence. Categorically, their concern resolves itself into the opposition of "girl/boy" classification versus "baby" classification (the latter designating children whose social behavior is problematic and who must be closely supervised). It is children's concern with being seen as socially competent that evokes their initial claims to gender identities:

> During the exploratory stage of children's socialization . . . they learn that only two social identities are routinely available to them, the identity of "baby," or, depending on the configuration of their external genitalia, either "big boy" or "big girl." Moreover, others subtly inform them that the identity of "baby" is a discrediting one. When, for example, children engage in disapproved behavior, they are often told "You're a baby" or "Be a big boy." In effect, these typical verbal responses to young children's behavior convey

to them that they must behaviorally choose between the discrediting identity of "baby" and their anatomically determined sex identity. (Cahill 1986a, p. 175)

Subsequently, little boys appropriate the gender ideal of "efficaciousness," that is, being able to affect the physical and social environment through the exercise of physical strength or appropriate skills. In contrast, little girls learn to value "appearance," that is, managing themselves as ornamental objects. Both classes of children learn that the recognition and use of sex categorization in interaction are not optional, but mandatory (see also Bem 1983).

Being a "girl" or a "boy" then, is not only being more competent than a "baby," but also being competently female or male, that is, learning to produce behavioral displays of one's "essential" female or male identity. In this respect, the task of four- to five-year-old children is very similar to Agnes's:

> For example, the following interaction occurred on a preschool playground. A 55-month-old boy (D) was attempting to unfasten the clasp of a necklace when a preschool aide walked over to him.
>   A: Do you want to put that on?
>   D: No. It's for girls.
>   A: You don't have to be a girl to wear things around your neck. Kings wear things around their necks. You could pretend you're a king.
>   D: I'm not a king. I'm a boy. (Cahill 1986a, p. 176)

As Cahill notes of this example, although D may have been unclear as to the sex status of a king's identity, he was obviously aware that necklaces are used to announce the identity "girl." Having claimed the identity "boy" and having developed a behavioral commitment to it, he was leery of any display that might furnish grounds for questioning his claim.

In this way, new members of society come to be involved in a *self-regulating process* as they begin to monitor their own and others' conduct with regard to its gender implications. The "recruitment" process involves not only the appropriation of gender ideals (by the valuation of those ideals as proper ways of being and behaving) but also *gender identities* that are important to individuals and that they strive to maintain. Thus gender differences, or the sociocultural shaping of "essential female and male natures," achieve the status of objective facts. They are rendered normal, natural features of persons and provide the tacit rationale for differing fates of women and men within the social order.

Additional studies of children's play activities as routine occasions for the expression of gender-appropriate behavior can yield new insights into how our "essential natures" are constructed. In particular, the transition from what

Cahill (1986a) terms "apprentice participation" in the sex-segregated worlds that are common among elementary school children to "bona fide participation" in the heterosocial world so frightening to adolescents is likely to be a keystone in our understanding of the recruitment process (Thorne 1986; Thorne and Luria 1986).

Gender and the Division of Labor

Whenever people face issues of *allocation*—who is to do what, get what, plan or execute action, direct or be directed, incumbency in significant social categories such as "female" and "male" seems to become pointedly relevant. How such issues are resolved conditions the exhibition, dramatization, or celebration of one's "essential nature" as a woman or man.

Berk (1985) offers elegant demonstration of this point in her investigation of the allocation of household labor and the attitudes of married couples toward the division of household tasks. Berk found little variation in either the actual distribution of tasks or perceptions of equity in regard to that distribution. Wives, even when employed outside the home, do the vast majority of household and child-care tasks. Moreover, both wives and husbands tend to perceive this as a "fair" arrangement. Noting the failure of conventional sociological and economic theories to explain this seeming contradiction, Berk contends that something more complex is involved than rational arrangements for the production of household goods and services:

> Hardly a question simply of who has more time, or whose time is worth more, who has more skill or more power, it is clear that a complicated relationship between the structure of work imperatives and the structure of normative expectations attached to work as *gendered* determines the ultimate allocation of members' time to work and home. (Berk 1985, pp. 195–96)

She notes, for example, that the most important factor influencing wives' contribution of labor is the total amount of work demanded or expected by the household; such demands had no bearing on husbands' contributions. Wives reported various rationales (their own and their husbands') that justified their level of contribution and, as a general matter, underscored the presumption that wives are essentially responsible for household production.

Berk (1985, p. 201) contends that it is difficult to see how people "could rationally establish the arrangements that they do solely for the production of household goods and services"—much less, how people could consider them "fair." She argues that our current arrangements for the domestic division of labor support *two* production processes: household goods and services (meals, clean children, and so on) and, at the same time, gender. As she puts it:

> Simultaneously, members "do" gender, as they "do" housework and child care, and what [has] been called the division of labor provides for the joint production of household labor and gender; it is the mechanism by which both the material and symbolic products of the household are realized. (1985, p. 201)

It is not simply that household labor is designated as "women's work," but that for a woman to engage in it and a man not to engage in it is to draw on and exhibit the "essential nature" of each. What is produced and reproduced is not merely the activity and artifact of domestic life, but the material embodiment of wifely and husbandly roles, and derivatively, of womanly and manly conduct (see Beer 1983, pp. 70–89). What are also frequently produced and reproduced are the dominant and subordinate statuses of the sex categories.

How does gender get done in work settings outside the home, where dominance and subordination are themes of overarching importance? Hochschild's (1983) analysis of the work of flight attendants offers some promising insights. She found that the occupation of flight attendant consisted of something altogether different for women than for men:

> As the company's main shock absorbers against "mishandled" passengers, their own feelings are more frequently subjected to rough treatment. In addition, a day's exposure to people who resist authority in a woman is a different experience than it is for a man. . . . In this respect, it is a disadvantage to be a woman. And in this case, they are not simply women in the biological sense. They are also a highly visible distillation of middle-class American notions of femininity. They symbolize Woman. Insofar as the category "female" is mentally associated with having less status and authority, female flight attendants are more readily classified as "really" females than other females are. (Hochschild 1983, p. 175)

In performing what Hochschild terms the "emotional labor" necessary to maintain airline profits, women flight attendants simultaneously produce enactments of their "essential" femininity.

Sex and Sexuality

What is the relationship between doing gender and a culture's prescription of "obligatory heterosexuality" (Rubin 1975; Rich 1980)? As Frye (1983, p. 22) observes, the monitoring of sexual feelings in relation to other appropriately sexed persons requires the ready recognition of such persons "before one can allow one's heart to beat or one's blood to flow in erotic enjoyment of that person." The appearance of heterosexuality is produced through emphatic and unambiguous indicators of one's sex, layered on in ever more conclusive fashion (Frye 1983, p. 24). Thus, lesbians and gay men concerned with passing as heterosexuals can rely on these indicators for camouflage; in contrast, those who would avoid the assumption of heterosexuality may foster ambiguous indicators of their categorical status through their dress, behaviors, and style. But "ambiguous" sex indicators are sex indicators nonetheless. If one wishes to be recognized as a lesbian (or heterosexual woman), one must first establish a categorical status as female. Even as popular images portray lesbians as "females who are not feminine" (Frye 1983, p. 129), the accountability of persons for their "normal, natural sexedness" is preserved.

Nor is accountability threatened by the existence of "sex-change operations"—presumably, the most radical challenge to our cultural perspective on sex and gender. Although no one coerces transsexuals into hormone therapy, electrolysis, or surgery, the alternatives available to them are undeniably constrained:

> When the transsexual experts maintain that they use transsexual procedures only with people who ask for them, and who prove that they can "pass," they obscure the social reality. Given patriarchy's prescription that one must be *either* masculine or feminine, free choice is conditioned. (Raymond 1979, p. 135, italics added)

The physical reconstruction of sex criteria pays ultimate tribute to the "essentialness" of our sexual natures—as women *or* as men.

GENDER, POWER, AND SOCIAL CHANGE

Let us return to the question: Can we avoid doing gender? Earlier, we proposed that insofar as sex category is used as a fundamental criterion for differentiation, doing gender is unavoidable. It is unavoidable because of the social consequences of sex-category membership: the allocation of power and resources not only in the domestic, economic, and political domains but also in the broad arena of interpersonal relations. In virtually any situation, one's sex category can be relevant, and one's performance as an incumbent of that category (i.e., gender) can be subjected to evaluation. Maintaining such pervasive and faithful assignment of lifetime status requires legitimation.

But doing gender also renders the social arrangements based on sex category accountable as normal and natural, that is, legitimate ways of organizing social life. Differences between women and men that are created by this process can then be portrayed as fundamental and enduring dispositions. In this light, the institutional arrangements of a society can be seen as responsive to the differences—the social order being merely an accommodation to the natural order. Thus if, in doing gender, men are also doing dominance and women are doing deference (cf. Goffman 1967, pp. 47–95), the resultant social order, which supposedly reflects "natural differences," is a powerful reinforcer and legitimator of hierarchical arrangements. Frye observes:

> For efficient subordination, what's wanted is that the structure not appear to be a cultural artifact kept in place by human decision or custom, but that it appear *natural*—that it appear to be quite a direct consequence of facts about the beast which are beyond the scope of human manipulation. . . . That we are trained to behave so differently as women and men, and to behave so differently toward women and men, itself contributes mightily to the appearance of extreme dimorphism, but also, the *ways* we act as women and men, and the *ways* we act toward women and men, mold our bodies and our minds to the shape of subordination and dominance. We do become what we practice being. (Frye 1983, p. 34)

If we do gender appropriately, we simultaneously sustain, reproduce, and render legitimate the institutional arrangements that are based on sex category. If we fail to do gender appropriately, we as individuals—not the institutional arrangements—may be called to account (for our character, motives, and predispositions).

Social movements such as feminism can provide the ideology and impetus to question existing arrangements, and the social support for individuals to explore alternatives to them. Legislative changes, such as that proposed by the Equal Rights Amendment, can also weaken the accountability of conduct to sex category, thereby affording the possibility of more widespread loosening of accountability in general. To be sure, equality under the law does not guarantee equality in other arenas. As Lorber (1986, p. 577) points out, assurance of "scrupulous equality of categories of people considered essentially different needs constant monitoring." What such proposed changes *can* do is provide the warrant for asking why, if we wish to treat women and men as equals, there needs to be two sex categories at all (see Lorber 1986, p. 577).

The sex category/gender relationship links the institutional and interactional levels, a coupling that legitimates social arrangements based on sex category and reproduces their asymmetry in face-to-face interaction. Doing gender furnishes the interactional scaffolding of social structure, along with a built-in mechanism of social control. In appreciating the institutional forces that maintain distinctions between women and men, we must not lose sight of the interactional validation of those distinctions that confers upon them their sense of "naturalness" and "rightness."

Social change, then, must be pursued both at the institutional and cultural level of sex category and at the interactional level of gender. Such a conclusion is hardly novel. Nevertheless, we suggest that it is important to recognize that the analytical distinction between institutional and interactional spheres does not pose an either/or choice when it comes to the question of effecting social change. Reconceptualizing gender not as a simple property of individuals but as an integral dynamic of social orders implies a new perspective on the entire network of gender relations:

> [T]he social subordination of women, and the cultural practices which help sustain it; the politics of sexual object-choice, and particularly the oppression of homosexual people; the sexual division of labor, the formation of character and motive, so far as they are organized as femininity and masculinity; the role of the body in social relations, especially the politics of childbirth; and the nature of strategies of sexual liberation movements. (Connell 1985, p. 261)

Gender is a powerful ideological device, which produces, reproduces, and legitimates the choices and limits that are predicated on sex category. An understanding of how gender is produced in social situations will afford clarification of the interactional scaffolding of social structure and the social control processes that sustain it.

NOTES

1. This definition understates many complexities involved in the relationship between biology and culture (Jaggar 1983, pp. 106–13). However, our point is that the determination of an individual's sex classification is a *social* process through and through.

2. This is not to say that gender is a singular "thing," omnipresent in the same form historically or in every situation. Because normative conceptions of appropriate attitudes and activities for sex categories can vary across cultures and historical moments, the management of situated conduct in light of those expectations can take many different forms.

3. Bernstein (1986) reports an unusual case of espionage in which a man passing as a woman convinced a lover that he/she had given birth to "their" child, who, the lover, thought, "looked like" him.

REFERENCES

Beer, William R. 1983. *Househusbands: Men and Housework in American Families*. New York: Praeger.

Bem, Sandra L. 1983. "Gender Schema Theory and Its Implications for Child Development: Raising Gender-Aschematic Children in a Gender-Schematic Society." *Signs: Journal of Women in Culture and Society* 8:598–616.

Berger, Joseph, Bernard P. Cohen, and Morris Zelditch, Jr. 1972. "Status Characteristics and Social Interaction." *American Sociological Review* 37:241–55.

Berger, Joseph, Thomas L. Conner, and M. Hamit Fisek, eds. 1974. *Expectation States Theory: A Theoretical Research Program*. Cambridge: Winthrop.

Berger, Joseph, M. Hamit Fisek, Robert Z. Norman, and Morris Zelditch, Jr. 1977. *Status Characteristics and Social Interaction: An Expectation States Approach*. New York: Elsevier.

Berk, Sarah F. 1985. *The Gender Factory: The Apportionment of Work in American Households.* New York: Plenum.

Bernstein, Richard. 1986. "France Jails 2 in Odd Case of Espionage." *New York Times* (May 11).

Blackwood, Evelyn. 1984. "Sexuality and Gender in Certain Native American Tribes: The Case of Cross-Gender Females." *Signs: Journal of Women in Culture and Society* 10:27–42.

Bourne, Patricia G., and Norma J. Wikler. 1978. "Commitment and the Cultural Mandate: Women in Medicine." *Social Problems* 25:430–40.

Cahill, Spencer E. 1982. "Becoming Boys and Girls." Ph.D. dissertation, Department of Sociology, University of California, Santa Barbara.

———. 1986a. "Childhood Socialization as Recruitment Process: Some Lessons from the Study of Gender Development." Pp. 163–86 in *Sociological Studies of Child Development,* edited by P. Adler and P. Adler. Greenwich, CT: JAI Press.

———. 1986b. "Language Practices and Self-Definition: The Case of Gender Identity Acquisition." *The Sociological Quarterly* 27:295–311.

Chodorow, Nancy. 1978. *The Reproduction of Mothering: Psychoanalysis and the Sociology of Gender.* Los Angeles: University of California Press.

Connell, R. W. 1983. *Which Way Is Up?* Sydney: Allen & Unwin.

———. 1985. "Theorizing Gender." *Sociology* 19:260–72.

Cucchiari, Salvatore. 1981. "The Gender Revolution and the Transition from Bisexual Horde to Patrilocal Band: The Origins of Gender Hierarchy." Pp. 31–79 in *Sexual Meanings: The Cultural Construction of Gender and Sexuality,* edited by S. B. Ortner and H. Whitehead. New York: Cambridge.

Firestone, Shulamith. 1970. *The Dialectic of Sex: The Case for Feminist Revolution.* New York: William Morrow.

Fishman, Pamela. 1978. "Interaction: The Work Women Do." *Social Problems* 25:397–406.

Frye, Marilyn. 1983. *The Politics of Reality: Essays in Feminist Theory.* Trumansburg, NY: The Crossing Press.

Garfinkel, Harold. 1967. *Studies in Ethnomethodology.* Englewood Cliffs, NJ: Prentice-Hall.

Gerson, Judith M., and Kathy Peiss. 1985. "Boundaries, Negotiation, Consciousness: Reconceptualizing Gender Relations." *Social Problems* 32:317–31.

Goffman, Erving. 1967 (1956). "The Nature of Deference and Demeanor." Pp. 47–95 in *Interaction Ritual.* New York: Anchor/Doubleday.

———. 1976. "Gender Display." *Studies in the Anthropology of Visual Communication* 3:69–77.

———. 1977. "The Arrangement Between the Sexes." *Theory and Society* 4:301–31.

Henley, Nancy M. 1985. "Psychology and Gender." *Signs: Journal of Women in Culture and Society* 11:101–119.

Heritage, John. 1984. *Garfinkel and Ethnomethodology.* Cambridge, England: Polity Press.

Hill, W. W. 1935. "The Status of the Hermaphrodite and Transvestite in Navaho Culture." *American Anthropologist* 37:273–79.

Hochschild, Arlie R. 1973. "A Review of Sex Roles Research." *American Journal of Sociology* 78:1011–29.

———. 1983. *The Managed Heart: Commercialization of Human Feeling.* Berkeley: University of California Press.

Hughes, Everett C. 1945. "Dilemmas and Contradictions of Status." *American Journal of Sociology* 50:353–59.

Humphreys, Paul, and Joseph Berger. 1981. "Theoretical Consequences of the Status Characteristics Formulation." *American Journal of Sociology* 86:953–83.

Jaggar, Alison M. 1983. *Feminist Politics and Human Nature.* Totowa, NJ: Rowman & Allanheld.

Kessler, S., D. J. Ashendon, R. W. Connell, and G. W. Dowsett. 1985. "Gender Relations in Secondary Schooling." *Sociology of Education* 58:34–48.

Kessler, Suzanne J., and Wendy McKenna. 1978. *Gender: An Ethnomethodological Approach.* New York: Wiley.

Kollock, Peter, Philip Blumstein, and Pepper Schwartz. 1985. "Sex and Power in Interaction." *American Sociological Review* 50:34–46.

Komarovsky, Mirra. 1946. "Cultural Contradictions and Sex Roles." *American Journal of Sociology* 52:184–89.

———. 1950. "Functional Analysis of Sex Roles." *American Sociological Review* 15:508–16.

Linton, Ralph. 1936. *The Study of Man.* New York: Appleton-Century.

Lopata, Helen Z., and Barrie Thorne. 1978. "On the Term 'Sex Roles.' " *Signs: Journal of Women in Culture and Society* 3:718–21.

Lorber, Judith. 1984. *Women Physicians: Careers, Status and Power.* New York: Tavistock.

———. 1986. "Dismantling Noah's Ark." *Sex Roles* 14:567–80.

Martin, M. Kay, and Barbara Voorheis. 1975. *Female of the Species.* New York: Columbia University Press.

Mead, Margaret. 1963. *Sex and Temperment.* New York: Dell.

———. 1968. *Male and Female.* New York: Dell.

Mithers, Carol L. 1982. "My Life as a Man." *The Village Voice* 27 (October 5):1ff.

Money, John. 1968. *Sex Errors of the Body.* Baltimore: Johns Hopkins.

———. 1974. "Prenatal Hormones and Postnatal Sexualization in Gender Identity Differentiation." Pp. 221–95 in *Nebraska Symposium on Motivation,* Vol. 21, edited by J. K. Cole and R. Dienstbier. Lincoln: University of Nebraska Press.

——— and John G. Brennan. 1968. "Sexual Dimorphism in the Psychology of Female Transsexuals." *Journal of Nervous and Mental Disease* 147:487–99.

——— and Anke, A. Erhardt. 1972. *Man and Woman/Boy and Girl.* Baltimore: John Hopkins.

——— and Charles Ogunro. 1974. "Behavioral Sexology: Ten Cases of Genetic Male Intersexuality with Impaired Prenatal and Pubertal Androgenization." *Archives of Sexual Behavior* 3:181–206.

——— and Patricia Tucker. 1975. *Sexual Signatures.* Boston: Little, Brown.

Morris, Jan. 1974. *Conundrum.* New York: Harcourt Brace Jovanovich.

Parsons, Talcott. 1951. *The Social System.* New York: Free Press.

——— and Robert F. Bales. 1955. *Family, Socialization and Interaction Process.* New York: Free Press.

Raymond, Janice G. 1979. *The Transsexual Empire.* Boston: Beacon.

Rich, Adrienne. 1980. "Compulsory Heterosexuality and Lesbian Existence." *Signs: Journal of Women in Culture and Society* 5:631–60.

Richards, Renee (with John Ames). 1983. *Second Serve: The Renee Richards Story.* New York: Stein and Day.

Rossi, Alice. 1984. "Gender and Parenthood." *American Sociological Review* 49:1–19.

Rubin, Gayle. 1975. "The Traffic in Women: Notes on the 'Political Economy' of Sex." Pp. 157–210 in *Toward an Anthropology of Women,* edited by R. Reiter. New York: Monthly Review Press.

Sacks, Harvey. 1972. "On the Analyzability of Stories by Children." Pp. 325–45 in *Directions in Sociolinguistics,* edited by J. J. Gumperz and D. Hymes. New York: Holt, Rinehart & Winston.

Schutz, Alfred. 1943. "The Problem of Rationality in the Social World." *Economics* 10:130–49.

Stacey, Judith, and Barrie Thorne. 1985. "The Missing Feminist Revolution in Sociology." *Social Problems* 32:301–16.

Thorne, Barrie. 1980. "Gender . . . How Is It Best Conceptualized?" Unpublished manuscript.

———. 1986. "Girls and Boys Together . . . But Mostly Apart: Gender Arrangements in Elementary Schools." Pp. 167–82 in *Relationships and Development,* edited by W. Hartup and Z. Rubin. Hillsdale, NJ: Lawrence Erlbaum.

————— and Zella Luria. 1986. "Sexuality and Gender in Children's Daily Worlds." *Social Problems* 33:176–90.

Tresemer, David. 1975. "Assumptions Made About Gender Roles." Pp. 308–39 in *Another Voice: Feminist Perspectives on Social Life and Social Science,* edited by M. Millman and R. M. Kanter. New York: Anchor/Doubleday.

West, Candace. 1984. "When the Doctor is a 'Lady': Power, Status and Gender in Physician-Patient Encounters." *Symbolic Interaction* 7:87–106.

————— and Bonita Iritani. 1985. "Gender Politics in Mate Selection: The Male-Older Norm." Paper presented at the Annual Meeting of the American Sociological Association, August, Washington, DC.

————— and Don H. Zimmerman. 1983. "Small Insults: A Study of Interruptions in Conversations Between Unacquainted Persons." Pp. 102–17 in *Language, Gender and Society,* edited by B. Thorne, C. Kramarae, and N. Henley. Rowley, MA: Newbury House.

Wieder, D. Lawrence. 1974. *Language and Social Reality: The Case of Telling the Convict Code.* The Hague: Mouton.

Williams, Walter L. 1986. *The Spirit and the Flesh: Sexual Diversity in American Indian Culture.* Boston: Beacon.

Wilson, Thomas P. 1970. "Conceptions of Interaction and Forms of Sociological Explanation." *American Sociological Review* 35:697–710.

Zimmerman, Don H., and D. Lawrence Wieder. 1970. "Ethnomethodology and the Problem of Order: Comment on Denzin." Pp. 287–95 in *Understanding Everyday Life,* edited by J. Denzin. Chicago: Aldine.

8   A Very Straight Gay: Masculinity, Homosexual Experience, and the Dynamics of Gender

R. W. CONNELL
University of California, Santa Cruz

I develop a conceptual approach to changes in masculinity that emphasizes the dynamics of the gender order as a whole. Homosexual masculinity is an important locus of these dynamics. After a critique of conventional discourses of masculinity I develop a theorized life-history method for researching gender. Analysis of eight life histories from an Australian gay community finds (1) initial engagement with hegemonic masculinity, (2) sexuality as the key site of difference, and (3) gradual closure based on relationships or on bodily experience that eroticizes similarity. Conventional masculinity is an aspect of the object of desire, yet is subverted by this object-choice; a contradictory masculinity is produced. Though the men in this study do not directly contest the gender order, the reification of "gayness" provides a social basis for sexual freedom, and the stabilization of a dissident sexuality opens possibilities for change in the social structure of gender.

Recent media attention to masculinity and male initiation, fueled in the United States by enormous sales of *Iron John: A Book About Men* (Bly 1990), does not represent a sudden discovery. Over the last 20 years, in the wake of the new feminism, debates on men's position in sexual politics have taken place in most Western countries, including Britain (Tolson 1977), Germany

AUTHOR'S NOTE: Direct all correspondence to R. W. Connell, Stevenson College, University of California, Santa Cruz CA 95064. I am deeply indebted to the men interviewed, to Norm Radican and Pip Martin for interviewing, and to colleagues Tim Carrigan, Gary Dowsett, Mark Davis, Rosemary Pringle, Marie O'Brien, Mike Messner, Alice Mellian, and the late John Lee. This research was supported by a grant from the Australian Research Grants Committee with supplementary funding from Macquarie University and Harvard University.

"A Very Straight Gay: Masculinity, Homosexual Experience, and the Dynamics of Gender" by R. W. Connell, in *American Sociological Review*, Vol. 57, pp. 735-751. © 1992 by the American Sociological Association. Reprinted with permission.

(Brzoska and Hafner 1990), Sweden (Bengtsson and Frykman 1987) and Australia (Lewis 1983). These debates have given rise to a body of descriptive research, termed "male sex role" or "masculinity" research in the United States (Kimmel 1987; Brod 1987).

Within this literature, changes in men's character or in the "male role" have most often been explained by the psychological discomfort of the individual or by generalized processes of modernization and technological change. I argue that we must focus on the social dynamics generated *within* gender relations. The gender order itself is the site of relations of dominance and subordination, struggles for hegemony, and practices of resistance.

I explore these issues by examining gender dynamics among a group of men who have sex with men. Using eight life histories I investigate their encounters with conventional masculinity, the contradictions of sexuality and identity, and the potential for change in the gender order that their social practice implies. Their homosexual masculinity simultaneously depends on and disrupts the existing gender order in ways that illuminate long-term possibilities of change in the structure of gender relations.

MASCULINITY IN GENDER DYNAMICS

The current popular literature "about men" has an unrelentingly psychological focus. Authors speak of archetypes and "father wounds," of men's pain and healing; they offer therapeutic programs to resolve crises of emotion and personal meaning. They have little to say about the social dimensions of these issues, and most are startlingly ethnocentric and class-bound in outlook. The research literature has a broader perspective—it has begun to document masculinities in a range of class and ethnic contexts. The conceptual framework is usually based on the idea of a "male sex role" (strictly, a masculine gender role) and masculine identity. The conceptualization of gender through role theory, however, reifies expectations and self-descriptions, exaggerates consensus, marginalizes questions of power, and cannot analyze historical change (Stacey and Thorne 1985; Connell 1987).

But gender is an area to which the classic sociological questions of power, institutionalized inequality, and dynamics of social change do apply. These questions have been posed in an international feminist literature centering on the concept of "patriarchy" (Walby 1989). Seeing gender as a structure of social power has immediate implications for research on men. To understand a system of inequality, we must examine its dominant group—the study of men is as vital for gender analysis as the study of ruling classes and elites is for class analysis. With this perspective the scope of research "about men" expands from the conventions of gender—the focus of gender-role studies— to the full range of ways in which men's social practices shape the gender order, including economic relations, institutions (such as the state), and sexuality (Segal 1990).

This is an important advance; yet masculinity cannot be treated as a simple reflex of patriarchal power, for two reasons. First, the concept of "patriarchy" has been sharply criticized within feminism (Rowbotham 1979) as ahistorical, implying an unchanging, universal domination of women by men. This is inconsistent with the historical record. Second, some of the very writing that identifies men as holders of social power (MacKinnon 1987) rests on a categorical model of gender that treats men as an undifferentiated class. This view is inconsistent with contemporary research, which documents a considerable range of masculinities, both in terms of cultural representations of men, and in terms of the institutionalized practices of men in gender relations. Differences are found not only across cultures (Herdt 1982) and through historical time (Roper and Tosh 1991), but also—a point vital for theory—within a particular culture at any given time, e.g., heterosexual and homosexual masculinities and the masculinities of different ethnic and age groups (Kimmel and Messner 1989).

The problems of change and difference are closely connected. The possibilities of historical change in a gender order are reflected in divisions among men as well as in the practices of women. At the same time, differences among men can only be understood with reference to the structure of the gender order. The recognition of multiple "masculinities" in recent research need not reduce the sociology of masculinity to a postmodern kaleidoscope of lifestyles. Rather, it points to the *relational* character of gender. Different masculinities are constituted in relation to other masculinities and to femininities—through the structure of gender relations (Connell 1987, pp. 175–88) and through other social structures (notably class and colonialism, Phillips 1987; ethnicity, Blauner 1989). In modern social formations, certain constructions of masculinity are hegemonic, while others are subordinated or marginalized.

My approach to social change is based on this relational perspective on masculinity. Relations of hegemony reflect and produce a social dynamic: struggles for resources and power, processes of exclusion and incorporation, splitting and reconstitution of gender forms. To analyze this dynamic is to explore the crisis tendencies of the gender order as a whole. (The concept of "crisis tendencies" is borrowed from Habermas [1976], who did not, however, apply it to gender.)

In the dynamics of hegemony in contemporary Western masculinity, the relation between heterosexual and homosexual men is central, carrying a heavy symbolic freight. To many people, homosexuality is a *negation* of masculinity, and homosexual men must be effeminate. Given that assumption, antagonism toward homosexual men may be used to define masculinity, a stance Herek (1986) summed up in the proposition that "to be 'a man' in contemporary American society is to be homophobic—that is, to be hostile toward homosexual persons in general and gay men in particular" (p. 563). The resulting oppression of gay men, as Pleck (1980) observed, provides a symbol for all cases of hierarchy among men.

While Herek's formulation is oversimplified, it captures the significance of heterosexual-versus-homosexual relations for *heterosexuality*. The emergence of "the homosexual" as a social type in the last two centuries of European and American culture and as documented in the new gay history (Kinsman 1987; Greenberg 1988) has a reciprocal. In the same historical process, erotic contact between men was expelled from the legitimate repertoire of dominant groups of men, and hegemonic masculinity was thus redefined as explicitly and exclusively heterosexual. The process of expulsion constructed hegemonic masculinity as homophobic, in Herek's sense. The view that homophobia is a means of policing the boundaries of a traditional male sex role (Lehne 1989) grasps the dynamic character of the process but misconstrues its history: Heterosexual masculinity did not predate homophobia but was historically produced along with it.

Herek's formulation misses the significance of gay masculinities. Some groups of openly gay men emphasize masculinity as part of their cultural style (Humphries 1985). Closeted gay men enjoy the general advantages of masculine gender, and even effeminate gay men may draw economic benefits from the overall subordination of women. In our culture, men who have sex with men are generally oppressed, but they are not definitively excluded from masculinity. Rather, they face *structurally-induced conflicts* about masculinity—conflicts between their sexuality and their social presence as men, about the meaning of their choice of sexual object, and in their construction of relationships with women and with heterosexual men. Out of these conflicts have come unusually sharp observations of heterosexual men and pioneering movements in sexual politics.

The experiences and practices of homosexual men, therefore, are important for understanding contemporary gender dynamics and the possibilities for change. Research on masculinity must explore how gender operates for those men most vehemently defined as unmasculine: how masculinity is constructed for them, how homosexual and heterosexual masculinities interact, and how homosexual men experience and respond to change in the gender order.

DISCOURSES OF HOMOSEXUALITY

These questions have *not* been central to the traditional discourses about "homosexuals" in the human sciences. (Using the term "homosexual" as a noun already reifies sexual object choice into a type of human being.) Yet there is a convergence with gender analysis, especially in recent critiques.

The disclosure of homosexuality most familiar to sociologists is the sociology of deviance. In classics of this field, one routinely encounters lists like "alcoholics, mentally disordered persons, stutterers, homosexuals, and systematic check forgers" (Lemert 1972:78; cf. Becker 1963; Goffman 1963). The "labeling" approach in the sociology of deviance raised useful questions about the apparatus of social control, the process of stigmatization, the moral entrepreneurs who stigmatized, and the need to negotiate assigned identities. But placing homosexuality within a "normality/deviance" framework virtually erased the dimension of gender and sexual politics. For example, Goffman (1963, pp. 98–99) quoted an episode in which a gay man was severely bashed for revealing his relationship with a man passing as straight, but dismissed the episode with a joke as an example of "disciplinary action," failing to see a dramatic and violent moment in the politics of masculinity. When Plummer (1975) applied interactionist labeling theory in fine detail to gay men, the result was a useful catalogue of pressures experienced in the individual life-course, but a conceptual retreat from the structural and dynamic questions being raised by gay movement theorists (Altman 1972).

Homosexual men have been the objects of a more individualistic discourse in psychiatry, psychoanalysis, and psychology. The focus here is the "etiology" of homosexuality—homosexuality being understood as a condition of the individual for which causes must be found, whether family pathology, gender aberration, or biological predisposition (Friedman 1988). Gender was emphasized by psychoanalysis, but the *social* dimension of gender was ignored. Lewes's (1988) remarkable history of psychoanalytic conceptions of homosexuality showed how Freud's radical but ambiguous formulations, which linked homosexuality to the universal bisexuality of human beings, were gradually displaced by a doctrine of homosexuality as a specific condition, and an inherently pathological one to boot. Psychoanalysis thus merged with the medical and juridical apparatus that treated male homosexuality as "other" to a "natural" heterosexuality.

This discourse was challenged in the 1960s and 1970s by therapists who found no particular pathology among homosexual men, though some among the homophobic (Weinberg 1973), and by gay liberationists, who considered psychiatrists attempting to "cure" homosexuality as direct agents of oppression. This position was given support by studies of sex that documented widespread same-sex experiences and failed to find pathology (Kinsey, Pomeroy, and Martin 1948; Bell and Weinberg 1978). Kinsey's positivist sexual science, however, left little space for desire, culture, or social relations. It was displaced in turn by social constructionist views, which saw homosexuality as scripted sexual performance (Gagnon and Simon 1974) or as the effect of an apparatus of surveillance and classification (Foucault 1980).

The social constructionist view of homosexuality (Plummer 1981; Greenberg 1988) has become the meeting point of sexology, sociology, anthropology, history, and gay theory. It has the conceptual power to integrate a wide range of evidence from a range of disciplines, and has become so accepted that it is now the target of dissenting polemics (Stein 1990). The central claim of social constructionism—that homosexual relations exist only within culture and show deep historical and cross-cultural variation—is now well established (Altman et al. 1989). Social constructionism underpins a widespread view of homosexuality as an *identity* formed gradually through a series of steps or stages (Troiden 1989) and as a *subculture* (or set of subcultures) maintained in a pluralistic society by socialization and boundary negotiation (Herdt 1992).

However, a focus on identity and subculture takes the emphasis off large-scale social structure, in this case structural questions about gender. In this respect, social constructionism has followed the sociology of deviance in leaching gender out of group process. Paradoxically (given the HIV epidemic) it also takes the emphasis off sexuality, which in much of this literature is primarily a criterion of group membership. These tendencies are clear in recent work on gay culture and identity in North America (Epstein 1987; Herdt 1992).

These trends have turned gay studies away from questions about masculinity and the large-scale dynamics of gender. There are, however, alternative versions of social constructionism. Blachford (1981) reflected on the interplay between the gay world and the culture of male dominance in society. He found both reproduction of that dominance, and resistance to it, in what is ultimately a "controlled space." Weeks (1986) recast social constructionism by treating sexuality as the domain of a complex and constantly changing political struggle. A post-structuralist view of social order allowed Weeks to see sexual subcultures as more diverse and having greater potential for change than did Blachford. Weeks also emphasized the agency of gay men in the construction of sexual subcultures. This brings Weeks closer to the Sartrean view of social process, which emphasizes collective practice in the making of history (Sartre 1976). Finally, even the subcultural approach can lead back to gender if it focuses on gay subcultures that dramatize gender issues. Klein (1990) and Levine (1992), studying hypermasculine bodybuilders and gay "clones" (a style of dress and interaction evolved in the 1970s), point to significant contradictions over masculinity within homosexual experiences and show the fruitfulness of exploring how those contradictions get resolved.

Although these debates about the nature of homosexuality have not focused on gender, they help refine the research agenda on gay masculinity. To understand the construction of homosexual masculinities requires an examination of gender relations in the family (the terrain of psychoanalytic discourse) and the shared social life of gay men (the terrain of subcultural studies). The construction of sexuality, in its problematic relationship with identity and subculture, must be on the agenda. Finally, the debates on etiology as well as some recent subcultural research indicate that contradictory social and emotional processes are likely to be involved.

METHOD

Four issues are the foci of this study: the construction of masculinity in the lives of gay men; the construction of sexuality and its relationship to identity and subculture; the interplay between heterosexual and homosexual masculinities; and the experience of change in gender relations.

This agenda requires close-focus methods. The classic approach to the dynamics of sexual object choice is through life-history case studies. Of these, Freud's (1955) "Wolf Man" case study remains the model exploration of internal contradictions in masculinity.

Life history studies are enjoying a revival as a way to include formerly unheard voices in public discourse (McCall and Wittner 1990). The method has problems, including the limitations of conscious memory (Rubin 1986), difficulties of corroboration, laborious data gathering, and time-consuming analysis. At the same time it has virtues as a tool of *verstehen* that is flexible in design and application (Plummer 1983). I chose the life-history method because of its capacity—less discussed in the methodological literature but clear in classic life-history research (Thomas and Znaniecki 1927)—to document social structure, collectivities, and institutional change at the same time as personal life. The fundamental connection between life-history and social structure has been theorized by Sartre (1963), whose conception of personal practice as a project developing through time underpins the method of this study.

To decode structural effects in personal practice, the basic unit of study must be the single case. Personal trajectories reveal the interplay of constraints and possibilities, and the interaction of structures. Accordingly, the single case is the basis of this study. However, if the research problem concerns the dynamics operating in a given social location, a group of cases from that location must be examined so that the range of practical possibilities and the character of collective practice become clear. Further, exploring a dynamic like the reconstruction of masculinity that operates across different social locations requires comparison of a range of groups. Accordingly, the study design had three levels: the single case, a group of cases from a particular location, and comparisons between groups in different locations. This report focuses on a group of cases from a particular location, but refers to the other levels.

This logic requires features of design and interpretation that take the life history well beyond unstructured narrative. The socially theorized life history, to give the approach a name, requires prior analysis of the social structure involved. Interviews in this study were based on an analysis of gender as a structure of social practice and of its three main substructures: the division of labor, the structure of power, and the structure of cathexis (Connell 1987), each realized at both collective and personal levels. For the substance of the autobiographical narrative, interviewers sought descriptions of concrete practices (e.g., what a boy and his father actually did in interaction, not just how the relationship was experienced). We used institutional transitions (e.g., entry to school, entry to workforce) as the framework for memory, and asked for descriptions of interactive practice in institutions (particularly families, schools, and workplaces). We explored the sequencing of relationships in order to understand the construction of gender as a project through time. To gain clues to emotional dynamics, we also sought accounts of early memories, family constellations, and relationship crises.

The mode of analysis in life-history research is as important as the interview design. In this study, the individual cases were intensively worked over and written up before the analysis of groups was undertaken. A standard format for the case studies was developed with three main components, each examining the whole interview material from a different point of view: (1) the life course (i.e., the narrative sequencing of events); (2) a structural analysis, using a grid of the substructures of gender relations defined by the theoretical model; and (3) a dynamic analysis that traced the construction (and deconstruction) of masculinity in the individual life.

After the case studies were completed, the group analysis began. The goal was to explore the similarities and differences between the trajectories of men in a given location and their collective involvement in the historical dynamic of gender. Cases were systematically compared by mapping them on a synoptic grid that, for each topic, kept all cases in view while preserving the gestalt of each life-course.

Because this project concerned contemporary transformations in masculinity, four social locations were chosen in which the institutionalization of masculinity was likely to be under pressure, and thus crisis tendencies might be decoded: urban gay community networks; environmental or "green" activism (a location with a strong feminist influence); unemployed working-class youth; and knowledge-based occupations outside the old professions. My approach is similar to what Glaser and Strauss (1967) called "theoretical sampling." I judged that about 10 cases from each location would reveal the diversity of dynamics without being unmanageable in terms of funding and reporting. Thirty-six case studies were completed.

This report presents the results for one location—a group of eight men recruited from an urban gay community in Sydney, Australia. The aim was to find respondents who had a reasonably well-defined, shared location in gender relations. This group reflects the social character of the Sydney gay community as established in a subsequent quantitative study (Connell et al. 1989). The group also reflects the predominant style of sexuality. It includes no drag queens, leathermen, or aficionados of sexual exotica. (Such sexual styles may be prominent on the gay cultural scene, but only a small proportion of the gay community is committed to them in practice [Connell and Kippax 1990].) Although representativeness is not measurable with a small group of case studies, I am confident that these cases are not atypical. Interviews, lasting one to two hours, were conducted from 1985 through 1986; interviews were tape recorded and transcribed.

Reporting on a study like this is difficult. The design emphasizes intensive analysis, rather than numbers of cases, while focusing on social process. Condensation is essential; but condensation can undermine the goal of the life-history method—to show life courses. In addition, a project on gender tensions related to sexuality can hardly avoid sensitive material that places ethical constraints on reporting. It is not easy to achieve a faithful representation of such data. My approach to writing this text is a compromise: For each research question, I select enough detail from one or a few cases to document the main process revealed by the full data set while giving enough of other cases to indicate variations or alternatives. Although all cases were considered in the analysis of each topic, not all cases are quoted.

Although the study is set in Australia, the analysis centers on topics having close parallels in North America and Western Europe. These regions are similar in the overall patterns of gender relations (Bottomley, de Lepervanche and Martin 1991) and the recent history of homosexual masculinities (Aldrich and Wotherspoon 1992) because of shared cultural history and contemporary global economic and media integration.

THE PARTICIPANTS

The participants were recruited by word of mouth through interpersonal networks in the Sydney gay community, inviting participation in a study of "changes in the lives of men." Participants came from mixed class and regional backgrounds, though their present lives converge.

Mark Richards is in his early twenties, unmarried, and a nurse trainee. The oldest child of a business family, his childhood was dominated by conflict between his parents, their separation, and his mother's illness and death. He bore heavy responsibilities early. Sent to a boys' private school, he formed his first long-term sexual relationship there and failed his exams. Rejecting social conservatism and a career, he went to live in a radical communal household. Women friends suggested nursing, and he started work in a hospice for the dying.

Dean Carrington is in his mid-twenties, unmarried, and works as a heavy-vehicle driver. The youngest child of a close-knit family that ran a small business, he had a religious upbringing but lost faith after a sibling died. His family migrated several times. (He is the only one of the eight men who was born outside Australia.) His parents encouraged education, but he failed university and then supported himself in a variety of manual jobs. He eventually migrated alone to join the gay community in Sydney.

Alan Andrews is in his late twenties, unmarried, works as a technician. He was a younger child in a large family in a small country town. His father, a tradesman in a family business, and his mother, a housewife, were embedded in an extended family. Successful in school, he moved away to attend college and began to break with country conservatism. He worked in the city because no jobs were available in the region. He linked up with gay social networks and eventually formed a long-term couple relationship.

Jonathan Hampden is in his late twenties, unmarried, and is a tradesman's assistant. The middle child in an affluent professional family, he was sent to private schools where he did poorly. His anxious relationship with an over-worked father meant that his father's death precipitated an emotional break-down as well as a family economic crisis. He made a slow recovery through a series of relationships and casual jobs. Recently he has been deeply involved in growth-movement therapy.

Damien Outhwaite is in his early thirties, unmarried, and is an unemployed taxi driver (works only occasionally). He was the middle child in a working-class family in a remote country town. He moved to the regional city for higher education and to escape country conservatism. A flamboyant student, he was pushed out of his professional course on suspicion of being gay. He moved to Sydney and discovered the gay community, but lost his white-collar job for being gay. Living on the dole and working periodically as a driver, he has become involved in creative arts.

Adam Singer is in his early thirties, unmarried, and works in the city office of a large organization as a professional specialist. His family was upwardly mobile from the working class; he was pushed toward a profession and succeeded at university, but lacks enthusiasm for the work. However, the environment is secure, and he has stayed with the same employer. His main enthusiasms lie in an active and varied sex life and a strong interest in the art world.

Gordon Anderson is in his early forties, divorced, a father, and is a company manager. He was the oldest child in a rural family that was disrupted by his father's alcoholism and supported by his mother's manual work. From school he went to white-collar work in the city, married, and started a family. He entered the "yuppie" (his word) social world, but disliked its snobbery. He became prominent working for a voluntary organization that had a high public profile. His marriage gradually broke down and separation followed; he keeps in touch with the children. He shifted his career to business management. He has established a long-term couple relationship, but remains closeted.

Gerry Lamont is in his late forties, married, a father, and is a professional in private practice. He was the oldest child in a working-class family marked by violent conflict. Rejecting this background he became upwardly mobile via schooling and religion. He entered a conventional marriage and built a successful, but increasingly unsatisfying, bureaucratic professional career. Personal crises and encounter groups led to a "period of transition" in which he consciously reconstructed his sexuality, personal relations, and working life. He formed gay relationships during and after this period.

CONSTRUCTING MASCULINITY

Traditional discourses of homosexuality have been preoccupied with the "causes" of homosexuality. The psychiatric discourse in particular has connected the "etiology" of homosexuality with some abnormality in family relations or gender development, although debate has raged about what that abnormality is. Recent opinion has been influenced by a San Francisco study that found little support for the seductive-mother/weak-father thesis (Bell, Weinberg, and Hammersmith 1981). However, homosexual men in the study often reported gender nonconformity in childhood.

Neither view of the origins of homosexuality throws light on the life histories in this study. All the men grew up in families with a conventional division of labor and a conventional power structure. Dean Carrington jokingly refers to his father as a "Victorian male." One-half of the fathers were physically abusive toward their wives. The mothers worked as housewives and child caregivers; a few had occasional paid jobs. The family constellations of these eight men clearly fell within the range of what was numerically "normal" or socially conventional in Australia in the 1950s and 1960s (Game and Pringle 1979).

There is little evidence of "gender nonconformity" either. The masculinizing practices in these families parallel those in the study's heterosexual life histories. What I have called the "moment of engagement" with hegemonic masculinity (Connell 1990) also occurred for these men. Their mothers put them in pants rather than skirts, their fathers taught them football, and they learned sexual difference. After leaving the family, they were inducted into the usual sex-typed peer groups, received the usual sexist informal sex education, were subjected to the gender dichotomies that pervade school life (Thorne forthcoming).

Jonathan Hampden's father, for example, was the dominant person in his household, although he increasingly withdrew as his energies focused on building up his professional business. Jonathan's father had been an academic and sporting success at the private boys' school to which he later sent Jonathan, and Jonathan was pressured to perform similarly. Rebellious and resentful in early adolescence, Jonathan became involved—even something of a leader—in a school-resisting peer network that engaged in heavy smoking, group sex play, playground fighting, antagonism toward teachers, and poor academic performance. In puberty, Jonathan grew physically large and became a successful footballer. He recalls episodes of violence on the football field in which he bashed opposing players, a practice that is in tune with rugby's hypermasculine culture (Dunning 1986).

Thus, Jonathan Hampden was engaged in the public construction of a hegemonic form of masculinity—entering a set of interpersonal and institutional practices that connected him to a public world and gave him a masculine position and stance within it. These practices are resilient: Jonathan remains socially masculinized, despite tremendous turbulence in his personal life since leaving school—his father died, his family faced economic disaster, and he suffered a near-psychotic episode. He is, for instance, working comfortably in a male-dominated manual trade. A similar social masculinization is seen with other men in the group. Dean Carrington drives heavy vehicles. Regardless of his sexual preference for men, Dean defines masculinity as sexual agency, i.e., taking an active and directing part. Gordon Anderson runs his office along conventional boss-and-secretary lines and has the controlled, authoritative manner that goes with the well-cut gray suit he wore when interviewed. Gordon is a skillful business tactician and a knowledgeable commentator on politics. He is as effective a participant in the public world of hegemonic masculinity in business as Jonathan Hampden was in the adolescent peer world of hegemonic masculinity as a rebel.

Yet psychoanalysis cautions us not to take such appearances for granted. The fundamental point of Freud's "Wolf Man" study is that adult masculinity is the product of a long, complex process that leaves a layered and contradictory structure of emotions. Institutional contradictions also emerge. For example, competitive sport institutionalizes masculinity in contemporary Australia as it does in North America. But if skill and success are masculine, most participants are distanced from hegemonic masculinity as well as inducted into it, because the hierarchy of competitive sport has many more places for the unsuccessful than for champions (Messner 1992).

Moreover, the existence of a masculinized public culture—in peer groups, schools, workplaces, sport organizations, media—makes gender a candidate for *resistance*. Resistance may mean seizing on a hypermasculine persona, as did Jonathan Hampden and others (Connell 1991). Resistance may also mean doing something outrageously unmasculine. Damien Outhwaite, who moved from a stifling rural background to college in the city, broke out by dying his hair, wearing hipster jeans, wearing nail-polish, and taking up knitting. Mark Richards, uncontrollable and hostile as a teenager, reversed gears as a young adult and became a nurse.

The current popular literature on masculinity argues that true masculinity is formed only by initiation among men and urges men to withdraw psychologically from women (Bly 1990; Keen 1991). The psychoanalytic discourse on homosexuality and Chodorow's (1978) psychoanalytic/sociological theory of the reproduction of gender have a more accurate perception of the importance of boys' and men's relations with women (especially their mothers) in the production of masculinity. But these relations should not be treated as deterministic. The eight cases in this study all show that the family setting is a field of relationships within which gender is negotiated—and the configuration of the field often changes. Given households with a conventional division of labor, relations with mothers and sisters are the primary means of marking sexual difference *and* the source of identifications that provide alternatives to identification with the father. Thus, the conventional structure of the patriarchal household opens up a range of possibilities in emotional relations and in the construction of gender.

Thus, in Jonathan Hampden's case, there is a powerful identification with his father, but also a distinct identification with his older sister—a relationship that developed as his father's affection was withdrawn. At a later stage, Jonathan vehemently repudiated the relation with his sister. Alan Andrews, a country boy like Damien Outhwaite, was always closer to his mother, had mainly girls as friends in childhood, and generally admires and feels close to women. While Alan had to be pushed out of the nest by his mother, Damien dodged his mother's control and escaped to the city, although he remains emotionally linked to her.

The construction of masculinity, then, is a powerful dynamic in these men's lives. Their homosexuality is clearly not built on a lack of masculinity. All the men had some engagement with hegemonic masculinity. But the construction of gender operates simultaneously through a variety of relationships and cultural processes (West and Zimmerman 1987). The complexity of the process allows it to be inflected in different ways. In these men's lives, the important occasion usually was a sexual experience—a discovery of sexuality, or a discovery in sexuality.

SEXUALITY AND IDENTITY

For the majority of the participants, the first major sexual encounters were heterosexual. Two have been married and have children, others have been close to marriage. For Alan Andrews, growing up in the country, sexuality was effectively defined as relationship with a girl. His mother and his peer group pressured him to find a girlfriend. His mates tried to find one for him. He tells a comic tale about being pushed into the girls' tent—one night when the peer group was camping out in the bush—and grabbing the wrong girl. What Rich (1980) called "compulsory heterosexuality" was taken for granted as part of growing up:

> There was a lot of pressure on boys at the age of 16 or 17 to not be virgins, and I was a virgin. So I always thought it will be really good when I meet the right girl. But it happened to be a boy.

The public discourse of sexuality is unreflectively heterosexual, but compulsory heterosexuality was not always realized in practice. The men's narratives document childhoods in which both same-gender and cross-gender experiences are common. Adam Singer recalls being "very sexual from as young as I can remember." He tells of sex games with peers of both genders in primary and secondary school, including a delightful vignette of a "nudist colony" set up by primary school boys in the bush just beyond the school fence. Likewise, Jonathan Hampden recalls childhood sex play with both genders, though less idyllic—he was caught.

Such childhood sexual experiences with partners of both genders appear in life histories of heterosexual adults as well as homosexual adults. Early sexual contact with boys or men does not in itself disrupt heterosexuality. General population surveys find that many more adults have had such contact than become wholly or mainly homosexual (Turner 1989). Freud (1953) pointed to free-form childhood sexuality (his joke about the "polymorphously perverse disposition" of the child is usually taken as a solemn theoretical statement), but confined it to early childhood. Cases like those of Adam Singer and Jonathan Hampden show polymorphous sexuality extending up to, and sometimes well into, adolescence.

Adult homosexuality, like adult heterosexuality, represents *closure* of this structured-but-open field. It is something that *happens,* that is *produced* by particular practices, and is not predetermined. The sexual closure involves choice of an object (in Freud's sense), and this narrowing of focus can be traced in some of the interviews. With Mark Richards, a period of severe adolescent unhappiness and rejection of authority was resolved by falling in love with a classmate after he was sent to an all-boys boarding school. He calls it "a classic boarding-house story . . . a very close friendship and on top of that . . . quite a strong sexual relationship as well." It was furtive, but intense:

> We didn't get caught—and where we didn't do it! I mean, under the Assembly Hall and under the stairs. He took up music lessons just because I was taking music lessons; we'd go out on the same days. . . .
> (*Did people in the school know about it?*)
> Oh God no. No. Absolutely not. I don't know how, but no.

From then on, Mark's choice of men as objects of cathexis was never in doubt. This choice was not a fetishistic fixation on a particular feature of the object; rather it represented a consolidation of Mark's sexuality around the *relationship,* creating a structure that Mark transferred to later attachments. Mark's sex life has, accordingly, been conducted through several relatively long-term relationships. He rejects fast-lane sexuality and speaks with heavy irony of the "wonderful" effects of AIDS, which "stop everyone fucking around everywhere."

Sexual closure can happen, as in Mark's case, without any reference to homosexual identity or any social definition as gay—the relationship itself is its basis. Adam Singer's sexuality, free-form to an extreme in childhood, also consolidated around emotional relationships, including relationships with women but placing much more emphasis on men. In high school Adam became sexually aware of the masculine aura of senior students: "They were students just like me, but their maleness was very, very strong." As an adult he expresses his desire, facetiously but effectively:

A big muscley man who I feel I can cuddle up to; and I love being nurtured.

The choice of object here is defined through a contradictory gender imagery— "muscley" conventionally contradicts "nurtured"—and this contradiction is not abstract, but embodied.

The social process here cannot be captured by notions of "homosexual identity" or a "homosexual role." The sexuality concerns gendered bodies— the giving and receiving of bodily pleasures. The social process is conducted mainly through touch. Yet it is unquestionably a *social* process, an interpersonal practice governed by the large-scale structure of gender.

Dean Carrington, who has had relationships with men and women, evokes a similar pattern. When asked about the difference, his answer focused on bodily sensation:

In the traditional sense it's been the same. I mean anal sex, or anything else: kissing, touching, sucking, licking, the whole works has been the same physically. But I've decided to think perhaps how much more exciting it is with a man. Because I know I can stimulate a man. I know how I like to be stimulated. And that's good, it's fantastic, I'm actually relating more. Whereas my lover B (female) never would say. She loved everything but she wouldn't point out one thing and say "I'd like you to do it this way, I'd like you to put pressure on, or do a certain thing, or wear certain clothes. . . . " I feel I can relate more to a man because his body's the same as mine. . . . Having sex with a man, I'm able to find out how I feel better. . . . I'm actually finding out more about my body. . . . I've developed two breasts, I know what they're like, these two tits there: They're not very big, they're very flat, but they're beautiful. And I've missed out on so many things. Such a shame, such a bloody waste.

Dean's answer rocks back and forth between similarity and difference. He experiences no categorical erotic difference between the sexes and does not engage in different practices with the two sexes. His answer is in accord with the conclusions of our quantitative study of the sexual repertoire among gay and bisexual men in this milieu (Connell and Kippax 1990): The most common practices in male-to-male sex in this culture (kissing, erotic hugging, and so on) are the same as those in female-to-male sex. What is different with a man, Dean makes clear, is the gestalt of the body—a configuration whose similarity is both disturbing and reassuring. The similarity allows exploration of another's body to be a means of exploring one's own.

A gendered sexuality, the evidence implies, is likely to be a gradual and provisional construction. But the social *identity* of being gay is another matter. The category is now so well-formed and readily available that it can be imposed on people. As a late-adolescent rebel, Damien Outhwaite experienced the process that labeling theory describes, when he was still actively interested in women:

> There was one guy at college that immediately identified me as being gay, and he used to give me a bit of a hassle about it . . . , used to identify things I would do to being gay. One of the things was that I was one of the first to wear hipster jeans when they came in—he thought of that as being gay. And the other thing that I did was that I used to carry my books around in a shoulder bag—he thought that was particularly gay too.

In due course, Damien embraced this definition of himself, which was confirmed by oppression—losing jobs—and by increasing embeddedness in gay social networks.

Gayness is now so reified that it is easy for men to experience the process of adopting this social definition as discovering a truth about themselves. Gordon Anderson speaks of having "realized" he was gay; Alan Andrews uses the same term. Alan offers a classic coming-out narrative encompassing six stages. *Prehistory:* Growing up in a country town; a relaxed, conservative family; no particular tensions. *Preparation:* Adolescent uncertainties— liking to be with girls, but not having a girlfriend; sex play with a boyfriend who backs off. *Contact:* Age 19, he stumbles across a beat (a venue for semipublic encounters, similar to the U.S. "tea-room") and has sex with men. Then he goes looking for beats, gets better at it, has a "wonderful" sex-filled beach holiday. *Acknowledgement:* Age 20, "I finally came to the conclusion I was gay, and I went to my first gay dance." *Immersion:* Does the bars on his own, has multiple relationships. *Consolidation:* Age 22, meets Mr. Right and settles into a couple relationship; has more gay male friends; joins some gay organizations; comes out to his parents.

Although these sound very much like the stages of "homosexual identity formation" in the models proposed by Cass (1990) and Troiden (1989), the neatness of the sequence is deceptive, and the outcome is not the homogeneous identity posited by the ego-psychology on which such models are based. Alan's first sexual experiences on the beat were disappointing—it took time for him to become skilled and to experience much pleasure. When he hit the bar scene in Sydney—"notoriously antisocial . . . , very cold places"—he was exploited. A big, handsome, slow-talking country boy, he must have been something of a phenomenon around the Sydney bars and did not lack for partners. He was looking for love and affection; his partners wanted sex. He even feels he was "raped" by a couple of partners—"I was forced into anal sex by them." He became critical of gay studs, interpreting their expertise as an overcompensation for insecurity. He learned to dissemble in heterosexual groups, to flirt surreptitiously. Coming out to his parents was hard and was not successful: His mother was upset, his father refused to talk, and both did their best to keep Alan's younger brother away from him, lest the corruption be passed on. Alan is not so hostile to them that this can pass without hurt.

In a story like this, "coming out" actually means coming *in* to an existing gay milieu. Gay theoreticians, especially those influenced by Foucault, have debated whether the collective identity sustained in this milieu is a means of "regulation" and ultimately a means of oppression (Sargent 1983; Weeks 1986). Certainly Damien Outhwaite's experience—being accused of gayness because of his jeans and his shoulder bag—could be read that way. So could Alan Andrews' passage through beats and bars. Mark Richards distances himself from the fast-track lifestyle and the gay subculture, from both effeminates and leathermen, in an implicit critique of what he sees as the conformities of the gay world.

But there is no doubt that Damien, Alan, and Mark also experienced their gay sexuality as freedom, as the capacity to do what they really wanted to do. This was not false consciousness. Dean Carrington vividly expresses the festival element in coming out:

> Rage, rage, rage! Let's do everything you've denied yourself for 25 years. Let's get into it and have a good time sexually. And go out partying and dancing and drinking.

Festival was a key part of the original experience of Gay Liberation (Altman 1979), and it remains in the post-AIDS era; the Lesbian and Gay Mardi Gras is always one of Sydney's largest popular gatherings of the year. For Gordon Anderson, who remains closeted for powerful reasons (he would certainly lose his job and probably lose access to his children), gay sexuality and friendship networks are less flamboyant, but nonetheless are experienced as a realm of freedom and pleasure outside the severe constraints of other departments of his life.

Sexual freedom, "partying" or "kicking up one's heels" (Gordon Anderson's phrase), important as it is, does not define the most wished-for kind of sexual connection. Adam Singer calls his first sexual experience with a man "not a relationship, but a sexual encounter." Most of the men recognize this distinction and agree with Adam in valuing the "relationship" far more. Their shared ideal is a long-term couple relationship, perhaps open to casual sex, but with an emphasis on a primary commitment. Its value is *both* in sexual pleasure and in "honesty . . . , caring and sharing and learning from each other," in Alan Andrews' words. Others mention mutual emotional involvement, common interests, and just sitting and listening to each other, as components of relationships that work.

How does the wish translate into practice? This is the most difficult part of the interview material to report, and for some participants it was the most difficult to discuss. Three of the men are currently living with male lovers in long-term relationships—11 years in one case. The most troubled of these relationships involves a large age difference, which makes mutuality hard to achieve. Three other participants are consciously searching for a long-term relationship—either rekindling an old flame or finding a new partner—and are making do with "encounters" or just waiting, as one of them put it, for "the drought" to break. Another has been involved mainly in short-term encounters with men (longer-term with women) and is now worrying about the ethics of short-term relationships. Only one of the eight men places the emotional emphasis on casual encounters, and he is trying to weave together a mainly gay erotic life with a continuing domestic relationship with the mother of his children.

Thus, the preferred pattern, as in the heterosexual world, is a committed long-term couple relationship; but such relationships are not easy to come by. Casual encounters (in beats, bars, saunas, and so on) remain an important part of the total experience. All the men have had short-term encounters— this was one path into gay sexuality—and "encounters" remain a significant possibility even after couple relationships are established.

RELATIONS BETWEEN HETEROSEXUAL
AND HOMOSEXUAL MASCULINITIES

A specific masculinity is not constituted in isolation, but in relation to other masculinities and to femininities. This relation is partly a question of differentiation, as in the distinctions only recently drawn between homosexuality (erotic attraction within the same gender), cross-dressing, and transsexuality (King 1981). But *difference* is only part of the story; institutional and personal *practices* are also vital. The relation between hegemonic masculinity and homosexual masculinity includes criminalization of male-to-male sex, homophobic speech and culture, and a bitter history of intimidation and violence (Greenberg 1988). Modern gay politics bears the collective memory of the Nazi final solution for homosexuals in the concentration camps (Plant 1986). At the time I began writing this paper a group of young Sydney men had recently been convicted for beating a gay man to death in an inner-city park. Attacks on gays are common enough that they have become an issue in Sydney's urban politics. Ethnographic research has documented deep homophobia in inner-city youth culture in the same area (Walker 1988).

None of the men interviewed in this study had been bashed, but some had been intimidated. Their conversation takes it for granted that they live in a homophobic environment. Damien Outhwaite has lost jobs, and Adam Singer stuck with a not very engaging career partly because it provided a safe milieu for a gay man. Gordon Anderson stays in the closet for fear of losing his job and his children:

> I don't want to stop what I am doing, I don't want to stop being a good father, I can never see myself being very prominent about my lifestyle. That's the price I suppose.

Gordon describes how the illusion of heterosexual masculinity is sustained when visiting businessmen have to be entertained. He has female friends who will come to his apartment and act as hostess, although the illusion wears thin when they have to ask him where he keeps the pepper.

Heterosexual masculinity, then, is encountered in everyday relations with straight men that often have an undercurrent of threat. Wariness, controlled disclosure, and turning inward to a gay network are familiar responses. However, legitimacy is not necessarily conceded to heterosexuality. Straight men may also be seen as pathetic bearers of outmoded ideas and a boring way of life. Dean Carrington went back to the country town of his childhood:

> I've seen friends, like a chap I went to school with. . . . He's now 25, third child, and he's stuck in a rut. I went back to see him. I did one of those terrible things of going back to your home town; and God, what an eye-opener! There's all these people grown up, and I hadn't got married and they had. They'd "done the right thing."

Alan Andrews had a similar experience watching his brother become a drunken boor. Compared with these images of hegemonic masculinity, gay masculinity is all sophistication and modernity. Negotiating the relation between the two is mainly a question of establishing cultural, and often physical, distance.

Personal relationships, however, do not exhaust the relation between masculinities. Hegemonic masculinity is also an institutional and cultural presence—*collective* practices are involved. A clear example is the football cult in Jonathan Hampden's school, which was sustained by school policy and institutionalized bodily confrontation and aggression. Masculinized authority in the workplace was a source of friction for Damien Outhwaite and Mark Richards, and Adam Singer and Gerry Lamont distanced themselves from male-dominated professions.

The institutional dimension of hegemonic masculinity gives it a social authority that shapes perceptions of gayness. Gordon Anderson, committed to his strategy of evasion, is critical of men who "flaunt" their gayness. Although Gordon sees this as characteristic of Australian gays, a similar criticism is made by "suburban homosexuals" in the United States (Lynch 1992). Adam Singer, Damien Outhwaite (despite his outrageousness), and Mark Richards reject hypermasculinity, but also dislike queens, i.e., effeminate gays. Mark puts the issue succinctly:

> If you're a guy why don't you just act like a guy? You're not a female, don't act like one. That's a fairly strong point. And leather and all this other jazz, I just don't understand it I suppose. That's all there is to it. I am a very straight gay.

Here Mark has identified a sexual/cultural dynamic of some importance. The choice of a man as sexual object is not just the choice of a-body-with-penis; it is the choice of embodied-masculinity. The cultural meanings of masculinity are (generally) part of the package. In this sense, most gays are "very straight." Being a "straight gay" is not just a matter of middle-class respectability—similar positions are taken by working-class men outside the gay community (Connell, Davis, and Dowsett forthcoming).

FACING CHANGE

Dean Carrington's story of his boyhood friends who had "done the right thing" says something about small-town life as well as masculinity. Dean moved to Sydney and immediately began to have sex with men, to come out as gay, and to "rage" around the bars and nightclubs. Movement between milieux is common, whether from country conservatism to the city lights, or, within the city, from the bourgeois school to the radical household (Mark Richards), from the business workplace to the gay social network (Gordon Anderson), from the professional career to the encounter groups of the therapeutic "growth movement" (Gerry Lamont).

The process of coming out, establishing oneself as homosexual in a homophobic world, almost necessarily gives this structure to the narratives.

The life history is experienced as a journey to one's current place. Contrary to Foucaultian arguments that see homosexual identity as regulation, I emphasize the agentic nature of this journey. Dean Carrington pictures it as both escape and self-exploration:

> And this is one of the big things that led to me coming [to Sydney], to be able to get away from my parents, to think, and to find out who I really am, and what I really want, and why I was doing these things over the years, why I was changing, what was I hiding from.

Contrary to the traditional psychiatric view that men's homosexuality results from disorders of relationships with parents, the majority of these cases show successful ego-development that allows separation from both mother and father. Most of the men still maintain as good relations with their parents as the parents allow.

Personal change may further take the shape of a deliberate reform of masculinity, of the kind now undertaken in certain countercultural and radical groups (Connell 1990). Damien Outhwaite, in particular, is working to overcome his "competitiveness" and dominance, and enjoys breaking conventions of masculinity. He has been to a "men's movement" event, and wants to pursue nonsexual physical closeness between men. Jonathan Hampden, despite an uncontrollable distaste for vegan coffee, has been living in a vegetarian household, has done "re-birthing" therapy, and now has the "dream" of setting up a center for workshops on sexuality.

Deliberate reform is only one possibility. A sense that gender relations are changing is widespread among the groups of men in this study, and a demand for change in masculinity does not require the support of the counterculture. It is widely believed that sex differences are lessening and that men are coming emotionally closer to women. Such a change may be occurring within gay masculinity as well. Damien Outhwaite recalls a party put on by a young gay man in a provincial city. The host had invited some women, and when they arrived, the older gay men at the party left. The older men's social network excluded women, and their outlook was misogynist—but this was not true of the young men. Consistent with this, the three youngest men among the group of eight—Mark Richards, Dean Carrington, and Alan Andrews—are the ones who most value and cultivate their friendships with women.

This consciousness of change has had few political effects. The dilution of Gay Liberation politics into an affirmation of gay identity and a consolidation of gay communities (Altman 1982) has had a containing effect. The men have little sense of being connected to a broad reform movement. The only commitment to a practice beyond the self is to a *therapeutic* practice

(Gerry Lamont's workshops, Jonathan Hampden's sexuality center) that assists other men in pursuing individualized reform projects.

The apolitical character of their outlook is indicated by their stance toward feminism. Although most of the men express some support for feminism, they disapprove "Those Who Go Too Far":

> I can't stand the butch dykes [who think] that males are shits. (Mark Richards)

> I have never had a personal conflict about it. I don't like extremisms of anything—the burn-bra thing sort of went over my head. (Gordon Anderson)

Their attitudes toward feminism and level of ignorance about it match the views of feminism among heterosexual groups interviewed.

CONCLUSION: THE HISTORICAL PROCESS

In the introduction to this paper, I posed the question of how homosexual masculinities are related to the historical dynamic of the gender order. The life histories discussed here show that familiar interpretations of homosexuality—both the traditional schema of "normal/deviant" and the newer schema of "dominant culture/subculture"—are too monolithic to capture the historical process. Subcultural diversity among gay men is important to recognize (Weeks 1986). The life-history material, however, shows another level of complexity beyond this, the internal complexity of the relationships through which a homosexual masculinity is constructed. Even the formula of "structurally-induced conflict" about masculinity is inadequate. The narratives reveal multilateral negotiations of emotional relations in the home and in the sexual marketplace, negotiations of economic and workplace relations, negotiations of authority relations and friendships. These relationships often push the person in different directions and are linked in different sequences for different men.

These observations do not deny the significance of social structure. Rather they underline the complexity of the social structuring of gender and of the ways individual lives are linked to this structure. These links are complex, but not random. Despite the variety of detail, the same logical "moments," or elements of historical process, appear in all these narratives: (1) an engagement with hegemonic masculinity, (2) a closure of sexuality around relationships with men, and (3) participation in the collective practices of a gay community.

These moments should not be construed as a new model of "homosexual identity formation." Many men who have sex with men never enter a gay community (Connell et al. forthcoming); some men who do enter a gay community have additional significant moments in the construction of sexuality, e.g., the "leather and all this other jazz" mentioned by Mark Richards. Rather, these are the logical components of the project that can be documented in this specific setting as the social making of a homosexual masculinity. This is not socialization into a stigmatized identity. Rather it is an agentic, multilevel collective project, of the kind analyzed in Sartre's (1976) theory of social process. Its outcome is not a necessary structure of personality, as mechanistic etiologies of homosexuality assume, but a historically realized configuration of practice. Analysis of how this configuration was realized illuminates other historical possibilities in the sandfield of social relations.

It is the interconnection of these three moments that defines the project. The closure of the sexual field around relationships with other men is determined by the engagement, however ambivalent, with hegemonic masculinity. Gay men are not free to invent new objects of desire any more than heterosexual men are—their choice of object is structured by the existing gender order. Adam Singer desires not a male body but a masculine body doing feminine things; Dean Carrington's eroticism revolves around bodily similarity seen in gender terms, e.g. his attention to breasts, a major gender symbol in our erotic culture. Such gendered eroticism underpins the urban gay community which currently defines what it is to be a gay man.

Relationships in this milieu are usually peer relationships marked by a higher level of reciprocity than that characterizing heterosexual relations. Reciprocity is emphasized as an ideal and is to a large extent practiced. The conditions for reciprocity include similar ages of partners, shared class position, and shared position in the overall structure of gender. Ironically, the difficulty of establishing long-term couple relationships may also push toward reciprocity in the sexual culture. In short-term encounters, in which giving and receiving pleasure is the only agenda, there is an approximate equality of position. Finally, there is the specific way the body is implicated in sexual practice—that mirroring of lover and beloved, naively but vigorously expressed by Dean Carrington, in which the exploration of another's body becomes the exploration of one's own.

What is the historical direction of a collective project structured in this way? What are the possibilities for transformation of social relations?

These men are more easily seen as products than producers of history. Their privatized politics offer little leverage on the state of gender relations. The life course shaped as a journey between milieux, exemplified by Dean Carrington's literal migration to the gay community, presupposes the history in which the milieux were formed. The men can adopt, negotiate, or reject a gay identity, a gay commercial scene, and gay sexual and social networks, all of which already exist. Although they are the inheritors of a world made by the gay liberationists and "pink capitalists" of the 1970s—the generation now devastated by AIDS—they have little awareness of, or commitment to, this history.

In these respects the picture resembles the "controlled space" theorized by Blachford (1981), who saw only limited social change effected by gay politics. The gendered eroticism of these men, their predominantly masculine social presence, their focus on private couple relationships, and their lack of solidarity with feminism, point in the same direction—there is no open challenge to the gender order here.

But in two ways, the processes documented here do point toward change. First, the reification of homosexuality that is usually theorized as a form of social regulation, is in these men's lives a condition of freedom. This reification is a necessary counterbalance to the institutionalized compulsory heterosexuality that surrounds them. It allows the realization of forbidden pleasure, the element of festival in their sexuality, and the building of long-term relationships with other gay men. The longest couple relationship in the group began at a beat—a site for casual encounters.

This is an effect specifically about homosexuality. Although most of these men have sexual experience with women, in this cultural context there is no positive social category of "the bisexual" on which a collective practice can be based. For these men, both object-choice and personality are formed within a framework of masculinity.

Second, the familiar heterosexual definition of homosexual men as effeminate is an inaccurate description of men like the ones interviewed here, who mostly do "act like a guy." But it is not wrong in sensing the outrage they do to hegemonic masculinity. A masculine object-choice subverts the masculinity of character and social presence. This subversion is a structural feature of homosexuality in a patriarchal society in which hegemonic masculinity is defined as exclusively heterosexual and its hegemony includes the formation of character in the rearing of boys. So it is not surprising to find, jammed in beside the elements of mainstream masculinity, items like Damien Outhwaite's flamboyant fingernails, Mark Richards's nursing, or Alan Andrews's and Jonathan Hampden's identifications with women.

Hence gay theorists (notably Mieli 1980) who see a necessary effeminacy in male homosexuality have a point, if not quite in the way they intend. At the same time, heterosexual men must deny desire except for the gendered Other, while making a hated Other of the men who desire them (or desire the embodied-masculinity they share). The historical exclusion of homosexual object-choice from heterosexual masculinity builds contradiction into the masculinity of *both* homosexual and heterosexual men.

Put in these abstract terms, this contradiction is merely a possible crisis tendency in a gender order structured in the way modern Western systems are. But the study of these men reveals that the possibility has been realized. The apolitical character of the group indicates the stabilization of a public alternative to hegemonic masculinity—they do not have to fight for their existence as gay men, in the way gay men in earlier generations did. This is all the more significant because the men started out within the framework of hegemonic masculinity. Their trajectories began in conventional settings and moved some distance toward hegemonic masculinity. "A very straight gay" neatly summarizes the contradiction introduced into the politics of gender.

Sexuality is the point of disruption of orderly gender relations. Under the influence of Foucault (1980) and Marcuse (1964), sexuality is taken to be a stabilizing force in social relations, or at least a site where social control is accomplished. It is time to revive the insight of Reich (1972) and Freud (1959), that sexuality is also disruptive and creative.

The creative possibilities can be seen in the shaping of sexual practice itself. Hegemonic heterosexuality, which eroticizes difference within a large structure of gender inequalities, hinders equality and mutuality in the conduct of sexual relations. Observed in earlier research (Rubin 1976), this has been rediscovered in studies of heterosexuality and AIDS prevention (Waldby, Kippax, and Crawford 1990). A higher degree of reciprocity has been created in gay men's sexual practice. The relative equality that permits this is not easily reproduced in heterosexual relations; but the contrast does suggest directions for action in heterosexual life.

Despite the lack of commitment to feminism, the younger men in the group studied here are already forming friendly, pacific relationships with young women in their workplaces and households. A more reciprocal sexuality and pacific everyday interactions are necessary if relations between men and women are to move beyond the current state of inequality, violence, and misogyny. Although far from revolutionary, this group of homosexual men defines possibilities and provides some models for major changes in the social relations of gender.

REFERENCES

Aldrich, R. and G. Wotherspoon, eds. 1992. *Gay Perspectives: Essays in Australian Gay Culture.* Sydney: University of Sydney.

Altman, Dennis. 1972. *Homosexual: Oppression and Liberation.* Sydney: Angus & Robertson.

———. 1979. *Coming Out in the Seventies.* Sydney: Wild and Woolley.

———. 1982. *The Homosexualization of America, the Americanization of the Homosexual.* New York: St. Martin's Press.

Altman, Dennis, et al. 1989. *Homosexuality, Which Homosexuality?* London: GMP.

Becker, Howard S. 1963. *Outsiders: Studies in the Sociology of Deviance.* New York: Free Press of Glencoe.

Bell, Alan P. and Martin Weinberg. 1978. *Homosexualities: A Study of Diversity Among Men and Women.* New York: Simon & Schuster.

Bell, Alan P., Martin Weinberg, and Sue Kiefer Hammersmith. 1981. *Sexual Preference: Its Development in Men and Women.* Bloomington: Indiana University Press.

Bengtsson, Margot and Frykman, Jonas. 1987. *Om Maskulinitet: Mannen som forskningsprojekt* (About Masculinity: The Male as a Research Project). Stockholm: Delegationen för Jämställdhetsforskning.

Blachford, Gregg. 1981. "Male Dominance and the Gay World." Pp. 184–210 in *The Making of the Modern Homosexual*, edited by K. Plummer. London: Hutchinson.

Blauner, Bob. 1989. *Black Lives, White Lives: Three Decades of Race Relations in America*. Berkeley: University of California Press.

Bly, Robert. 1990. *Iron John: A Book About Men*. Reading, PA: Addison-Wesley.

Bottomley, Gillian, Marie de Lepervanche, and Jeannie Martin, eds. 1991. *Intersexions: Gender/Class/Culture/Ethnicity*. Sydney: Allen and Unwin.

Brod, Harry, ed. 1987. *The Making of Masculinities: The New Men's Studies*. Boston: Allen and Unwin.

Brzoska, Georg and Gerhard Hafner. 1990. "Männer in Bewegung?" (A Men's Movement?). *Sozialistische Praxis* 90(5):4–6.

Cass, Vivienne C. 1990. "The Implications of Homosexual Identity Formation for the Kinsey Model and Scale of Sexual Preference." Pp. 239–66 in *Homosexuality/Heterosexuality: Concepts of Sexual Orientation*, edited by D. P. McWhirter, S. A. Sanders, and J. M. Reinisch. New York: Oxford University Press.

Chodorow, Nancy. 1978. *The Reproduction of Mothering: Psychoanalysis and the Sociology of Gender*. Berkeley: University of California Press.

Connell, R. W. 1987. *Gender and Power: Society, The Person and Sexual Politics*. Palo Alto, CA: Stanford University Press.

———. 1990. "A Whole New World: Remaking Masculinity in the Context of the Environmental Movement." *Gender & Society* 4:452–78.

———. 1991. "Live Fast and Die Young: The Construction of Masculinity Among Young Working-Class Men on the Margin of the Labour Market." *Australian and New Zealand Journal of Sociology* 27:141–71.

Connell, R. W., June Crawford, Susan Kippax, G. W. Dowsett, Don Baxter, Lex Watson, and R. Berg. 1989. "Facing the Epidemic: Changes in the Sexual Lives of Gay and Bisexual Men in Australia and Their Implications for AIDS Prevention Strategies." *Social Problems* 36:384–402.

Connell, R. W., M. Davis, and G. W. Dowsett. Forthcoming, "A Bastard of a Life: Homosexual Desire and Practice Among Men in Working-Class Milieux." *Australian and New Zealand Journal of Sociology*.

Connell, R. W. and Susan Kippax. 1990. "Sexuality in the AIDS Crisis: Patterns of Sexual Practice and Pleasure in a Sample of Australian Gay and Bisexual Men." *Journal of Sex Research* 27:167–98.

Dunning, Eric. 1986. "Sport as a Male Preserve: Notes on the Social Sources of Masculine Identity and its Transformations." *Theory Culture and Society* 3:79–89.

Epstein, Steven. 1987. "Gay Politics, Ethnic Identity: The Limits of Social Constructionism." *Socialist Review* 93/94:9–54.

Foucault, Michel. 1980. *The History of Sexuality, vol. 1: An Introduction*. New York: Vintage.

Freud, Sigmund. 1953. "Three Essays on the Theory of Sexuality." Pp. 125–243 in *Complete Psychological Works*, standard ed., vol. 7. London: Hogarth Press.

———. 1955. "From the History of an Infantile Neurosis." Pp. 3–122 in *Complete Psychological Works*, standard ed., vol. 17. London: Hogarth Press.

———. 1959. " 'Civilized' Sexual Morality and Modern Nervous Illness." Pp. 177–204 in *Complete Psychological Works*, vol. 9. London: Hogarth.

Friedman, Richard C. 1988. *Male Homosexuality: A Contemporary Psychoanalytic Perspective*. New Haven: Yale University Press.

Gagnon, John H. and William Simon. 1974. *Sexual Conduct: The Social Sources of Human Sexuality*. London: Hutchinson.

Game, Ann and Rosemary Pringle. 1979. "Sexuality and the Suburban Dream." *Australian and New Zealand Journal of Sociology* 15:4–15.

Glaser, Barney G. and Anselm Strauss. 1967. *The Discovery of Grounded Theory: Strategies for Qualitative Research.* New York: Aldine.

Goffman, Erving. 1963. *Stigma: Notes on the Management of Spoiled Identity.* New York: Simon and Schuster.

Greenberg, David F. 1988. *The Construction of Homosexuality.* Chicago: University of Chicago Press.

Habermas, Juergen. 1976. *Legitimation Crisis.* London: Heinemann.

Herdt, Gilbert. 1982. *Rituals of Manhood: Male Initiation in Papua New Guinea.* Berkeley: University of California Press.

————. ed. 1992. *Gay Culture in America: Essays From the Field.* Boston: Beacon Press.

Herek, Gregory M. 1986. "On Heterosexual Masculinity: Some Psychical Consequences of the Social Construction of Gender and Sexuality." *American Behavioral Scientist* 29:563–77.

Humphries, Martin. 1985. "Gay Machismo." Pp. 70–85 in *The Sexuality of Men,* edited by A. Metcalf and M. Humphries. London: Pluto.

Keen, Sam. 1991. *Fire in the Belly: On Being a Man.* New York: Bantam.

Kimmel, Michael S., ed. 1987. *Changing Men: New Directions in Research on Men and Masculinity.* Newbury Park, CA: Sage.

Kimmel, Michael S. and Michael A. Messner, eds. 1989. *Men's Lives.* New York: Macmillan.

King, Dave. 1981. "Gender Confusions: Psychological and Psychiatric Conceptions of Transvestism and Transsexualism." Pp. 155–83 in *The Making of the Modern Homosexual,* edited by K. Plummer. London: Hutchinson.

Kinsey, Alfred C., Wardell B. Pomeroy, and Clyde E. Martin. 1948. *Sexual Behavior in the Human Male.* Philadelphia: Saunders.

Kinsman, Gary. 1987. *The Regulation of Desire: Sexuality in Canada.* Montreal, Quebec: Black Rose Books.

Klein, Alan M. 1990. "Little Big Man: Hustling, Gender Narcissism, and Bodybuilding Subculture." Pp. 127–39 in *Sport, Men, and the Gender Order,* edited by M. A. Messner and D. F. Sabo. Champaign, IL: Human Kinetics.

Lehne, Gregory K. 1989. "Homophobia Among Men: Supporting and Defining the Male Role." Pp. 416–29 in *Men's Lives,* edited by M. S. Kimmel and M. A. Messner. New York: Macmillan.

Lemert, Edwin M. 1972. *Human Deviance, Social Problems, and Social Control.* 2d ed. Englewood Cliffs, NJ: Prentice-Hall.

Levine, Martin P. 1992. "The Life and Death of Gay Clones." Pp. 68–86 in *Gay Culture in America,* edited by G. Herdt. Boston: Beacon.

Lewes, Kenneth. 1988. *The Psychoanalytic Theory of Male Homosexuality.* New York: Simon and Schuster.

Lewis, Glen. 1983. *Real Men Like Violence.* Sydney: Kangaroo Press.

Lynch, Frederick R. 1992. "Nonghetto Gays: An Ethnography of Suburban Homosexuals." Pp. 165–201 in *Gay Culture in America,* edited by G. Herdt. Boston: Beacon Press.

McCall, Michal M. and Judith Wittner. 1990. "The Good News About Life History." Pp. 46–89 in *Symbolic Interaction and Cultural Studies,* edited by H. S. Becker and M. M. McCall. Chicago: University of Chicago Press.

MacKinnon, Catharine A. 1987. *Feminism Unmodified: Discourses on Life and Law.* Cambridge, MA: Harvard University Press.

Marcuse, Herbert. 1964. *One Dimensional Man.* London: Routledge and Kegan Paul.

Messner, Michael A. 1992. *Power at Play: Sports and the Problem of Masculinity.* Boston: Beacon Press.

Mieli, Mario. 1980. *Homosexuality and Liberation: Elements of a Gay Critique.* London: Gay Men's Press.

Phillips, Jock. 1987. *A Man's Country? The Image of the Pakeha Male, A History.* Auckland, Australia: Penguin.

Plant, Richard. 1986. *The Pink Triangle: The Nazi War Against Homosexuals.* New York: Holt.

Pleck, Joseph H. 1980. "Men's Power with Women, Other Men, and in Society." Pp. 417–33 in *The American Man,* edited by E. H. Pleck and J. H. Pleck. Englewood Cliffs, NJ: Prentice-Hall.

Plummer, Kenneth. 1975. *Sexual Stigma: An Interactionist Account.* London: Routledge and Kegan Paul.

———. ed. 1981. *The Making of the Modern Homosexual.* London: Hutchinson.

———. 1983. *Documents of Life: An Introduction to the Problems and Literature of a Humanistic Method.* London: Allen and Unwin.

Reich, Wilhelm. 1972. *Sex-Pol Essays 1929–1934.* New York: Vintage Books.

Rich, Adrienne. 1980. "Compulsory Heterosexuality and Lesbian Existence." *Signs* 5:631–60.

Roper, Michael and John Tosh, eds. 1991. *Manful Assertions: Masculinities in Britain Since 1800.* London: Routledge.

Rowbotham, Sheila. 1979. "The Trouble With 'Patriarchy.' " *New Statesman* 28 Dec.

Rubin, D. C., ed. 1986. *Autobiographical Memory.* Cambridge, England: Cambridge University Press.

Rubin, Lillian B. 1976. *Worlds of Pain: Life in the Working-Class Family.* New York: Basic Books.

Sargent, Dave. 1983. "Reformulating (Homo)sexual Politics: Radical Theory and Practice in the Gay Movement." Pp. 163–82 in *Beyond Marxism?,* edited by J. Allen and P. Patton. Sydney: Intervention.

Sartre, Jean-Paul. 1963. *The Problem of Method.* London: Methuen.

———. 1976. *Critique of Dialectical Reason.* London: New Left Books.

Segal, Lynne. 1990. *Slow Motion: Changing Masculinities, Changing Men.* London: Virago.

Stacey, Judith and Barrie Thorne. 1985. "The Missing Feminist Revolution in Sociology." *Social Problems* 32:301–16.

Stein, Edward, ed. 1990. *Forms of Desire: Sexual Orientation and the Social Constructionist Controversy.* New York: Garland.

Thomas, William I. and Florian Znaniecki. 1927. *The Polish Peasant in Europe and America.* New York: Knopf.

Thorne, Barrie. Forthcoming. *Gender Play: Girls and Boys in School.* New Brunswick: Rutgers University Press.

Tolson, Andrew. 1977. *The Limits of Masculinity.* London: Tavistock.

Troiden, Richard R. 1989. "The Formation of Homosexual Identities." *Journal of Homosexuality* 17:43–73.

Turner, Charles F. 1989. "Research on Sexual Behaviors that Transmit HIV: Progress and Problems." *AIDS* 3 (Supplement I):S63–S69.

Walby, Sylvia. 1989. "Theorising Patriarchy." *Sociology* 23:213–34.

Waldby, Cathy, Susan Kippax, and June Crawford. 1990. "Theory in the Bedroom: A Report from the Macquarie University AIDS and Heterosexuality Project." *Australian Journal of Social Issues* 25:177–85.

Walker, J. C. 1988. *Louts and Legends: Male Youth Culture in an Inner-City School.* Sydney: Allen and Unwin.

Weeks, Jeffrey. 1986. *Sexuality.* London: Horwood and Tavistock.

Weinberg, George H. 1973. *Society and the Healthy Homosexual.* New York: Anchor.

West, Candace and Don H. Zimmerman. 1987. "Doing Gender." *Gender & Society* 1:125–51.

9 The Missing Feminist Revolution in Sociology*

JUDITH STACEY
University of California, Davis

BARRIE THORNE
Michigan State University

Feminists have made important contributions to sociology, but we have yet to transform the basic conceptual frameworks of the field. A comparison of sociology with anthropology, history, and literature—disciplines which have been more deeply transformed—suggests factors that may facilitate or inhibit feminist paradigm shifts. The traditional subject matter of sociology fell into a co-optable middle ground, neither as thoroughly male centered as in history or literature, nor as deeply gendered as in anthropology. In addition, feminist perspectives have been contained in sociology by functionalist conceptualizations of gender, by the inclusion of gender as a variable rather than as a theoretical category, and by being ghettoized, especially in Marxist sociology. Feminist rethinking is also affected by under-lying epistemologies (proceeding more rapidly in fields based on interpretive rather than positivist understanding), and by the status and nature of theory within a discipline.

A decade ago feminist sociologists shared with our counterparts in other disciplines an optimistic vision about the intellectual revolution a feminist perspective promised to bring to all our fields. As Arlene Daniels (1975:349) proclaimed in her contribution to *Another Voice:*

> . . . the women's movement contributes far more to sociology than a pass-ing interest would. The development of a feminist perspective in sociology offers an important contribution to the sociology of knowledge. And through this contribution, we are forced to rethink the structure and organization

of sociological theory in all the traditional fields of theory and empirical research.

By now there has been an extraordinary amount of sociological work on gender. It is likely that more gender-sensitive research has been "main-streamed" in sociological periodicals and conferences than in those of most other disciplines. Feminists can point with pride to important, even cutting-edge contributions such work has made to our understanding of society. Feminist perspectives have helped correct androcentric biases in established lines of work and have inspired much better research in the study, for example, of organizations,[1] occupations (e.g., Epstein, 1981; Glenn, in press; Kahn-Hut et al., 1982), criminology (Leonard, 1982; Smart, 1977), deviance (Millman, 1975; Piven and Cloward, 1979), health (Scully, 1980), and stratification (Acker, 1980; Blumberg, 1978). Feminist sociologists have helped revitalize the study of mothering (e.g., Bernard, 1974; Chodorow, 1978), housework (Berk, 1980; Glazer-Malbin, 1976), rape (Holmstrom and Burgess, 1978; Russell, 1982), contraception (Luker, 1975), marriage (Bernard, 1982), divorce (Weitzman, 1981), widowhood (Lopata, 1973), and the life cycle (Giele, 1980; Rossi, 1980)—topics which previously had been devalued or studied in distorted ways. And by attending to women's experiences, feminists have opened new topics for research, such as sexual harrassment (McKinnon, 1979), wife battering (Breines and Gordon, 1983; Dobash and Dobash, 1979), compulsory heterosexuality (March, 1982; Rich, 1980), lesbian communities (Krieger, 1982), the feminization of poverty (Pearce, 1979), and the sociology of childbirth (Rothman, 1982). Feminists have also provided new insight into relationships between family and work institutions (Voydanoff, 1983), and women's and men's different experiences of being fat (Millman, 1980), of conversation (West and Zimmerman, 1981), of intimacy (Rubin, 1983), and of emotions like anger and love (Hochschild, 1983).

These are impressive achievements. And yet, we find that the impact of feminist thought on sociology, and the current relationship between femi-nism and the discipline as a whole, seem to fall short when measured against the optimistic vision of a decade ago. Peggy McIntosh (1983; also see Tetreault, in press) has identified several stages in feminist transformations of knowledge. The initial period is one of filling in gaps—correcting sexist biases and creating new topics out of women's experiences. Over time, however, feminists discover that many gaps were there for a reason, i.e., that existing paradigms systematically ignore or erase the significance of women's experiences and the organization of gender. This discovery, McIntosh suggests, leads feminists to rethink the basic conceptual and theoretical frameworks of their respective fields.

Feminists have done extensive and extremely valuable work in uncovering and filling gaps in sociological knowledge. This work has demonstrated systematic flaws in traditional sociological theory and method. However, feminist sociologists—especially when compared with our counterparts in anthropology, history, and literature—have been less successful in moving to the next stage of reconstructing basic paradigms of the discipline.[2] Other fields, notably psychology, political science, and economics, have also resisted feminist transformation.

The process of paradigm shifting, by which we mean changes in the orienting assumptions and conceptual frameworks which are basic to a discipline,[3] involves two separable dimensions: (1) the transformation of existing conceptual frameworks; and (2) the acceptance of those transformations by others in the field. As we discuss later, of all the disciplines, feminist anthropology has been the most successful in both of these dimensions. Feminists in history and literary criticism have accomplished significant conceptual transformations, but have been far less successful than feminist anthropologists in influencing mainstream work in their fields.

Feminist sociology, however, seems to have been both co-opted and ghettoized, while the discipline as a whole and its dominant paradigms have proceeded relatively unchanged. Sociological teaching and professional life reflect this ambiguous relationship to feminism. Courses on "sex roles," gender, and women abound. But rare are the courses on sociological theory or methodology that even include feminist literature, let alone those that attempt to use feminist questions to rethink sociological canons. When we design courses in the sociology of gender or especially in feminist theory, we find ourselves assigning very little work by sociologists, while our feminist colleagues who teach comparable courses in history or anthropology are comfortable assigning readings primarily from within their own disciplines. Likewise, sociological work is underrepresented in *Feminist Studies* and in *Signs*—feminist journals which emphasize theory.

Not everyone shares our belief that a feminist revolution in sociology—a revolution we once anticipated and still desire—has been averted or forestalled. But this has been our persistent observation, and one we seek to understand. This paper is part of an extended dialogue, inviting reflection across disciplines on the process of feminist transformations of knowledge. We begin by comparing feminist transformations in anthropology, history, and literature—the fields in which we believe the most impressive feminist conceptual shifts have occurred. We hope to mitigate some of the difficulties of analyzing a "negative case" by examining the nature and effects of feminist reconstruction in comparatively successful cases. How would we recognize a feminist revolution in sociology if one had occurred, and how can we identify factors that cause the absence of such a revolution? An analysis of the comparative success of feminist rethinking in other disciplines helps to identify the nature of feminist paradigm shifts, and it provides insight into factors that facilitate or inhibit such shifts.

Next we examine sociology, a discipline in which strategies for transforming knowledge similar to the ones employed by feminists in anthropology, history, and literature have had more contradictory and, we believe, less radical effects. Here we attempt to identify some of the obstacles that confront sociologists who are trying to effect basic conceptual changes in the discipline. Our comparison of disciplines suggests that feminist transformation may be facilitated, or impeded, by the traditional subject matter of a given field of inquiry, by its underlying epistemologies, and by the status and nature of theory within each discipline, and within feminist thought.

PUTTING WOMEN AT THE CENTER
OF KNOWLEDGE: A COMPARISON OF DISCIPLINES

Feminist scholars begin by placing women at the center, as subjects of inquiry and as active agents in the gathering of knowledge. This strategy makes women's experiences visible, reveals the sexist biases and tacitly male assumptions of traditional knowledge, and (as we will explain later) opens the way to gendered understanding. This basic feminist strategy has been notably successful in history, literature, and anthropology.

History

Writing in 1979, historian Nancy Schrom Dye (1979:28) made a claim similar to the statement by Arlene Daniels with which we began:

> By restoring women to the historical narrative and by uncovering women's unique experiences in the past, women's history revolutionizes the scope of historical inquiry.

Placing women at the center of historical inquiry has (for those aware of this work) begun to transform the grounding of the discipline as a whole. Social history, which attends to the lives of humble people such as peasants and workers, opened the way for the challenge women's history has made to the discipline. As the late Joan Kelly (1977) pointed out in her article, "Did Women Have a Renaissance?", starting analysis with women's experiences has helped challenge the central assumption that history is primarily about politics, public policy, and famous individuals. This, in turn, has led to rethinking historical periodization itself. Historical turning points are not necessarily the same for women as for men; women's status, for example, did not improve during the Renaissance.

Centering on women, which necessitates a focus on everyday life and the "private" sphere, has helped fuel the ascendance of social history in the discipline. In fact, Dye suggests that the discipline's traditional emphasis on politics and public life may have been more a consequence than a cause of history's having been, until recently, so profoundly male-centered. The extreme sex segregation of their social class and period permitted the 19th century male founders of history as an academic discipline in the West to be particularly ignorant of female culture and experience.

Feminist historians have begun to reconceptualize basic understandings of social class and politics by questioning the assumed division between public and private life. For example, in a study of family and community life in the 19th century in New York state, Mary Ryan (1981) has analyzed the relationship between changing gender and family organization and the making of the U.S. middle class. Her analysis suggests the centrality of gender to class formation and the nature of "the political."

Literature

Literature, like history, has almost totally excluded women from its traditions of study. As in history, a tacitly male, white, and class-privileged universe has been represented as *the* universe worth studying, in this case in the form of traditional literary canons, which deemed certain writers, texts, and genres as central, and which included few, if any, women writers. Feminists have recovered and re-evaluated the work of such writers as Kate Chopin and Zora Neale Hurston, and the value of sources such as diaries and letters. This process of recovery has raised the question of why women (as well as working-class and Black) writers were omitted from literary canons in the first place.

Although presented as absolute, literary canons are socially constructed and historically changing, and feminist literary criticism has led to inquiries into the process by which canons were formed and transmitted. Paul Lauter (1983), for example, traced the historical development of the canon of American literature. He found that the exclusion of Blacks, white women, and all working-class writers consolidated in the 1920s with the professionalization of the teaching of literature (controlled by a small group of elite white men) and the consolidation of formalist critical traditions and conventions of periodicization, which further narrowed the canon. For example, emphasis on "Puritanism" as a founding period exaggerated the significance of a New England, predominantly male theocratic tradition.

In questioning literary canons and the relations of inequality they enshrine, feminists have developed new interpretive strategies which emphasize the effects of gender on literary creation. For example, in *The Madwoman in the Attic* Sandra Gilbert and Susan Gubar (1979) explore the effects of patriarchal literary traditions on the work of 19th century women writers. They argue that the "anxiety of authorship" expressed by Emily Dickinson, George Eliot, and the Brontës is grounded in the historic denial of literary creation to women. Feminists have also begun to rethink aesthetic standards which have diminished the value of women's experiences and writing. Like their colleagues in history, feminist literary critics have begun to reshape their discipline in fundamental ways.[4]

The overwhelmingly male definitions of traditional history and literature helped provoke feminist transformation. The act of starting with women's experiences had dramatic analytical consequences because the traditional fields were so thoroughly male-centered, and because women were clearly there to be discovered and valued as participants in history, and as writers and readers. These two fields have made noteworthy progress on the first dimension of successful paradigm shifting—the transformation of core theoretical assumptions. But, it should be emphasized, the efforts of feminist historians and literary critics to influence mainstream work in their disciplines have met with considerable indifference and hostility.

Anthropology

Feminist gains in anthropology are impressive in both dimensions of paradigm shifting. We believe that the transformation of the core domain assumptions of the discipline has been more radical than in any other field. And these conceptual breakthroughs have achieved greater acceptance by many of the prominent scholars in the field.

These exemplary gains seem to have a source different from those made by feminist historians and literary critics. In contrast with the thoroughly male-centered fields of literature and history, there was a significant female imprint on the anthropological pavements from the discipline's earliest days. Thus Carol McCormack (1981) titled her contribution to *Men's Studies Modified* (an anthology that assesses the impact of feminism on the disciplines), "Anthropology—A Discipline with a Legacy."[5]

The legacy is twofold. From the beginning, there have been more women in the ranks of prominent anthropologists than in the other social sciences. In addition, the favored subject matter of anthropology—small, pre-literate societies where kinship is central to all of social life—has always encouraged anthropologists, even those concerned with law, religion, politics, and the economy, to attend to the sexual division of labor and structural and symbolic dimensions of gender relationships. As Anna Tsing and Sylvia Yanagisako (1983:511) put it: "the centrality of kinship in anthropological inquiry places the feminist re-examination of gender at the heart of the discipline." While there were deep male biases that led to androcentric theories, traditional anthropology, more than any other social science, took gender centrally into account. Perhaps that is why our feminist colleagues in anthropology appear less alienated from their discipline than those in any other field.[6]

Although traditional anthropology offered feminists a rich legacy, there too the strategy of placing women at the center of inquiry has elicited dramatic conceptual shifts. Perhaps the best example is the feminist discourse on the "Man the Hunter" thesis of human evolution. The female-centered strategy led initially to the development of a counter-thesis of "Woman-the-Gatherer," an important compensatory corrective that reclaimed for women an active, and possibly dominant role in the development of human intelligence and culture (Slocum, 1975; Tanner and Zihlman, 1976). Now the discussion has reached a more sophisticated, nuanced stage. Feminist anthropologists have suggested that the myth that "Man the Hunter" rather than "Woman the Gatherer" as the central cultural figure is one shared by members of contemporary foraging-hunting societies as well (Collier and Rosaldo, 1981).

This recognition—involving close attention to ideologies of gender in the context of social structure—is an example of the maturation of feminist thought from being female-centered to developing what we would call a more fully "gendered" understanding of all aspects of human culture and relationships. Such "gendered knowledge" has involved profound paradigm shifts within anthropology, such as the questioning of the division between public and domestic life and of conventional methods of categorizing pre-state societies.[7] Anthropology seems to provide the best example of a discipline that is benefitting from a feminist "revolution." Anthropologists have begun to move beyond the woman-centered strategy to decipher the gendered basis of all of social and cultural life, tracing the significance of gender organization and relations in all institutions and in shaping men's as well as women's lives.

THE CONTAINMENT OF
FEMINISM WITHIN SOCIOLOGY

Within sociology the feminist strategy of putting women at the center of knowledge has yielded valuable new insights and redirections of inquiry, as we detailed in the introduction. But we believe the results have been more contradictory and less successful, on the whole, than in anthropology, history, or literature. Specific subfields have been challenged, and many new topics added, but there has been less rethinking of basic conceptual frameworks. This may be due, in part, to the traditional subject matter of sociology, which was neither as gender-sensitive as in anthropology nor as dramatically male-centered as in history or literature.

In contrast with history and literature, the discipline of sociology was not organized around formal canons or narrowing definitions (e.g., history defined in terms of the politically powerful) which clearly excluded entire groups. Margaret Andersen (1983) and Helen Roberts (1981b) have each noted that the "bedrock" assumptions of the field commit sociologists, at least *in theory*, to understanding all institutions and the experiences of their members, which in turn produces beneficial potential for including women in their analyses. *In practice*, however, the standpoints of the privileged (western, white, upper-middle class, heterosexual men) infuse traditional sociological knowledge.

In traditional sociology, sexual divisions of labor and gender-related issues were considered primarily in the subfields of family, demography, and community studies, where the presence of women could not be ignored. However, sociologists of occupations, politics, law, religion, formal organizations, and even social stratification and social movements virtually ignored women; they tacitly or explicitly assumed male experience without including gender as a category of analysis. The fact that gender was explicitly present in a few subfields—albeit present in distorted, androcentric ways—probably contributed to the containment of feminism within sociology; and note that the presence of *women,* not men, made gender a visible issue. Because the subject matter of traditional sociology was neither totally male-centered nor basically gender-sensitive, it fell into a co-optable middle ground.

Over a decade ago feminist sociologists began to raise fresh questions about gender and social life, but our queries have been co-opted in several basic ways. We are glossing enormous complexity by sketching these patterns of co-optation, and even by speaking of sociology as a discipline. Sociology is large and fragmented: since the 1960s, when functionalism was undermined as the dominant paradigm, sociology has been a field without a center (Becker, 1979). This fragmentation suggests that a unitary "feminist revolution" is unlikely; the conceptual transformations we might hope for would have to be multiple and diverse. Feminist transformations of the paradigms of sociology have been contained in three major ways: by the limiting assumptions of functionalist conceptualizations of gender, by the inclusion of gender as a variable rather than as a central theoretical concept, and by the ghettoization of feminist insights, especially within Marxist sociology.

Functionalist Co-optation

In the United States the sociological study of gender originated in functionalist family sociology and has been deeply shaped by the concepts developed by Talcott Parsons. Parsons (Parsons and Bales, 1955) translated gender divisions into the (female) "expressive role" and the (male) "instrumental role" within the traditional nuclear family. His analysis of the family (and hence, of gender) emphasized the function of "socialization," understood as integral to maintaining a smoothly functioning social order. This way of casting the subject matter has left a lasting imprint on the sociology of gender, shaping basic concepts (e.g., the language of "sex roles") and assumptions (for example, that gender is more central to the family than to other institutions, and that gender arrangements function primarily to insure social maintenance and reproduction).

Early on, contemporary feminists recognized the influence and limitations of functionalism as a framework for understanding gender. Several of the founding works of the contemporary women's movement criticized Parsons for what Betty Friedan (1963) called "the functionalist freeze," which tacitly legitimized women's subordination and their encapsulation within the family. Feminist sociologists have cleared away many of Parsons' blind spots by attending to gender in work and politics, as well as in families, and by emphasizing gender hierarchies. Yet functionalism has continued to exert a significant and, we believe, inhibiting effect on the development of feminist sociology.

Much of feminist sociology is cast in the language of roles ("sex roles," "the male role," "the female role") and emphasizes the process of "sex role socialization." This approach to the analysis of gender retains its functionalist roots, emphasizing consensus, stability, and continuity (Thorne, 1978). The notion of "role" focuses attention more on individuals than on social structure, and implies that "the female role" and "the male role" are complementary (i.e., separate or different but equal). The terms are depoliticizing; they strip experience from its historical and political context and neglect questions of power and conflict. It is significant that sociologists do not speak of "class roles" or "race roles." Functionalist assumptions linger more deeply in sociological conceptualizations of gender than of other forms of inequality. These functionalist assumptions have posed significant obstacles to feminist rethinking of basic orienting assumptions within sociology.

Gender as a Variable

Within the last decade an increasing number of empirical sociological studies have included attention to gender. For those working in more quantitative research traditions where problems are conceptualized in terms of variables, gender, understood as the division between women and men, has been relatively easy to include. Whether one is a man or a woman, after all, is highly visible; as it is socially constructed, the division encompasses the entire population and sorts neatly into a dichotomy.

A growing number of surveys (e.g., research on status attainment) now include gender (as well as factors like race, education, and income) as a variable, as do experimental studies (e.g., of processes of attribution). Here, as in other research traditions, sensitivity to gender has resulted in important revisionist work. For example, in status attainment research, measures of occupational prestige and socioeconomic position have been found to account more adequately for data about men—from whom the measures were derived—than for data about women (see review in Acker, 1980). Feminist sociologists working in this tradition have pursued fresh topics and developed new measures (e.g., to assess the occupational status of housewives [Bose, 1980]) suggested by attention to women's lives. The use of quantitative methods has provided information crucial to documenting problems such as gender segmentation of the labor force and the feminization of poverty (see literature reviewed in Ferber, 1982).

Much of this literature, however, is unreflective about the nature of gender as a social category. Gender is assumed to be a property of individuals and is conceptualized in terms of sex difference, rather than as a principle of social organization. Reducing social life to a series of measurable variables diminishes the sense of the whole that is crucial to theoretical understanding of social, including gender, relationships. The use of gender as a variable, rather than as a basic theoretical category, is a prime example of the co-optation of feminist perspectives.

The Containment of Feminism
Within Marxist Sociology

The development of feminist sociology has been contained not only by inadequate conceptualizations of gender, but also by ghettoization within dominant sociological traditions. Ghettoization is especially dramatic, and perhaps surprising, within Marxist sociology, where feminist theorizing has flourished, but apart from and with little influence on the "mainstream."

The relationship between feminism and Marxism is more complex and contradictory than the relationship of feminism to other sociological paradigms. On the one hand, feminist theory maintains its traditional status within Marxism as a continuation of the "Woman Question." On the other hand, feminists have generated a body of "Marxist-Feminist" theory that operates primarily outside "mainstream" Marxist discourse in the social sciences.

It can be argued that Marxist sociology has been even less affected by feminist thought than have more mainstream bodies of sociological theory. Analysis of sex and gender is not easily absorbed within a Marxist conceptual framework. The central Marxist categories which focus on production, labor, and class—as defined through men's relationship to production and labor—are more obviously androcentric than categories like "roles" or "social system."

It is possible, of course, to study women in traditional Marxist terms as is evident in the literature and debate about "domestic labor" and in the significant renaissance of interest in women's labor force participation (see literature reviewed in J. Smith, 1982; Sokoloff, 1980; and see Vogel, 1984). But such analyses, at their best, provide only partial understanding of women or of our relationships to men. And they do little to challenge or revise the epistemological or even conceptual foundations of Marxist thought.

On the positive side, Marxism has been subjected to full-scale critical scrutiny by feminists who have made a self-conscious, sustained attempt to develop a Marxist-Feminist theoretical paradigm that augments the theoretical effectiveness of both perspectives without subordinating one to the other (e.g., Eisenstein, 1979; Hartmann, 1981; Kuhn and Wolpe, 1978). In part this has happened because Marxism, a critical paradigm, tends to incite critical reflection on its own conceptual system. Thus feminists who work within a Marxist tradition begin with a critical stance as well as with a strong commitment to theoretical knowledge. More importantly, Marxist-Feminist work emerged in a political context that encouraged theoretical effort. Socialist-feminists who participated in the development of an autonomous women's movement sought to develop a relatively autonomous body of theory as a guide to political practice.

Somewhat ironically, however, this has allowed the ghettoization of the "Woman Question" tradition to continue, now in the form of "hyphen" literature.[8] Marxist-Feminists have succeeded in developing entirely autonomous and almost exclusively female institutions, conferences, and publications. Resistance of many Marxists to engage with this increasingly sophisticated body of literature has left the rest of contemporary Marxist thought remarkably untransformed. For example, Immanuel Wallerstein's (1979) influential book, *The Capitalist World Economy,* ignores sexual divisions of labor and is uninformed even by feminist critiques of sexist language. Using Marxist definitions of social class, Erik Wright and his colleagues (Wright, Costello, Hachen, and Sprague, 1982) recently reported an empirical finding that "a sizable majority of the U.S. working class is composed of women and minorities." Yet they pursue none of the implications this suggests for rethinking Marxist theories of class to take more specific account of race and gender.

INTERPRETIVE VS. POSITIVIST KNOWLEDGE

Having briefly discussed the containment of feminist thinking within sociology, we return to the comparative question: What are the obstacles to feminist transformation within different disciplines? In addition to its traditional subject matter and conceptual frameworks, the basic epistemology of a discipline may affect its congeniality or resistance to feminist rethinking.

We have observed that feminist thinking has made the most headway in fields (anthropology, literature, and history) with strong traditions of interpretive understanding. In contrast, fields more deeply anchored in positivist epistemologies—sociology, psychology, political science (excepting political theory), and economics—have posed more obstacles to feminist transformation.[9]

Why has feminist thinking been more successful in revamping interpretive rather than positivist traditions? For one thing, interpretive approaches are more reflexive about the circumstances in which knowledge is developed. They are thus more open to the question: What are the effects of the social and political circumstances in which knowledge is created and received? Feminists modify this question to ask: What are the effects of the gender of the researcher, the audience, or those studied or written about? Positivist knowledge, in contrast, is phrased in abstract, universal terms. It claims to be "objective" and "unrelated to a particular position or a particular sex as its source and standpoint" (Smith, 1978:283).

Values and interests *do,* of course, infuse positivist knowledge, as critics of positivism long have argued. Max Weber initiated a line of analysis, continued by critical theorists like Jürgen Habermas, which connects positivist science to processes of rationalization and control in industrial society. Specifically, Habermas (1971) argues that the attitude of technical and instrumental rationality, which is at the core of positivist social science, serves dominant groups' interests in mastery and control.

Feminists have built upon this critique to argue that positivist knowledge serves the interests not only of dominant social classes (the focus of critical theorists), but also the interests of men, the dominant gender. Evelyn Fox Keller (1982; 1983), Dorothy Smith (1978; 1979), and Nancy Hartsock (1983a) have each developed theories connecting masculine standpoints and interests to the structure of knowledge. They argue that the sexual division of labor and male dominance produce fundamental differences in the lives and experiences of women and men, with important consequences for knowledge. Using feminist revisions of psychoanalytic theories of development, Keller (1982; 1983) and Hartsock (1983a) suggest that rationality divorced from feelings, and sharp separation between the knower and the known—an objectifying stance basic to positivist social science—may be founded in the organization of gender. This stance is characteristic of a rigidly autonomous personality that, for reasons of social organization and family structure, is more often found among men than women. "To what extent," Keller (1983:18) asks, "does the disjunction of subject and object carry an intrinsic implication of control and power?"

Feminist theorists, among others, are reconsidering the relationship between knower and known to develop a method of inquiry that will preserve the presence of the subject as an actor and experiencer. This approach, as

Dorothy Smith (1979) has theorized it, embodies "the standpoint of women," a standpoint rooted in the production and maintenance activities of everyday life. Nancy Hartsock (1983a) proposes the development of "a feminist standpoint," an achieved and critical perspective on those activities. By preserving the agency of female subjects, feminist epistemological theory promises significant contributions to the hermeneutic and neo-Marxist critiques of positivist social science. This critique may help to clarify the barriers to feminist transformation of knowledge posed by the positivist tradition.

THE STATE OF FEMINIST THEORY

Not all of the barriers to feminist reconstruction stand within the disciplines. Feminist theory is a fledgling endeavor; perhaps greater maturation is necessary before sociology can reap the full intellectual harvest it promises. It is unsurprising, but somewhat ironic, that thus far the major achievements of feminist theory have been grounded in analyses of family, kinship, and "domestic" relationships. Feminist theorists make the legitimate claim that analyses of the far-from "private" sphere have important theoretical implications for all other arenas of social life, but we have only begun to reconceptualize conventionally-defined political or economic relationships such as the nature of the state, revolutions, social class, or power.[10] That is, we have only recently begun the work of developing knowledge that is "gendered" rather than androcentric or largely limited to the institutions associated with women.

We believe that this underdevelopment of feminist theory has more serious repercussions in sociology than it does in the fields where feminist thought has made more radical progress. This is due to the paradoxical status of theory in sociology. On the one hand, much mainstream sociological work is atheoretical. The aversion to developing theory, which is present among many sociologists, is certainly part of the problem. Although gender may be readily incorporated as a variable, or as a source of research topics, this does little to advance theoretical reconstruction. On the other hand, the subject matter of most sociological inquiry may make the adequacy of one's theoretical perspective especially important. Complex contemporary societies cannot be grasped, or even studied, whole. At the same time, the potential sources of accessible data are overwhelming. Yet a holistic view gives greater analytical significance to description.

Perhaps that is another reason why anthropology—where the favored subjects of inquiry are small societies which allow one to retain a sense of the whole (e.g., to conceptualize and later reconsider a public-domestic dichotomy)—has been such a fruitful site for feminist scholarship. Because anthropologists have a more holistic (and gendered) view of society, they have been in a better position than sociologists to question overall assumptions, such as the division between public and private (Rosaldo, 1980; Tsing and Yanagisako, 1983). Sociologists have yet to fully problematize the "public/domestic" division, which separates the study of the family from the study of occupations, the labor force, and politics.

In history as in anthropology, empirical depth can be a profound theoretical statement. As E. P. Thompson (1979) notes, close historical attention to the complex process and details of social change can generate analytical concepts sufficiently elastic to capture the irregularities and particularities of patterns of human experience. Thompson contrasts empirical depth with empiricism, which fetishizes facts as the only valid objects of knowledge.

However, in most sociological work, "thick description" will not suffice.[11] This might have been less true had more feminist sociologists worked within the tradition of ethnography and community studies, but, for reasons unclear to us, few feminists are doing such work, and those few are mostly anthropologists (e.g., Stack, 1976; Whitehead, 1976). More conscious and developed theory may be necessary to produce equally compelling treatments of the complex, contemporary social world. Generally sociologists study only a part, and often a small part, of that world. We need theory to help us situate the part in the whole.

CONCLUSION

We wrote this paper in a spirit of invitation, rather than final statement. Our starting point, and immediate concern, is the state of feminist thinking within sociology. But this concern has taken us to a larger set of questions that deserve fuller discussion. With over a decade of work behind us, what is the relative impact of feminist theory on the construction of knowledge in different disciplines? And how have different disciplines contributed to feminist theory? We hope this essay will provide further discussion of these questions.

Questions like these rightfully take us across disciplines; feminist scholarship has always had a healthy disrespect for boundaries, and interdisciplinary work has provided critical perspectives on more narrowly defined fields of inquiry. This is an important corrective for the way we have cast our argument. By focusing on sociology as if it were a bounded endeavor, we have given the false impression that feminist sociologists, historians, or anthropologists mine in separate disciplinary tunnels. Comparison of feminist work in different disciplines must be sensitive to effects of disciplinary training, but it also should more fully probe our shared terrain.

Our analysis has emphasized the organization of knowledge and methods of inquiry of different disciplines. Perhaps ironically, we have neglected the sociological dimensions of this question. Feminist transformations of knowledge are surely affected by factors such as the demographic composition of a given discipline, its internal organization and structure of opportunities, the availability and forms of research funding, and the relation of the discipline to the making of public policy.

We want to emphasize another, crucial corrective. A feminist critique of knowledge is not the only missing revolution in sociology, nor could it, by itself, produce an adequate epistemology. Scholars (e.g., Ladner, 1973; Rich, 1980; Wolf, 1982) have also begun to analyze the effects on the discipline of the traditional erasure and distortion of the experiences of other subordinated groups—Blacks, Chicana/os, Native Americans, Asian-Americans, homosexuals, working-class people, the peoples of the Third World—half of whom are women. Our focus on gender was necessary to analyze the limitations of feminist efforts to transform sociology, but it may have given the impression that gender is *the* central category of analysis. Feminist theory has itself been charged, justifiably we believe, with falsely universalizing the category of "woman." Too often the experience of white, middle-class, heterosexual, Euro-American women has served as the basis for analyses that seek to generalize about the experience of WOMAN.[12] The inclusive knowledge we seek would as equally attend to race, class, and sexuality as to gender. The paradigm shifts we hope for are much broader, and more complex, than we have implied.

Feminists have begun to seek a more complicated understanding of both unity and diversity among women, and among men. We have also begun to recognize some of the dilemmas that attend our analytic stance. Central to feminist scholarship is belief in the deep importance of gender, not only for understanding areas specific to the experiences of women, such as mothering or rape, but also for understanding class structure, the state, social revolutions, or militarism—phenomena which are also shaped by the organization of gender, although this point has been obscured by prior conceptualizations. Yet in our efforts to restore agency to women and to develop knowledge sensitive to gender, sexuality, race, and class, feminists often have employed frameworks that essentialize differences rather than understanding that differences are socially constructed and historically changing. Thus much feminist work has unintentionally reinforced the dichotomizing ideologies of contemporary Western culture. The challenge to feminist theory has been succinctly described by feminist scientist and theorist, Evelyn Fox Keller (1982:593–94):

> . . . the task of a feminist theoretic in science is twofold: to distinguish that which is parochial from that which is universal in the scientific impulse, reclaiming for women what has historically been denied to them; and to legitimate those elements of scientific culture that have been denied precisely because they are defined as female.

Thus far, feminist tools have worked better to criticize than to reconstruct most bodies of theoretical knowledge. It is time, we believe, to follow the lead of our colleagues in anthropology who have begun to reconstruct the core theoretical frameworks and conceptual systems in their field. Feminist sociologists have a crucial role to play in this project, because sociological theory has significance far beyond our disciplinary borders. Many "applied" fields like speech communication, criminology, education, and social work rely upon sociological frameworks. And feminist scholars in literature, history, philosophy, and other fields turn frequently to sociology and anthropology either to organize and interpret their data or to situate abstract ideas. If we can effect a feminist revolution in sociology, the results will be far-reaching indeed.

NOTES

* The two authors contributed equally to this paper, which we presented at the 1984 annual meetings of the American Sociological Association, San Antonio, Texas. Our thinking was enhanced by discussions following presentations at the Bay Area Faculty Women's Research Forum, and at the Universities of California, Berkeley and Santa Cruz; Stanford University; and Carleton College. We would like to thank the following people who provided critical written comments on earlier drafts: Margaret Andersen, Jane Atkinson, Howard Becker, Nancy Chodorow, Arlene Daniels, Cathy Davidson, Jane Flax, Nona Glazer, Gary Hamilton, Barbara Laslett, Lyn Lofland, Sherry Ortner, Karen Paige, Beverly Purrington, Shula Reinharz, Dorothy Smith, Malcolm Spector, Avril Thorne, Gaye Tuchman, and Candace West. Correspondence to: Thorne, Department of Sociology, Michigan State University, East Lansing, MI 48824.

1. For example, in *Men and Women of the Corporation,* Rosabeth Kanter (1977) showed that the sociology of organizations was tacitly skewed towards male experience. By analyzing women's experiences as secretaries, wives, and tokens in occupations where men predominate, she demonstrated the centrality of gender in the structure of formal organizations.

2. Our overall argument is that paradigm-shifting has proceeded more slowly in sociology than in some other fields. But we want to emphasize that feminist sociological work *does* provide promising leads for theoretical reconstruction. To give two examples: feminist work in psychoanalytic sociology, especially by Nancy Chodorow (1978) and by Jessica Benjamin (1980), provides transformative theoretical insight into relations between the organization of gender and personality formation. And feminist critiques of theories of social stratification (e.g., Acker, 1980; Milkman, 1982) have suggested leads for developing a historically anchored, gendered theory of social class.

3. The general notion of paradigm is developed by Thomas Kuhn (1964) in *The Structure of Scientific Revolutions.* Margaret Masterman (1970) notes that Kuhn uses "paradigm" in at least 21 different ways. Our use of the term is also very flexible. We generally equate paradigm with the basic conceptual frameworks and orienting assumptions of a body of knowledge.

4. For a sampling of the issues involved in feminist literary criticism see Abel (1982); Kolodny (1980); and B. Smith (1982).

5. The titles of the other essays in *Men's Studies Modified* (Spender, 1981) are much less upbeat, for example, "Some of the Boys Won't Play Anymore: The Impact of Feminism on Sociology" (by Helen Roberts); "Toward the Emasculation of Political Science: The Impact of Feminism" (by Joni Lovenduski); "Psychology and Feminism—If You Can't Beat Them, Join Them" (by Beverly M. Walker); and "The Oldest, the Most Established, the Most Quantitative

of the Social Sciences—and the Most Dominated by Men: The Impact of Feminism on Economics" (by Marianne A. Ferber and Michelle L. Teiman).

6. Jane Monnig Atkinson's (1982) recent review essay offers a good example. The citations, which refer to articles in mainstream anthropology journals, convey the legitimacy of feminist anthropology, and her writing exudes a positive feeling about the relationship between feminism and the discipline. Similarly, anthropologists who attended a 1982 conference on Feminism and Kinship Theory "stressed the relevance of the analysis of gender for broad areas of anthropological investigation" and saw the promise of feminist rethinking of the discipline as its ability to "transform the apparently known into an area of exciting new inquiry" (Tsing and Yanagisako, 1983:511).

7. The culture-bound nature of public/private dichotomies is analyzed in Rosaldo (1980) and in Collier, Rosaldo, and Yanagisako (1982). In work that builds upon her earlier collaboration with the late Michelle Rosaldo, Jane Collier is developing a framework for analyzing and classifying systems of inequality in pre-state societies that rejects traditional kinship or economic categories in favor of brideservice/bridewealth systems of marital exchange.

8. The term "hyphen literature" refers to the hyphen in "Marxist-feminism" or "socialist-feminism": see Petchesky (1979).

9. Various feminists have lamented their slow progress in transforming the more positivist disciplines; for psychology, see Sherif (1979); Walker (1981); and Wine (1982); for political science see Keohane (1983) and Vickers (1982). It is not by chance that feminist methodological critiques, emphasizing alternatives to positivism, emerged in psychology and sociology, for example, Reinharz (1981); Reinharz, Bombyk, and Wright (1983); Cook and Fonow (forthcoming); and Roberts (1981a).

As Candace West has aptly noted, the hegemony of positivism within sociology is reflected in the naming of journals. Those with a qualitative or theoretical emphasis bear explicit names (e.g., *Qualitative Sociology, Theory and Society*), but journals with a quantitative and methodological focus, like *American Sociological Review,* more often have general names.

10. For feminist analyses of the state, see Diamond (1983) and Ortner (1978); on revolutions, Stacey (1983); on militarism, Enloe (1983) and Ruddick (1983); on gender and social class, see Rapp (1982) and Ryan (1981); on power, see Hartsock (1983b).

11. Clifford Geertz (1973) uses the term "thick description" to characterize the knowledge of ethnographic anthropology. His analysis echoes E. P. Thompson's point about interpretive knowledge being close to the ground and honed by the case at hand.

12. For analyses of racist bias in feminist writings, see hooks (1981); Simons (1979); and Zinn (1982). On heterosexual bias, see Rich (1980).

REFERENCES

Abel, Elizabeth. 1982. *Writing and Sexual Difference.* Chicago: University of Chicago Press.

Acker, Joan. 1980. "Women and stratification: a review of recent literature." *Contemporary Sociology* 9:25–29.

Andersen, Margaret L. 1983. "Thinking about women and rethinking sociology." Working Paper Series, Wellesley College Center for Research on Women.

Atkinson, Jane Monnig. 1982. "Review essay: anthropology." *Signs* 8:232–58.

Becker, Howard S. 1979. "What's happening to sociology?" *Society* 15,5:19–24.

Benjamin, Jessica. 1980. "The bonds of love: rational violence and erotic domination." *Feminist Studies* 6:144–74.

Berk, Sarah Fenstermaker, (ed.) 1980. *Women and Household Labor.* Beverly Hills: Sage.

Bernard, Jessie. 1974. *The Future of Motherhood.* New Haven: Yale University Press.

———. 1982. *The Future of Marriage.* 2nd edition. New Haven: Yale University Press.

Blumberg, Rae Lesser. 1978. *Stratification: Socioeconomic and Sex Equality*. Dubuque, IA: Wm. C. Brown.

Bose, Christine E. 1980. "Social status of the homemaker." Pp. 69–87 in Sarah Fenstermaker Berk (ed.), *Women and Household Labor*. Beverly Hills: Sage.

Breines, Winni and Linda Gordon. 1983. "Review essay: the new scholarship on family violence." Signs 8:490–531.

Chodorow, Nancy. 1978. *The Reproduction of Mothering*. Berkeley: University of California Press.

Collier, Jane F. and Michelle Z. Rosaldo. 1981. "Politics and gender in simple societies." Pp. 275–329 in Sherry B. Ortner and Harriet Whitehead (eds.), *Sexual Meanings: The Cultural Construction of Gender and Sexuality*. New York: Cambridge University Press.

Collier, Jane, Michelle Z. Rosaldo, and Sylvia Yanagisako. 1982. "Is there a family? New anthropological views." Pp. 25–39 in Barrie Thorne, with Marilyn Yalom (eds.), *Rethinking the Family: Some Feminist Questions*. New York: Longman.

Cook, Judith A. and Mary Margaret Fonow. Forthcoming. "Knowledge and women's interests: feminist methodology in the field of sociology." *Sociological Inquiry.*

Daniels, Arlene Kaplan. 1975. "Feminist perspectives in sociological research." Pp. 340–70 in Marcia Millman and Rosabeth Moss Kanter (eds.), *Another Voice: Feminist Perspectives on Social Life and Social Science*. Garden City, NY: Anchor.

Diamond, Irene, (ed.) 1983. *Families, Politics and Public Policy: A Feminist Dialogue on Women and the State*. New York: Longman.

Dobash, R. Emerson and Russell Dobash. 1979. *Violence Against Wives*. New York: Free Press.

Dye, Nancy Shrom. 1979. "Clio's American daughters: male history, female reality." Pp. 9–31 in Julia A. Sherman and Evelyn T. Beck (eds.), *The Prism of Sex: Essays in the Sociology of Knowledge*. Madison: University of Wisconsin Press.

Eisenstein, Zillah, (ed.) 1979. *Capitalist Patriarchy and the Case for Socialist Feminism*. New York: Monthly Review Press.

Enloe, Cynthia. 1983. *Does Khakhi Become You? Militarism in Women's Lives*. Boston: South End Press.

Epstein, Cynthia Fuchs. 1981. *Women in Law*. New York: Basic Books.

Ferber, Marianne A. 1982. "Women and work: issues of the 1980's." Signs 8:273–95.

Friedan, Betty. 1963. *The Feminine Mystique*. New York: Norton.

Geertz, Clifford. 1973. *The Interpretation of Cultures*. New York: Basic Books.

Giele, Janet. 1982. *Women in the Middle Years*. New York: John Wiley.

Gilbert, Sandra M. and Susan Gubar. 1979. *The Madwoman in the Attic: The Woman Writer and the Nineteenth-Century Imagination*. New Haven, CT: Yale University Press.

Glazer-Malbin, Nona. 1976. "Review essay: housework." Signs 1:905–22.

Glenn, Evelyn Nakano. In press. *Japanese American Women and Domestic Service, 1905–40*. Philadelphia: Temple University Press.

Habermas, Jürgen. 1971. *Knowledge and Human Interests*. Boston: Beacon Press.

Hartmann, Heidi. 1981. "The unhappy marriage of Marxism and feminism: toward a more progressive union." Pp. 1–42 in Lydia Sargent (ed.), *Women and Revolution*. Boston: South End Press.

Hartsock, Nancy. 1983a. "The feminist standpoint: developing the ground for a specifically feminist historical materialism." Pp. 283–310 in Sandra Harding and Merrill B. Hintikka (eds.), *Discovering Reality*. Amersterdam: D. Reidel Publishing Co.

———. 1983b. *Money, Sex and Power*. New York: Longman. To be reissued by Northeastern University Press, Boston.

Hochschild, Arlie Russell. 1983. *The Managed Heart*. Berkeley: University of California Press.

Holmstrom, Lynda L. and Ann W. Burgess. 1978. *The Victim of Rape: Institutional Reactions*. New York: John Wiley & Sons.

hooks, bell. 1981. *Ain't I a Woman? Black Women and Feminism*. Boston: South End Press.

Kahn-Hut, Rachel, Arlene K. Daniels, and Richard Colvard, (eds.) 1982. *Women and Work.* New York: Oxford.

Kanter, Rosabeth Moss. 1977. *Men and Women of the Corporation.* New York: Basic Books.

Keller, Evelyn Fox. 1982. "Feminism and science." *Signs* 7:589–602.

———. 1983. "Feminism as an analytic tool for the study of science." *Academe* 69, 5:15–21.

Kelly-Gadol, Joan. 1977. "Did women have a Renaissance?" Pp. 139–63 in Renate Bridenthal and Claudia Koonz (eds.), *Becoming Visible: Women in European History.* Boston: Houghton Mifflin.

Keohane, Nannerl O. 1983. "Speaking from silence: women and the science of politics." Pp. 86–100 in Elizabeth Langland and Walter Gove (eds.), *A Feminist Perspective in the Academy.* Chicago: University of Chicago Press.

Kolodny, Annette. 1980. "Dancing through the minefield: some observations on the theory, practice, and politics of a feminist literary criticism." *Feminist Studies* 6:1–26.

Krieger, Susan. 1982. "Review essay: lesbian identity and community: recent social science literature." *Signs* 8:91–108.

Kuhn, Annette and Ann Marie Wolpe, (eds.) 1978. *Feminism and Materialism.* London: Routledge & Kegan Paul.

Kuhn, Thomas. 1964. *The Structure of Scientific Revolutions.* Chicago: University of Chicago Press.

Ladner, Joyce. 1973. *The Death of White Sociology.* New York: Random House.

Lauter, Paul. 1983. "Race and gender in the shaping of the American literary canon: a case study from the twenties." *Feminist Studies* 9:435–64.

Leonard, Eileen B. 1982. *Women, Crime and Society: A Critique of Theoretical Criminology.* New York: Longman.

Lopata, Helena Z. 1973. *Widowhood in an American City.* Cambridge, MA: Schenkman.

Luker, Kristen. 1975. *Taking Chances—Abortion and the Decision Not to Contracept.* Berkeley: University of California Press.

March, Artemis. 1982. *The Changing Structure of Control of Female Sexuality.* Unpublished Ph.D. dissertation, University of California, Santa Cruz.

Masterman, Margaret. 1979. "The nature of a paradigm." Pp. 59–89 in Imre Lakatos and Alan Musgrave (eds.), *Criticism and the Growth of Knowledge.* New York: Cambridge University Press.

McCormack, Carol P. 1981. "Anthropology—a discipline with a legacy." Pp. 99–110 in Dale Spender (ed.), *Men's Studies Modified.* New York: Pergamon Press.

McIntosh, Peggy. 1983. "Interactive phases of curricular re-vision: a feminist perspective." Working Paper Series, Wellesley College Center for Research on Women.

McKinnon, Catharine. 1979. *Sexual harrassment of working women.* New Haven: Yale University Press.

Milkman, Ruth. 1982. "Redefining 'women's work': the sexual division of labor in the auto industry during World War II." *Feminist Studies* 8:337–72.

Millman, Marcia. 1975. "She did it all for love: a feminist view of the sociology of deviance." Pp. 251–79 in Marcia Millman and Rosabeth Kanter (eds.), *Another Voice.* Garden City, NY: Anchor.

———. 1980. *Such a Pretty Face: Being Fat in America.* New York: Norton.

Ortner, Sherry B. 1978. "The virgin and the state." *Feminist Studies* 4:19–36.

Parsons, Talcott and Robert F. Bales. 1955 *Family, Socialization and Interaction Process.* New York: Free Press.

Pearce, Diana. 1979. "Women, work and welfare: the feminization of poverty." Pp. 103–24 in Karen Feldstein (ed.), *Working Women and Families.* Beverly Hills: Sage.

Petchesky, Rosalind. 1979. "Dissolving the hyphen: a report on Marxist-Feminist Groups 1–5." Pp. 373–90 in Zillah Eisenstein (ed.), *Capitalist Patriarchy and the Case for Socialist Feminism.* New York: Monthly Review Press.

Piven, Frances Fox and Richard A. Cloward. 1979. "Hidden protest: the channeling of female innovation and resistance." *Signs* 4:651–70.

Rapp, Rayna. 1982. "Family and class in contemporary America: notes toward an understanding of ideology." Pp. 168–87 in Barrie Thorne, with Marilyn Yalom (eds.), *Rethinking the Family: Some Feminist Questions.* New York: Longman.

Reinharz, Shulamit. 1981. "Dimensions of the feminist research methodology debate." Unpublished paper given at annual meetings of the American Psychological Association.

Reinharz, Shulamit, Marti Bombyk and Janet Wright. 1983. "Methodological issues in feminist research: a bibliography of literature in women's studies, sociology and psychology." *Women's Studies International Forum* 6:437–54.

Rich, Adrienne. 1980. "Compulsory heterosexuality and lesbian existence." *Signs* 5:631–60.

Roberts, Helen, (ed.) 1981a. *Doing Feminist Research.* London: Routledge & Kegan Paul.

———. 1981b "Some of the boys won't play any more: the impact of feminism on sociology." Pp. 73–82 in Dale Spender (ed.), *Men's Studies Modified.* New York: Pergamon Press.

Rosaldo, Michelle Z. 1980. "Use and abuse of anthropology: reflections on feminism and cross-cultural understanding." *Signs* 5:389–417.

Rossi, Alice. 1980. "Life-span theories and women's lives." *Signs* 6:4–32.

Rothman, Barbara Katz. 1982. *In Labor: Women and Power in the Birthplace.* New York: Norton.

Rubin, Lillian. 1983. *Intimate Strangers.* New York: Harper & Row.

Ruddick, Sara. 1983. "Pacifying the forces: drafting women in the interests of peace." *Signs* 8:471–89.

Russell, Diana E. H. 1982. *Rape in Marriage.* New York: Macmillan.

Ryan, Mary. 1981. *Cradle of the Middle Class: The Family in Oneida County, New York, 1790–1865.* New York: Cambridge University Press.

Scully, Diana. 1980. *Men Who Control Women's Health.* Boston: Houghton Mifflin.

Sherif, Carolyn Wood. 1979. "Bias in psychology." Pp. 93–133 in Julia Sherman and Evelyn T. Beck (eds.), *The Prism of Sex: Essays in the Sociology of Knowledge.* Madison: University of Wisconsin Press.

Simons, Margaret A. 1979. "Racism and feminism: a schism in the sisterhood." *Feminist Studies* 4:384–401.

Slocum, Sally. 1975. "Woman the gatherer: male bias in anthropology," Pp. 36–50 in Rayna R. Reiter (ed.), *Toward an Anthropology of Women.* New York: Monthly Review Press.

Smart, Carol. 1977. *Women, Crime and Criminology: A Feminist Critique.* London: Routledge & Kegan Paul.

Smith, Barbara. 1982. "Towards a Black feminist criticism." Pp. 152–75 in Gloria T. Hull, Patricia Bell Scott, and Barbara Smith (eds.), *But Some of Us Are Brave: Black Women's Studies.* Old Westbury, NY: Feminist Press.

Smith, Dorothy E. 1978. "A peculiar eclipsing: women's exclusion from man's culture." *Women's Studies International Quarterly* 1:281–95.

———. 1979. "A sociology for women." Pp. 135–87 in Julia A. Sherman and Evelyn T. Beck (eds.), *The Prism of Sex: Essays in the Sociology of Knowledge.* Madison: University of Wisconsin Press.

Smith, Joan. 1982. "The way we were: women and work." *Feminist Studies* 8:437–56.

Sokoloff, Natalie J. 1980. *Between Money and Love: The Dialectics of Women's Home and Market Work.* New York: Praeger.

Spender, Dale (ed.) 1981. *Men's Studies Modified: The Impact of Feminism on the Academic Disciplines.* New York: Pergamon Press.

Stacey, Judith. 1983. *Patriarchy and the Socialist Revolution in China.* Berkeley: University of California Press.

Stack, Carol. 1976. *All Our Kin: Strategies for Survival in a Black Community.* New York: Harper & Row.

Tanner, Nancy and Adrienne Zihlman. 1976. "Women in evolution, Part I: innovation and selection in human origins." *Signs* 1:585–608.

Tetreault, Mary Kay. In Press. "Feminist phase theory: An experience derived evaluation model." *The Journal of Higher Education.*

Thompson, E. P. 1979. *The Poverty of Theory and Other Essays.* New York: Monthly Review Press.

Thorne, Barrie. 1978. "Gender . . . how is it best conceptualized?" Unpublished paper given at annual meetings of the American Sociological Association.

Tsing, Anna Lowenhaupt and Sylvia Junko Yanagisako. 1983. "Feminism and kinship theory." *Current Anthropology* 24:511–16.

Vickers, Jill McCalla. 1982. "Memoirs of an ontological exile: the methodological rebellions of feminist research." Pp. 27–46 in Angela Miles and Geraldine Finn (eds.), *Feminism in Canada.* Montreal: Black Rose Books.

Vogel, Lise. 1984. *Marxism and the Oppression of Women.* New Brunswick, NJ: Rutgers University Press.

Voydanoff, Patricia, (ed.) 1983. *Work and Family.* Palo Alto, CA: Mayfield.

Walker, Beverly M. 1981. "Psychology and feminism—if you can't beat them, join them!" Pp. 111–24 in Dale Spender (ed.), *Men's Studies Modified.* New York: Pergamon Press.

Wallerstein, Immanuel. 1979. *The Capitalist World Economy.* New York: Cambridge University Press.

Weitzman, Lenore J. 1981. *The Marriage Contract.* New York: Free Press.

West, Candace and Don Zimmerman. 1983. "Small insults: a study of interruptions in cross-sex conversations between unacquainted persons." Pp. 103–18 in Barrie Thorne, Cheris Kramarae, and Nancy Henley (eds.), *Language, Gender and Society.* Rowley, MA: Newbury House Publishers.

Whitehead, Ann. 1976. "Sexual antagonism in Herefordshire." Pp. 169–203 in Diana L. Barker and Sheila Allen (eds.), *Dependence and Exploitation in Work and Marriage.* London: Longman.

Wine, Jeri Dawn. 1982. "Gynocentric values and feminist psychology." Pp. 67–88 in Angela Miles and Geraldine Finn (eds.), *Feminism in Canada.* Montreal: Black Rose Books.

Wolf, Eric. 1982. *Europe and the People Without History.* Berkeley: University of California Press.

Wright, Erik Olin, Cynthia Costello, David Hachen, and Joey Sprague. 1982. "The American class structure." *American Sociological Review* 47:709–26.

Zinn, Maxine Baca. 1982. "Mexican American women in the social sciences." *Signs* 8:259–72.

Challenging the Self With Feminist Scholarship[1]

DOUGLAS MASON-SCHROCK

Most of the chapters in this section were originally published while I was a high school student in a rural, one-stoplight Indiana town where half the people were Amish and relied on horses and buggies to get around. I lived with my mom, a sixth-grade teacher, my dad, who ran a small real estate business, and my older sister, whom I looked up to for the way she always stood her ground. I don't recall ever hearing the words *feminist* or *sociologist* there. As a white, middle-class male who did pretty well in school without caring much for it, I didn't have much incentive to become either. I was going to be a pro-basketball player. However, sitting on the bench in high school led me to switch dreams. I started spending hours a day alone, strumming guitars and writing songs. Music, as I now see it, opened me up to emotions other than anger and helped me trust them. A few years later, as an undergraduate trying (unsuccessfully) to create an independent major for guitar playing, I took a few sociology courses that taught me about oppression, most of which I had never experienced. I was emotionally disturbed by the injustices these professors told me about; I wanted to find out more, so I became a sociology major.

As my recognition and disgust of oppression increased, I became more concerned with understanding how I colluded in or resisted it in my personal life. A year before I started graduate school, Marcy, my partner, and I moved in together. Although we had been dating for 4 years and had been friends since high school, this new living arrangement brought about a whole new set of problems and compromises, mainly regarding the doing of household tasks. Reading feminist works in graduate school led me to think more clearly about this relationship, as well as friendships with other women and men. As a man, I started becoming uncomfortably self-aware. The more I learned about feminism, the more masculinist habits I recognized in myself.

I read the articles reprinted here as part of a sociology of gender course taught by Barbara Risman. I knew gender inequality existed and was morally unjustified, but I was just beginning to learn about what gender actually is. While I was taking Barbara's class, I was also trying to make sense out of data I was collecting for my master's thesis, which (eventually) examined how transsexuals worked together to construct a differently gendered "true self." It became pretty clear at the transgender support group meetings I was attending that the very notion of gender was being worked out. The authors of the chapters in this section were also trying to figure out what gender means, and some of their ideas helped to me understand the transsexuals sociologically.

To be honest, though, it's hard to point my finger at this or that chapter and say it affected me in this or that way, because doing so takes things out of context. During the gender class, I read a variety of feminist sociology. I worked most closely with my mentor, Michael Schwalbe, on my master's thesis and later met with him once a week to talk about feminist works dealing with men and masculinity, as part of an individualized readings course. During this same general time period, I was forming friendships with other students interested in feminism and learned much from them. I really can't disentangle whether my life was affected more by the chapters I'm going to comment on, feminist works not included here, conversations in coffee shops and class-rooms, or discussions with Marcy. My guess would be that the whole, not any particular part, was most important, but I do see ideas brought up in the chapters that can be tied to changes in my thinking and will try to highlight some of those links.

Coming to grips with the idea that gender has virtually nothing to do with biology was my first step toward fundamentally changing the way I thought about gender. All of the writings in this section helped me understand this, because they point out or imply that there are no biological triggers that inexorably lead us to be gendered in this or that way. Unlike the writers of some feminist works, West and Zimmerman, Connell, and Stacey and Thorne don't leave much room in their theories for such myths. As a student, I think disconnecting biology and gender was essential to understanding gender sociologically. As a man, this decoupling made useless one of the strongest ideological justifications for male supremacy. Learning to disregard biological essentialism was not easy; these faulty assumptions about gender had been growing in the nooks and crannies of my mind for 20-some years, but through reading and talking with feminists, they were gradually uprooted.

Without fully understanding that biology is ideology when applied to gender issues, I would have thought about transsexuals vastly differently. The trans-sexuals I studied relied on essentialist rhetoric to legitimate their gender switching. If I had been holding on tight to similar assumptions, I would have asked vastly different questions about what they were doing. I probably would have tried to understand how they "cope" with being born in wrong-sexed bodies, for example, instead of examining how they created this *idea*. Biological essentialism would thus have led to psychological reductionism, which would have moved my analysis away from the political context and gotten me in trouble with my thesis advisor.

The feminist sociologists highlighted here also guard against such psychologizing by challenging the idea that gender is inherently embedded in our psyches. West and Zimmerman argue that gender is something we do. Although Connell sees that desire can be rooted in the body, he also emphasizes that gender is constructed through concrete actions, or, as he puts it, "practice." Reading these chapters made me realize that gender is largely something we create in interaction, not something merely inside of us.

The emphasis on interaction in the chapters suggests to me that if interaction is where gender is accomplished, sociologists interested in gender ought to be examining how people do gender in everyday life. In the beginning stages of my fieldwork, this helped me see that one angle for understanding what the transsexuals were doing was to figure out how they worked together to construct gender. The general importance the chapters placed on interaction also fit with my understanding of how most of the world's work gets done: through interaction, as Erving Goffman once said. The feminist pieces reprinted here also helped me realize that critics who argue that so-called microlevel perspectives are politically conservative are off the mark. I think the apolitical character of much of the research using a symbolic interactionist or similar framework has more to do with the lack of consciousness of particular interactionists than it does with the perspective per se. In fact, as Judith Stacey and Barrie Thorne argue, an interpretive approach is more amenable to feminist thought than positivism.

At the time Stacey and Thorne wrote their chapter, quantitative researchers had begun readily to incorporate gender as a variable. Such descriptions of gender inequality are important because policymakers probably pay closer attention to numbers generated "scientifically" than to interpretations derived from "mere" observation. But Stacey and Thorne point out that research based on methodological individualism is often "unreflective about the nature of gender as a social category." Although some feminists are now developing ways to address this problem, much sociological research still tells us more about the association between variables than it does about the larger gender order.

On the other hand, interpretive approaches don't automatically lead to critical inquiries about gender. Stacey and Thorne tell us we need theory to understand how topics we study are connected to the larger society. Obviously, it is a dose of *feminist* theory that is needed. Connell shows that doing this, even if you're studying the life histories of only eight people, can provide more sociological insights about gender than many studies that gather information from thousands of people selected randomly. One way he accomplished this was to address how the men he studied both challenge and reinforce the larger gender order. It was perhaps this general analytic strategy, also prominent in my mentor's work on the mythopoetic men's movement, that led me to theorize how transgenderists both reproduce and threaten gender ideologies.

This brings out another aspect of Connell's work that I find especially important when studying gender: his examination of contradictions, which are old Marxist and interactionist ways of thinking. He points out that the self can be contradictory, versions of masculinity can be contradictory, and the effects of one's actions can be contradictory. Understanding that social life is often contradictory helps sociologists avoid dichotomous thinking—that is, it allows us to see the "both/and" of reality instead of squeezing diversity into an "either/or" framework.

For example, early on in my research, I noticed that male transsexuals told stories at support group meetings about being lousy at sports (implying they were failures at masculinity). If I had taken this at face value, it would have suppressed important contradictions, because some of the born males I interviewed admitted that they were actually quite successful at sports. Without allowing myself to recognize this contradiction, I might have falsely understood doing poorly at sports as a common biographical event that somehow leads them to question their gender identity, or I might have just discounted the contradictory data. Instead, examining these contradictions led me to see sports failure stories as a way the group collectively used ideal images of gender to mask real behavior.

These readings point out that believing in gender differences leads people to see gender differences where none exist. This has led me to reflect on my own perceptions of the actions of women and men I know in my life. I've asked myself: Would I or others perceive the actions of various people differently if they appeared to be in a different sex category? Also: If someone presents herself or himself in a masculine way, do I or others take the person more seriously than if she or he acts in ways considered feminine? I think addressing these questions is important, because our faulty perceptions have real consequences for the way we treat others.

Sometimes an assumption has to be violated before we remember to ask ourselves these sorts of questions. For example, when I recently co-taught a senior-level class, there were two students (a woman and a man) who seemed to understand the material far better than others. In discussing the weekly readings, they always presented themselves in a rational, logical manner. After grading the first essay exams "blindly" (i.e., turning the cover page over so I could not tell whose exam I was grading), I was a bit shocked when three other students, all women, turned in exams that were considerably better than the two "gifted" students'. In trying to figure out why I had misjudged the three students who turned in almost perfect exams, I noticed that although they talked as frequently as others, they did *not* present themselves in a linear or deductive fashion and thus sometimes appeared to be working out their thoughts as they spoke. In thinking about why I had misjudged the students, I realized that I had devalued their input because of the androcentric value academics place on masculine-rational posturing.

I have also noticed similar episodes in graduate classes, where faculty members often give more credit to skilled rational posers than to students unwilling to play that game, who are sometimes just ignored. I began listening more closely to students who did not present themselves in stereotypically masculine ways—both those I was teaching and peers—and noticed that the content of what they said was as valuable and oftentimes more valuable than what was being offered by the rational posers. After figuring this out, I regularly began to affirm the importance of the classroom contributions made by students who didn't present themselves in a masculine-rational fashion before their input could be ignored.

When I first read about the doing of gender, I started thinking a lot about the difference between the content of talk and the meaning of actions. The emphasis on the interactional construction of gender reminded me of the old saying, "actions speak louder than words." Although I noticed feminist values becoming more central in things I wrote about and discussed with others, this helped me realize I needed to take a closer look at my actions. Although Marcy assures me I was never a male chauvinist, I knew that growing up in our male-supremacist society leads many men to develop masculinist habits. By reflecting on and questioning my actions, I recognized myself, at times, having impulses to fish for praise for any housework I did (when I did it), discounting women's contributions, and being unnecessarily competitive with other men. Through critical self-reflection and the help of those close to me, I've tried to change my actions and have hoped that will change my impulses—which I now understand can't always be trusted because they are sometimes tainted with male supremacy.

Reflecting on this makes me think that women and men travel different paths to feminism. Women's lives are full of countless instances where they've been ignored, objectified, discounted, and hurt by men, just because they are women. These experiences are emotionally disturbing to women, and feminism helps them make sense of these troubling events and can empower them to try to change the world. But feminism doesn't empower men in the same way. Often, when men who take feminism seriously look at their biographies, they recognize the damage they have done to women, and this can initially lead to guilt and shame, as it did for me. I think male academics usually come to feminism because they believe in social justice, and their feminism develops through reading, writing, hearing, and thinking about women's oppression, which is much different, no doubt, than living it. Because of this, I and other men who believe in feminism have to reflect continually on the morality of our behaviors.

There are two final issues brought up in the chapters that I'd like to comment on. Both Connell and West and Zimmerman (by implication) suggest that studying men as gendered beings is consistent with the goals of feminist scholarship. I think it's still essential to understand the experiences of women, but studying men is crucial because understanding how their collective actions reproduce women's oppression is necessary to end women's oppression. The chapters also remind me that feminist scholarship should be tied to social change.

These final issues helped in my decision to start dissertation research on an antibattering program for men. To understand more fully why men abuse, it's necessary to talk to them and to understand their subjectivities. Another reason this project appealed to me was that it seemed a way to combine the academic and social change goals of feminism. Studying an organization that seems to have a political agenda similar to my own should make the antibattering program more likely to take seriously any criticism I may offer. By being an active participant in the program, I'm learning about the interactional process through which men change or resist change, and this will allow me to give practical advice to those who work on a daily basis trying to change men. By writing sociologically about such matters in ways that are understandable and useful to those inside and outside of academia, and by talking with students, family, and friends about the connections between masculinity and violence, I hope to influence others to make feminist sense of their lives.

Although I've spoken here to my personal transformation, I don't think my experience is unique. I first read these and other feminist writings while participating in a semester-long seminar on the sociology of gender, and I was not alone in the class. There were several of us that semester who learned a lot and were changed through what we read and discussed each week. We created friendships and a sense of togetherness that helped us learn more about feminism than we could have by working in isolation. We also found other students and faculty members with similar concerns and linked ourselves to a larger network of feminists. To us, and other students in other departments elsewhere, the ways of thinking developed by feminist sociologists, whether included or excluded from this reader, motivated us to become feminist sociologists ourselves. Over time, the knowledge they worked so hard to create has become our starting point. Now it is up to us to push the boundaries farther while creating the knowledge from which our students will someday proceed.

NOTE

1. Through conversations about and comments on previous drafts, the following people helped me with this chapter: Sandra Godwin, Shealy Hale, Daphne Holden, Jacqueline Johnson, Marcy Mason-Schrock, Barbara Risman, Michael Schwalbe, Elizabeth Strugatz, Danette Sumerford, Michelle Wolkomir, Beth Wright, and Mary Wyer.

Discourses on Women, Sex, and Gender[1]

ESTHER NGAN-LING CHOW

My intellectual journey as a feminist in sociology is rooted in my past experience growing up in Hong Kong and pursuing my academic career as a graduate student in the United States during the social turbulence of the 1960s. The latter circumstance offered me opportunities to be politically involved in the civil rights, women's, and antiwar movements as well as other student demonstrations on the UCLA campus. As an international student, I was devastated by what many perceived to be the pervasive social problems of racism, sexism, classism, ageism, imperialism, and neocolonialism in this country. I saw these problems manifest themselves in different forms of inequality and injustice as disempowered and disadvantaged groups who experienced these sought change through political mobilization and action. This revelation, perplexing as it was, led me to reexamine many basic assumptions about U.S. society and to raise questions about the intricate relationships between social institutions and individuals, seeking to undertake the main task of the sociological imagination as C. Wright Mills (1956) suggested.

Feminism transformed the intellectual landscape of different academic disciplines at an uneven rate, in different forms, and with varying force. In the 1960s, my subfields of concentration in sociology—complex organizations and industrial sociology—were predominantly male bastions basically untouched by feminist critiques. There were very few women sociologists to serve as role models for me or with whom to engage in feminist discourse. At the beginning, my enlightenment by American feminism was the result of personal pursuit. Not until I taught my first highly enrolled course, "Women and Society," in the fall of 1973 at the American University (AU), did I begin to join forces with other feminist colleagues to transform knowledge in sociology as well as women's studies.

The concepts of "sex" and "gender" have been contested and redefined as several phases of transforming curriculum occurred in women's studies specifically and in the social sciences and humanities generally (McIntosh, 1984; Schuster & Van Dyne, 1985; Tetreault, 1985). In most of these phases, "women" rather than "gender" was the focus, along with such major concepts as sex differences, sex roles, and sex role socialization. Several textbooks I used had *Women* in the title, including *Woman's Place* by Cynthia Fuchs Epstein (1970), *Woman in Sexist Society* edited by Vivian Gornick and Barbara Moran (1971), *Woman in a Man-Made World* edited by Nona Glazer and Helen Y. Waehrer (1971), and *Changing Women in a Changing Society* edited by Joan Huber (1973).

Critical of the "traditional" phase of scholarship that ignored and excluded women, feminist scholars in the 1960s began projects to search for the missing or invisible women in fields and disciplines where women as subject matter and creators of knowledge were underrepresented. In two "searching" and "discovery" phases, women were viewed as a subordinate group with devalued roles, and their experience was considered problematic. These phases conceptualized women primarily as victims by demonstrating systematic and pervasive discrimination against them in all aspects of social life. This was followed by a "women-centered" phase of scholarship development in which women were studied on their own terms and their experience was validated as a main source of knowledge. Scholarly inquiry began to raise new questions to illuminate the experience of diverse groups of women. The final phase of curriculum transformation was what is called "multifocal scholarship" (Tetreault, 1985) or "inclusive" scholarship (Schuster & Van Dyne, 1985). In this phase, a gender-balanced curriculum was emphasized to study women in relation to men. The inclusive vision takes into account the variety of complex human experience based on difference and diversity as gender intersects with race, ethnicity, class, sexual orientation, age, disability, and other factors.

Debates emerged surrounding the intellectual and political implications when women-centered concerns were replaced by gender-centered ones in curriculum transformation. Women-centered proponents, on the one hand, have argued that the process of discovering women after millennia of their omission from human knowledge takes time. Feminist challenges to the tacitly male, white, class, and homophobic biases of traditional scholarship in terms of its assumptions, theories, concepts, and knowledge base will be a long, continuous process if herstory is to be told and women's experience and writing are to be validated. Rigorous effort was thus urged to place women at the center, as subjects of inquiry, as cores of theoretical thinking, and as active agents in knowledge production. Shifting the focus from women to gender, some feared, would divert time, effort, and resources from women's key concerns and would further reduce women's significance. Some have even worried that a political process of co-optation of gender issues by men may create backlashes that make women still more invisible and powerless in both knowledge and society and that render transformations by feminist scholarship less effectual.

On the other hand, gender is seen increasingly as *relational* in that women's position vis-à-vis men's is contextualized as a gender relationship enveloped in a complex system of domination (Chow, 1996c). For many, women's problematic subordinated status and their disadvantages cannot be fully understood and effectively changed without men's involvement in change. Men obviously have gender too (Connell, Chapter 8 in this volume). Inclusive knowledge, therefore, accounts for both women's and men's experiences. Wrestling with the convincing logic on both sides of the debate, collective decisions were made at AU to change the title of my course "Women and Society" to "Women, Men, and Social Change" and the name of the "Women's Studies" program to "Women's and Gender Studies."

Stacey and Thorne point out that anthropology has begun "to move beyond the women-centered strategy to decipher the gendered basis of all of social and cultural life, tracing the significance of gender organization and relations in all institutions and in shaping men's as well as women's lives" (p. 225). In "Doing Gender," West and Zimmerman suggest a new understanding of gender as a routine accomplishment embedded in everyday interaction that involves women and men. Bob Connell, in particular, has made a strong case for expanding the study of gender to include men and sexuality. He argues that "to understand a system of inequality, we must examine its dominant group—the study of men is as vital for gender analysis as the study of ruling classes and elites is for class analysis" (p. 192). My cautionary note is that the oppressed tend to know more about their oppressor than the other way around. However, Connell's contribution lies in his insightful analysis of differences among men, of how a multiplicity of masculinities are constituted in relation to each other and to femininities through a structure of gender relations that is highly fluid.

How sex and gender are conceptualized has been vital in feminist scholarship. Sex, a biological construction, refers to what is ascribed by biology to determine one's femaleness and maleness, whereas gender, a social construction, refers to socially learned sets of normative expectations and behavior that are associated with the two sexes (Epstein, 1985; West & Zimmerman, 1987). Sex and gender very often are debated around issues of nature versus nurture or biology versus culture. On the basis of recent research, female and male sex are viewed as existing on a single continuum

rather than as two opposite, mutually exclusive categories, because biolo-
gists and physical scientists have found out that not everyone fits into one or
the other category as neatly as they had previously assumed (Lorber &
Farrell, 1991). Most so-called sex differences are actually distributed widely
throughout the population, and the variability within one gender is usually
found to be larger than the mean difference between the genders (Andersen,
1993). Ample research evidence points to the fact that social environment
and culture exert a greater influence on individuals than nature and biology,
although the interplay between biology and culture is generally recognized.
As Epstein (1985) explains,

> the biological differences between men and women have little or no relevance
> to their behavior and capacities apart from the sexual and reproductive roles;
> even the effects of early gender socialization may be reversed by adult experi-
> ences. . . . That conditions vary for men and women has more to do with
> divisions of power in society than with innate sex differences. (p. 441)

The American Sociological Association has for years had a section on
"Sex and Gender" that recognizes the intellectual importance of this as a
subfield specialty. The usage of the gender concept has come to include
sex. In 1987, Sociologists for Women in Society (SWS), a feminist caucus
group in sociology, published its new scholarly journal, *Gender & Society,*
contributing the sociological perspective to research and theory on gender.
Lorber (1987) proclaimed in the journal's inauguration issue that "women
and men are not automatically compared; rather, gender categories themselves are questioned, and the situational and institutional processes that
construct gender are the focus of analysis" (p. 3). Critical of the existing
perspectives on sex and gender, West and Zimmerman further propose
important distinctions among sex (birth classification), sex category (social
membership), and gender (processual validation of that membership).
Recognition of an analytical independence among these three concepts is
essential for understanding the pervasiveness of "doing gender" in the
social interaction processes of everyday practice.

Gender as an analytical category has been conceptualized in a variety of
ways over time at both the micro-interaction and macro-structural levels of
analysis.[2] I underscore these evolving conceptual meanings as I understand
them in the following approaches as I relate them to the three chapters
included in Part III of this book. The gender approaches identified here are
for analytical discussion. All authors primarily emphasize the social construction of gender, although in varying degrees and with slightly different foci and
meanings in defining gender.

GENDER AS SEX DIFFERENCES

Strongly influenced by the psychological paradigm, this approach conceptualizes gender as individual attributes resulting from biology, socialization,
or some interaction of the two (Hochschild, 1973). The traits of masculinity
and femininity as ascribed characteristics become the basis of one's gender
identity, personality, and self-concept. A general consensus among the
authors in Part III is that this approach is too biologically deterministic, too
psychological, and too individualistic. They question the approach's basic
assumption that the defining characteristics of gendered behavior are the
results of internalized traits of individuals. This thinking tends to neglect social
situations, ongoing interactions, and institutional factors that influence the
formation, boundaries, imagery, and dynamics of gender relations. These
authors also cast doubt on the assumption that sex differences make women
and men "separate but equal," ignoring that the very fact of difference implies
rankings of inferiority or superiority as a basis for justifying and perpetuating
gender inequality. Studies of sex differences generally tend to stress differences rather than similarities between women and men, misconceptualiz-
ing them as binary opposites. When sex differences are found, "sex/gender"
is assumed to account for the findings, misconstruing description for explanation.[3]

GENDER AS STATUS AND ROLE

Influenced by the "functionalist" and "role theory" traditions, this approach
sees "gender" as an achieved status accompanied by a particular set of
expectations and patterned behavior that is called a "role."[4] When study of
gender first began, the field was often called "Sex Roles." In this approach,
sex difference is used as a basis for division of the world into men's and
women's roles that are highly institutionalized in society's values, cultural
practices, and structures. All authors in Part III find this approach inadequate
for explaining power, conflict, and change. In particular, the notion of gender
as role is too individualistic, for it obscures "the work that is involved in
producing gender in everyday activities" (West & Zimmerman, Chapter 7 in
this volume, p. 169). Echoing the criticisms of this approach, Stacey and
Thorne (Chapter 9) and Connell (Chapter 8 and 1992) add that role theory
tends to reify expectations and self-description, to overlook historical change,
to overemphasize consensus and social order, and to marginalize the politics
of power structure. Thorne (1980) goes so far as to assert that gender, like
the concepts of race and class, is not in itself a role (though it links to other

specific roles for women and men) because it is void of a specific site or organizational context.[5]

GENDER AS A SYSTEM OF RELATIONSHIPS

Informed by the sociological perspective that emphasizes relationships between social structure and the individual, this approach considers gender as a system of relations rather than individual properties. The emphasis is shifted from individual to structural explanations. Gender relationships cut across race, class, age, and institutional boundaries. These relationships are structurally embedded and ideologically enforced in all aspects of social life. Gender relations are unequal and asymmetric, for differences are not only conceptually but also structurally related to domination and subordination. Accordingly, opportunities, valued resources, power, and privileges as well as responsibilities are distributed unequally. Developing a conceptual framework to study changes in masculinity and homosexuality, Connell focuses on the dynamics of gender relations in the gender order as a whole. To him, the gender order is the site of relations of dominance and subordination, struggle for hegemony, and practice of resistance.[6]

GENDERING AS A PROCESS

The constructionist framework for studying gender is sometimes criticized as too static, though the stress on the dynamics of gender relations varies among scholars. Using an ethnomethodological approach, West and Zimmerman add a processual dimension in reconceptualizing gender as situated doing, constituted through social interaction. Once the differences have been constructed through "doing" gender, they are used to reinforce the "essentialness" of gender and are further enacted in gender behavior and legitimized as institutionalized arrangements. However, theoretical discussion by West and Zimmerman (and also West & Fenstermaker, 1995) using this approach tends to focus more on gendering as an interaction process and less convincingly discusses how this process is specifically and intricately linked to social structure. Studies by Connell (Chapter 8 in this volume) offer a better understanding of both dynamics and structure in systems of gender relations.

All the chapters in Part III address how the ways in which sex and gender are conceptualized and reconceptualized have profound implications for social change through research, teaching, policy, and collective action. Transforming knowledge is a major vehicle for social change. The chapter by Stacey and Thorne is particularly thought-provoking, and has challenged me intellectually since 1985. Two of my recent edited books, *Women, Family, and Policy: A Global Perspective* (with Catherine White Berheide, 1994) and *Race, Class, and Gender: Common Bonds, Different Voices* (with Doris

Wilkinson and Maxine Baca Zinn, 1996) are the results of joining in scholarly effort with others to respond to these challenges. However, conceptualizing gender is not enough; theorizing gender is of paramount importance. The paradigm shift that Stacey and Thorne envision for sociology will require much more critique, debate, and rigorous thinking that relate gender to linkages between individual and social structure, self and others, biography and history, theory and research, and idea and praxis at both micro and macro levels of analysis.

At least three major attempts at paradigm shifts that have had far-reaching impact on the theorizing of gender are worth mentioning here. The first sees *gender as a dimension of multiple systems of domination.* Gender is compounded by interlocking systems of relationships with other variables such as race, ethnicity, class, age, sexual orientation, disability, and nationality as distinctive dimensions in systems of oppression and domination (Andersen & Collins, 1995; Baca Zinn & Thornton Dill, 1994; Brewer, 1993; Chow et al., 1996; Collins, 1991; Dill, 1979; King, 1988). As Collins (1991) proclaims, "Black feminist thought fosters a fundamental paradigmatic shift that rejects additive approaches to oppression" in favor of studying the interconnection of race, class, and gender (p. 222). Instead of starting with gender as an entry point, this approach places gender along with other dimensions of difference that form the bases of the matrix of domination.

In 1979, I worked on two federally funded projects on the acculturation and occupational attainment of Asian American women. I also began in that year to work on the intersection of race, class, and gender when I served as the coordinator and instructor of the First HANNA (Hispanic, Asian, and Native Americans) Summer Institute at AU. My intellectual thinking on this triple bind was enormously benefited by my participation in 1983 as an instructor and group leader in the Summer Institute on Teaching, Researching, and Writing About Women of Color sponsored by the Center for Research on Women at Memphis State University. I was very much inspired by the other women-of-color participants, their intellectual promise as well as political commitment. Such inspiration led me to write my article on "The Development of Gender Consciousness Among Asian American Women," which was published in *Gender & Society* in 1987. Since then, I have worked on various projects and writings related to the intersection of race, class, and gender. In my recent book (Chow, 1996c), I moved away from seeing gender in terms of categories. I conceptualized race, class, and gender as basic principles of social organization and of the human interaction process, principles that constitute basic social relationships, patterns of inequality, and systems of meanings that influence social structures and affect the life experience of diverse kinds of women and men.

West and Fenstermaker (1995) take on the second challenging task of expanding *doing gender* to *doing difference* by using an ethnomethodological approach to theorize about race, class, and gender. Their theoretical formulation moves these three dimensions away from the additive and inter-active model. Instead, they reconceptualize relationships of race, class, and gender through "doing difference" as ongoing interactional and institutional accomplishments that result in multiple forms of domination. Both admirers and detractors of this perspective have found it a stimulus to fresh theoretical thinking.[7] Furthermore, Connell brought sexuality back into gender analysis, seeing it as the key site of difference. This approach by no means de-centers the importance of gender, but rather enriches its conceptual complexity, fluidity, and relevance to understanding diverse women and men and a multiplicity of masculinities and femininities.

The third attempt at a new paradigm is suggested by Lorber (1994), who offers *gender as a social institution,* not as individual attributes or interpersonal relations. Focusing on gender as a social structure, Lorber (1994) sees it

> as an institution that establishes patterns of expectations for individuals, orders the social processes of everyday life, is built into the major social organizations of society, such as the economy, ideology, the family, and politics, and is also an entity in and of itself. (p. 1)

As a sequel to their first article on the missing revolution in sociology, Stacey and Thorne (1996) admitted that their comparative report card approach used in 1985 now seems flawed. Developing feminist scholarship is "trans-disciplinary" and across subfields of study, with differing ways of devising, producing, and organizing appropriate principles, domains, and practices in the division of intellectual labor. They modestly conclude that feminism has had an enormous impact on sociology but that impact is not the same as revolution. Although their outlook is rather pessimistic, their critical insights have stimulated responses to their charges over the past decade. To name a few, works in rethinking family and work (Hochschild, 1983, 1989; Jones, 1985; Kanter, 1977b; Risman, 1987), development and economy (Blumberg, 1991), organizations (Acker, 1990; Kanter, 1977a; Ferree & Martin, 1995), women's and human rights (Bunch, 1990, 1995), masculinity (Brod & Kaufman, 1994; Connell, 1987), and gendered state theories (Connell, 1990; MacKinnon, 1982, 1983, 1989) have pushed the intellectual frontiers to transcend disciplinary boundaries. To say that some of these works and the three recent reconceptualizations of gender have merely had an impact is perhaps an understatement, because the intellectual scrutiny and assessment of their implications and utility is still in progress. Intellectual work is a continuous revolution, which does not halt or suspend at a given time and space.

My participation in the NGO (Non-Governmental Organization) Forum on Women and the Fourth United Nations World Conference on Women as an official NGO observer representing SWS in 1995 was an eye-opening experience for me intellectually as well as politically. The debates over whether to use the term *gender* in the Platform for Action document prepared for the UN conference on women held in Beijing signaled the ongoing tensions concerning focus on women or gender and conceptualizing sex and gender.[8] As the world has become interdependently linked, gender understanding in sociology needs globalizing. American sociology is not universal, but one particular lens through which systems of gender relationships and structural inequality are seen in the ever-changing world. Catharine MacKinnon (1982) argues that sex and gender are a worldwide system of domination of women by men in sexuality and reproduction through sex/gender systems of control. In a recent paper (Chow, 1996b), I argue that sociologists can play a critically important role in this globalization of gender understanding by transforming sociological knowledge through theory, research, teaching, and praxis. If a feminist revolution is to take place in the discipline of sociology as Stacey and Thorne hope, we need to integrate global feminist thinking, including Third World perspectives, into gender analyses and to broaden feminist discourse to explore a possible paradigm shift across disciplines, not only in the U.S. context, but also in the global and socio-historical ones.[9]

NOTES

1. I especially thank Barrie Thorne for her generosity in sharing ideas and references with me and also Elaine Stahl Leo for her editorial assistance.

2. Only a brief description of each approach with its merits and weaknesses is presented in this discussion. Consult relevant readings to obtain a detailed understanding of how each approach conceptualizes gender.

3. See more detailed discussion in Thorne (1980) and Connell (1985, 1987).

4. This approach is very much influenced by the "functionalist" and "role theory" traditions, which see a social system primarily as an arrangement of statuses and roles (Linton, 1936; Parsons, 1951). *Status* refers to position in the social system, whereas *role,* the dynamic aspect of status, describes the patterns of expected behavior, structured around specific rights and duties, that are associated with a particular status. In Lorber's early work (1987), she conceptualized gender as relational social statuses that are integral parts of social orders.

5. See thoughtful discussions of this approach in Hochschild (1973), Lopata and Thorne (1978), Thorne (1980), Connell (1985, 1987), and Lorber (1994). Thorne (1980) points out that no such terms as *racial role* or *class role* exist in sociological usage.

6. Bob Connell may have dismissed the concept of patriarchy prematurely, in favor of a more general concept of "gender order" that dilutes the reality that patriarchy is the predominant gender order throughout the world today. In view of global women's issues ranging from poverty to gender-based violence and sexuality, the concept of

patriarchy is still considered by many feminist scholars, especially Third World ones, to be conceptually useful.

7. A collection of five responses to "Doing Difference" published in the August issue of Volume 9, *Gender & Society* (1995), followed with a response by West and Fenstermaker.

8. The global discourse on women, sex, and gender is more complicated than I have explained in these personal reflections. If the term *gender,* including women and men, is used, men may also be viewed as subject to gender inequality. There was concern that women's struggle for survival, social equity, sustainable development, democracy, political governance, peace, and environmental justice may turn out to advantage men and further disadvantage women. Opposition also came from Catholics, religious fundamentalists, and countries with conservative dogmas and authoritarian regimes that argue against the language of gender in favor of the biological construction of sex.

9. Feminist scholarship has been quite successful in shifting the international human rights paradigm to include women's rights along with men's (Bunch, 1990, 1995; also see Chow, 1996a).

Part IV

Gender in the Machine:
Structured Inequality

In this genre, feminist writers apply the assumption of social construction of gender to the institutional level of analysis, arguing that gender is more than individual behavior or identity. These scholars show how gender is built into structures and how this helps to create and maintain gender inequality. These chapters are important for many reasons; as the analytical focus is shifted from the individual, the argument that women are oppressed because of personal deficiencies, incomplete socialization, biology, or human capital deficits is destroyed. Instead, gender inequality is understood as being built into organizations and formal power structures, thereby systematically advantaging men over women. This genre impedes victim blaming. The authors shine a spotlight on rules, organizations, and hierarchies as enabling gender inequality. They freely acknowledge that gender inequality exists because men, as a group, benefit; and gender inequality will persist until the less powerful force change. These writings provide intellectual support for government programs and policies that actively confront power imbalances in our institutions.

10   The Impact of Hierarchical Structures on the Work Behavior of Women and Men

ROSABETH MOSS KANTER
Harvard Law School and Brandeis University

This paper makes the case for an absence of sex differences in work behavior, arguing instead that work attitudes and work behavior are a function of location in organizational structures. The structures of opportunity (e.g., mobility prospects) and power (e.g., influence upward), along with the proportional representation of a person's social type, define and shape the ways that organization members respond to their jobs and to each other. In hierarchical systems like large corporations, the relative disadvantage of many women with respect to opportunity and power results in behaviors and attitudes (such as limited aspirations, concern with co-worker friendships, or controlling leadership styles) that are also true of men in similarly disadvantaged positions. The structure of power in organizations, rather than inherent sexual attitudes, can also explain why women sometimes appear to be less preferred as leaders. It is concluded that it is not the nature of women but hierarchical arrangements that must be changed if we are to promote equity in the workplace.

This paper proposes that structural conditions, particularly those stemming from the nature of hierarchy, shape apparent "sex differences" in the workplace and in organizations. Findings about behavior of and toward women in organizations can be explained by a number of structural variables that *also* can account for the behavior of and toward men in similar situations.

AUTHOR'S NOTE: Revised version of "Women and Hierarchies," read at the 1975 meetings of the American Sociological Association, San Francisco. Zick Rubin, Barry Stein, and Nancy Chodorow made helpful comments.

This conclusion has been reached after field work in two corporations, interviews with "token" women in professional and management positions and secretaries and secretarial supervisors, and an extensive review of the social psychological and sociological literatures on work orientations and leadership behavior.

Underlying this analysis is a conception of an organization as a total system. Occupations, work behavior, and work relations are too often studied as if they exist in a vacuum—each occupation or office or departmental unit considered as an isolated entity—and not within complex systems that define the position of interacting parties with respect to larger distributions of opportunity, power, and numerical ratios of social types. The hierarchical systems in which most work relations occur define which people are mobile, which will advance, which positions lead to other positions, and how many opportunities for growth and change occur along a particular chain of positions. Organizational systems also define a network of power relations outside of the authority vested in formal positions; the power network defines which people can be influential beyond the boundaries of their positions. Finally, the distribution of social types and social characteristics among personnel in different positions (and especially such ascribed characteristics as age, race, and sex) define whether people of a given type are relatively rare or relatively common.

These three structural variables—the opportunity structure, the power structure, and the sex ratio—shape the behavior of women in organizations, just as they shape the behavior of men. If women sometimes have lower aspirations, lesser involvement with work, and greater concern with peer group relations—so do men in positions of limited or blocked mobility. If women are sometimes less preferred as leaders, generate lower morale among subordinates, and use directive-interfering leadership styles—so are men with relatively little organizational or system-wide power. If women in managerial or professional positions are sometimes isolated, stereotyped, overly visible, and cope by trying to limit their visibility—so are men who are "tokens" and therefore rare among a majority of another social type.

In other words, structural position can account for what at first glance appear to be "sex differences" and perhaps even explain more of the variance in the behavior of women and men. It becomes important to understand how women and men get distributed across structural positions and how this differential distribution affects behavior—not how women differ from men. In this analysis, sex is one criterion for social placement, one sorting mechanism among others, that accounts for which positions and roles are considered appropriate for people. Women may be more likely to face discrimination than men, and more women than men may be found at the bottom of opportunity and power hierarchies. If given opportunity, women may more often find themselves alone among other-sex peers. But the behavior of women at the bottom (or alone) should be seen as a function of *being* at the bottom, and not primarily as a function of being a woman.

This paper considers two structural effects of hierarchical systems on behavior: the opportunity structure and the power structure. It deals primarily with the behavioral consequences of disadvantaged positions. To explain fully the behavior and problems of women in more advantaged positions requires the introduction of the third variable, the sex ratio, for women more highly placed in hierarchies are often "tokens" in groups numerically dominated by men; the effects of tokenism on women and men is discussed at length elsewhere (Kanter, 1975a and forthcoming).

WORK ORIENTATIONS, ASPIRATIONS, AND LOCATION IN AN OPPORTUNITY STRUCTURE

It is tempting to conclude, on the basis of research evidence and common-sense observations, that women's work orientations, on the average, differ from those of men's. Isn't this, after all, compatible with the "primary" socialization of women for family roles and men for work roles? Women, this thesis goes, tend to be less involved in their work and committed to it than men, interrupting their careers whenever they can; they are more concerned about their relationships with other people than the task or reward aspects of their jobs; and they have lower levels of aspiration. I review some of the evidence for these statements below. But I also argue, instead, that all of these findings can be explained by the nature of the *opportunity structure* in which people find themselves in an organization, whether they are men or women. People in low-mobility or blocked-mobility situations tend to limit their aspirations, seek satisfaction in activities outside of work, dream of escape, and create sociable peer groups in which interpersonal relationships take precedence over other aspects of work. When women occupy low-mobility positions, they tend to exhibit these characteristics; since most of the women studied in organizations tend to be disadvantageously placed in the organization's opportunity structure, they confirm the generalizations made about "women's organizational behavior." Yet, when we observe *men* disadvantageously located in the opportunity structure, they tend to demonstrate the same characteristics. What one line of thought considers a "sex difference," I consider a structural phenomenon. (See Laws, 1976, for a psychological version of a similar argument.) This is consistent with the prevalent finding in organizational behavior that people at upper levels of organizations tend routinely to be more motivated, involved, and interested in their jobs than those at lower levels (Tannenbaum et al., 1974:1).

**Opportunity and
Limited Aspirations**

The evidence for women's more limited aspirations and greater concern with peer relationships comes from a variety of sources. Several studies conclude that women more than men tend to be concerned with local and immediate relationships, remaining loyal to the local work group even as professionals, rather than identifying with the field as a whole and aspiring to promotions which might cause them to leave the local environment. Several studies of male professionals in organizations have found a correlation between professionalism and a "cosmopolitan" rather than a "local" orientation, using Merton's terms. The one exception was a study of nurses by Bennis and colleagues (1958b). In this *female* group, the more professionally oriented nurses "did not differ from others in their loyalty to the hospital, and they were *more* apt than others, not less, to express loyalty to the local work groups" (Blau and Scott, 1962:69). While Blau and Scott conclude that this is due to the limited visibility of the nurses' professional competence, it is also compatible with the response of people to a professional opportunity structure characteristic of nursing which does not offer much mobility out of the current organization and in which good peer relationships are likely to be an important component of competent work performance. Similarly, Constantini and Craik (1972) found that women politicians in California were oriented intraparty and locally more than men, while the men were much more often oriented toward higher office. The difference in the opportunity structures for women and men in politics at the time this research was carried out is well known, making the women's preferences understandable on structural rather than characterological grounds.

In a recent dissertation research project on a major corporation, Homall (1974) surveyed 111 non-exempt (i.e., hourly) employees on their attitudes toward promotion. Using an expectancy-value theory, she found that men show greater motivation to be promoted than women and perceive greater overall desirability and likelihood of the possible consequences following a promotion. The men also perceived themselves to be more competent in basic managerial skills than the women did and to receive more encouragement from superiors to improve and advance. But newer employees were also more likely than older to show high motivation for promotion, and the better educated more likely than the more poorly educated, indicating that not only sex but also other characteristics affecting the employee's real advancement opportunities played a part in the results.

Homall also found that *neither* men nor women *reported* perceiving many real advancement opportunities for themselves. Yet, in this company, like most, the differences in the *actual* opportunities for men and women, and the mobility hierarchies in which they are located, are quite striking and dramatic. About two-thirds of the women non-exempts in the company unit from which the sample was drawn were secretaries. The secretarial hierarchy is a short one, with increased rank reflecting the status of the boss rather than the secretary's work, and leading to executive secretary as the highest position. Until recently, practically no executive secretary was ever promoted into the exempt (salaried) ranks, and those promoted represent a minuscule proportion of either secretaries or exempt personnel. The other women in Homall's sample were predominantly clerks in dead-end jobs. It is not surprising that the aspirations of women in such an organizational situation should be limited, that they should not think highly of their own management skills, and that they should turn to other sources of satisfaction. Indeed, in a study of the values of 120 occupational groups, secretaries (the only predominantly female category studied) were unique in placing their highest priorities on security, love, responsibility and happiness—not job advancement (Sikula, 1973). The men in Homall's sample, on the other hand, were a much smaller proportion of the non-exempt population. The majority worked as accounting clerks or in the international exports department in a customer relations function that led directly into the exempt ranks of the company. Their mobility prospects were strong.

There is evidence that, in general, the jobs held by most women workers tend to have shorter chains of opportunity associated with them, to contain fewer advancement opportunities. In a study of 11 industries employing about 17% of the U.S. work force (motor vehicles and parts, basic steel, communications, department and variety stores, commercial banking, insurance carriers, and hotels and motels), a consulting group found that as the amount of progression possible in non-supervisory jobs increased—the number of steps of opportunity it contained—the proportion of women declined markedly (Grunker et al., 1970). Women represented 46% of all non-supervisory workers, but they were a whopping 64% of workers in the "flattest" jobs (least advancement opportunities) and a minuscule 5% of workers in the highest opportunity jobs (see Table 10.1).

Thus, the Homall results and others showing women's "lower" work involvement and aspirations can be more profitably read as reflecting a response on both the part of employees and their managers to the worker's placement in an opportunity structure. Those who are disadvantageously placed limit their aspirations and are less likely to be perceived as promotable, thus completing a vicious cycle. Those who are more advantageously placed are likely to maintain higher aspirations and to be encouraged in keeping them. The sex-typing of jobs in this major corporation, like others, means that a *social structural effect* might be misleadingly interpreted as a sex difference. My own interviews, in the same company Homall studied, with women who are advantageously placed in a high-mobility opportunity structure (as sales personnel in a hierarchy that regularly leads directly to

TABLE 10.1 Percentage of Men and Women in Jobs with Long and Short Opportunity Structures in Eleven Industries

Upgrading Category	Number of Non-supervisory Workers	Percent Male	Percent Female	Percent of Workers to Total
1. Craft or craft type progression	1,350,000	95	5	19
2. Long, narrow pyramid progression—at least 6 steps normally	1,235,000	68	32	18
3. Moderate pyramid progression—3 to 5 steps normally	2,045,000	39	61	29
4. Flat pyramid progression—at most 2 steps normally	2,390,000	36	64	34
	7,020,000	54% (average)	46% (average)	100%

SOURCE: William J. Grunker et al. *Climbing the Job Ladder,* New York: E. F. Shelley and Co., 1970, p. 13.

management positions) indicates that they are highly motivated and aspire to top management positions.

But it is not only women who respond to blocked mobility by limiting their aspirations, lowering work commitment, and dreaming of escape. Men poorly placed in an opportunity structure tend to behave in similar ways. A number of classic studies of male blue-collar workers indicate that work commitment and aspirations are both low where advancement opportunities also are low. Dubin (1956) concluded that work is not a "central life interest" of industrial workers. Chinoy's (1955) study of automobile workers revealed some interesting parallels between the men's response to their work and that of female clerical workers or the telephone company women observed by Langer (1970). The younger men, first, tended to define their jobs as temporary and, instrumentally, as means to immediate out-of-work pleasure through the purchase of consumer goods. Hope for or interest in promotion was extremely limited, especially for those men over 35. When workers hoped for "better" jobs, they tended to mean those that were easier or cleaner, rather than those that advanced them in the hierarchy. Almost four-fifths had at some time contemplated leaving; they dreamed of escape into their own small business. As Riesman put it: "Chinoy's interviews show work to be regarded as a form of daily part-time imprisonment, through which one pays off the fines incurred by one's pursuit of the good, or rather the 'good time,' life at home and on vacations" (1955:xix).

Other research confirms this finding. Purcell (1960) studied male workers in three meat packing plants. Around half were negative about their chances for advancement, and many denied that they would ever *want* to be foremen. Bonjean and his associates (1967) also found that individuals with negative mobility perceptions tend to have low aspirations. Where work is boring or repetitive and chances for mobility low, people tend to develop little attachment to work and seek their major satisfactions in the family realm. They also seek to leave the organization whenever possible. Mayer and Goldstein (1964) and others offer evidence that the "interrupted career" pattern is true for men as well as women; blue-collar men leave organizations to start small businesses and then return when (as is statistically likely) the business fails.

Concern with Peer Group Relationships

Along with more limited aspirations, women are said to be more concerned than men with interpersonal relationships on the job, more involved with other people than with the intrinsic nature of the task. In attitudinal studies attempting to distinguish job aspects motivating increased performance ("motivating" factors) from those merely preventing dissatisfaction ("hygiene" factors), attitudes toward interpersonal relations with peers constituted the only variable differentiating men and women. (The women in two major studies include those in both relatively high-level and relatively low-level jobs.) For women, peer relationships were a motivational factor, spurring them on, whereas for men they were only a hygiene factor, which the men would miss if it were not there but which did not push them to perform (Davis, 1967:35–6).[1] One of the few significant sex differences found by University of Michigan researchers in their national survey of the attitudes of 1472 working men and women lay also in this area. More women (68%) than men (61%) indicated that it was very important to them that their coworkers be friendly and helpful (Crowley, Levitin, and Quinn, 1973). And Johnston (1975), in a more limited survey of workers in an Australian soap factory, found that men and women differed in the reasons they most often gave for liking their jobs. Women mentioned "coworkers are friendly" with greatest frequency; "the job is interesting" came in second, tied with "the immediate boss is kind." For men, the listing was nearly reversed. "The job is interesting" received the most frequent mentions, with friendly coworkers tied for second place, and the kind boss coming in fifth.

Some laboratory studies also suggest that the tendency of more women than men to be concerned with the quality of relationships affects those women's behavior and performance. Female game-playing strategy, in a series of experiments, tended on the average to be "accommodative," including rather than excluding, and oriented toward other people rather than toward winning, whereas the male strategy was more often "exploitative" and success-oriented (Vinacke, 1959; Uesugi and Vinacke, 1963). But even here, later investigators have challenged the sex differences interpretation and offered an explanation based on situational characteristics. Lirtzman and Wahba (1972) have pointed out that the Vinacke experiments used minimally competitive social games with uncertainty and risk reduced once coalitions were formed, permitting any sort of partnership relationship. In their own experiments, using a highly competitive game with high uncertainty about the consequences of behavior, sex differences disappeared. Women as well as men behaved competitively, aggressively, and exploitatively, trying to maximize their chances of winning. In other words, the context shapes organizational behavior. A concern with relationships tends to arise for women in low-risk, low-uncertainty environments, where opportunities will not be lost if one accommodates to others.

The opportunity structure is an important part of the context that defines for organization members how important good, accommodative relationships with peers ought to be, and whether or not minimizing peer relations in favor of competition or distance has a "pay-off" in mobility. High-mobility situations foster rivalry, instability in the composition of work groups, comparisons upward in the hierarchy, and concern with intrinsic aspects of the job. Low-mobility situations, however—those characteristic of most of the working women studied—foster camaraderie, stably composed groups, and more concern with extrinsic rewards, social and monetary. In a classic piece of sociological analysis, Merton (1968:233) argued that amount of upward mobility as an institutionalized characteristic of a social system generates either vertical or horizontal orientations. When people face favorable advancement opportunities, they compare themselves upward in rank, with one foot already out of the current peer group in the process he called "anticipatory socialization." Unfavorable advancement opportunities, on the other hand, lend themselves to comparison with peers, and concern with peer solidarity. Pennings' (1970) study of white collar workers with high or low mobility opportunities (measured by promotion rates) offers confirmation. The importance attached to intrinsic job characteristics, to the nature of the job itself as opposed to such external factors as relationships with coworkers, varied with promotion rates.

Work-value orientations and the importance of interpersonal relations, then, are a function of the structure of opportunity facing people in different parts of the organization by virtue of the category into which they fall. There is evidence that men as well as women turn to relationships with work peers as an alternative interest when mobility opportunities are limited or blocked. Under such circumstances, men, like women, form strong peer groups that value solidarity and loyalty within the group and look with suspicion upon fellow workers who identify or interact with anyone outside the group. One example is the men in the bank wiring room group in the Hawthorne studies (Roethlisberger and Dickson, 1939) who created a strong peer group which restricted work output. Burns' (1955) observations of a factory in an uncertain, changing environment, showed dramatically the differences in interpersonal orientations of low- and high-mobility men. The older men, considered "over the hill" and in positions outside of the main career advancement ladders, formed "cliques" oriented toward protection and reassurance; these peer groups represented, to Burns, organized retreats from occupational status into the realm of intimacy. The younger men, on the other hand, who still had opportunities, formed a very different kind of group, "cabals" which plotted an increase in their status. The younger men oriented themselves around power, while the older ones substituted intimacy and support. Tichy (1973) hypothesizes that in no-mobility systems friendship needs are the primary pressure for group formation, and that lack of ability to envision other rewards in the future encourages people to seek more immediate socio-emotional rewards in the present situation.

A laboratory study of communication in experimentally created hierarchies offers supportive evidence for the importance of peer relationships in low-opportunity situations. Cohen (1958) put male subjects into high-power (management-like) or low-power (subordinate-like) task groups, varying the opportunity structure for the two low-power groups. One condition offered no opportunities for mobility into the high-power group; the other created the possibility for mobility during the experimental situation. The mobile groups showed greater concern with task, suppressed irrelevant communications, were less critical of the upper groups, and were more oriented toward the high-power groups than toward members of their own peer group. They were careful about criticism, stayed more with the task, and tended to be less attracted to members of their own group than to the high-power people. The non-mobiles, on the other hand, centered their affect and attention on the members of their own group, neglecting the high-power people, because "for them, communication and interaction cannot be instrumental to mobility" (Cohen, 1958:49). The non-mobiles were also significantly more likely to feel that their "social validity" was received from their own rather than the upper group, to send "cohesiveness-building content" to their own group, and to be openly critical of the upper group.

Tichy has further theorized that the peer groups formed by non-mobile people tend to quickly become closed:

> Members of no-mobility organizations tend not to be interested in instrumental relationships, since they offer very little possibility of changing the indi-

vidual's status in any way; once a member is satisfactorily adapted to a clique, he is under no pressure to look for other relationships. This tends to create cliques which are closed (1973:205–6).

As a member of a closed peer group, the individual is under further pressure to remain loyal to the immediate group of workmates and to see leaving the group, even for a promotion, as an act of "disloyalty." We can speculate with some confidence that the rare man who is offered an advancement opportunity out of a low-mobility peer group will experience some of the same conflict as the rare secretary who is ambivalent about the promotion she is offered because it will mean "leaving her friends." (For a woman, the conflict is probably more severe, because as she rises in an organization she is likely to find fewer and fewer female peers, whereas men find a male peer group at every level of the system.)

And thus the circle is closed. Initial placement in an opportunity structure helps determine whether a person will develop the aspirations and orientations that make further mobility possible. Women in low-mobility organizational situations develop attitudes and orientations said to be characteristic of "women as a group" but which can more profitably be seen as human responses to blocked opportunities. (Some of these responses, of course, may have positive rather than negative social value.)

LEADERSHIP ATTITUDES, BEHAVIOR
AND THE POWER STRUCTURE

There is no research evidence that yet proves a case for sex differences in either leadership aptitude or style. A wide variety of investigations, from field studies of organizations to paper-and-pencil tests, indicate that the styles of men and women vary over the same range, and there are no conclusive sex-related preferences (Crozier, 1956:126; Day and Stogdill, 1972; Rousell, 1974; Bartol, 1974, 1975). In an organizational simulation using college students, Bartol found that sex of the leader did not by itself affect follower satisfaction, even when female leaders were characterized by high dominance, a trait most likely to "offend" male subordinates (Bartol, 1974, 1975).

Even attempts to prove that women leaders are perceived and evaluated differently from men—a not unlikely occurrence—have resulted in very few significant results. In a study of high school departments, Rousell (1974) found that teachers' ratings of their department heads' aggressiveness, suggestibility, and professional knowledge did not discriminate between the sexes. Bartol and Butterfield (1974) asked subjects to make judgments about male and female leaders exhibiting a variety of styles. The evaluations of men and women did not differ significantly on most variables, including such critical ones as "production emphasis," but there was a tendency to give higher ratings to men than to women when they "initiated structure" and higher to women than men when they showed "consideration," demonstrating some propensity for raters to "reward" people for sex-role-appropriate behavior. Rosen and Jerdee (1973) used a different set of categories but had nearly identical results. Students and bank supervisors judged stories involving male and female leaders using four different styles. The "reward" style was rated somewhat more effective when used by men, but the "friendly-dependent" style (which the researchers hoped would capture a female stereotype) was rated high for *either* sex when used with the opposite sex. The use of "threat" was considered ineffective for both sexes, though there was a slight but not significant tendency to let men get away with it more than women. Thus, sex-role stereotypes seem to play only a very small role, if any, in responding to the style of a leader, and leadership styles themselves do not show much differentiation by sex.

On the other hand, there is considerable evidence for a general cultural attitude that men make better leaders. A large number of studies have concluded that neither men nor women want to work for a woman (although women are somewhat more ready to do so than men, and people who have already worked under a woman are much likelier to be favorable toward doing so). In a 1965 *Harvard Business Review* survey of 1000 male and 900 female executives, for example, an educated and experienced sample, over two thirds of the men and nearly one fifth of the women reported that they themselves would not feel comfortable working for a woman. Very few of either sex (9 percent of the men and 15 percent of the women) felt that *men* feel comfortable working for a woman; and a proportion of the male respondents said that women did not belong in executive positions. A total of 51 percent of the men responded that women were "temperamentally unfit" for management, writing comments such as, "They scare male executives half to death . . . As for an efficient woman manager, this is cultural blasphemy . . ." (Bowman, Worthy, and Greyser, 1965). At the same time, there is a prevalent stereotype of the "woman boss" as rigid, petty, controlling, and too prone to interfere in personal affairs of subordinates. (See Laird, 1942. My own interviews confirm this stereotypic picture.)

It is too easy to explain these findings only by reference to abstract notions of sex discrimination. Here, too, I want to invoke a structural explanation that can account for a preference for male leaders and for women's occasional use of authoritarian-controlling leadership styles. Both of these phenomena are understandable given the current distribution of men and women in the power structure of organizations. The nature of the power structure of the organization as a *total* system can account for (a) which leaders are preferred and considered effective by subordinates; and (b) which leaders are likely to use and be perceived as using overly directive, overly interfering styles.

Leadership Effectiveness and Power Position

What makes leaders effective with subordinates? Attempts to distinguish more effective and less effective styles have generally failed, in part because there are trade-offs associated with emphasizing one or another forms of supervision, as early studies of authoritarian, democratic, and laissez-faire leaders showed. While human relations skills are considered important if coupled with a production emphasis, the evidence is mixed enough to permit few conclusions about leader traits alone (Tannenbaum, 1966:78–9). Marcus and House (1973), for example, tried to differentiate instrumental and expressive exchanges between superiors and subordinates as a way to predict interaction and group process. The distinction was not ultimately very useful. Subordinates reported getting about equally as much job-related information whether the leaders tended to be instrumental or expressive, and they found very little relationship between styles of leadership behavior and subordinate group process. This is one of a number of studies that fail to demonstrate that leader strategy alone makes much difference and, as I have already indicated, there is no firm evidence that men and women differ in characteristic choice of style anyway.

But what *does* seem to make a difference is the leader's own position in the power structure of the wider organizational system. Early theory in organizational behavior assumed a direct relation between leader behavior and group satisfaction and morale, as if each organizational sub-group existed in a vacuum. However, Pelz (1952) discovered in the early 1950's that perceived influence *outside* the work group and upward in the organization was a significant intervening variable. He compared high- and low-morale work groups to test the hypothesis that the supervisor in high-morale groups would be better at communicating, more supportive, and more likely to recommend promotion. Yet, when he analyzed the data, the association seemed to be nonexistent or even reversed. In some cases, supervisors who frequently recommended people for promotion and offered sincere praise for a job well done had *lower* morale scores. The differentiating variable that Pelz finally hit upon was whether or not the leaders had power outside and upward: influence on their own superiors and how decisions were made in the department as a whole. The combination of good human relations *and* power was associated with high morale. Human-relations skills and low power (a likely combination for women leaders) sometimes had negative effects on morale.

High external status, sometimes taken as a shorthand symbol for potential or actual power and influence also contributes to leader effectiveness. It adds a power base outside of the legitimate authority vested in the current office. Subordinates are more likely to inhibit aggression and negativity toward a demanding person of higher than lower status (Thibaut and Riecken, 1955).

People who come into a group with higher external status tend to be liked more, talk more often, and receive more communications (Hurwitz, Zander, and Hymovitch, 1968). Leaders with higher-status characteristics are generally assumed to be capable of greater influence in other parts of the organization. This gives people of higher credentials and higher-status ascribed characteristics an obvious initial advantage over those with lesser assets, and, to belabor the obvious, gives men an edge over women on this variable.

An advantageous location in the power structure has real as well as symbolic pay-offs. It gives leaders more rewards to dispense to subordinates, as they may have more claim over the resources of the organization. It means that the leader can more effectively back up both promises and threats and can, indeed, make changes in the situation of subordinates. Such organizational power comes from several factors that are themselves structural: (a) close contact and good relations with other power-holders in the system; (b) advantageous location in the opportunity structure and favorable mobility prospects. The first guarantees influence through present relations and present interactions; the second through bets about future increases in power, giving subordinates a chance to capitalize on the success of a "comer" in the organization (see Stein, 1976).

Women are currently likely to be disadvantaged on both grounds and thus less likely to act as though they have, and be perceived by subordinates as having, organizational power. In business organization, those systems in which the most negative attitudes toward working for women are consistently expressed, women are both numerically rare and structurally isolated as managers or supervisors of any kind. Statistically, they represent about three percent of all managers and officials in the most recent U.S. census, but even within this category they tend to be concentrated in staff rather than line positions where they often lack supervisory responsibility (Kanter, 1975b). Accumulating evidence indicates that women leaders, under such circumstances, may be excluded from the informal network of organization managers (Cussler, 1958), just as they may be excluded from the influential networks of professional peers in male-dominated professions (Epstein, 1970). Even if she occupies a leadership position, then, a woman may have less influence in the wider organizational situation because of her rarity and isolation, and this may interfere with her effective exercise of leadership, with subordinate satisfaction, or with the likelihood of subordinates to prefer her to a man, *regardless* of her own style or competence. This proposition may account for evidence of the importance of a male sponsor in the success of women executives (Cussler, 1958; Hennig, 1970). A high-status man bringing a woman leader up behind him may provide the visible sign needed by subordinates that the woman does have influence outside and upward. While sponsors serve multiple functions (such as coaching and socialization in the informal routines), the "reflected power" they offer may be even more important for women than for men who are proteges. Indeed, the dozen women I interviewed who are the first to sell industrial chemicals (on a sales force of over 300) reported that their influence with customers is partly a function of how much their manager indicates he will back up and support their decisions. They can be more effective at selling if they look like they have organizational power.

Power, Powerlessness, and Leadership Style

Leaders with favorable mobility prospects are also likely to please their subordinates more than those who appear stuck. Here there is a complex interaction between leader power, leader behavior, and subordinate perception. People well-placed in the opportunity structure are already likely to be paying more attention to those upward in the organization and to be less critical of them, and thus to be making the connections that give them organizational power. They are also likely to be less rigid, directive, and authoritarian than low-mobility leaders (Metzler, 1955). And, they offer more opportunity to subordinates to move up right along with them. Under such circumstances, we can guess that leader actions are likely to be seen as helping rather than hindering the group's performance and that morale would be high.

The only significant sex-linked difference found in a study of high school department heads lay in just these group climate characteristics, and they can be traced directly to differences in the organizational power of the men and women leaders, even though the researcher does not herself make this interpretation. Rousell (1974) studied 205 teachers and 40 department heads, 25 male and 15 female, working with small departments of roughly equal sex distribution. Departments headed by men were perceived as higher in "esprit and intimacy"—a good indicator of morale—and those headed by women in "hindrance"—an indicator that the leader was seen as getting in the way rather than promoting subordinates' interests. But mobility prospects and the likelihood that leaders would be moving up in the organization also appear to have been very different for the men and the women. For one thing, there were no women *above* the level of department head in the whole county. Secondly, the women seemed to have risen to their last position. They had moved to this position more slowly than the men (they were older, more experienced, and had spent a longer time in their previous positions) and they had more limited aspirations (one-seventh of the women, as contrasted with half of the men expressed a desire for further promotions).

Levenson (1961) has also suggested that the fact of promotability itself influences style of supervision and subordinate attitudes, evoking good leadership practices. *Promotable* supervisors are more likely to adopt a participatory style in which they share information, delegate, train, and allow latitude and autonomy—in order to show that they are not indispensable in their current jobs and to fill the vacancy created by their promotion with someone they have trained. *Unpromotable* supervisors, on the other hand, may try to retain control and restrict the opportunities for their subordinates' learning and autonomy, as they themselves are not moving up, and a capable subordinate represents a serious replacement threat.

Thus, when people in "middle management" positions have lower advancement potential and a less favorable position in the power structure (because of their age, ascribed characteristics, or present achievements), they tend to "take it out" on their subordinates in the form of greater directiveness and increased control. So do people who feel relatively powerless or relatively insecure in their jobs. In other words, under these circumstances, more likely to be encountered by women than by men, *men as well as women* begin to act in those ways said to characterize the negatively stereotyped "woman boss."

Hetzler (1955) conducted an attitude survey of male Air Force officers. He found that leaders of lower status and advancement potential favored more directive, rigid, and authoritarian techniques of leadership, seeking control over subordinates. Subordinates were their primary frame of reference for their own status assessment and enhancement, and so they found it important to "lord it over" group members, just as some women have complained women supervisors do to them. They also did not help talented members of the group get ahead (perhaps finding them too threatening), selecting immediate assistants of mediocre rather than outstanding talent. A series of laboratory experiments confirm these field observations. People who find themselves relatively powerless, because they lack confidence in their own abilities, or because they encounter resistance from their targets of influence, tend to use more coercive rather than persuasive power (Goodstadt and Kipnis, 1970). Furthermore, the "psychologically powerless"—as people who know they are going no further in an organization are likely to be—are more likely to use coercive power to elevate their own sense of worth and dignity, especially when their control over subordinates is threatened by someone's "poor attitude" (Goodstadt and Hjelle, 1973).

Finally, people who feel vulnerable and insecure are most likely to be authoritarian-controlling leaders. The behavior attributed to women supervisors is likely to be characteristic of new and insecure supervisors generally. Gardner (1945) noted this during World War II when the demands of war production brought women into formerly all-male positions. Even women, he observed, complained that women supervisors were unfriendly, too critical, too concerned with petty details, and too strict in disciplining them. But Gardner concluded that newly promoted men given supervisory jobs without sufficient training also showed these tendencies:

> Any new supervisor who feels unsure of himself, who feels that his boss is watching him critically, is likely to demand perfect behavior and performance

from his people, to be critical of minor mistakes, and to try too hard to please his boss. A woman supervisor, responding to the insecurity and uncertainty of her position as a woman, knowing that she is being watched both critically and doubtfully, feels obliged to try even harder. And for doing this she is said to be 'acting just like a woman.' (Gardner, 1945:270–1)

We again come full circle. Those favorably placed in the power structure are more likely to be effective as leaders and thus likely to gain even more power. The attitudes toward women leaders in organizations where they are most likely to have an unfavorable position in the power structure, despite the authority of their office, become understandable not just as an example of sex discrimination but as an example of a general organizational process that can also affect men. If some women respond, as some men do, by turning to control over subordinates as their internal measure of "success," this reaction is also understandable as a response to structural circumstances.

CONCLUSION

It is time to move beyond "sex differences" and "sex roles" in our understanding of the observed behavior of women in organizations, and to return to classic and emerging social psychological and structural theories that explain behavior as a function of position in a network of hierarchical relations. By looking at the larger organizational context in which relationships and interactions occur, we can account for the behavior of both men and women who find themselves in similar positions in an opportunity or power structure or in a similar sex ratio. Tannenbaum and colleagues reach this conclusion in another context in their study of 50 plants in 5 nations: that social structure rather than interpersonal relations is the more substantial basis for understanding outcomes such as the distribution of reactions and adjustments within a system (1974:205).

We thus avoid the "blame the victim" approach that locates explanations for work behavior in dispositions in the individual (whether planted there by temperament or socialization). The real villain of the piece in a structuralist model turns out to be the very nature of hierarchy. Complex organizations whose opportunity and power structures routinely disadvantage some kinds of people (whether women or men) are likely to generate the behavioral consequences of such disadvantaging. On the other hand, the creation of a class of advantaged who are offered the prospects for increasing their opportunities and power does not itself always lead to desirable consequences, for those people may become more involved with the politics of climbing than with the human side of the organization or the personal side of life.

The structuralist perspective that I have outlined here suggests a different kind of social policy and intervention strategy for the elimination of sex discrimination than the "sex differences" or "sex roles" schools of thought (Kanter, 1976a). Instead of retraining women (or men) as individuals to acquire work-appropriate behavior, attitudes, and motivation, or providing different models of socialization, change strategies would focus on the structure of the organization as a total system. It is much easier, of course, to approach the individual, the family, or the school with change policies and research programs, as these are relatively small and powerless elements of the society compared to work organizations. But I argue that it is those complex organizations that more critically shape the prospects for the work life of adults, and it is thus those systems we must investigate and understand. It is the nature, form, and degree of hierarchy that should bear the burden of change.

NOTE

1. While the dual-factor theory of motivation has been challenged recently, these results stand independently of the theory.

REFERENCES

Bartol, Kathryn M. 1974. "Male versus female leaders: the effect of leader need for dominance on follower satisfaction." *Academy of Management Journal* 17(June):225–33.

———. 1975. "The effect of male versus female leaders on follower satisfaction and performance." *Journal of Business Research* 3(January):33–42.

Bartol, Kathryn M. and D. Anthony Butterfield. 1974. "Sex effects in evaluating leaders," Working Paper #74-10, University of Massachusetts School of Business Administration.

Bennis, Warren G., Norman Berkowitz, Mona Affinito, and Mary Malone. 1958a. "Authority, power, and the ability to influence." *Human Relations* 11:143–55.

———. 1958b. "Reference groups and loyalties in the outpatient department." *Administrative Science Quarterly* 2:481–500.

Blau, Peter M. and W. Richard Scott. 1962. *Formal Organizations.* San Francisco: Chandler.

Bonjean, Charles M., Grady D. Bruce, and Allen J. Williams, Jr. 1967. "Social mobility and job satisfaction: a replication and extension." *Social Forces* 46(June):492–501.

Bowman, G. W., N. B. Worthy, and S. A. Greyser. 1965. "Are women executives people?" *Harvard Business Review* 43(July–August): 14–30.

Burns, Tom. 1955. "The reference of conduct in small groups: cliques and cabals in occupational milieux." *Human Relations* 8:467–86.

Cattell, Raymond B. and Edwin D. Lawson. 1962. "Sex differences in small group performance." *Journal of Social Psychology* 58:141–45.

Chinoy, Ely. 1955. *Automobile Workers and the American Dream.* New York: Doubleday.

Cohen, Arthur R. 1958. "Upward communication in experimentally created hierarchies." *Human Relations* 11:41–53.

Constantini, Edmond and Kenneth H. Craik. 1972. "Women as politicians: the social background, personality, and political careers of female party leaders." *Journal of Social Issues* 28(2):217–36.

Coser, Rose Laub and Gerald Rokoff. 1970. "Women in the occupational world: social disruption and conflict." *Social Problems* 18:535–54.

Crowley, Joan E., Teresa E. Levitan, and Robert P. Quinn. 1973. "Seven deadly half-truths about women." *Psychology Today* 6(April):94–96.

Crozier, Michel. 1965. *The World of the Office Worker.* Trans. David Landau. Chicago: University of Chicago Press, 1971.

Cussler, Margaret. 1958. *The Woman Executive.* New York: Harcourt Brace.

Davis, Keith. 1967. *Human Relations at Work.* New York: McGraw-Hill.

Day, D. R. and R. M. Stogdill. 1972. "Leader behavior of male and female supervisors: a comparative study." *Personnel Psychology* 25:353–60.

Dittes, J. D. and H. H. Kelley. 1956. "Effects of difference conditions of acceptance upon conformity to group norms." *Journal of Abnormal and Social Psychology* 53:100–107.

Dubin, Robert. 1956. "Industrial workers' worlds." *Social Problems* 3(January):131–42.

Epstein, Cynthia Fuchs. 1970. *Woman's Place: Options and Limits on Professional Careers.* Berkeley: University of California Press.

Gardner, Burleigh B. 1945. *Human Relations in Industry.* Chicago: Richard D. Irwin.

Goodstadt, Barry E. and Larry A. Hjelle. 1973. "Power to the powerless: focus of control and the use of power." *Journal of Personality and Social Psychology* 27(July):190–6.

Goodstadt, B. and D. Kipnis. 1970. "Situational influences on the use of power." *Journal of Applied Psychology* 54:201–7.

Grunker, William J., Donald D. Cooke, and Arthur W. Kirsch. 1970. *Climbing the Job Ladder: A Study of Employee Advancement in Eleven Industries.* New York: Shelley and Co.

Hennig, Margaret. 1970. "Career development for women executives." Unpublished doctoral dissertation, Harvard Business School.

Hetzler, Stanley A. 1955. "Variations in role-playing patterns among different echelons of bureaucratic leaders." *American Sociological Review* 20(December):700–6.

Homall, Geraldine M. 1974. "The motivation to be promoted among non-exempt employees: An expectancy theory approach." Unpublished M.S. Thesis, Cornell University.

Hurwitz, Jacob I., Alvin F. Zander, and Bernard Hymovich. 1968. "Some effects of power on the relations among group members." In D. Cartwright and A. Zander (eds.), *Group Dynamics.* New York: Harper and Row.

Johnston, Ruth. 1975. "Pay and job satisfaction: a survey of some research findings." *International Labour Review* 3(May):441–9.

Kanter, Rosabeth Moss. 1975a. "The problems of tokenism." Working Paper, Center for Research on Women in Higher Education and the Professions, Wellesley College.

———. 1975b. "Women and the structure of organizations: explorations in theory and behavior." In M. Millman and R. M. Kanter (eds.), *Another Voice: Feminist Perspectives on Social Life and Social Science.* New York: Doubleday.

———. 1976a. "Research styles and intervention strategies: an argument for a social structural model." *Signs: A Journal of Women in Culture and Society* 2(Spring). And in M. Blaxall and B. Reagan (eds.), *Women and the Workplace.* Chicago: University of Chicago Press.

———. 1976b. "Women and organizations: sex roles, group dynamics, and change strategies." In A. G. Sargent (ed.), *Beyond Sex Roles.* St. Paul, Minnesota: West.

———. forthcoming. *Men and Women of the Corporation.* New York: Basic Books.

Laird, Donald A. and Eleanor C. Laird. 1942. The Psychology of Supervising the Working Woman. New York: McGraw-Hill.

Langer, Elinor. 1970. "Inside the New York Telephone Company." In W. L. O'Neil (ed.), *Women at Work.* Chicago: Quadrangle.

Laws, Judith Long. 1976. "Work aspirations in women: false leads and new starts." *Signs: A Journal of Women in Culture and Society* 2(Spring). And in M. Blaxall and B. Reagan (eds.), *Women and the Workplace.* Chicago: University of Chicago Press.

Levenson, Bernard. 1961. "Bureaucratic succession." Pp. 362–75 in A. Etzioni (ed.), *Complex Organizations: A Sociological Reader.* New York: Holt, Rinehart and Winston.

Lirtzman, Sidney I. and Mahmoud A. Wahba. 1972. "Determinants of coalitional behavior of men and women: sex roles or situational requirements?" *Journal of Applied Psychology* 56(5):406–11.

Marcus, Philip M. and James S. House. 1973. "Exchange between superiors and subordinates in large organizations." *Administrative Science Quarterly* 18:209–222.

Mayer, Kurt B. and Sidney Goldstein. 1964. "Manual workers as small businessmen." Pp. 537–50 in A. Shostak and W. Gomberg (eds.), *Blue Collar World.* Englewood Cliffs, New Jersey: Prentice-Hall.

Menzel, Herbert. 1957. "Public and private conformity under different conditions of acceptance in the group." *Journal of Abnormal and Social Psychology* 55:398–402.

Merton, Robert K. 1968. *Social Theory and Social Structure.* New York: Free Press.

Millman, Marcia and Rosabeth Moss Kanter (eds.) 1975. *Another Voice: Feminist Perspectives on Social Life and Social Science.* New York: Doubleday.

Pelz, Donald C. 1952. "Influence: a key to effective leadership in the first-line supervisor." *Personnel* 29:3–11.

Pennings, J. M. 1970. "Work-value systems of white-collar workers." *Administrative Science Quarterly* 15:397–405.

Purcell, Theodore V. 1960. *Blue Collar Man: Patterns of Dual Allegiance in Industry.* Cambridge: Harvard University Press.

Riesman, David. 1955. "Introduction." In Ely Chinoy, *Automobile Workers and the American Dream.* New York: Doubleday.

Roethlisberger, F. J. and William J. Dickson. 1939. *Management and the Worker.* Cambridge: Harvard University Press.

Rosen, Benson and Thomas H. Jerdee. 1973. "The influence of sex-role stereotypes on evaluations of male and female supervisory behavior." *Journal of Applied Psychology* 5(1):44–8.

Rousell, Cecile. 1974. "Relationship of sex of department head to department climate." *Administrative Science Quarterly* 19(June):211–20.

Sikula, Andrew F. 1973. "The uniqueness of secretaries as employees." *Journal of Business Education* 48(Fall):203–5.

Stein, Barry A. 1976. "Patterns of managerial promotion." Working Paper, Center for Research on Women in Higher Education and the Professions, Wellesley College.

Tannenbaum, Arnold S. 1966. *Social Psychology of the Work Organization.* Belmont, California: Wadsworth.

Tannenbaum, Arnold S., Bogdan Kavcic, Menachem Rosner, Mino Vianello and Georg Wieser. 1974. *Hierarchy in Organizations: An International Comparison.* San Francisco: Jossey-Bass.

Thibaut, John W. and Henry W. Riecken. 1955. "Authoritarianism, status, and the communication of aggression." *Human Relations* 8:95–120.

Tichy, Noel. 1973. "An analysis of clique formation and structure in organizations." *Administrative Science Quarterly* 18:194–207.

Uesugi, Thomas K. and W. Edgar Vinacke. 1963. "Strategy in a feminine game." *Sociometry* 26:35–88.

Vinacke, W. Edgar. 1959. "Sex roles in a three-person game." *Sociometry* 22(December): 343–60.

Waters, L. K. and Carrie Wherry Waters. 1969. "Correlates of job satisfaction and job dissatisfaction among female clerical workers." *Journal of Applied Psychology* 53(5):388–91.

Wild, Ray. 1969. "Job needs, job satisfaction, and job behavior of women manual workers." *Journal of Applied Psychology* 54(2):157–62.

11 Bringing the Men Back In: Sex Differentiation and the Devaluation of Women's Work

BARBARA F. RESKIN
University of Illinois, Urbana

To reduce sex differences in employment outcomes, we must examine them in the context of the sex-gender hierarchy. The conventional explanation for wage gap—job segregation—is incorrect because it ignores men's incentive to preserve their advantages and their ability to do so by establishing the rules that distribute rewards. The primary method through which all dominant groups maintain their hegemony is by differentiating the subordinate group and defining it as inferior and hence meriting inferior treatment. My argument implies that neither sex-integrating jobs nor implementing comparable worth will markedly improve women's employment status because men can subvert these mechanisms or even change the rules by which rewards are allocated. As evidence, I show that occupational integration has failed to advance

AUTHOR'S NOTE: This article is a revised version of the Cheryl Allyn Miller Lecture on Women and Social Change, presented at Loyola University on May 1, 1987. I am grateful to Sociologists for Women in Society and the friends and family of Cheryl Allyn Miller who prompted me to develop these ideas. The present version owes a great deal to Judith Lorber and Ronnie Steinberg for their extensive comments. I also wish to thank James Baron, Cynthia Epstein, Lowell Hargens, Mary Jackman, Kathleen Much, Deborah Rhode, Patricia Roos, and an anonymous reviewer for their helpful suggestions, but I ask readers to remember that I did not always take their advice and that they will not necessarily agree with my final conclusions. This article was partly prepared while I was a Fellow at the Center for Advanced Study in the Behavioral Sciences, where I was supported in part by a grant from the John D. and Catherine T. MacArthur Foundation. Grants from the National Science Foundation (SES-85-12452) and the Rockefeller Foundation Program on the Long-Term Implications of Changing Gender Roles supported the larger study that contributed to my developing these ideas.

women appreciably, and I argue that comparable worth is not likely to be much more effective. Instead, we must seek political analyses and political solutions.

One of the most enduring manifestations of sex inequality in industrial and postindustrial societies is the wage gap.[1] In 1986, as in 1957, among full-time workers in the United States, men earned 50 percent more per hour than did women. This disparity translated to $8,000 a year in median earnings, an all-time high bonus for being male. Most sociologists agree that the major cause of the wage gap is the segregation of women and men into different kinds of work (Reskin and Hartmann 1986). Whether or not women freely choose the occupations in which they are concentrated, the outcome is the same: the more proportionately female an occupation, the lower its average wages (Treiman and Hartmann 1981). The high level of job segregation (Bielby and Baron 1984) means that the 1963 law stipulating equal pay for equal work did little to reduce the wage gap.[2]

This "causal model"—that the segregation of women and men into different occupations causes the wage gap—implies two possible remedies. One is to equalize men and women on the causal variable—occupation—by ensuring women's access to traditionally male occupations. The other is to replace occupation with a causal variable on which women and men differ less, by instituting comparable-worth pay policies that compensate workers for the "worth" of their job regardless of its sex composition.

I contend, however, that the preceding explanation of the wage gap is incorrect because it omits variables responsible for the difference between women and men in their distribution across occupations. If a causal model is incorrect, the remedies it implies may be ineffective. Lieberson's (1985, p. 185) critique of causal analysis as it is commonly practiced explicates the problem by distinguishing between *superficial* (or surface) causes that *appear to* give rise to a particular outcome and *basic* causes that *actually* produce the outcome. For example, he cites the belief that the black-white income gap is due to educational differences and thus can be reduced by reducing the educational disparity. As Lieberson pointed out, this analysis misses the fact that "the dominant group . . . uses its dominance to advance its own position" (p. 166), so that eliminating race differences in education is unlikely to reduce racial inequality in income because whites will find another way to maintain their income advantage. In other words, what appear in this example to be both the outcome variable (the black-white income gap) and the imputed causal variable (the black-white educational disparity) may stem from the same basic cause (whites' attempt to maintain their economic advantage). If so, then if the disparity in education were eliminated, some other factor would arise to produce the same economic consequence (Lieberson 1985, p. 164).

Dominant groups remain privileged because they write the rules, and the rules they write "enable them *to continue to write the rules*" (Lieberson 1985, p. 167; emphasis added). As a result, they can change the rules to thwart challenges to their position. Consider the following example. Because Asian American students tend to outscore occidentals on standard admissions tests, they are increasingly overrepresented in some university programs. Some universities have allegedly responded by imposing quotas for Asian students (Hechinger 1987, p. C1) or weighing more heavily admissions criteria on which they believe Asian Americans do less well.[3]

How can one tell whether a variable is a superficial or a basic cause of some outcome? Lieberson offered a straightforward test: Does a change in that variable lead to a change in the outcome? Applying this rule to the prevailing causal theory of the wage gap, we find that between 1970 and 1980 the index of occupational sex segregation declined by 10 percent (Beller 1984), but the wage gap for full-time workers declined by just under 2 percent (computed from data in Blau and Ferber 1986, p. 171). Although its meaning may be equivocal,[4] this finding is consistent with other evidence that attributing the wage gap to job segregation misses its basic cause: men's propensity to maintain their privileges. This claim is neither novel nor specific to men. Marxist and conflict theory have long recognized that dominant groups act to preserve their position (Collins 1975). Like other dominant groups, men are reluctant to give up their advantages (Goode 1982). To avoid having to do so, they construct "rules" for distributing rewards that guarantee them the lion's share (see also Epstein 1985, p. 30). In the past, men cited their need as household heads for a "family wage" (May 1982) and designated women as secondary earners. Today, when millions of women who head households would benefit from such a rule, occupation has supplanted it as the principle for assigning wages.

Neoclassical economic theory holds that the market is the mechanism through which wages are set, but markets are merely systems of rules (Marshall and Paulin n.d., p. 15) that dominant groups establish for their own purposes. When other groups, such as labor unions, amassed enough power, they modified the "market" principle.[5] Steinberg (1987) observed that when consulted in making comparable-worth adjustments, male-dominated unions tended to support management over changes that would raise women's salaries (see also Simmons, Freedman, Dunkle, and Blau 1975, pp. 115–36; Hartmann 1976).

In sum, the basic cause of the income gap is not sex segregation but men's desire to preserve their advantaged position and their ability to do so by establishing rules to distribute valued resources in their favor.[6] Figure 11.1 represents this more complete causal model. Note that currently segregation

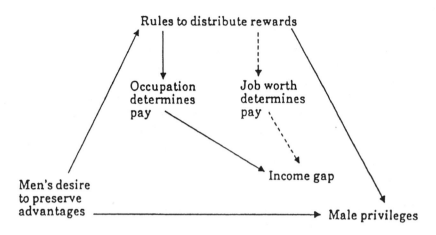

Figure 11.1. Heuristic Model of the Wage Gap

is a superficial cause of the income gap, in part through "crowding" (Bergmann 1974), but that some other distributional system such as comparable-worth pay could replace it with the same effect.

With respect to income, this model implies that men will resist efforts to close the wage gap. Resistance will include opposing equalizing women's access to jobs because integration would equalize women and men on the current superficial cause of the wage gap—occupation. Men may also try to preserve job segregation because it is a central mechanism through which they retain their dominance in other spheres, and because many people learn to prefer the company of others like them. My theory also implies that men will resist efforts to replace occupation with alternative principles for assigning pay that would mitigate segregation's effect on women's wages (as pay equity purports to do).

Before I offer evidence for these claims, let us examine how dominant groups in general and men in particular maintain their privileged position. I formulate my analysis with reference to dominant groups to emphasize that the processes I discuss are not specific to sex classes. It also follows that, were women the dominant sex, the claims I make about men's behavior should hold for women.

DIFFERENTIATION, DEVALUATION, AND HIERARCHY

Differentiation—the practice of distinguishing categories based on some attribute—is the fundamental process in hierarchical systems, a logical necessity for differential evaluation and differential rewards. But differentiation involves much more than merely acting on a preexisting difference. In a hierarchical context, differentiation assumes, amplifies, and even creates psychological and behavioral differences in order to ensure that the subordinate group differs from the dominant group (Epstein 1985, p. 36; Jagger 1983, pp. 109–10; MacKinnon 1987, p. 38; West and Zimmerman 1987, p. 137), "because the systematically differential delivery of benefits and deprivations require[s] making no mistake about who was who" (MacKinnon 1987, p. 40) and because "differences are inequality's post hoc excuse" (MacKinnon 1987, p. 8).

Differentiated status characteristics influence evaluations of people's behavior and their overall worth (Berger, Cohen, and Zelditch 1972; Pugh and Wahrman 1983). In hierarchical systems in which differentiation takes the form of an Aristotelian dichotomy, individuals are classified as either A ("the subject") or Not-A ("the other"). But these two classes are not construed as natural opposites that both have positive qualities; instead, A's characteristics are valued as normal or good and Not-A's as without value or negative (de Beauvoir 1953, p. xvi; Jay 1981).

The official response to the influx of south- and central-eastern European immigrants to the United States early in this century, when people assumed that each European country represented a distinct biological race (Lieberson 1980, p. 24), illustrates differentiation's central role in dominance systems. A congressionally mandated immigration commission concluded that "innate, ineradicable race distinctions separated groups of men from one another" and agreed on the

> necessity of classifying these races to know which were most worthy of survival. The immediate problem was to ascertain "whether there may not be certain races that are inferior to other races . . . to discover some test to show whether some may be better fitted for American citizenship than others." (Lieberson 1980, pp. 2–26)

Thus differentiation in all its forms supports dominance systems by demonstrating that superordinate and subordinate groups differ in essential ways and that such differences are natural and even desirable.

"Sex differentiation" versus "gender differentiation": a note on terminology. Scholars speak of both "sex" and "gender" differentiation: the former when biological sex or the "sex category" into which people are placed at birth (West and Zimmerman 1987, p. 127) is the *basis for* classification and differential treatment; the latter to refer to the *result* of that differential treatment. In order to emphasize that the initial biological difference (mediated through sex category) is the basis for differential treatment, I use the terms *sex differentiation* and *sex segregation.* This usage should not obscure

the fact that the process of converting sex category into gender is a social one or that most differences that are assumed to distinguish the sexes are socially created. I agree with Kessler and McKenna (1978) that the "gender attribution process" assumes dimorphism and seeks evidence of it to justify classifying people as male and female and treating them unequally. This article examines how and why those differences are produced.

Sex differentiation and devaluation. Probably no system of social differentiation is as extensive as that based on sex category. Its prevalence led anthropologist Gayle Rubin to claim that there is "a taboo against the sameness of men and women, a taboo dividing the sexes into two mutually exclusive categories, a taboo which exacerbates the biological differences between the sexes and thereby *creates* gender" (1975, p. 178). Moreover, although femaleness is not always devalued, its deviation from maleness in a culture that reserves virtues for men has meant the devaluation of women (Jay 1981). Bleier's research on biological scientists' study of sex differences illustrates this point: the "search for the truth about differences, [implies] that difference means *different from the white male norm and, therefore, inferior"* (1987, p. 2; emphasis added). In consequence, men's activities are typically valued above women's, regardless of their content or importance for group survival (Goode 1964; Mead 1949; Schur 1983, pp. 35–48), and both sexes come to devalue women's efforts (Major, McFarlin, and Gagnon 1984). Thus it should be no surprise that women's occupations pay less at least partly *because* women do them (Treiman and Hartmann 1981).

In short, differentiation is the sine qua non of dominance systems. Because of its importance, it is achieved through myriad ways:

> To go for a walk with one's eyes open is enough to demonstrate that humanity is divided into two classes of individuals whose clothes, faces, bodies, smiles, gaits, interests and occupations are manifestly different. (de Beauvoir 1953, p. xiv)

We differentiate groups in their location, appearance, and behavior, and in the tasks they do. Now let us turn to how these mechanisms operate to differentiate women and men.

PHYSICAL SEGREGATION

Dominant groups differentiate subordinate groups by physically isolating them—in ghettos, nurseries, segregated living quarters, and so on. Physical segregation fosters unequal treatment, because physically separate people can be treated differently and because it spares members of the dominant group the knowledge of the disparity and hides it from the subordinate group.

Although women and men are integrated in some spheres, physical separation continues to differentiate them (e.g., see Goffman 1977, p. 316).

Cohn's (1985) vivid account of women's physical segregation in the British Foreign Office in the nineteenth century illustrates the extent to which organizations have gone to separate the sexes. The Foreign Office hid its first female typists in an attic, but it failed to rescind the requirement that workers collect their pay on the ground floor. When payday came, managers evacuated the corridors, shut all the doors, and then sent the women running down the attic stairs to get their checks and back up again. Only after they were out of sight were the corridors reopened to men.

This account raises the question of *why* managers segregate working men and women. What licentiousness did the Foreign Office fear would occur in integrated hallways? Contemporary answers are markedly similar to turn-of-the-century fears. Compare the scenario expressed in a 1923 editorial in the *Journal of Accountancy* ("any attempt at heterogeneous personnel [in after-hours auditing of banks] would hamper progress and lead to infinite embarrassment" [p. 151]) with recent reactions to the prospect of women integrating police patrol cars, coal mines, and merchant marine vessels (e.g., Martin 1980). At or just below the surface lies the specter of sexual liaisons. For years, McDonald's founder Ray Kroc forbade franchisees to hire women counter workers because they would attract "the wrong type" of customers (Luxenburg 1985). The U.S. Army ended sex-integrated basic training to "facilitate toughening goals" (National Organization for Women 1982), and the Air Force reevaluated whether women could serve on two-person Minuteman missile-silo teams because "it could lead to stress" (*New York Times* 1984).

My thesis offers a more parsimonious alternative to these ad hoc explanations—men resist allowing women and men to work together *as equals* because doing so undermines differentiation and hence male dominance.

BEHAVIORAL DIFFERENTIATION

People's behavior is differentiated on their status-group membership in far too many ways for me to review the differences adequately here. I concentrate in this section on differentiation of behaviors that occur in the workplace: task differentiation and social differentiation.

Task differentiation assigns work according to group membership. It was expressed in the extreme in traditional Hindu society in which caste virtually determined life work. Task assignment based on sex category—the sexual division of labor—both prescribes and proscribes assorted tasks to each sex, and modern societies still assign men and women different roles in domestic work (Pleck 1985), labor-market work (Reskin and Hartmann 1986), and emotional and interpersonal work (Fishman 1982; Hochschild 1983).[7] Task differentiation generally assigns to lower-status groups the least desirable, most poorly rewarded work: menial, tedious, and degraded tasks, such as cleaning, disposing of waste, and caring for the dying.[8] This practice symbolizes and legitimates the subordinate group's low status, while making it appear to have an affinity for these undesirable tasks. As an added benefit, members of the dominant group don't have to do them! Important to discussions of the wage gap, because modern law and custom permit unequal pay for different work, task differentiation justifies paying the subordinate group lower wages, thereby ensuring their economic inferiority. Women's assignment to child care, viewed as unskilled work in our society, illustrates these patterns. Women are said to have a "natural talent" for it and similar work; men are relieved from doing it; society obtains free or cheap child care; and women are handicapped in competing with men. As researchers have shown, sex-based task differentiation of both nonmarket and market work legitimates women's lower pay, hinders women's ability to succeed in traditionally male enterprises, and, in general, reinforces men's hegemony (Coverman 1983).

Social differentiation is achieved through norms that set dominant and subordinate groups apart in their appearance (sumptuary rules) or behavior (etiquette rules [van den Berghe 1950]). When applied to sex, Goffman's (1976) concept of "gender display" encompasses both. Sumptuary rules require certain modes of dress, diet, or life-style of members of subordinate groups as emblems of their inferior status, and reserve other modes to distinguish the dominant group. For example, Rollins (1985) discovered that white female employers preferred black domestic employees to dress shabbily to exaggerate their economic inferiority. Sex-specific sumptuary rules are epitomized in norms that dictate divergent dress styles that often exaggerate physical sex differences and sometimes even incapacitate women (Roberts 1977).[9] An extreme example is the *burqua* fundamentalist Muslim women wear as a symbol of their status and as a portable system of segregation (Papanek 1973).

Etiquette rules support differentiation by requiring subordinate group members to display ritualized deference toward dominants. Relations between enlistees and officers (van den Berghe 1960) or female domestic workers and their employers (Rollins 1985) illustrate their role. Although typically it is the subordinate group that must defer, gender etiquette that requires middle- and upper-class men to display deference to women of the same classes preserves differentiation by highlighting women's differentness. Women who do not express gratitude or who refuse to accept the deference are faced with hostility, shattering the fiction that women hold the preferred position.

Physical segregation, behavioral differentiation, social separation, and even hierarchy are functional alternatives for satisfying the need for differentiation in domination systems. For example, when their physical integration with the dominant group means that a subordinate group's status differences might otherwise be invisible, special dress is usually required of them, as servants are required to wear uniforms. Physical separation can even compensate for the absence of hierarchy, a point acknowledged in the black folk saying that southern whites don't care how close blacks get if they don't get too high, and northern whites don't care how high blacks get if they don't get too close (Lukas 1985).

This substitutability explains why men will tolerate women in predominantly male work settings if they work in "women's" jobs and accept women doing "men's" jobs in traditionally female settings, but resist women doing traditionally male jobs in male work settings (e.g., Schroedel 1985). Physical proximity per se is not threatening as long as another form of differentiation sets women apart. But the absence of *any* form of differentiation precludes devaluation and unequal rewards and hence threatens the sex-gender hierarchy. Because of the centrality of differentiation in domination systems, dominant groups have a considerable stake in maintaining it.

DOMINANTS' RESPONSE TO CHALLENGES

Dominants respond to subordinates' challenges by citing the group differences that supposedly warrant differential treatment (Jackman and Muha 1984). Serious challenges often give rise to attempts to demonstrate biological differences scientifically.

The nineteenth-century antislavery and women's rights movements led reputable scientists to try to prove that women's and blacks' brains were underdeveloped (Bleier 1987). The Great Migration to the United States in the first two decades of this century fueled a eugenics movement that purported to establish scientifically the inferiority of south- and central-eastern Europeans (Lieberson 1980, pp. 25–26). The civil rights movement of the 1960s stimulated renewed efforts to establish racial differences in intelligence. And we are once again witnessing a spate of allegedly scientific research seeking a biological basis for presumed sex differences in cognitive ability and, specifically, for boys' higher average scores on math questions in some standardized tests. As Bleier pointed out, "The implication if not purposes of [such] research is to demonstrate that the structure of society faithfully reflects the natural order of things" (1987, p. 11; see also Epstein 1985, pp. 32, 35, for a similar pattern in the social sciences). According to Bleier, reputable journals have published studies that violate accepted standards of proof, and the scientific press has given dubious findings considerable attention (as in the news story in *Science* that asked, "Is There a Male

Math Gene?"). Although subsequently these studies have been discredited, the debate serves its purpose by focusing attention on how groups differ.[10]

MEN'S RESPONSE TO OCCUPATIONAL INTEGRATION

An influx of women into male spheres threatens the differentiation of men and women, and men resist (Goode 1982). One response is to bar women's entry. Women have had to turn to the courts to win entry into Little League sports, college dining clubs, private professional clubs, and the Rotary (Anderson 1987; Association of American Colleges 1985, p. 11; Schafran 1981). Recently, University of North Carolina trustees decried the fact that women are now a majority of UNC students, and some proposed changing the weights for certain admission criteria to restore the male majority (Greene 1987).[11] Twice since a shortage of male recruits forced the army to lift its quota on women, it has reduced the number of jobs open to women (Becraft 1987, p. 3).

Numerous studies have documented men's resistance to women entering "their" jobs (e.g., see Hartmann 1976 on cigar makers; Schroedel 1985 on a cross-section of trades). Sometimes the resistance is simply exclusion; at other times it is subtle barriers that block women's advancement or open harassment (Reskin 1978). Now that more women hold managerial jobs, one hears of "a glass ceiling" that bars middle-management women from top-level positions (e.g., Hymowitz and Schellhardt 1986), and Kanter (1987) claimed that organizations are changing the rules of what one must do to reach the top in order to make it more difficult for women to succeed.

My thesis implies that men will respond to women's challenge in the workplace by emphasizing how they differ from men. Especially common are reminders of women's "natural" roles as wife, mother, or sexual partner. Witness the recent—and subsequently disputed—claims that women who postponed marriage and childbearing to establish their careers had a negligible chance of finding husbands and were running the risk that their "biological clocks" would prevent pregnancy, and accounts of women dropping out of middle management to spend more time with their children.[12]

Men who cannot bar women from "male" jobs can still preserve differentiation in other spheres. Their attempts to do so may explain why so few husbands of wage-working women share housework (Pleck 1985, p. 146), as well as elucidating Wharton and Baron's (1987) finding that among men working in sex-integrated jobs, those whose wives were employed were more dissatisfied than unmarried men or men married to homemakers.

Another response to women's challenge is to weaken the mechanisms that have helped women advance in the workplace. Since 1980, the Reagan administration has sought to undermine equal-opportunity programs and affirmative-action regulations, and the campaign has partly succeeded. Efforts to dilute or eliminate Equal Employment Opportunity (EEO) programs are advanced by claims that sex inequality has disappeared (or that men now experience "reverse discrimination"). For example, the *New York Times* (Greer 1987, pp. C1, 10) recently described the Department of Commerce announcement that women now compose the majority in professional occupations as a "historic milestone," adding that "the barriers have fallen."

THE ILLUSION OF OCCUPATIONAL INTEGRATION

If male resistance is so pervasive, how can we explain the drop in the index of occupational sex segregation in the 1970s and women's disproportionate gains in a modest number of male-dominated occupations (Rytina and Bianchi 1984)? In order to answer this question, Patricia Roos and I embarked on a study of the changing sex composition of occupations (Reskin and Roos forthcoming). The results of our case studies of a dozen traditionally male occupations in which women made disproportionate statistical gains during the 1970s cast doubt on whether many women can advance economically through job integration.

The case studies revealed two general patterns. First, within many occupations nominally being integrated, men and women remain highly segregated, with men concentrated in the highest-status and best-paying jobs. For example, although women's representation in baking grew from 25 percent in 1970 to 41 percent in 1980, men continue to dominate production baking. The increase in women bakers is due almost wholly to their concentration in proliferating "in-store" bakeries (Steiger 1987). Although women now make up the majority of residential real estate salespersons, men still monopolize commercial sales (Thomas and Reskin 1987).

The second pattern shows that women often gained access to these occupations after changes in work content and declines in autonomy or rewards made the work less attractive to men (Cockburn 1986, p. 76). In some occupations, the growth of functions already socially labeled as "women's work" (e.g., clerical, communications, or emotional work) spurred the change. For example, computerization and the ensuing clericalization prompted women's entry into type-setting and composing (Roos 1986) and insurance adjusting and examining (Phipps 1986). An increasing emphasis on communicating and interpersonal or emotional work contributed to women's gains in insurance sales (Thomas 1987), insurance adjusting and examining (Phipps 1987), systems analysis (Donato 1986), public relations (Donato 1987), and bank and financial management (Bird 1987).

Brief summaries of our findings for two occupations illustrate these processes.[13] First, women's disproportionate gains in pharmacy have been largely confined to the retail sector (male pharmacists work disproportionately in research and management) and occurred after retail pharmacists lost professional status and entrepreneurial opportunities. After drug manufacturers took over the compounding of drugs, pharmacists increasingly resembled retail sales clerks; their primary duties became dispensing and record keeping. As chain and discount-store pharmacies supplanted independently owned pharmacies, retail pharmacy no longer offered a chance to own one's own business, reducing another traditional attraction for men. The resulting shortages of male pharmacy graduates eased women's access to training programs and retail jobs (Phipps 1987).

Second, book editing illustrates how declining autonomy and occupational prestige contributed to feminization of an occupation. For most of this century, the cultural image of publishing attracted bright young men and women despite very low wages. But during the 1970s, multinational conglomerates entered book publishing, with profound results. Their emphasis on the bottom line robbed publishing of its cultural aura, and the search for blockbusters brought a greater role for marketing people in acquisition decisions, thereby eroding editorial autonomy. As a result, editing could no longer compete effectively for talented men who could choose from better opportunities. Because women's occupational choices are more limited than men's, editing still attracted them, and the occupation's sex composition shifted accordingly (Reskin 1987).

In sum, although sex integration appears to have occurred in the 1970s among census-designated detailed occupations (Beller 1984), our findings indicate that within these occupations, women are segregated into certain specialties or work settings and that they gained entry because various changes made the occupations less attractive to men. The nominal integration that occurred in the 1970s often masks within-occupation segregation or presages resegregation of traditionally male occupations as women's work. In short, the workplace is still overwhelmingly differentiated by sex. Moreover, our preliminary results suggest that real incomes in the occupations we are studying declined during the 1970s; so reducing segregation at the occupational level appears to have been relatively ineffective in reducing the wage gap—and certainly not the remedy many experts predicted. This brings us to the other possible remedy for the wage gap—comparable worth.

IMPLICATIONS FOR COMPARABLE WORTH

The comparable-worth movement calls for equal pay for work of equal worth. Worth is usually determined by job-evaluation studies that measure the skill, effort, and responsibility required, but in practice, assessing worth often turns on how to conceptualize and measure skill.

Although some objective criteria exist for assessing skill (e.g., how long it takes a worker to learn the job [see Spenner 1985, pp. 132–136]), typically the designation of work as skilled is socially negotiated. Workers are most likely to win it when they control social resources that permit them to press their claims, such as a monopoly over a labor supply or authority based on their personal characteristics such as education, training, or sex (Phillips and Taylor 1980). As a result, the evaluation of "skill" is shaped by and confounded with workers' sex (Dex 1985, p. 100).

Groups use the same power that enabled them to define their work as skilled to restrict competition by excluding women (among others) from training for and practicing their trade or profession (Dex 1985, p. 103; see also Hartmann 1976), as Millicent Fawcett recognized almost a hundred years ago when she declared, "Equal pay for equal work is a fraud for women." Because men use their power to keep women "from obtaining equal skills, their work [cannot be] equal" (Hartmann 1976, p. 157). Roos's (1986) case history of the effect of technological change on women's employment in typesetting illustrates these points. When a Linotype machine was developed that "female typists could operate," the International Typographical Union (ITU) used its labor monopoly to force employers to agree to hire as operators only skilled printers who knew *all* aspects of the trade. By denying women access to apprenticeships or other channels to become fully skilled and limiting the job of operating the Linotype to highly skilled printers, the ITU effectively barred women from the new Linotype jobs. In short, the ITU used its monopoly power both to restrict women's access to skills and credentials and to define its members as "uniquely skilled" to operate the Linotype.

Excluded from occupations male workers define as skilled, women are often unable, for several reasons, to press the claim that work in traditionally female occupations is skilled. First, as I have shown, the devaluation of women's work leads whatever work women do to be seen as unskilled. Second, women's powerlessness prevents their successfully defining their work—caring for children, entering data, assembling microelectronic circuits—as skilled. Third, because many female-dominated occupations require workers to acquire skills before employment, skill acquisition is less visible and hence unlikely to be socially credited. Fourth, the scarcity of apprenticeship programs for women's jobs and women's exclusion from other programs denies women a credential society recognizes as denoting skill (Reskin and Hartmann 1986). Finally, "much of women's work involves recognizing and responding to subtle cues" (Feldberg 1984, p. 321), but the notion of "women's intuition" permits men to define such skills as inborn and hence not meriting compensation. Thus women are both kept from acquiring socially valued skills and not credited for those they do acquire (Steinberg 1984–85). As a result, the sex of the majority of workers in an occupation influences whether or not their work is classified as skilled (Feldberg 1984; Gregory 1987).

In view of these patterns, how effective can comparable worth be in reducing the wage gap? As with the Equal Pay Act, implementing it has symbolic value. Moreover, it would bar employers from underpaying women relative to their job-evaluation scores, the practice alleged in *AFSCME v. Washington State* (1985). But setting salaries according to an occupation's worth will reduce the wage gap only to the extent that (1) women have access to tasks that society values, (2) evaluators do not take workers' sex into account in determining a job's worth, and (3) implementers do not sacrifice equity to other political agendas.

Neither of the first two conditions holds. As I have shown, men already dominate jobs society deems skilled. Moreover, the tendency to devalue women's work is embedded in job-evaluation techniques that define job worth (Steinberg 1984–85); so such techniques may yield biased evaluations of traditionally female jobs and lower their job-evaluation scores (Treiman and Hartmann 1981; Marshall and Paulin n.d., p. 5). Beyond these difficulties is the problem of good-faith implementation. Acker (1987), Brenner (1987), and Steinberg (1987) have documented the problems in implementing comparable-worth pay adjustments. According to Steinberg (p. 8), New York State's proposed compensation model *negatively* values working with difficult clients, work performed in historically female and minority jobs (in other words, workers lose pay for doing it!), and Massachusetts plans to establish separate comparable-worth plans across sex-segregated bargaining units. For these reasons, the magnitude of comparable-worth adjustments have been about half of what experts expected—only 5 percent to 15 percent of salaries (Steinberg 1987).

Moreover, to the extent that equity adjustments significantly raise salaries in women's jobs, men can use their power to monopolize them. It is no accident that the men who integrated the female semiprofessions moved rapidly to the top (Grimm and Stern 1974). The recent experience of athletic directors provides an additional illustration. Title IX required college athletic programs to eliminate disparities in resources between women's and men's programs, including salaries. Within ten years the proportion of coaches for women's programs who were male grew from 10 percent to 50 percent (Alfano 1985). Finally, men as the primary implementers of job evaluation have a second line of defense—they can and do subvert the process of job evaluation.

CONCLUSION

Integrating men's jobs and implementing comparable-worth programs have helped some women economically and, more fully implemented, would help others. But neither strategy can be broadly effective because both are premised on a flawed causal model of the pay gap that assigns primary responsibility to job segregation. A theory that purports to explain unequal outcomes without examining the dominant group's stake in maintaining them is incomplete. Like other dominant groups, men make rules that preserve their privileges. With respect to earnings, the current rule—that one's job or occupation determines one's pay—has maintained white men's economic advantage because men and women and whites and nonwhites are differently distributed across jobs.[14]

Changing the allocation principle from occupation to job worth would help nonwhites and women if occupation were the pay gap's *basic* cause. But it is not. As long as a dominant group wants to subordinate others' interests to its own and is able to do so, the outcome—distributing more income to men than women—is, in a sense, its own cause, and tinkering with superficial causes will not substantially alter the outcome. Either the rule that one's occupation determines one's wages exists *because* men and women hold different occupations, or men and women hold different occupations because we allocate wages according to one's occupation. Obviously the dominant group will resist attempts to change the rules. In *Lemons v. City and County of Denver* (1980), the court called comparable worth "pregnant with the possibility of disrupting the entire economic system" (Steinberg 1987). "Disrupting the entire white-male dominance system" would have been closer to the mark.

If men's desire to preserve their privileges is the basic cause of the wage gap, then how can we bring about change? The beneficiaries of hierarchical reward systems yield their privileges only when failing to yield is more costly than yielding. Increasing the costs men pay to maintain the status quo or rewarding men for dividing resources more equitably may reduce their resistance.

As individuals, many men will gain economically if their partners earn higher wages. Of course, these men stand to lose whatever advantages come from outearning one's partner (Hartmann 1976; Kollock, Blumstein, and Schwartz 1985). But more important than individual adjustments are those achieved through organizations that have the power to impose rewards and penalties. Firms that recognize their economic stake in treating women equitably (or can be pressed by women employees or EEO agencies to act as if they do) can be an important source of pressure on male employees. Employers have effectively used various incentives to overcome resistance to affirmative action (e.g., rewarding supervisors for treating women fairly [Shaeffer and Lynton 1979; Walshok 1981]). Employers are most likely to use such mechanisms if they believe that regulatory agencies are enforcing equal-opportunity rules (Reskin and Hartmann 1986). We can attack men's resistance through political pressure on employers, the regulatory agencies that monitor them, and branches of government that establish and fund such agencies.

Analyses of sex inequality in the 1980s implicitly advance a no-fault concept of institutionalized discrimination rather than fixing any responsibility on men. But men *are* the dominant group, the makers and the beneficiaries of the rules. Of course, most men do not consciously oppose equality for women (Kluegel and Smith 1986) or try to thwart women's progress. When men and women work together, both can gain, as occurred when the largely male blue-collar union supported the striking Yale clerical and technical workers (Ladd-Taylor 1985; see also Glazer 1987). But as a rule, this silent majority avoids the fray, leaving the field to those who do resist to act on behalf of all men (Bergmann and Darity 1981). It is time to bring men back into our theories of economic inequality. To do so does not imply that women are passive agents. The gains we have made in the last two decades in the struggle for economic equality—redefining the kinds of work women can do, reshaping young people's aspirations, and amassing popular support for pay equity despite opponents' attempt to write it off as a "loony tune" idea—stand as testimony to the contrary. Just as the causal model I propose views the dominant group's self-interest as the source of unequal outcomes, so too does it see subordinate groups as the agents of change.

NOTES

1. Women's incomes are not depressed uniformly. Women of color continue to earn less than white women, particularly when their hours of work are controlled. As I indicate below, the same general social processes that subordinate women as a group—differentiation and devaluation—operate to preserve the advantages of white men *and women*.

2. Workplace segregation occurs across occupations and, within occupations, across jobs. For convenience, I speak primarily of occupational segregation because most segregation and income data are for occupations, but my remarks apply as well to jobs.

3. My informant said his campus now weighs the admissions essay more heavily for this reason.

4. For example, Smith and Ward (1984) attributed the wage gap's failure to narrow to the influx of less-experienced women into the labor force during the 1970s.

5. Some employers do reward productivity, as neoclassical economists predict, but for the most part, wages are attached to occupations—the proximate cause of workers' wages.

6. Of course, only a subset of men—predominantly upper-class whites—actually make rules, and the rules they make protect class- and race- as well as sex-based interests.

7. A full explanation of the specific forces that produce the sexual division of labor is beyond the scope of this article, but social-control systems, including gender ideology, "custom," socialization, and myriad institutionalized structures, shape the preferences of wives and husbands, workers and employers, women and men (Reskin and Hartmann 1986). These preferences in turn are played out in concert with institutional arrangements (training programs, personnel practices, child-care facilities, informal organization) to give rise to the task differentiation we observe in the home and workplace.

8. This is not to say that all tasks assigned to subordinate groups are unimportant or undesirable. Many, such as reproducing, socializing the young, and burying the dead, are essential. Others are more intrinsically pleasant (e.g., office work) than the work some domi-

nant-group members do (which has led economists to argue that men's wages are higher than women's partly to compensate them for doing less desirable jobs [Filer 1985]).

9. This perspective elucidates the importance that the media attached to the wearing, spurning, and burning of bras in the early 1970s. Shedding or burning these symbols of women's sex (and hence their status) constituted insubordination.

10. For example, at the 1987 meetings of the American Educational Research Association, 25 sessions reported research on sex differences in interest or achievement in math and science (Holden 1987, p. 660).

11. Trustee John Pope remarked, "Any time you get over 50 percent, it's becoming more and more a girl's school . . . and I don't think favoritism should be given to the females" (Greene 1987). It apparently did not strike him as favoritism when the rules produced a male majority.

12. The return in the late 1970s of feminine dress styles following the entry of large numbers of women into professional and managerial jobs is probably not coincidental. Although caution is in order in drawing conclusions about changing dress styles, a quick trip through a department store should persuade readers that dresses and skirts have supplanted pants for women (see Reskin and Roos 1987). Although fashion is ostensibly a woman's choice, most women are aware of the sanctions that await those who fail to dress appropriately.

13. Limited space forces me to condense sharply the causes of women's disproportional gains in these occupations. For a full account, see the complete studies.

14. It also serves the interest of the economically dominant classes by legitimating a wide disparity in income. Comparable-worth pay would largely preserve that disparity, in keeping with the class interests of its middle-class proponents and its implementers (Brenner 1987).

REFERENCES

Acker, Joan. 1987. "Sex Bias in Job Evaluation: A Comparable-Worth Issue." Pp. 183–96 in *Ingredients for Women's Employment Policy,* edited by Christine Bose and Glenna Spitze. Albany: SUNY University Press.

AFSCME v. State of Washington. 1985. 770 F.2d 1401. 9th Circuit.

Alfano, Peter. 1985. "Signs of Problems Amid the Progress." *New York Times* (December 14):25, 28.

Anderson, Susan Heller. 1987. "Men's Clubs Pressed to Open Doors for Women." *New York Times* (February 1).

Association of American Colleges. 1985. "Princeton's All-Male Eating Clubs Eat Crow." *Project on the Status and Education of Women* (Fall):11.

Becraft, Carolyn. 1987. "Women in the Military." Pp. 203–7 in *The American Woman: A Report in Depth,* edited by Sara Rix. New York: W. W. Norton.

Beller, Andrea. 1984. "Trends in Occupational Segregation by Sex and Race." Pp. 11–26 in *Sex Segregation in the Workplace: Trends, Explanations, Remedies,* edited by Barbara F. Reskin. Washington, DC: National Academy Press.

Berger, Joseph, Bernard P. Cohen, and Morris Zelditch. 1972. "Status Characteristics and Social Interaction." *American Sociological Review* 37:241–55.

Bergmann, Barbara R. 1974. "Occupational Segregation, Wages and Profits When Employers Discriminate by Race or Sex." *Eastern Economic Journal* 1:103–10.

Bergmann, Barbara R. and William Darity. 1981. "Social Relations, Productivity, and Employer Discrimination." *Monthly Labor Review* 104:47–9.

Bielby, William T. and James N. Baron. 1984. "A Woman's Place Is with Other Women." Pp. 27–55 in *Sex Segregation in the Workplace: Trends, Explanations, Remedies,* edited by Barbara F. Reskin. Washington, DC: National Academy Press.

Bird, Chloe. 1987. "Changing Sex Composition of Bank and Financial Managers." Unpublished manuscript. University of Illinois, Urbana.

Blau, Francine D. and Marianne A. Ferber. 1986. *The Economics of Women, Men and Work.* Englewood Cliffs, NJ: Prentice-Hall.

Bleier, Ruth. 1987. "Gender Ideology: The Medical and Scientific Construction of Women." Lecture presented at the University of Illinois, Urbana.

Brenner, Johanna. 1987. "Feminist Political Discourses: Radical vs. Liberal Approaches to the Feminization of Poverty and Comparable Worth." *Gender & Society* 1:447–65.

Cockburn, Cynthia. 1986. "The Relations of Technology: Implications for Theories of Sex and Class." Pp. 74–85 in *Gender and Stratification,* edited by Rosemary Crompton and Michael Mann. Cambridge, England: Polity Press.

Cohn, Samuel. 1985. *The Process of Occupational Sex Typing.* Philadelphia: Temple University Press.

Collins, Randall. 1975. *Conflict Sociology.* New York: Academic Press.

Coverman, Shelley. 1983. "Gender, Domestic Labor Time, and Wage Inequality." *American Sociological Review* 48:623–37.

de Beauvoir, Simone. 1953. *The Second Sex.* New York: Knopf.

Dex, Shirley. 1985. *The Sexual Division of Work.* New York: St. Martin's Press.

Donato, Katharine M. 1986. "Women in Systems Analysis." Paper presented at Annual Meetings, American Sociological Association, New York.

———. 1987. "Keepers of the Corporate Image: Women in Public Relations." Paper presented at Annual Meetings, American Sociological Association, Chicago.

Epstein, Cynthia F. 1985. "Ideal Roles and Real Roles or the Fallacy of the Misplaced Dichotomy." *Research in Social Stratification and Mobility* 4:29–51.

Feldberg, Roslyn L. 1984. "Comparable Worth: Toward Theory and Practice in the U.S." *Signs: Journal of Women in Culture and Society* 10:311–28.

Filer, Randall K. 1985. "Male-Female Wage Differences: The Importance of Compensating Differentials." *Industrial & Labor Relations Review* 38:426–37.

Fishman, Pamela. 1982. "Interaction: The Work Women Do." Pp. 170–80 in *Women and Work,* edited by Rachel Kahn-Hut and Arlene Kaplan Daniels. New York: Oxford University Press.

Glazer, Nona Y. 1987. "Where Are the Women? The Absence of Women as Social Agents in Theories of Occupational Sex Segregation." Paper presented at Annual Meetings, American Sociological Association, Chicago.

Goffman, Erving. 1976. "Gender Display." *Studies in the Anthropology of Visual Communication* 3:69–77.

———. 1977. "The Arrangement Between the Sexes." *Theory and Society* 4:301–31.

Goode, William C. 1964. *The Family.* Englewood Cliffs, NJ: Prentice-Hall.

———. 1982. "Why Men Resist." Pp. 121–50 in *Rethinking the Family,* edited by Barrie Thorne with Marilyn Yalom. New York: Longman.

Greene, Elizabeth. 1987. "Too Many Women? That's The Problem at Chapel Hill, Say Some Trustees." *Chronicle of Higher Education* (January 28):27–8.

Greer, William R. 1987. "In Professions, Women Now a Majority." *New York Times* (March 19):C1, 10.

Gregory, R. G. 1987. Lecture, Labor and Industrial Relations Institute, University of Illinois, Urbana.

Grimm, James W. and Robert N. Stern. 1974. "Sex Roles and Internal Labor Market Structures: The Female Semi-Professions." *Social Problems* 21:690–705.

Hartmann, Heidi. 1976. "Capitalism, Patriarchy, and Job Segregation by Sex." *Signs: Journal of Women in Culture and Society* 1, (Part 2):137–69.

Hechinger, Fred M. 1987. "The Trouble with Quotas." *New York Times* (February 10):C1.

Hochschild, Arlie. 1983. *The Managed Heart.* Berkeley, CA: University of California Press.

Holden, Constance. 1987. "Female Math Anxiety on the Wane." *Science* 236: 660–61.

296 STRUCTURED INEQUALITY

Hymowitz, Carol and Timothy D. Schellhardt. 1986. "The Glass Ceiling." *The Wall Street Journal* (March 24):Section 4, 1.

Jackman, Mary and Michael Muha. 1984. "Education and Intergroup Attitudes." *American Sociological Review* 49:751–69.

Jagger, Allison M. 1983. *Feminist Politics and Human Nature.* Totowa, NJ: Rowman & Allanheld.

Jay, Nancy. 1981. "Gender and Dichotomy." *Feminist Studies* 7:38–56.

Journal of Accountancy. 1984. "J of A Revisited: Women in Accountancy." 158:151–2.

Kanter, Rosabeth Moss. 1987. "Men and Women of the Change Master Corporation (1977–1987 and Beyond): Dilemmas and Consequences of Innovations of Organizational Structure." Paper presented at Annual Meetings, Academy of Management, New Orleans.

Kessler, Suzanne and Wendy McKenna. 1978. *Gender: An Ethnomethodological Approach.* New York: John Wiley.

Kluegel, James R. and Eliot R. Smith. 1986. *Beliefs about Inequality.* New York: Aldine de Gruyter.

Kollock, Peter, Philip Blumstein, and Pepper Schwartz. 1985. "Sex and Power in Interaction." *American Sociological Review* 50:34–46.

Ladd-Taylor, Molly. 1985. "Women Workers and the Yale Strike." *Feminist Studies* 11:464–89.

Lemon v. City and County of Denver. 1980. 620 F.2d 228. 10th Circuit.

Lieberson, Stanley. 1980. *A Piece of the Pie.* Berkeley: University of California Press.

———. 1985. *Making It Count.* Berkeley: University of California Press.

Lukas, J. Anthony. 1985. *Common Ground.* New York: Knopf.

Luxenberg, Stan. 1985. *Roadside Empires.* New York: Viking.

MacKinnon, Catharine. 1987. *Feminism Unmodified.* Cambridge, MA: Harvard University Press.

Major, Brenda, Dean B. McFarlin, and Diana Gagnon. 1984. "Overworked and Underpaid: On the Nature of Gender Differences in Personal Entitlement." *Journal of Personality and Social Psychology* 47:1399–1412.

Marshall, Ray and Beth Paulin. N.D. "Some Practical Aspects of Comparable Worth." Unpublished manuscript.

Martin, Susan E. 1980. *Breaking and Entering.* Berkeley: University of California Press.

May, Martha. 1982. "Historical Problems of the Family Wage: The Ford Motor Company and the Five Dollar Day." *Feminist Studies* 8:395–424.

Mead, Margaret. 1949. *Male and Female.* New York: Morrow.

National Organization for Women. 1982. *NOW Times,* July.

New York Times. 1984. "Air Force Studies Male-Female Missile Crews." December 12.

———. 1987. "Dispute on Sex Ratio Troubles Women at North Carolina University." March 22.

Papanek, Hanna. 1973. "Purdah: Separate Worlds and Symbolic Shelter." *Comparative Studies in Society and History* 15:289–325.

Phillips, Anne and Barbara Taylor. 1980. "Sex and Skill." *Feminist Review* 6:79–88.

Phipps, Polly. 1986. "Occupational Resegregation: A Case Study of Insurance Adjusters, Examiners and Investigators." Paper presented at Annual Meetings, American Sociological Association, New York.

———. 1987. "Women in Pharmacy: Industrial and Occupational Change." Paper presented at Annual Meetings, American Sociological Association, Chicago.

Pleck, Joseph H. 1985. *Working Wives, Working Husbands.* Beverly Hills, CA: Sage.

Pugh, M. D. and Ralph Wahrman. 1983. "Neutralizing Sexism in Mixed-Sex Groups: Do Women Have to Be Better than Men?" *American Journal of Sociology* 88:746–62.

Reskin, Barbara F. 1978. "Sex Differentiation and the Social Organization of Science." *Sociological Inquiry* 48:6–36.

————. 1987. "Culture, Commerce and Gender: The Changing Sex Composition of Book Editors." Unpublished manuscript.

———— and Heidi I. Hartmann. 1986. *Women's Work, Men's Work, Sex Segregation on the Job.* Washington, DC: National Academy Press.

Reskin, Barbara F. and Patricia A. Roos. 1987. "Sex Segregation and Status Hierarchies." Pp. 1–21 in *Ingredients for Women's Employment Policy,* edited by Christine Bose and Glenna Spitze. Albany: SUNY University Press.

————. Forthcoming. *Gendered Work and Occupational Change.*

Roberts, Helene E. 1977. "The Exquisite Slave: The Role of Clothes in the Making of the Victorian Woman." *Signs: Journal of Women in Culture and Society* 2:554–69.

Rollins, Judith. 1985. *Between Women.* Philadelphia: Temple University Press.

Roos, Patricia A. 1986. "Women in the Composing Room: Technology and Organization as the Determinants of Social Change." Paper presented at Annual Meetings, American Sociological Association, New York.

Rubin, Gayle. 1975. "The Traffic in Women: Notes on the 'Political Economy' of Sex." Pp. 157–210 in *Toward an Anthropology of Women,* edited by Rayna R. Reiter. New York: Monthly Review Press.

Rytina, Nancy F. and Suzanne M. Bianchi. 1984. "Occupational Reclassification and Changes in Distribution by Gender." *Monthly Labor Review* 107:11–17.

Schafran, Lynn Hecht. 1981. *Removing Financial Support from Private Clubs that Discriminate Against Women.* New York: Women and Foundations Corporate Philanthropy.

Schroedel, Jean Reith. 1985. *Alone in a Crowd.* Philadelphia: Temple University Press.

Schur, Edwin M. 1983. *Labeling Women Deviant.* New York: Random House.

Shaeffer, Ruth Gilbert and Edith F. Lynton. 1975. *Corporate Experience in Improving Women's Job Opportunities.* Report no. 755. New York: The Conference Board.

Simmons, Adele, Ann Freedman, Margaret Dunkle, and Francine Blau. 1975. *Exploitation from 9 to 5.* Lexington, MA: Lexington.

Smith, James P. and Michael Ward. 1984. *Women's Wages and Work in the Twentieth Century.* R-3119 NICHD. Santa Monica, CA: Rand Corporation.

Spenner, Kenneth I. 1985. "The Upgrading and Downgrading of Occupations: Issues, Evidence, and Implications for Education." *Review of Educational Research* 55 (Summer): 125–54.

Steiger, Thomas. 1987. "Female Employment Gains and Sex Segregation: The Case of Bakers." Paper presented at Annual Meetings, American Sociological Association, Chicago.

Steinberg, Ronnie J. 1984–85. "Identifying Wage Discrimination and Implementing Pay Equity Adjustments." In *Comparable Worth: Issues for the 80s.* Vol. 1. Washington, DC: U.S. Commission on Civil Rights.

————. 1987. "Radical Challenges in a Liberal World: The Mixed Successes of Comparable Worth." *Gender & Society* 1:466–75.

Thomas, Barbara J. 1987. "Changing Sex Composition of Insurance Agents." Unpublished manuscript.

———— and Barbara F. Reskin. 1987. "Occupational Change and Sex Integration in Real Estate Sales." Paper presented at the Annual Meetings, American Sociological Association, Chicago.

Treiman, Donald J. and Heidi Hartmann. 1981. *Women, Work and Wages.* Washington, DC: National Academy Press.

van den Berghe, Pierre. 1960. "Distance Mechanisms of Stratification." *Sociology and Social Research* 44:155–64.

Walshok, Mary Lindenstein. 1981. "Some Innovations in Industrial Apprenticeship at General Motors." Pp. 173–82 in *Apprenticeship Research: Emerging Findings and Future Trends* edited by Vernon M. Briggs, Jr., and Felician Foltman. Ithaca: New York State School of Industrial Relations.

West, Candace and Don H. Zimmerman. 1987. "Doing Gender." *Gender & Society* 1:125–51.
Wharton, Amy and James Baron. 1987. "The Impact of Gender Segregation on Men at Work."
    American Sociological Review 52:574–87.

12   Hierarchies, Jobs, Bodies:
A Theory of Gendered Organizations

JOAN ACKER
University of Oregon and Arbetslivscentrum, Stockholm

In spite of feminist recognition that hierarchical organizations are an important location of male dominance, most feminists writing about organizations assume that organizational structure is gender neutral. This article argues that organizational structure is not gender neutral; on the contrary, assumptions about gender underlie the documents and contracts used to construct organizations and to provide the commonsense ground for theorizing about them. Their gendered nature is partly masked through obscuring the embodied nature of work. Abstract jobs and hierarchies, common concepts in organizational thinking, assume a disembodied and universal worker. This worker is actually a man; men's bodies, sexuality, and relationships to procreation and paid work are subsumed in the image of the worker. Images of men's bodies and masculinity pervade organizational processes, marginalizing women and contributing to the maintenance of gender segregation in organizations. The positing of gender-neutral and disembodied organizational structures and work relations is part of the larger strategy of control in industrial capitalist societies, which, at least partly, are built upon a deeply embedded substructure of gender difference.

Most of us spend most of our days in work organizations that are almost always dominated by men. The most powerful organizational positions are almost entirely occupied by men, with the exception of the occasional

AUTHOR'S NOTE: Presented at the American Sociological Association Annual Meetings, Chicago, August 1987. I wish to thank Judith Lorber, Pat Martin, and Ronnie Steinberg, who contributed a great deal to this article through their careful and insightful comments and suggestions. Conversations with Harriet Holter, Carole Pateman, and Dorothy Smith also helped my thinking.

biological female who acts as a social man (Sorenson 1984). Power at the national and world level is located in all-male enclaves at the pinnacle of large state and economic organizations. These facts are not news, although sociologists paid no attention to them until feminism came along to point out the problematic nature of the obvious (Acker and Van Houten 1974; Moss Kanter 1975, 1977). Writers on organizations and organizational theory now include some consideration of women and gender (Clegg and Dunkerley 1980; Mills 1988; Morgan 1986), but their treatment is usually cursory, and male domination is, on the whole, not analyzed and not explained (Hearn and Parkin 1983).

Among feminist social scientists there are some outstanding contributions on women and organizations, such as the work of Moss Kanter (1977), Feldberg and Glenn (1979), MacKinnon (1979), and Ferguson (1984). In addition, there have been theoretical and empirical investigations of particular aspects of organizational structure and process (Izraeli 1983; Martin 1985), and women's situations have been studied using traditional organizational ideas (Dexter 1985; Wallace 1982). Moreover, the very rich literature, popular and scholarly, on women and work contains much material on work organizations. However, most of this new knowledge has not been brought together in a systematic feminist theory of organizations.

A systematic theory of gender and organizations is needed for a number of reasons. First, the gender segregation of work, including divisions between paid and unpaid work, is partly created through organizational practices. Second, and related to gender segregation, income and status inequality between women and men is also partly created in organizational processes; understanding these processes is necessary for understanding gender inequality. Third, organizations are one arena in which widely disseminated cultural images of gender are invented and reproduced. Knowledge of cultural production is important for understanding gender construction (Hearn and Parkin 1987). Fourth, some aspects of individual gender identity, perhaps particularly masculinity, are also products of organizational processes and pressures. Fifth, an important feminist project is to make large-scale organizations more democratic and more supportive of humane goals.

In this article, I begin by speculating about why feminist scholars have not debated organizational theory. I then look briefly at how those feminist scholars who have paid attention to organizations have conceptualized them. In the main part of the article, I examine organizations as gendered processes in which both gender and sexuality have been obscured through a gender-neutral, asexual discourse, and suggest some of the ways that gender, the body, and sexuality are part of the processes of control in work organizations. Finally, I point to some directions for feminist theory about this ubiquitous human invention.

WHY SO LITTLE FEMINIST DEBATE ON ORGANIZATIONS?

The early radical feminist critique of sexism denounced bureaucracy and hierarchy as male-created and male-dominated structures of control that oppress women. The easiest answer to the "why so little debate" question is that the link between masculinity and organizational power was so obvious that no debate was needed. However, experiences in the feminist movement suggest that the questions are not exhausted by recognizing male power.

Part of the feminist project was to create nonhierarchical, egalitarian organizations that would demonstrate the possibilities of nonpatriarchal ways of working (Gould 1979; Martin 1990). Although many feminist organizations survived, few retained this radical-democratic form (Martin 1990). Others succumbed to the same sorts of pressures that have undermined other utopian experiments with alternative work forms (Newman 1980), yet analyses of feminist efforts to create alternative organizations (Freeman 1975; Gould 1979) were not followed by debates about the feasibility of nonpatriarchal, nonhierarchical organization or the relationship of organizations and gender. Perhaps one of the reasons was that the reality was embarrassing; women failing to cooperate with each other, taking power and using it in oppressive ways, creating their own structures of status and reward were at odds with other images of women as nurturing and supportive.

Another reason for feminist theorists' scant attention to conceptualizing organizations probably lies in the nature of the concepts and models at hand. As Dorothy Smith (1979) has argued, the available discourses on organizations, the way that organizational sociology is defined as an area or domain "is grounded in the working worlds and relations of men, whose experience and interests arise in the course of and in relation to participation in the ruling apparatus of this society" (p. 148). Concepts developed to answer managerial questions, such as how to achieve organizational efficiency, were irrelevant to feminist questions, such as why women are always concentrated at the bottom of organizational structures.

Critical perspectives on organizations, with the notable exception of some of the studies of the labor process (Braverman 1974; Knights and Willmott 1985), although focusing on control, power, exploitation, and how these relations might be changed, have ignored women and have been insensitive to the implications of gender for their own goals. The active debate on work democracy, the area of organizational exploration closest to feminist concerns about oppressive structures, has been almost untouched by feminist insights (Rothschild 1987; Rothschild-Whitt, 1979). For example, Carole Pateman's influential book, *Participation and Democratic Theory* (1970), critical in shaping the discussions on democratic organization in the 1970s, did not consider women or gender. More recently, Pateman (1983a, 1983b, 1988) has examined the fundamental ideas of democracy from a feminist perspective, and other feminist political scientists have criticized theories of democracy (Eisenstein 1981), but on the whole, their work is isolated from the main discourse on work organization and democracy.

Empirical research on work democracy has also ignored women and gender. For example, in the 1980s, many male Swedish researchers saw little relation between questions of democracy and gender equality (Acker 1982), with a few exceptions (Fry 1986). Other examples are studies of Mondragon, a community in the Spanish Basque country, which is probably the most famous attempt at democratic ownership, control, and organization. Until Sally Hacker's feminist study (1987), researchers who went to Mondragon to see this model of work democracy failed to note the situation of women and asked no questions about gender. In sum, the absence of women and gender from theoretical and empirical studies about work democracy provided little material for feminist theorizing.

Another impediment to feminist theorizing is that the available discourses conceptualize organizations as gender neutral. Both traditional and critical approaches to organizations originate in the male, abstract intellectual domain (Smith 1988) and take as reality the world as seen from that standpoint. As a relational phenomenon, gender is difficult to see when only the masculine is present. Since men in organizations take their behavior and perspectives to represent the human, organizational structures and processes are theorized as gender neutral. When it is acknowledged that women and men are affected differently by organizations, it is argued that gendered attitudes and behavior are brought into (and contaminate) essentially gender-neutral structures. This view of organizations separates structures from the people in them.

Current theories of organization also ignore sexuality. Certainly, a gender-neutral structure is also asexual. If sexuality is a core component of the production of gender identity, gender images, and gender inequality, organizational theory that is blind to sexuality does not immediately offer avenues into the comprehension of gender domination (Hearn and Parkin 1983, 1987). Catharine MacKinnon's (1982) compelling argument that sexual domination of women is embedded within legal organizations has not to date become part of mainstream discussions. Rather, behaviors such as sexual harassment are viewed as deviations of gendered actors, not, as MacKinnon (1979) might argue, as components of organizational structure.

FEMINIST ANALYSES OF ORGANIZATIONS

The treatment of women and gender most assimilated into the literature on organizations is Rosabeth Kanter's *Men and Women of the Corporation* (1977). Moss Kanter sets out to show that gender differences in organizational behavior are due to structure rather than to characteristics of women and men as individuals (1977, 291-92). She argues that the problems women have in large organizations are consequences of their structural placement, crowded in dead-end jobs at the bottom and exposed as tokens at the top. Gender enters the picture through organizational roles that "carry characteristic images of the kinds of people that should occupy them" (p. 250). Here, Moss Kanter recognizes the presence of gender in early models of organizations:

> A "masculine ethic" of rationality and reason can be identified in the early image of managers. This "masculine ethic" elevates the traits assumed to belong to men with educational advantages to necessities for effective organizations: a tough-minded approach to problems; analytic abilities to abstract and plan; a capacity to set aside personal, emotional considerations in the interests of task accomplishment; a cognitive superiority in problem-solving and decision making. (1974, 43)

Identifying the central problem of seeming gender neutrality, Moss Kanter observes: "While organizations were being defined as sex-neutral machines, masculine principles were dominating their authority structures" (1977, 46).

In spite of these insights, organizational structure, not gender, is the focus of Moss Kanter's analysis. In posing the argument as structure *or* gender, Moss Kanter also implicitly posits gender as standing outside of structure, and she fails to follow up her own observations about masculinity and organizations (1977, 22). Moss Kanter's analysis of the effects of organizational position applies as well to men in low-status positions. Her analysis of the effect of numbers, or the situation of the "token" worker, applies also to men as minorities in women-predominant organizations, but fails to account for gender differences in the situation of the token. In contrast to the token woman, White men in women-dominated workplaces are likely to be positively evaluated and to be rapidly promoted to positions of greater authority. The specificity of male dominance is absent in Moss Kanter's argument, even though she presents a great deal of material that illuminates gender and male dominance.

Another approach, using Moss Kanter's insights but building on the theoretical work of Hartmann (1976), is the argument that organizations have a dual structure, bureaucracy and patriarchy (Ressner 1987). Ressner argues that bureaucracy has its own dynamic, and gender enters through patriarchy, a more or less autonomous structure, that exists alongside the bureaucratic structure. The analysis of two hierarchies facilitates and clarifies the discussion of women's experiences of discrimination, exclusion, segregation, and low wages. However, this approach has all the problems of two systems theories of women's oppression (Young 1981; see also Acker 1988): the central theory of bureaucratic or organizational structure is unexamined, and patriarchy is added to allow the theorist to deal with women. Like Moss Kanter, Ressner's approach implicitly accepts the assumption of mainstream organizational theory that organizations are gender-neutral social phenomena.

Ferguson, in *The Feminist Case Against Bureaucracy* (1984), develops a radical feminist critique of bureaucracy as an organization of oppressive male power, arguing that it is both mystified and constructed through an abstract discourse on rationality, rules, and procedures. Thus, in contrast to the implicit arguments of Moss Kanter and Ressner, Ferguson views bureaucracy itself as a construction of male domination. In response to this overwhelming organization of power, bureaucrats, workers, and clients are all "feminized," as they develop ways of managing their powerlessness that at the same time perpetuate their dependence. Ferguson argues further that feminist discourse, rooted in women's experiences of caring and nurturing outside bureaucracy's control, provides a ground for opposition to bureaucracy and for the development of alternative ways of organizing society.

However, there are problems with Ferguson's theoretical formulation. Her argument that feminization is a metaphor for bureaucratization not only uses a stereotype of femininity as oppressed, weak, and passive, but also, by equating the experience of male and female clients, women workers, and male bureaucrats, obscures the specificity of women's experiences and the connections between masculinity and power (Brown 1984; see also Martin 1987; Mitchell 1986; Ressner 1986). Ferguson builds on Foucault's (1979) analysis of power as widely diffused and constituted through discourse, and the problems in her analysis have their origin in Foucault, who also fails to place gender in his analysis of power. What results is a disembodied, and consequently gender-neutral, bureaucracy as the oppressor. That is, of course, not a new vision of bureaucracy, but it is one in which gender enters only as analogy, rather than as a complex component of processes of control and domination.

In sum, some of the best feminist attempts to theorize about gender and organizations have been trapped within the constraints of definitions of the theoretical domain that cast organizations as gender neutral and asexual. These theories take us only part of the way to understanding how deeply embedded gender is in organizations. There is ample empirical evidence: We know now that gender segregation is an amazingly persistent pattern and that the gender identity of jobs and occupations is repeatedly reproduced, often in new forms (Bielby and Baron 1987; Reskin and Roos 1987; Strober and Arnold 1987). The reconstruction of gender segregation is an integral part of the dynamic of technological and organizational change (Cockburn 1983, 1985; Hacker 1981). Individual men and particular groups of men do not always win in these processes, but masculinity always seems to symbolize self-respect for men at the bottom and power for men at the top, while confirming for both their gender's superiority. Theories that posit organization and bureaucracy as gender neutral cannot adequately account for this continual gendered structuring. We need different theoretical strategies that examine organizations as gendered processes in which sexuality also plays a part.

ORGANIZATION AS GENDERED PROCESSES

The idea that social structure and social processes are gendered has slowly emerged in diverse areas of feminist discourse. Feminists have elaborated gender as a concept to mean more than a socially constructed, binary identity and image. This turn to gender as an analytic category (Connell 1987; Harding 1986; Scott 1986) is an attempt to find new avenues into the dense and complicated problem of explaining the extraordinary persistence through history and across societies of the subordination of women. Scott, for example, defines gender as follows: "The core of the definition rests on an integral connection between two propositions; gender is a constitutive element of social relationships based on perceived differences between the sexes, and gender is a primary way of signifying relationships of power" (1986, 1067).

New approaches to the study of waged work, particularly studies of the labor process, see organizations as gendered, not as gender neutral (Cockburn 1985; Game and Pringle 1984; Knights and Willmott 1985; Phillips and Taylor 1986; Sorenson 1984) and conceptualize organizations as one of the locations of the inextricably intertwined production of both gender and class relations. Examining class and gender (Acker 1988), I have argued that class is constructed through gender and that class relations are always gendered. The structure of the labor market, relations in the workplace, the control of the work process, and the underlying wage relation are always affected by symbols of gender, processes of gender identity, and material inequalities between women and men. These processes are complexly related to and powerfully support the reproduction of the class structure. Here, I will focus on the interface of gender and organizations, assuming the simultaneous presence of class relations.

To say that an organization, or any other analytic unit, is gendered means that advantage and disadvantage, exploitation and control, action and emotion, meaning and identity, are patterned through and in terms of a distinction between male and female, masculine and feminine. Gender is not an addition to ongoing processes, conceived as gender neutral. Rather, it is an integral part of those processes, which cannot be properly understood without an analysis of gender (Connell 1987; West and Zimmerman 1987). Gendering occurs in at least five interacting processes (cf. Scott 1986) that, although analytically distinct, are, in practice, parts of the same reality.

First is the construction of divisions along lines of gender—divisions of labor, of allowed behaviors, of locations in physical space, of power, including the institutionalized means of maintaining the divisions in the structures of labor markets, the family, the state. Such divisions in work organizations are well documented (e.g., Moss Kanter 1977) as well as often obvious to casual observers. Although there are great variations in the patterns and extent of gender division, men are almost always in the highest positions of organizational power. Managers' decisions often initiate gender divisions (Cohn 1985), and organizational practices maintain them—although they also take on new forms with changes in technology and the labor process. For example, Cynthia Cockburn (1983, 1985) has shown how the introduction of new technology in a number of industries was accompanied by a reorganization, but not abolition, of the gendered division of labor that left the technology in men's control and maintained the definition of skilled work as men's work and unskilled work as women's work.

Second is the construction of symbols and images that explain, express, reinforce, or sometimes oppose those divisions. These have many sources or forms in language, ideology, popular and high culture, dress, the press, television. For example, as Moss Kanter (1975), among others, has noted, the image of the top manager or the business leader is an image of successful, forceful masculinity (see also Lipman-Blumen 1980). In Cockburn's studies, men workers' images of masculinity linked their gender with their technical skills; the possibility that women might also obtain such skills represented a threat to that masculinity.

The third set of processes that produce gendered social structures, including organizations, are interactions between women and men, women and women, men and men, including all those patterns that enact dominance and submission. For example, conversation analysis shows how gender differences in interruptions, turn taking, and setting the topic of discussion recreate gender inequality in the flow of ordinary talk (West and Zimmerman 1983). Although much of this research has used experimental groups, qualitative accounts of organizational life record the same phenomena: Men are the actors, women the emotional support (Hochschild 1983).

Fourth, these processes help to produce gendered components of individual identity, which may include consciousness of the existence of the other three aspects of gender, such as, in organizations, choice of appropriate work, language use, clothing, and presentation of self as a gendered member of an organization (Reskin and Roos 1987).

Finally, gender is implicated in the fundamental, ongoing processes of creating and conceptualizing social structures. Gender is obviously a basic constitutive element in family and kinship, but, less obviously, it helps to frame the underlying relations of other structures, including complex organizations. Gender is a constitutive element in organizational logic, or the underlying assumptions and practices that construct most contemporary work organizations (Clegg and Dunkerley 1980). Organizational logic appears to be gender neutral; gender-neutral theories of bureaucracy and organizations employ and give expression to this logic. However, underlying both academic theories and practical guides for managers is a gendered substructure that is reproduced daily in practical work activities and, somewhat less frequently, in the writings of organizational theorists (cf. Smith 1988).

Organizational logic has material forms in written work rules, labor contracts, managerial directives, and other documentary tools for running large organizations, including systems of job evaluation widely used in the comparable-worth strategy of feminists. Job evaluation is accomplished through the use and interpretation of documents that describe jobs and how they are to be evaluated. These documents contain symbolic indicators of structure; the ways that they are interpreted and talked about in the process of job evaluation reveal the underlying organizational logic. I base the following theoretical discussion on my observations of organizational logic in action in the job-evaluation component of a comparable-worth project (Acker 1987, 1989, 1990).

Job evaluation is a management tool used in every industrial country, capitalist and socialist, to rationalize the organizational hierarchy and to help in setting equitable wages (International Labour Office 1986). Although there are many different systems of job evaluation, the underlying rationales are similar enough so that the observation of one system can provide a window into a common organizational mode of thinking and practice.

In job evaluation, the content of jobs is described and jobs are compared on criteria of knowledge, skill, complexity, effort, and working conditions. The particular system I observed was built incrementally over many years to reflect the assessment of managers about the job components for which they were willing to pay. Thus today this system can be taken as composed of residues of these judgments, which are a set of decision rules that, when followed, reproduce managerial values. But these rules are also the imagery out of which managers construct and reconstruct their organizations. The rules of job evaluation, which help to determine pay differences between jobs, are not simply a compilation of managers' values or sets of beliefs, but are the underlying logic or organization that provides at least part of the blueprint for its structure. Every time that job evaluation is used, that structure is created or reinforced.

Job evaluation evaluates jobs, not their incumbents. The job is the basic unit in a work organization's hierarchy, a description of a set of tasks, competencies, and responsibilities represented as a position on an organizational chart. A job is separate from people. It is an empty slot, a reification that must continually be reconstructed, for positions exist only as scraps of paper until people fill them. The rationale for evaluating jobs as devoid of actual workers reveals further the organizational logic—the intent is to assess the characteristics of the job, not of their incumbents who may vary in skill, industriousness, and commitment. Human beings are to be motivated, managed, and chosen to fit the job. The job exists as a thing apart.

Every job has a place in the hierarchy, another essential element in organizational logic. Hierarchies, like jobs, are devoid of actual workers and based on abstract differentiations. Hierarchy is taken for granted, only its particular form is at issue. Job evaluation is based on the assumption that workers in general see hierarchy as an acceptable principle, and the final test of the evaluation of any particular job is whether its place in the hierarchy looks reasonable. The ranking of jobs within an organization must make sense to managers, but it is also important that most workers accept the ranking as just if the system of evaluation is to contribute to orderly working relationships.

Organizational logic assumes a congruence between responsibility, job complexity, and hierarchical position. For example, a lower-level position, the level of most jobs filled predominantly by women, must have equally low levels of complexity and responsibility. Complexity and responsibility are defined in terms of managerial and professional tasks. The child-care worker's responsibility for other human beings or the complexity facing the secretary who serves six different, temperamental bosses can only be minimally counted if the congruence between position level, responsibility, and complexity is to be preserved. In addition, the logic holds that two jobs at different hierarchical levels cannot be responsible for the same outcome; as a consequence, for example, tasks delegated to a secretary by a manager will not raise her hierarchical level because such tasks are still his responsibility, even though she has the practical responsibility to see that they are done. Levels of skill, complexity, and responsibility, all used in constructing hierarchy, are conceptualized as existing independently of any concrete worker.

In organizational logic, both jobs and hierarchies are abstract categories that have no occupants, no human bodies, no gender. However, an abstract job can exist, can be transformed into a concrete instance, only if there is a worker. In organizational logic, filling the abstract job is a disembodied worker who exists only for the work. Such a hypothetical worker cannot have other imperatives of existence that impinge upon the job. At the very least, outside imperatives cannot be included within the definition of the job. Too many obligations outside the boundaries of the job would make a worker unsuited for the position. The closest the disembodied worker doing the abstract job comes to a real worker is the male worker whose life centers on his full-time, life-long job, while his wife or another woman takes care of his personal needs and his children. While the realities of life in industrial capitalism never allowed all men to live out this ideal, it was the goal for labor unions and the image of the worker in social and economic theory. The woman worker, assumed to have legitimate obligations other than those required by the job, did not fit with the abstract job.

The concept of "a job" is thus implicitly a gendered concept, even though organizational logic presents it as gender neutral. "A job" already contains the gender-based division of labor and the separation between the public and the private sphere. The concept of "a job" assumes a particular gendered organization of domestic life and social production. It is an example of what Dorothy Smith has called "the gender subtext of the rational and impersonal" (1988, 4).

Hierarchies are gendered because they also are constructed on these underlying assumptions: Those who are committed to paid employment are "naturally" more suited to responsibility and authority; those who must divide their commitments are in the lower ranks. In addition, principles of hierarchy, as exemplified in most existing job-evaluation systems, have been derived from already existing gendered structures. The best-known systems were developed by management consultants working with managers to build methods of consistently evaluating jobs and rationalizing pay and job classifications. For example, all managers with similar levels of responsibility in the firm should have similar pay. Job-evaluation systems were intended to reflect the values of managers and to produce a believable ranking of jobs based on those values. Such rankings would not deviate substantially from rankings already in place that contain gender typing and gender segregation of jobs and the clustering of women workers in the lowest and the worst-paid jobs. The concrete value judgments that constitute conventional job evaluation are designed to replicate such structures (Acker 1989). Replication is achieved in many ways; for example, skills in managing money, more often found in men's than in women's jobs, frequently receive more points than skills in dealing with clients or human relations skills, more often found in women's than in men's jobs (Steinberg and Haignere 1987).

The gender-neutral status of "a job" and of the organizational theories of which it is a part depend upon the assumption that the worker is abstract, disembodied, although in actuality both the concept of "a job" and real workers are deeply gendered and "bodied." Carole Pateman (1986), in a discussion of women and political theory, similarly points out that the most fundamental abstraction in the concept of liberal individualism is "the abstraction of the 'individual' from the body. In order for the individual to appear in liberal theory as a universal figure, who represents anyone and everyone, the individual must be disembodied" (p. 8). If the individual were not abstracted from bodily attributes, it would be clear that the individual represents one sex and one gender, not a universal being. The political fiction of the universal "individual" or "citizen," fundamental to ideas of democracy and contract, excluded women, judging them lacking in the capacities necessary for participation in civil society. Although women now have the rights of citizens in democratic states, they still stand in an ambiguous relationship to the universal individual who is "constructed from a male body so that his identity is always masculine" (Pateman 1988, 223). The worker with "a job" is the same universal "individual" who in actual social reality is a man. The concept of a universal worker excludes and marginalizes women who cannot, almost by definition, achieve the qualities of a real worker because to do so is to become like a man.

ORGANIZATIONAL CONTROL, GENDER, AND THE BODY

The abstract, bodiless worker, who occupies the abstract, gender-neutral job has no sexuality, no emotions, and does not procreate. The absence of sexuality, emotionality, and procreation in organizational logic and organizational theory is an additional element that both obscures and helps to reproduce the underlying gender relations.

New work on sexuality in organizations (Hearn and Parkin 1987), often indebted to Foucault (1979), suggests that this silence on sexuality may have historical roots in the development of large, all-male organizations that are the primary locations of societal power (Connell 1987). The history of modern organizations includes, among other processes, the suppression of sexuality in the interests of organization and the conceptual exclusion of the body as a concrete living whole (Burrell 1984, 1987; Hearn and Parkin 1987; Morgan 1986).

In a review of historical evidence on sexuality in early modern organizations, Burrell (1984, 98) suggests that "the suppression of sexuality is one of the first tasks the bureaucracy sets itself." Long before the emergence of the very large factory of the nineteenth century, other large organizations, such as armies and monasteries, which had allowed certain kinds of limited participation of women, were more and more excluding women and attempting to banish sexuality in the interests of control of members and the organization's activities (Burrell 1984, 1987; Hacker and Hacker 1987). Active sexuality was the enemy of orderly procedures, and excluding women from certain areas of activity may have been, at least in part, a way to control sexuality. As Burrell (1984) points out, the exclusion of women did not eliminate homosexuality, which has always been an element in the life of large all-male organizations, particularly if members spend all of their time in the organization. Insistence on heterosexuality or celibacy were ways to control homosexuality. But heterosexuality had to be practiced outside the organization, whether it was an army or a capitalist workplace. Thus the attempts to banish sexuality from the workplace were part of the wider process that differentiated the home, the location of legitimate sexual activity, from the place of capitalist production. The concept of the disembodied job symbolizes this separation of work and sexuality.

Similarly, there is no place within the disembodied job or the gender-neutral organization for other "bodied" processes, such as human reproduction (Rothman 1989) or the free expression of emotions (Hochschild 1983). Sexuality, procreation, and emotions all intrude upon and disrupt the ideal functioning of the organization, which tries to control such interferences. However, as argued above, the abstract worker is actually a man, and it is the man's body, its sexuality, minimal responsibility in procreation, and conventional control of emotions that pervades work and organizational processes. Women's bodies—female sexuality, their ability to procreate and their pregnancy, breast-feeding, and child care, menstruation, and mythic "emotionality"—are suspect, stigmatized, and used as grounds for control and exclusion.

The ranking of women's jobs is often justified on the basis of women's identification with childbearing and domestic life. They are devalued because women are assumed to be unable to conform to the demands of the abstract job. Gender segregation at work is also sometimes openly justified by the necessity to control sexuality, and women may be barred from types of work, such as skilled blue-collar work or top management, where most workers are men, on the grounds that potentially disruptive sexual liaisons should be avoided (Lorber 1984). On the other hand, the gendered definition of some jobs "includes sexualization of the woman worker as a part of the job" (MacKinnon 1979, 18). These are often jobs that serve men, such as secretaries, or a largely male public (Hochschild 1983).

The maintenance of gendered hierarchy is achieved partly through such often-tacit controls based on arguments about women's reproduction, emotionality, and sexuality, helping to legitimate the organizational structures created through abstract, intellectualized techniques. More overt controls, such as sexual harassment, relegating childbearing women to lower-level mobility tracks, and penalizing (or rewarding) their emotion management also conform to and reinforce hierarchy. MacKinnon (1979), on the basis of an extensive analysis of legal cases, argues that the willingness to tolerate sexual harassment is often a condition of the job, both a consequence and a cause of gender hierarchy.

While women's bodies are ruled out of order, or sexualized and objectified, in work organizations, men's bodies are not. Indeed, male sexual imagery pervades organizational metaphors and language, helping to give form to work activities (see Hearn and Parkin 1987, for an extended discussion). For example, the military and the male world of sports are considered valuable training for organizational success and provide images for teamwork, campaigns, and tough competition. The symbolic expression of male sexuality may be used as a means of control over male workers, too, allowed or even encouraged within the bounds of the work situation to create cohesion or alleviate stress (Collinson 1988; Hearn and Parkin 1987). Management approval of pornographic pictures in the locker room or support for all-male work and play groups where casual talk is about sexual exploits or sports are examples. These symbolic expressions of male dominance also act as significant controls over women in work organizations because they are per se excluded from the informal bonding men produce with the "body talk" of sex and sports.

Symbolically, a certain kind of male heterosexual sexuality plays an important part in legitimating organizational power. Connell (1987) calls this hegemonic masculinity, emphasizing that it is formed around dominance over women and in opposition to other masculinities, although its exact content changes as historical conditions change. Currently, hegemonic masculinity is typified by the image of the strong, technically competent, authoritative leader who is sexually potent and attractive, has a family, and has his emotions under control. Images of male sexual function and patriarchal paternalism may also be embedded in notions of what the manager does when he leads his organization (Calas and Smircich 1989). Women's bodies cannot be adapted to hegemonic masculinity; to function at the top of male hierarchies requires that women render irrelevant everything that makes them women.

The image of the masculine organizational leader could be expanded, without altering its basic elements, to include other qualities also needed, according to many management experts, in contemporary organizations, such as flexibility and sensitivity to the capacities and needs of subordinates. Such qualities are not necessarily the symbolic monopoly of women. For example, the wise and experienced coach is empathetic and supportive to his individual players and flexibly leads his team against devious opposition tactics to victory.

The connections between organizational power and men's sexuality may be even more deeply embedded in organizational processes. Sally Hacker (1989) argues that eroticism and technology have common roots in human sensual pleasure and that for the engineer or the skilled worker, and probably for many other kinds of workers, there is a powerful erotic element in work processes. The pleasures of technology, Hacker continues, become harnessed to domination, and passion becomes directed toward power over nature, the machine, and other people, particularly women, in the work hierarchy. Hacker believes that men lose a great deal in this transformation of the erotic into domination, but they also win in other ways. For example, many men gain economically from the organizational gender hierarchy. As Crompton and Jones (1984) point out, men's career opportunities in white-collar work depend on the barriers that deny those opportunities to women. If the mass of female clerical workers were able to compete with men in such work, promotion probabilities for men would be drastically reduced.

Class relations as well as gender relations are reproduced in organizations. Critical, but nonfeminist, perspectives on work organizations argue that rational-technical systems for organizing work, such as job classification and evaluation systems and detailed specification of how work is to be done, are parts of pervasive systems of control that help to maintain class relations (Edwards 1979). The abstract "job," devoid of a human body, is a basic unit in such systems of control. The positing of a job as an abstract category, separate from the worker, is an essential move in creating jobs as mechanisms of compulsion and control over work processes. Rational-technical, ostensibly gender-neutral, control systems are built upon and conceal a gendered substructure (Smith 1988) in which men's bodies fill the abstract jobs. Use of such abstract systems continually reproduces the underlying gender assumptions and the subordinated or excluded place of women. Gender processes, including the manipulation and management of women's and men's sexuality, procreation, and emotion, are part of the control processes of organizations, maintaining not only gender stratification but contributing also to maintaining class and, possibly, race and ethnic relations. Is the abstract worker white as well as male? Are white-male-dominated organizations also built on underlying assumptions about the proper place of people with different skin colors? Are racial differences produced by organizational practices as gender differences are?

CONCLUSION

Feminists wanting to theorize about organizations face a difficult task because of the deeply embedded gendering of both organizational processes and theory. Commonsense notions, such as jobs and positions, which constitute the units managers use in making organizations and some theorists use in making theory, are posited upon the prior exclusion of women. This underlying construction of a way of thinking is not simply an error, but part of processes of organization. This exclusion in turn creates fundamental inadequacies in theorizing about gender-neutral systems of positions to be filled. Creating more adequate theory may come only as organizations are transformed in ways that dissolve the concept of the abstract job and restore the absent female body.

Such a transformation would be radical in practice because it would probably require the end of organizations as they exist today, along with a redefinition of work and work relations. The rhythm and timing of work would be adapted to the rhythms of life outside of work. Caring work would be just as important and well rewarded as any other; having a baby or taking care of a sick mother would be as valued as making an automobile or designing computer software. Hierarchy would be abolished, and workers would run things themselves. Of course, women and men would share equally in different kinds of work. Perhaps there would be some communal or collective form of organization where work and intimate relations are closely related, children learn in places close to working adults, and work-mates, lovers, and friends are all part of the same group. Utopian writers and experimenters have left us many possible models (Hacker 1989). But this brief listing begs many questions, perhaps the most important of which is how, given the present organization of economy and technology and the pervasive and powerful, impersonal, textually mediated relations of ruling (Smith 1988), so radical a change could come about.

Feminist research and theorizing, by continuing to puzzle out how gender provides the subtext for arrangements of subordination, can make some contributions to a future in which collective action to do what needs doing—producing goods, caring for people, disposing of the garbage—is organized so that dominance, control, and subordination, particularly the subordination of women, are eradicated, or at least minimized, in our organization life.

REFERENCES

Acker, Joan. 1982. Introduction to women, work and economic democracy. *Economic and Industrial Democracy* 3(4):i-viii.
———. 1987. Sex bias in job evaluation: A comparable worth issue. In *Ingredients for women's employment policy,* edited by Christine Bose and Glenna Spitze. Albany: SUNY Press.
———. 1988. Class, gender and the relations of distribution. *Signs* 13:473-97.
———. 1989. *Doing comparable worth: Gender, class and pay equity.* Philadelphia: Temple University Press.
———. 1990. The Oregon case. In *State experience and comparable worth,* edited by Ronnie Steinberg. Philadelphia: Temple University Press.
Acker, Joan, and Donald Van Houten. 1974. Differential recruitment and control: The sex structuring of organizations. *Administrative Science Quarterly* 19:152-63.
Bielby, William T., and James N. Baron. 1987. Undoing discrimination: Job integrations and comparable worth. In *Ingredients for women's employment policy,* edited by Christine Bose and Glenna Spitze. Albany: SUNY Press.
Braverman, Harry. 1974. *Labor and monopoly capital.* New York: Monthly Review Press.
Brown, Wendy. 1984. Challenging bureaucracy. *Women's Review of Books* 2 (November):14-17.
Burrell, Gibson. 1984. Sex and organizational analysis. *Organization Studies* 5:97-118.
———. 1987. No accounting for sexuality. *Accounting, Organizations and Society* 12:89-101.
Calas, Marta B., and Linda Smircich. 1989. Voicing seduction to silence leadership. Paper presented at the Fourth International Conference on Organizational Symbolism and Corporate Culture in Fountainbleau, France.
Clegg, Stewart, and David Dunkerley. 1980. *Organization, class and control.* London: Routledge & Kegan Paul.
Cockburn, Cynthia. 1983. *Brothers: Male dominance and technological change.* London: Pluto Press.
———. 1985. *Machinery of dominance.* London: Pluto Press.

Cohn, Samuel. 1985. *The process of occupational sex-typing.* Philadelphia: Temple University Press.

Collinson, David L. 1988. Engineering humour: Masculinity, joking and conflict in shop-floor relations. *Organization Studies* 9:181-99.

Connell, R. W. 1987. *Gender and power.* Stanford, CA: Stanford University Press.

Crompton, Rosemary, and Gareth Jones. 1984. *White-collar proletariat: deskilling and gender in clerical work.* Philadelphia: Temple University Press.

Dexter, Carolyn R. 1985. Women and the exercise of power in organizations: From ascribed to achieved status. In *Women and work: An annual review,* Vol. 1, edited by Laurie Larwood, Ann H. Stromberg, and Barbara A. Gutek. Beverly Hills, CA: Sage.

Edwards, Richard. 1979. *Contested terrain.* New York: Basic Books.

Eisenstein, Zillah R. 1981. *The radical future of liberal feminism.* New York: Longman.

Feldberg, Roslyn, and Evelyn Nakano Glenn. 1979. Male and female: Job versus gender models in the sociology of work. *Social Problems* 26:524-38.

Ferguson, Kathy E. 1984. *The feminist case against bureaucracy.* Philadelphia: Temple University Press.

Foucault, Michel. 1979. *The history of sexuality,* Vol. 1. London: Allen Lane.

Freeman, Jo. 1975. *The politics of women's liberation.* New York: Longman.

Fry, John. 1986. *Toward a democratic rationality.* Aldershot: Gower.

Game, Ann and Rosemary Pringle. 1984. *Gender at work.* London: Pluto Press.

Gould, Meredith. 1979. When women create an organization: The ideological imperatives of feminism. In *The international yearbook of women's studies 1979,* edited by D. Dunkerley and G. Salaman. London: Routledge & Kegan Paul.

Hacker, Barton C., and Sally Hacker. 1987. Military institutions and the labor process: Noneconomic sources of technological change, women's subordination, and the organization of work. *Technology and Culture* 28:743-75.

Hacker, Sally. 1981. The culture of engineering women: Women, workplace and machine. *Women's Studies International Quarterly* 4:341-54.

———. 1987. Women workers in the Mondragon system of industrial cooperatives. *Gender & Society* 1:358-79.

———. 1989. *Pleasure, power and technology.* Boston: Unwin Hyman.

Harding, Sandra. 1986. *The science question in feminism.* Ithaca, NY: Cornell University Press.

Hartmann, Heidi. 1976. Capitalism, patriarchy and job segregation by sex. *Signs* 1:137-70.

Hearn, Jeff, and P. Wendy Parkin. 1983. Gender and organizations: A selective review and critique of a neglected area. *Organization Studies* 4:219-42.

———. 1987. *Sex at work.* Brighton: Wheatsheaf.

Hochschild, Arlie R. 1983. *The managed heart: Commercialization of human feeling.* Berkeley: University of California Press.

International Labour Office. 1986. *Job evaluation.* Geneva: ILO.

Izraeli, Dafna N. 1983. Sex effects or structural effects? An empirical test of Kanter's theory of proportions. *Social Forces* 61:153-65.

Kanter, Rosabeth Moss. 1975. Women and the structure of organizations: Explorations in theory and behavior. In *Another voice,* edited by Rosabeth Kanter and Marcia Millman. New York: Doubleday.

———. 1977. *Men and women of the corporation.* New York: Basic Books.

Knights, David, and Hugh Willmott. 1985. *Gender and the labour process.* Aldershot: Gower.

Lipman-Blumen, Jean. 1980. Female leadership in formal organizations: Must the female leader go formal? In *Readings in managerial psychology,* edited by Harold J. Leavitt, Louis R. Pondy, and David M. Boje. Chicago: University of Chicago Press.

Lorber, Judith. 1984. Trust, loyalty, and the place of women in the organization of work. In *Women: A feminist perspective,* 3d ed., edited by Jo Freeman. Palo Alto, CA: Mayfield.

MacKinnon, Catharine A. 1979. *Sexual harassment of working women.* New Haven, CT: Yale University Press.

———. 1982. Feminism, Marxism, method and the state: An agenda for theory. *Signs* 7:515-44.

Martin, Patricia Yancey. 1985. Group sex composition in work organizations: A structural-normative view. In *Research in the sociology of organizations,* edited by S. A. Bacharach and R. Mitchell. Greenwich, CT: JAI.

———. 1987. A commentary on *The feminist case against bureaucracy. Women's Studies International Forum* 10:543-48.

———. 1990. Rethinking feminist organizations. *Gender & Society* 4:182-206.

Mills, Albert J. 1988. Organization, gender and culture. *Organization Studies* 9(3):351-69.

Mitchell, Diane. 1986. Review of Ferguson, *The feminist case against bureaucracy.* Unpublished manuscript.

Morgan, Gareth. 1986. *Images of organization.* Beverly Hills, CA: Sage.

Newman, Katherine. 1980. Incipient bureaucracy: The development of hierarchies in egalitarian organizations. In *Hierarchy and society,* edited by Gerald R. Britan and Ronald Cohen. Philadelphia: Institute for the Study of Human Issues.

Pateman, Carole. 1970. *Participation and democratic theory.* Cambridge: Cambridge University Press.

———. 1983a. Feminist critiques of the public private dichotomy. In *Public and private in social life,* edited by S. I. Benn and G. F. Gaus. Beckenham, Kent: Croom Helm.

———. 1983b. Feminism and democracy. In *Democratic theory and practice,* edited by Graeme Duncan. Cambridge: Cambridge University Press.

———. 1986. Introduction: The theoretical subversiveness of feminism. In *Feminist challenges,* edited by Carole Pateman and Elizabeth Gross. Winchester, MA: Allen & Unwin.

———. 1988. *The sexual contract.* Cambridge, MA: Polity.

Phillips, Anne, and Barbara Taylor. 1986. Sex and skill. In *Waged work,* edited by Feminist Review. London: Virago.

Reskin, Barbara F., and Patricia Roos. 1987. Status hierarchies and sex segregation. In *Ingredients for women's employment policy,* edited by Christine Bose and Glenna Spitze. Albany: SUNY Press.

Ressner, Ulla. 1986. Review of K. Ferguson, *The feminist case against bureaucracy. Economic and Industrial Democracy* 7:130-34.

———. 1987. *The hidden hierarchy.* Aldershot: Gower.

Rothman, Barbara Katz. 1989. *Recreating motherhood: Ideology and technology in a patriarchal society.* New York: Norton.

Rothschild, Joyce. 1987. Do collectivist-democratic forms of organization presuppose feminism? Cooperative work structures and women's values. Paper presented at Annual Meetings, American Sociological Association, Chicago.

Rothschild-Whitt, Joyce. 1979. The collectivist organization. *American Sociological Review* 44:509-27.

Scott, Joan. 1986. Gender: A useful category of historical analysis. *American Historical Review* 91:1053-75.

Smith, Dorothy E. 1979. A sociology for women. In *The prism of sex: Essays in the sociology of knowledge,* edited by Julia A. Sherman and Evelyn Torten Beck. Madison: University of Wisconsin Press.

———. 1988. *The everyday world as problematic.* Boston: Northeastern University Press.

Sorenson, Bjorg Aase. 1984. The organizational woman and the Trojan horse effect. In *Patriarchy in a welfare society,* edited by Harriet Holter. Oslo: Universitetsforlaget.

Steinberg, Ronnie, and Lois Haignere. 1987. Equitable compensation: Methodological criteria for comparable worth. In *Ingredients for women's employment policy,* edited by Christine Bose and Glenna Spitze. Albany: SUNY Press.

Strober, Myra H., and Carolyn L. Arnold. 1987. Integrated circuits/segregated labor: Women in computer-related occupations and high-tech industries. In *Computer chips and paper clips: Technology and women's employment,* edited by H. Hartmann. Washington, DC: National Academy Press.

Wallace, Phyllis A., ed. 1982. *Women in the workplace.* Boston: Auburn House.

West, Candace, and Don H. Zimmerman. 1983. Small insults: A study of interruptions in conversations between unacquainted persons. In *Language, gender and society,* edited by B. Thorne, C. Kramerae, and N. Henley. Rowley, MA: Newbury House.

———. 1987. Doing gender. *Gender & Society* 1:125-51.

Young, Iris. 1981. Beyond the unhappy marriage: A critique of dual systems theory. In *Women and revolution,* edited by L. Sargent. Boston: South End Press.

Personal Reflection on Three Gender and Work Articles

IRENE PADAVIC

Ever since I was a child I have known how important work is in people's lives—for better or for worse. My mother would wake up with the alarm on weekdays and make her way to the kitchen, lean on the countertop, and groan at the thought of another day as a clerical worker. The electrician in the apartment next door was injured on his job. My baby-sitter took in other families' ironing and was on her feet for hours on end, hot and sweaty, while I did my homework and watched. I lived in a world where work seemed to damage people.

For my part, even though I'd worked in various service sector jobs since I was 16—candy seller at a movie theater, waitress in many places, telephone solicitor, door-to-door salesperson—I didn't groan at the thought of going to work until I worked full-time after college as a paralegal. It wasn't a particularly terrible job, as jobs go. It was just monotonous. The thought of doing that kind of work for 40 years panicked me. I went to graduate school—less to get a PhD than to leave the workforce.

In my initial years as a graduate student in sociology at the University of Michigan, I learned that the key to understanding why work made people miserable was power, particularly the power of bosses over workers. Actually, I learned mostly about what caused misery for men workers; in the early 1980s, the hot issues centered on the labor process involved in men's jobs. I became a labor process junkie. I couldn't get enough of lectures and readings about workplace relations. Women's work wasn't an issue we learned much about. The only exception was Kanter's book. Her idea that structure, not gender, shapes behavior was very liberating for me. My mother groaned about her job because she was a secretary, not because of some-thing intrinsic to her femaleness or her personality. I loved to teach Kanter to undergraduates—its logic is compelling and it was very rewarding to me to open students' eyes to the revolutionary idea that structure matters.

It wasn't until the end of graduate school that I arrived at the view that power relations between women and men are as important as power relations between bosses and workers. Why did it take me most of my graduate career to see this fairly obvious point? My blindness speaks to the fundamental Kanterian truth: The opportunity structure limited my exposure to such ideas. There were no women professors who specialized in the sociology of work. When the university hired Barbara Reskin, I finally had the opportunity to learn another way of thinking about power and work. "Bringing the Men Back In" is a courageous piece. This article applied the technique that I'd learned in male labor process studies: The bottom-line question is, "Whose interests are being served?" This chapter straightforwardly and logically targets men as the beneficiaries of a system of dominance. Almost 10 years after it was published, I still find this piece relevant for my research. In a paper that a colleague and I just finished about sexual harassment, we used this article to back up our claim that the main reason men harass is to maintain male dominance over women at work and in society in general. From this article— and from Barbara Reskin herself—I learned that as long as you can back up your claim, it is fine to identify who is hurt and who gains by what goes on in the workplace.

Acker's chapter also shows how male dominance is a basic part of what goes on at work. Stereotypes about women and men—as taken-for-granted, built-in aspects of most people's jobs—have a huge effect.

My brother-in-law recently told me that more than half of the new associates hired every year into his large and prestigious law firm are women. They perform just as well as men, but few rise to partner status because "they quit after the birth of their second child"! It turns out that men and women alike are expected to work 70 hours a week for years on end. As Acker notes, the job doesn't say "men only," but men—few of whom have homefront responsibilities on a par with women—come closest to being employers' version of an ideal worker. Women who quit from that law firm don't leave the labor force altogether; instead they take "in-house council" jobs, which means they work for corporations on a 9-to-5 schedule for less pay and less prestige than offered by the big law firm. Another encounter, this one a casual conversation with a manager at a huge corporation, also taught me how sheltered I am from stereotypes and ill treatment compared to most women and, again, how right Acker is. In a completely matter-of-fact way, the manager described how he would never hire someone he didn't know or who hadn't been recommended by someone he knows. While this makes sense at one level, in practice it usually rules out most women and minorities from high-level jobs. This is because, more often than not, workers' friends are their same sex and race. Thus, as long as the best jobs are staffed by white men and as long as employers rely on informal recruiting methods, then white men will continue to fill new openings. As far as he was concerned, this is probably just as well, because women are "high maintenance" (as opposed to "zero maintenance"). By this he meant that women employees take up more of their supervisors' time, either because their presence causes problems in the ranks (if co-workers give them a hard time, for example) or because they are more "emotional," requiring supervisors to deal with their supposed emotional needs. Just as Acker notes, this kind of stereotyped thinking is grounds for excluding women.

These chapters, my own life, and the interviews I've done with women workers all point to the importance of work in shaping the basic contours of adults' lives. I recall as a college student trying to decide what were the most important ingredients for personal happiness. Was it who you spent your life with, where you were located, or what you did that mattered most? I acted on the "what" and let the other two fall in line on their own, and think that was the right decision. Just as when I was a child, I still think that work is the most important determinant of the quality of people's lives. Since then, though, I've learned that by and large women's quality of work life is not equal to men's. Now that I'm an adult, I have the chance to try to understand why and to try to change it. Chapters like these three have helped me further that project.

Gender and Organizations

PATRICIA YANCEY MARTIN

Sociological models of family and work (e.g., structural-functionalism theory) that were dominant for decades prior to the 1970s argued that girls are reared to accommodate others' needs and boys are reared to be assertive, competitive, and aggressive. The modern family requires a division of labor in which the man represents the family in the harsh, competitive world of commerce and the woman stays home to rear children, support husband, and run the household. Women who enter the world of work (note that this model presumes that most women *do not* enter the work world) will be unprepared due to their nature or "sex role" socialization to compete effectively with men. If women want to compete effectively with men, they must be resocialized, or trained, to show the right behaviors and attitudes, that is, the behaviors and attitudes of men!

Kanter rejects such reasoning and solutions by focusing on "the behavioral consequences of disadvantaged positions" (p. 261) in the organization. The implication of Kanter's argument, which for the time was quite radical, is that nothing is wrong with women. Granted that women act differently and have different attitudes at work compared to men, Kanter asks if the explanation for these differences lies in their "sex" or in their organizational locations. Her answer: organizational locations. Men who are situated in locations like women's display behaviors and attitudes similar to women's. Women's lesser status and rewards reflect their organizational placement—not innate sex differences or attitudes and behaviors learned through "sex role socialization." In Kanter's model, gender is an ascribed status characteristic that people bring to work and that, due to cultural biases against women as leaders or managers, fosters sex discrimination against women and sex preference for men. To understand these dynamics, we need to study how women and men are distributed differently across positions and how this differential distribution affects behavior (p. 260). Kanter called for study of the processes by which men and women are sorted into different jobs and of the workplace as a "total system of organization." One of Kanter's major contributions for the time was to decenter gender as the explanation for women's disadvantage and men's privilege at work.

A few years later, Reskin recentered gender to account for women's disadvantage and men's privilege at work by conceptualizing it as political, not as biology or socialization nor as a consequence of organization structure. According to Reskin, gender politics account for women's relative disadvantage at work. Men act qua men to preserve their privilege by making rules that differentiate women from men and allow men to prefer men to women. Her conception of men as an interest group in and for itself gives agency to men, disputing the claim that they act in disinterested ways as gender-free people, for example, for the good of the organization, without concern for gender. The income gap is, for example, a result of men's intentional creation and use of rules that reward men more. Reskin argues that the dominant group in a hierarchy will act to preserve its privilege, and she emphasizes that differentiation is the primary dynamic by which dominant groups pursue this goal. If women were dominant, Reskin says, they would make rules to preserve their privilege also. In contrast to Kanter and Acker, Reskin gives little attention to the work organization.

For Acker, gender is a central dynamic in work organizations. This situation is hard to see because organization and management theories—and societal ideologies about gender—say otherwise. Claiming that work organizations are suffused with gender, Acker shows how gendered processes are enacted through organization processes; and organization processes through gender. The premises upon which organizations are based reflect men's lives and bodies more than women's lives and bodies, thus privileging men. The alleged "gender-free" worker is free of pregnancy, breast-feeding, sleepless nights, and family and other nonwork obligations so she or he can prioritize work over other loyalties, work late or at odd hours, or travel at the employer's discretion. Because their lives often prevent them from making work the centerpiece of their identities and labor, women are disadvantaged relative to men even before they enter a workplace.

Acker's focus on the body and sexuality puzzled me when I first encountered it. As a captive to organization theory's depiction of jobs as "disembodied" empty slots waiting to be filled by the most qualified worker, sexuality as having no place at work, bodies as irrelevant to work organizations, procreation and sex as something one did "away from work," and heterosexuality as so normative as to preclude challenge, I assumed that bodies, sexuality, procreation, emotions, and sexuality truly were irrelevant to the social organization of work. I no longer make such assumptions. I view organizations as social contexts in which people systematically socially construct gender inequality as well as sexual and other inequalities. Acker's focus on the social construction of gender follows Kanter's advice to study processes by which women and men are allocated to different locations and Reskin's lead in framing men as agents who actively create gender hierarchy at work. In framing gender as a "complex component of processes of control and domination" (p. 304), Acker shows how work organizations perpetuate women's economic and cultural disadvantages. Her focus on the society's gender order shows how the social organization of life beyond the workplace is embedded in the workplace. Finally, her call for "theoretical strategies that examine organizations as gendered processes in which sexuality also plays a part" (p. 305) will, if heeded, produce very different understandings of work organizations as well as different organization theory.

Reactions. I cannot recall not knowing that organizations are "political," although I only recently learned to characterize them that way. I knew that employers routinely used their power beyond the workplace door to interfere in workers' "personal" lives. The cotton mill that occupied the center of life in the small Alabama town where I grew up taught me these lessons. My parents worried about what people in the mill would say about me as much as they worried about what I did; a girl's reputation could be ruined in a day if "they talked bad about her in the mill." Married men found to have "girlfriends" in addition to their wives were told to straighten up or lose their jobs, which some did. The mill employed no white women in supervisory positions and no black women, period. White women were hired only as machine operators, office clerks, and clinic nurses. Black men were restricted to janitorial and heavy lifting jobs and were not allowed to be machine operators, much less supervisors. The mill meant business; and everyone, including us kids, knew it.

All three chapters confirm these and other of my life experiences. After becoming a faculty member, I saw Kanter's thesis at work in the academy; women's failure to be promoted or awarded merit raises had little to do with their talents, skills, or behavior. Reskin's thesis was confirmed when men colleagues differentiated themselves from women and made interpretations and decisions that gave themselves or other men the bulk of grants, honors, awards, promotions, and tenure. Acker's claim that organizations are premised on men's lives and bodies helped me understand my university's failures to affirm women's childbearing and child-rearing responsibilities with supportive policies or to develop workable guidelines for sanctioning sexual harassers.

In 1971, I joined with eight other women to bring a class action lawsuit in federal court against Florida State University and the Florida State University System. I had received my PhD in 1969 and was in my second year of teaching. The impetus for our action was a university-wide self-study from which I learned that three men in my academic unit who were hired when I was or shortly afterwards were earning $10,000, $6,000, and $4,000 a year more than I. Besides hurting my feelings, this knowledge embarrassed me. Later, it made me angry, and when geneticist Margaret Menzel called women together for a meeting with some civil rights attorneys, I was one of nine who joined the suit. The suit lasted 7 years and was settled out of court, with the result that case law was never made. I nevertheless believe it had good effects on the university, and it gave me two small "back pay" sums of money. I was promoted and tenured on time, furthermore, instead of being fired or banned from campus as were many women across the nation who brought similar suits at the time.

Among other lessons I drew from this experience, these three chapters, and my research on organizations is this one: Work organizations are, at bottom, political. Yes, they are bureaucracies to an extent; they are meritocracies to an extent; but they are permeated by politics. Politics in the university concerns gender, sexuality, race/ethnicity, age, and social class as well as publications, teaching, rank, discipline, college, and profession. Rather than be depressed by this knowledge, I try to be informed by it, standing ready to resist as well as to wage political battle. I have been very fortunate, but I have also fought the good fight—and I have no intention of stopping.

For the 1987 American Sociological Association meetings, I organized a session on "A Feminist Critique of Bureaucracy" and invited Joan Acker to present a paper, which she did. That paper developed into "hierarchies, jobs, and bodies," the chapter in this collection. I am proud of my (minimalist) role in producing this pathbreaking work. I had no part in bringing into existence the stellar research on men and women of the corporation by Rosabeth Moss Kanter and the theorization of men's political agency by Barbara Reskin. I can accord this work the respect it is due, however, by testing and extending it into new areas of inquiry. The work of Rosabeth Kanter, Barbara Reskin, and Joan Acker instructs me in what I should know, and these women and their overall work inspire and direct me to follow through.

Part V

Panning to the Margins

Putting this section at the end of the book is potentially problematic. You may examine the layout of this book and think how typical it is to put the contributions of lesbians and women of color where they always are: last. We placed this genre last because we see it as a culmination of intellectual progression. This intellectual genre has presented the most formidable challenges to sociology as a discipline so far: These scholars question our assumptions, our methods, and our theories. They turn sociology on its head, forcing us all to confront our myriad roles in the perpetuation of inequality in the discipline and in society. They show us that gender as a system of oppression does not exist in a vacuum. Gender oppression is inextricably interwoven with racism, economic inequality, and homophobia. This genre forces sociologists to confront the potential of multiculturalism whereby differences will be used as building blocks rather than divisive tools.

Some questions remain: Why do these works constitute a genre of their own? Why not incorporate these ideas into other genres instead of bundling them together? These works constitute their own genre because they have only recently been recognized in sociology at all, and they continue to be marginalized by mainstream sociologists who are made uncomfortable by their analyses. We would very much like to see scholarship by traditionally marginalized people incorporated into the mainstream. We want to get rid of the intellectual ghettos in sociology (Stacey & Thorne, Chapter 9, this volume). Exploring diverse experiences: that is the future of sociology. While we run the risk of reifying the ghetto due to the way we've organized this work, we hope to spotlight this genre as essential to the future development of sociology and to the emancipation of all people.

13 Women's Culture
and Lesbian Feminist
Activism: A Reconsideration
of Cultural Feminism

VERTA TAYLOR
Ohio State University

LEILA J. RUPP
Ohio State University

The rise of cultural feminism within the U.S. women's movement, according to the current feminist orthodoxy, spelled the death of radical feminism. Because cultural feminism is based on an essentialist view of the differences between women and men and advocates separatism and institution building, it has, say its critics, led feminists to retreat from politics to "life-style." Alice Echols, the most prominent critic of cultural feminism, credits Redstockings member Brooke Williams with introducing the term *cultural feminism* in

AUTHORS' NOTE: We are full coauthors and have listed our names in reverse alphabetical order. We would like to thank Phyllis Gorman and Kelly McCormick for helpful discussions of current developments in the Columbus lesbian community; Nancy Whittier, whose contributions to this article are legion; Myra Marx Ferree, Mary Margaret Fonow, Roberta Ash Garner, Susan M. Hartmann, Joan Huber, Carol Mueller, Laurel Richardson, Barbara Ryan, and Beth Schneider, whose comments on earlier drafts were extremely helpful; the participants in the conference "New Theoretical Directions in the Study of the Women's Movement," Aarhus, Denmark, October 28—November 1, 1990, for fruitful discussions of this research; the anonymous reviewers for *Signs,* whose comments helped us immeasurably in the long process of revision; and Kate Tyler for her perceptive editorial work.

1975 to describe the depoliticization of radical feminism (Echols 1989, 301). "Cultural feminism is the belief that women will be freed via an alternate women's culture. It . . . has developed at the expense of feminism, even though it calls itself 'radical feminist' " (Williams 1975, 79).[1] Since 1975, denunciations of cultural feminism have become common-place. From all sides—from socialist feminists, black feminists, postmodern feminists, and especially from radical feminists who reject cultural feminism as a betrayal of their early ideas—come charges that cultural feminism represents the deradicalization and demobilization of the women's movement.[2] In Echols's words, "radical feminism was a political movement dedicated to eliminating the sex-class system, whereas cultural feminism was a countercultural movement aimed at reversing the cultural valuation of the male and the devaluation of the female" (1989, 6).

Implicit in most discussions of cultural feminism is the centrality of lesbianism to the process of depoliticization. The critique of cultural feminism sometimes is a disguised—and within the women's movement more acceptable—attack on lesbian feminism. By *lesbian feminism,* we mean a variety of beliefs and practices based on the core assumption that a connection exists between an erotic and/or emotional commitment to women and political resistance to patriarchal domination. Cultural feminism's three greatest "sins"—essentialism, separatism, and an emphasis on building an alternative culture—are strongly associated with the lesbian feminist communities that grew up in U.S. cities and towns in the 1970s and 1980s. Williams, herself lesbian, identified the development of cultural feminism with the growth of lesbianism; later critics have strengthened this association. Echols sees cultural feminism as growing out of lesbian feminism but modifying it, "so that male values rather than men were vilified and female bonding rather than lesbianism was valorized" (1989, 244). In the context of the 1980s "sex wars"—the struggle over sexual expressiveness and regulation between, on one side, feminists who emphasized the dangers of sexuality and the need to fight pornography as a form of violence against women and, on the other side, those who stressed its pleasures—cultural feminism came to stand for an "antisex" variety of lesbian feminism.[3] Although lesbian voices are among those raised in condemnation of cultural feminism, the boundary in common usage between cultural feminism and lesbian feminism is highly permeable, if it exists at all.

Our goal here is to reposition what has been called "cultural feminism" as one tendency within dynamic and contested contemporary U.S. lesbian feminist communities. By shifting our focus from the ideology of cultural feminism to concrete social movement communities, we make explicit the central role of lesbians in what is often euphemistically called the "women's community" and we emphasize that a movement's culture is more than a formal ideological position.[4] To understand the culture of any group requires attention to the contexts in which it is produced, so we turn our gaze to the communities that give birth to "women's culture."

Lesbian feminist communities in the United States are made up of women with diverse views and experiences. They encompass "cultural feminists"— significantly, this is not a label that any women, as far as we know, apply to themselves—and their critics, as well as "antisex" and "pro-sex" feminists and separatists and antiseparatists. In contrast to critics who view lesbian feminist communities as embodying the evils of cultural feminism, we see the debate over essentialism, separatism, sexuality, and so on taking place within these communities. As Jan Clausen has pointed out, even critics of the racism and Eurocentrism of "the women's community" remain identified with it (1992, 9).

Our intent is not to defend the ideological position that has been described as "cultural feminism" but to change the terms of the debate by focusing on the consequences for feminist activism of lesbian feminist culture and communities. We identify four elements of lesbian feminist culture that promote survival of the women's movement during periods of waning activity: female values, separatism, the primacy of women's relationships, and feminist ritual. The culture of lesbian feminist communities both serves as a base of mobilization for women involved in a wide range of protest activities aimed at political and institutional change and provides continuity from earlier stages of the women's movement to the future flowering of feminism. Rather than depoliticizing the radical feminist attack on the multiple roots of women's oppression, lesbian feminist communities preserve that impulse.

Our argument is shaped by historical analyses of women's culture and by theories of social movement continuity. From a historical perspective, Echols's and others' indictment of cultural feminism is curious, given that women's culture and intimate bonds between women have generally played a benevolent role in the development of the women's movement.[5] As Estelle Freedman explains in her classic article "Separatism as Strategy," the decline of the U.S. women's movement in the 1920s can be partly attributed to the devaluation of women's culture and the decline of separate women's institutions (1979). And Blanche Cook argues persuasively that female networks of love and support were vital to women's political activism in the early twentieth century (1977). Although no monolithic women's culture has developed across lines of race, class, and ethnicity, women involved in a wide array of collective action—from food riots in immigrant neighborhoods, to labor strikes, to protests against the lynching of African-American men, to suffrage demonstrations—have shaped oppositional cultures that sustained their struggles.[6] These women were motivated by what Nancy Cott has distinguished as three forms of consciousness: feminist consciousness, female consciousness, and communal consciousness (1989).[7] The lesbian feminist culture we explore here is such an oppositional culture.

Recent work on social movements by sociologists also points to a positive relationship between the culture of lesbian feminist communities and the persistence of feminist activism. Focusing on the sixties, scholars have documented the role that preexisting organizations and activist networks from earlier rounds of protest played in the emergence of all of the so-called new social movements such as the civil rights, student, and gay rights movements.[8] These studies illuminate the importance of studying movements in differing stages of mobilization and in various organizational forms. To conceptualize periods of the U.S. women's movement that previously have been overlooked, we draw on the concept of "abeyance stages" in social movements (Taylor 1989b). The term *abeyance* depicts a holding process by which activists sustain protest in a hostile political climate and provide continuity from one stage of mobilization to another. Abeyance functions through organizations that allow members to build their lives around political activity. Such groups ensure the survival of a visionary core of the movement, develop a strategy or project for realizing the movement's vision, and allow activists to claim an identity that opposes the dominant order. We see lesbian feminist communities as fulfilling this function for the radical branch of the women's movement in the 1980s and early 1990s.

The argument we develop here is based on preliminary research for a larger study of lesbian feminist communities and on our own extensive participation in the Columbus, Ohio, lesbian feminist community. Although we use published movement writings, formal and informal interviews with members of various communities, and participant observation in Columbus and at national events, we see this article as less an empirical study than a conceptual piece.[9] Our perspective is, of course, shaped by our identities as white, middle-class, academic lesbians immersed in the issues we discuss. But we try to use our experience to reproduce for nonparticipants the flavor of involvement in a lesbian feminist community. Much of what we report will be familiar to other participants, even those from quite different communities. Columbus is a noncoastal but urban community where developments in New York, Washington, D.C., Boston, San Francisco, and Los Angeles are played out later and on a smaller scale. In that sense, Columbus both reflects national trends and typifies smaller communities that have been less studied by feminist scholars.[10]

LESBIAN FEMINIST COMMUNITIES: A MOVEMENT IN ABEYANCE

The late 1960s and early 1970s brought the full flowering of both the liberal and radical branches of the women's movement. Radical feminism— which is what concerns us here—emerged as women within the civil rights movement and the New Left (the antiwar and student movements) began to apply a leftist analysis to their own situation as women. In contrast to "politicos" who thought that a socialist revolution would automatically liberate women, radical feminists blamed both capitalism and male supremacy for women's oppression and conceptualized women as a "sex class." With its use of consciousness-raising and dramatic "zap actions" designed to expose sexist practices, radical feminism had a profound effect on both leftist politicos and liberal feminists. But increasingly the concept of a sex class foundered on differences of race, class, and sexuality among women (Spelman 1988; Gordon 1991).

No issue proved more volatile than sexuality. The surfacing of the "lesbian question" in both the liberal and radical branches of the women's movement resulted in part from the gay/lesbian liberation movement emerging in the late sixties and paved the way for the emergence of lesbian feminist groups such as Radicalesbians in 1970 and The Furies in 1971. As more women came out as lesbians within the radical branch of the women's movement, radical feminism and lesbian feminism became conflated. Small groups that were motivated by the radical feminist vision and composed primarily of lesbians sprang up in a variety of locations, including, by the 1980s, smaller communities, especially those with major colleges and universities.

Since the 1970s, feminists who view fundamental change as necessary to the eradication of male domination have faced an increasingly unfriendly social milieu. The civil rights movement and New Left, which gave birth to the radical branch of the women's movement, began to ebb in the 1970s, while the gay liberation movement was, like the other sixties movements, more congenial for men than for women. As liberal feminism became more institutionalized, explicit antifeminism emerged in the late 1970s as a major foundation of the ultraconservative New Right; the election of President Ronald Reagan reflected the influence of that countermovement. The early 1980s saw the failure of the Equal Rights Amendment to the U.S. Constitution and increasing challenges to reproductive freedom. That, and complacency among some young women who saw no further need for feminism, prompted the media gleefully to proclaim the death of feminism.[11] The heyday of the contemporary women's movement gave way, by the early 1980s, to a period of abeyance. Most recently, the media-fanned attack by conservatives on "political correctness" and multiculturalism has targeted radical feminism. Given all this, what critics of cultural feminism have portrayed as deradicalization can be viewed instead as survival in a climate of backlash and declining opportunities.[12]

Since 1980, the women's rights branch of the women's movement, forming policy networks at the national and local levels, has gained influence in such traditional arenas as electoral politics, academic institutions, and the professions (Boles 1991). At the same time, the alternative institutions founded by early radical feminists—including rape crisis centers, battered women's shelters, bookstores, newspapers, publishing and recording companies, recovery groups, support groups concerned with health and identity issues, spirituality groups, restaurants and coffeehouses, and other women-owned businesses—have increasingly come to be driven by the commitment of lesbians and women in the process of coming out. Women find in this world a social context supportive of lesbian relationships and identity that was unavailable in early feminist organizations or in the predominantly male gay liberation movement. This is not to say that feminist counterinstitutions are solely the preserve of lesbians. The commonly used term *women's community* emphasizes access for all women even if feminist institutions fail to include women of every race, class, and sexual identity. Nevertheless, the base of mobilization of the "women's community" stems primarily from interpersonal networks and organizational ties in the lesbian world.[13]

The history of the Columbus community illustrates developments at the national level and provides a model of the kinds of institutions, organizations, and events that undergird the lesbian feminist community.[14] The radical branch of the women's movement in Columbus emerged in 1970 out of Women's Liberation at Ohio State University, made up of women from the civil rights and New Left movements. This group fought for changes on campus, including the establishment of a women's studies program. In 1971, it sponsored a consciousness-raising group that gave birth to the Women's Action Collective, an off-campus umbrella organization that became the heart of the women's community. The collective sheltered a variety of groups, including Women Against Rape, the Women's Co-op Garage, Lesbian Peer Support, Single Mothers' Support Group, *Womansong* newspaper, and Fan the Flames Feminist Book Collective. A large proportion of early Women's Action Collective members were lesbian; more members came out throughout the 1970s until the collective was almost entirely lesbian. Outside the Women's Action Collective, women in Columbus formed Central Ohio Lesbians; the Women's Music Union, which produced feminist concerts; and Feminists in Self-Defense Training, which grew in part out of the self-defense workshops sponsored by Women Against Rape. Heterosexual women found the local chapter of the National Organization for Women (NOW) a haven for radical feminist activity; in what became a local cause célèbre, five NOW members were arrested in 1979 for spray-painting antirape slogans on a freeway sound barrier covered with misogynist graffiti.

By the late 1970s, Women Against Rape had come to dominate the Women's Action Collective, largely as a result of a major grant from the National Institute for Mental Health for a community rape prevention project. This grant, which paid indirect costs to the collective, funded a paid staff and the rental of a house in the university area for offices, meeting rooms, and a bookstore. As Women Against Rape expanded its operations and grew in size, a number of other original collective groups dissolved. At the same time, the late seventies and early eighties witnessed the start of a variety of short-lived feminist organizations and two enduring ones, the Child Assault Prevention project (spawned by Women Against Rape) and Women's Outreach to Women, a twelve-step recovery group. But in the increasingly antifeminist climate of the early 1980s, both members and funds began to disappear. The end of the grant that had catapulted Women Against Rape to local (and national) prominence had dire effects on the entire community. When the Women's Action Collective found itself devoting more time to maintaining the house than to engaging in political activity, its remaining members moved to a smaller space in 1983 and a year later disbanded the collective.

But these changes meant abeyance and not death for the lesbian feminist community. Women Against Rape and Fan the Flames Feminist Book Collective (which moved from the Ohio State campus area to a downtown location and, in early 1993, to a neighborhood with a relatively high lesbian population) survived the death of their parent organization and continue to thrive, as has Women's Outreach to Women, which sponsors groups for incest survivors as well as for women recovering from substance abuse. The Child Assault Prevention project developed into the National Assault Prevention Center, based in Columbus, and the Women's Music Union continued to produce feminist concerts until 1990. In 1990, a revived Take Back the Night march to protest violence against women (an annual event in the late 1970s) led to the establishment of an on-going Take Back the Night organization. A lesbian support group, Sisters of Lavender, continues; a Lesbian Business Association publishes a local lesbian newsletter titled *The Word Is Out!;* lesbian mothers and lesbians hoping to bear children have formed a group called Momazons that has launched a national newsletter; and members of the lesbian feminist community have moved into pro-choice and lesbian/gay community organizations. Stonewall Union, for example, central Ohio's gay/lesbian advocacy group, has had lesbian feminists as president, executive director, and head of its antiviolence project in the 1990s.

What this history suggests is that the lesbian feminist community is characterized by a shifting core. In Columbus, the nucleus of the community moved from the university women's liberation group, to the university-area Women's Action Collective, to the more focused Women Against Rape and Women's Outreach to Women; perhaps Take Back the Night is in the process of becoming a new core. The organizations and the personnel have changed, but the basic character of lesbian feminist culture has remained. Thus the demise of a radical feminist organization may represent less the "death" of radical feminism than a movement of members and resources to a new local movement core.

In a climate of increasing political opposition, decreasing funding, and lower levels of mobilization, the Columbus community never lost sight of its political goals. Rape prevention workshops, which might have become a depoliticized community service, continued to interpret rape as a "pillar of patriarchy" and to advocate strategies to prevent rape as a means of knocking out one support of the system (Community Action Strategies to Stop Rape 1978). Even the growth of the recovery movement and a turn to feminist spirituality, associated by critics of cultural feminism with a sacrifice of politics for life-style, did not depoliticize the community. Lesbian feminists devoted to recovery from incest or substance abuse, for example, argued the political ramifications of their work (Direen 1991). And when the Women's Action Collective newsletter appeared in the fall of 1982 with a new title, *Womoon Rising,* whose explanation was suffused with references to matriarchy and spirituality, the change met with resistance from collective members who insisted that a "Womoon . . . certainly doesn't sound like a political activist" (*Womoon Rising* 1982). The newsletter ceased publication soon after its change of title; feminist spirituality may have sparked heated debates, but it never replaced politics in the Columbus community.

THE CULTURE OF LESBIAN FEMINIST COMMUNITIES

Lesbian feminist communities do show signs of the essentialism, separatism, and "life-style politics" that cultural feminism's critics view as anathema to radical feminism. But a closer examination of the ideas, separatist strategies, primary relationships, and symbolic practices of community members reveals that these elements of lesbian feminist culture are what sustain and nourish feminist activism.

Female Values

The question of whether women are fundamentally different from men is central throughout the women's movement. Although a variety of individuals and groups assert the existence of "female values," this position is closely associated with contemporary lesbian feminists, who are more forthright than earlier feminists in proclaiming the superiority of women's values over men's. This is also the aspect of cultural feminism that is most disputed, in part because the notion of universal female values sits uneasily with the recognition of differences among women.

Critics of cultural feminism denounce belief in female values as essentialist, that is, based on biological determinism. According to Linda Alcoff, "cultural feminism is the ideology of a female nature or female essence reappropriated by feminists in an effort to revalidate undervalued female attributes" (1988, 408). Some lesbian feminists do see female values as linked to women's biological capacity to reproduce, but others take a social constructionist position and attribute differences between female and male values to differences in women's and men's socialization and prescribed roles. Explanations aside, belief in fundamental differences between female and male values permeates lesbian feminist communities. Indeed, this emphasis on difference serves to justify the existence of a "women's community."

Lesbian feminists find support for the belief in female values in a large body of scholarly and popular writing that valorizes egalitarianism, collectivism, an ethic of care, respect for knowledge derived from experience, pacifism, and cooperation as female traits. In contrast, an emphasis on hierarchy, oppressive individualism, an ethic of individual rights, abstraction, violence, and competition are denounced as male. Not all such works are written by lesbian women or by women who would identify with the lesbian feminist community, but they set forth positions embraced by lesbian feminists.[15]

On one end of the female values continuum lies Mary Daly's later work, which dismisses men as death-dealing necrophiliacs draining female energy, both figuratively and literally, in order to stay alive (Daly 1978, 1984; Daly and Caputi 1987). Audre Lorde, in an open letter to Daly, criticizes what she sees as Daly's assumption that all women suffer the same oppression and calls for recognition of the creative function of differences among women (Lorde 1984a). In a spoof of arguments such as Daly's, Margot Sims's *On the Necessity of Bestializing the Human Female* purports to prove that women and men belong to different species (1982). The biological underpinnings of Daly's work, or of Adrienne Rich's early work on motherhood, fuel the charge of essentialism hurled by cultural feminism's critics (Rich 1976).

But an essentialist view of female values is only one perspective. To move to the other end of the continuum, Patricia Hill Collins, whose work is influential in the academic sector of the lesbian feminist community, draws parallels between the standpoints of African-American and white feminists, suggesting that both share values that are different from, and superior to, those of the dominant white male culture (1989, 1990). Although this is a social constructionist argument, to critics of cultural feminism it might still smack of an unwarranted emphasis on difference between women and men, or at least between women and white men.

Exposed to these intellectual debates through books, periodicals, and women's studies classes, lesbian feminists often find support for their belief in superior female values. As one community member explained, "We've been acculturated into two cultures, the male and the female culture. And luckily we've been able to preserve the ways of nurturing by being in this alternative culture."[16] Even women who intellectually reject the notion of male and female difference are apt to use *male* as a term of derision. It is common in the Columbus community to hear everything from controlling and aggressive behavior to impersonal relationships and hierarchical organizational structures characterized in casual conversation as "male." Our point here is that while most lesbian feminists do not embrace biological explanations of sex differences, such drawing of boundaries between male and female values promotes the kind of oppositional consciousness necessary for organizing one's life around feminism.

Separatism

Lesbian feminist communities advocate both separatism as strategy and separatism as goal, but it is total separation from men as an end in itself that has proven most controversial and that has given the impression that radical feminism has evolved into a politics of identity.[17] Some groups have attempted to withdraw from all aspects of male control by forming rural self-sufficient communes, but these are the exception. Sally Gearhart glorifies such communities in her popular fiction, which portrays separatist communities of women fighting the death-dealing patriarchy with extraordinary and distinctively female mental and physical powers (1978, 1991). Critics of such total separatism point to the race and class bias inherent in the assumption that women want to and can separate from men in this way (Jaggar 1983; hooks 1984).

In general, however, the lesbian feminist community endorses temporally and spatially limited separatism. The Columbus Women's Action Collective statement of philosophy asserted plainly that "the work of the women's movement must be done by women. Our own growth can only be fostered by solving our problems among women."[18] Often men, and even male children over a very young age, are explicitly excluded from participation in groups and events. Some early lesbian feminist communes included male children but barred them from decision making and social events on the grounds that "male energy" violates women's space.[19] This tradition continues at the annual Michigan Womyn's Music Festival in Hart, Michigan, where male children over the age of three are not permitted in the festival area but must stay at a separate camp. Men were not permitted to attend any sessions at the National Lesbian Conference in Atlanta in 1991 (Stevens 1991). In Columbus, the annual Take Back the Night march welcomes men at the kickoff rally but permits only women to march, a source of ongoing controversy. Supporters of this policy maintain that women gain a liberating sense of power specifically from separating from men for the march, reclaiming the right to walk the streets at night with no vestiges of male "protection."

The importance of such limited separatism is asserted even by critics of total separation from men and boys. Lesbian women of color, working-class lesbian women, and Jewish lesbian women with an interest in working politically within their own racial, class, and ethnic communities argue for separate space to organize and express solidarity apart both from men and from lesbian women who are white or middle-class or Christian.[20] The very structure of the National Women's Studies Association embodies separatism as strategy: caucuses for women of color, lesbian women, Jewish women, and working-class and poor women reflect women's different and competing interests. The need for this kind of organizing within the lesbian feminist community was illustrated at the National Lesbian Conference in Atlanta, at which women of color caucused separately in an attempt to make the conference deal more directly with issues of racism (Sharon, Elliott, and Latham 1991). Separatism in the lesbian feminist community has come to mean organizing around one's identity.

Separately organized caucuses or groups may, then, work politically with women of different interests or with men. Although some lesbian feminist groups, especially in the early years of the community, refused to work at all with heterosexual women, coalitions across the lines of both sexual identity and gender are increasingly common. Barbara Epstein argues that lesbian feminists have played a significant role in mixed-gender nonviolent direct action since the mid-1970s because the lesbian feminist movement has matured and succeeded in creating space for lesbianism within the broader radical community (1991).[21] Many participants in lesbian communities consider the women's movement their primary allegiance but work actively in movements for gay and lesbian rights, AIDS education and advocacy, Latin American solidarity, environmental causes, peace, animal rights, reproductive freedom, and labor unions, and movements against racism, apartheid, and nuclear weapons. Nevertheless, separatist events and caucuses remain important for women who are disenchanted with the politics of the mainstream; separatism is a means of both drawing sustenance and maintaining feminist identity.

The Primacy of Women's Relationships

Lesbian feminist communities view heterosexuality as an institution of patriarchal control and lesbian relationships as a means of subverting male domination. Relationships between women are considered not only personal affairs but also political acts, as captured in the often-repeated slogan, "Feminism is the theory and lesbianism is the practice."[22] The statement of philosophy of the Columbus Women's Action Collective, for example, defined lesbianism as a challenge to male domination.[23] It was no accident that the coming out of a large number of radical feminists in Columbus coincided with the founding of the Women's Action Collective and Women Against Rape. That lesbian women were central in the antirape movement undoubtedly shaped the feminist analysis of rape as an act representing one end of the continuum of what Susan Cavin calls "heterosex" (1985).

For some community members, lesbianism is defined by overriding identification with women and by resistance to patriarchy rather than by sexual
attraction to or involvement with women. As one woman put it, lesbianism
is "an attempt to stop doing what you were taught—hating women."[24] Rich's
classic article "Compulsory Heterosexuality and Lesbian Existence" introduced the notion of the "lesbian continuum," which embraces women who
resist male control but are not sexual with women (1980). Earlier writers had
also accepted what were originally known in the movement as "political
lesbians." Ti-Grace Atkinson, for example, denounced married women who
engaged in sexual relations with women as "collaborators" and praised
women who had never had sex with women but who lived a total commitment
to the women's movement as "lesbians in the political sense" (1973, 12).
More recently, Marilyn Frye, in an address to the 1990 National Women's
Studies Association conference titled "Do You Have to Be a Lesbian to Be a
Feminist?" equated lesbianism with rebellion against patriarchal institutions.
Frye was willing to imagine truly radical feminist women—what she called
"Virgins" in the archaic sense of autonomous women—in erotic relationships
with men, but she insisted that they would be exceptional (1990).

Lesbian feminist communities indeed include some women who are oriented toward women emotionally and politically but not sexually; they are
sometimes referred to as "political dykes" or "heterodykes" (Clausen 1990;
Smeller 1992; Bart 1993). Some are women in the process of coming out,
and some are "going in," or moving from lesbian to heterosexual relationships. For example, singer and political activist Holly Near explains in her
autobiography that she continues to call herself lesbian even though she is
sometimes heterosexually active because of the importance of lesbian feminism as a political identity (1990). In the same vein, a feminist support group
sprang up in 1989 at Ohio State University for "Lesbians Who Just Happen
to Be in Relationships with Politically Correct Men." What is significant is
that lesbian identity is so salient to involvement in the women's community
that even women who are not, or no longer, involved sexually with women
claim such an identity.

Most lesbians are, of course, erotically attracted to other women, and a
strong current within the community criticizes those who downplay sexuality. The popularity of lesbian sex expert JoAnn Loulan, who spoke to a large
and enthusiastic audience in Columbus in 1991, signals that the erotic aspects
of lesbian relationships have not been completely submerged (Loulan 1990).
The "sex wars" of the early 1980s have spawned an assertively sexual style
on the part of some members of the lesbian feminist community (Stein 1989;
Echols 1991). Advocates of sexual expressiveness, including champions of
"butch-femme" roles and sadomasochism (S/M), challenge the less sexual
style of what S/M practitioners call "vanilla lesbians" and denounce any
notion of "politically correct" sex (see, e.g., Califia 1981; Dimen 1984). The

lines are explicitly drawn by the very titles of the periodicals associated with each camp: *off our backs,* the classic radical feminist newspaper, now confronts the magazine *On Our Backs* with its sexual "bad girl" style. But the role of politics in structuring relationships is undisputed, even for those who emphasize sexual pleasure over the use of (hetero)sexuality as a means of social control of women. The defense of S/M, for example, argues the superiority of sexual interactions and relationships that explicitly play with power (Califia 1979, 1980; Samois 1979).[25]

In other words, the lesbian feminist community includes both women who emphasize relationships between women as a form of political resistance and women who stress the sexual pleasures of lesbianism. The sex wars are fought within the community over who best deserves the label "feminist." Although advocates of lesbian S/M and associated sexual practices experience exclusion from some community events, the nature of lesbian sexuality is contested openly at community conferences and in movement publications (Califia 1981). Even smaller communities have been affected by the national debate. In Columbus, when a gay bar placed ads featuring S/M imagery in a local gay/lesbian publication, lesbian members of Columbus's women's S/M group, Briar Rose, came to blows, metaphorically, with antipornography lesbian feminists offended by the depiction of what they perceived as violence.[26]

Although lesbian feminist communities are riven by conflict over the nature and proper expression of lesbian sexuality, relationships hold communities together. Highly committed activists tend to form partnerships with each other because, as one woman noted, otherwise "there's too much political conflicts."[27] Political organizing, meetings, and conferences become occasions for meeting potential lovers or for spending time with a partner. Even an academic women's studies conference can provide a safe place to show affection in public. Women's relationships often structure their entire social worlds. Within the community, lesbian couples or groups of single and paired lesbian women construct family-like ties with one another, together celebrating holidays, birthdays, commitment ceremonies, births, and anniversaries. Former lovers are often part of lesbian networks, at least in smaller communities like Columbus. In contrast to the New Left in the 1960s, where women no longer in relationships with male leaders often found themselves marginalized in the movement, lesbian feminists' tendency to remain friends with their ex-lovers provides stability in the lesbian world (Pearlman 1987; Epstein 1991, 181–82).

Lesbian feminist communities make explicit—and sexual—the ties that bind women. The contemporary antifeminist charge that one "has to be a lesbian to be a feminist" is in an odd way an acknowledgment of the central role that lesbians play in the contemporary women's movement and that women with primary bonds to other women played in earlier stages of feminism.[28] It is no coincidence that self-identified "gay women" who reject the label "lesbian" often associate it with feminism and political activism.[29] Women's relationships are especially crucial to the maintenance of the women's movement when mass support for feminism ebbs; such bonds tie together groups of women who are unlikely to find acceptance for their relationships outside the movement. Furthermore, lesbian feminist communities provide fertile ground for recruiting young lesbian women into feminism. Thus, the relationship between activism and woman-bonding (lesbian or otherwise) is a symbiotic one: women with primary commitments to other women find support within the women's movement and, in turn, pour their energies into it.

Feminist Ritual

Among lesbian feminists, both public and private rituals are important vehicles for constructing feminist models of community and expressing new conceptions of gender. Public rituals are local or national cultural events such as concerts, films, poetry readings, exhibitions, plays, and conferences. Most prominent nationally is the annual Michigan Womyn's Music Festival, a five-day celebration that attracts several thousand women for musical performances, workshops, support groups, political strategy sessions, "healing circles," and the sale of woman-made crafts, clothing, and other goods. The National Women's Studies Association (NWSA) conference is another annual cultural event; it goes far beyond the usual parameters of an academic conference by providing a forum for feminist performances and by featuring open and often highly charged debate over issues central to the women's movement.[30] Dozens of specialized national and regional conferences and festivals take place each year. Other local events, such as antiviolence marches and pro-choice rallies, occur in much the same way in different communities. Publicity in national publications and participation in national demonstrations foster a common culture of protest across the country; chants and songs, for example, spread from one community to another. Lesbian feminist events in Columbus mirror those in both larger and smaller communities. The Women's Action Collective for many years sponsored an annual Famous Feminist Day to raise money and educate the community about feminist foremothers; Stonewall Union or Women's Outreach to Women bring nationally known performers to town (as the Women's Music Union did until 1990); the Lesbian Business Association puts on an annual Ohio Lesbian Festival; and Take Back the Night continues to sponsor an annual march and rally.

What is known among contemporary feminists as "women's culture"—women's music, literature, and art—plays a central role in recruiting women and raising their feminist consciousness.[31] Musicians such as Meg Christian,

Holly Near, and Sweet Honey in the Rock, as well as dozens of other feminist performers, have introduced issues as well as songs to communities across the country. For example, in Columbus as in other areas, Near introduced the lesbian feminist community to sign language interpretation of concerts. Now no feminist—or even mainstream—event is without such interpretation for the hearing impaired. Likewise, Christian brought discussion of alcoholism and the recovery movement to the Columbus community by performing such songs as "Turning It Over" and talking of the Alcoholism Center for Women in Los Angeles. And Sweet Honey in the Rock exposed Columbus audiences composed primarily of white women to an Afrocentric perspective and African-American history and culture. Women in local communities read many of the same lesbian novels and poetry and listen to the same music. At the 1979 gay/lesbian march in Washington, women at the rally joined in to sing and sign when lesbian performers came on stage, while gay men in the crowd, lacking such unifying rituals, seemed to wonder how all of the women knew the words.

Private ritual or the politicization of everyday life is, in many respects, the hallmark of the lesbian feminist community and the most damning aspect of cultural feminism in the eyes of its critics. Through the tenet that "the personal is political," every aspect of life—where one lives, what one eats, how one dresses—can become an expression of politics (Hanisch 1978). The sale at feminist bookstores, conferences, concerts, and festivals of feminist T-shirts, jewelry (especially labryses), books, music, and bumper stickers means that women can adorn and surround themselves with their politics.

The most significant displays challenge conventional standards of gender behavior that subordinate women. In the early years of lesbian feminism, comfortable, practical, less "feminine" styles of dress, unshaved legs and armpits, and extremely short hair were de rigueur. Although flannel shirts, jeans, and boots are no longer a uniform, the dominant mode of presentation is still unisex or what Holly Devor has termed a deliberate "gender blending" (1989). In the Columbus community, attire at cultural events has changed markedly over the past fifteen years. What was once a fairly monolithic crowd has become more diverse. Although most women remain "gender blended," some appear in leather and mohawks and some in skirts, lipstick, and long hair. At one feminist event, billed as "Girls Just Want to Have Fun," members of the community participated in a fashion show, albeit one that included political commentary on style. The use of the term *girls* (previously anathema), the emphasis on fun rather than serious politics, the reference to a mainstream popular song (Cyndi Lauper's "Girls Just Want to Have Fun") rather than women's music, and attention to clothing, including traditional women's attire, all marked this event as a new departure for the community.

Such changes in self-presentation are in part a consequence of the sex wars and in part an expression of the preferences of working-class women, women of color, and young women. "Antifeminine" styles associated with the downplaying of sexuality are under attack from advocates of sexual expressiveness who sometimes adopt fashions associated with the sex trade (Stein 1989). "Pro-sex" lesbian feminists sport high-heeled shoes, short skirts, low-cut tops, and other items of clothing denounced by "antisex" lesbian feminists as the paraphernalia of oppression. In addition, some working-class women and women of color criticize the "politically correct" styles of the dominant faction as an imperialist imposition of white, middle-class standards. And young lesbian feminist women have brought their own ideas on fashion and self-presentation, including the grunge and punk styles, to the community.

The intensity of the debate over cultural expression is an indication of the significance of ritual for distinguishing who is and is not a feminist—just as lesbian women historically have developed cultural codes to identify one another while remaining "hidden" to the mainstream culture that stigmatized them (see, e.g., Faderman 1991). Feminist ritual reaffirms commitment to the community and openly embraces resistance to the dominant society. Thus, what Echols and other critics of cultural feminism have denounced as a "profoundly individualistic" retreat to life-style has political consequences (Echols 1989, 251).

CONCLUSION: THE POLITICAL
FUNCTIONS OF LESBIAN FEMINIST COMMUNITIES

Our reconsideration of cultural feminism in the context of lesbian feminist communities suggests a number of interpretations that run counter to the standard view. First, cultural feminism, as it has been defined by its critics, represents just one ideological position within lesbian feminist communities. Second, these communities have forged a rich and complex resistance culture and style of politics that nourishes rather than betrays the radical feminist vision. Third, the dynamics of lesbian feminist communities are shaped at least in part by the politics of the Right that dominated the period of abeyance or maintenance in which the women's movement found itself in the 1980s. And, finally, the lesbian feminist community intersects with many contemporary struggles for political and institutional change and carries a feminist legacy that will shape the future of the women's movement itself.

In our earlier collaborative work on the U.S. women's rights movement in the period from 1945 to the 1960s, we argued that a small group of white, well-educated, economically privileged old women, primarily recruited to the women's movement during the suffrage struggle, greatly influenced the resurgent liberal branch of the women's movement. We showed that the women's rights movement that hung on in the doldrum years provided activist networks, the ultimately unifying goal of the Equal

Rights Amendment, and a feminist identity that maintained a focus on women's subordination. Yet this group of committed feminists sustained their vision in a homogeneous community that did not and could not attract women of color, working-class women, or young women. Although the women's movement that blossomed in the 1960s differed in fundamental ways from the more limited women's rights movement that preceded it, the legacy, both positive and negative, of that early activism lingered (Rupp and Taylor 1987).

In the same way, lesbian feminist communities both sustain the women involved in them now and also have consequences for the next round of mass feminist activism. Perhaps a new wave of the women's movement is already taking shape; witness the ground swell of outrage at Anita Hill's treatment in the U.S. Senate confirmation hearings for Supreme Court Justice Clarence Thomas in October 1991 and the huge turnout for the pro-choice march on Washington, D.C., in April 1992. Since the presidential election of 1992 and the passage of antigay/lesbian legislation in Colorado, the National Organization for Women has decided to make lesbian and gay rights a priority in the 1990s.[32]

Our discussion of the culture of lesbian feminist communities has emphasized how belief in female difference, the practice of limited or total separatism, belief in the primacy of women's relationships, and the practice of feminist ritual create a world apart from the mainstream in which women can claim feminism as a political identity. At the same time, of course, the ideas and practices of lesbian feminist communities can exclude potential participants. Most heterosexual feminists may not find the lesbian world congenial. The association of feminism and lesbianism, as several scholars have found, alienates some young heterosexual women from feminist identification.[33] Our experience suggests that there is, even among older women, a widespread sense of the "lesbianization" of the women's movement. The revelation by Patricia Ireland, president of the National Organization for Women, that she lives with a "female companion" undoubtedly reinforced that perception (Minkowitz 1992). One feminist quoted in the Washington *Post* commented on the public view of NOW as "a gay front group" (*off our backs* 1992a). Participants at the 1992 NOW conference report that it had the feel of a lesbian conference.[34] The 1992 Bloomington (Indiana) Women's Music Festival offered a workshop on "Networking for Straight Women in a Lesbian World."[35] At the local level, one lesbian-affirming heterosexual Columbus woman went to a local NOW meeting with a profeminist male friend involved in a men against rape group and reported feeling completely unwelcome because of her association with a man.[36] Equally as important, the dominance of white, middle-class, Christian women creates barriers to the achievement of a truly multicultural lesbian feminist community despite the ongoing community dialogue about race, class, ethnic, and other differences. As Judit

Moschkovich, a Jewish Latina, put it, the assumption that she should reject her Latin culture means accepting "the American culture of French Fries and Hamburgers (or soyburgers), American music on the radio (even if it's American women's music on a feminist radio show), not kissing and hugging every time you greet someone" (Moschkovich 1981).

Our point is not that the lesbian feminist community is a pure expression of radical feminism. Rather, we want to highlight its political and transformative functions. A wide variety of struggles have been influenced by the involvement of lesbian feminists or by ideas and practices characteristic of the community (Whittier 1991, esp. chap. 7). Direct action movements concerned with peace and other issues have adopted from the lesbian feminist community a view of revolution as an ongoing process of personal and social transformation, an emphasis on egalitarianism and consensus decision making, an orientation toward spirituality, and a commitment to shaping present action according to the values desired in an ideal future world (Epstein 1991; *off our backs* 1992b). Similarly, the ongoing dialogue in the lesbian feminist community about diversity has carried over into the gay/lesbian movement, and the radical feminist analysis of rape shapes the struggle against anti-gay/lesbian violence (Vaid 1991). Further, the AIDS movement has been driven by the radical feminist definition of control of one's body and access to health care as political issues (Hamilton 1991). Lesbians also have played a leading role in the development of the recovery movement for survivors of incest (Galst 1991). In short, lesbian feminist cultures of resistance have had political impact not only by sheltering battle-weary feminists but also by influencing the course of other social movements.

Finally, lesbian feminist communities affect a younger generation of women who hold the future of the women's movement in their hands. In our research on women's rights activists of the 1940s and 1950s, we found these women longing for "young blood" but unwilling to accept the new ideas and new strategies that young women brought with them (Rupp and Taylor 1987). An aging generation of activists may always long for fresh recruits who will be drawn to their cause but will not change anything about their movement; such an inclination, in part, lies behind the cultural clash between Meg Christian fans and Madonna devotees within the lesbian feminist community (Echols 1991; Yollin 1991; Starr 1992; Stein 1993). The next round of the women's movement is likely to take a different course, but it will not be untouched by the collective processes, consciousness, and practices of lesbian feminism. One of the major mechanisms of transmittal is women's studies, which mobilizes young women who identify as feminists (Dill 1991; Houppert 1991; Kamen 1991).

Some young activists identify themselves as a "third wave" of feminism, thus making a connection to the first two waves and at the same time claiming responsibility for a new resurgence. "I am not a postfeminism feminist. I am the Third Wave," writes Rebecca Walker, a student at Yale University and a contributing editor to *Ms.* (Walker 1992, 41).[37] Already we can see elements of change and continuity in the activities of a new generation. Young lesbians attracted to the gay/lesbian protest group Queer Nation, for example, reject the tradition of nonviolence and female pacifism when they adopt the "Queers bash back" response to violence against lesbians and gay men. At the same time, the formation of women's caucuses in Queer Nation and the AIDS activism group ACT-UP echoes the struggles of earlier generations of women within male-dominated organizations (Faderman 1991; Hamilton 1991; Yollin 1991). Lesbians engaging in direct action tactics are transforming the face of activism. In Columbus, female Queer Nation members, in a protest reminiscent of the early radical feminist zap actions, have engaged in kiss-ins at local shopping centers and the city zoo as a means of challenging heterosexual privilege. The Lesbian Avengers, founded in New York City in 1992, engage in "creative activism: loud, bold, sexy, silly, fierce, tasty and dramatic" ("Dyke Manifesto" 1993). In their first action, they marched into a Queens, N.Y., school board meeting to the tune of "When the Dykes Come Marching In" and handed out lavender balloons inscribed "Ask about Lesbian Lives" to first graders to protest the board's refusal to allow a multicultural curriculum that included discussion of lesbians and gay men ("Dyke Manifesto" 1993; Jule and Marin 1993).

In the climate of the 1980s and early 1990s, then, the culture of lesbian feminist communities has not just served to comfort, protect, and console activists in retreat. It also has nourished women involved in myriad protests, both within and outside the women's movement, whose vision of feminist transformation goes beyond political and economic structures to a broad redefinition of social values. Rather than squelching mobilization, we see lesbian feminist communities as sustaining the radical feminist tradition and bequeathing a legacy, however imperfect, to feminists of the future.

NOTES

1. Redstockings was a radical feminist action group founded in New York City in 1969. On cultural feminism versus radical feminism, see also Echols 1983a, 1983b, 1984.

2. For a critique of total separatism from a socialist feminist perspective, see Jaggar 1983; for a black feminist critique of the race and class bias of cultural feminism, see hooks 1984; for postmodern critiques, see Alcoff 1988—juxtaposing the cultural feminist and poststructuralist answers to the problem of defining the category of women—and Young 1990—rejecting the ideal of "community" as unable to encompass difference. For attacks on cultural feminism as a betrayal of radical feminism, from a radical feminist perspective, see Atkinson 1984; Willis 1984; and Ringelheim 1985. Other commentaries on cultural feminism can be found in Eisenstein 1983 (she does not use the term *cultural feminism* but warns of reactionary tendencies in what she calls "the new essentialism" [xvii]); Donovan 1985 (she traces cultural feminism to its nineteenth-century roots); and Buechler 1990 (he identifies cultural feminism as a variant of radical feminism).

3. The "sex wars" became a national issue after the 1982 "Scholar and the Feminist IX" conference at Barnard College, New York City. The conference, which focused on women's sexual autonomy, choice, and pleasure, included speakers who advocated sadomasochism, sexual role-playing, and pornography, provoking an attack by Women against Pornography, Women against Violence against Women, and New York Radical Feminists. See the discussion and bibliography in Vance 1984, 441–53; and see Segal and McIntosh 1993. The two major feminist anthologies associated with the "pro-sex" position (Snitow, Stansell, and Thompson 1983; Vance 1984) both included essays by Alice Echols in which she looked critically at the development of cultural feminism; see Echols 1983b, 1984. See also Echols 1991.

4. Our thinking on movement culture is influenced by Rick Fantasia's study of mergent cultures of resistance within the labor movement (1988).

5. The basic positions on the nature of women's culture and its relationship to feminism are clearly stated in an exchange between Ellen DuBois and Carroll Smith-Rosenberg (DuBois et al. 1980). DuBois defines women's culture as "the broad-based commonality of values, institutions, relationships, and methods of communication, focused on domesticity and morality and particular to late eighteenth- and nineteenth-century women" (29). For her, women's culture and feminism stand in a dialectical relationship. In contrast, Smith-Rosenberg questions the use of the term *women's culture* to describe the acceptance of mainstream cultural values and insists that a culture must have "its own autonomous values, identities, symbolic systems, and modes of communication" (58). Eschewing the word *culture,* she argues that feminism cannot develop outside a "female world" in which women create rituals and networks, form primary ties with other women, and develop their own worldview (61).

6. Scholars of African-American and working-class women, in particular, have rejected the notion of a universal women's culture. But their evidence suggests that various groups of women—enslaved African-American women, mill workers, and working-class housewives—did create "women's cultures," albeit multiple ones that often supported men of their groups. See Hewitt 1985. See Pascoe 1990 for a recent work that attacks the idea that there is a women's culture based on women's values.

7. Feminist consciousness involves a critique of male supremacy, the will to change it, and the belief that change is possible. (Cott 1989 draws on Gordon 1986, 29, in defining feminist consciousness.) Female consciousness, which Cott bases on Kaplan's (1982) exploration of working-class food protests and strikes, is rooted in women's acceptance of the division of labor by sex. Communal consciousness is based on solidarity with men of the same group. Feminist consciousness is necessarily oppositional, while female and communal consciousness can support the status quo or can lead women to engage in a variety of kinds of protest.

8. For a discussion of "new social movements," see Klandermans and Tarrow 1988. On the civil rights movement, see Morris 1984; McAdam 1988. On the New Left, see Gittlin 1987; Isserman 1987; Whalen and Flacks 1987; and Hayden 1988. On the gay rights movement, see D'Emilio 1983.

9. Written sources include books, periodicals, and narratives by community members, and newsletters, position papers, and other documents from lesbian feminist organizations. We also have made use of twenty-one in-depth, open-ended interviews with informants from Provincetown, Boston, and the rural Berkshire region of western Massachusetts; Portland, Maine; Washington, D.C.; New York City; St. Petersburg, Fla.; Columbus, Yellow Springs, Cleveland, and Cincinnati, Ohio; Minneapolis; Chicago; Denver; and Atlanta, conducted between 1987 and 1989, mostly by Nancy E. Whittier 1988) but also by Verta Taylor (Taylor and Whittier 1992). In addition, we have both been a part of the lesbian feminist community in Columbus since the late 1970s, have attended national events such as conferences, cultural events, and marches in Washington, D.C., and have over the past fifteen years interviewed informally lesbian feminists in a variety of communities across the country. All of these interviews were conducted with the understanding that quotations would not be attributed to named individuals.

10. Columbus is the largest city in Ohio, the state capital, and the home of the largest university campus in the country, Ohio State University. The lesbian feminist community is overwhelmingly, although not exclusively, white and middle class, with a large proportion of students and professionals. Most scholarship on the women's movement focuses on developments in large cities. See, e.g., Freeman 1975; Cassell 1977; Wolf 1979; Echols 1989; Staggenborg 1991; Ryan 1992. A notable exception is Krieger 1983.

11. See, e.g., Bolotin 1982; Friedan 1985; Davis 1989; Ebeling 1990.

12. On the institutionalization of liberal feminism, see Gelb and Palley 1982; Mueller 1987; Buechler 1990; Katzenstein 1990; Schlozman 1990; Davis 1991. On the climate of antifeminism, see Luker 1984; Ferree and Hess 1985; Mansbridge 1986; Chafetz and Dworkin 1987; Taylor 1989a; Matthews and De Hart 1990; Faludi 1991. For examples of the attack on "political correctness," see Charon 1992, which focuses on what she calls "rad-fems"; D'Souza 1991; and Taylor 1991. On the radical branch, see Hole and Levine 1971; Freeman 1975; Evans 1979; Ferree and Hess 1985; Echols 1989; Ryan 1989; Buechler 1990; Castro 1990; Davis 1991; Taylor and Whittier 1993.

13. The concept of "social movement community" comes from Buechler 1990; literature documenting the nature of lesbian feminist communities includes Barnhart 1975; Ponse 1978; Lewis 1979; Wolf 1979; Krieger 1983; Lockard 1986; Phelan 1989; Cavin 1990; Esterberg 1990; Zimmerman 1990; Penelope 1992.

14. This discussion is heavily indebted to Whittier 1991. In addition, we draw on other unpublished research on Columbus, including Haller 1984; Matteson 1989; Dill 1991; Wilkey 1991; Gorman 1992; McCormick 1992. Finally, our account is shaped by our own involvement, since both of us were peripheral members of the Women's Action Collective and have attended meetings, marches, demonstrations, concerts, and community conferences for the past fifteen years.

15. See, e.g., Walker 1974; Rich 1976; Chodorow 1978; Daly 1978, 1984; Dworkin 1981; Gilligan 1982; Cavin 1985; Johnson 1987; MacKinnon 1987.

16. Interview conducted by Nancy Whittier, August 1987, Stockbridge, Mass.

17. On separatism, see Frye 1983; Hoagland and Penelope 1988.

18. Women's Action Collective "Statement of Philosophy," adopted by consensus May 21, 1974, in the personal papers of Teri Wehausen, Columbus, Ohio.

19. Interview conducted by Verta Taylor, April 1989, Columbus, Ohio.

20. See, for a variety of perspectives, Beck 1980; Moraga and Anzaldúa 1981; Hull, Scott, and Smith 1982; Smith 1983; Bulkin, Pratt, and Smith 1984; Lorde 1984a, 1984b; Anzaldúa 1990; Trujillo 1991.

21. See also Cavin 1990; Whittier 1991; and Gorman 1992.

22. This statement is attributed to Ti-Grace Atkinson in Koedt 1973. Echols points out that Sidney Abbott and Barbara Love record the original version of this remark quite differently: in 1970, Atkinson addressed the lesbian group Daughters of Bilitis in New York and commented that "Feminism is a theory; but Lesbianism is a practice" (Abbott and Love 1972, 117; Echols 1989, 238). In any case, the phrase has been widely quoted within lesbian feminist communities.

23. Women's Action Collective "Statement of Philosophy."

24. Interview conducted by Nancy Whittier, September 1987, Washington, D.C.

25. For the opposing position, see Linden et al. 1982.

26. Interview conducted by Leila Rupp, May 1992, Columbus, Ohio.

27. Interview conducted by Verta Taylor, May 1987, Columbus, Ohio.

28. See Faderman 1981, 1991; Rupp 1989a, 1989b; Lützen 1990.

29. Interviews conducted by Verta Taylor and Leila Rupp, April 1992, Columbus, Ohio.

30. The issue of racism within the organization blew apart the twelfth annual NWSA conference, "Feminist Education: Calling the Question," held in Akron, Ohio, June 20–24, 1990. See Ruby, Elliott, and Douglas 1990.

31. Zimmerman 1990 analyzes the impact of lesbian fiction on the development of the lesbian community.

32. Communication from Jo Reger, Columbus, Ohio, 1992.

33. See Schneider 1986, 1988; Dill 1989; Kamen 1991.

34. Interview conducted by Verta Taylor and Leila Rupp, February 1992, Columbus, Ohio.

35. Communication from Suzanne Staggenborg, Bloomington, Ind., 1992.

36. Interview conducted by Verta Taylor, May 1992, Columbus, Ohio.

37. At the American Sociological Association meetings in Cincinnati, August 23–27, 1991, a group of women issued a call for an ad hoc discussion of "third wave feminism." See also Kamen 1991.

REFERENCES

Abbott, Sidney, and Barbara Love. 1972. *Sappho Was a Right-on Woman: A Liberated View of Lesbianism.* New York: Stein & Day.

Alcoff, Linda. 1988. "Cultural Feminism versus Post-Structuralism: The Identity Crisis in Feminist Theory." *Signs: Journal of Women in Culture and Society* 13(3):405–36.

Anzaldúa, Gloria. 1990. *Making Face, Making Soul—Haciendo Caras: Creative and Critical Perspectives by Women of Color.* San Francisco: Aunt Lute.

Atkinson, Ti-Grace. 1973. "Lesbianism and Feminism." In *Amazon Expedition: A Lesbian Feminist Anthology,* ed. Phyllis Birkby et al., 11–14. New York: Times Change Press.

———. 1984. "Le nationalisme feminin." *Nouvelles questions feministes* 6–7: 35–54.

Barnhart, Elizabeth. 1975. "Friends and Lovers in a Lesbian Counterculture Community." In *Old Family, New Family,* ed. N. Glazer-Malbin, 90–115. New York: Van Nostrand.

Bart, Pauline B. 1993. "Protean Woman: The Liquidity of Female Sexuality and the Tenaciousness of Lesbian Identity." In *Heterosexuality: A Feminism and Psychology Reader,* ed. Sue Wilkinson and Celia Kitzinger, 246–52. London: Sage.

Beck, Evelyn Torton. 1980. *Nice Jewish Girls: A Lesbian Anthology.* Watertown, Mass.: Persephone.

Boles, Janet K. 1991. "Form Follows Function: The Evolution of Feminist Strategies." *Annals of the American Academy of Political and Social Science* 515 (May): 38–49.

Bolotin, Susan. 1982. "Voices from the Post-Feminist Generation." *New York Times Magazine,* October 17, 28–31+.

Buechler, Steven M. 1990. *Women's Movements in the United States.* New Brunswick, N.J.: Rutgers University Press.

Bulkin, Elly, Minnie Bruce Pratt, and Barbara Smith. 1984. *Yours in Struggle: Three Feminist Perspectives on Anti-Semitism and Racism.* Brooklyn, N.Y.: Long Haul Press.

Califia, Pat. 1979. "A Secret Side of Lesbian Sexuality." *Advocate,* December 27, 19–23.

———. 1980. *Sapphistry: The Book of Lesbian Sexuality.* Tallahassee, Fla.: Naiad.

———. 1981. "Feminism and Sadomasochism." *Heresies* 12:30–34.

Cassell, Joan. 1977. *A Group Called Women: Sisterhood and Symbolism in the Feminist Movement.* New York: McKay.

Castro, Ginette. 1990. *American Feminism: A Contemporary History.* New York: New York University Press.

Cavin, Susan. 1985. *Lesbian Origins.* San Francisco: Ism Press.

———. 1990. "The Invisible Army of Women: Lesbian Social Protests, 1969–1988." In *Women and Social Protest,* ed. Guida West and Rhoda Lois Blumberg, 321–32. New York: Oxford University Press.

Chafetz, Janet Saltzman, and Anthony Gary Dworkin. 1987. "In the Face of Threat: Organized Antifeminism in Comparative Perspective." *Gender & Society* 1(1):33–60.

Charon, Mona. 1992. "Shrill, Leftist Thought Police Still Seek to Govern Nation's Campuses." *Columbus Dispatch,* May 5.

Chodorow, Nancy. 1978. *The Reproduction of Mothering: Psychoanalysis and the Sociology of Gender.* Berkeley: University of California Press.

Clausen, Jan. 1990. "My Interesting Condition." *Outlook* 7 (Winter): 10–21.

———. 1992. "A Craving for Community." *Women's Review of Books* 9 (March): 8–9.

Collins, Patricia Hill. 1989. "The Social Construction of Black Feminist Thought." *Signs* 14(4):745–73.

———. 1990. *Black Feminist Thought: Knowledge, Consciousness, and the Politics of Empowerment.* Boston: Unwin Hyman.

Community Action Strategies to Stop Rape. 1978. "Freeing Our Lives: A Feminist Analysis of Rape Prevention." Community Action Strategies to Stop Rape, Women Against Rape, Columbus, Ohio.

Cook, Blanche Wiesen. 1977. "Female Support Networks and Political Activism: Lillian Wald, Crystal Eastman, Emma Goldman." *Chrysalis* 3:43–61.

Cott, Nancy F. 1989. "What's in a Name? The Limits of 'Social Feminism'; or, Expanding the Vocabulary of Women's History." *Journal of American History* 76(3):809–29.

Daly, Mary. 1978. *Gyn-Ecology: The Metaethics of Radical Feminism.* Boston: Beacon.

———. 1984. *Pure Lust: Elemental Feminist Philosophy.* Boston: Beacon.

Daly, Mary, in cahoots with Jane Caputi. 1987. *Websters' First New Intergalactic Wickedary of the English Language.* Boston: Beacon.

Davis, Flora. 1991. *Moving the Mountain: The Women's Movement in America since 1960.* New York: Simon & Schuster.

Davis, Sally Ogle. 1989. "Is Feminism Dead?" *Los Angeles,* February.

D'Emilio, John. 1983. *Sexual Politics, Sexual Communities: The Making of a Homosexual Minority in the U.S., 1940–1970.* Chicago: University of Chicago Press.

Devor, Holly. 1989. *Gender Blending: Confronting the Limits of Duality.* Bloomington: Indiana University Press.

Dill, Kim. 1989. "Qualified Feminism and Its Influence on College Women's Identification with the Women's Movement." Unpublished manuscript, Columbus, Ohio.

———. 1991. "Feminism in the Nineties: The Influence of Collective Identity and Community on Young Feminist Activists." M.A. thesis, Ohio State University.

Dimen, Muriel. 1984. "Politically Correct? Politically Incorrect?" In Vance 1984, 138–48.

Direen, Brenda. 1991. "The Politics of Recovery." *Feminisms* (newsletter of the Center for Women's Studies, Ohio State University) 4 (March/April): 6–7.

Donovan, Josephine. 1985. *Feminist Theory: The Intellectual Traditions of American Feminism.* New York: Ungar.

D'Souza, Dinesh. 1991. *Illiberal Education: The Politics of Race and Sex on Campus.* New York: Free Press.

DuBois, Ellen, Mari Jo Buhle, Temma Kaplan, Gerda Lerner, and Carroll Smith-Rosenberg. 1980. "Politics and Culture in Women's History." *Feminist Studies* 6(1):26–64.

Dworkin, Andrea. 1981. *Pornography: Men Possessing Women.* New York: Perigee.

"Dyke Manifesto." 1993. Flyer handed out at the March on Washington for Lesbian, Gay, and Bisexual Rights and Liberation, April 25, 1993, in possession of the authors.

Ebeling, Kay. 1990. "The Failure of Feminism." *Newsweek* 116 (November 19): 9.

Echols, Alice. 1983a. "Cultural Feminism and the Anti-Pornography Movement." *Social Text* 7:34–53.

———. 1983b. "The New Feminism of Yin and Yang." In Snitow, Stansell, and Thompson 1983, 439–59.

———. 1984. "The Taming of the Id: Feminist Sexual Politics, 1968–83." In Vance 1984, 50–72.

———. 1989. *Daring to Be Bad: Radical Feminism in America, 1967–1975*. Minneapolis: University of Minnesota Press.

———. 1991. "Justifying Our Love? The Evolution of Lesbianism through Feminism and Gay Male Politics." *Advocate,* March 26, 48–53.

Eisenstein, Hester. 1983. *Contemporary Feminist Thought.* Boston: G. K. Hall.

Epstein, Barbara. 1991. *Political Protest and Cultural Revolution: Nonviolent Direct Action in the 1970s and 1980s.* Berkeley and Los Angeles: University of California Press.

Esterberg, Kristin Gay. 1990. "Salience and Solidarity: Identity, Correctness, and Conformity in a Lesbian Community." Paper presented at the annual meeting of the American Sociological Association, Washington, D.C., August 11–15.

Evans, Sara. 1979. *Personal Politics: The Roots of Women's Liberation in the Civil Rights Movement and the New Left.* New York: Knopf.

Faderman, Lillian. 1981. *Surpassing the Love of Men.* New York: Morrow.

———. 1991. *Odd Girls and Twilight Lovers: A History of Lesbian Life in Twentieth-Century America.* New York: Columbia University Press.

Faludi, Susan. 1991. *Backlash: The Undeclared War against American Women.* New York: Crown.

Fantasia, Rick. 1988. *Cultures of Solidarity: Consciousness, Action, and Contemporary American Workers.* Berkeley and Los Angeles: University of California Press.

Ferree, Myra Marx, and Beth B. Hess. 1985. *Controversy and Coalition: The New Feminist Movement.* Boston: Twayne.

Freedman, Estelle. 1979. "Separatism as Strategy: Female Institution Building and American Feminism, 1870–1930." *Feminist Studies* 5(3):512–52.

Freeman, Jo. 1975. *The Politics of Women's Liberation.* New York: Longman.

Friedan, Betty. 1985. "How to Get the Women's Movement Moving Again." *New York Times Magazine,* November 3, 26–29+.

Frye, Marilyn. 1983. "Some Reflections on Separatism and Power." In her *The Politics of Reality: Essays in Feminist Theory,* 95–109. Trumansburg, N.Y.: Crossing Press.

———. 1990. "Do You Have to Be a Lesbian to Be a Feminist?" *off our backs* 20 (August/September): 21–23.

Galst, Liz. 1991. "Overcoming Silence." *Advocate,* December 3, 60–63.

Gearhart, Sally Miller. 1978. *The Wanderground: Stories of the Hill Women.* Watertown, Mass.: Persephone.

———. 1991. "The Chipko." *Ms.* 2 (September-October): 64–69.

Gelb, Joyce, and Marian Lief Palley. 1982. *Women and Public Policy.* Princeton, N.J.: Princeton University Press.

Gilligan, Carol. 1982. *In a Different Voice.* Cambridge, Mass.: Harvard University Press.

Gittlin, Tod. 1987. *The Sixties.* New York: Bantam.

Gordon, Linda. 1986. "What's New in Women's History." In *Feminist Studies/Critical Studies,* ed. Teresa de Lauretis. Bloomington: Indiana University Press.

———. 1991. "On 'Difference.' " *Genders* 10 (Spring): 91–111.

Gorman, Phyllis. 1992. "The Ohio AIDS Movement: Competition and Cooperation between Grassroots Activists and Professionally Sponsored Organizations." Ph.D. dissertation, Ohio State University.

Haller, Mary. 1984. "Decline of a Social Movement Organization: The Women's Action Collective." Unpublished manuscript, Columbus, Ohio.

Hamilton, Amy. 1991. "Women in A.I.D.S. Activism." *off our backs* 21 (November): 4–5.

Hanisch, Carol. 1978. "The Personal Is Political." In *Feminist Revolution,* ed. Redstockings of the Women's Liberation Movement, 204–15. New York: Random House.

Hayden, Tom. 1988. *Reunion.* New York: Random House.

Hewitt, Nancy A. 1985. "Beyond the Search for Sisterhood: American Women's History in the 1980s." *Social History* 10(3):299–321.

Hoagland, Sarah Lucia, and Julia Penelope. 1988. *For Lesbians Only: A Separatist Anthology.* London: Onlywomen.

Hole, Judith, and Ellen Levine. 1971. *Rebirth of Feminism.* New York: Quadrangle/New York Times.

hooks, bell. 1984. *Feminist Theory: From Margin to Center.* Boston: South End.

Houppert, Karen. 1991. "Wildflowers among the Ivy: New Campus Radicals." *Ms.* 2 (September/October): 52–58.

Hull, Gloria T., Patricia Bell Scott, and Barbara Smith. 1982. *All the Women Are White, All the Blacks Are Men, but Some of Us Are Brave: Black Women's Studies.* Old Westbury, N.Y.: Feminist Press.

Isserman, Maurice. 1987. *If I Had a Hammer: The Death of the Old Left and the Birth of the New Left.* New York: Basic.

Jaggar, Alison M. 1983. *Feminist Politics and Human Nature.* Totowa, N.J.: Rowman & Allanheld.

Johnson, Sonia. 1987. *Going Out of Our Minds: The Metaphysics of Liberation.* Freedom, Calif.: Crossing Press.

Jule, Ilsa, and Laurie Marin. 1993. "The Lesbian Avengers." *Deneuve,* May/June, 42–44.

Kamen, Paula. 1991. *Feminist Fatale: Voices from the "Twentysomething" Generation Explore the Future of the Women's Movement.* New York: Donald I. Fine.

Kaplan, Temma. 1982. "Female Consciousness and Collective Action: The Case of Barcelona, 1910–1918." *Signs* 7(3):545–66.

Katzenstein, Mary Fainsod. 1990. "Feminism within American Institutions: Unobtrusive Mobilization in the 1980s." *Signs* 16(1):27–54.

Klandermans, Bert, and Sidney Tarrow. 1988. "Mobilization into Social Movements: Synthesizing European and American Approaches." In *From Structure to Action: Comparing Social Movement Research across Cultures,* ed. Bert Klandermans, Hanspeter Kriesi, and Sidney Tarrow, 1–38. International Social Movement Research, vol. 1. Greenwich, Conn.: JAI.

Koedt, Anne. 1973. "Lesbianism and Feminism." In *Radical Feminism,* ed. Anne Koedt, Ellen Levine, and Anita Rapone, 246–58. New York: Quadrangle.

Krieger, Susan. 1983. *The Mirror Dance: Identity in a Women's Community.* Philadelphia: Temple University Press.

Lewis, Sasha Gregory. 1979. *Sunday's Women.* Boston: Beacon.

Linden, Robin Ruth, Darlene R. Pagano, Diana E. H. Russell, and Susan Leigh Star. 1982. *Against Sadomasochism: A Radical Feminist Analysis.* East Palo Alto, Calif.: Frog in the Well.

Lockard, Denyse. 1986. "The Lesbian Community: An Anthropological Approach." In *The Many Faces of Homosexuality,* ed. Evelyn Blackwood, 83–95. New York: Harrington Park.

Lorde, Audre. 1984a. "An Open Letter to Mary Daly." In her *Sister Outsider: Essays and Speeches,* 66–71. Trumansburg, N.Y.: Crossing Press.

————. 1984b. "The Master's Tools Will Never Dismantle the Master's House." In her *Sister Outsider: Essays and Speeches,* 110–13. Trumansburg, N.Y.: Crossing Press.

Loulan, JoAnn Gardner. 1990. *The Lesbian Erotic Dance: Butch, Femme, Androgyny, and Other Rhythms.* San Francisco: Spinsters.

Luker, Kristin. 1984. *Abortion and the Politics of Motherhood.* Berkeley and Los Angeles: University of California Press.

Lützen, Karin. 1990. *Was das Herz begehrt: Liebe und Freundschaft zwischen Frauen.* Hamburg: Ernst Kabel.

McAdam, Doug. 1988. *Freedom Summer.* New York: Oxford University Press.

McCormick, Kelly, 1992. "Moms without Dads: Women Choosing Children." Ph.D. dissertation, Ohio State University.

MacKinnon, Catharine A. 1987. *Feminism Unmodified: Discourses on Life and Law.* Cambridge, Mass.: Harvard University Press.

Mansbridge, Jane J. 1986. *Why We Lost the ERA.* Chicago: University of Chicago Press.

Matteson, Gretchen. 1989. "The History of the Women's Action Collective, a Successful Social Movement Organization, 1971–1984." Unpublished manuscript, Columbus, Ohio.

Matthews, Donald G., and Jane Sherron De Hart. 1990. *Sex, Gender, and the Politics of ERA: A State and the Nation.* New York: Oxford University Press.

Minkowitz, Donna. 1992. "The Newsroom Becomes a Battleground." *Advocate,* May 19, 31–37.

Moraga, Cherríe, and Gloria Anzaldúa, eds. 1981. *This Bridge Called My Back: Writings by Radical Women of Color.* Watertown, Mass.: Persephone.

Morris, Aldon. 1984. *The Origins of the Civil Rights Movement: Black Communities Organizing for Change.* New York: Free Press.

Moschkovich, Judit. 1981. " 'But I Know You, American Woman.' " In Moraga and Anzaldúa 1981, 79–84.

Mueller, Carol McClurg. 1987. "Collective Consciousness, Identity Transformation and the Rise of Women in Public Office in the U.S." In *The Women's Movements of the United States and Western Europe: Consciousness, Political Opportunity and Public Policy,* ed. Mary Fainsod Katzenstein and Carol McClurg Mueller, 89–111. Philadelphia: Temple University Press.

Near, Holly. 1990. *Fire in the Rain, Singer in the Storm.* New York: Morrow.

off our backs. 1992a. "The News That 'Rocked the Feminist Community.' " *off our backs* 22 (January): 2.

———. 1992b. "Queer Notions." *off our backs,* October, 12–15.

Pascoe, Peggy. 1990. *Relations of Rescue: The Search for Female Moral Authority in the American West, 1874–1939.* New York: Oxford University Press.

Pearlman, Sarah F. 1987. "The Saga of Continuing Clash in Lesbian Community, or Will an Army of Ex-Lovers Fail?" In *Lesbian Psychologies: Explorations and Challenges,* ed. Boston Lesbian Psychologies Collective, 313–26. Urbana: University of Illinois Press.

Penelope, Julia. 1992. *Call Me Lesbian: Lesbian Lives, Lesbian Theory.* Freedom, Calif.: Crossing Press.

Phelan, Shane. 1989. *Identity Politics: Lesbian Feminism and the Limits of Community.* Philadelphia: Temple University Press.

Ponse, Barbara. 1978. *Identities in the Lesbian World: The Social Construction of Self.* Westport, Conn.: Greenwood.

Rich, Adrienne. 1980. "Compulsory Heterosexuality and Lesbian Existence." *Signs* 5(4):631–60.

———. 1976. *Of Woman Born.* New York: Norton.

Ringelheim, Joan. 1985. "Women and the Holocaust: A Reconsideration of Research." *Signs* 10(4):741–61.

Ruby, Jennie, Farar Elliott, and Carol Anne Douglas. 1990. "NWSA: Troubles Surface at Conference." *off our backs* 1 (August/September): 10–16.

Rupp, Leila J. 1989a. "Feminism and the Sexual Revolution in the Early Twentieth Century: The Case of Doris Stevens." *Feminist Studies* 15(2):289–309.

———. 1989b. " 'Imagine My Surprise': Women's Relationships in Mid-Twentieth Century America." In *Hidden from History: Reclaiming the Gay and Lesbian Past,* ed. Martin Bauml Duberman, Martha Vicinus, and George Chauncey, Jr., 395–410. New York: New American Library.

Rupp, Leila J., and Verta Taylor. 1987. *Survival in the Doldrums: The American Women's Rights Movement, 1945 to the 1960s.* New York: Oxford University Press.

Ryan, Barbara. 1989. "Ideological Purity and Feminism: The U.S. Women's Movement from 1966 to 1975." *Gender & Society* 3(2):239–57.

———. 1992. *Feminism and the Women's Movement*. New York: HarperCollins.

Samois. 1979. *What Color Is Your Handkerchief? A Lesbian S/M Sexuality Reader*. Berkeley, Calif.: Samois.

Schlozman, Kay Lehman. 1990. "Representing Women in Washington: Sisterhood and Pressure Politics." In *Women, Politics, and Change,* ed. Louise A. Tilly and Patricia Gurin, 339–82. New York: Sage.

Schneider, Beth. 1986. "Feminist Disclaimers, Stigma, and the Contemporary Women's Movement." Unpublished manuscript, Santa Barbara, Calif.

———. 1988. "Political Generations in the Contemporary Women's Movement." *Sociological Inquiry* 58(1):4–21.

Segal, Lynne, and Mary McIntosh. 1993. *Sex Exposed: Sexuality and the Pornography Debate*. New Brunswick, N.J.: Rutgers University Press.

Sharon, Tanya, Farar Elliott, and Cecile Latham. 1991. "The National Lesbian Conference." *off our backs,* June, 1–4, 18–19.

Sims, Margot. 1982. *On the Necessity of Bestializing the Human Female*. Boston: South End.

Smeller, Michele M. 1992. "Crossing Over: The Negotiation of Sexual Identity in a Social Movement Community." Unpublished manuscript, Columbus, Ohio.

Smith, Barbara. 1983. *Home Girls: A Black Feminist Anthology*. New York: Kitchen Table; Women of Color Press.

Snitow, Ann, Christine Stansell, and Sharon Thompson. 1983. *Powers of Desire: The Politics of Sexuality*. New York: Monthly Review Press.

Spelman, Elizabeth V. 1988. *Inessential Woman: Problems of Exclusion in Feminist Thought*. Boston: Beacon.

Staggenborg, Suzanne. 1991. *The Pro-Choice Movement*. New York: Oxford University Press.

Starr, Victoria. 1992. "The Changing Tune of Women's Music." *Advocate,* June 2, 68–71.

Stein, Arlene. 1989. "All Dressed Up but No Place to Go? Style Wars and the New Lesbianism." *Out/Look* 1(4):34–42.

———. 1993. *Sisters, Sexperts, Queers: Beyond the Lesbian Nation*. New York: Plume.

Stevens, Robin. 1991. "Style vs. Substance at the National Lesbian Conference." *Out/Look* 14:51–53.

Taylor, John. 1991. "Are You Politically Correct?" *New York,* January 21, 33–40.

Taylor, Verta. 1989a. "The Future of Feminism: A Social Movement Analysis." In *Feminist Frontiers II: Rethinking Sex, Gender, and Society,* ed. Laurel Richardson and Verta Taylor, 473–90. New York: Random House.

———. 1989b. "Social Movement Continuity: The Women's Movement in Abeyance." *American Sociological Review* 54 (October): 761–75.

Taylor, Verta, and Nancy E. Whittier. 1992. "Collective Identity in Social Movement Communities: Lesbian Feminist Mobilization." In *Frontiers of Social Movement Theory,* ed. Aldon Morris and Carol Mueller, 104–29. New Haven, Conn.: Yale University Press.

———. 1993. "The New Feminist Movement." In *Feminist Frontiers III: Rethinking Sex, Gender, and Society,* ed. Laurel Richardson and Verta Taylor, 533–48. New York: Random House.

Trujillo, Carla. 1991. *Chicana Lesbians: The Girls Our Mothers Warned Us About*. Berkeley: Third Woman.

Vaid, Urvashi. 1991. "Let's Put Our Own House in Order." *Out/Look* 14 (Fall): 55–57.

Vance, Carole S., ed. 1984. *Pleasure and Danger: Exploring Female Sexuality*. Boston: Routledge & Kegan Paul.

Walker, Alice. 1974. *In Search of Our Mothers' Gardens*. New York: Harcourt Brace Jovanovich.

Walker, Rebecca. 1992. "Becoming the Third Wave." *Ms.* 2 (January/February): 39–41.

Whalen, Jack, and Richard Flacks. 1987. *Beyond the Barricades: The Sixties Generation Grows Up*. Philadelphia: Temple University Press.

Whittier, Nancy E. 1988. "The Construction of a Politicized Collective Identity: Ideology and Symbolism in Contemporary Lesbian Feminist Communities." M.A. thesis, Ohio State University.

———. 1991. "Feminists in the 'Post-Feminist' Age: Collective Identity and the Persistence of the Women's Movement." Ph.D. dissertation, Ohio State University.

Wilkey, Cindy. 1991. "The Role of Women in Local Radical Organizations." Unpublished manuscript, Columbus, Ohio.

Williams, Brooke. 1978. "The Retreat to Cultural Feminism." In *Feminist Revolution,* ed. Redstockings of the Women's Liberation Movement. New York: Random House.

Willis, Ellen. 1984. "Radical Feminism and Feminist Radicalism." In *The '60's without Apology,* ed. Sonya Sayres, Anders Stephanson, Stanley Aronowitz, and Fredric Jameson. Minneapolis: University of Minnesota Press.

Wolf, Deborah Goleman. 1979. *The Lesbian Community*. Berkeley and Los Angeles: University of California Press.

Womoon Rising. 1982. Columbus, Ohio, Women's Action Collective newsletter. September/October and November/December.

Yollin, Patricia. 1991. "Painting the Town Lavender." *Image* (San Francisco *Examiner*), March 10, 18–29.

Young, Iris Marion. 1990. "The Ideal of Community and the Politics of Difference." In *Feminism/Postmodernism,* ed. Linda J. Nicholson, 300–323. New York: Routledge.

Zimmerman, Bonnie. 1990. *The Safe Sea of Women: Lesbian Fiction, 1969–1989*. Boston: Beacon.

14 Mexican-American Women in the Social Sciences

MAXINE BACA ZINN
University of Michigan, Flint

The treatment of minority women in social science literature has long reflected the surrounding society's sexual and racial differentiation. Dorothy Smith's contention that women have been "outside the frame" of social science investigation is especially true of minority women.[1] As a consequence of erroneous assumptions and limited empirical research, Mexican-American women have been particularly misconstrued. The image of Chicanas in the social sciences has been narrow and biased. They have been portrayed as long-suffering mothers who are subject to the brutality of insecure husbands and whose only function is to produce children—as women who themselves are childlike, simple, and completely dependent on fathers, brothers, and husbands. Machismo and its counterpart of female submissiveness are assumed to be rooted in a distinctive cultural heritage.[2]

The portrait of the passive Mexican-American woman has been successfully challenged in the wave of revisionist scholarship about minorities and women. The recent publication of several book-length works on Mexican-American women should be hailed as a significant development. The research has demonstrated that, like women in all social categories, Chicanas can be active, adaptive human beings despite their subordination. However, the causes and dynamics of that subordination have remained ambiguous. Less attention has been devoted to explaining the social worlds and behaviors of Chicanas than to describing them. This is true of the growing body of social science literature on Chicanas, as well as feminist works that deal with

357

minority women. The inclusion of minority women in feminist works, Margaret Simons contends, is confined to the level of pretheoretical presentation of concrete problems.[3] Yet a central goal of feminist scholarship is that of analysis. According to Judith Laws, "feminist scholarship goes beyond simple descriptions of the status quo, seeking systematic explanation."[4]

Applying the new conceptual developments in social science, especially feminist social science, will advance our understanding of Chicanas' past, present, and future in this society. We cannot afford to ignore recent advances made in the study of women. That is not to say that feminist theoretical constructs should be uncritically applied to the study of Chicanas. Given the eclipse of minority women in feminist scholarship, much theorizing about women will undoubtedly fall short in its application to Chicanas. However, an integration of insights generated in feminist social science with scholarship about Mexican-American women is both timely and intellectually challenging.

This essay focuses on analytic issues in the study of Chicanas. The intent is to narrow the gap between social science works on Chicanas and feminist social science. This will be accomplished by reviewing three books on Mexican-American women that treat Chicanas from different social science perspectives. They are Alfredo Mirandé and Evangelina Enriquez's *La Chicana: The Mexican-American Woman*,[5] Margarita B. Melville's *Twice a Minority: Mexican American Women*,[6] and Magdelina Mora and Adelaida R. Del Castillo's *Mexican Women in the United States: Struggles Past and Present*.[7] Other works offering new evidence on the social worlds of Chicanas will also be examined.

THE NEW SCHOLARSHIP ON CHICANAS

The publication of full-length books, numerous articles, and several bibliographic essays about Chicanas in the past few years indicates that, after decades of neglect, Mexican-American women have suddenly become a legitimate subject of scholarly concern. Much of this new scholarship is reviewed in an essay on reference works by Cordelia Candelaria[8] and in an exhaustive bibliographic survey by Catherine Loeb.[9] Both of these outstanding reviews appear in *Frontiers: A Journal of Women Studies,* in an issue devoted to "Chicanas in the National Landscape." Loeb does a superb job of providing a sweeping introduction to the literature on Chicanas and grouping the works according to such topics as history, literature, economic and social profile, the family, and politics. An earlier review of historical sources by Judith Sweeney provides a useful division of works into three major periods: the colonial period (1519–1821), the nineteenth century (1821–1910), and the contemporary period (1910–76).[10]

La Chicana is a long-awaited, first full-length book about Mexican-American women. Mirandé and Enriquez account for the contemporary status of Chicanas by presenting an interdisciplinary analysis of sociohistorical conditions. Using historical, literary, and sociological literature, they assemble a comprehensive account of Mexican-American women. The basic thesis of the book is that a full understanding of Chicanas can only be gained through an examination of their colonial heritage in Mexico and the United States. The central proposition is that the present-day cultural mandates impinging on Chicanas originated in ancient Indian and Mexican culture. A major contribution of the book lies in its correction of the erroneous notion that Chicanas have been absent from history. The authors are especially effective in presenting accounts of individual women who actively shaped the history of Mexico and the Southwest. *La Chicana* should remain a significant and seminal work for years to come.

The Melville book, *Twice a Minority,* is the first anthology of empirical studies about Mexican-American women. "Its purpose," according to the editor, "is to modify the stereotypes of Mexican-American women found in much of the social science literature which often views females as passive sufferers."[11] This collection of primarily anthropological studies of Chicanas is divided into three sections: status of womanhood, changes in gender roles, and cultural conflict. The picture that emerges "is that of a population of women who attempt with varying degrees of success to fit into the mainstream of American life without losing their identity as Mexicans." The merit of this collection lies in the abundance of original material that establishes Chicanas' social worlds as worthy of the serious attention of social scientists.

Mora and Del Castillo's collection is intended to "document and appraise Mexican women's participation in the struggle against national oppression, class exploitation, and sexism."[12] Included are essays on the general topic of women's activism as well as articles on the history of women's involvement in political and class movements in Mexico. These works provide background and context for the essays specifically addressed to the political activism of Chicanas. The book's title, *Struggles Past and Present,* suggests that its subject is the collective struggle of Mexican women in the United States. However, the scope of the collection is somewhat broader since many of the essays are concerned with the societal conditions that have generated those struggles. The book makes a genuine contribution to our understanding of the "leadership, courage, tenacity and creativity" of Mexican women in the United States. Furthermore, it provides a corrective to the scholarly preoccupation with women's domesticity by highlighting their participation in formal institutional structures.

Taken together, these three works have filled large gaps in the social science of Mexican-American women. The task now at hand involves grappling with analytic concerns.

"Critical work," Meredith Gould posits, "is that which develops strategies for locating women within a sociocultural context and then explains the existence and consequence of that location."[13] Such a definition prompts the following question, How successful have we been at explaining the existence and consequences of the location of Chicanas? Despite recent advances, much explanatory work lies ahead. Few recent works are explicitly explanatory in intent, but most offer interpretations that have significant implications for dealing with questions about the social location of Chicanas.

Two conceptual features characterize most social science literature related to Chicanas: (1) the guiding interpretive framework is cultural and (2) interpretations are uninformed by current conceptualizations on gender. Consequently, several problems plague the literature. Until they are resolved, theoretical progress will be hampered.

THE OVERRELIANCE ON CULTURE

The most serious problem in the existing literature is one that has characterized the study of Chicanos in general. Too great an emphasis has been placed on culture while other dimensions of social organization have been ignored.[14] The difficulties associated with a cultural analysis are most clearly revealed in the Mirandé and Enriquez book. Their consistent adherence to a cultural framework both in the presentation and interpretation of data makes for a coherent and sustained work. However, it also generates serious flaws in treating issues of causality. A summary quotation from Mirandé and Enriquez captures the essence of their approach: "One of our theses is that a number of present day cultural mandates which impinge on the contemporary Chicana originated in ancient Indian and Mexican culture. Some cultural expectations of Chicanos date back to Aztec models, such as being heart of the home, bearing and rearing children, being clean and tidy, dedicating oneself to a husband, and preserving one's respectability in the eyes of the community."[15]

The authors' revision of Chicana history in Mexico and the United States, their descriptions of Chicanas in contemporary institutions, and their exploration of Chicana feminism are all rooted in an adherence to Mexican cultural antecedents. They consider these antecedents responsible for women's subjugation, women's position in families, and girls' lack of competitiveness in school. Chicana feminism is, thus, traced to a distinctive Mexican cultural heritage.

The authors do acknowledge that race and gender, as sources of oppression in the society at large, have an effect on Chicanas; their framework is not totally culturally deterministic. Still, the focus on culture tends to deemphasize sources of subordination and control in contemporary societal institutions. Through a focus on "internal oppression by a cultural heritage," it can be reasoned that Chicano culture is itself responsible for the oppression of Chicanas.

THE SIGNIFICANCE OF STRUCTURE

The failure to distinguish between structural and cultural dimensions of social organization has resulted in serious misunderstandings about women in Chicano communities. In order to ground this review in a general structural framework, I will draw upon the distinction between structure and culture provided by Peter M. Blau and W. Richard Scott. Structure refers to the networks of social relations and the status structure defined by them, while culture refers to a system of shared beliefs and orientations that serve as standards for human conduct.[16] This distinction has important ramifications when applied to the study of Chicanos in general and to the study of Chicanas in particular.

It may be argued that the social location of Chicanas (as well as the causes and consequences of that location) springs from and is shaped by structural arrangements of American society that have excluded Chicanos (both women and men) from full and equal participation in its public institutions. Institutional processes affect Chicanos in important ways; for one, they create the need for distinctive institutional arrangements among Chicano people. Evidence in support of structural explanations for life conditions of Chicanas is mounting. For example, recent scholarship in the Melville collection points to the importance of institutional accessibility in understanding the fertility behavior of Chicanas. Works by Sally Andrade and Maria Luisa Urdaneta provide evidence that high fertility cannot be explained primarily by ethnic-specific or cultural factors.[17] Rather, economic considerations, availability of birth control services, and attitudes and behaviors toward minority women by service personnel all account for restricted fertility control.

Broad societal processes also affect institutional forms within Chicano communities. Chicanos have been characterized as being highly oriented toward close-knit kinship patterns, a preference generally explained in cultural terms. Increasingly, researchers recognized that this orientation may represent an adaptation to conditions of exclusion, socioeconomic marginality, and hostility in the larger society. Kinship networks operate as mechanisms of social exchange and support among Chicanos, and this gives women resources not available elsewhere. Research by Roland Wagner and Diane Schaffer reveals that, for single Chicanas with dependent children, the kinship network can be a primary means of coping with their difficult circumstances.[18] They found that women turn to parents for some types of assistance and to siblings and other kin for other types. Such "resource specialization" represents an important survival strategy for women who are economically vulnerable.

It is important that we ask how close-knit patterning affects women. One theory suggests that for married women there is a relationship between such patterning and the segregation of husbands' and wives' activities and roles.

That theory, proposed by Elizabeth Bott, holds that highly connected kinship and friendship networks operate to sustain conjugal segregation.[19] This provides evidence that the pattern of segregated conjugal roles among Chicanos could have its source in a certain type of social network rather than in their cultural orientations, as past interpretations have suggested.

Changes in family lives of married Chicanas are closely linked to their involvement in social networks outside family settings. Linda Whiteford's study of innovative behavior among Mexican-American women gives detailed attention to changes occurring among women pursuing jobs outside of the home.[20] The study revealed that certain structural conditions were associated with departures from traditional behaviors. Among the most significant preconditions for change were social networks that connect women to jobs offering new options and generating innovative behaviors.

There is also evidence that married Chicanas' activities outside the family enhance their power within the family. Richard Griswold Del Castillo, in his historical work on the Los Angeles barrio from 1850 to 1890, finds that increased female involvement outside the family altered the role of women in the household as well as relations between women and men.[21] My own study of Chicano families reveals that wives' education and employment gives them power by providing them with extradomestic resources.[22] Similarly, Lea Ybarra finds that Chicano couples in which both partners are in the labor force are more egalitarian than couples in which only the husband is employed.[23] These findings support the resource theory of family power, which proposes that power rests on economic and other resources external to the marriage. If married women's status and power is linked to their acquisition of resources in extradomestic settings, it is crucial that we further our understanding about social conditions within which Chicanas carry out their extradomestic activities.

The broad issue of societal conditions surrounding women's work is most notably addressed in separate works by Albert Camarillo, Mario Garcia, and Mario Barrera. Camarillo's analysis of Chicanos in southern California from 1848 to 1930 presents evidence that the "subordinate socioeconomic and political status of Mexicans emanated from the establishment of the dominant Anglo society in Southern California and the corresponding growth of the capitalist economic system during the late nineteenth century."[24] Mexicans became disproportionately placed at the bottom of the capitalist labor market; Chicanas' entrance into the labor market contributed to this occupational placement. The confinement of Chicanas to the home changed after 1880 when they began to concentrate in domestic service and, later, agricultural work. Between 1900 and 1930, the majority of Chicanas were restricted to four general types of employment: (1) domestic services, (2) cannery and packing houses, (3) the textile industry, and (4) agricultural work. Thus, the

Chicana occupational structure was characterized by a concentration in semiskilled and unskilled employment.

Garcia finds that domestic service occupations were the largest female employment sectors in El Paso from 1890 to 1920. This period revealed a persistent increase in the number of women working for wages. While the two largest occupations were servants and laundresses, Mexican-American women were also employed as production workers in El Paso's garment factories and as cooks and dishwashers in restaurants.[25]

While Camarillo and Garcia give historical descriptions of the Chicana worker, Barrera provides an interpretation of this occupational placement as part of his larger theory of racial inequality. This theory, a synthesis of internal-colonialist and Marxist-structuralist perspectives, relies heavily on the concept of labor-market segmentation. He contends that Chicanos have been incorporated into the United States' political economy as subordinate ascriptive class segments and that historically they have occupied such a low structural position at all class levels.[26] According to Barrera, ascriptive class segments can be based on race or sex or both. Chicanas in the labor force generally find themselves in not one, but two, subordinate class segments— one based on race and another on sex—with their place in the occupational structure representing an intersection of the two kinds of class segments. Racial and sexual subordination combine to place Chicanas at the bottom of the occupational hierarchy.[27]

Recent historical analyses of women's work and Barrera's model of labor-market segmentation together have begun to illuminate sources of Chicana inequality apart from those located in cultural phenomena.

As a reservoir of exploitable labor, Chicanas are increasingly indispensable to certain labor segments. The collection of articles by Mora and Del Castillo contains a good deal of information on the relationship of Chicana laborers to the capitalist system of production. Five articles describe in detail the exploitive working conditions in the apparel and electronics industries as well as the ways in which Chicanas have attempted to change these conditions. Especially noteworthy is the report by Laurie Coyle, Gayle Hershatter, and Emily Honing, "Women at Farah: An Unfinished Story." This essay recounts the organized opposition of garment workers at Farah plants in El Paso, Texas, between 1972 and 1974.[28] The works included in this collection make it clear that just as Mexican women in the United States have been constantly exploited and controlled, so have they continually engaged in struggles to end such domination. Dialectically, Chicanas' struggles— past, present, and future—are rooted in the structural conditions of Chicanas' lives and are a persistent feature of their presence in American society.

The emphasis by Mora and Del Castillo in this volume is clearly on capitalist exploitation and control of Mexican women in the United States and on their participation in class struggles. Not all of the authors adopt the perspective of class analysis, and the editorial treatment of diverse perspectives is insufficient. Still, for the editors, class is at the heart of both subordination and liberation. In their introduction they state: "Understandably, the question of female liberation and its implications for Mexican women becomes crucial. But Mexican women are inevitably forced to analyze liberation within the context of national oppression and class conflict. For her, liberation is primarily a political question linked to the liberation of her people and her class."[29] Missing from the collection is an examination of the relationship between capitalism and patriarchy and the ways in which they interact to maintain the oppression of Chicanas. An earlier historical materialist approach by Linda Apodaca does acknowledge these two sources of Chicana subjugation.[30] However, her essay devotes less attention to patriarchy and greater attention to changes in relations of production in pre-Aztec Mexican society, through Spanish colonial feudalism and U.S. imperialism, and the impact of those changes on Chicanas.

Joan Acker's review of recent literature on women and stratification identifies the integration of capitalism and patriarchy as an important analytic strategy in contemporary Marxist perspectives. This strategy proposes that there are "two structures, capitalism and patriarchy, that are interrelated in complex ways and that they must be analyzed together in order to understand the position of women."[31] Chicanas are subordinated not only by class relations of production but also by the sexually hierarchical relations of production that socialist-feminist scholarship now terms "capitalist patriarchy."[32] As Catharine Stimpson puts it, "Patriarchy refers both to families that fathers dominate and large structures like the state that men regulate. Many patriarchal worlds tend to consist of two subworlds. The analysis of two subworlds becomes far more complex when race and class are included."[33] It must be emphasized that patriarchy is deeply entrenched in broad societal conditions affecting Chicanos as well as in their ethnic institutions. When the subordination of Chicanas is seen against a backdrop of patriarchy in society, the cause of subordination cannot be located in Chicano culture alone, but in broader dimensions of social organization.

The observation that race adds to the complexity of women's subordination is crucial in this regard. Chicanas are women who are defined as culturally different. Therefore, their subordination can be more easily justified. A study of nonconsenting sterilization of Mexican women in the Los Angeles County Medical Center reveals that such abuse is justified by an "ideology of cultural differences" whereby differential treatment of Mexican women is institutionalized.[34] The victimization and abuse of Mexican women in this manner provides support for Juliet Mitchell's contention that reproduction, like production, can be used to control women.[35] More importantly, it offers insight into the racial and cultural dynamics of such control.

A complete understanding of how capitalism, patriarchy, and racism operate together to subordinate women of color awaits conceptual development and empirical study. The ascribed characteristics of race and sex, together with class, are significant at all levels of analysis. The social identity of Chicanas, their conceptions of gender and gender roles, their placement in ethnic networks and in institutions of the larger society must be examined against a background of three stratification axes: those of race, sex, and class. Attention to the consequences of such stratification for Chicanas should remain central in any analysis. Attempts to deal with these issues will necessarily involve different levels of analysis and conceptualization. To argue for refinement of structural frameworks is not to slight microlevel analyses of the lives of Chicanas. Indeed, everyday worlds should be the beginning of inquiry about Chicanas, just as they should be for all women. But as we inquire about these everyday worlds, we must make the effort to examine how they are linked to and determined by social organization. In short, we must make a conscious effort to "locate social experiences in a set of *social* relations" (emphasis added).[36]

CHICANA SUBORDINATION AND
THE DOMESTIC/PUBLIC SPLIT

Assumptions about Chicanas' roles and status need to be examined in the context of recent discussions concerning the universality of women's subordination.[37] It could be argued that extreme sex segregation among Chicanos is due not to culture per se but to the differentiation between men's and women's activities that is found in all societies. Ann Oakley has argued that women's subordination can be explained in terms of the division of labor between domestic and public spheres of society: "Increasingly it seems that the opposition between domestic and public domains in most if not all cultures is the main structural component of gender differentiation. Materially, socially, symbolically, ideologically, men and women are separated through their differential commitments in and outside the home."[38] Women's child-bearing abilities limit their participation in public sphere activities and allow men the freedom to participate in and control the public sphere. While it may be true, as Mirandé and Enriquez speculate, that cultural expectations date back to Aztec models, domestic and maternal expectations are imposed on most women in most societies. Of course, specific sociocultural expectations may differ, but the point is that a basic organizational feature of all societies generates sexual inequality.

Theoretical consideration about the character of the domestic/public split and its application to gender differentiation among blacks has pertinent implications for Chicanos as well. Diane Lewis acknowledges the general usefulness of the notion of a structural opposition between the domestic and public spheres.[39] Nevertheless, she argues that it is limited in explaining the differential participation of minority men and women because black men and black women have both been excluded from participation in public sphere institutions. Lewis asserts: "What the black experience suggests is that differential participation in the public sphere is a symptom rather than a cause of structural inequality. While inequality is manifested in the exclusion of a group from public life, it is actually generated in the group's unequal access to power and resources in a hierarchically arranged social order. Relationships of dominance and subordination, therefore, emerge from a basic structural opposition between groups which is reflected in exclusion of the subordinate group from public life."[40] Clearly, an important source of minority women's subordination lies in their exclusion from the public life of society at large. The insight should not lead us to overlook the causal significance of domesticity. The extent to which domesticity characterizes the lives of Chicanas may well be an important indicator of their social position. Melville's collection of works is largely confined to women's involvement in domestic events, activities, and interests. This focus seems to parallel the predominant concern in the literature on women generally. In a recent review of feminist sociological works, Oakley found the largest number of pieces concerned motherhood and aspects of gender-role differentiation.[41] According to Oakley this highlights the central significance of the domestic domain and of social division between the sexes in influencing the status of women.

Some feminist works have specifically identified motherhood, that is, women's mothering role, as the primary feature in accounting for the universal secondary status of women.[42] This argument, while controversial,[43] deserves the attention of those seeking to sort out sources of Chicanas' oppression, particularly in light of the high birth rate among Chicanas. Melville contends that Mexican-American women are expected to be wives and mothers first and foremost,[44] and Carlos Velez asserts that childbearing is a primary source of social identity for certain women of Mexican descent.[45] This raises the issue of interpreting "tradition" among ethnic women. Elsewhere I have argued that ethnic traditions should not be seen as responsible for subordination of women but rather as expressive of distinctive life-styles that can exist along with modern behaviors and orientations.[46] That position notwithstanding, it is worthwhile to recognize that some traditions can be oppressive.[47]

Comparative attention to motherhood within the Chicana population and in other groups of women will enable us to distinguish between ethnic-specific and generalized consequences of motherhood. Keeping in mind the importance of domesticity and motherhood in understanding women's position, we should recognize as well that Chicanas, like other groups of women in this society, have long been workers outside of the home. The long-standing myth of the homebound Chicana has proven resistant to challenge. Melville's collection of works runs the risk of reinforcing the assumption that Chicanas' subordination rests in a cultural relegation of women to domestic and familial activities.

Melville acknowledges the omission of studies on Chicana labor-force participation, but this does not overcome the limitation inherent in this omission. The limitation is rendered even more problematic in light of the dramatic increase in Chicanas' extradomestic roles during the past decade. This is not to say that studies of family planning, childbirth, breast-feeding, and traditional medicine are less significant than studies of Chicanas' activities in the public sphere. Clearly, they are of equal significance. Still, emphasis and selection have substantive import. The focus on traditional gender and cultural roles tends to reinforce a one-dimensional view of Chicanas.

The distinction between the gender-roles approach and an institutional approach is crucial in this regard. According to Nona Glazer, the difference lies in the emphasis given to factors that characterize individuals (acquired by individuals during the course of socialization) versus the organization of social institutions (including the concentration of power, the legal system, organizational barriers, and other factors external to individuals that generate and maintain the hierarchical relationship between the sexes).[48] Melville recognizes that the subordination of Chicanas is a consequence of social and economic conditions. Similarly, many of the studies support the premise that the minority experience is as important as cultural and domestic roles in maintaining the secondary status of Chicanas. Yet this very important distinction can become blurred unless findings are incorporated into an analytic framework. The point requires affirmation and conceptual elaboration.

CONCLUSION

The quest for explanations of the causes and consequences of Chicanas' social locations will require continued careful and rigorous analysis. Greater conceptual and theoretical precision may be achieved by locating Chicanas in precise organizational contexts, distinguishing between macro and micro levels of analysis, separating social structural from cultural phenomena, and examining the relevance of emerging theoretical perspectives in the social science literature on women. The distinctive conditions of Chicanas' social lives will remain central in our analyses. Nevertheless, our study of Chicanas must be as far-reaching as the study of all women in society.

NOTES

1. Dorothy E. Smith, "Some Implications of a Sociology for Women," in *Woman in a Man-made World,* ed. Nona Glazer and Helen Youngelson Waehrer, 2d ed. (Chicago: Rand McNally, 1977).

2. The term "machismo" has gained popular usage in American society, referring to exaggerated masculinity, physical prowess, and male chauvinism. In the social science literature about Mexicans and Chicanos, machismo is the primary concept used to explain family structure and inadequate personality development. It is based on the assumption that exaggerated masculinity represents a compensation for cultural inferiority. See the following critiques of traditional social science uses of the term "machismo": Alfredo Mirandé, "Machismo: Rucas, Chingasos, y Chingaderas," *De Colores, Journal of Chicano Expression and Thought* 6, nos. 1 and 2 (1982): 17–31; and Maxine Baca Zinn, "Chicano Men and Masculinity," *Journal of Ethnic Studies* 10, no. 2 (1982): 29–44.

3. Margaret A. Simons, "Racism and Feminism: A Schism in the Sisterhood," *Feminist Studies* 4, no. 2 (1979): 384–401.

4. Judith Long Laws, "Feminism and Patriarchy: Competing Ways of Doing Social Science" (paper presented at the American Sociological Association, San Francisco, 1978).

5. Alfredo Mirandé and Evangelina Enriquez, *La Chicana: The Mexican-American Woman* (Chicago: University of Chicago Press, 1979).

6. Margarita B. Melville, ed., *Twice a Minority: Mexican American Women* (St. Louis: C. V. Mosby Co., 1980).

7. Magdelina Mora and Adelaida R. Del Castillo, eds., *Mexican Women in the United States: Struggles Past and Present* (Los Angeles: University of California, Chicano Studies Center Publications, 1980).

8. Cordelia Candelaria, "Six Reference Works on Mexican-American Women: A Review Essay," *Frontiers: A Journal of Women Studies* 5, no. 2 (Summer 1980): 75–80.

9. Catherine Loeb, "La Chicana: A Bibliographic Survey," *Frontiers: A Journal of Women Studies* 5, no. 2 (Summer 1980): 59–74.

10. Judith Sweeney, "Chicana History: A Review of the Literature," in *Essays on La Mujer,* ed. Rosaura Sanchez and Rosa Martinez Cruz (Los Angeles: University of California, Chicano Studies Center Publications, 1977).

11. Melville, p. 1.

12. Mora and Del Castillo, eds., p. 1.

13. Meredith Gould, "Review Essay: The New Sociology," *Signs: Journal of Women in Culture and Society* 5, no. 3 (Spring 1980): 459–67, esp. 461.

14. Maxine Baca Zinn, "Sociological Theory in Emergent Chicano Perspectives," *Pacific Sociological Review* 24, no. 2 (April 1981): 225–71.

15. Mirandé and Enriquez, p. 15.

16. Peter M. Blau and W. Richard Scott, *Formal Organizations* (San Francisco: Chandler Publishing Co., 1962).

17. Sally J. Andrade, "Family Planning Practices of Mexican Americans," in Melville, ed., pp. 17–32; Maria Luisa Urdaneta, "Chicana Use of Abortion: The Case of Alcala," in Melville, ed., pp. 35–51.

18. Roland M. Wagner and Diane M. Schaffer, "Social Networks and Journal Strategies: An Exploratory Study of Mexican American, Black and Anglo Female Family Heads in San Jose, California," in Melville, ed., pp. 173–90.

19. Elizabeth Bott, *Family and Social Network* (New York: Free Press, 1957).

20. Linda Whiteford, "Mexican American Women as Innovators," in Melville, ed., pp. 109–26.

21. Richard Griswold Del Castillo, *The Los Angeles Barrio, 1850–1890* (Berkeley and Los Angeles: University of California Press, 1979).

22. Maxine Baca Zinn, "Employment and Education of Mexican American Women: The Interplay of Modernity and Ethnicity in Eight Families," *Harvard Educational Review* 50, no. 1 (February 1980): 47–62.

23. Lea Ybarra, "When Wives Work: The Impact on the Chicano Family," *Journal of Marriage and the Family* 44, no. 1 (February 1982): 169–78.

24. Albert Camarillo, *Chicanos in a Changing Society: From Mexican Pueblos to American Barrios in Santa Barbara and Southern California, 1848–1930* (Cambridge, Mass.: Harvard University Press, 1979).

25. Mario Garcia, *Desert Immigrants: The Mexicans of El Paso, 1890–1920* (New Haven, Conn.: Yale University Press, 1981). Also, see his "The Chicana in American History: The Mexican Women of El Paso, 1880–1920: A Case Study," *Pacific Historical Review* 49, no. 2 (1980): 315–37. A study of women's labor-market participation in three cities during the Great Depression provides some information about the occupational segregation of Mexican women; see Julia Kirk Blackwelder, "Women in the Work Force: Atlanta, New Orleans, and San Antonio, 1930 to 1940," *Journal of Urban History* 4, no. 3 (1978): 331–58.

26. Mario Barrera, *Race and Class in the Southwest: A Theory of Racial Inequality* (Notre Dame, Ind.: Notre Dame University Press, 1979), p. 212.

27. Ibid., p. 99.

28. Laurie Coyle, Gayle Hershatter, and Emily Honing, "Women at Farah: An Unfinished Story," in Mora and Del Castillo, eds. (n. 7 above), pp. 117–44.

29. Mora and Del Castillo, eds., p. 2.

30. Maria Linda Apodaca, "The Chicana Woman: An Historical Materialist Perspective," *Latin American Perspectives* 4, nos. 1/2 (Winter/Spring 1977): 70–89.

31. Joan R. Acker, "Women and Stratification: A Review of Recent Literature," *Contemporary Sociology* 9 (January 1980): 25–39.

32. Zillah R. Eisenstein, *Capitalist Patriarchy and the Case for Socialist Feminism* (New York: Monthly Review Press, 1979).

33. Catharine R. Stimpson, "The New Scholarship about Women: The State of the Art," *Annals of Scholarship: Metastudies of the Humanities and Social Sciences* 1, no. 2 (Summer 1980): 2–14.

34. Carlos G. Velez-I, "Se me acabo la cancion: An Ethnography of Non-consenting Sterilizations among Mexican Women in Los Angeles," in Mora and Del Castillo, eds., pp. 65–70.

35. Juliet Mitchell, "Women: The Longest Revolution," *New Left Review* 30 (November/December 1996): 11–37.

36. Gould (n. 13 above), p. 466. Gould makes the point that Dorothy Smith's work uses insights formulated by Marx, Engels, Mannheim, and others to create a feminist methodology that consciously locates social experience in a set of social relations.

37. Michelle Zimbalist Rosaldo, "Woman, Culture, and Society: A Theoretical Overview," in *Woman, Culture, and Society,* ed. Michelle Zimbalist Rosaldo and Louise Lamphere (Stanford, Calif.: Stanford University Press, 1974), pp. 17–42; Sherry B. Ortner, "Is Female to Male as Nature Is to Culture?" in Rosaldo and Lamphere, eds., pp. 67–68. See, also, Michelle Zimbalist Rosaldo, "The Use and Abuse of Anthropology: Reflections on Feminism and Cross-cultural Understanding," *Signs: Journal of Women in Culture and Society* 5, no. 3 (Spring 1980): 389–417.

38. Ann Oakley, "Review Essay: Feminism and Sociology—Some Recent Perspectives," *American Journal of Sociology* 84, no. 5 (1979): 1259–65.

39. Diane K. Lewis, "A Response to Inequality: Black Women, Racism, and Sexism," *Signs: Journal of Women in Culture and Society* 3, no. 2 (Winter 1977): 339–61.

40. Ibid., p. 342.

41. Oakley, p. 1260.

42. Nancy Chodorow, "Family Structure and Feminine Personality," in Rosaldo and Lamphere, eds., pp. 43–66, and *The Reproduction of Mothering: Psychoanalysis and the Sociology of Gender* (Berkeley and Los Angeles: University of California Press, 1978).

43. See, e.g., Judith Lorber, Rose Laub Coser, Alice Rossi, and Nancy Chodorow, "On *The Reproduction of Mothering:* A Methodological Debate," *Signs: Journal of Women in Culture and Society* 6, no. 3 (Spring 1981): 482–514.

44. Melville, p. 11.

45. Carlos G. Velez-I, "The Nonconsenting Sterilization of Mexican Women in Los Angeles: Issues of Psychocultural Rupture and Legal Redress in Paternalistic Behavioral Environments," in Melville, ed., pp. 235–48.

46. Baca Zinn, "Employment and Education of Mexican American Women: The Interplay of Modernity and Ethnicity in Eight Families" (n. 22 above).

47. Rayna Rapp, "Review Essay: Anthropology," *Signs: Journal of Women in Culture and Society* 4, no. 3 (Spring 1979): 497–513.

48. Nona Glazer, "Introduction: Part Two," in Glazer and Waehrer, eds. (n. 1 above), pp. 101–13.

15   The Social Construction
of Black Feminist Thought

PATRICIA HILL COLLINS
University of Cincinnati

Sojourner Truth, Anna Julia Cooper, Ida Wells Barnett, and Fannie Lou Hamer are but a few names from a growing list of distinguished African-American women activists. Although their sustained resistance to Black women's victimization within interlocking systems of race, gender, and class oppression is well known, these women did not act alone.[1] Their actions were nurtured by the support of countless, ordinary African-American women who, through strategies of everyday resistance, created a powerful foundation for this more visible Black feminist activist tradition.[2] Such support has been essential to the shape and goals of Black feminist thought.

The long-term and widely shared resistance among African-American women can only have been sustained by an enduring and shared standpoint among Black women about the meaning of oppression and the actions that Black women can and should take to resist it. Efforts to identify the central concepts of this Black women's standpoint figure prominently in the works of contemporary Black feminist intellectuals.[3] Moreover, political and epistemological issues influence the social construction of Black feminist thought. Like other subordinate groups, African-American women not only have developed distinctive interpretations of Black women's oppression

AUTHOR'S NOTE: Special thanks go out to the following people for reading various drafts of this manuscript: Evelyn Nakano Glenn, Lynn Weber Cannon, and participants in the 1986 Research Institute, Center for Research on Women, Memphis State University; Elsa Barkley Brown, Deborah K. King, Elizabeth V. Spelman, and Angelene Jamison-Hall; and four anonymous reviewers at *Signs*.

but have done so by using alternative ways of producing and validating knowledge itself.

A BLACK WOMEN'S STANDPOINT

The Foundation of Black Feminist Thought

Black women's everyday acts of resistance challenge two prevailing approaches to studying the consciousness of oppressed groups.[4] One approach claims that subordinate groups identify with the powerful and have no valid independent interpretation of their own oppression.[5] The second approach assumes that the oppressed are less human than their rulers and, therefore, are less capable of articulating their own standpoint.[6] Both approaches see any independent consciousness expressed by an oppressed group as being not of the group's own making and/or inferior to the perspective of the dominant group.[7] More important, both interpretations suggest that oppressed groups lack the motivation for political activism because of their flawed consciousness of their own subordination.

Yet African-American women have been neither passive victims of nor willing accomplices to their own domination. As a result, emerging work in Black women's studies contends that Black women have a self-defined standpoint on their own oppression.[8] Two interlocking components characterize this standpoint. First, Black women's political and economic status provides them with a distinctive set of experiences that offers a different view of material reality than that available to other groups. The unpaid and paid work that Black women perform, the types of communities in which they live, and the kinds of relationships they have with others suggest that African-American women, as a group, experience a different world than those who are not Black and female.[9] Second, these experiences stimulate a distinctive Black feminist consciousness concerning that material reality.[10] In brief, a subordinate group not only experiences a different reality than a group that rules, but a subordinate group may interpret that reality differently than a dominant group.

Many ordinary African-American women have grasped this connection between what one does and how one thinks. Hannah Nelson, an elderly Black domestic worker, discusses how work shapes the standpoints of African-American and white women: "Since I have to work, I don't really have to worry about most of the things that most of the white women I have worked for are worrying about. And if these women did their own work, they would think just like I do—about this, anyway."[11] Ruth Shays, a Black inner city resident, points out how variations in men's and women's experiences lead to differences in perspective: "The mind of the man and the mind of the woman is the same. But this business of living makes women use their minds in ways that men don't even have to think about."[12] Finally, elderly domestic worker Rosa Wakefield assesses how the standpoints of the powerful and those who serve them diverge: "If you eats these dinners and don't cook 'em, if you wears these clothes and don't buy or iron them, then you might start thinking that the good fairy or some spirit did all that. . . . Blackfolks don't have no time to be thinking like that. . . . But when you don't have anything else to do, you can think like that. It's bad for your mind, though."[13]

While African-American women may occupy material positions that stimulate a unique standpoint, expressing an independent Black feminist consciousness is problematic precisely because more powerful groups have a vested interest in suppressing such thought. As Hannah Nelson notes, "I have grown to womanhood in a world where the saner you are, the madder you are made to appear."[14] Nelson realizes that those who control the schools, the media, and other cultural institutions are generally skilled in establishing their view of reality as superior to alternative interpretations. While an oppressed group's experiences may put them in a position to see things differently, their lack of control over the apparatuses of society that sustain ideological hegemony makes the articulation of their self-defined standpoint difficult. Groups unequal in power are correspondingly unequal in their access to the resources necessary to implement their perspectives outside their particular group.

One key reason that standpoints of oppressed groups are discredited and suppressed by the more powerful is that self-defined standpoints can stimulate oppressed groups to resist their domination. For instance, Annie Adams, a southern Black woman, describes how she became involved in civil rights activities.

> When I first went into the mill we had segregated water fountains. . . . Same thing about the toilets. I had to clean the toilets for the inspection room and then, when I got ready to go to the bathroom, I had to go all the way to the bottom of the stairs to the cellar. So I asked my boss man, "What's the difference? If I can go in there and clean them toilets, why can't I use them?" Finally, I started to use that toilet. I decided I wasn't going to walk a mile to go to the bathroom.[15]

In this case, Adams found the standpoint of the "boss man" inadequate, developed one of her own, and acted upon it. In doing so, her actions exemplify the connections between experiencing oppression, developing a self-defined standpoint on that experience, and resistance.

The Significance of Black Feminist Thought

The existence of a distinctive Black women's standpoint does not mean that it has been adequately articulated in Black feminist thought. Peter Berger

and Thomas Luckmann provide a useful approach to clarifying the relationship between a Black women's standpoint and Black feminist thought with
the contention that knowledge exists on two levels.[16] The first level includes
the everyday, taken-for-granted knowledge shared by members of a given
group, such as the ideas expressed by Ruth Shays and Annie Adams. Black
feminist thought, by extension, represents a second level of knowledge, the
more specialized knowledge furnished by experts who are part of a group
and who express the group's standpoint. The two levels of knowledge
are interdependent; while Black feminist thought articulates the taken-for-
granted knowledge of African-American women, it also encourages all
Black women to create new self-definitions that validate a Black women's
standpoint.

Black feminist thought's potential significance goes far beyond demonstrating that Black women can produce independent, specialized knowledge. Such thought can encourage collective identity by offering Black
women a different view of themselves and their world than that offered by
the established social order. This different view encourages African-American women to value their own subjective knowledge base.[17] By taking
elements and themes of Black women's culture and traditions and infusing
them with new meaning, Black feminist thought rearticulates a consciousness that already exists.[18] More important, this rearticulated consciousness
gives African-American women another tool of resistance to all forms of
their subordination.[19]

Black feminist thought, then, specializes in formulating and rearticulating
the distinctive, self-defined standpoint of African-American women. One
approach to learning more about a Black women's standpoint is to consult
standard scholarly sources for the ideas of specialists on Black women's
experiences.[20] But investigating a Black women's standpoint and Black
feminist thought requires more ingenuity than that required in examining the
standpoints and thought of white males. Rearticulating the standpoint of
African-American women through Black feminist thought is much more
difficult since one cannot use the same techniques to study the knowledge of
the dominated as one uses to study the knowledge of the powerful. This is
precisely because subordinate groups have long had to use alternative ways
to create an independent consciousness and to rearticulate it through specialists validated by the oppressed themselves.

THE EUROCENTRIC MASCULINIST
KNOWLEDGE-VALIDATION PROCESS[21]

All social thought, including white masculinist and Black feminist, reflects the interests and standpoint of its creators. As Karl Mannheim notes,
"If one were to trace in detail . . . the origin and . . . diffusion of a certain

thought-model, one would discover the . . . affinity it has to the social position of given groups and their manner of interpreting the world."[22] Scholars, publishers, and other experts represent specific interests and credentialing processes, and their knowledge claims must satisfy the epistemological and political criteria of the contexts in which they reside.[23]

Two political criteria influence the knowledge-validation process. First, knowledge claims must be evaluated by a community of experts whose members represent the standpoints of the groups from which they originate. Second, each community of experts must maintain its credibility as defined by the larger group in which it is situated and from which it draws its basic, taken-for-granted knowledge.

When white males control the knowledge-validation process, both political criteria can work to suppress Black feminist thought. Since the general culture shaping the taken-for-granted knowledge of the community of experts is one permeated by widespread notions of Black and female inferiority,[24] new knowledge claims that seem to violate these fundamental assumptions are likely to be viewed as anomalies.[25] Moreover, specialized thought challenging notions of Black and female inferiority is unlikely to be generated from within a white-male-controlled academic community because both the kinds of questions that could be asked and the explanations that would be found satisfying would necessarily reflect a basic lack of familiarity with Black women's reality.[26]

The experiences of African-American women scholars illustrate how individuals who wish to rearticulate a Black women's standpoint through Black feminist thought can be suppressed by a white-male-controlled knowledge-validation process. Exclusion from basic literacy, quality educational experiences, and faculty and administrative positions has limited Black women's access to influential academic positions.[27] Thus, while Black women can produce knowledge claims that contest those advanced by the white male community, this community does not grant that Black women scholars have competing knowledge claims based in another knowledge-validation process. As a consequence, any credentials controlled by white male academicians can be denied to Black women producing Black feminist thought on the grounds that it is not credible research.

Those Black women with academic credentials who seek to exert the authority that their status grants them to propose new knowledge claims about African-American women face pressures to use their authority to help legitimate a system that devalues and excludes the majority of Black women.[28] One way of excluding the majority of Black women from the knowledge-validation process is to permit a few Black women to acquire positions of authority in institutions that legitimate knowledge and to encourage them to work within the taken-for-granted assumptions of Black female inferiority shared by the scholarly community and the culture at large. Those

Black women who accept these assumptions are likely to be rewarded by their institutions, often at significant personal cost. Those challenging the assumptions run the risk of being ostracized.

African-American women academicians who persist in trying to rearticulate a Black women's standpoint also face potential rejection of their knowledge claims on epistemological grounds. Just as the material realities of the powerful and the dominated produce separate standpoints, each group may also have distinctive epistemologies or theories of knowledge. It is my contention that Black female scholars may know that something is true but be unwilling or unable to legitimate their claims using Eurocentric masculinist criteria for consistency with substantiated knowledge and Eurocentric masculinist criteria for methodological adequacy.

For any particular interpretive context, new knowledge claims must be consistent with an existing body of knowledge that the group controlling the interpretive context accepts as true. The methods used to validate knowledge claims must also be acceptable to the group controlling the knowledge-validation process.

The criteria for the methodological adequacy of positivism illustrate the epistemological standards that Black women scholars would have to satisfy in legitimating alternative knowledge claims.[29] Positivist approaches aim to create scientific descriptions of reality by producing objective generalizations. Since researchers have widely differing values, experiences, and emotions, genuine science is thought to be unattainable unless all human characteristics except rationality are eliminated from the research process. By following strict methodological rules, scientists aim to distance themselves from the values, vested interests, and emotions generated by their class, race, sex, or unique situation and in so doing become detached observers and manipulators of nature.[30]

Several requirements typify positivist methodological approaches. First, research methods generally require a distancing of the researcher from her/his "object" of study by defining the researcher as a "subject" with full human subjectivity and objectifying the "object" of study.[31] A second requirement is the absence of emotions from the research process.[32] Third, ethics and values are deemed inappropriate in the research process, either as the reason for scientific inquiry or as part of the research process itself.[33] Finally, adversarial debates, whether written or oral, become the preferred method of ascertaining truth—the arguments that can withstand the greatest assault and survive intact become the strongest truths.[34]

Such criteria ask African-American women to objectify themselves, devalue their emotional life, displace their motivations for furthering knowledge about Black women, and confront, in an adversarial relationship, those who have more social, economic, and professional power than they. It seems unlikely, therefore, that Black women would use a positivist epistemological stance in rearticulating a Black women's standpoint. Black women are more likely to choose an alternative epistemology for assessing knowledge claims, one using standards that are consistent with Black women's criteria for substantiated knowledge and with Black women's criteria for methodological adequacy. If such an epistemology exists, what are its contours? Moreover, what is its role in the production of Black feminist thought?

THE CONTOURS OF AN
AFROCENTRIC FEMINIST EPISTEMOLOGY

Africanist analyses of the Black experience generally agree on the fundamental elements of an Afrocentric standpoint. In spite of varying histories, Black societies reflect elements of a core African value system that existed prior to and independently of racial oppression.[35] Moreover, as a result of colonialism, imperialism, slavery, apartheid, and other systems of racial domination, Blacks share a common experience of oppression. These similarities in material conditions have fostered shared Afrocentric values that permeate the family structure, religious institutions, culture, and community life of Blacks in varying parts of Africa, the Caribbean, South America, and North America.[36] This Afrocentric consciousness permeates the shared history of people of African descent through the framework of a distinctive Afrocentric epistemology.[37]

Feminist scholars advance a similar argument. They assert that women share a history of patriarchal oppression through the political economy of the material conditions of sexuality and reproduction.[38] These shared material conditions are thought to transcend divisions among women created by race, social class, religion, sexual orientation, and ethnicity and to form the basis of a women's standpoint with its corresponding feminist consciousness and epistemology.[39]

Since Black women have access to both the Afrocentric and the feminist standpoints, an alternative epistemology used to rearticulate a Black women's standpoint reflects elements of both traditions.[40] The search for the distinguishing features of an alternative epistemology used by African-American women reveals that values and ideas that Africanist scholars identify as being characteristically "Black" often bear remarkable resemblance to similar ideas claimed by feminist scholars as being characteristically "female."[41] This similarity suggests that the material conditions of oppression can vary dramatically and yet generate some uniformity in the epistemologies of subordinate groups. Thus, the significance of an Afrocentric feminist epistemology may lie in its enrichment of our understanding of how subordinate groups create knowledge that enables them to resist oppression.

The parallels between the two conceptual schemes raise a question: Is the worldview of women of African descent more intensely infused with the overlapping feminine/Afrocentric standpoints than is the case for either African-American men or white women?[42] While an Afrocentric feminist epistemology reflects elements of epistemologies used by Blacks as a group and women as a group, it also paradoxically demonstrates features that may be unique to Black women. On certain dimensions, Black women may more closely resemble Black men, on others, white women, and on still others, Black women may stand apart from both groups. Black feminist sociologist Deborah K. King describes this phenomenon as a "both/or" orientation, the act of being simultaneously a member of a group and yet standing apart from it. She suggests that multiple realities among Black women yield a "multiple consciousness in Black women's politics" and that this state of belonging yet not belonging forms an integral part of Black women's oppositional consciousness.[43] Bonnie Thornton Dill's analysis of how Black women live with contradictions, a situation she labels the "dialectics of Black womanhood," parallels King's assertions that this "both/or" orientation is central to an Afrocentric feminist consciousness.[44] Rather than emphasizing how a Black women's standpoint and its accompanying epistemology are different than those in Afrocentric and feminist analyses, I use Black women's experiences as a point of contact between the two.

Viewing an Afrocentric feminist epistemology in this way challenges analyses claiming that Black women have a more accurate view of oppression than do other groups. Such approaches suggest that oppression can be quantified and compared and that adding layers of oppression produces a potentially clearer standpoint. While it is tempting to claim that Black women are more oppressed than everyone else and therefore have the best standpoint from which to understand the mechanisms, processes, and effects of oppression, this simply may not be the case.[45]

African-American women do not uniformly share an Afrocentric feminist epistemology since social class introduces variations among Black women in seeing, valuing, and using Afrocentric feminist perspectives. While a Black women's standpoint and its accompanying epistemology stem from Black women's consciousness of race and gender oppression, they are not simply the result of combining Afrocentric and female values—standpoints are rooted in real material conditions structured by social class.[46]

Concrete Experience as a Criterion of Meaning

Carolyn Chase, a thirty-one-year-old inner city Black woman, notes, "My aunt used to say, 'A heap see, but a few know.' "[47] This saying depicts two types of knowing, knowledge and wisdom, and taps the first dimension of an Afrocentric feminist epistemology. Living life as Black women requires wisdom since knowledge about the dynamics of race, gender, and class subordination has been essential to Black women's survival. African-American women give such wisdom high credence in assessing knowledge.

Allusions to these two types of knowing pervade the words of a range of African-American women. In explaining the tenacity of racism, Zilpha Elaw, a preacher of the mid-1800s, noted: "The pride of a white skin is a bauble of great value with many in some parts of the United States, who readily sacrifice their intelligence to their prejudices, and possess more knowledge than wisdom."[48] In describing differences separating African-American and white women, Nancy White invokes a similar rule: "When you come right down to it, white women just *think* they are free. Black women *know* they ain't free."[49] Geneva Smitherman, a college professor specializing in African-American linguistics, suggests that "from a black perspective, written documents are limited in what they can teach about life and survival in the world. Blacks are quick to ridicule 'educated fools,' . . . they have 'book learning' but no 'mother wit,' knowledge, but not wisdom."[50] Mabel Lincoln eloquently summarizes the distinction between knowledge and wisdom: "To black people like me, a fool is funny—you know, people who love to break bad, people you can't tell anything to, folks that would take a shotgun to a roach."[51]

Black women need wisdom to know how to deal with the "educated fools" who would "take a shotgun to a roach." As members of a subordinate group, Black women cannot afford to be fools of any type, for their devalued status denies them the protections that white skin, maleness, and wealth confer. This distinction between knowledge and wisdom, and the use of experience as the cutting edge dividing them, has been key to Black women's survival. In the context of race, gender, and class oppression, the distinction is essential since knowledge without wisdom is adequate for the powerful, but wisdom is essential to the survival of the subordinate.

For ordinary African-American women, those individuals who have lived through the experiences about which they claim to be experts are more believable and credible than those who have merely read or thought about such experiences. Thus, concrete experience as a criterion for credibility frequently is invoked by Black women when making knowledge claims. For instance, Hannah Nelson describes the importance that personal experience has for her: "Our speech is most directly personal, and every black person assumes that every other black person has a right to a personal opinion. In speaking of grave matters, your personal experience is considered very good evidence. With us, distant statistics are certainly not as important as the actual experience of a sober person."[52] Similarly, Ruth Shays uses her concrete experiences to challenge the idea that formal education is the only route to knowledge: "I am the kind of person who doesn't have a lot of education, but both my mother and my father had good common sense. Now, I think that's all you need. I might not know how to use thirty-four words where three would do, but that does not mean that I don't know what I'm talking about . . . I know what I'm talking about because I'm talking about myself. I'm talking about what I have lived."[53] Implicit in Shay's self-assessment is a critique of the type of knowledge that obscures the truth, the "thirty-four words" that cover up a truth that can be expressed in three.

Even after substantial mastery of white masculinist epistemologies, many Black women scholars invoke their own concrete experiences and those of other Black women in selecting topics for investigation and methodologies used. For example, Elsa Barkley Brown subtitles her essay on Black women's history, "how my mother taught me to be an historian in spite of my academic training."[54] Similarly, Joyce Ladner maintains that growing up as a Black woman in the South gave her special insights in conducting her study of Black adolescent women.[55]

Henry Mitchell and Nicholas Lewter claim that experience as a criterion of meaning with practical images as its symbolic vehicles is a fundamental epistemological tenet in African-American thought-systems.[56] Stories, narratives, and Bible principles are selected for their applicability to the lived experiences of African-Americans and become symbolic representations of a whole wealth of experience. For example, Bible tales are told for their value to common life, so their interpretation involves no need for scientific historical verification. The narrative method requires that the story be "told, not torn apart in analysis, and trusted as core belief, not admired as science."[57] Any biblical story contains more than characters and a plot—it presents key ethical issues salient in African-American life.

June Jordan's essay about her mother's suicide exemplifies the multiple levels of meaning that can occur when concrete experiences are used as a criterion of meaning. Jordan describes her mother, a woman who literally died trying to stand up, and the effect that her mother's death had on her own work:

> I think all of this is really about women and work. Certainly this is all about me as a woman and my life work. I mean I am not sure my mother's suicide was something extraordinary. Perhaps most women must deal with a similar inheritance, the legacy of a woman whose death you cannot possibly pinpoint because she died so many, many times and because, even before she became your mother, the life of that woman was taken. . . . I came too late to help my mother to her feet. By way of everlasting thanks to all of the women who have helped me to stay alive I am working never to be late again.[58]

While Jordan has knowledge about the concrete act of her mother's death, she also strives for wisdom concerning the meaning of that death.

Some feminist scholars offer a similar claim that women, as a group, are more likely than men to use concrete knowledge in assessing knowledge claims. For example, a substantial number of the 135 women in a study of women's cognitive development were "connected knowers" and were drawn to the sort of knowledge that emerges from first-hand observation. Such women felt that since knowledge comes from experience, the best way of understanding another person's ideas was to try to share the experiences that led the person to form those ideas. At the heart of the procedures used by connected knowers is the capacity for empathy.[59]

In valuing the concrete, African-American women may be invoking not only an Afrocentric tradition, but a women's tradition as well. Some feminist theorists suggest that women are socialized in complex relational nexuses where contextual rules take priority over abstract principles in governing behavior. This socialization process is thought to stimulate characteristic ways of knowing.[60] For example, Canadian sociologist Dorothy Smith maintains that two modes of knowing exist, one located in the body and the space it occupies and the other passing beyond it. She asserts that women, through their child-rearing and nurturing activities, mediate these two modes and use the concrete experiences of their daily lives to assess more abstract knowledge claims.[61]

Amanda King, a young Black mother, describes how she used the concrete to assess the abstract and points out how difficult mediating these two modes of knowing can be:

> The leaders of the ROC [a labor union] lost their jobs too, but it just seemed like they were used to losing their jobs. . . . This was like a lifelong thing for them, to get out there and protest. They were like, what do you call them—intellectuals. . . . You got the ones that go to the university that are supposed to make all the speeches, they're the ones that are supposed to lead, you know, put this little revolution together, and then you got the little ones . . . that go to the factory everyday, they be the ones that have to fight. I had a child and I thought I don't have the time to be running around with these people. . . . I mean I understand some of that stuff they were talking about, like the bourgeoisie, the rich and the poor and all that, but I had surviving on my mind for me and my kid.[62]

For King, abstract ideals of class solidarity were mediated by the concrete experience of motherhood and the connectedness it involved.

In traditional African-American communities, Black women find considerable institutional support for valuing concrete experience. Black extended families and Black churches are two key institutions where Black women experts with concrete knowledge of what it takes to be self-defined Black women share their knowledge with their younger, less experienced sisters.

This relationship of sisterhood among Black women can be seen as a model for a whole series of relationships that African-American women have with each other, whether it is networks among women in extended families, among women in the Black church, or among women in the African-American community at large.[63]

Since the Black church and the Black family are both woman-centered and Afrocentric institutions, African-American women traditionally have found considerable institutional support for this dimension of an Afrocentric feminist epistemology in ways that are unique to them. While white women may value the concrete, it is questionable whether white families, particularly middle-class nuclear ones, and white community institutions provide comparable types of support. Similarly, while Black men are supported by Afrocentric institutions, they cannot participate in Black women's sisterhood. In terms of Black women's relationships with one another then, African-American women may indeed find it easier than others to recognize connectedness as a primary way of knowing, simply because they are encouraged to do so by Black women's tradition of sisterhood.

The Use of Dialogue in Assessing Knowledge Claims

For Black women, new knowledge claims are rarely worked out in isolation from other individuals and are usually developed through dialogues with other members of a community. A primary epistemological assumption underlying the use of dialogue in assessing knowledge claims is that connectedness rather than separation is an essential component of the knowledge-validation process.[64]

The use of dialogue has deep roots in an African-based oral tradition and in African-American culture.[65] Ruth Shays describes the importance of dialogue in the knowledge-validation process of enslaved African-Americans: "They would find a lie if it took them a year . . . the foreparents found the truth because they listened and they made people tell their part many times. Most often you can hear a lie. . . . Those old people was everywhere and knew the truth of many disputes. They believed that a liar should suffer the pain of his lies, and they had all kinds of ways of bringing liars to judgement."[66]

The widespread use of the call and response discourse mode among African-Americans exemplifies the importance placed on dialogue. Composed of spontaneous verbal and nonverbal interaction between speaker and listener in which all of the speaker's statements or "calls" are punctuated by expressions or "responses" from the listener, this Black discourse mode pervades African-American culture. The fundamental requirement of this interactive network is active participation of all individuals.[67] For ideas to be tested and validated, everyone in the group must participate. To refuse to join in, especially if one really disagrees with what has been said is seen as "cheating."[68]

June Jordan's analysis of Black English points to the significance of this dimension of an alternative epistemology.

> Our language is a system constructed by people constantly needing to insist that we exist. . . . Our language devolves from a culture that abhors all abstraction, or anything tending to obscure or delete the fact of the human being who is here and now/the truth of the person who is speaking or listening. Consequently, *there is no passive voice construction possible in Black English.* For example, you cannot say, "Black English is being eliminated." You must say, instead, "White people eliminating Black English." The assumption of the presence of life governs all of Black English . . . every sentence assumes the living and active participation of at least two human beings, the speaker and the listener.[69]

Many Black women intellectuals invoke the relationships and connectedness provided by use of dialogue. When asked why she chose the themes she did, novelist Gayle Jones replied: "I was . . . interested . . . in oral traditions of storytelling—Afro-American and others, in which there is always the consciousness and importance of the hearer."[70] In describing the difference in the way male and female writers select significant events and relationships, Jones points out that "with many women writers, relationships within family, community, between men and women, and among women—from slave narratives by black women writers on—are treated as complex and significant relationships, whereas with many men the significant relationships are those that involve confrontations—relationships outside the family and community."[71] Alice Walker's reaction to Zora Neale Hurston's book, *Mules and Men,* is another example of the use of dialogue in assessing knowledge claims. In *Mules and Men,* Hurston chose not to become a detached observer of the stories and folktales she collected but instead, through extensive dialogues with the people in the communities she studied, placed herself at the center of her analysis. Using a similar process, Walker tests the truth of Hurston's knowledge claims: "When I read *Mules and Men* I was delighted. Here was this perfect book! The 'perfection' of which I immediately tested on my relatives, who are such typical Black Americans they are useful for every sort of political, cultural, or economic survey. Very regular people from the South, rapidly forgetting their Southern cultural inheritance in the suburbs and ghettos of Boston and New York, they sat around reading the book themselves, listening to me read the book, listening to each other read the book, and a kind of paradise was regained."[72]

Their centrality in Black churches and Black extended families provides Black women with a high degree of support from Black institutions for invoking dialogue as a dimension of an Afrocentric feminist epistemology. However, when African-American women use dialogues in assessing knowledge claims, they might be invoking a particularly female way of knowing as well. Feminist scholars contend that males and females are socialized within their families to seek different types of autonomy, the former based on separation, the latter seeking connectedness, and that this variation in types of autonomy parallels the characteristic differences between male and female ways of knowing.[73] For instance, in contrast to the visual metaphors (such as equating knowledge with illumination, knowing with seeing, and truth with light) that scientists and philosophers typically use, women tend to ground their epistemological premises in metaphors suggesting speaking and listening.[74]

While there are significant differences between the roles Black women play in their families and those played by middle-class white women, Black women clearly are affected by general cultural norms prescribing certain familial roles for women. Thus, in terms of the role of dialogue in an Afrocentric feminist epistemology, Black women may again experience a convergence of the values of the African-American community and woman-centered values.

The Ethic of Caring

"Ole white preachers used to talk wid dey tongues widdout sayin' nothin', but Jesus told us slaves to talk wid our hearts."[75] These words of an ex-slave suggest that ideas cannot be divorced from the individuals who create and share them. This theme of "talking with the heart" taps another dimension of an alternative epistemology used by African-American women, the ethic of caring. Just as the ex-slave used the wisdom in his heart to reject the ideas of the preachers who talked "wid dey tongues widdout sayin' nothin'," the ethic of caring suggests that personal expressiveness, emotions, and empathy are central to the knowledge-validation process.

One of three interrelated components making up the ethic of caring is the emphasis placed on individual uniqueness. Rooted in a tradition of African humanism, each individual is thought to be a unique expression of a common spirit, power, or energy expressed by all life.[76] This belief in individual uniqueness is illustrated by the value placed on personal expressiveness in African-American communities.[77] Johnetta Ray, an inner city resident, describes this Afrocentric emphasis on individual uniqueness: "No matter how hard we try, I don't think black people will ever develop much of a herd instinct. We are profound individualists with a passion for self-expression."[78]

A second component of the ethic of caring concerns the appropriateness of emotions in dialogues. Emotion indicates that a speaker believes in the validity of an argument.[79] Consider Ntozake Shange's description of one of the goals of her work: "Our [Western] society allows people to be absolutely neurotic and totally out of touch with their feelings and everyone else's feelings, and yet be very respectable. This, to me, is a travesty. . . . I'm trying to change the idea of seeing emotions and intellect as distinct faculties."[80] Shange's words echo those of the ex-slave. Both see the denigration of emotion as problematic, and both suggest that expressiveness should be reclaimed and valued.

A third component of the ethic of caring involves developing the capacity for empathy. Harriet Jones, a sixteen-year-old Black woman, explains why she chose to open up to her interviewer: "Some things in my life are so hard for me to bear, and it makes me feel better to know that you feel sorry about those things and would change them if you could."[81]

These three components of the ethic of caring—the value placed on individual expressiveness, the appropriateness of emotions, and the capacity for empathy—pervade African-American culture. One of the best examples of the interactive nature of the importance of dialogue and the ethic of caring in assessing knowledge claims occurs in the use of the call and response discourse mode in traditional Black church services. In such services, both the minister and the congregation routinely use voice rhythm and vocal inflection to convey meaning. The sound of what is being said is just as important as the words themselves in what is, in a sense, a dialogue between reason and emotions. As a result, it is nearly impossible to filter out the strictly linguistic-cognitive abstract meaning from the sociocultural psycho-emotive meaning.[82] While the ideas presented by a speaker must have validity, that is, agree with the general body of knowledge shared by the Black congregation, the group also appraises the way knowledge claims are presented.

There is growing evidence that the ethic of caring may be part of women's experience as well. Certain dimensions of women's ways of knowing bear striking resemblance to Afrocentric expressions of the ethic of caring. Belenky, Clinchy, Goldberger, and Tarule point out that two contrasting epistemological orientations characterize knowing—one, an epistemology of separation based on impersonal procedures for establishing truth, and the other, an epistemology of connection in which truth emerges through care. While these ways of knowing are not gender specific, disproportionate numbers of women rely on connected knowing.[83]

The parallels between Afrocentric expressions of the ethic of caring and those advanced by feminist scholars are noteworthy. The emphasis placed on expressiveness and emotion in African-American communities bears marked resemblance to feminist perspectives on the importance of personality in connected knowing. Separate knowers try to subtract the personality of an individual from his or her ideas because they see personality as biasing those ideas. In contrast, connected knowers see personality as adding to an individual's ideas, and they feel that the personality of each group member enriches a group's understanding.[84] Similarly, the significance of individual uniqueness, personal expressiveness, and empathy in African-American communities resembles the importance that some feminist analyses place on women's "inner voice."[85]

The convergence of Afrocentric and feminist values in the ethic-of-care dimension of an alternative epistemology seems particularly acute. While white women may have access to a women's tradition valuing emotion and expressiveness, few white social institutions except the family validate this way of knowing. In contrast, Black women have long had the support of the Black church, an institution with deep roots in the African past and a philosophy that accepts and encourages expressiveness and an ethic of caring. While Black men share in this Afrocentric tradition, they must resolve the contradictions that distinguish abstract, unemotional Western masculinity from an Afrocentric ethic of caring. The differences among race/gender groups thus hinge on differences in their access to institutional supports valuing one type of knowing over another. Although Black women may be denigrated within white-male-controlled academic institutions, other institutions, such as Black families and churches, which encourage the expression of Black female power, seem to do so by way of their support for an Afrocentric feminist epistemology.

The Ethic of Personal Accountability

An ethic of personal accountability is the final dimension of an alternative epistemology. Not only must individuals develop their knowledge claims through dialogue and present those knowledge claims in a style proving their concern for their ideas, people are expected to be accountable for their knowledge claims. Zilpha Elaw's description of slavery reflects this notion that every idea has an owner and that the owner's identity matters: "Oh, the abominations of slavery! . . . every case of slavery, however lenient its inflictions and mitigated its atrocities, indicates an oppressor, the oppressed, and oppression."[86] For Elaw, abstract definitions of slavery mesh with the concrete identities of its perpetrators and its victims. Blacks "consider it essential for individuals to have personal positions on issues and assume full responsibility for arguing their validity."[87]

Assessments of an individual's knowledge claims simultaneously evaluate an individual's character, values, and ethics. African-Americans reject Eurocentric masculinist beliefs that probing into an individual's personal viewpoint is outside the boundaries of discussion. Rather, all views expressed and actions taken are thought to derive from a central set of core beliefs that cannot be other than personal.[88] From this perspective, knowledge claims made by individuals respected for their moral and ethical values will carry more weight than those offered by less respected figures.[89]

An example drawn from an undergraduate course composed entirely of Black women, which I taught, might help clarify the uniqueness of this portion of the knowledge-validation process. During one class discussion, I assigned the students the task of critiquing an analysis of Black feminism advanced by a prominent Black male scholar. Instead of dissecting the rationality of the author's thesis, my students demanded facts about the author's personal biography. They were especially interested in concrete details of his life such as his relationships with Black women, his marital status, and his social class background. By requesting data on dimensions of his personal life routinely excluded in positivist approaches to knowledge validation, they were invoking concrete experience as a criterion of meaning. They used this information to assess whether he really cared about his topic and invoked this ethic of caring in advancing their knowledge claims about his work. Furthermore, they refused to evaluate the rationality of his written ideas without some indication of his personal credibility as an ethical human being. The entire exchange could only have occurred as a dialogue among members of a class that had established a solid enough community to invoke an alternative epistemology in assessing knowledge claims.[90]

The ethic of personal accountability is clearly an Afrocentric value, but is it feminist as well? While limited by its attention to middle-class, white women, Carol Gilligan's work suggests that there is a female model for moral development where women are more inclined to link morality to responsibility, relationships, and the ability to maintain social ties.[91] If this is the case, then African-American women again experience a convergence of values from Afrocentric and female institutions.

The use of an Afrocentric feminist epistemology in traditional Black church services illustrates the interactive nature of all four dimensions and also serves as a metaphor for the distinguishing features of an Afrocentric feminist way of knowing. The services represent more than dialogues between the rationality used in examining biblical texts/stories and the emotion inherent in the use of reason for this purpose. The rationale for such dialogues addresses the task of examining concrete experiences for the presence of an ethic of caring. Neither emotion nor ethics is subordinated to reason. Instead, emotion, ethics, and reason are used as interconnected, essential components in assessing knowledge claims. In an Afrocentric feminist epistemology, values lie at the heart of the knowledge-validation process such that inquiry always has an ethical aim.

EPISTEMOLOGY AND BLACK FEMINIST THOUGHT

Living life as an African-American woman is a necessary prerequisite for producing Black feminist thought because within Black women's communities thought is validated and produced with reference to a particular set of historical, material, and epistemological conditions.[92] African-American women who adhere to the idea that claims about Black women must be substantiated by Black women's sense of their own experiences and who anchor their knowledge claims in an Afrocentric feminist epistemology have produced a rich tradition of Black feminist thought.

Traditionally, such women were blues singers, poets, autobiographers, storytellers, and orators validated by the larger community of Black women as experts on a Black women's standpoint. Only a few unusual African-American feminist scholars have been able to defy Eurocentric masculinist epistemologies and explicitly embrace an Afrocentric feminist epistemology. Consider Alice Walker's description of Zora Neale Hurston: "In my mind, Zora Neale Hurston, Billie Holiday, and Bessie Smith form a sort of unholy trinity. Zora *belongs* in the tradition of Black women singers, rather than among 'the literati.' . . . Like Billie and Bessie she followed her own road, believed in her own gods, pursued her own dreams, and refused to separate herself from 'common' people."[93]

Zora Neale Hurston is an exception for, prior to 1950, few Black women earned advanced degrees, and most of those who did complied with Eurocentric masculinist epistemologies. While these women worked on behalf of Black women, they did so within the confines of pervasive race and gender oppression. Black women scholars were in a position to see the exclusion of Black women from scholarly discourse, and the thematic content of their work often reflected their interest in examining a Black women's standpoint. However, their tenuous status in academic institutions led them to adhere to Eurocentric masculinist epistemologies so that their work would be accepted as scholarly. As a result, while they produced Black feminist thought, those Black women most likely to gain academic credentials were often least likely to produce Black feminist thought that used an Afrocentric feminist epistemology.

As more Black women earn advanced degrees, the range of Black feminist scholarship is expanding. Increasing numbers of African-American women scholars are explicitly choosing to ground their work in Black women's experiences, and, by doing so, many implicitly adhere to an Afrocentric feminist epistemology. Rather than being restrained by their "both/and" status of marginality, these women make creative use of their outsider-within status and produce innovative Black feminist thought. The difficulties these women face lie less in demonstrating the technical components of white male epistemologies than in resisting the hegemonic nature of these patterns of thought in order to see, value, and use existing alternative Afrocentric feminist ways of knowing.

In establishing the legitimacy of their knowledge claims, Black women scholars who want to develop Black feminist thought may encounter the often conflicting standards of three key groups. First, Black feminist thought must be validated by ordinary African-American women who grow to womanhood "in a world where the saner you are, the madder you are made to appear."[94] To be credible in the eyes of this group, scholars must be personal advocates for their material, be accountable for the consequences of their work, have lived or experienced their material in some fashion, and be willing to engage in dialogues about their findings with ordinary, everyday people. Second, if it is to establish its legitimacy, Black feminist thought also must be accepted by the community of Black women scholars. These scholars place varying amounts of importance on rearticulating a Black women's standpoint using an Afro-centric feminist epistemology. Third, Black feminist thought within academia must be prepared to confront Eurocentric masculinist political and epistemological requirements.

The dilemma facing Black women scholars engaged in creating Black feminist thought is that a knowledge claim that meets the criteria of adequacy for one group and thus is judged to be an acceptable knowledge claim may not be translatable into the terms of a different group. Using the example of Black English, June Jordan illustrates the difficulty of moving among epistemologies: "You cannot 'translate' instances of Standard English preoccupied with abstraction or with nothing/nobody evidently alive into Black English. That would warp the language into uses antithetical to the guiding perspective of its community of users. Rather you must first change those Standard English sentences, themselves, into ideas consistent with the person-centered assumptions of Black English."[95] While both worldviews share a common vocabulary, the ideas themselves defy direct translation.

Once Black feminist scholars face the notion that, on certain dimensions of a Black women's standpoint, it may be fruitless to try to translate ideas from an Afrocentric feminist epistemology into a Eurocentric masculinist epistemology, then the choices become clearer. Rather than trying to uncover universal knowledge claims that can withstand the translation from one epistemology to another, time might be better spent rearticulating a Black women's standpoint in order to give African-American women the tools to resist their own subordination. The goal here is not one of integrating Black female "folk culture" into the substantiated body of academic knowledge, for that substantiated knowledge is, in many ways, antithetical to the best interests of Black women. Rather, the process is one of rearticulating a preexisting Black women's standpoint and recentering the language of existing academic discourse to accommodate these knowledge claims. For those Black women scholars engaged in this rearticulation process, the social construction of Black feminist thought requires the skill and sophistication to decide which knowledge claims can be validated using the epistemological assumptions of one but not both frameworks, which claims can be generated in one framework and only partially accommodated by the other, and which claims can be made in both frameworks without violating the basic political and epistemological assumptions of either.

Black feminist scholars offering knowledge claims that cannot be accommodated by both frameworks face the choice between accepting the taken-for-granted assumptions that permeate white-male-controlled academic institutions or leaving academia. Those Black women who choose to remain in academia must accept the possibility that their knowledge claims will be limited to those claims about Black women that are consistent with a white male worldview. And yet those African-American women who leave academia may find their work is inaccessible to scholarly communities.

Black feminist scholars offering knowledge claims that can be partially accommodated by both epistemologies can create a body of thought that stands outside of either. Rather than trying to synthesize competing worldviews that, at this point in time, may defy reconciliation, their task is to point out common themes and concerns. By making creative use of their status as mediators, their thought becomes an entity unto itself that is rooted in two distinct political and epistemological contexts.[96]

Those Black feminists who develop knowledge claims that both epistemologies can accommodate may have found a route to the elusive goal of generating so-called objective generalizations that can stand as universal truths. Those ideas that are validated as true by African-American women, African-American men, white men, white women, and other groups with distinctive standpoints, with each group using the epistemological approaches growing from its unique standpoint, thus become the most objective truths.[97]

Alternative knowledge claims, in and of themselves, are rarely threatening to conventional knowledge. Such claims are routinely ignored, discredited, or simply absorbed and marginalized in existing paradigms. Much more threatening is the challenge that alternative epistemologies offer to the basic process used by the powerful to legitimate their knowledge claims. If the epistemology used to validate knowledge comes into question, then all prior knowledge claims validated under the dominant model become suspect. An alternative epistemology challenges all certified knowledge and opens up the question of whether what has been taken to be true can stand the test of alternative ways of validating truth. The existence of an independent Black women's standpoint using an Afrocentric feminist epistemology calls into question the content of what currently passes as truth and simultaneously challenges the process of arriving at that truth.

NOTES

1. For analyses of how interlocking systems of oppression affect Black women, see Frances Beale, "Double Jeopardy: To Be Black and Female," in *The Black Woman,* ed. Toni Cade (New York: Signet, 1970); Angela Y. Davis, *Women, Race and Class* (New York: Random House, 1981);

Bonnie Thornton Dill, "Race, Class, and Gender: Prospects for an All-Inclusive Sisterhood," *Feminist Studies* 9, no. 1 (1983): 131–50; bell hooks, *Ain't I a Woman? Black Women and Feminism* (Boston: South End Press, 1981); Diane Lewis, "A Response to Inequality: Black Women, Racism, and Sexism," *Signs: Journal of Women in Culture and Society* 3, no. 2 (Winter 1977): 339–61; Pauli Murray, "The Liberation of Black Women," in *Voices of the New Feminism,* ed. Mary Lou Thompson (Boston: Beacon, 1970), 87–102; and the introduction in Filomina Chioma Steady, *The Black Woman Cross-Culturally* (Cambridge, Mass.: Schenkman, 1981), 7–41.

2. See the introduction in Steady for an overview of Black women's strengths. This strength-resiliency perspective has greatly influenced empirical work on African-American women. See, e.g., Joyce Ladner's study of low-income Black adolescent girls, *Tomorrow's Tomorrow* (New York: Doubleday, 1971); and Lena Wright Myer's work on Black women's self-concept, *Black Women: Do They Cope Better?* (Englewood Cliffs, N.J.: Prentice-Hall, 1980). For discussions of Black women's resistance, see Elizabeth Fox-Genovese, "Strategies and Forms of Resistance: Focus on Slave Women in the United States," in *In Resistance: Studies in African, Caribbean and Afro-American History,* ed. Gary Y. Okihiro (Amherst, Mass.: University of Massachusetts Press, 1986), 143–65; and Rosalyn Terborg-Penn, "Black Women in Resistance: A Cross-Cultural Perspective," in Okihiro, ed., 188–209. For a comprehensive discussion of everyday resistance, see James C. Scott, *Weapons of the Weak: Everyday Forms of Peasant Resistance* (New Haven, Conn.: Yale University Press, 1985).

3. See Patricia Hill Collins's analysis of the substantive content of Black feminist thought in "Learning from the Outsider Within: The Sociological Significance of Black Feminist Thought," *Social Problems* 33, no. 6 (1986): 14–32.

4. Scott describes consciousness as the meaning that people give to their acts through the symbols, norms, and ideological forms they create.

5. This thesis is found in scholarship of varying theoretical perspectives. For example, Marxist analyses of working-class consciousness claim that "false consciousness" makes the working class unable to penetrate the hegemony of ruling-class ideologies. See Scott's critique of this literature.

6. For example, in Western societies, African-Americans have been judged as being less capable of intellectual excellence, more suited to manual labor, and therefore as less human than whites. Similarly, white women have been assigned roles as emotional, irrational creatures ruled by passions and biological urges. They too have been stigmatized as being less than fully human, as being objects. For a discussion of the importance that objectification and dehumanization play in maintaining systems of domination, see Arthur Brittan and Mary Maynard, *Sexism, Racism and Oppression* (New York: Basil Blackwell, 1984).

7. The tendency for Western scholarship to assess Black culture as pathological and deviant illustrates this process. See Rhett S. Jones, "Proving Blacks Inferior: The Sociology of Knowledge," in *The Death of White Sociology,* ed. Joyce Ladner (New York: Vintage, 1973), 114–35.

8. The presence of an independent standpoint does not mean that it is uniformly shared by all Black women or even that Black women fully recognize its contours. By using the concept of standpoint, I do not mean to minimize the rich diversity existing among African-American women. I use the phrase "Black women's standpoint" to emphasize the plurality of experiences within the overarching term "standpoint." For discussions of the concept of standpoint, see Nancy M. Hartsock, "The Feminist Standpoint: Developing the Ground for a Specifically Feminist Historical Materialism," in *Discovering Reality,* ed. Sandra Harding and Merrill Hintikka (Boston: D. Reidel, 1983), 283–310, and *Money, Sex, and Power* (Boston: Northeastern University Press, 1983); and Alison M. Jaggar, *Feminist Politics and Human Nature* (Totowa, N.J.: Rowman & Allanheld, 1983), 377–89. My use of the standpoint epistemologies as an organizing concept in this essay does not mean that the concept is problem-free. For a helpful

critique of standpoint epistemologies, see Sandra Harding, *The Science Question in Feminism* (Ithaca, N.Y.: Cornell University Press, 1986).

9. One contribution of contemporary Black women's studies is its documentation of how race, class, and gender have structured these differences. For representative works surveying African-American women's experiences, see Paula Giddings, *When and Where I Enter: The Impact of Black Women on Race and Sex in America* (New York: William Morrow, 1984); and Jacqueline Jones, *Labor of Love, Labor of Sorrow: Black Women, Work, and the Family from Slavery to the Present* (New York: Basic, 1985).

10. For example, Judith Rollins, *Between Women: Domestics and Their Employers* (Philadelphia: Temple University Press, 1985); and Bonnie Thornton Dill, " 'The Means to Put My Children Through': Child-Rearing Goals and Strategies among Black Female Domestic Servants," in *The Black Woman*, ed. LaFrances Rodgers-Rose (Beverly Hills, Calif.: Sage Publications, 1980), 107–23, report that Black domestic workers do not see themselves as being the devalued workers that their employers perceive and construct their own interpretations of the meaning of their work. For additional discussions of how Black women's consciousness is shaped by the material conditions they encounter, see Ladner (n. 2 above); Myers (n. 2 above); and Cheryl Townsend Gilkes, " 'Together and in Harness': Women's Traditions in the Sanctified Church," *Signs* 10, no. 4 (Summer 1985): 678–99. See also Marcia Westkott's discussion of consciousness as a sphere of freedom for women in "Feminist Criticism of the Social Sciences," *Harvard Educational Review* 49, no. 4 (1979): 422–30.

11. John Langston Gwaltney, *Drylongso: A Self-Portrait of Black America* (New York: Vintage, 1980), 4.

12. Ibid., 33.

13. Ibid., 88.

14. Ibid., 7.

15. Victoria Byerly, *Hard Times Cotton Mill Girls: Personal Histories of Womanhood and Poverty in the South* (New York: ILR Press, 1986), 134.

16. See Peter L. Berger and Thomas Luckmann, *The Social Construction of Reality* (New York: Doubleday, 1966), for a discussion of everyday thought and the role of experts in articulating specialized thought.

17. See Michael Omi and Howard Winant, *Racial Formation in the United States* (New York: Routledge & Kegan Paul, 1986), esp. 93.

18. In discussing standpoint epistemologies, Hartsock, in *Money, Sex, and Power*, notes that a standpoint is "achieved rather than obvious, a mediated rather than immediate understanding" (132).

19. See Scott (n. 2 above); and Hartsock, *Money, Sex, and Power* (n. 8 above).

20. Some readers may question how one determines whether the ideas of any given African-American woman are "feminist" and "Afrocentric." I offer the following working definitions. I agree with the general definition of feminist consciousness provided by Black feminist sociologist Deborah K. King: "Any purposes, goals, and activities which seek to enhance the potential of women, to ensure their liberty, afford them equal opportunity, and to permit and encourage their self-determination represent a feminist consciousness, even if they occur within a racial community" (in "Race, Class and Gender Salience in Black Women's Womanist Consciousness" [Dartmouth College, Department of Sociology, Hanover, N.H., 1987, typescript], 22). To be Black or Afrocentric, such thought must not only reflect a similar concern for the self-determination of African-American people, but must in some way draw upon key elements of an Afrocentric tradition as well.

21. The Eurocentric masculinist process is defined here as the institutions, paradigms, and any elements of the knowledge-validation procedure controlled by white males and whose purpose is to represent a white male standpoint. While this process represents the interests of

powerful white males, various dimensions of the process are not necessarily managed by white males themselves.

22. Karl Mannheim, *Ideology and Utopia: An Introduction to the Sociology of Knowledge* (New York: Harcourt, Brace, 1936, 1954), 276.

23. The knowledge-validation model used in this essay is taken from Michael Mulkay, *Science and the Sociology of Knowledge* (Boston: Allen & Unwin, 1979). For a general discussion of the structure of knowledge, see Thomas Kuhn, *The Structure of Scientific Revolutions* (Chicago: University of Chicago Press, 1962).

24. For analyses of the content and functions of images of Black female inferiority, see Mae King, "The Politics of Sexual Stereotypes," *Black Scholar* 4, nos. 6–7 (1973): 12–23; Cheryl Townsend Gilkes, "From Slavery to Social Welfare: Racism and the Control of Black Women," in *Class, Race, and Sex: The Dynamics of Control*, ed. Amy Smerdlow and Helen Lessinger (Boston: G. K. Hall, 1981), 288–300; and Elizabeth Higginbotham, "Two Representative Issues in Contemporary Sociological Work on Black Women," in *But Some of Us Are Brave*, ed. Gloria T. Hull, Patricia Bell Scott, and Barbara Smith (Old Westbury, N.Y.: Feminist Press, 1982).

25. Kuhn.

26. Evelyn Fox Keller, *Reflections on Gender and Science* (New Haven, Conn.: Yale University Press, 1985), 167.

27. Maxine Baca Zinn, Lynn Weber Cannon, Elizabeth Higginbotham, and Bonnie Thornton Dill, "The Cost of Exclusionary Practices in Women's Studies," *Signs* 11, no. 2 (Winter 1986): 290–303.

28. Berger and Luckmann (n. 16 above) note that if an outsider group, in this case African-American women, recognizes that the insider group, namely, white men, requires special privileges from the larger society, a special problem arises of keeping the outsiders out and at the same time having them acknowledge the legitimacy of this procedure. Accepting a few "safe" outsiders is one way of addressing this legitimation problem. Collins's discussion (n. 3 above) of Black women as "outsiders within" addresses this issue. Other relevant works include Franz Fanon's analysis of the role of the national middle class in maintaining colonial systems, *The Wretched of the Earth* (New York: Grove, 1963); and William Tabb's discussion of the use of "bright natives" in controlling African-American communities, *The Political Economy of the Black Ghetto* (New York: Norton, 1970).

29. While I have been describing Eurocentric masculinist approaches as a single process, there are many schools of thought or paradigms subsumed under this one process. Positivism represents one such paradigm. See Harding (n. 8 above) for an overview and critique of this literature. The following discussion depends heavily on Jaggar (n. 8 above), 355–58.

30. Jaggar, 356.

31. See Keller, especially her analysis of static autonomy and its relation to objectivity (67–126).

32. Ironically, researchers must "objectify" themselves to achieve this lack of bias. See Arlie Russell Hochschild, "The Sociology of Feeling and Emotion: Selected Possibilities," in *Another Voice: Feminist Perspectives on Social Life and Social Science*, ed. Marcia Millman and Rosabeth Kanter (Garden City, N.Y.: Anchor, 1975), 280–307. Also, see Jaggar.

33. See Norma Haan, Robert Bellah, Paul Rabinow, and William Sullivan, eds., *Social Science as Moral Inquiry* (New York: Columbia University Press, 1983), esp. Michelle Z. Rosaldo's "Moral/Analytic Dilemmas Posed by the Intersection of Feminism and Social Science," 76–96; and Robert Bellah's "The Ethical Aims of Social Inquiry," 360–81.

34. Janice Moulton, "A Paradigm of Philosophy: The Adversary Method," in Harding and Hintikka, eds. (n. 8 above), 149–64.

35. For detailed discussions of the Afrocentric worldview, see John S. Mbiti, *African Religions and Philosophy* (London: Heinemann, 1969); Dominique Zahan, *The Religion, Spirituality, and Thought of Traditional Africa* (Chicago: University of Chicago Press, 1979); and

Mechal Sobel, *Trabelin' On: The Slave Journey to an Afro-Baptist Faith* (Westport, Conn.: Greenwood Press, 1979), 1–76.

36. For representative works applying these concepts to African-American culture, see Niara Sudarkasa, "Interpreting the African Heritage in Afro-American Family Organization," in *Black Families,* ed. Harriette Pipes McAdoo (Beverly Hills, Calif.: Sage, 1981); Henry H. Mitchell and Nicholas Cooper Lewter, *Soul Theology: The Heart of American Black Culture* (San Francisco: Harper & Row, 1986); Robert Farris Thompson, *Flash of the Spirit: African and Afro-American Art and Philosophy* (New York: Vintage, 1983); and Ortiz M. Walton, "Comparative Analysis of the African and the Western Aesthetics," in *The Black Aesthetic,* ed. Addison Gayle (Garden City, N.Y.: Doubleday, 1971), 154–64.

37. One of the best discussions of an Afrocentric epistemology is offered by James E. Turner, "Foreword: Africana Studies and Epistemology; a Discourse in the Sociology of Knowledge," in *The Next Decade: Theoretical and Research Issues in Africana Studies,* ed. James E. Turner (Ithaca, N.Y.: Cornell University Africana Studies and Research Center, 1984), v–xxv. See also Vernon Dixon, "World Views and Research Methodology," summarized in Harding (n. 8 above), 170.

38. See Hester Eisenstein, *Contemporary Feminist Thought* (Boston: G. K. Hall, 1983). Nancy Hartsock's *Money, Sex, and Power* (n. 8 above), 145–209, offers a particularly insightful analysis of women's oppression.

39. For discussions of feminist consciousness, see Dorothy Smith, "A Sociology for Women," in *The Prism of Sex: Essays in the Sociology of Knowledge,* ed. Julia A. Sherman and Evelyn T. Beck (Madison: University of Wisconsin Press, 1979); and Michelle Z. Rosaldo, "Women, Culture, and Society: A Theoretical Overview," in *Woman, Culture, and Society,* ed. Michelle Z. Rosaldo and Louise Lamphere (Stanford, Calif.: Stanford University Press, 1974), 17–42. Feminist epistemologies are surveyed by Jaggar (n. 8 above).

40. One significant difference between Afrocentric and feminist standpoints is that much of what is termed women's culture is, unlike African-American culture, created in the context of and produced by oppression. Those who argue for a women's culture are electing to value, rather than denigrate, those traits associated with females in white patriarchal societies. While this choice is important, it is not the same as identifying an independent, historic culture associated with a society. I am indebted to Deborah K. King for this point.

41. Critiques of the Eurocentric masculinist knowledge-validation process by both Africanist and feminist scholars illustrate this point. What one group labels "white" and "Eurocentric," the other describes as "male-dominated" and "masculinist." Although he does not emphasize its patriarchal and racist features, Morris Berman's *The Reenchantment of the World* (New York: Bantam, 1981) provides a historical discussion of Western thought. Afrocentric analyses of this same process can be found in Molefi Kete Asante, "International/Intercultural Relations," in *Contemporary Black Thought,* ed. Molefi Kete Asante and Abdulai S. Vandi (Beverly Hills, Calif.: Sage, 1980), 43–58; and Dona Richards, "European Mythology: The Ideology of 'Progress,' " in Asante and Vandi, eds., 59–79. For feminist analyses, see Hartsock, *Money, Sex, and Power.* Harding also discusses this similarity (see chap. 7, "Other 'Others' and Fractured Identities: Issues for Epistemologists," 163–96).

42. Harding, 166.

43. D. King (n. 20 above).

44. Bonnie Thornton Dill, "The Dialectics of Black Womanhood," *Signs* 4, no. 3 (Spring 1979): 543–55.

45. One implication of standpoint approaches is that the more subordinate the group, the purer the vision of the oppressed group. This is an outcome of the origins of standpoint approaches in Marxist social theory, itself a dualistic analysis of social structure. Because such approaches rely on quantifying and ranking human oppressions—familiar tenets of positivist approaches—they are rejected by Blacks and feminists alike. See Harding (n. 8 above) for a

discussion of this point. See also Elizabeth V. Spelman's discussion of the fallacy of additive oppression in "Theories of Race and Gender: The Erasure of Black Women," *Quest* 5, no. 4 (1982): 36–62.

46. Class differences among Black women may be marked. For example, see Paula Giddings's analysis (n. 9 above) of the role of social class in shaping Black women's political activism; or Elizabeth Higginbotham's study of the effects of social class in Black women's college attendance in "Race and Class Barriers to Black Women's College Attendance," *Journal of Ethnic Studies* 13, no. 1 (1985): 89–107. Those African-American women who have experienced the greatest degree of convergence of race, class, and gender oppression may be in a better position to recognize and use an alternative epistemology.

47. Gwaltney (n. 11 above), 83.

48. William L. Andrews, *Sisters of the Spirit: Three Black Women's Autobiographies of the Nineteenth Century* (Bloomington: Indiana University Press, 1986), 85.

49. Gwaltney, 147.

50. Geneva Smitherman, *Talkin and Testifyin: The Language of Black America* (Detroit: Wayne State University Press, 1986), 76.

51. Gwaltney, 68.

52. Ibid., 7.

53. Ibid., 27, 33.

54. Elsa Barkley Brown, "Hearing Our Mothers' Lives" (paper presented at the Fifteenth Anniversary Faculty Lecture Series, African-American and African Studies. Emory University, Atlanta, 1986).

55. Ladner (n. 2 above).

56. Mitchell and Lewter (n. 36 above). The use of the narrative approach in African-American theology exemplifies an inductive system of logic alternately called "folk wisdom" or a survival-based, need-oriented method of assessing knowledge claims.

57. Ibid., 8.

58. June Jordan, *On Call: Political Essays* (Boston: South End Press, 1985), 26.

59. Mary Belenky, Blythe Clinchy, Nancy Goldberger, and Jill Tarule, *Women's Ways of Knowing* (New York: Basic, 1986), 113.

60. Hartsock, *Money, Sex and Power* (n. 8 above), 237; and Nancy Chodorow, *The Reproduction of Mothering* (Berkeley and Los Angeles: University of California Press, 1978).

61. Dorothy Smith, *The Everyday World as Problematic* (Boston: Northeastern University Press, 1987).

62. Byerly (n. 15 above), 198.

63. For Black women's centrality in the family, see Steady (n. 1 above); Ladner (n. 2 above); Brown (n. 54 above); and McAdoo, ed. (n. 36 above). See Gilkes, " 'Together and in Harness' " (n. 10 above), for Black women in the church; and chap. 4 of Deborah Gray White, *Ar'n't I a Woman? Female Slaves in the Plantation South* (New York: Norton, 1985). See also Gloria Joseph, "Black Mothers and Daughters: Their Roles and Functions in American Society," in *Common Differences: Conflicts in Black and White Feminist Perspectives,* ed. Gloria Joseph and Jill Lewis (Garden City, N.Y.: Anchor, 1981), 75–126. Even though Black women play essential roles in Black families and Black churches, these institutions are not free from sexism.

64. As Belenky et al. note, "Unlike the eye, the ear requires closeness between subject and object. Unlike seeing, speaking and listening suggest dialogue and interaction" (18).

65. Thomas Kochman, *Black and White: Styles in Conflict* (Chicago: University of Chicago Press, 1981); and Smitherman (n. 50 above).

66. Gwaltney (n. 11 above), 32.

67. Smitherman, 108.

68. Kochman, 28.

69. Jordan (n. 58 above), 129.

70. Claudia Tate, *Black Women Writers at Work* (New York: Continuum, 1983), 91.

71. Ibid., 92.

72. Alice Walker, *In Search of Our Mothers' Gardens* (New York: Harcourt Brace Jovanovich, 1974), 84.

73. Keller (n. 26 above); Chodorow (n. 60 above).

74. Belenky et al. (n. 59 above), 16.

75. Thomas Webber, *Deep Like the Rivers* (New York: Norton, 1978), 127.

76. In her discussion of the West African Sacred Cosmos, Mechal Sobel (n. 35 above) notes that Nyam, a root word in many West African languages, connotes an enduring spirit, power, or energy possessed by all life. In spite of the pervasiveness of this key concept in African humanism, its definition remains elusive. She points out, "Every individual analyzing the various Sacred Cosmos of West Africa has recognized the reality of this force, but no one has yet adequately translated this concept into Western terms" (13).

77. For discussions of personal expressiveness in African-American culture, see Smitherman (n. 50 above); Kochman (n. 65 above), esp. chap. 9; and Mitchell and Lewter (n. 36 above).

78. Gwaltney (n. 11 above), 228.

79. For feminist analyses of the subordination of emotion in Western culture, see Hochschild (n. 32 above); and Chodorow.

80. Tate (n. 70 above), 156.

81. Gwaltney, 11.

82. Smitherman, 135 and 137.

83. Belenky et al. (n. 59 above), 100–130.

84. Ibid., 119.

85. See ibid., 52–75, for a discussion of inner voice and its role in women's cognitive styles. Regarding empathy, Belenky et al. note: "Connected knowers begin with an interest in the facts of other people's lives, but they gradually shift the focus to other people's ways of thinking. . . . It is the form rather than the content of knowing that is central. . . . Connected learners learn through empathy" (115).

86. Andrews (n. 48 above), 98.

87. Kochman (n. 65 above), 20 and 25.

88. Ibid, 23.

89. The sizable proportion of ministers among Black political leaders illustrates the importance of ethics in African-American communities.

90. Belenky et al. discuss a similar situation. They note, "People could critique each other's work in this class and accept each other's criticisms because members of the group shared a similar experience. . . . Authority in connected knowing rests not on power or status or certification but on commonality of experience" (118).

91. Carol Gilligan, *In a Different Voice* (Cambridge, Mass.: Harvard University Press, 1982). Carol Stack critiques Gilligan's model by arguing that African-Americans invoke a similar model of moral development to that used by women (see "The Culture of Gender: Women and Men of Color," *Signs* 11, no. 2 [Winter 1986]: 321–24. Another difficulty with Gilligan's work concerns the homogeneity of the subjects whom she studied.

92. Black men, white women, and members of other race, class, and gender groups should be encouraged to interpret, teach, and critique the Black feminist thought produced by African-American women.

93. Walker (n. 72 above), 91.

94. Gwaltney (n. 11 above), 7.

95. Jordan (n. 58 above), 130.

96. Collins (n. 3 above).

97. This point addresses the question of relativity in the sociology of knowledge and offers a way of regulating competing knowledge claims.

Finding Myself Among the Long-Haired Women: Reflections of Gender, Race, Sexuality, and Feminist Identity[1]

JACQUELINE JOHNSON

When I was a child, I believed that women who had long hair were the most admired and most powerful women in the world! From Barbie to Wonder Woman, images of the long-haired women who dominated my books, television, and playtime seemed to be self-reliant, confident, exciting, and free. They wore their hair in long ponytails, which they would toss defiantly into the face of anyone who crossed them. I would simulate long, flowing locks by tying my grandmother's brown sweater on my head and pretend to drive down a deserted highway in a convertible at top speed, the wind blowing through my hair. Sometimes I would ride the range on horseback, with my hair blowing in the wind like my horse's mane and tail. Of course, all of the women I saw on television, read about in books, or saw in public who could toss their hair in such a manner were white. So, as a young African American girl, I thought that if I wanted to join this group there were only two things that I could do: (a) study hard in school, get a good job, and buy a convertible; and (b) pray for long hair.

I was about 10 years old when the women's liberation movement of the early seventies became public knowledge in rural North Carolina. Because watching the evening news was a family event in my household, at six o'clock the long-haired women who protested male oppression and privilege would come into my home. I remember thinking how liberating it must be for women to have the freedom to speak out and to stand up for what they believe; how wonderful to have the time to attend protest rallies, organizational meetings, and enlightenment seminars. However, I also remember thinking, "Where are the women of my family in this fight for equality?" I mean, if the women on television were fighting to gain access to the paid labor force, the women of my family were already out there. If the fight was for equality, what about the women with short, kinky hair, who were already trapped in low-wage, domestic jobs? When they said "sisterhood is global," did they also mean to include us?

Although I never purchased a convertible, studying hard as a child did have an important benefit: It allowed me to attend college. Despite the fact that I had good grades and had taken college preparatory classes, my guidance counselor tried to convince me that I would not do well in a large, predominantly white institution. He recommended that I limit my college applications to the smaller, historically black institutions, arguing that they would be the best places for me to study. When I insisted, he refused to give me application materials. In other words, he was telling me that I had no place among the long-haired women.

What he did not know, however, is that I was supported by a large collective of women who encouraged me to make my own college choices. They included my mother, sister, three college-educated aunts, and several "Other mothers" from my community who had themselves resisted counselors like mine. The common view of this collective was that the act of getting a college education was, for African Americans, itself an act of resistance to racial and gender oppression. I was taught that I could change my world through education and that a place among the long-haired women was mine if I wanted to claim it. This was "the dream" of the civil rights movement, and it was also the ideology embraced by members of my community. So, contrary to the wishes of my guidance counselor, my women's collective helped me to complete my college applications and sent me off to college.

I later learned that this struggle for inclusiveness would continue throughout my life. I entered college with the strength of my women's collective supporting me, but continued to struggle with individuals who, like my guidance counselor, seemed determined to maintain and reproduce a limited and negative view of African American women. A particularly disturbing incident occurred during my second year in college. I was enrolled in a history course titled "Women in U.S. History" and was very excited because my previous course on "U.S. History" had been quite male-centered. However, while the professor did a good job of discussing the accomplishments of *white* women throughout U.S. history, women of color were mentioned only in the contexts of slavery, poverty, and welfare programs. When I asked him about this, he argued that this was not a course about *race,* but was one about *history,* and referred me to a special topics course titled "Afro-Americans in U.S. History" to fill in my gaps of knowledge. Clearly, his perception of history was that women's experiences are completely separate from men's and that the history of African Americans is separate from mainstream or whites'. In other words, the message that I received from this professor is that African Americans are located so far out on the margins of mainstream society that our historical experiences are hardly worth mentioning except within the confines of a separate, special topics course. Once again, I was assured that I had no place among the long-haired women.

Relief was in sight, however, and it came to me within the context of a sociology course that I took in my senior year of college, titled "Sex Roles." It was here that I first read *The Dialectics of Black Womanhood,* by Bonnie Thornton Dill (1979). In her four-point critique of studies on African American families, Dill argues that because traditional studies tend to address African American culture as if it were created and maintained in complete isolation from mainstream white, Western culture, African Americans are viewed as outside of white culture, not only in terms of residential and economic segregation, but also in terms of their cultural and personal values. As a result of these misinterpretations and historical inaccuracies, the economic plight of African Americans has often been explained in terms of their own personal deficiencies.

During the same year that I read Dill's work, I also learned that many of the same historical inaccuracies and misconceptions levied on African American women have also been applied to other women of color. In *Mexican-American Women in the Social Sciences* (Chapter 14, this volume), Maxine Baca Zinn argues that social structural and cultural phenomena are often intertwined within most mainstream social science research about Chicana families. As a result, these studies tend to portray Mexican American women as the passive victims of culturally determined female sex roles and male machismo. Her review points out several revisionist studies that place Mexican American women in particular structural contexts. These studies suggest that the social location of Chicanos is mostly a function of structural arrangements that have restricted the access of both men and women to full and equal participation in American institutions, such as the labor force. Zinn concludes that to move beyond the descriptive examinations and misconceptions of most Chicana studies, researchers must operate within an analytic framework that separates social structure from cultural phenomena, locates Chicanas in specific organizational contexts, distinguishes between macro and micro levels of analysis, and relates studies of Mexican American women to mainstream feminist scholarship.

The work of Dill (1979) and of Zinn made a very dramatic contribution to my life as an African American woman and as a scholar. In addition to providing me with a framework for conducting feminist research, this work helped me to locate myself among a larger group of feminist scholars, sociologists, and activists. Although Dill addressed many of my personal concerns with traditional scholarship, Zinn showed me that other women of color share my concerns. By challenging the racist assumptions maintained by scholars like my history professor, I came to think of Dill and Zinn as my personal advocates. I have located them within the community of my women's collective, as "Other mothers" who fight for me against racist and sexist ideology and support and encourage me through their scholarship.

When I attended graduate school, I discovered other African American women who also gained inspiration from the work of Dill and Zinn. One such woman, Patricia Hill Collins, draws on the work of feminists such as Dill and Zinn to discuss the subordinate nature of black feminist epistemology within mainstream social science in *The Social Construction of Black Feminist Thought*. I first read this work in a graduate sociology course called the "Sociology of Gender." Not only has Collins expanded social science discourse by advancing feminist research and standpoint theory in sociology, her work lies at the center of new courses devoted specifically to black feminist theory. Moreover, this work has captured the attention of scholarship outside sociology and currently appears on reading lists for psychology, women's studies, and African American studies courses.

For me, much of Collins's work reads like a journal of my personal and professional life. She articulates the feelings that I have as an African American woman intellectual in the academy. She also showed me that my women's collective operates within a larger historical context of intellectual thought, resistance to oppression, and humanism widely embraced by African American women.

Her basic argument is that African American women have developed a body of knowledge concerning our own subordination that is not widely recognized or known, but that is shaped by historical, social, and economic factors. She explains that the dominant voices in sociological discussions, most often white men's, typically assume that their theories are generalizable to all people, especially the oppressed who are incapable of "legitimately" speaking for themselves. She asserts that this view is elitist and inaccurate. It is not that African American women are not able to express themselves; rather, our ways of expression are not valued or legitimated within mainstream intellectual discourse. Collins maintains that African American women have a distinct point of view as a result of their collective experiences within simultaneous matrices (race, class, gender) of domination. So, the voices of African American women do not need to be changed to fit the mainstream, nor should it be assumed that we cannot speak for ourselves. Rather, we need to challenge and change the traditional ways of knowing that have suppressed our voices.

I also found direct parallels with my own experiences in Collins's discussion of the centrality of wisdom to black feminist thought. She contends that because African American extended families and churches are both women-centered and Afrocentric, they are key sources of private and public transference and validation of women's concrete lived experiences and knowledge claims. Furthermore, because African American women scholars and academicians also value these ways of knowing, we face considerable resistance from the "Eurocentric, masculinist, knowledge-validation process," which represents the collective interests of their leaders and members, who are most often white men. They can be particularly harmful to the development of black feminist epistemology because, like values and emotions, lived experiences and wisdom are not valued as conventional sources of scientific knowledge. Hence, Collins argues that because we often work from the margins, African American feminist scholars must be particularly diligent in their quest for black feminist scholarship, which values concrete experience, as well as knowledge claims gained through dialogue and ethics of caring and personal accountability.

Other scholars maintain that women of color are not the only ones working from the margins of sociological discourse. These scholars challenge the heterosexism of mainstream feminist scholarship, arguing that lesbian and bisexual women also have unique standpoints as a result of their social location within patriarchal structures. In *Women's Culture and Lesbian Feminist Activism* (Chapter 13 in this volume), Verta Taylor and Leila J. Rupp address attacks by critics who accuse lesbian feminists of betraying the radical feminist movement and the goals of cultural feminism. These critics argue that the central concerns of cultural feminism, which are based on the notions of essential differences between women and men and on separatism, have changed from political activism to issues involving "lifestyles," female sexuality, and eroticism.

Taylor and Rupp maintain that rather than betraying radical feminism, lesbian feminist communities have played a central role in supporting and protecting activists, thereby sustaining radical feminist tradition, both within and outside lesbian communities. Their investigation of lesbian feminist communities includes extensive participation in the lesbian feminist community of Columbus, Ohio, and examines the contributions of these women within specific historical and social locations. This study uncovered three main components of cultural feminism that are mirrored in lesbian feminist communities: a focus on essential differences between women and men; support for separatism; and emphasis on building an alternative, woman-centered culture. Therefore, Taylor and Rupp call for mainstream feminists both to acknowledge and to legitimize the work of lesbian feminists and their continuing support of the radical movement.

I gained such inspiration and knowledge from the work of Collins and of Taylor and Rupp that I have placed them beside Zinn—and Dill—among my extended group of "Other mothers." These scholars have shown me that my women's collective extends far beyond the boundaries of kinship and hometown boarders. Their chapters reflect a tone of inclusiveness, legitimation, and empowerment for women who are often rendered invisible because they operate on the margins of mainstream epistemology. This tone is quite political and has been very influential in changing the tide of traditional discourse and scholarship within mainstream social science. Their work is especially important today, as conservative backlashes operate to silence voices outside of the mainstream.

This group of "Other mothers" continue to work toward women-centered, feminist epistemology at the center of social science. Their work motivates me to question the status quo and to challenge racist, classist, sexist, and heterosexual assumptions within mainstream knowledge. They showed me that I do have a place among the long-haired women and invited me to join them on my own terms—as a powerful, important woman with wonderful short and nappy hair.

NOTE

1.   This reflection is based on three articles: "Mexican-American Women in the Social Sciences," Maxine Baca Zinn (1982); "Social Construction of Black Feminist Thought," Patricia Hill Collins (1989); and "Women's Culture and Lesbian Feminist Activism," Verta Taylor and Leila J. Rupp (1993).

Reflections on Transformations in Feminist Sociology— and in Myself

NANCY WHITTIER

I began college as a Women's Studies major in 1983. One of my first exposures to women's studies was the National Women's Studies Association conference at Ohio State University in 1983, the summer before my freshman year. The conference was thrilling, and it challenged my thinking as it erupted into conflict over racism and exclusion in women's studies. I vividly remember listening to Barbara Smith eloquently and angrily call white women to account for their own racism and demand that white women take responsibility for learning and thinking about women of color and intersections among race, class, and gender. As a white woman raised in a liberal middle-class family, I was both inspired and intimidated by this challenge. It shaped my focus as an undergraduate, as I wrestled with questions of differences among women.

Bonnie Thornton Dill's (1979) classic article, "The Dialectics of Black Womanhood," which I first encountered as an undergraduate, was a lightning bolt of clarity. Strange as it sounds now, I had not been able to conceptualize the intersections between race and gender in a concrete way: I understood that women of color experienced racial as well as gender discrimination, but that was as far as I got. Dill showed so clearly how black women's work and family lives were constructed by their structural position, white culture and racism, and black culture, and she showed how and why dominant sociological interpretations of black women's lives were wrong. Reading Dill, and hearing her speak at Ohio State in the mid-1980s, I "got it": There is no such thing as "femininity," no such category as "women." Instead, there are racialized, class-specific constructions of womanhood. And more: Black womanhood is not simply a more oppressed version of "general" (read "white")

403

womanhood. Instead, it is a qualitatively different construction that carries its own distinct perils and advantages.

Wow! This was truly exciting stuff, and it irrevocably changed how I approached the study of gender and the pursuit of social change. Writing this, I feel a little sheepish admitting that I held such simplistic views of race and gender. But I know that I was not alone. In fact, my perspective paralleled that of the discipline overall; my transformations matched the larger transformation of feminist sociology. Between the 1970s and the 1990s, feminist sociology changed from a field that largely took race for granted and assumed white women's experiences as the norm, to a field that is now at the forefront of thinking about intersections among gender, race, class, and sexuality.

When I started graduate school in sociology in 1986, the notion that gender was not monolithic, but rather varied according to race and class, was firmly implanted in my mind. Imagine my surprise to discover that this conceptualization was not taken for granted in some of my classes! In some classes, race and gender were simply variables to be "thrown into the equation"; others dichotomized race as "white" and "nonwhite"; others deemed it complicated enough to take account of either race or gender, and far too complicated to consider both simultaneously. I felt sometimes as though I were being asked to unlearn or abandon the perspective I had adopted as an undergraduate in women's studies. The classes I took from Verta Taylor were a breath of fresh air, as she continually pushed us students. It was not enough to say that race was important, or that the experiences of women of color differed from those of white women. "HOW does race affect women's activism?" she would demand. "What effects did white hegemony have on the women's movement?"

Patricia Hill Collins's work sent shivers up my spine with the recognition of another level at which race, class, and gender intersected. Her clear discussion of how different epistemologies promote the interests of different groups, and how oppositional knowledge is suppressed subtly at the epistemological level, made me feel as though I had at last received glasses that enabled me to see the borders and contours of hegemony clearly. I read her work in graduate school shortly after reading Kuhn's (1970) *The Structure of Scientific Revolutions,* and together these works brought home the socially constructed nature of knowledge. This was exciting for thinking about connections among race, class, and gender, to be sure, but it was also exciting on a more abstract level of sociological knowledge. Collins showed me how knowledge is linked to power, how social hierarchies produce scholarship that justifies their existence, and how theory can be redefined to include the knowledge that marginalized groups produce outside the academy.

Although Maxine Baca Zinn's chapter was first published in 1982, I did not read it until 10 years later when, as a beginning faculty member, I was looking for articles on Latinas to include in my Sex and Gender syllabus. This is telling.

For much of my college and graduate school years, race was conceptualized primarily in terms of black/white differences. If Latinas, Asian Americans, Native Americans, or women of other ethnic/racial groups were discussed at all, it was often assumed that their experiences were similar or analogous to those of African American women. Women of color had "race," and white women did not. Baca Zinn challenged this simplistic notion by detailing the specific contexts of Mexican American women and showing how their structural and cultural position produced particular constructions of gender. By showing how, for example, Chicanas' various types of kinship connections affect their resources and social power, Baca Zinn accomplished two important tasks. First, she advanced a more sophisticated analysis of Chicanas' lives and social position. Second, she showed how a complex and context-specific analysis is necessary to understand the institutional positions of any group of women. Work such as Baca Zinn's makes it impossible to make sweeping statements about "the oppression of women of color" as if that oppression always took the same shape. Her precision in specifying the questions to be asked about Chicanas' positions in families, the labor force, and daily life moved us toward a more nuanced conception of racialized capitalist patriarchy.

Verta Taylor and Leila Rupp's chapter represents an additional level of thinking about the intersections of gender with other systems of domination. A growing body of sociological work on sexual orientation emerged during the late 1970s and the 1980s. Most of this work focused on documenting lesbian and gay experiences; examining differences among lesbians, gay men, and heterosexuals; and analyzing lesbian or gay communities. Taylor and Rupp's chapter on lesbian feminism took the next step in sociological work on sexuality by asking how our conceptualizations of the radical women's movement change if we make lesbians central to our inquiry. They suggest that criticisms of cultural feminism ignore its grounding in lesbian feminist communities and argue that those communities are a diverse context within which cultural feminism is hotly debated. It is only when lesbianism is left invisible that cultural feminism can be viewed in the ideological abstract and thus oversimplified and dismissed.

It is a bit odd to write about Taylor and Rupp, as my own work is intimately tied up with theirs: Verta Taylor was my dissertation adviser, and both Taylor and Rupp remain my intellectual collaborators and friends. Over many dinners, Taylor, Rupp, my historian partner Kate Weigand, and I lamented the invisibility of lesbianism in the accounts of the demise of radical feminism and decried the assumption that cultural politics are apolitical. As I progressed in my dissertation research on the radical women's movement in Columbus, Ohio, I uncovered considerable evidence about the overlap between supposedly "cultural" forms of organizing and political confrontation, and it became clear that lesbian organizing was central to this overlap. So I was delighted when Taylor and Rupp pulled together such a strong argument for reconceptualizing the contribution of lesbian feminism. It has also been important to me as a less-established lesbian sociologist to have respected feminist sociologists who are both open about being lesbians and who help legitimate lesbian research topics. Although the transformation of the discipline into a nonhomophobic arena is far from complete, and although too many authors still fail to consider sexual orientation, work such as Taylor and Rupp's helps move us in that direction.

Together, these chapters represent a real transformation in the discipline of sociology. As a sociologist trained during this transformation, I cannot really conceive of a sociology of gender in which race, class, and sexuality are not central. Yet looking over what I have written here, I realize that it is an account of "progress" in the sociology of gender. Although I certainly believe that new conceptualizations of race, class, sexuality, and gender as intersecting are an improvement, it is important to emphasize that these approaches do not represent an inevitable scholarly progression, but are a product of a particular intellectual and historical context. Organizing by women of color outside of the academy in the late 1970s pushed white feminists to begin considering racism and exclusion within the women's movement. It was this same organizing that filtered into academia, as feminist sociologists like Bonnie Thornton Dill, Patricia Hill Collins, and Maxine Baca Zinn illuminated the previously invisible assumptions of white normalcy. A few years later, the growing strength and recognition of the lesbian and gay movement legitimated academic research on lesbian organizing and made it possible for scholars such as Verta Taylor and Leila Rupp (and me) to come out as lesbians within the academy. These academic developments do not occur in a vacuum, and they do not represent a transcendent "Truth." Rather, they reflect and refract the political changes occurring within the social movements that have always supported and pushed feminist sociology.

That said, how have these works transformed feminist sociology? They have done so much the same way they have transformed me as a feminist sociologist. They refuse to stop with acknowledging that race has an effect on gender, and ask instead HOW gender varies by race. They refuse to leave lesbianism invisible in analysis, and ask instead HOW making lesbianism central changes our conceptualizations. They show how sociological knowledge is historically contingent on and shaped by systems of racial, class, gender, and sexual dominance. No longer can we write about women as if white, middle-class, heterosexual womanhood were the norm. For that matter, no longer can we write about white, middle-class, heterosexual women as if they were unaffected by race, class, and sexuality.

These changes are not confined to academic theory. They also affect how we work for social change in the broader world. Like many feminist sociologists, I hope that my research, teaching, and activism will contribute to progressive social change. The chapters in this section help make clear to me the necessity for coalitions—and careful listening—across lines of race, class, sexual orientation, and gender. They remind me that feminist goals cannot be conceptualized in terms of the needs and interests of white women, or middle-class women, or heterosexual women. They give me tools to teach my students a complex view of gender as mediated by other systems of domination. They should remind all of us, on the one hand, of the vast transformations in the academy that make consideration of race, class, gender, and sexual orientation not only acceptable but, in some cases, expected. On the other hand, they should remind us of the strength of the backlash against multiculturalism and the need to reassert the complexities of multiple systems of domination and resistance in women's (and men's) lives.

Conclusion: The Philosophy of Feminist Knowledge: Contemplating the Future of Feminist Thought

In this edited collection, we catalog some of our "feminist foundations" in sociology. As we said earlier, we hope our efforts will stimulate and widen the existing community of feminist scholars. In this conclusion, we do not wish to summarize progress, canonize articles, or reinterpret reflectors' thoughts. Rather, we pose a simple question: What next? Where do feminists go from here?

We think that the future of feminist thought is tied to opening conduits of information between the intellectual margins and the center of sociological knowledge. bell hooks (1984) writes that a particularly insightful standpoint comes from living life in "the margins" as opposed to "the center," referring specifically to racial divisions in residential areas, jobs, and education. The center is where people who are economically and racially privileged reside. Major policy decisions are made by and for people in the center, and the policies they make allow them to continue making policies (these powerful policymakers also tend to be men; see Reskin, Chapter 11 in this volume). The margins are where the "others" live—those people systematically excluded from material privileges as well as myriad other resources—people of color, poor people, and people who are gay and lesbian. In a broader sense, the margins also include people with disabilities, people deemed "too old" or "too young," and even women.

In this book, we have applied hooks's language of margins and centers to the processes of intellectual production. According to this analogy, the *center* is where work becomes legitimated, paradigmatic, and sometimes canonized. Scholarship in the center influences future work and sets the guidelines for "quality" scholarship. The intellectual *margins* are the places where new ideas are born. Here, scholars react critically to work at the center as well as in the margins, and they build on each others' endeavors. For intellectual production to remain fluid, we require both the margins and the centers. Exciting work takes place in the margins, but in order to transform knowledge, we must bring the work from the margins to the center. When this occurs in sociology, we experience what Popper (1968) calls a "paradigmatic shift."

All of the intellectual genres included in this book have made the journey from margin to center. For example, consider the journals that originally published these articles. Some of the articles were first published smack in the middle of the center in sociology: in the *American Sociological Review* and in the *American Journal of Sociology*. Some were published in other mainstream journals, such as *Social Problems*. Other articles were published in journals that represent the new field of gender sociology—while perhaps ghettoized—that are the top journals for the sub-area: *Gender & Society* and *Signs*. Some articles here were published in journals with a much smaller circulation, such as *Daedalus*. Still, most of these articles were published in journals relatively central to "legitimate" intellectual production. In bringing the ideas, concepts, and data from the margins to the center, scholars are able to influence future feminist work.

The process of bringing knowledge from margin to center—of creating a paradigmatic shift—is affected by the political climate of the academy in particular and society in general. Radical thought is generated in the margins. Yet unless the political atmosphere allows this thought to be included in/with the mainstream—which would validate this theory and research—then it *remains* in the margins, where it goes largely unheard. Marginal scholars end up "preaching to the choir" unless their work transcends the margins. Entering the center allows scholars to better reach other scholars, both allies and opponents. Work in the margins only reaches the center when the political constraints abate, and when those at the center—the gatekeepers of knowledge—allow it in. Understanding the political context of feminist thought helps us to understand why black feminist thought, for example, has only recently begun to infiltrate the center even though it has existed in various forms for decades.

This brings us to the link between the academy and politics: Why do we care about changing the discipline? Surely *not* because we are sociological entrepreneurs interested in the greater glory of the American Sociological Association. We care about studying inequality because we want to eradicate it—both in the discipline and in society as a whole. We hope this book helps in the quest for equality in many ways. We want this book to be used as a teaching tool, for teaching can be a revolutionary act. When we go into classrooms, expand the knowledge of our students, and open their minds to feminist scholarship and critical thinking, we affect their futures. Few of our students are likely to become sociologists, but they *will* take these ideas with them into their personal and professional lives. By affecting students, we affect the political climate in which thought is produced. Thus, teaching can be seen as a dialectical process: We teach our students about the development of feminist thought; they take progressive ideas with them and affect the social world in which thought is produced; then, their contributions to the political climate will help move future works from the margin to the center. Sharing feminist thought with students is centrally important to transforming sociology and society.

Like our students, we academics take our feminist knowledge into our everyday lives: inside and outside of the academy. We bring our feminist standpoints to the school systems where our children are enrolled, and we work with teachers and administrators to transform primary and secondary education. We worship through feminist lenses and affect the practices of our religious institutions. When we become politically involved on our campuses and in our communities, our activism is guided by our feminist convictions. Feminism informs our struggle for equality within our intimate and familial relationships. Feminist thought is embedded in our behaviors and ideologies as well as our intellectual endeavors. Not only is the personal political, but so is the intellectual.

We can also take our feminist sociological imaginations and knowledge and become policymakers ourselves. As the federal government increasingly decentralizes policy decision making, opportunities for "lay people" to become involved in politics are increasing. This may be one of the only silver linings in the ominous cloud of the "contract with America." As individual social scientists, we may have little access to the federal level, but we may have stronger networks and more access to decision makers at the state and local levels. We can use our expertise and our contacts to affect policy. For progressive changes to occur, it takes more of us willing to get involved.

Although we use the language of *feminist thought* and *feminism,* there is not one and only one conceptualization of what is feminist. There is not a "Feminism" with a capital *F.* We conceptualize multiple feminisms, which are informed by multiple standpoints. In the same vein, we should also problematize our use of *we* in reference to ourselves and other feminists. There is no monolithic group of feminists, nor is there a unified "them" (Thompson & Walker, 1995). If the future of sociology is to include diverse experiences, then the future of feminist thought must also take a relativist approach to the construction of knowledge. There should be *multiple* conduits of information from the margins to the center—and back to the margins. Allowing a diverse knowledge base, however, creates tensions in the discipline because it confounds our ability to draw conclusive lines between genres of thought. Opening the doors to diverse experiences means that many of us will have to step outside of our intellectual comfort zones. This process is not going to be uncomplicated, but we all have to work together.

Finally, those feminists who make it to the center must remember their roots. If we want to open multiple conduits, we need people in positions of power and influence to help bridge the gaps. Feminists in the center can help in many ways. First, they can continue to collect and read scholarship from the margins. It is important that those edging to the center keep up with critical work at the margins and keep ideas percolating toward the center. A second, related strategy for feminists closer to the center is to use their influence to take stock of feminist progress in the discipline or sub-discipline(s). As Thompson and Walker (1995) write in their examination of feminist thought in family studies, "taking stock is an essential practice for feminist scholars who want to work at the center, yet retain the right to be critical, of their discipline" (p. 847). Thompson and Walker resist being co-opted by the conservative center; they claim space to critique the center, even while they benefit from being there. Last, feminists in the center should use their relative security to help build bridges among sub-areas within the center, as well as to the margins. Working together and pooling their resources, feminist sociologists can help to transform the discipline of sociology and, more important, our society in general.

Reflection References

Acker, J. (1980). Women and stratification: A review of the recent literature. *Contemporary Sociology, 9,* 25-39.

Andersen, M. (1993). *Thinking about women* (3rd ed.). New York: McGraw-Hill.

Andersen, M. L., & Collins, P. H. (Eds.). (1995). *Race, class, and gender: An anthology* (2nd ed.). Belmont, CA: Wadsworth.

Anderson, C., Myers, K., & Price, J. (1995). The re-production of feminist theory in sociology graduate programs. *Journal of Creative Social Discourse, 1,* 30-41.

Baca Zinn, M., & Thornton Dill, B. (Eds.). (1994). *Women of color in U.S. society.* Philadelphia: Wadsworth.

Blackwell, J. (1992). Minorities in the liberation of the ASA? *The American Sociologist, 23,* 11-17.

Blau, P., & Duncan, O. D. (1967). *The American occupational structure.* New York: John Wiley.

Blumberg, R. L. (1991). The "triple overlap" of gender stratification, economy, and the family. In Rae Lesser Blumberg (Ed.), *Gender, family, and economy: The triple overlap* (pp. 7-32). Newbury Park, CA: Sage.

Brewer, R. M. (1993). Theorizing race, class, and gender: The new scholarship of black feminist intellectuals and black women's labor. In A. P. A. Busia & S. M. James (Eds.), *Theorizing black feminism: The visionary pragmatism of black women.* New York: Routledge.

Brod, H., & Kaufman, M. (Eds.). (1994). *Theorizing masculinities.* Thousand Oaks, CA: Sage.

Bunch, C. (1990). Women's rights as human rights: Toward a re-vision of human rights. *Human Rights Quarterly, 12,* 486-498.

Bunch, C. (1995). Transforming human rights from a feminist perspective. In J. Peters & A. Wolper (Eds.), *Women's rights, human rights: International feminist perspectives.* New York: Routledge.

Campbell, M., & Manicom, A. (1995). *Knowledge, experience and ruling relations: Studies in the social organization of knowledge.* Toronto: University of Toronto Press.

Chafetz, J. S. (1974). *Masculine/feminine or human? An overview of the sociology of sex roles.* Itasca, IL: F. E. Peacock.

Chafetz, J. S. (1984). *Sex and advantage: A comparative, macro-structural theory of sex stratification.* Totowa, NJ: Rowman & Allanheld.

Chafetz, J. S. (1988). *Feminist sociology: An overview of contemporary theories.* Itasca, IL: F. E. Peacock.

Chafetz, J. S. (1990). *Gender equity: A theory of stability and change.* Newbury Park, CA: Sage.

Chafetz, J. S. (1997). Feminist theory and sociology: Ignored contributions for mainstream theory. In John Hagan (Ed.), *Annual review of sociology.* Palo Alto, CA: Annual Reviews.

Chafetz, J. S. (in press). The varieties of gender theory in sociology. In J. S. Chafetz (Ed.), *Handbook on gender sociology*. New York: Plenum.

Chafetz, J. S., & Dworkin, A. G. (1986). *Female revolt: Women's movements in world and historical perspective*. Totowa, NJ: Rowman & Allanheld.

Chow, E. N. L. (1996a). Making waves, moving mountains: Reflections on Beijing '95 and Beyond. *Signs: Journal of Women in Culture and Society, 22,* 185-192.

Chow, E. N. L. (1996b). *Toward a globalization of gender understanding: Lessons learned from Beijing '95 and Beyond*. Paper presented at the Annual Meeting of the American Sociological Association, New York City.

Chow, E. N. L. (1996c). Transforming knowledge: Race, class, and gender. In E. N. L. Chow, D. Y. Wilkinson, & M. Baca Zinn (Eds.), *Race, class, and gender: Common bonds, different voices* (pp. xix-xxvi). Thousand Oaks, CA: Sage.

Chow, E. N. L., & White Berheide, C. (Eds.). (1994). *Women, the family, policy: A global perspective*. Albany: State University of New York Press.

Chow, E. N. L., Wilkinson, D. Y., & Baca Zinn, M. (Eds.). (1996). *Race, class, and gender: Common bonds, different voices*. Thousand Oaks, CA: Sage.

Collins, P. H. (1991). *Black feminist thought: Knowledge, consciousness, and the politics of empowerment*. New York: Routledge.

Connell, R. W. (1985). Theorizing gender. *Sociology, 19,* 260-272.

Connell, R. W. (1987). *Gender and power: Society: The person and sexual politics*. Palo Alto, CA: Stanford University Press.

Connell, R. W. (1990). The state, gender, and sexual politics: Theory and appraisal. *Theory and Society, 19,* 507-544.

Coser, R. L. (1975). Stay home, little Sheba: On placement, displacement, and social change. *Social Problems, 22,* 470-480.

Coser, R. L. (1986). Cognitive structure and the use of social space. *Sociological Forum, 1,* 1-26.

Dill, B. T. (1979). The dialectics of black womanhood. *Signs: Journal of Women in Culture and Society, 4,* 543-569.

England, P. (Ed.). (1993). *Theory on gender/Feminism on theory*. New York: Aldine de Gruyter.

Epstein, C. F. (1970). *Woman's place: Options and limits in professional careers*. Berkeley: University of California Press.

Epstein, C. F. (1985). Ideal images and real roles. *Dissent,* 441-447.

Ferree, M. M., & Martin, P. Y. (Eds.). (1995). *Feminist organizations: Harvest of the new women's movement*. Philadelphia: Temple University Press.

Feyerabend, P. K. (1978). *Against method: Outline of an anarchistic theory of knowledge*. London: Verso.

Friedan, B. (1963). *The feminine mystique*. New York: Norton.

Glazer, N., & Waehrer, H. Y. (Eds.). (1971). *Woman in a man-made world* (2nd ed.). Chicago: Rand McNally.

Gornick, V., & Moran, B. K. (Eds.). (1971). *Woman in sexist society: Studies in power and powerlessness*. New York: Basic Books.

Hochschild, A. (1973). A review of research on sex roles. *American Journal of Sociology, 78,* 1011-1029.

Hochschild, A. (1983). *The managed heart: Commercialization of human feelings*. Berkeley: University of California Press.

Hochschild, A. (1989). *The second shift: Working parents and the revolution at home*. New York: Viking.

hooks, b. (1984). *Feminist theory: From margin to center*. Boston: South End.

Huber, J. (Ed.). (1973). *Changing women in a changing society*. Chicago: University of Chicago Press.

Huber, J. (1976). Toward a sociotechnological theory of the women's movement. *Social Problems, 23,* 371-388.

Huber, J. (1988). A theory of family, economy, and gender. *Journal of Family Issues, 9,* 9-26.

Huber, J. (1991). Macro-micro links in gender stratification. In J. Huber (Ed.), *Macro-micro linkages in sociology* (pp. 11-25). Newbury Park, CA: Sage.

Johnson, J., & Risman, B. J. (1997). *Feminist scholarship and sociology: Transforming the discipline*. Baltimore, MD: National Center for Curriculum Transformation Resources on Women.

Jones, J. (1985). *Labor of love, labor of sorrow: Black women, work, and the family from slavery to the present*. New York: Basic Books.

Kanter, R. M. (1977). *Work and family in the United States: A critical review and agenda for research and policy*. New York: Russell Sage.

King, D. (1988). Multiple jeopardy, multiple consciousness: The contexts of a black feminist ideology. *Signs: Journal of Women in Culture and Society, 14,* 42-72.

Kuhn, T. (1970). *The structure of scientific revolutions*. Chicago: University of Chicago Press.

Lakatos, I., & Musgrave, A. (1970). *Criticism and the growth of knowledge*. Cambridge, UK: Cambridge University Press.

Linton, R. (1936). *The study of man*. New York: Appleton-Century.

Lopata, H. Z., & Thorne, B. (1978). On the term "sex roles." *Signs: Journal of Women in Culture and Society, 3,* 718-721.

Lorber, J. (1987). From the editor. *Gender & Society, 1,* 3-5.

Lorber, J. (1994). *Paradoxes of gender*. New Haven, CT: Yale University Press.

Lorber, J., & Farrell, S. A. (Eds.). (1991). *The social construction of gender*. Newbury Park, CA: Sage.

MacKinnon, C. A. (1982). Feminism, Marxism, method, and the state: An agenda for theory. *Signs: Journal of Women in Culture and Society, 7,* 515-544.

MacKinnon, C. A. (1983). Feminism, Marxism, method, and the state: Toward feminist jurisprudence. *Signs: Journal of Women in Culture and Society, 8,* 635-658.

MacKinnon, C. A. (1989). *Toward a feminist theory of the state*. Cambridge, MA: Harvard University Press.

McIntosh, P. (1984). Interactive phases of curricular re-vision. In B. Spanier, A. Gloom, & D. Boroviak (Eds.), *Toward a balanced curriculum* (pp. 25-34). Cambridge, MA: Schenkman.

Mills, C. W. (1956). *The sociological imagination*. New York: Oxford University Press.

Parsons, T. (1951). *The social system*. New York: Free Press.

Popper, K. (1968). *The logic of scientific discovery*. New York: Harper & Row.

Risman, B. J. (1987). Intimate relationships from a microstructural perspective: Mothering men. *Gender & Society, 1,* 6-32.

Risman, B. J., & Schwartz, P. (1989). *Gender in intimate relationships: A microstructural approach*. Belmont, CA: Wadsworth.

Roby, P. (1992). Women and the ASA: Degendering organizational structures and processes, 1964-1974. *The American Sociologist, 23,* 18-48.

Schuster, M. R., & Van Dyne, S. R. (Eds.). (1985). *Women's place in the academy: Transforming the liberal arts curriculum*. Totowa, NJ: Rowman & Allanheld.

Sprague, J. (1997). Holy men and big guns: The can[n]on and social theory. *Gender & Society, 11,* 88-107.

Stacey, J. & Thorne, B. (1985). The missing feminist revolution in sociology. *Social Problems, 32,* 301-316.

Stacey, J., & Thorne, B. (1996). Is sociology still missing its feminist revolution? *The ASA (American Sociological Association) Theory Section Newsletter, 18,* 1-3.

Tetreault, M. K. T. (1985). Feminist phase theory: An experience-derived evaluation model. *Journal of Higher Education, 56,* 363-384.

Thompson, L., & Walker, A. (1995). The place of feminism in family studies. *Journal of Marriage and the Family, 57,* 847-865.

Thorne, B. (1980). *Gender . . . how is it best conceptualized?* Paper presented at the Annual Meetings of the American Sociological Association.

Wallace, R. (Ed.). (1989). *Feminism and sociological theory.* Newbury Park, CA: Sage.

West, C., & Fenstermaker, S. (1995). Doing difference. *Gender & Society, 9,* 8-37.

Index

About the Editors

Cynthia Anderson is Assistant Professor of Sociology at Iowa State University. Her research interests include work, community, and inequality. Her publications appear in *Gender & Society, Work and Occupations,* and *Perspectives on Social Problems.* For her dissertation at North Carolina State University, she completed an extended case study of social impacts of change in a southern textile mill community. Anderson is co-winner of the 1996 SWS C.A. Miller Award.

cda@iastate.edu

Kristen Myers is Assistant Professor of Sociology at Northern Illinois University. She received her PhD from North Carolina State University in 1996, under the direction of Barbara Risman. Her dissertation research was a case study of an interracial women's organization, concentrating particularly on the intersection of race, class, and gender. She is concerned with the social construction of oppression as it is manifested in the different axes of the matrix of domination. She has an article coming out with Barbara Risman in 1997 on the social construction of gender among children, in the *Journal of Qualitative Sociology.*

kmyers@niu.edu

Barbara J. Risman is Professor of Sociology at North Carolina State University, where she was also the Founding Director of Women and Gender Studies. Professor Risman is currently coeditor of *Contemporary Sociology.* She has served as the Chair of the American Sociological Association's Sex and Gender Section, and the Chair of the Committee on the Status of Women. She has a book titled *Gender Vertigo: American Families in Transition* (1998) in which she argues that gender must be reconceptualized as a social structure, and one that currently retards feminist social change in intimate relationships. Her current research focuses on understanding the development of women's movements in post-Soviet Russia. She is a coauthor (with Judy Howard, Mary Romero, and Joey Sprague) of the disciplinary transformation series titled Gender Lens, published jointly by Sage and Pine Forge Press.

barbara_risman@ncsu.edu

About the Reflectors

Christine Bose is Associate Professor of Sociology (with joint appointments in the Departments of Latin American and Caribbean Studies and Women's Studies) at the University at Albany. Her academic interests lie in the areas of stratification, labor market studies, development issues, and gender studies. She has published in the areas of occupational prestige, gender and status attainment, employment and poverty among Latinas, the social impact of household technology, and, most recently, two coedited books (with Edna Acosta-Belén) titled *Women in the Latin American Development Process* and *Researching Women in Latin America and the Caribbean.* She is currently working on a book titled *Gateway to the Twentieth Century: Women and the U.S. Political Economy in 1900.* She is active in a variety of professional organizations: She has been Chair of the Sex and Gender Section of the ASA, and was a founding Associate Editor for the journal *Gender & Society.* She was also the founding Director of her university's Institute for Research on Women and is part of the *Latino Review of Books* editorial group there.

C.Bose@Albany.edu

Toni M. Calasanti is Associate Professor of Sociology and a faculty affiliate of both Women's Studies and the Center for Gerontology. Her research focuses on diversity and aging, both nationally and internationally, particularly in relation to the intersections of work/family/retirement. Her most recent publications include "Incorporating Diversity: Meaning, Levels of Research, and Implications for Theory" (*The Gerontologist,* 1996), "Gender and Life Satisfaction in Retirement: An Assessment of the Male Model" (*Journal of Gerontology: Social Sciences,* 1996), and an article forthcoming (with Anna Zajicek) exploring the effects of economic restructuring in Poland on gender, work, and retirement. She is currently working on an examination of the intersections of ageism, sexism, and other systems of oppression, and spends most of her time trying to "balance" work and family.

toni@vt.edu

Janet Saltzman Chafetz is Professor of Sociology and departmental chairperson at the University of Houston, where she has been since 1973. She has written numerous books, book chapters, and articles concerning gender inequality and gender theory, including *Sex and Advantage: A Comparative, Macrostructural Theory of Sex Stratification; Female Revolt: Women's Movements in World and Historical Perspective* (with A. G. Dworkin); *Feminist Sociology: An Overview of Contemporary Theories;* and *Gender Equity: An Integrated Theory of Stability and Change.*

JSChafetz@uh.edu

Esther Ngan-ling Chow received a PhD from the University of California at Los Angeles and is a Professor of Sociology at the American University. She is a feminist scholar, researcher, and community activist. Her research interests span gender, work, and family; race, ethnicity, and immigration; gender and development; industrial sociology; organizational studies; state and social policy; and feminist theory and methodology. She is a coeditor of a special issue of *Gender & Society* (1992) on race, class, and gender. She is a coauthor and coeditor of *Women, the Family, and Policy: A Global Perspective* (1994) and *Race, Class, and Gender: Common Bonds, Different Voices* (1996).

echow@american.edu

Jacqueline Johnson received a PhD in sociology from North Carolina State University in Raleigh and is currently Assistant Professor of Sociology at Syracuse University. Her research interests include gender and racial inequality in job search and hiring processes. She writes about feminist sociology and curriculum development and transformation (J. Johnson & B. Risman, 1997, *Feminist Scholarship and Sociology: Transforming the Discipline*).

jjohns04@maxwell.syr.edu

Patricia Yancey Martin is Professor of Sociology and Daisy Parker Flory Alumni Professor at Florida State University. She teaches and does research on gender and organizations, focusing on the social construction of masculinities and femininities in the workplace. She recently coedited (with Myra Marx Ferree) a collection of essays on feminist organizations

(*Feminist Organizations: Harvest of the New Women's Movement*) and is writing a monograph on the politics of rape work based on data from 130 Florida organizations in 28 communities (including rape crisis centers, police, prosecutors, judges, hospitals, and defense attorneys). She is working with David Collinson on a book about gender and organizations for the Pine Forge Gender Lens Series.

pmartin@coss.fsu.edu

Douglas Mason-Schrock is a doctoral student in sociology at North Carolina State University. His ongoing dissertation research is an ethnographic study of a court-mandated antibattering program for men. He is investigating the links between masculinity and violence, the interactional dynamics of state-enforced therapy, and how abusive men work toward and/or resist self-change.

Doug_mason-schrock@server.sasw.ncsu.edu

Irene Padavic is Associate Professor of Sociology at Florida State University. Her research has been in the areas of gender and work, economic restructuring, and the labor process. Before becoming a professor, she had been a candy seller at a movie theater, a food waitress, a cocktail waitress, a telephone solicitor, a door-to-door promoter of real estate, a paralegal, and a coalhandler at a power plant.

ipadavic@coss.fsu.edu

Nancy Whittier is Assistant Professor of Sociology at Smith College. Her areas of interest are gender and social movements. She is the author of *Feminist Generations: The Persistence of the Radical Women's Movement,* which traces the evolution of radical feminist activism from the late 1960s through the early 1990s, and is coeditor of *Feminist Frontiers IV.* She is currently working on a study of the social movements around child sexual abuse, including survivors' organizing, child abuse prevention, and countermovement mobilization.

nwhittie@smith.smith.edu

Doris Wilkinson is Professor of Sociology at the University of Kentucky. She received her degrees from Case Western Reserve and Johns Hopkins University. She is a former Executive Associate for Careers, Minorities and Women at the American Sociological Association. She is also the author of numerous publications on race, class, and gender and has served as vice president of the ASA and president of the DCSS, SSSP, and ESS. In 1992, she was selected by her university as the Distinguished Arts & Sciences

Professor. Two of her recent critical theoretical essays have been selected as landmark articles: "Americans of African Identity" (1990, 1998) and "Gender and Social Inequality: The Prevailing Significance of Race" (1995).

soc166@ukcc.uky.edu